*Through*

*Your*

*Dreams*

To: Joan,

Best wishes.

Paul Edward Napora

## Canada

The Publishers gratefully acknowledge the financial assistance of the
Government of Canada through the Book Publishing Industry Development Program
(BPIDP) for our publishing activities.


**National Library of Canada Cataloguing in Publication Data**

Napora, Paul Edward, 1939-
    You through your dreams / Paul Edward Napora.

Includes index.
ISBN 0-88887-325-5 (bound).— ISBN 0-88887-324-7 (pbk.)


    1. Dream interpretation–Dictionaries–New Age–Metaphysical–
Spiritual–Self-help–Psychology–Positive Living.  I. Title.

BF1091.N36 2006              154.6'303              C2006-904768-5

*Cover design by Bull's Eye Design, Ottawa*
*Printed and bound in Canada on acid free paper.*

# You
# Through
# Your
# Dreams

Paul Edward Napora

Borealis Press,
Ottawa, Canada
2006

DEDICATION

WITH ALL THE LOVE IN MY SOUL,
I HUMBLY DEDICATE THIS BOOK
…TO YOU.

# INTRODUCTION

The dream code has persistently puzzled Mankind through the centuries. YOU THROUGH YOUR DREAMS—a psychic interpretation of dreams, which took eleven years to write—hopes to solve some of that puzzle!

What is a dream? A dream is the communication line—the link—between our subconscious mind and our conscious mind. Some people (i.e., psychics, mediums, mystics) are more finely attuned to their subconscious mind than others. Everyone, however, possesses some measure of psychic ability. This ability is often released by the subconscious mind into a dream state which can reveal prophecy and forewarnings, when required.

A tension dream merely involves the gamut of our daily thoughts, actions, and deeds. There are no limits to this kind of dream because everyone is unique.

A prophetic dream, however, is different. If a dream repeats itself many times over a period of two weeks or longer, then whatever was shown in that dream is very likely to take place. Sometimes prophetic dreams are good omens; sometimes they are direct forewarnings. It is up to the dreamer to heed the warnings. Unfortunately, not everyone does.

Everyone dreams. Some people can remember their dreams; others cannot. If you cannot, relax; you obviously are managing your daily life relatively well, at least for the moment. In many respects, your subconscious mind is trying to tell you not to worry about what you cannot remember from your dreams and to continue your daily quests with confidence and hope.

Times will come, however, when—out of the blue—you will remember a dream or two. When this happens, your subconscious mind is trying to tell you something. What is it trying to tell you? Perhaps it is trying to tell you something about your physical, mental, spiritual, psychic, or sexual state. Perhaps it is trying to help you through a quandary you may be experiencing. There is obviously a message being given to you. Sort it out, analyze it, and—hopefully—heed it. YOU THROUGH YOUR DREAMS was written to help you in good times and in troubled times.

Dreams can encourage, console, forewarn, confirm, or enlighten a person. Sometimes, they can also frighten a person. You are advised not to take your troubles to sleep with you. A clear mind and a clear conscience will not only help you sleep better, they can also produce better dreaming!

The "buffer zone" symbolisms within this book are as follows: ARROWHEAD, BUTTERFLY, CELESTIAL, CONE, CRUCIFIX, CRY, DOG, FLYING, FLYING SAUCER, GOD, HEAVEN, HOLY MOTHER, JESUS, KNIFE, LEVITATION, MAGI, MOSES, PEACEMAKER, PRAYER, QUASAR, SAINT and clear WATER. These very special lifeline symbolisms all act as a buffer zone to anything negative within a dream. So, if you have a very negative dream but somewhere in your dream state you happen to see any one of the abovementioned symbolisms, then you can allay your fears; better times are ahead for you, not bad times. These limited, special symbolisms should be respected and cherished. They offer you love and courage when you need it most!

The ability to decode dreams was given to me many years ago by a Cosmic Master and Guide, Oscar Camille. Everyone has a guide (a guardian angel). Unfortunately, not everyone is able to effect direct communication with his or hers. At one point in my lengthy tutorship, Oscar symbolically and humbly presented me with a golden key, stating that I "would help unlock many doors for Mankind".

I, in turn, now humbly present you, the dreamer, with a golden key—this book. It will unlock many mysteries and truths for you.

May the Light of God shine upon you, now and always.

Paul Edward Napora

**ABANDONMENT** (i.e., to desert a person or thing) (also see **DEFEATIST** or **DEFECTOR**)

Being abandoned by a stranger or a group of people within a dream implies that a very close friend has some doubts about your integrity and loyalty. At this moment, do not alarm yourself over this revelation, but rather consider how you can improve this relationship. The best friendships can survive the test of time with honesty, respect, and forgiveness.

Abandoning members of your family, a friend, acquaintance, or stranger advises you to stop being so stubborn and overconfident in life. You may take your loved ones and others around you for granted, but be wary of this negative action, for everything you do wrongful to others has a day of reckoning! The final outcome of your dominance towards others could inevitably leave you isolated and abandoned by the very same people whom you once took for granted.

To abandon your faith, enthusiasm, or courage within a dream advises the dreamer to treat other races of people with equality and compassion. By utilizing more humility, kindness, and spiritual harmony within yourself, your sometimes biased and prejudiced attitudes will commence to disappear. Bear in mind, as well, that you are here to love and help your fellow man—not to hate and degrade your fellow man.

**ABBEY** (see **CONVENT** or **MONASTERY**)

**ABBESS** (see **CONVENT** or **MONASTERY**)

**ABBOTT** (see **MONK** or **MONASTERY**)

**ABDICATION** (see **RESIGNATION**)

**ABDUCTION** (see **KIDNAPPING**)

**ABNORMALITY** (see **DEFORMITY**, **FREAK**, **INSANITY**, or **SEX**)

**ABOLISHMENT** (see **DESTRUCTION**)

**ABORTION** (see *also* **FAILURE**, **FETUS**, or **MISCARRIAGE**)

Any of the following definitions may be applicable: A) that you had an abortion at one time, and to this very day you either have great remorse towards this action or show great indifference towards this action; or B) that you know of someone who is contemplating an abortion; or C) that you personally know someone who performs abortions; or D) that your pro-abortion thinking has changed drastically over the years; or E) that this act is basically wrong, simply because life should not be wasted, eliminated, or harmed, but should be cherished and protected, at all costs; or F) that you feel the act of abortion, whether right or wrong, should be an individual decision to make; or G) that you feel the decisions people make regarding the matter of abortion can and do affect them profoundly into the future; or H) that you feel the preoccupation with sex nowadays will always make abortion a threatening substitute for human responsibility; or I) that your mind is laden with remorse or guilt over some advice you gave someone who either contemplated abortion or who had an abortion; or J) that you often wonder how many great souls this world has lost because of abortion; or K) that you see abortion as a grave holocaust upon this planet, as long as people tend to ignore the wisdom, sanctity, and purity of God's Better Judgment and Laws; or L) that there may be decent, logical, and conceivable reasons for some abortions (e.g., extreme, life-threatening situations), but-for the vast majority of cases, there appear to be selfish, one-sided motivations behind this action; or M) that you feel decent-minded individuals are compelled to do the wrong things in life (e.g., abortion) because they succumb to outside pressures, rather than utilize introspective common sense; or N) that you feel no one is immune from making some unpleasant decisions within their lifetime, but in matters of abortion itself, one must weigh the consequences of their heart, mind, and soul with foresight, not with hindsight; or O) that no one should judge another person's actions in these difficult matters unless they, too, have walked the same road; or P) that you feel there are enough adoptive parents who would be very willing to accept the vast majority of these unwanted births, if given the opportunity; or Q) that this dream has absolutely no relevance to you at this time.

**ABORTIONIST** (see **EVILDOER** or **CRIMINAL**)

**ABRIDGEMENT** (see **REDUCTION**)

**ABSENTMINDEDNESS** (see **NEGLECTFULNESS**)

**ABSTINENCE** (see **FAST**, **LENT**, or **PREVENTION**)

**ABSTRUSENESS** (see **MYSTERY**)

**ABSURDITY** (see *also* **BABBLE**)
There is a certain amount of mental confusion and lack of self-control concerning your lifestyle or your immediate plans. Your compulsive behaviour often leads you towards heartaches and resentful disappointments. Nonetheless, the state of being foolish or nonsensical within a dream advises you and/or a loved one to be especially careful about personal investments or about physical or mental overwork. It also advises you to be especially careful where untimely or unnecessary travel is concerned. Neglect or misuse of one's better judgment in this regard may result in monetary loss, mental anguish, or unfavorable travel conditions. Heeding this warning, on the other hand, may avert some needless discomforts!

**ABUNDANCE** (see *also* **BILLIONAIRE, FORTUNE, HAPPINESS, MILLIONAIRE,** or **OWNERSHIP**)
There are occasions when you are very grateful for all your earthly and spiritual wealth; but, there are occasions when you simply go overboard where materialistic wants are concerned. The "buy now, starve later" attitude will simply place you deeper in debt, whereas learning to handle a sound budget will give you a greater sense of responsibility and peace of mind. Remember, there will always be an occasion or two when you will be further tempted to go beyond your financial means! At this juncture, be guided by good common sense until you can honestly afford to buy an item. A day or two down the road may teach you that inner patience in all matters of life is the wisest policy to uphold!

**ABUSE** (see **BLASPHEMY, CRUELTY, CURSE, DISAPPROVAL, FIGHT, MASOCHISM, MISCHIEF, MOCKERY, PERSECUTION,** or **PUNISHMENT**)

**ABYSS** (see **HOLE**)

**ACADEMY** (see **SCHOOL**)

**ACCELERATION** (see **QUICKNESS**)

**ACCIDENT** (see **COLLISION** or **INJURY**)

**ACCLAMATION** (see **APPLAUSE** or **PRAISE**)

**ACCOMMODATION** (see **HOSTEL, HOTEL, LODGING, MOTEL,** or **RENT**)

**ACCORDION** (see **INSTRUMENT**)

**ACCOUNTABILITY** (see **RESPONSIBILITY**)

**ACCUSATION** (see *also* **BLASPHEMY, COMPLAINER, DISAPPROVAL, LAWSUIT,** or **LIBEL**)

Accusing another person of some wrongs they may have done signifies that, at times, you tend to be moody, short-tempered, and disagreeable, with no just cause to be so. You also expect a sympathetic ear from other people, but you seldom offer comfort to others in return. Bear in mind that the love and understanding you give to others is basically the love and respect you will receive in return. This dream symbolism directs you to adopt a more calm disposition through love, prayer, patience, and humility, and by admitting your own weaknesses and limitations. In summation, any form of self-improvement people make within their life is not only for the betterment of "one", but for the betterment of "all" concerned.

**ACHIEVEMENT** (see **COMPLETION, DETERMINATION, HEROISM,** or **OWNERSHIP**)

**ACID**

Although you may have experienced great disappointments in your past, you should not harbour despairing or indifferent views about your present or future! This dream urges you to adopt a more assured, positive attitude about yourself through prayer and by maintaining worthy actions and deeds towards others. Self-pity is not your answer in forging ahead; but, hard work and concentrated efforts in making your world better is certainly a step in the right direction. Note, as well, that the peace of mind you seek will be yours when you are ready, willing, and able to finally let go of those unwholesome obstacles which you somehow deem so important (e.g., failure, distractions, fear, temptations, despair, pride).

**ACKNOWLEDGEMENT** (i.e., a mental, verbal, or written confirmastion of a fact receipt)

Acknowledging someone or something within a dream symbolizes a sudden change of plan, which could be beneficial to you, and/or a journey, which could be both rewarding and educational for you. Your immediate future looks steadfast and fulfilling, simply because your determination and faith reveal a mature fixity of purpose! As you go on in life, the challenges and difficulties you may face should be triumphantly mastered with truth, farsightedness, and the keeping of a one-to-one relationship with God.

**ACORN** (see **CONE**)

**ACQUAINTANCE** (see **FRIEND**)

**ACQUITTAL** (see **LIBERATION**)

**ACREAGE** (see *also* **MEASUREMENT**)

You have great visions of being rich and worldly, yet you fail to overcome one of your greatest weaknesses in life—namely, your idleness in bringing this vision to fruition. People who are famous or rich do not necessarily become this way overnight. On the contrary, it sometimes takes years of self-sacrifice, struggle, and pain before they commence to enjoy the due rewards of their labor! Your desires in life may be achieved when you decide to settle down within yourself; when you commence to gain a firm grip on your talent(s) or aim(s); and when you finally decide to carry out your goal(s) with a never ending, positive stand. However, if your visions are mere pipe dreams with absolutely no hope of attainment in sight, then resign yourself to what you have now, and be as happy as you can. Your dreams can become a reality or remain a fantasy; this depends entirely on you.

**ACROBAT** (e.g., a skilled gymnast, aerialist, stuntman)

Any of the following revelations may be applicable: A) that some major or minor repairs to your home, garage, or cottage will be fulfilled before too long; or B) that major purchase such as a car, boat, or house will be made soon; or C) that an eventual tour to another country or state will give you much satisfaction and food for thought; or D) that a promotion or raise in pay concerning your job or career is just around the corner; or E) that your friendships or marital status will commence to be more harmonious, communicative, and support-ive; or F) that this dream has no significance to you at this time.

**ACROPHOBIA** (i.e., a fear of great heights)
Experiencing this phobia within a dream could very well imply how you actually feel during your wake state. You may, in fact, suffer from acrophobia. However, if this is not the case, then this dream implies that you are striving to attain a career, position, or some facet of work that offers satisfying and open-minded challenges. Persistence, courage, and perhaps taking a course or two in your area of interests will assist you in your quest. You will find the success you want in life, but be prepared for an uphill struggle!

**ACTIVITY** (see **QUICKNESS**)

**ACTOR**
Seeing yourself or someone else as a stage actor or actress infers that a pending business venture will prove to be both productive and profitable for you. By choice, you may wish to remain a silent partner, but you will eventually own this company, by mutual agreement.
Seeing yourself or someone else as a movie actor or actress reveals that you are talented in any of the following: architecture, dancing, acting, literature, music, painting, or sculpture. You may certainly excel in any one or two of these chosen fields simply because your ambition, persistence, love, and sincerity are glowing attributes of your charismatic personality!

**ACTRESS** (see **ACTOR**)

**ACUPUNCTURE** (see **NATUROPATHY**)

**ADDER** (see **SNAKE**)

**ADDICT** (see **DRUG ADDICT**)

**ADDRESS** (see **HOME** or **LECTURE**)

**ADJUDICATION** (i.e., the decision of a judge)
This dream gives promise of an advancement in what you are presently doing. Even though your world may appear to be falling apart

from time to time, hold on to your present aspirations, for they are not a lost cause. Giving up now would be tantamount to admitting defeat-something you would later regret. You can master all your problems, provided you have the courage and stamina to accept the challenges and barriers in front of you. Your difficulties may appear insurmountable today; yet, tomorrow they can vanish into thin air because of your faith, self-sacrifice, and lasting endurance. Remember, you have the ability to rise over and above the nadir of your despair by utilizing the inner forces of wisdom and truth within the very depths of your mind-soul!

**ADMINISTRATOR** (*see* **CAPTAIN, CLERGYMAN, CONDUCTOR, CORONER, DEPUTY, DICTATOR, ENGINEER, FOREMAN, GOVERNOR, HERDSMAN, HUSBAND, JUDGE, LEADERSHIP, MANAGER, MASTER OF CEREMONIES, MAYOR, PEACE OFFICER, POLITICIAN, PRESIDENT, PRIME MINISTER, PRINCIPAL, SECRETARY, SHEIKH, SUPERVISOR,** or **WARDEN**)

**ADMIRAL** (see **LEADERSHIP** or **NAVY**)

**ADMIRATION** (see **ACKNOWLEDGEMENT, CERTIFICATE, COMPLIMENT, IDOLATRY, LOVE,** or **PRAYER**)

**ADOLESCENT** (i.e., a minor or juvenile)
    To see yourself as an adolescent or to dream of an adolescent who is a stranger to you reveals that you have a tendency to exaggerate and project overconfidence when you are with or around people. These overpowering, negative traits have led you into difficulty in the past and will certainly continue to do so in the future, unless you curb these unwholesome tendencies. The truth may hurt at times, but you have a choice: be silent and passive when you are with a group of people, instead of attempting to hold your audience captive with vanity and self-deception.

**ADOPTION**
    To adopt a person, animal, place, or thing within a dream denotes that you are discontent with your present status due to the fact that you either lack the education required for job advancement and/or you lack the willpower and initiative required for job advancement. In

either case, you may at times feel subordinate or limited in your present line of work. No outstanding promotion or advancement is foreseen, unless you decide to upgrade your education or commence to show more interest and willingness to get ahead with success in mind.

**ADORNMENT** (see **DECORATION**)

**ADULATION** (i.e., showing great flattery or fawning over someone or something)
    This act within a dream reveals that a vacation, a retreat, a short journey, a visit, or a minor celebration will not be as pleasurable as you hoped it might be. Disappointments will beset you in a variety of ways, thus leaving you perplexed and disgusted. This dream symbolism advises you to nullify or postpone any of the above measures for a later date, if possible. If this is not possible, then you must carry on, with the deepest hopes that this warning will pass you by.

**ADULTERY** (i.e., the act of a married person having a sexual relationship with a person other than his or her spouse; an act of infidelity) (see *also* **AFFAIR, INTERCOURSE, MISTRESS,** or **SEX**)
    The act of adultery within a dream can imply that you are or were having an adulterous relationship with someone. Hence, your dream is simply personifying the happiness, sadness, or guilt that you are presently experiencing in life. However, if the above-mentioned entry is not applicable to you, then your dream about adultery reveals that your love and loyalty towards your married partner will continue to blossom and flourish! This dream also foretells that you will triumph over people who will make attempts to besmirch your happiness and reputation. It appears that the more good you try to do for appreciative people, the more static you receive from others who have nothing better to do than revel in criticism, hatred, and jealousy. You will master your disappointments in others with common sense and a fair amount of isolation.

**ADVERTISEMENT** (e.g., billboard, handbill, commercial, want ad, brochure) (see *also* **ANNOUNCEMENT, BOOK JACKET, POSTER, PUBLICITY,** or **SIGNBOARD**)
    A neat looking, rational advertisement infers eventual prestige and honour in your present endeavours. This, of course, will not be

handed to you on a silver platter, but will result from a combination of hard work, being dependable, and thoroughly enjoying your profession, skill, or craftsmanship.

Seeing an advertisement that is obscure, old looking, torn, smeared, or damaged in any way reveals dissatisfaction either at home, at work, or perhaps in some educational pursuit. This dilemma should be corrected in time with serious insight and with much needed encouragement and wholesome communication. Failing to correct any measure of personal unhappiness could invariably prompt you to seek satisfaction elsewhere.

**ADVICE** (see **ADVERTISEMENT, ANNOUNCEMENT, CONFERENCE, DISAPPROVAL, FOREWARNING, INQUIRY, LEARNING, LECTURE,** or **MESSENGER**)

**AERIAL** (see **ANTENNA**)

**AERIALIST** (see **ACROBAT**)

**AERONAUT** (i.e., the pilot of a balloon or dirigible) (see *also* **BALLOON** or **DIRIGIBLE**)
     If the sky is relatively calm and clear while piloting a balloon or dirigible, then be assured that you are striving for greater self-discipline and self-discovery within your being. It appears that many past mistakes, failings, and sad memories haunt you quite frequently, but you are not about to make the same mistakes again. This dream further reveals a possible change of residence or occupation or a complete change of character that will finally enable you to reestablish your worth and purpose in life.
     Seeing a sky that is dark and foreboding while piloting a balloon or dirigible intimates that you will continue to have lasting perseverance and good friendships, no matter what misfortune or hardships you may encounter. Your very strength of character suggests that you have already surpassed many trials and tribulations with flying success!

**AFFAIR** (i.e., a sexual relationship between two people not married to each other) (see *also* **ADULATION, INTERCOURSE, MISTRESS,** or **SEX**)
     To see or to have a love affair within a dream intimates that you sometimes overindulge in passionate thoughts or actions concerning the

opposite sex. Perhaps, at times, you regard the opposite sex as merely a means or tool for your own personal needs and gratification. Only you have the concrete or superficial answers for your thoughts, reasons, and actions in life. But whatever your reasons may be in this regard, you are strongly urged to respect the opposite sex with inner honesty and with substantial control of mental and physical temptations. Realize, as well, the importance of acknowledging intelligent friendships and intelligent love, as opposed to immature friendships and immature love.

**AFFIDAVIT** (see **DOCUMENT** or **PROMISE**)

**AFTERBIRTH** (i.e., the placenta and membranes which are expelled from the womb after birth)
     You have been working to the point of exhaustion. Yet, stubbornly, you will not admit this fact to yourself or to your loved ones! Continuing in this manner could result in a complete mental and physical breakdown, which would force you into a more passive lifestyle. This dream by no means advises you not to work in life; however, it cautions you to slow down and to keep your earthly priorities and obligations in order. A good rest, a trip, a leave of absence, or getting some additional assistance are but a few suggestions recommended to the beholder of this dream symbolism.

**AFFLUENCE** (see **ABUNDANCE, BILLIONAIRE, FORTUNE, HAPPINESS, MILLIONAIRE,** or **OWNERSHIP**)

**AFTERLIFE** (see *also* **HEAVEN** or **HELL**)
     To see visions of afterlife within a dream is a very favourable sign. This implies that you are slowly becoming aware of your true inner needs in life. This does not imply wealth or materialistic prosperity, but rather a mind-soul spiritual awakening. You often think about the next world to come—a thought that very often leaves mankind mystified, fearful, and somewhat narrow-minded. You are beginning to show an uncanny sixth sense awareness about people, places, and events. This places you in a rather unique position among your fellow man. In essence, this dream augurs spiritual advancement and understanding.

**AGE** (see **OLD AGE**)

**AGGRAVATION** (see **ANGER** or **ANNOYANCE**)

**AGENDA** (see **PROGRAM**)

**AGENT** (i.e., actor's agent, author's agent, press agent, or a person who acts as a proxy for someone else)

Seeing an agent who represents you or someone else within a dream denotes you are a talented person with a very compassionate mind. Try putting your thoughts down on paper once in a while, and keep compiling these thoughts until you feel this material could be put into book form. Why not? Your thoughts are beautiful, uplifting, and often awe-inspiring! This world could use some of your thought-provoking ideas and idealism. Just think—somewhere on this planet, someone may need the inspiration you possess! Whoever you are, may God enlighten your road and guide you towards a fulfilling life of noble thoughts, actions, and deeds.

Being an agent within a dream or seeing an agent who refuses to represent you or someone else infers that you will assist a member of your family or a friend who appears to need your comfort and guidance. Sometimes, you are judged and misjudged by others but, true to form, whenever the need arises, you are always there to lend a helping hand! The understanding spirit of your heart and mind should tell you that you are, indeed, an angel of mercy.

**AGGRESSION** (see **ANGER, HATRED,** or **INVASION**)

**AGNOSTIC** (i.e., a skeptic; or a person who has doubts about the existence of God, about man's purpose or destiny, or about the existence of supernatural phenomena)

Being or seeing an agnostic within a dream infers lack of responsibility from time to time, showing little faith in your convictions, and becoming somewhat clingy or dependent upon people around you. These mind-based insecurities are not wholesome to the soul and should be recognized as being rather immature. By being faithful and responsible to self and others, you will create a better road, a greater vision, and a worthy image of self upon entering into a more assured, enriched future.

**AGORAPHOBIA** (i.e., an unnatural fear of open places or public places)

Possessing this phobia within a dream denotes that you have an inferiority complex. Bear in mind that we cannot all be gifted, beautiful, handsome, or wealthy on earth! One of your biggest setbacks is that you compare yourself to others far too frequently. The results of these comparisons can only leave you dejected, forlorn, and maintaining inferior thoughts about yourself. When you feel inferior or unworthy, it is simply because you are allowing your emotional state complete control of your thoughts. First, begin to construct your life in a positive way, as though you were building a cathedral from a foundation to a spire. Then, commence to feel and believe deep within yourself that you do belong to the Universal Order of Life, no matter how subordinate you act or feel. Next, acknowledge this fact: no one on this planet should feel inferior or superior, no matter who they are. They should, rather, feel natural in their rightful frame of mind, body, and surroundings. Follow these simple recommendations: commence to improve or update your dress apparel, hair style, or whatever you deem necessary in this regard; make some attempts to meet new people with mutual interests, by joining a club, association, fellowship, etc.; do some charitable work; and read good books offering inspiration and ideas for further self-improvement.

**AIM** (e.g., a purpose, plan, project, or ambition) (see *also* **DETERMINATION** or **LIFEWORK**)

Aiming towards something positive infers that you possess good foresight in what you do and in what you say. Being levelheaded in life has its advantages, in that you are generally able to cope with your problems without too much hassle or difficulty. This symbolism indicates that your present state of being will improve for the better, and your hopeful plans or ambitions will eventually be achieved.

Aiming towards something negative infers that you can expect some difficult times ahead (e.g., mental or physical stress, difficulty with an employer or employee, a financial loss). However, in spite of this forewarned setback, you can master your losses, shortcomings, and impediments through faith, prayer, and an ample amount of gutsy determination!

**AIRBOAT** (see **BOAT**)

**AIRFIELD** (see **AIRPORT**)

**AIR FORCE**

To see yourself or someone else partaking in some air force activity, or to save your country, state, village, a person, or a group of people, and so on, under the air force banner implies that you are presently undergoing some very sensitive, soul-searching thoughts about your successes and failures in life. If you weigh this out very carefully, you must admit that you have more successes than failures to your credit. You are also undergoing some monetary stress; this, by the way, is not a permanent situation. Strive to advance your mind through education, in reading philosophical books concerning self-confidence, and perhaps books and testimonials about saints and heroes who have fought and mastered earthly obstacles. Begin to gain a greater insight into the world around you by channeling your thoughts and actions through compassion and love towards your fellow man. By thinking less of self and more of others, you will invariably receive much honour and esteem—a personal success that cannot be weighed or measured by dollars and cents, but rather by an intimate feeling of well-being, intensified and sanctified by your actions and deeds.

Working against the air force banner, on the other hand, intimates that you are presently discouraged and dissatisfied with your life style. The peace of mind you seek cannot come unless you strive very hard to heal your wounds from some past or present heartache or from some wrong actions against you (e.g., being rejected as a child; marital or romantic problems; difficulty with a family member or friend; inability to hold down a job or to achieve some personal goal[s]). Whatever your problems may be, you are strongly urged to settle down by utilizing more forgiveness and renewal of purpose within the portals of your heart, mind, and soul. Fight your inner battles now like you have never fought before, and you will victoriously find the peace of mind and new beginning you rightfully deserve!

**AIRPLANE** (i.e., a propeller airplane or jet airplane) (see *also* **AERONAUT, FRAMEWORK,** or **PROPELLER**)

Being on board an airplane with other passengers, or finding it difficult to board an airplane, or being too late to board an airplane, or piloting an airplane signifies that you are overanxious to attain financial security in life. You certainly may achieve this goal in life, but not without patience and perseverance. It is natural to want to feel secure in life. However, one should not forget the true and meaningful joys of living (e.g., family life, the wonders of nature, making new friendships and keeping old friendships as well, seeking inner happiness through good deeds). Should you decide that your work and time have no need for the better things in life that are relatively free, then you will one day realize that all the sweat and toil you reserved for that almighty dollar bill was not really worth the time and effort.

Seeing an airplane heading towards a crash landing but failing to see the airplane actually crash infers that you will surmount some personal annoyance or disappointments concerning business, home, or career opportunities(e.g., loss of business revenue; being unemployed; misunderstanding with a spouse, offspring or relative; losing a promotion for some reason or other). This problem will eventually clear up and settle but not necessarily without some sadness, tears, anguish, and sleepless nights on your part.

Seeing an airplane crash or seeing a midair collision reveals that sudden disappointments, interruptions, demands, or losses within your life should be handled with logic and wisdom, not with fear and frustration. This dream cautions the dreamer or a family member to be extremely careful when traveling with a vehicle, bike, motorbike, boat, or airplane and/or to be more heedful where mental and physical care is concerned. Injury, escape from death, sickness, or mental stresses are foretold by this dream. An earnest prayer for guidance and protection is advised. Hopefully this revelation may be averted.

(*Note*: A repetitive dream concerning an airplane crash could mean the demise of someone whom you know, or—prophetically—you are receiving a dream vision about an airplane crash that will actually take place somewhere on earth with, perhaps, many lives lost.)

Seeing an airplane being destroyed, shot down, or losing a propeller, wing, or some other vital parts reveals that you are behaving in a very impetuous, temperamental manner. Instead of being your own best friend at this time, you appear to be your own worst enemy! Before you fly off the handle, so to speak, think twice about your thoughts and actions and about the effect you are having on others around you. Tranquilize your mind and actions with an unselfish, patient, and humble attitude instead of displaying pride and disrespect. In simple terms, be nice and kind to yourself and to others, and your world will be kind to you as well.

## AIRPORT (see *also* CONTROL TOWER or HANGAR)

Seeing an airport that appears peaceful and in order or one that is relatively busy and natural looking intimates that you desperately wish to be understood by others. There are many occasions when people place you in the "nutty plus" category because of your high ideals and futuristic thinking. Be happily aware that, although you may feel misunderstood and left out by others around you, you are still loved and appreciated by some precious beings who do care about your welfare! It is quite obvious by this dream that you are headed towards a bright future where personal success is concerned. This may involve leadership in medicine, law, theology, engineering, teaching, and so on. Bear in mind, as well, that your self-confidence will be the deciding factor to the basic heights you intend to reach in your lifetime.

Seeing an airport that is rather obscure, ominous-looking, untidy, is being protected by law officials, or any other form of unusualness means that you are presently undergoing some marital indifferences, and/or you are experiencing some emotional discord with someone or something within your life. The feeling to leave all your troubles behind is quite prevalent here; there are times when you would simply like to pack your bags and go away forever. This disharmony you are experiencing stems from some foolish, nonsensical attitudes and differences of opinion, which can easily be solved through humility and compromises. Do not be too proud to say "I'm sorry" or to admit that you were wrong in some situation. Life is much too short for any type of pettiness. Furthermore, if you cannot handle the small, needless problems on earth, how will you ever master the major ones?

**AIRSICKNESS** (see **NAUSEOUSNESS** or **SICKNESS**)

**AISLE** (see **PASSAGEWAY**)

**ALBUM** (see **AUTOGRAPH**, **LOOSE-LEAF**, **PHOTOGRAPH**, **POSTAGE STAMP**, or **RECORD**)

**ALCHEMY** (i.e., the infant state of chemistry)

The practice of alchemy within a dream (e.g., making gold out of metal or concocting an elixir of youth) forewarns the dreamer not to be too complacent where healthy, realistic attitudes are concerned. The body, mind, and soul must be properly nourished in order to maintain some sane equilibrium in life. Neglect or creating a phobia in any one of these vital matters can, and will, upset the balance of things within your system. In essence, this dream symbolism is urging you to always strive to maintain a sensible balance of thought and action, both within and around you.

**ALCOHOLIC** (see **DRUNKENNESS**)

**ALGEBRA** (see **MATHEMATICS**)

**ALIBI** (i.e., an excuse)
Giving an alibi within a dream reveals that you are not facing the truth about yourself, another person, or about some situation in your life. Whatever it may be, you would be wise to realize that truth surpasses all falsehood, and love supersedes bitterness, hate, and revenge. Remember, you are very worthy and needed upon this planet, but you must commence to face reality with trust, faith, and unvarnished sincerity. Failing to utilize and accept this fact of life could eventually give you a guilt-ridden conscience heaped with inner conflicts, sadness, and much sorrow.

**ALIMONY** (see **ALLOWANCE**)

**ALLEY** (e.g., a back street or lane)
To walk naked down an alley indicates that the dreamer may have leanings towards homosexuality or bisexuality. If you are homosexual (gay or lesbian) or bisexual, then this dream simply reaffirms your needs and wants in life. If, however, you have a tendency to lean towards this form of sexuality but do not want any part of this activity at all, then by all means continue to fight your temptations with courage, strength, and perhaps some professional guidance.
Seeing yourself or someone else in an alley clothed implies that you are experiencing some insecurity and emotional upsets with your life style. This matter will be solved in due course. Be patient, for the darkness you foresee ahead will turn to unparalleled calmness and satisfaction!

**ALLIGATOR**
You tend to be very childish and critical when minor situations are not to your liking. It appears that you will simply have to learn to cope with the fact that there will always be some pleasant or unpleasant matters around you. Not everything will go your way in life, no matter how upset you become! Basically, by keeping calm, cool, and collected in any predicament, you will begin to show more maturity, and you will also begin to give other people a better impression about you.

**ALLOWANCE** (see *also* **PENSION**)

Receiving an allowance from someone reveals you have a rather selfish, one-sided attitude about people, places, and things. This attitude can be rectified by realizing that there is more to life than just your own little world and that your embitterment and selfish ways are of no use to yourself or to the people around you. Lacking the spirit of kindness and sharing has repeatedly held you back in life and will continue to do so until you decide to change. By focusing your mind on the good of life around you, by grasping the inner peace within you that so desperately wishes to be known and utilized, and by realizing that we are all dependent upon one another on this planet, you will slowly commence to improve your ways, living for a better today and tomorrow.

Giving an allowance to someone, on the other hand, reveals your refusal to be angered or provoked by an insult or accusation. Obviously, you have great self-control and tolerance. This dream also reveals that you are a creature of habit. Being so allows you the fortitude to hold your ground and your feelings on various matters. You have a winning personality and a courageous, enduring, and competitive spirit. Being a good friend towards your fellow man, you also display an excellent sense of fairness and justice.

**ALMANAC** (see **BOOK** or **CHRONICLE**)

**ALMOND** (see **KERNEL**)

**ALMSHOUSE** (see **POORHOUSE** or **POVERTY**)

**ALPHABET**

Travel throughout various parts of the world is indicated when you see an alphabet within a dream. You will gain immeasurable knowledge with regard to the language, habits, and cultures of other people. Perhaps, later in life, you will place your worldly experiences within a book, a play, poetry, art, or music. Whatever you decide in this matter, one thing stands out: your life, in time to come, will bring you great spiritual satisfaction and worldly wisdom.

**ALTAR**

An altar of a church is always a good sign. This foretells that you, the dreamer, will gain through meditation, prayer, leading a good life, and by reading books about Far Eastern Masters, Biblical characters, and U.F.O. material, written and researched by authorities in their chosen work. Your quest is sincere, but your thirst for knowledge will go unquenched until you piece together certain facts about ancient history (this has perplexed you for quite some time). With your acute sense of judgment and analytical mind, you are bound to uncover certain facts that you, as well as others, should know.

## ALTAR BOY

Being or seeing an altar boy within a dream advises you to settle some longstanding dispute or hatred towards another person (e.g., parent, brother, sister, friend). The sooner you take steps to rectify this situation, the better off you will feel. The procedure for peace is relatively simple: reconcile with sincerity, and apologize with love and peace in your heart.

## AMBASSADOR (see MESSENGER or POLITICIAN)

## AMBITION (see AIM, DETERMINATION, or LIFEWORK)

## AMBULANCE

Seeing an ambulance is a direct indication that you or someone within the family will be ill for a very brief period of time, but will recover. This illness could be the mumps, chicken pox, measles, influenza, or some other illness.

## AMBUSH

To see or to be a part of an ambush within a dream indicates that you will be asked to invest in some worthy project. Although you will not be the only investor in this project, it is revealed that this venture will be both rewarding and gratifying to you. You have an excellent business mind!

## AMNESIA (i.e., loss of memory)

Mockery, criticism, or some form of disrespect will be shown towards you if you have a dream about amnesia. This misunderstanding will not be long-lasting and will probably be solved through common sense reasoning on your part. Be strong in forgiveness, but be greater in forgetting the wrongs done to you.

**AMOEBA** (i.e., one of the simplest animals)

You tend to give up too easily in life, often resigning yourself to an attitude of hopeless despair and self-pity. Commence to see what you can do for others by seriously tuning in to the needs and wants of your fellow man. There are needy people around you at all times; seek ways in which to help them (e.g., volunteer work at a hospital, old age home, or orphanage; be an uncle or aunt at large for a young boy or girl). The small amoeba you dreamed about struggles and cooperates so hard to exist; you, too, should strive equally hard! You should commence to arouse and utilize the usefulness of your spirit rather than hinder your spirit through downhearted attitudes and self-pity.

**AMPUTATION** (see *also* **SURGERY**)

This low-cycle dream unhappily suggests any of the following: sickness, accident, mental or physical collapse, or a suicide attempt may be carried out by someone whom you know. Extreme caution is especially advised when traveling with a vehicle. Carelessness in this matter could bring about serious results! Hopefully, this negative revelation will pass you by unscathed, but in heeding this dream's warning, you are urged to pray—from the very depths of your soul—for the guidance, protection, and safety of yourself and your loved ones!

**AMULET** (see **TALISMAN**)

**ANACONDA** (see **SNAKE**)

**ANATOMY** (i.e., the human body) (see *also* **ANKLE, ARM, ARMPIT, BLOOD, BRAIN, BREAST, BUTTOCK, CHEST, EAR, ELBOW, EYE, EYEBROW, EYELASH, FEET, FORE-HEAD, GENITALS, HAIR, HAND, HEAD, INTESTINE, LEG, MOUTH, NIPPLE, NOSE, SKELETON, STOMACH, TEETH,** or **TOE**)

Seeing the entire human anatomy within a dream infers that you will begin to experience a new outlook on life before too long. Through some good circumstance of events, you will begin to feel an urgency to fulfill some of your better hopes and aspirations. This is a high soul-cycle dream which will augur greater happiness and progress (e.g., completion of one's education, learning through travel, successful marriage, planning a family, good investments).

Seeing a portion, half, or perhaps three-quarters of the human anatomy implies that you tend to be too old-fashioned and unmoved by modern progress. Your actions and feelings seem to belong to another time, a bygone era. Life will continue to move on, no matter how you think or act. You should at least try to belong to that progress. By adopting a more young-at-heart attitude, your colorless, boring life could become more interesting and inspiring. One is never too old to transform; nor is one ever too young to reform!

A disfigured or distorted anatomy suggests you need to exert greater concern and attention where home, business, legal, or health matters are involved. Lack of care in any of these matters could create some untimely discomforts! It is never too late to try to improve and rectify any uncomfortable situations both within and around you.

## ANCESTRY (see BIRTH, FAMILY, FAMILY TREE, or RELATIVE)

## ANCHOR

Dreaming about an anchor infers that you will lead a happy, challenging, and productive life. You are sincere and determined, you have an assured attitude about your single or married status, and your better thoughts and actions are to be praised and encouraged.

## ANESTHETIC

Using or seeing this drug or gas within a dream suggests that you have some latent fears about being sick, feeling pain, or dying. Remember that there isn't a person on this planet who is not living on borrowed time, or who has not been sick in some way, or who has not experienced some form of pain in life. Your basic concern should be to lead a normal, constructive life, accepting your God-given destiny or fate with an open mind, rather than harboring needless phobias and unprofitable anxieties.

## ANGEL (see CELESTIAL or MESSENGER)

## ANGER (see *also* ANNOYANCE or HATRED)

Showing anger within a dream indicates that an undue amount of verbal and mental stress is taking place at home or at work, bringing you much irritability and vexation. Learning to accept some of these difficulties may be fine up to a point, but to continuously live in an atmosphere of unpredictable hostilities is certainly something that should be modified or rectified. If you, the dreamer, are the direct cause of some of these stressful difficulties, then be a little wiser by showing good judgment, calmness, and patience towards those around you. If someone else is the direct cause of this difficulty, then have a heart-to-heart talk with that person, with the sole purpose of bringing about peace. You might be amazed at what a little bit of faith, hope, determination, and forgiveness can do for you!

**ANGUISH** (i.e., excessive pain of body and mind; heartache)

You are mulling over a very important decision in your life but, due to a variety of uncertainties within and around you, it becomes very difficult to let go of old insecurities and hang-ups. Be prepared to be more flexible in your thinking by attuning your mind, heart, and soul towards the decision to be made, think about the positive possibilities, and then think about the negative possibilities where your final answer is concerned. Then, come what may, make your final decision and never look back! Sometimes we make the right decision, and sometimes we make the wrong decision in life; but, whatever happens either way, we must learn to accept ourselves and our losses and gains with courage and sensibility. Perhaps, as you reflect upon this dream symbolism at a later date, you will more than likely be grateful that you made the right decision!

**ANIMAL** (see *also* **ANTELOPE, APE, BEAR, BEAVER, BOBCAT, BULL, CALF, CAMEL, CAT, CATTLE, DEER, DOG, DONKEY, ELEPHANT, FOX, GIRAFFE, GOAT, HOG, HORSE, KANGAROO, LAMB, LION, LLAMA, MAMMOTH, MINK, MOLE, MONGOOSE, MOOSE, MOUSE, OTTER, PET, PLATYPUS, PORCUPINE, RABBIT, RACCOON, RAT, RHINOCEROS, SHEEP, SHREW, SKUNK, SLOTH, SQUIRREL, TIGER, UNICORN, WEASEL, WOLF,** or **ZEBRA**)

Basically, an animal within a dream infers that you are harboring a conscious or subconscious fear, hatred, or love towards that specific animal you happen to see, and/or it infers that you are presently feeling, expressing, or repressing a conscious or subconscious fear, hatred, or love towards yourself, a person, a place, or a thing. For example, a ferocious animal may imply that you are vexed and angered over someone or something; an animal about to attack could imply that someone has attacked your good character; a wounded animal may suggest that you or someone whom you know is not feeling too well.

Seeing a calm animal may suggest a lull before a storm or that some unforeseen events and changes are about to occur in your life. Try to identify or locate your fears, phobias, or hang-ups through your animal dreams. This may be difficult to do at first; but, if you reflect hard enough upon waking up, you may be amazed at how close your animal dreams reveal behavioural characteristics about yourself or about people whom you know.

(*Note*: The above selected animal entries warranted attention because of their symbolic importance within a dream.)

## ANKLE

To dream of an ankle urges you to exercise extreme care where the following are concerned: running, jogging, skipping, hopping, skating, skiing, climbing, surfing, and so on. This symbolism also advises you to be sure-footed on any other type of slippery surface such as a stairway, sidewalk, bathtub, shower bath, road, or other surface. An accident symbolism is shown here, which could result in a sprained or broken ankle, leg, foot, or toe. Note, as well, that the dreamer may also be suffering from some previous ankle injury and/or may be suffering from arthritic pain to the hands, legs, or feet.

## ANNIVERSARY (see CELEBRATION)

## ANNOUNCEMENT

An announcement of any nature signifies good news from a distance either by telephone, telegram, cablegram, letter, or package. This news may relate to any of the following: a birth, a wedding, possibility of travel, acceptance at a school/college/university, a contract, winning of a scholarship, acceptance of employment, some money being sent to you, an inheritance, or other event. Whatever the good tidings may be, you can be sure that you will be very delighted and relieved!

## ANNOUNCER

You are very reliable, energetic, and persistent in life. Demands placed upon you are always met with vigour and are executed to the fullest extent. You have both the magnetism and know-how to choose the friends and happiness you desire in life. Your shrewd, unsentimental actions have saved the day for you on more than one occasion! You may be uncompromising where religion or politics are concerned, but you certainly have a tender and loving heart where family matters are concerned. Your future is quite secure simply because you know yourself very well, and you project a sense of love and duty towards your fellow man.

## ANNOYANCE (see *also* MISCHIEF or PERSECUTION)

This dream symbolism advises you to take stock of your unpredictable, moody nature. Sometimes your verbal and/or physical tantrums go beyond rational sensibility! The fact remains that there is absolutely no need for you to abuse or misuse your high intelligence in this manner. Think twice before you get carried away with any type of anger or hatred. Commence to accentuate the good that is already in you!

## ANT

Dreaming about ants signifies a fear of heights, pain, or loneliness. These fears or phobias could well stem from childhood days or from some recent traumatic experience. These anxieties should be ignored, if possible; otherwise, you will continue to cling to your mind-labeled fears for many years to come. We all dread certain facets and experiences within our life; but, in harbouring our worst fears beyond rational thinking, we tend to hinder our progress, thoughts, and actions. In retrospect, by eliminating your worst fears in life, you will have eliminated your worst stresses in life, as well!

## ANTEATER (see ANIMAL)

## ANTELOPE

Seeing an antelope or herd of antelopes romping or grazing in a valley or field signifies travel or a move to another country, state, or city. This gesture on your part will prove both culturally stimulating and progressively beneficial to you, as time will reveal.

On the other hand, should the antelope or antelopes show fear or are being chased by an enemy, then be prepared for some low-cycle activity around you. In other words, you will commence to experience some low-key happiness, prosperity, and inactivity—which, by the way, you will endure and surmount!

## ANTENNA

Seeing an antenna by itself or on a roof of a building symbolizes your great compassion to serve your fellow man in a positive manner.

You are a unique individual who truly has much to offer, providing you never become too discouraged or indifferent in your chosen profession or goals. In time, your leadership potential may bring you outstanding honour and prestige!

Seeing an aerial on a vehicle, boat, or other form of transport denotes that you are having emotional and financial upsets at home. Less demanding attitudes should be adopted here, with more feelings of gratitude and thankfulness. By showing more strength of maturity and civility during these trials and tribulations you are experiencing, you will ultimately earn the peace and harmony for a better, prosperous future.

## ANTHILL

An anthill symbolizes inner anxieties about being rejected by people around you and about being a failure in life. Well, to begin with, you are not being rejected by others, nor are you a failure in life. In reality, you are making a mountain out of an anthill! This inner turmoil you possess should be rejected as you would a virus; and you can, when you commence to let go of your self-conscious attitudes and doubts about your self-worth. Think positive and you will be positive in all your ideals, actions, and successes in life.

## ANTHOLOGY (see **BOOK**)

## ANTICHRIST

To dream of an antichrist reveals that your wake state will be filled with mixed emotions and hurtful remarks from other people. After having a dream of this nature, it might be advisable to simply stay at home for the day, lock the door, and try to avoid contact with anyone. This, of course, is up to you. If avoiding contact with people is simply impossible for you to do, then grit your teeth and try to maintain a calm, cool, and collected attitude throughout the entire day.

## ANTIDOTE (i.e., a remedy or cure)

Seeing or using an antidote within a dream suggests that some unpleasant fears about life, death, poor health conditions, imagined tragedies, or other worries beset you, from time to time. Those unpleasant fears are some measure of your own insecurities and feelings of being helpless during your mental, physical, or spiritual depressions. This dream is trying to tell you to be very strong whenever you are beset with these troublesome thoughts. In their place, say a prayer or two for "inner peace and comfort". Those unnecessary and unwarranted thoughts should also commence to disappear when you utilize more gratitude, hope, love, goodness, and wisdom in your life (e.g., reading good books, keeping yourself pleasantly busy, being optimistic, getting along with others). You will find the peace of mind you desire, but not necessarily without some holy efforts on your part.

## ANTIQUE

Dreaming of an antique or relic reveals that you possess very strong humane qualities. For example, if someone you know shows prejudice towards other human beings, you quickly make attempts to correct their negative thinking. If someone shows cruelty towards animals in any way, you make your feelings known, so that the person involved will actually commence to think about such negative conduct. It is quite obvious that you love all life and strive in every way possible to make the world around you a more pleasant place in which to live. You have an inner gift; you have the gift of being a peacemaker!

## ANTI-SEMITISM (see GHETTO, HATRED, PERSECUTION, or PREJUDICE)

## ANVIL (i.e., an iron block to hammer metal into shape)

You will have to maintain a more determined outlook in your present position or situation in life. If you allow unscrupulous people to talk and walk all over you, then they will do just that and more! Just as an anvil is hit by a hammer, so you, too, are likened unto an anvil in your dream. This dream is not advising you to be vicious or cruel to anyone; it merely suggests that you take a few positive steps in the right direction. For example, do not always be swayed by the thoughts and actions of others, but reason situations out for yourself; act and do more for yourself; and, finally, speak your mind with sincerity for your own beliefs and truths. All in all, this dream counsels you to be yourself by maintaining more insight and control over your life.

## APARTHEID (see GHETTO, HATRED, PERSECUTION, or PREJUDICE)

## APARTMENT (see *also* LODGING)

Being in an apartment with other people present suggests you are currently undergoing a spiritual uplifting of good will within your life.

Through introspection and meditation, you are slowly beginning to realize that petty jealousies, greed, hatred, or materialistic gains are not the answer to your happiness, but that love, humility, self-sacrifice, and kindness towards your fellow man are the truest measures to fulfill in this lifetime.

If someone or something holds you back from entering an apartment, then you will be successful in your immediate plans or wishes. Do not be disappointed with someone's attempt to discourage you; rather, realize that your determination could very well lead you towards limitless happiness and success!

Seeing an apartment that looks deserted or run-down implies that you will rise over and above your present depression with the help of those around you. Sometimes you have the feeling that your life is nothing more than a big mistake! This is not true! Your basic confidence, hope, and faith will be restored through the kindness and understanding of your family and true friends.

**APATHY** (i.e., indifference)

You tend to feel very restless where recent personal problems are concerned. You must gather your forces together, get your head "back on", and commence to pray and concentrate for better things to happen. Your main goals at this time should be to courageously forge on, no matter what the consequences may be; to live in peace with good intentions; and to shout from the depths of your soul for the harmony, joy, and happiness you so earnestly desire. This earthly life may be short, but we must all try to improve ourselves for a better tomorrow—a better tomorrow that will come through our own perseverance and patience. Be still sometimes, and gather your strength there; pray sometimes, and gather your strength there; and, above all, be grateful sometimes for all that has happened to you in life, and gather your strength there as well, until you are finally heard and guided the rest of your way.

**APE** (e.g., chimpanzee, gorilla, orangutan, gibbon, monkey)

Discontented, disloyal, or unfriendly overtones of thought and action are characterized by you towards someone you know. In either situation where you or this other person is concerned, there is a measure of stubbornness without any thoughts of compromise. This dream urges you to take hold of this situation with a firm grip, and begin to mentally and spiritually discern the harm that is being done—not only to yourself, but to the other person involved, as well. By being less overpowering and overbearing with other people, you may find that your unsatisfied expectations with life and self will slowly begin to be satisfied and fulfilled.

**APOSTLE** (see **BIBLE, DISCIPLE,** or **MISSION**)

**APPAREL** (see **CLOTHES**)

**APPARITION** (see **GHOST** or **PHANTOM**)

**APPENDICITIS** (see **SICKNESS**)

**APPLAUSE**
You take too much for granted! You have yet to discover that you are a very fortunate person who has never really suffered too much in life. Hopefully, your passage in life will remain benevolent and rewarding to you, but you should always remember to be thankful for all your blessings. By having "hope" in your fellow man, "faith" in yourself, and by expressing "charity" where the need is the greatest, you will become more attuned to the supreme part of your being—your soul! Learn to be appreciative for just being you and for being an important, integral part of this vast Universe.

**APPLE** (see **FRUIT**)

**APPLIANCE** (e.g., iron, mixer, toaster, vacuum cleaner) (see *also* **BLENDER, COFFEEPOT, KETTLE, FREEZER,** or **STOVE**)
You may be dealing with someone who is habitually foolish, stubborn, or simply wayward. Some negative habits are very hard to unshackle; but, whoever it is that you are dealing with, you are strongly urged not to nag, annoy, or demand immediate results from this individual. Your philosophic output in this matter appears to be generally wholesome and sound. However, how often does a foolish, stubborn, or wayward person listen to good, sound advice? Be patient and allow this person time to grow up in order to see the rights and wrongs of their ways. Nothing is absolutely hopeless on this earth plane, for we are all God's vehicles, and it is God who will eventually repair the damage, one way or another. Too often people tend to give up on troubled souls, not realizing that they failed to bring God into

*application* *30*

the picture. Prayer, respect, gratitude, and a deep loyalty towards God will always bring results. Remember this well: it is His Will that shall be done—not yours.

**APPLICATION** (see **DOCUMENT**, **QUALIFICATION**, or **RÉSUMÉ**)

**APPOINTMENT** (see **EMPLOYMENT**, **NOMINATION**, **ORDAINMENT**, or **PROMOTION**)

**APPRENTICE** (see **LEARNING**)

**AQUALUNG**
Exercise is advised for you if you happen to dream about an aqualung. Too often you preoccupy yourself with other matters, failing to realize that your body needs special care and attention. Whenever you find yourself bored or depressed, or your body appears "stiff and creaky", so to speak, do some exercise (e.g., go for a long walk, skip, swim). You would be amazed at how much better you will feel, both mentally and physically!

**AQUARIUM**
This dream reveals that a change of attitude is in store for you. By all that is good and glorious, you will commence to see why other people are more happy than you and why they appear to be more successful than you. These happier, successful people do not mope, whine, or procrastinate but are "get-up-and-go" people with specific aims and achievements in mind. Good luck, happiness, and prosperity will come your way when you finally decide to replace your old attitudinal hang-ups with more action, determination, and self-confidence within your daily life.

**ARCHANGEL** (see **CELESTIAL** or **MESSENGER**)

**ARCHBISHOP** (see **CLERGYMAN**)

**ARCHDEACON** (see **CLERGYMAN**)

**ARCHERY** (see **BOWMAN** or **GAME**)

## ARCHITECT

Being or seeing an architect within a dream augurs peace in marriage, blessings with children, and much fulfillment and pleasures in life. Obviously, you are a very deserving person, sharing your spiritual good will, tenderness, and harmony wherever you go. May God continue to enrich your pathway with all the goodness you so admirably merit!

## ARCHWAY

You try very hard to improve your life conditions, but it appears that the harder you try, the worse situations become. Your quest for peace, gratitude, and love are sensible requests or desires, but the missing link is your faith and hope for a better tomorrow. Although you may be on the verge of throwing your hands in the air and giving up, this dream urges you to pray hard, meditate, concentrate, and feel the advent of a better tomorrow coming to you. Believe above anything else that God loves you more than you honestly know, and that He has not abandoned you! Visualize yourself walking down a lonely pathway in order that you might experience and learn the true value of being you, of knowing more about yourself, and finally finding the real "you" emerging knowledgeable and fulfilled, with an inner wisdom no man could possibly take away. The cross you carry is never perpetual; before you know it, the inner and outer battle will cease to exist, resulting in peace and love. Be very patient, be strong, and be willing to fight through your trials and tribulations until you know, beyond any shadow of a doubt, that you are victorious! A hidden door that is closed within your soul will eventually open, giving forth inspirational knowledge and wisdom that you personally cannot perceive at this time. This Cosmic Knowledge and Wisdom is gained only through perseverance, honesty, and—above all—your positive belief that your "bitter" times are just a mere interlude in comparison to the "better" times shown ahead.

## ARENA (i.e., amphitheatre)

Some emotional or verbal exchanges with another person (e.g., spouse, offspring, friend, employer, employee) are strongly revealed by this dream symbolism. If a settlement is not possible at this time, then remain very calm and patient with this individual. This misunderstanding is temporary, and should be solved within a very short period of time.

## ARGUMENT (see CONTRADICTION or QUARREL)

**ARISTOCRAT** (see **NOBLEMAN**)

**ARITHMETIC** (see **MATHEMATICS**)

**ARM**

An arm basically symbolizes strength of character and a willingness to let go of the past for a better, more enriched future. There is no need to dally in one spot when you personally know the horizon is a little brighter just over that hill or mountain. And, it appears that you do move on, both in thought and action, simply because your creative, inventive, and technical mind will not allow you to stifle or stall for long periods of time. Whether in leisure time or work time, you are a person who expresses a great amount of wit, charm, and originality!

Seeing an arm that appears to be pointing in a special direction (e.g., north, south, east, or west) suggests that you will travel in that direction. The journey may be to a village, town, city, state, or country, but you will travel in that direction. The purpose of this journey may involve business, pleasure, or being a participant or spectator in some competitive sport.

Seeing an arm that appears to be mauled or decayed advises you to pay closer attention to your mental and physical well-being. Bad eating habits, coupled with excessive working habits, may be at the crux of your problem. A common sense attitude should be adopted here, otherwise you may regret your neglect in these vital matters.

Seeing an arm covered with worms, slime, bruises, sores, or anything else that appears repulsive to the mind suggests that you will undergo an operation in time to come. Even though this operation may appear traumatic to you, you will survive the ordeal with flying colors!

Seeing an arm covered with paint, chalk, wax, gauze, paper, and so on suggests you can look forward to better days ahead (e.g., love, peace, prosperity, happiness, travel). This "high cycle" dream may have been long overdue, but today will be rather special simply because it will be a new beginning for someone like you—who are very deserving!

**ARMED FORCES** (see **AIR FORCE, ARMY, DRAFTEE, NAVY,** or **OUTPOST**)

**ARMPIT**

Hidden factors in your past may hold you back from expressing yourself fully and completely where sexual matters are concerned. In matters of marriage, "sexual compatibility" may not necessarily be a priority, but it certainly helps in maintaining a fair, satisfying relationship. The roots of your sexual hang-ups may stem from your childhood stages into your puberty stages of development. However, the entire concept of this dream is to advise you to be "levelheaded" with your fears, phobias, and seclusion in this matter. Sometimes people <u>fear</u> the wrong things simply because they choose to <u>remember</u> the wrong things. Nonetheless, there are times when they must mature and accept their God-given abilities with expressive wants and needs, instead of suppressive wants and needs.

Seeing an armpit that is devoid of hair or shaven suggests that you are a well-balanced, mature individual where sexual matters are concerned. Being a levelheaded, understanding individual allows you to cope with certain situations that others would likely not be able to handle. In matters of marriage, your positive attitude could only lead to greater love, peace, and harmony with your chosen mate.

## ARMY (see *also* BATTALION, BRIGADE, or CADET)

You are commencing to project an avid concern about the welfare of your planet when you dream about an army. Reading about or witnessing the many tragic misunderstandings, contradictions, and failures of people to communicate in a peaceful, loving, brotherly way makes you wonder just what on earth is happening to mankind! Will there ever be lasting peace, joy, and comfort for you and others like you who wish only peace and good fellowship? What can you do, at least, to try to assist mankind in understanding the folly of needless battles and the use of destructive weaponry? Pray for the sinners of this world, for they are truly in a deep mire and must come out of their tragic state; pray for the warmongers to stop their insatiable desires to create havoc, pain,and long-lasting hell on earth; pray for the peacemakers, so that they may humbly win their battle against the Godless foe; and, finally, pray for the guidance and protection of all your loved ones. Until mankind sees the Hand of God take over to finally eradicate the evil forces that do exist, the meek, loving souls of this planet must continue their vigil with hope, faith, and prayer.

## ARREST (i.e., being apprehended by a legal authority, or citizen's arrest)

Being arrested within a dream suggests that someone or a group of people will tempt you into doing something that is illegal or something totally bizarre and out of character. Be wary of bad company! By keeping on the right track of life, you will be sure-footed in life. Someday you may perform a valorous deed which will bring you much praise and honour!

**ARROW** (see *also* **ARROWHEAD**)

If the arrow you see is pointed in a horizontal direction, then you can be sure you will do an inestimable amount of learning and travel in your lifetime. This wonderful opportunity will bring you the joy and happiness that you rightfully deserve!

Should the arrow be pointed in a skyward direction, then you can be sure that your immediate hopes and plans will be fulfilled. There may be a brief waiting period for you in this regard, but the end results will prove to be both inspiring and beneficial to your future.

Should the arrow be pointed in a downward direction, then be advised that someone rather close to you has some serious reservations about your honesty and integrity. It seems that you were contradictory about something, and/or you were not practicing what you were preaching, which consequently upset this person. Maybe you were not quite justified in doing what you did, but everyone has a right to change their mind freely from time to time.

**ARROWHEAD**

Seeing an arrowhead within a dream is always an auspicious sign, especially where spiritual awareness and attunement to the higher elements of life are concerned. You obviously are becoming more psychically or mystically aware about the seen or unseen forces around you. In time, you should be able to walk into a room with the ability to sense the good or bad elements present. With this level of sensitivity, you should consider meditation from time to time; it will assist you with your ability. The gift of prophecy should never be treated lightly. Always remember that this sixth sense awareness should be used wisely, humbly, and with thankfulness.

(*Note*: You may also have the pleasure of knowing that if, for example, you are experiencing a very negative dream but at the very end of your dream sequence or anywhere during your dream sequence you happen to see an arrowhead, then this arrowhead symbolism takes precedence over your entire negative dream. Consequently, you have nothing to worry about, simply because the arrowhead acts as a "buffer zone" to anything negative within a dream.)

**ARSONIST** (i.e., a person who sets fire to buildings, etc.; a pyromaniac)

To see or to be an arsonist within a dream reveals that you are a very troubled individual (e.g., this could be emotional, spiritual, physical) You appear to lack the willpower, direction, and know-how as to what to do or where to go to assess your problem and/or be assisted in your dilemma. You will never be assisted unless you are totally honest with yourself and are willing to tell the truth to someone who may be in a position to help you, such as a clergyman or doctor. Your dream has attempted to assist you by telling you to improve your ways, turn over a new leaf, and begin to harmonize with life around you.

**ARTIFICIAL RESPIRATION** (see **RESUSCITATION**)

**ARTIST** (see **DRAFTSMAN, ILLUSTRATOR, MUSICIAN, PAINTER, SCULPTOR,** or **STUDIO**)

**ASHES**

Someone whom you are attempting to teach, assist, or respect does not appear to believe in your abilities, intelligence, or sincerity. Do not panic! Continue your fine work and assistance, and you will soon see a miraculous change within that individual. There are many routes to take in order to reach the heart, mind and soul of a person. In your case, you must continue to be strong with your faith and convictions in order to prove your worth and purpose to those around you. The end results will prove that you are not only an excellent teacher or helper, but a true friend, as well!

**ASSASSIN** (see **EVILDOER, KILL,** or **MURDER**)

**ASSASSINATION** (see **KILL** or **MURDER**)

**ASSEMBLAGE** (see **CONFERENCE, CONVENTION, CROWD,** or **MEETING**)

**ASSISTANCE** (e.g., to help or lend a hand, give charity aid)

Receiving or giving assistance within a dream signifies that your future looks active, harmonious, and prosperous providing you maintain an optimistic outlook on life. Although storms may hinder you now and then, these obstacles can be overcome with responsibility, self-sacrifice, and loyalty towards those whom you love and appreciate. You are a strong-willed individual who knows about the hardcore realities of life; yet, come what may, you are willing to plod onwards without looking back. You are a fine example of a human being who deserves sound spiritual progress, the highest form of happiness, and ultimate respect for your persistence and generous attitude.

## ASTEROID

Are you destined to do very well in your lifetime? Will you be successful and happy in spite of your hardships and struggles? The answer to all this and more is a resounding yes! This auspicious dream reveals fulfillment and mastery in your endeavours through compassion for your fellow man; the utilization of your God-given inspiration and talents for the good of everyone concerned; and the sharing of your mature ideas and actions with philosophical insight. You have much to offer your fellow man, and your fellow man accepts you wholeheartedly; but, in this world of greed, jealousies, and false promises, you must never forget that the Source of All Good comes from the Christ-Light which abides in each and every one of us. The more good you do upon this planet, the greater this Light becomes. It acts like a cresset, guiding you and others less fortunate than yourself through the highways and byways of life. Also, as you rise over and above your pit of loneliness and despair to reach out to some luckless soul who appears to need your Light, your words of encouragement, and your love and understanding, then inner peace and the virtue of charity will be revealed to you.

## ASTROLOGY (see *also* HOROSCOPE)

This dream shows that your immediate desires or aims will not be fulfilled to your precise specifications. By waiting patiently and learning to control your rash decisions, you will discover that a better future awaits you. Through this "wait and see" process, you will gain more decisive maturity, independence, and perceptivity about yourself and about life in general. But, do not expect too much change in your style of living if you persist in trying to climb a mountain from its summit instead of its base.

## ASTRONAUT (see SPACEMAN)

## ASTRONOMY

You are a person who shows much truth, inventiveness, and stability. You deplore any type of negativity simply because you realize this type of action is both idiotic and senseless! This dream reveals that you can look forward in doing some humanitarian work. It is here that your sincere thoughts and actions will affect people in a remarkable way!

## ASYLUM (see INSANITY or REFUGE)

## ATHEIST (i.e., a person who believes that there is no God)

Being or seeing an atheist within a dream reveals that you appear to be too selfishly opinionated in life. You strive much too hard to be the center of attention; hence, you lose the respect and confidence of others around you. This attitude is a sure-fire guarantee on how to lose friendships without really trying! You can, however, repair your actions by simply giving others a chance to speak and a chance to share an idea or two with you. You must learn to be more flexible and understanding in the realization that people with whom you associate have good, sound ideas, too!

## ATHLETE

Your groundless fears about your present or future successes or failures are not conducive to a better sense of judgment. Of course you will rise over and above your greatest obstacles, depressions, or rejections in life, but always remember that your greatest moment of weakness should also be your greatest moment of strength! Why even bother to worry about tomorrow when today has barely begun? Go forth in life, cheerful and realistic, knowing that you will have your share of success and failure, no matter who you are or what you do. It is these sweet and bitter scenarios of life which actually build your character with self-confidence, self-control, and self-discovery.

## ATLAS

You are headed towards a decision-making storm in your life. However, when your inner and outer battle is finally victorious in this matter, you will begin to perceive a greater tomorrow. Your past and present dreams, hopes, and wishes have been stifled and shattered many times, thus making it almost impossible for you to share your talents, knowledge, or expertise properly and proficiently. This new beginning will at last give you the liberty to know yourself and to express yourself.

## ATOMIC BOMB

You are likened unto a person who, upon occasion, gets into a boat with one oar and simply goes around in circles! You will create displeasure in your lifetime—not only for yourself, but for others as well—unless you maintain a more diligent approach to your wants and needs in life. At times, you do what you emphatically say you will never do; at times you emphatically say you will do something special, but this, too, never appears to transpire. Much too often, you are deceived by your emotional wants and needs versus your realistic wants and needs. The change you need must come from within you, not from outside the portals of your heart, mind, and soul. Your dream's revelation is trying to show you the way to achieve more inner happiness, peace, comfort, and stability.

## ATTACHE CASE (see BRIEFCASE)

## ATTACK (see ANGER, FIGHT, HATRED, INVASION, or PERSECUTION)

## ATTIC

You appear to be carrying the weight of this world upon your shoulders, with hopeless feelings that there is no one to turn to in your hour of need. There is Someone very special who has been waiting to hear from you for quite some time! This dream counsels you to unshackle your troubles and woes by placing your hope, faith, and strength totally upon God. So often in difficult times, we earthlings fail to put our complete trust and belief in His Love and Care. You will be looked after in ways that you could not dream possible when you finally accept God with the simple innocence, purity, and faith as that of a child. Remember, your life can be filled with prosperity, hope, and love, providing you become move observant to your true "soul" needs instead of your doubtful "mind" needs.

## AUCTION

Your keen sense of judgment tells you immediately what is right or wrong, and your instinctive timing should always place you in the right place at the right time. You are slated to go through some good and some unpleasant occurrences within your lifetime; however, you will always express a deep strength and sureness, which others will appreciate and admire.

## AUDIENCE

Seeing or mingling with an audience implies that you are a very strong-willed individual, quite capable of thinking and doing more for yourself "your way" than that of another person. This is not to imply that you would not heed the advice of another person; you simply find it more expedient to think and to do things in your own way and in your own time. You also realize that you would have nobody else to blame for your mistakes but yourself. You are basically a no-nonsense type of person who appreciates the good, realistic sensibilities around you. This dream also infers that you could be very successful in some new business venture, should you decide to go this route.

## AUDITORIUM

Do not be too vexed when matters around you appear to be confusing, boring, or exhausting. This dream infers that matters pertaining to the heart will be mastered and solved with aplomb (e.g., marriage, romance, career, education, spiritual peace). This dream also suggests that you have to work exceedingly hard for anything that you want in life. However, when you actually do achieve the final product of your sweat, toil, and initiative, you also appreciate the intrinsic value and importance of having done something from scratch to finish. Your belief in self has proven to you over and over again that, sooner or later, your aims or goals do become a reality!

## AUNT

If you dream about an aunt who is alive on this earth plane, then consider your dream as an exchange of love, warmth, and deep feelings towards her. Note, as well, that your aunt may be thinking or dreaming about you as you dreamt about her. By coincidence, you may also be meeting, writing, or talking to your aunt before too long. The adage that good minds think alike certainly may be applicable here!

Dreaming about an aunt who has passed away strongly advises you to say a prayer for her. She has come to you for some reason; respond by showing an expression of love and kindness towards her through thought and prayer. Remember, people on the other side of life require prayers and loving thoughts just as we do! As well, do not forget to tell her to "ask for the Light"!

## AURA (See AUREOLE)

**AUREOLE** (i.e., a phenomenal light emanation that surrounds a person or thing; a halo)

You have made some quantum leaps in maturity over the past several years. It appears that your many experiences and hardships during this period of time have taught you to become more patient, understanding, and compassionate towards all things around you. You have become move attuned to your inner and outer self with remarkable insight and fortitude! You will continue to flourish in this mental, physical, and spiritual manner for many years to come.

**AURORA BOREALIS** (i.e., Northern Lights)

You will always be fascinated by the so-called mysteries of life. This could involve ancient writings, drawings, or artifacts about past civilizations; U.F.O. landings or sightings on earth; man's outer space explorations; learning more about life after death, and so on. This world is full of seen and unseen mysteries (e.g., Bermuda Triangle, Easter Island, Black Forest, hauntings) which appear to defy scientific logic; nonetheless, they do exist. Your interest and quest in these matters are most sincere and wholesome. Who knows—maybe you will unlock a phenomenal mystery or two in your lifetime. Why not? You certainly are endowed with an analytical, searching mind.

**AUTHOR**

Being or seeing an author within a dream implies that you have great ambitions or latent desires to become worldly successful. This could imply being an author, doing some other great work in the creative arts, and/or doing some great inventive or scientific work to assist your fellow man. Of course, to climb the ladder of fame, you have to be prepared for hard work, sweat, and tears all the way. In any event, this dream emphatically reveals that you actually can become known and successful, providing you are ready, willing, and able to devote your time and energy unselfishly towards your inspired and mighty goal.

**AUTHORESS** (see **AUTHOR**)

**AUTOBIOGRAPHY**

Seeing an autobiography that is clear, concise, and neatly written infers that you are neglecting to do something that can bring you more peace of mind, such as paying a long overdue debt, completing some unfinished work at home or at work, apologizing to someone for something you said or did, and so forth. Whatever it is that you are neglecting to do, this dream symbolism is merely trying to instill some positive action on your part. Hopefully, your adherence to this matter will bring you the peace and comfort you so richly deserve.

On the other hand, seeing an autobiography that is not clear, concise, and neatly written suggests that, although you are an interesting and intelligent individual, you often fail to carry out your better hopes and wishes. A lack of self-confidence and a lack of money appear to be the two major setbacks in your life. In both cases, you must maintain an optimistic outlook through your hardships before you can commence to see better days ahead. Feeling hopeless in anything will merely prolong your agony; feeling hopeful will bring about new changes, both within and around you.

## AUTOGRAPH

Autographing a book, an album, a piece of paper, and so on reveals an improvement in your financial and emotional state of affairs. Your fear of being financially defeated for some reason or other should be tossed aside. In its place, concentrate more optimistically on your well-being. Even if you do lose or fail in something from time to time, do not feel that you are washed-up or unsuccessful. On the contrary! The greatest losers can become the greatest winners if they choose to do so. However, they must first discard their attitudinal fears and self-pity and adopt more worthy traits, such as positive determination and self-confidence.

## AUTOMOBILE (see CAR)

## AUTOPSY

Seeing an autopsy of a person or animal cautions you to pay special attention to any health problems that you may be experiencing. If you are experiencing persistent physical pain for some reason or other, then you are advised to seek medical attention. In seeking this attention, you will have gained the satisfaction and peace of mind that everything is all right. Should the problem be a bit more serious, hopefully some medication or a common operative procedure will repair the damage.

## AUTUMN (see SEASON)

## AVALANCHE (see *also* LANDSLIDE)

This dream urges you to try to assist a family member who has caused you and other members of your family much hardship and grief (e.g., drugs, alcohol, negative attitude). Do not give up on this individual! Several members of your family could perhaps get together on this matter to persuade this individual to seek professional guidance. He or she may not listen at first; however, if enough words of encouragement are spoken by you and others around you, then rest assured that some positive action and changes will take place. It would be such a great pity and waste should this member of the family fail to receive the help required. A much better future is revealed for this member when he/she decides to mend the error of his/her ways.

## AWARD (see MEDAL or PRIZE)

## AWNING

Make the best of what you have today in spite of your whims, notions, wants, and needs. Tomorrow is another day, with perhaps another outlook and another realization that you are a lot more fortunate than you could possibly realize. Even the angels know about your truest needs. Understand, however, that the simplest things in life are by far the greatest things in life! Someday soon, or perhaps someday far away, you will have some of your fondest wishes realized. First, though, you must learn to work for and wait for those earthly and spiritual blessings.

## AXE (see *also* HATCHET)

In reading books, magazines, or newspapers of a "doom and gloom" nature, you have created a fixation of fear about your future. Your fears are about world problems, such as brother against brother, nation against nation, and the possibility of man destroying all life upon the face of this globe. It is true that various backward nations will not change their warmonger attitudes immediately. But, for a moment or two, let us at least give credence to those positive nations and union of peacemakers who do strive for world harmony. Be strong, faithful, and thankful to God that you are able to share some of your knowledge, goodness, and kindness with others around you. Tomorrow will come, and the future will come, with its world tranquility, as men of past centuries have prophesied. But, first mankind must rebuild each nation with a God-like framework of peace and love. War, the axe of Hell, is not the way to peace, and if the Laws of God are continuously defied, then it is the souls of the barbaric warmongers who will suffer in the end. Then, at last, the meek will inherit the earth!

**BABBLE** (i.e., making meaningless sounds like a baby)

Babbling in your dream is a symptom that you are not being comforted by those whom you love in life. There appears to be a disunion in communication and understanding with your family at this time; and it is not for lack of trying on your part. First, avoid anxieties by keeping your mind and heart centered upon the positive things in life and by feeling an inner fixity of thought towards God. Ask for His help, and believe implicitly that His help will come. The missing link in this entire matter is a lack of spiritual love, kindness, and forgiveness by those who have misjudged you and who conceivably abused your better intentions towards them. Do not give up or resign yourself to a fate of defeat, as this loveless state you are presently experiencing is a learning phase for you as well as for those who have done you wrong. Showing gratitude for the grace that God will eventually bring you and your loved ones will augment the peace and tranquility which you all rightfully deserve!

**BABOON** (see **APE**)

**BABY**

You can give a big sigh of relief when you dream about a baby. This good sign augurs much contentment and happiness for you. Your immediate difficulties where school, employment, or home life conditions are concerned will improve beyond your wildest hopes!

**BABY CARRIAGE**

This is a classic "good luck" dream! If you are a young girl or unmarried woman who happens to dream about a baby carriage, then you can expect a rich and wholesome marriage in time to come. If a young boy or man dreams of a baby carriage, then he can look forward to a successful, professional career. Being married and dreaming of a baby carriage indicates a financial upswing in your present state of affairs.

**BABY SITTER**

Being a baby sitter or seeing a baby sitter within a dream intimates your great impatience to have things happen suddenly and quickly in your life. In other words, when you set your mind on something, you simply cannot bear to wait to consummate your better wishes or desires (e.g., purchases, travel, romance). Anything wished or hoped for, or anything accomplished upon this earth, takes time; you must learn to accept this simple fact. By using emotional judgment instead of mental foresight, you readily place yourself in a mental, spiritual, or financial bind. You simply cannot have everything you see, nor can you hope to achieve any sound happiness, by forcing your wishes upon someone who chooses to wait for some reason or other. In order to gain more peace of mind, success, and future happiness, you must be more patient with yourself and with others. Strive to understand the inner needs of others, and don't offend those who honestly care about you. Basically, you are a wonderful person, but you must learn to curb your strong desires to have everything your way or no way at all!

## BACHELOR

You can look forward to a busy year ahead if you dream of a bachelor whom you know. You will be called upon, perhaps on more than one occasion, to give some sound advice to people who respect and think highly of your good judgment (e.g., lecture, symposium, conference). Your concern for the welfare of others is most sincere. Normally, you never impose your authority, nor do you impart knowledge to others unless you are asked to do so.

## BACKACHE

Experiencing a backache within a dream could very well imply that you are having back pains while asleep! However, if this is not the case, then this symbolism advises you to be very cautious throughout the week. There are strong indications here that you could fall off a roof or a ladder; you could fall down a flight of stairs; or you could fall on a slippery sidewalk, road, and so on. By being careful and sure-footed and heeding this warning, you may totally avert an accident, thus saving yourself much anguish and needless pain.

## BACON

To see bacon in its raw state implies you will be facing difficult emotional times ahead, with little or no reprieve forthcoming unless you are willing to change. Some people admire you for what you are; however, they also avoid you for the same reason, especially your forceful domination over them. You cannot buy friendships; nor should you impose your authority over others. The sooner you disband some of these negative "quirks", the better off you will be.

Seeing cooked bacon reveals confusion and total shock where the actions of a loved one are concerned. Anger and spite will not solve this problem! What is required, at this time, is a deep-felt understanding towards your loved one, with a willingness on your part to uplift this troubled soul. This problem should be solved in time, but you must be strong and willing to accept the consequences concerning some past moments or lost moments which should have been shared with this family member. Be patient and calm; and, above all, maintain your determination to bring about a more loving, ideal tomorrow.

**BADGE** (see **SYMBOL**)

**BAG** (i.e., paper bag) (see *also* **SACK**)
You are inclined to feel envious of a friend, a neighbour, or simply anyone who happens to be more prosperous than you. This form of thinking obviously stems from your earlier years. You know better, but you fail to think better! The crux of your problem is that you have centered your life style towards materialistic gain, not realizing that your soul is what really counts here, today and forever. How can you correct your mode of thinking? Well, for a start, begin to search within your being for the real you—the positive you that exists now. By praying, asking, and demanding for the correct values of your heart, mind, and soul to come forth with God's Love, you will commence to realize that your jealousies will cease to exist. You will at last come out of your mind's imprisonment and arrive at a greater place known as self-improvement and self-realization.

**BAGGAGE** (e.g., luggage, suitcase, trunk)
You yearn to change your present position in life. It appears that, no matter how hard you try, you do not feel the happiness, contentment, or achievement you would hope to accomplish on this earth plane. Your activities are diverse and, because you scatter your thoughts and actions in so many directions, it appears you get lost in a void and never really accomplish that one specific goal you have in mind. Sometimes, you feel you would like to move entirely away from the tedious work and the daily, monotonous routine you have thus far accepted. Perhaps a trip or an inspired change would balance the hum-

drum activities of your existence. Remember: it is up to you to make your life as interesting—or as dull—as you allow it to be. Give yourself some extra time and space to do what you want to do, rather than becoming bored and robotic with the pressures of life around you.

## BAGPIPE (see INSTRUMENT)

## BAKER

You should pay more heed to your food habits. According to this dream symbolism, you do not take care of your body and mind as properly as you should. Good food habits, some exercise, and strong-mindedness to uphold these good intentions will make you a happier person.

## BAKERY

Before too long, you will meet a person who will attempt to befriend you. However, it is revealed that this person may or may not meet up to your standards as a friend. This dream, on the surface, does not appear to be too important at this stage; however, as time goes by, it will be vitally important for you to be aware of some hurtful outcome, should you decide to go into this friendship. You will be able to recognize this individual by his or her habitual cynicism towards people, places, and things.

## BALCONY

A balcony with people on it reveals you show strong love and solidarity within your home life. You share a spirit of firmness and understanding with your immediate family, thus making life for those around you more meaningful and thankful.

A balcony devoid of people implies that you have a tendency, from time to time, to stretch the truth. You can resist this temptation only through your willingness to think twice before saying something that is not necessarily true or reliable. The result of any falsehood is always distasteful. Perhaps the only way to shock yourself into believing this fact is to hear yourself a bit more closely when you add bits and pieces of fantasy to an otherwise true story or statement.

Seeing yourself or someone else fall off a balcony implies that you will be confronted and humiliated at a gathering by someone whom you know. This disturbing event may lead to other ramifications unless apologies are made quickly or unless distance separates you and your agitator.

## BALDNESS

You have great fears of being a disappointment to people around you. However, people around you do not feel this way at all! You strive too hard to be accepted. Consequently, you tend to disappoint yourself with your own actions, thoughts, and basic insecurities. If you ease up a bit and try to adopt a more natural, calm, or relaxed state of mind in these matters, the fears you feel and express will automatically dissipate.

## BALL

To see, to throw, or to pitch a ball implies that you often expound and act in a very unrealistic manner. You have the capacity to tease a person into believing you are someone you are not. Playing with other people's emotions can in time have dire consequences for you. This symbolism advises you to take stock of your actions and mannerisms now, or you may be negatively stigmatized by others. This could unduly harm your position and standing in life.

## BALLERINA

Dreaming of being a ballerina means that you have the ability to excel in fields such as the following: dancer, singer, model, fashion designer, writer, sculptor. Your artistic temperament merely adds to your make-up as a person gifted in the arts. Hard work, perseverance, and a positive outlook can lead you to the very heights in any one or two of the above-mentioned or related fields.

## BALLET

Seeing a ballet performance wherein the performers are dressed in beautifully coloured costumes (except black costumes) intimates that you are headed towards more peaceful and prosperous times. Your remarkable ability to weather the bad times with a strong heart and a good disposition and your great willingness to make others smile and laugh in spite of your trials and tribulations are most commendable!

Ballet dancers dressed in black forewarns you of a possible accident with an automobile, plane, or train, and/or a great misadventure with fire. This warning can be totally averted if you are explicitly discerning in where and how you travel within the next several weeks or so. As well, show great caution and action, if necessary, in improving any fire hazards within your home. Showing prudence here can make a world of a difference to you.

**BALLOT** (see **VOTE**)

**BALLOON**

An array of coloured balloons (except the black balloon) predicts an upgrade in your employment stature after you take an academic or technical course. You will be both proud and happy by the decision you make regarding this matter.

Seeing a black balloon suggests that you are treading on someone's personal business. This could lead to serious ramifications. While you are still ahead of the game, you are strongly advised to "back off" before trouble, not at all to your liking, ensues.

**BANANA** (see **FRUIT**)

**BANDAGE**

This symbolism implies that you may be duped into signing a contract, a will, or a document which you may have second thoughts about later. If someone literally badgers you into signing something you are not sure about, then hold back and think twice! There may be future repercussions that would involve certain legalities—at your expense—to undo the wrong you may be cajoled into doing.

**BANDIT** (see **CRIMINAL** or **THIEVERY**)

**BANISHMENT**

To be banished, exiled, or deported suggests that you are vexed or troubled over some venture you are presently undertaking. The end results can be enlightening, but first get rid of your hopeless thoughts about this venture. This dream reveals overall success ahead for you, but you must be willing to make it happen! Do not dwell on the negative aspects of this venture; think, instead, of the higher spirit of your being mastering your present state of depression. Right now your feelings should be centered upon prayer, trust, hope, and faith in self and in your Creator's willingness to see you through this trying time. Nothing is impossible to you, providing you utilize the highest measure of your being with confidence and unbroken concentration!

**BANJO**

Your hopes and aspirations in devoting your time to the music profession or to some other artistic endeavour may be totally thwarted due to your present obligations and commitments, such as home life, business, other educational interests, and other obligations. In time, your hopes may be realized, but perhaps on a lesser scale.

## BANK

Walking into a bank portends a loss in some business venture or some investment that looks very promising. Be exceedingly careful at this time not to commit yourself to some long-range business project or some other enticing investment(s).

Walking out of a bank, on the other hand, indicates an improved financial state is in store for you. You can breathe a little easier now simply because you appear to be on the verge of better and more prosperous times!

## BANKRUPTCY

You are scattering your mental and physical forces in all directions without really attaining your special goal in life. You have so many things you would like to do, but you fail to focus on that one goal! First of all, slow down, sit back, and commence to think very seriously on how you can map your way out of the detours in which you have placed yourself. Then gently come out of your maze of thoughts and actions with new hope, vigor, and foresight. This dream offers you hope—hope to reestablish yourself with courage, persistence, and a greater command of self. You deserve more happiness and success in life. Attaining it, however, depends upon your willingness to change.

## BANNER (see FLAG or NEWSPAPER)

## BANQUET

Attending a banquet whereby people appear to be mocking you, laughing, or joking in hilarious tones implies that a friend may turn against you through spite or sudden hatred. This indignity will hurt you deeply. If your forgiveness is greater than your pride, this friendship will continue. If, however, your forgiveness is weaker than your pride, then this friendship will cease to exist.

Being at a banquet where people appear to be sad or weeping implies that it is very difficult for you to refuse someone a favor. One of the kindest gestures a person can do is to help other people. However, having friends who constantly demand some service from you is another matter! Be honest and firm with people who assume that your time is more valuable to them than it should be to yourself. If they are true friends, they will understand; if they are not true friends, then consider yourself very fortunate to have discovered this fact now instead of much later!

## BAPTISM

To see or to be a part of this ceremony is a very auspicious dream. Inner peace and harmony, communication with interesting people, travel, adventure, and plenty of good luck are in the offing for you. All this is well deserved. You have had your share of bitterness and toil! You show honesty and integrity and always try to beam your light of encouragement upon less fortunate people. Your friendliness and love towards your fellow man is an inspiration for all to accept, cherish, and follow. We should thank God for miracles—and we should also thank Him for people like you!

**BARBELL** (i.e., a metal bar with adjustable weights at each end used for weight lifting exercises)

Merely seeing a barbell within a dream indicates you are very displeased with a person's persistent need to tell you all his or her intimate problems. This does not imply that you are not kindhearted or sympathetic to this person's needs, but you sense that you are being used as a leaning post for this person's "ills and pills" in life. This dream counsels you to be gentle but firm with this individual in suggesting that professional help (e.g., clergy, doctor, psychologist) be sought.

Lifting a barbell intimates that it is very difficult for you to face certain facts of life (e.g., sickness, death, failure). There comes a time in everyone's life whereby we must all contend with various inevitable situations. We may not always like what we experience on this earth plane, but these are facts of life we simply have to accept. You cannot continually run away from a world that is literally filled with "veiled elements" we must all, in some way, forge through. There is not a living creature on this planet who is not affected by some struggle, which supposedly is either won or lost! Always face life with thankfulness in spite of your pain, your struggles, and your anxieties. Someday you may reflect back and realize that, in reality, you were always victorious because of your persistence and faith.

Dropping a barbell implies that you expect too much perfection from others around you. No two beings are alike on earth; what appears to be very simple and adequate for you to perform may not necessarily be as easy for another person. Your expectations of others are much too high. This often leaves you in a state of confusion, depression, and rejection. Bear in mind that nobody is perfect on earth. Even you make mistakes! The important thing is to never be afraid to admit that you are imperfect in something or to make a mistake once in a while, for this, too, is good for the mind and soul! We all learn from our mistakes, as we continue on our way to self-improvement.

## BARBERSHOP (see *also* HAIR or HAIRCUT)

Entering a barbershop implies that your immediate health and financial state of affairs will take a turn for the better.

Leaving a barbershop indicates new opportunities, goals, and achievements are in store for you. You will succeed at what you are presently doing. Moreover, a "new way" will be shown to you so that you can improve upon the venture you are now undertaking.

## BARBWIRE

As hard as you try to progress, the results sometimes appear futile and depressing in areas, for example, such as money problems, illness, lack of friendships, being forced to move, and other changes. This dream informs you that, whatever your problem(s) may be, you will eventually come out of this low state. However, you must make further spiritual contact through prayer. Express your inner needs for contentment, and believe that what you are praying for will be fulfilled sooner or later. You are likened unto a person who now sees the brightest array of stars in the deepest valley and who, in some strange way, is being shown a route on earth towards enlightened wisdom and understanding.

## BARGAIN (see NEGOTIATION)

## BARMAID

You can expect better harmony within your home life if you see or if you are a barmaid within a dream. This symbolism gives promise of better understanding, compromise, and love with your immediate family members.

## BARN

You are advised to be exceedingly cautious throughout the week that you dream about a barn. The accident or injury symbolism shown here points to carelessness in driving a vehicle, or experiencing some malfunction or flaw within a vehicle; this may lead to an accident. The dream also warns you against possibly being very absent-minded when you are walking, running, jogging, repairing, or doing something which may lead to an injury. By having one's vehicle professionally examined and by being prudent and alert in your other affairs, you will be successful in preventing an accident or injury.

## BARNYARD

An eventual move from your present location is indicated by seeing a barnyard with an animal or two present. You may be happy where you are presently living now, but an offer of better employment elsewhere could make a change of residence much more attractive to accept.

Seeing a barnyard devoid of any animals reveals that you need space to think things over concerning some past or present events. It appears as though you are being forced to make a sudden decision which may or may not be to your satisfaction. This symbolism strongly urges you to bring peace to yourself and others by simply compromising and by not being upset over some possible losses involving materialistic gain (e.g., inheritance, sibling rivalry over some property, losses pertaining to some bad investment).

## BAROMETER

You have experienced many weather changes in your life. This dream reveals that you can change like the wind, as well. Your disregard for other peoples' feelings may put you in a complete category all by yourself. Sarcasm, derision, and anger directed at others is no way to achieve understanding and good fellowship! You have created enemies. Cool it! One's time on this earth plane is far too short to be bitter and hotheaded. Your time should be spent doing good upon this planet. You have so much good in you begging to come through your being; however, this can only happen when you are ready, willing, and able to open the portals of your mind to this fact.

## BARREL

A pleasant family reunion is revealed if you dream of seeing a barrel. There will be many happy moments at this reunion, with many positive surprises involving some family members (e.g., birth, marriage, travel, education).

Hiding in or behind a barrel intimates that you will hear some very disheartening news about a friend's announcement of a divorce. This news will be very shocking and difficult to believe for days to come!

## BARTENDER

The things you tell one person may not be the same story you tell another person. This kind of behaviour can lead to some very embarrassing moments, if it is not curbed. The more you yield to the temptations of bragging or falsifying facts, the worse off you will be. Try to think, act, and speak in a positive, constructive way. By eliminating your false pride in these matters, you will discover that you will have more freedom to do what is right and just within your life.

Seeing a child as a bartender implies that a young member of your family is endowed with a very brilliant mind. This young member may one day be well-known in some chosen profession (e.g., science, medicine, law, cinema, television, sports). One thing is certain: you will be very proud of this family member in time to come!

## BASEBALL (see GAME)

## BASEMENT

Your inherent knowledge and patience will continue to serve you well in life. Your intuitive feelings, which appear to be phenomenally accurate, have allowed you to assist others in their time of need. Sometimes you are misunderstood by those who assume to know you. However, with your fine attunement and possible mediumship capabilities, you have overcome these minor difficulties rather well! You are slated for many great moments and events within your life. Perhaps only you and God are capable of comprehending these. You are, indeed, a wise soul!

## BASIN

Employment changes and financial improvements are ahead for you if you see a basin within a dream. These auspicious changes should allow you to pay off some of your old debts and even allow you to take a long-awaited trip or two.

A broken basin, however, advises you to prepare yourself for some unforeseen events which can take you by surprise. This dream is not a happy one; it reveals sickness, injury, or death to an elderly person you know. Hopefully, through prayer and positive thinking, this entire "dark cloud" symbolism will pass by quickly without fulfilling its prophecy.

## BASKET

Seeing an empty basket within a dream suggests that ill health may befall you and/or a close member of your family. This health problem will be solved through prompt medical attention.

A basket full of food, fruit, or anything else reveals that you should disengage your emotional outbursts and learn to show more gratitude towards people who honestly care about you. By embarrassing those close to you in public places, you are lowering yourself to a state of selfish immaturity. Since you are highly intelligent but somewhat spoiled in your own way and fashion, you would be wise do some serious introspection on how you can improve your ways. Then simply follow your "good" rules with the God-given maturity you were always meant to utilize!

## BAT (i.e., a flying mammal)

You will be asked to give a lecture and/or participate in some event. However, you will apparently refuse to do so. Circumstances, being what they are at this time, would make it very unwise to take part in this public or social event. Have no regrets; you will have made the right decision.

## BATH (i.e., shower bath, steam bath, sun bath, whirlpool bath, etc.)

Difficulties that arise from time to time will always be solved through common sense, a certain amount of wit, and a bit of foresight. This dream also suggests that you have a very imaginative mind which occasionally places you in a mental or spiritual turmoil. Unbecoming visions or imaginings of the mind tend to make you very nervous and uncomfortable. Many times, you do not really know who or where to turn to for help during these traumatic moments. Turn to prayer and good, wholesome, inspirational books—and you will slowly come out of this low soul-cycle state with flying colours!

## BATHROOM (see *also* OUTHOUSE)

You are cautioned not to pay heed to any hearsay about a very close friend. You know and trust this friend. Should someone come to you and attempt to degrade your friend, either through jealousy or spite, simply ignore the statements made. Petty gossip is not really your style, so you should be able to handle this situation rather admirably.

**BATHTUB** (See **BATHROOM**)

**BATTALION** (i.e., a large group of soldiers ready for battle)
There appears to be a lack of understanding and communication between you and a parent. This dream does not reveal which parent you are having difficulties with, but it strongly emphasizes that you reconsider your stand or position in this matter. Your parents have guided you and love you the best way that they are capable of doing. Basically, their experience has been their teacher! Smile and be kind to the one parent who you are certain has created some difficulty in your life; and, within a month or two, you will begin to realize a wonderful change in your relationship. You will change, and so will your parent! If you really care and want a better family relationship, then commence to show respect towards everyone around you. Before you know it, a miracle will take place in your life. Thank God for small miracles and united families!

**BATTERY** (i.e., cells which generate or store electricity)
The financial, mental, physical, and spiritual crisis you are presently experiencing will not be permanent; improved times are indicated in this dream for you. Why the panic? Why the anxiety? The best way to control your fear and worry is through self-discipline. First, control your temper when someone close to you offers you encouragement. Be thankful that someone really cares! Second, gather your inner forces and begin to think optimistically about your future. Be honest to all people, no matter what your situation in life happens to be. Life, as you know, is not entirely a paradise; sometimes you must weather certain unpleasant tribulations. But, remember that when your trials and tribulations appear almost insurmountable, something strange and wonderful should happen to you. That glorious event is called humility. Consequently, when you reach this state of being, your pride will be vanquished, thus giving you the leverage to carry on and prosper in life.

**BATTLE**
A battle between any opposing forces intimates that you should not overstep the bounds of your authority upon anyone. Sometimes

you get carried away with your importance, position, or rank in life and assume everyone must obey your beck and call. Not so! There is a right and a wrong way to ask or demand something from somebody; but, to merely believe that a person should jump at your command is totally wrong! By disbanding this attitude, your acclaim or recognition will be more appreciated and acknowledged, not only by self but by others, as well.

**BATTLEFIELD** (i.e., a place where a battle is fought)

You will do everything in your power to assist two people (family members or close friends) from going their separate ways (i.e. divorce, misunderstanding between two friends, etc.). You feel that these two people have not made a sincere effort to patch things up or to seek help in this entire matter. Do your very best for these people; if your plan does not work, however, be satisfied in knowing that you did the right thing.

**BAZAAR**

Dreaming about a bazaar portends good luck (e.g., lottery ticket, raffle ticket, bingo, winning something on a radio or television program). This dream may change your entire life style. However, what is important here is that if you do happen to receive a great winning, then you should not allow greed or money power any room to control your life. Money can buy you many things, but it will never give you peace of mind if used wrongly in any way!

**BEACH** (see **SHORE**)

**BEACON** (see **LIGHTHOUSE**)

**BEAR**

A peaceful or docile bear counsels you to watch your intake of pastry, junk food, or candy. Health problems could arise if you "go overboard" in these matters. To stay healthy, eat nutritious foods, exercise, and think positively about yourself.

A ferocious bear implies that you have a witty and quick sense of humour and that, in most instances, you are an extrovert. It saddens you, however, to know that the world around you fails to see the importance of working together for peace, spiritual illumination, and knowledge. It appears that people are so wrapped up in their mundane, earthly activities that they fail to see the importance of loving, sharing, laughing, and harmonizing with one another. Sometimes you feel as though you do not belong to this planet. However, you do know that you will continue to share your good blessings and tidings with others, no matter how indifferent some people may appear to you.

## BEARD

You wish to enlighten and bring happiness to others through your chosen profession, charitable work, or through some form of inventive or creative endeavours. Generally, you finish what you start out to do! That alone is a vital step in fulfilling your good wishes. As well, the recent changes within your home life should give you the inner incentive to never look back, but to go forward until your life's dream is fulfilled!

## BEARSKIN

You will receive a gift, a prize, or a token; or, some other acquisition will be yours when you dream about a bearskin. Whatever it is that you will receive, you can be sure that you will be both proud and honoured to be the lucky recipient!

## BEATING (see PUNISHMENT)

## BEAUTY PARLOUR (see PARLOUR)

## BEAVER

There is plenty of good work ahead for you as your future unfolds; you can be sure that you will see many productive and prosperous days ahead! Perish the thought of defeat! Your road to progress has met many dead ends in the past, but your present and your future will commence to change in your favour. It is your inner belief in self, in God, and in all the good things that exist now and forevermore, and it is your patience and unbending spirit that will allow you to rise over and above your sad, difficult life.

## BED

Dreaming of a bed augurs an offensive attack on your personality by a person who has clashed with you in the past. If you are strong and levelheaded, you will simply ignore the entire provocation. Fighting back now would be the precise act your oppressor wishes from you. Love and pray for your enemy, but do not associate with your enemy until you know, beyond any shadow of a doubt, that a positive change has taken place within the mind and soul of your oppressor.

Seeing a broken bed within a dream admonishes you to improve your thoughts and actions towards the opposite sex. Perhaps you are inconsiderate, cruel, or dislike the opposite sex. Whatever your problem may be, you would be wise to seek professional assistance, and completely change your attitude where this matter is concerned. Failing to change your attitude can only bring you inner frustration and continued self-hatred!

To make up a bed, such as placing coverings on it, suggests that you have a knack for wanting to know everything about people around you. Actually, it is all right to be genuinely concerned about those whom you know, but to pry in the affairs of people whom you know or do not know is taboo. You may avoid future arguments and humiliation by showing more respect, tact, and diplomacy toward people around you.

## BEDCLOTHES (see **BLANKET** or **CLOTHES**)

## BEDROOM

Seeing the interior of a bedroom within a dream advises you not to lose hope in someone or not to despair over some personal matter. Before too long, your troubles will simply vanish into thin air; then you can wonder why you struggled with your heart, mind, and soul so needlessly. You are not alone! Many people do the same thing, in their own worrisome ways, only to realize much later that their worries were a total waste of time.

Leaving a bedroom implies that you should be aware of any "double your money back" schemes. Be wary and alert! Someone may try to entice you into investing your money in some scheme which could be totally false.

Standing outside a bedroom implies that someone will confide in you with the utmost secrecy. Unfortunately, you will betray that confidence with an absent-minded slip of the tongue.

## BEE

Fighting or running away from a swarm of bees cautions you to be wary of the company you keep. Choose your friends as though they were the most precious flowers on earth. Nourish your friendships with the utmost respect and cordiality. If you, in turn, are not treated with the sincerity which you have shown a friend, or you feel totally unwanted or abused by this friend, then you will know that a brotherly love has come to a standstill—or to an end.

Being stung by a bee or by a swarm of bees implies that, in an unguarded moment, you may lose a sum of money. This action may come about by losing your purse or wallet or by being shortchanged at a store, bank, and so on. This entire matter may be averted by being on your guard for about a week or so.

Seeing a bee or a swarm of bees attempting but failing to alight upon your fingers, hands, feet, or any other part of your body indicates that you are under a certain amount of stress. What you are experiencing is a situation wherein you feel obligated to say yes to some important matter; but, deep within your mind, you are inclined to say no. You are bound to surface from this temporary ordeal with good taste, clever observation, and gutsy truth!

## BEER

You wish to be in total seclusion at this time of your life. You have recently been unduly affected by other people's actions around you. For a brief period of time, you would like to think and walk alone to sort things out. It appears as though you are beginning to see life around you for the very first time! With patience, self-confidence, and inner spiritual strength, you are bound to rise above your present state.

## BEETLE

You will be asked by a friend for a small loan of money. This communication may come verbally or by letter, telegram, electronic mail, or telephone. The answer should be affirmative, as this friend is very trustworthy.

Dreaming of being bitten by a beetle or beetles suggests that you will eventually embark upon a beautiful voyage to a tropical paradise. This trip will be a true source of inspiration for you!

## BEGGAR

Begging for food, shelter, or money is a very good sign. What must a person go through in life in order to see better, more prosperous times? It seems that you have lived through the gamut of troubled times, only to hope and pray that somewhere, somehow you will live to see a few happy moments in your life. These moments have arrived, for soon you will experience that inner joy and peace which rightfully belongs to you! This high-cycle dream involves success and happiness with home life, business, education, traveling, or career opportunities.

Refusing a beggar warm hospitality and comfort, on the other hand, suggests difficulties involving legal matters or some dispute over a purchase. You may win the battle in this entire matter—but not necessarily the war.

## BELIEF (see DOCTRINE)

## BELL

To hear or to ring a bell implies that you will be asked to pay an old debt. There may be a threat of court action against you where this matter is concerned. If you are unable to pay this debt, you should at least meet your creditor half way with some small payment or some positive indication of your good intentions.

Seeing a bell but not hearing the bell signifies that you will be disappointed due to some minor sickness (e.g., flu, backache, upset stomach). This untimely sickness will not allow you to pursue some urgent plans. Inevitably, these plans will have to be postponed for another time.

Seeing a broken, old-looking, or abandoned bell signifies that you are mentally debating whether or not to go to a meeting or celebration. The dream reveals that you will attend this meeting or celebration and, to your surprise, will have a splendid time!

## BELL BUOY (i.e., a buoy with a warning bell which rings by the movement of water)

You will go back on your word regarding a promise made to a relative, friend, or acquaintance (e.g., a loan of money, investing in some business, changing your mind about a trip). This uneventful situation may be taken very seriously by the person directly involved. Hopefully, an apology on your part will suffice. Should this not be sufficient, then you will have to bear the consequences until the person involved is willing to forgive and forget the whole affair.

## BELLMAN (i.e., a man or boy hired by a hotel, club, or other employer to carry luggage and run errands)

You may find yourself at a gathering, before too long, where an enraged battle or dispute will take place. Do not get tangled in this situation! Some physical harm to you may result, should you decide to join forces with this rowdy group of people.

**BELLOWS** (i.e., a device for producing and directing a current of air)
Seeing this instrument in working order reveals that a very close friend will be getting engaged. The marriage to follow will be a good and prosperous one!

Bellows that do not work, however, infer that you will have to start and finish some task in order to see a good wish fulfilled. Merely sitting back and musing about your good intentions will not bring you closer to any realization; you must actually do something about it!

**BELT**
Seeing or wearing a belt indicates a short, relaxing trip in store for you. Upon your return from this trip, there will be several good surprises in store for you!

Using a belt for punishment purposes (e.g., thrashing a child, adult) suggests that your anxieties and frustrations seem to be centered upon poor sleeping habits. Keeping late hours and having little rest can prove to be very discomfiting to you after a period of time. Sooner or later, your mind and your body rebel, thus making you irritable and extremely high-strung. Obviously, you need more rest than you are now receiving or willing to admit!

**BENCH** (i.e., a long seat with or without a back)
You show good will towards your fellow man. Oftentimes, however, you are the object of criticism from others who have neither the gumption, the ability, nor the know-how to do what you do. As long as you are able to maintain your good values, sense of humour, and stability in everything you do, then continue your life style without changing a thing. Pay no mind to people who tend to be envious of you. You are a humanitarian in the truest sense of the word and are endowed with an enriched soul!

**BEQUEST** (i.e., leaving a legacy such as property, etc., to someone by last will and testament)
Leaving all your worldly possessions to a relative, friend, or stranger within a dream merely endeavours to teach you that any materialistic wealth on earth is simply "borrowed" wealth on "bor-

rowed" time. Even if you live to be one hundred and five years old, you will eventually discover that you cannot take your materialistic belongings to the other side of life. In essence, your dream is trying to tell you not to place too much emphasis on earthly wealth but to concentrate more on spiritual wealth, such as your soul, your mind, your good intentions, your self-sacrifice, and so on.

**BESTIALITY** (i.e., sexual relations between a person and an animal) (see *also* **SEX**)

Seeing or partaking in this brutal, perverted sexual activity implies that you are often dictatorial and unreasonable—not only to self, but to others as well. You seem to be treading forbidden waters, where this attitude is concerned. Unless you commence to curb this attitude, there could be some serious and unpleasant future ramifications (e.g., display of uncontrolled violence, nervous stresses creating sickness, using liquor or drugs to hide your problem). Being totally honest and sincere with yourself, praying, and perhaps seeking some outside help in this matter of rash judgments and losing control of one's temper should assist you with peace of soul and human respect.

**BEST MAN**

Your hasty judgment towards a family member, friend, relative, or stranger may produce negative results. Be careful in your accusations or insinuations, where other people are concerned. Discretion of the highest order should be utilized in this regard, even when you do have all the facts together. A false accusation is like trying to build a house without a foundation!

**BET** (i.e., a wager)

Making a bet at a sports event suggests you will have a challenging year, with some good and some bad times. Your bad times may be small or great; but, if you maintain an optimistic confidence about the days yet to come, then you will be able to walk over those small, troublesome pebbles or walk around that great, troublesome mountain with illuminating results!

**BETRAYER**

You should show more loyalty and concern towards members of your family and people who honestly care about you. A million personal excuses cannot pardon you for ignoring your obligations, duties, and love where this matter is concerned. An uncaring person is likened unto a bird with a broken wing—a troubled soul who outwardly appears free but inwardly becomes a slave to a weakness or fear. Strive to place your priorities and perspectives of life in order, so that when tomorrow comes (and it will), you will be grateful for the blessings right in front of you.

## BIBLE

Reading a Bible or seeing a Bible that is in good condition promises continued happiness in what you are presently doing. There are some forthcoming changes for you within the next several months that will be an asset to your present living conditions (e.g., a raise in pay, adding a new feature to your home, early retirement). Whatever this change may be, you can be sure that good luck, health, and prosperity will follow you.

Destroying a Bible or seeing a Bible in poor condition infers that you have been troubled with menacing thoughts about your past or your present. Sometimes you feel that God just does not care what you are presently going through. Believe me, He knows and He cares more than you know! And, yes, He has heard your prayers in this matter; but, before He can relieve you of this guilt or regret you are inwardly nursing, you must first forgive yourself. Not only must you forgive yourself, but you must also forget that certain element of your past or present, once and for all time! Let it go! God has forgiven you many times regarding this matter, but you have refused to believe in that possibility. When you pray again, believe with all your being that you have been forgiven. Never turn back, but go forward in your life with peace, gratitude, and a closer kinship with God.

## BIBLIOGRAPHY (i.e., a book containing, or the study of, the editions, dates, authorship, etc. of books and other writings)

Reading a bibliography within a dream reveals that you are a very determined, mature individual. When you set your mind to something, nothing could stop you! These admirable traits will one day bring you much honour and prestige in life.

Compiling a bibliography intimates that you are a perfectionist, in the truest sense of the word. Seeing the world through your eyes can be a very beautiful sight! Your sensitive awareness of people, places, and things; your meticulous reading habits and insatiable desire to learn as much as you can about life itself; your appreciation for good music, theatre, etc.; and your charitable work within your society are all glowing facets of your being. You are a well-admired, ambitious person who is destined to achieve the better things in life.

Seeing the pages of a bibliography being torn or ripped implies that you are being held back in life through someone's incessant put-downs or strong will over you (e.g., spouse, parent, sister, brother, friend). It appears that no matter what you would like to do or where you want to go, there are warning signs of great discouragement given to you by this individual. Remember, this individual may mean well, but he or she is petrified that something may happen to you. In fact, it is this individual who is more insecure than you will ever be! Comfort them and assure them of your well-being but, by the same token, commence to assert yourself. Everything you do on earth may be a risk; however, as long as you are dominated by the thoughts and actions of other people, your own learning processes in life can be shattered. Be firm in life, and slowly commence to be the special person you were always destined to be; namely, you!

## BICYCLE

Merely seeing a bicycle infers that you have recently become very despondent, bored, and simply fed up with the mundane routine of your life (e.g., household chores, place of employment). It appears that your outside interests are very limited because of the demands placed upon you at home or at work. Besides, by the time you finish your work load at the end of the day, you are simply too exhausted to think of anything but a personal moment of relaxation. Such is the life of a very dedicated, loyal person! There must be more to life than what you are experiencing. There is; however, you must be willing to explore the possibilities open to you. For example: taking a course at the university or college level, learning a handicraft, taking a computer course or a mechanics course, learning to play an instrument, joining a club or organization, learning to swim or play tennis or golf and so forth. If you search long enough, you will find another outlet in your life which will give you a new release from your present mundane existence.

Riding a bicycle implies that you have a very creative imagination which should be utilized (e.g., writing, painting, music, inventing). In fact, there are no heights that you could not master within your lifetime, providing you do not neglect or ignore the gifts that are within you.

**BIER** (i.e., a portable framework or platform on which a coffin or corpse is placed)

Seeing this device implies that you are depressed over a personal matter which you would like to discuss with someone, but you do not have the courage to do so. Whether you do or do not reveal this dilemma to anyone, it is shown that you will come out of your quandary with courage and common sense.

**BIGAMY** (i.e., having two wives or two husbands at the same time)

You are laughing on the outside but crying on the inside! Often, you blame your upbringing for the unhappiness you are experiencing today. Since you cannot relive the hour that has already passed, what good will it do you to keep delving into, and whining over, your past? Think, instead, about today and tomorrow and about how you can improve your state of affairs. Keep yourself occupied with things you like to do. Commence to appreciate yourself for who and what you are, and never forget to give yourself a pat on the back once in a while for just being alive and well! Remember also that you cannot possibly like and love anything in life if you fail to like and love yourself. In essence, this dream symbolism is telling you that you have not tried hard enough to appreciate your life through logic, through faith, and from lessons of experience.

**BIGOT** (see **PREJUDICE**)

**BILL** (see **DEBT**)

**BILLBOARD** (see **ADVERTISEMENT** or **SIGNBOARD**)

**BILLIARDS**

You appear to be playing two roles in life: one pleasant, the other not so pleasant. For example, when guests are present, you appear to be rather nice and hospitable; however, when they leave, the bear comes out of you, and the growling begins! You are failing to place yourself at the receiving end of this attitude. You can change if you want to! Some serious introspection is advised here, with the advent of making some positive changes both within and around you. Grumbling and complaining will get you nowhere; but a little bit of kindness, affection, and love will go a very long way.

## BILLIONAIRE

If you are in fact a billionaire and dream of being one, then your dream is merely reflecting upon your present position or status in life. However, if you are not a billionaire and dream of being one, then this symbolism implies that some plan or project you are contemplating may fall short of being successful. Perhaps, at a later time, something better will come your way with better, more flourishing results.

## BINOCULAR

Dreaming about a binocular means that a debt owed by you will be paid in full (e.g., the final mortgage payment on your home, automobile, trailer, boat). Whatever your debt may be, you will be comforted and relieved to be free of this burden!

## BIOGRAPHY (i.e., a life story of a person described by someone else; a memoir)

Seeing a biography that is neat, clear, and concise infers that you have a knack for exerting influence upon the political issues of your community. Your good ideas and intentions can be utilized, thus enabling your community to grow and prosper. Here's a suggestion: perhaps you will implement the idea of having an orphanage situated right next door to a seniors residence. Just think of the positive results this could bring into the lives of the children at the orphanage, as well as to the lonely people in the seniors home! Their get-togethers would be awe inspiring! The many deeds you are capable of conceiving will have a momentous impact upon your own good future.

Seeing a biography that is not neat, clear, or concise implies that you will be pleased with some matter that appears to be very promising at first; however, later you will be shocked and disappointed to discover that your expectations will not be realized. Sometimes, when things do not turn out in our favour, we fail to realize that there is a reason for this being so. We only realize the value and importance of things not turning in our favour at a much later date. Then we are grateful they turned out the way they did!

## BIRD

Birds showing a peaceful display of merriment and song intimates that you are beginning to search within your being for the peace, joy, and comfort you are entitled to have. Silent meditation, prayer, and assisting your fellow man in some positive way is certainly the right road to finding and knowing yourself.

Assisting a bird or a flock of birds in some difficulty implies that you will be compensated for something destroyed, lost, or stolen (e.g., insurance, government or community funding). You will be totally appeased in this matter.

Being attacked by a bird or a flock of birds means that you will go beyond your budget with some major purchase. This will set you back financially for a period of time but, come what may, you will be very satisfied with your actions.

Destroying a bird or a flock of birds symbolizes that you are loyal, hard-working, and content with your life. You have an innate talent to create peace wherever you go. In many ways, you are always welcome wherever you go; your charisma is like a rainbow after a storm!

Seeing a dead bird or a flock of dead birds within a dream implies that you are very concerned about the upbringing of a child and/or the welfare of an older member of your family. In both instances your fears and hang-ups will dissipate as the future progresses. Nothing is as bad or as negative as you sometimes concoct within your mind and heart. Be faithful and positive in this entire matter; you will then see the good changes resulting from your action.

## BIRDBATH

A birdbath signifies making adjustments where some change is concerned. This could be a new rule at work, a change of residence, adhering to some medical advice, and so on. You will adjust, but not necessarily without some minor incidents, complaints, and personal sentiment.

## BIRDHOUSE

A birdhouse devoid of any bird activity reveals that you will experience an unnerving event that will convince you that life on other planets appears to be very factual. This could involve having a direct encounter with a flying saucer, or seeing a figure emerge from one, or having a conversation with a person from outer space. Too incredible? Time will tell!

Seeing bird activity both within and around a birdhouse denotes that you will travel a great distance to visit a certain country or some family and friends. This trip will be eventful and should take place within a year of this dream.

**BIRTH** (see *also* **BABY, CAESARIAN SECTION, CHILDHOOD, FETUS, ILLEGITIMACY, MISCARRIAGE, NATIVITY,** or **PREGNANCY**)

Seeing the miracle of birth, be it that of a human being or that of an animal, is a very promising dream for you. A state of good will, along with your most important ambitions, will be fulfilled within your lifetime.

If there appears to be great stress or some ominous difficulty shown with the birth of a human being or that of an animal, then you are advised to fortify your heart, mind, and soul against a luckless two-week period that is about to follow. Be careful where and how you travel; avoid impulsive thoughts and actions which could lead you into danger; do not stray to an unwholesome area where difficulty could be lurking, and so on. This critical two-week period may pass by without a single incident, if you heed this warning. Your dream symbolism is not attempting to frighten you; rather, it is wishing to guide you away from some pending pitfall.

**BIRTHDAY** (see **CELEBRATION**)

**BIRTHPLACE**

Wandering back to the place of your birth with peace and contentment implies that you are a very good-natured, mature individual. Your inexhaustible tolerance level towards others less knowledgeable than you is astounding! Be thankful in knowing that all your yesterdays, todays, and tomorrows will lead you towards a life enriched with courage, honour, and wisdom.

Seeing a birthplace in a state of clownish amusement implies that you are not acting your age, nor are you willing to cope with responsibility. Your actions are often childish, without any regard as to how you are affecting people around you. As soon as you let go of your self-pity, your self-complacency, and your many disbeliefs where personal courage is concerned, you will commence to see a tremendous transformation within your life. A better "you" will emerge from this change, to face a better future with maturity, hope, and inner security!

Revisiting a birthplace but finding many unusual changes from the way you had once known it to be signifies that you have to clarify your intentions with someone (e.g., spouse, family members). This could involve educational plans, employment intentions, improving living conditions or harmony around you, or desiring to work or travel abroad. Since some of your ideas may not be in accord with those around you, you must show strong faith and patience with your cherished desires in life. The forces of good are working with you, not against you; and, in time, your fondest wishes will come true.

**BIRTHSTONE** (i.e., a jewel associated with the month of one's birth)

Seeing one birthstone in a dream implies that a gift will be given to you. This gift will symbolize love from your benefactor. You obviously are being admired by someone who really cares!

Seeing more than one birthstone, however, cautions you to control your sexual and emotional wants and needs in life. Be wary of any individual(s) who may attempt to involve you in some acts of sexual depravity. Do not be gullible; rather, use all your better judgment and common sense in matters of this nature.

**BISEXUALISM** (i.e., being sexually attracted to both sexes)

If you are a bisexual who dreams about having sexual relationships with both sexes, then your dream is a subconscious expression of your inner desires and activities. Only time and spiritual growth could perhaps lead you away from your impaired behaviour (e.g., prayer, meditation, faith). Above all, a willingness to forgive and forget some of the wrongs that have been done to you in your past is a vital factor in putting your life in order.

If you are not a bisexual yet dream of being one, then this symbolism implies that you are either over-sexed or undersexed. Should your life be too stressful in either case, then you are strongly advised to seek some professional help such as through a medical doctor, a psychologist, or other professional.

**BISHOP**

A bishop dressed in black or white or who simply argues within a dream portends a day of strife and bitterness for you. Try not to annoy anyone today, if at all possible. If someone else aggravates you for some reason, simply bow out of the situation in a polite way. Failing to adhere to these positive courses of action will regrettably bring you the negative consequences of this day.

Seeing a bishop who smiles or talks pleasantly to you or to someone else within a dream signifies that you tend to mistrust people. Obviously, you must have been affected by some people who were not very honest and aboveboard towards you. Do not judge all people to be dishonest or unkind. There are more good people upon this planet than negative ones! Soon, you will come out of your bitter attitude; you will realize that you were a bit premature in your condemnation of all people simply because of the sadly disappointing actions of a few.

## BLACKBIRD (see BIRD)

## BLACKBOARD

Your determination and competence at work will eventually lead you towards an outstanding promotion. You would be pleased to see this happen, but you also realize that you would never allow success to go to your head in any way. You also realize that anyone who tries hard enough in life will be eventually rewarded for their labours.

## BLACK MAGIC (i.e., magic with an evil purpose)

Performing or merely seeing the art of black magic within a dream is a bad omen! You may be deceived into doing something against your better judgment. If you are in the midst of bad company, then be wary of listening to or acting on false information. Not all good or bad people heed sound advice, but if you have enough courage to heed this warning, then you may be averting some serious trouble looming on the horizon!

## BLACKMAIL

Two people whom you know will attempt to oppose you secretly. Their hypocritical action will eventually be revealed to you by a third party. Eventually, these two people will attempt to rekindle their friendship or dealings with you; but this, of course, will not be realized. You will probably forgive them. However, you will have no more dealings with them.

Opposing any form of blackmail within a dream indicates that an unpleasant business venture may bring about a foreclosure on your holdings or estate. This could be averted, but you must have enough good business judgment and belief in yourself in order to counteract this negative revelation. Remember that to be forewarned is to be prepared for any difficulty which may ensue.

## BLACK MARKET (see CHEATING, DECEPTION, or STORE)

## BLACKSMITH

You are advised not to make any major purchases at this particular time simply because difficulties and needless hassles are foreseen in this regard. Furthermore, your soul cycle is not at its peak at this moment, so you would be strongly advised to wait for a period of two or three months before you invest your money. Of course, the final choice in this entire matter is yours to make.

A blacksmith working under stress is a favourable sign. You will journey to many places in time to come, with the possibility of actually living in a foreign country for a brief period of time.

## BLAME (see ACCUSATION, BLASPHEMY, COMPLAINER, DISAPPROVAL, LAWSUIT, or LIBEL)

## BLANKET

A clean blanket that appears new implies that you are very sensitive with respect to people's feelings about you. Sometimes you get carried away in these matters by creating unwarranted suspicions and accusations towards a friend or two. Friendships are broken in this manner quite easily! First, learn to trust people around you, and realize that no one is absolutely perfect on this earth plane. Second, be more forgiving towards people whom you know simply because they, too, have their many failings and successes and are capable of laughing and crying, just like you. They can be just as sensitive and just as easily offended as you. Third, commence to express yourself in a thankful manner just for being alive and well and for being more worthy towards your fellow man. A good soul will always be patient, helpful, and understanding in all matters of life; an agitated soul will not only hinder his own progress in life, but will also make sure others around him suffer, as well!

Should the blanket be soiled and torn, then the first three months of the year yet to come will be difficult ones for you. Spiritual and financial upheavals will bring about an all-time low in your life. You will survive this testing period with merit, understanding, and inner vision.

Seeing a blanket or blankets draped over furniture, a vehicle, a house, or any other such object suggests that there are reasonable possibilities that you may make a spectacle of yourself at some social gathering, wedding, or casual party. To avoid this possible embarrassment, simply maintain a calm, cool, and collected attitude at any forthcoming function. You may come out of this smelling like a rose!

**BLASPHEMY** (i.e., profane speech, writing, or action concerning God or anything held as sacred)

To blaspheme the Almighty God within a dream implies that, at times, you are too talkative and cynical. This weakness has often left you standing alone, looking rather foolish in the eyes of other people. You are trying too hard to be the center of attention wherever you go. This insecure action is neither wholesome nor wise. Be a good listener. You may learn from the next person who may be very knowledgeable about what he or she is talking about. Do not mock or sneer at anyone's appearance or manner of speech. For all you know, this person could be the wisest person you could ever hope to meet! In summation, do not treat other people as though you were judge and jury; rather, treat others as you would want others to treat you.

**BLENDER** (i.e., an electrical appliance that chops, whips, mixes, liquefies foods)

Using or merely seeing this appliance within a dream indicates that some behavioural habits or attitudes of a family member have bewildered you. Apparently, this individual has changed so drastically that you simply find the new personality becoming totally alien to your common sense thinking. This family member is strongly influenced by the company he or she keeps. Pleading or begging for them to change at this time will prove totally futile! Be strong in this entire matter; and within ten months of this dream, you will begin to see a positive change take place in this individual.

**BLINDFOLD**

Using a blindfold or seeing another person use one implies that you will be buying clothes for a very special occasion. This occasion will be a very happy event!

If the blindfold slips off or is forced off your face, then you are advised not to take advantage of someone's kindness towards you. By being honest and fair in your dealings with others, you will prosper; but by using others for selfish reasons, you will struggle with your conscience.

**BLINDNESS**

If you are, in fact, blind and dream of being blind, then you are merely expressing your present state of being. However, if you are not blind and dream of being in this state, then this symbolism reveals that you appear to be a punching bag for someone else's frustration (mentally, physically, and so on). The biggest mistake of your life is to allow anyone a chance to use or misuse your God-given body and soul! Be strong and seek the help you need before unpleasant consequences occur! Talk to someone (e.g., clergy, doctor, lawyer, friend) about your problem, and you will be assisted in the best possible way.

To cause blindness in another person in your dream suggests that you have an annoying habit of expressing all forms of morbidities to people who generally shy away from such topics. Your actions may appear to be inconsequential to you; but to the next person, these thoughts can bring about mental fear and anguish. When reading about certain disastrous or bizarre events that occur on earth, you would be wise to keep these horrifying topics to yourself. Do not revel or express happy feelings over the sad state of affairs of people much less fortunate than you. Since you know better, try harder to act wiser.

## BLIZZARD

To be in a blizzard or to walk out of a blizzard signifies that you often feel second-best or fourth-rate in things that you try to do. You are trying too hard to compare yourself to others around you. Be natural, and do the best that you are humanly capable of doing. Success in life is more than just being number one in everything a person hopes to accomplish. Personally, you are acknowledged for many fine things that you do very adequately and admirably! The simple truth is that you fail to give yourself a pat on the back once in a while. You deserve this praise; you have earned it!

To be lost in a blizzard reveals that, quite frequently, you cannot make up your mind on various matters. Your indecisiveness need not be a problem when you begin to realize that only one decision should be made at a time. Do not clutter your mind when you are about to make a decision. More often than not, your first thought or impulse is the correct answer to any decision-making problems.

## BLOCKADE (see OBSTRUCTION)

## BLOOD (see *also* BLOOD POISONING, KILL, MURDER, NOSEBLEED, or TRANSFUSION)

You can expect the dawn of a better tomorrow if you dream specifically about blood. Better times will now allow you to go on in life with ease and assurance. You have been struggling for a very long time;

but, with the courage of your own convictions and undaunted faith, you will soon see the results of your good work prosper and flourish. Who said that faith cannot move a mountain?

## BLOOD POISONING

Dreaming about having some poisonous matter in your blood reveals that you are a hardheaded individual who often refuses to admit that you are or can be wrong in certain matters. If you can honestly admit that you are one hundred percent correct in all that you do or say, then you have to be one of the most unusual individuals on the face of this globe. As a matter of fact, you would be quite alone in this matter. Do not be afraid to admit that you are wrong in anything, for doing so is wholesome for the mind and soul. The simple fact is that what you do know about life should give you the incentive to learn more about the things which you do not know.

## BLOTTER (i.e., paper used for absorbing ink)

A clean blotter signifies that you will be undertaking a business or creative course. This advanced course will offer you greater possibilities and positive challenges, where your future is concerned.

A blotter with ink stains on it reveals that you have the capacity to reach inestimable heights of recognition within your lifetime. You could, perhaps, play a major role in advancing or updating the fundamental basics in your profession, or perhaps you will create or invent something very special for this world to enjoy and cherish. Whatever it is that you are destined to do, this symbolism reveals your leadership potential in almost anything you wish to accomplish in life. You are special, unique, and gifted!

## BLOWGUN (i.e., a long, tube-like weapon through which darts or pellets are blown)

You are not budgeting your earnings; this suggests you are biting off more than you can chew. Being unable to pay your debts should alert you that something is wrong in the way you are handling your finances. Sometimes people have to make a sacrifice or two in order to settle their debts, but once this is accomplished, they profit from their experience. They not only learn to budget their money, but they also have the great satisfaction of having fulfilled their financial obligation(s).

## BLOWTORCH

This dream advises you to always maintain a good, positive attitude about people around you, no matter what your gifts, talents, or occupation may be in life. Do not make the foolish mistake of strutting your self-importance to anyone in life. There is not a single person on earth who is not as important as another; but man must yet learn to mature and accept life in this understanding manner. Unfortunately, many people allow their vanity, ego, pride, greed, wealth, and fame to have complete control over themselves and the basic truths of life. They eventually get lost in the void with their earthly importance—with themselves, with God, and with their fellow man. Always be a shining example of a human being, no matter what fate may bring you. Never lose touch with the realities of your purpose to seek your worth here on earth and your purpose to share your love with your fellow man.

Seeing a blowtorch that fails to work advises you to be wary of your rowdiness and temper in life. Involvement with the law is strongly indicated by this symbolism, so do not stretch your luck too far in this matter. Remember, any harm you do to others, you also do to yourself. For your future's sake, curb some of your negative actions now.

## BLUEPRINT

A clear, neat looking blueprint suggests you will be encouraged to build onto your present home or be inspired to move away from your present location to a larger, more spacious dwelling. There should be no impediments in your way, once you have made up your mind in bringing about any one of these possible changes within your life.

An unclear, messy looking blueprint suggests that the time and labour you are exerting over some project at home or at work will beset you in a mental and physical way. You are advised to slow down, otherwise dire consequences may compel you to cease this work for a very long period of time. One of the reasons you are so anxious is that you see a finished project in your mind. But, in reality, you must be patient for its completion. Why fret over something that will have its hour and its day of glory? Think about these matters seriously in the hope that you will sail with the waves of life—rather than against the waves of life.

**BLUSH**

Blushing in a dream implies that you are a trustworthy and generous individual. You also know your limitations and shortcomings in life; this is an admirable trait! Your future may lead you to many great but strange places, as well. Your adaptability to unusual situations is an inspiration for others. Before too long, an event will provide you with an opportunity to fulfill a long-forgotten wish!

**BOA** (see **SNAKE**)

**BOARDINGHOUSE** (see **HOSTEL**, **HOTEL**, **LODGING**, **MOTEL**, or **RENT**)

**BOARDINGSCHOOL**

To dream of this type of school predicts that you should be involved with the publishing industry in some way. This dream also reveals that you could be successful at being a published author, an editor or an executive of a prestigious publishing house, or a very successful literary agent. If you already know that one of these fields applies to you, then be confident that you are on the right road in life. However, if you are undecided as to what field you should follow in life, then perhaps your dream has provided you with an answer.

**BOARD ROOM** (i.e., a room where a board of administrators or directors hold regular meetings)

Dreaming about a board room with or without someone present implies that you are overtaxing your mind with so many earthly problems that your mind is literally playing little tricks on you. In other words, you are beginning to imagine certain problems that do not even exist! Allay your fears, phobias, and trepidations with calmness and inner faith. For the moment, you are over-estimating your problems with short-sighted attention. Once you get a grip on yourself, everything will turn out all right. No matter how troublesome life may present itself to you, be at peace with yourself and with the world around you. Remember, also, that no storms in life are ever permanent!

**BOARDWALK**

You do everything to conceal the fact that you are a lonely person. Someone or something has made you lonely, but perhaps you can look upon your state of being as a blessing in disguise. We all grow from certain experiences within our lives. Even though we may not see the hidden miracles behind the experiences at first, we eventually begin to comprehend the "whys" and the "wherefores" of our sadness or trauma with an open mind. Utter a prayer or two, and call upon the Good Forces of Life and Heaven to grant you the peace and tranquility you rightfully deserve.

There is no prayer, big or small, that will not be answered providing it is sincere, humble, and blessed with thankful intentions. Let this dream symbolism be your realization that, somewhere in the highest reaches of Heaven, your call for help will be heard, until the very essence of your soul becomes joyful.

## BOAT (see *also* FERRY, FIREBOAT, GONDOLA, HOVERCRAFT, PROPELLER, or RAFT)

Rowing, sailing, or cruising in a boat indicates that some past miscalculation or illogical thinking has caused you much grief to this present day. Cast your past anxieties to the wind! By living for today and tomorrow, your yesterdays will vanish like a cloud dissipating in the sky; and, once again, you will begin to see, feel, taste, and live within the positive forces of life.

Acting foolish or careless aboard a boat cautions you or a younger member of your family to be exceedingly careful when swimming, sailing, or fishing, and/or driving carelessly by land. Adhering to this dream's warning would be wholesome and wise; it is, indeed, better to be safe now than sorry later.

A boat appearing to be in danger, such as being destroyed, colliding, or sinking reveals that you often see the futility in worrying and fretting over others around you, but that it is part of your nature to be concerned about your loved ones, one way or another. Of course, you must be wary about being over-stressed with certain matters which may unduly affect you. Do not forget to look after yourself, as well. This is not being selfish; this is being logical. Your loved ones need and love you as much as you need and love them. Learn to be more calm, placid, and inwardly trusting whenever it rains and storms in your life. With this attitude, you will experience a more peaceful ending to a troubled story.

## BOATHOUSE (i.e., a building for storing a boat)

A common household appliance will malfunction during the week of this dream. This could be any of the following: coffee maker, blender, portable oven, hair dryer, toaster, dishwasher, clothes dryer, clothes washer, stove, refrigerator, freezer, water heater, iron, sewing machine, radio, record player, or television. As inconsequential as this dream symbolism may appear, you will admit that a breakdown of any of these appliances can be an unpleasant experience or just a plain nuisance.

Seeing a boathouse sink into muddy water is a foreboding dream. Some structural weakness or problem concerning your home could have some serious ramifications (e.g., walls, roof, basement, furnace, electrical system). There appears to be no rest for the good on earth, so be kind to yourself by heeding this warning.

## BOBBY PIN

You are a very sensible person who rarely becomes intimidated by the threats, betrayals, or foolishness of people. Over the years, you have learned to cope with life and all its ups and downs with steadfast determination and an inner compulsion to push onwards. Life may be hard at times; but, with a song and a prayer, you have always mastered those mighty waves very efficiently! Your future will be the good harvest of your life, with the advent of pleasure, rest, and travel ahead for you.

## BOBCAT

Should this animal appear relatively calm, then you will hear some distressing news from a distance. It appears that you will make a sudden trip to the place in which this news originated.

An accident or death is symbolized by this dream. Remember we are all here on borrowed time; eventually we must all leave this planet, one way or another. When God calls us, we must leave this state of being for another place—a place more beautiful than words could describe!

A ferocious bobcat, on the other hand, suggests that you will console the offended feelings of a spouse or family member. If you are the cause of your loved one's grief or sadness, then be more aware of your actions towards them, as well as their sensitivity towards you. If you are not the prime cause of their grief or sadness, then it is with deep foresight and affection that you console them.

## BODY (see ANATOMY)

## BODYGUARD

This symbolism reveals that you are obsessed with a fear of being a victim of someone's diabolical intentions towards you. No one appears to be after you; it is only the created fantasies of your own mind causing the fear. The more you rely on the sanctity of your mind, body, and soul being protected by God, the greater are your chances of having little or no fears in life. The roots of your problem appear to be loneliness, self-pity, and fears of being unwanted or rejected by people. No one wishes to harm you; but as you can already see, you are doing a very good job of this yourself!

**BODY SNATCHER** (i.e., a person who removes dead bodies from graves)

As you begin to perceive life and its true meaning a bit more clearly, you will try harder to maintain peace, common sense, poise, and humility wherever you go. The good forces of life are far more meaningful and masterful than all the evils put together. As you wander through your many experiences in life, you will note that there will be many worldly and personal situations not to your liking. It is within these dissatisfied periods of your life that your strength and faith should be the strongest. This would be equivalent to walking into a deep valley for the very first time, only to be awe inspired by the brightness of the stars overhead! Such is this life with all its goodness, surprises, and trials and tribulations. There is not an experience within your life that will not have some lesson attached to it. Accept this life; challenge this life. Above all, center your attention upon God.

**BOG** (see **SWAMP**)

**BOIL** (e.g., boiling water or other liquids)

Seeing foodstuff in boiling water is a direct health warning to you. Proper attention to your food habits is strongly urged here. Your body needs just as much attention as anything else in your life.

To see mice, snakes, lizards, frogs, turtles, or anything else most unusual in boiling water is a foreboding dream. An elderly family member or family friend will experience ill health. The passing of life is a possibility here. Hopefully, with prayer, faith, and good medical attention, everything will turn out all right.

**BOLT** (i.e., a bar used to fasten a door)

A bolt fastened to a door is a sign of improved conditions concerning family relationships, business ventures, educational pursuits, or settling some legal matters. This dream symbolism could not be more timely!

Seeing a bolt broken or partially unfastened on a door suggests that you will be successful in a venture or project you had hoped would succeed. However, be prepared for a brief financial setback just before the completion of this project or venture.

**BOMB** (e.g., high explosive bomb, smoke bomb, hand grenade, torpedo or stink bomb) (see *also* **ATOMIC BOMB**, **HYDROGEN BOMB**, **MINE DETECTOR**, **MINE FIELD**, or **MISSILE**)

To merely see a bomb implies that you should be more punctual where personal appointments, invitations, or regulated time schedules are concerned (e.g., a doctor's appointment, visiting a friend, attending school). It appears that you are arriving late for various occasions which require more promptness on your behalf.

An exploding bomb, on the other hand, intimates that someone will make some serious accusations in order to ruin your fine reputation. You may be at the heights of your career when this takes place, so hopefully you will have your defenses up in order to refute this person's jealousy and hatred.

Diffusing a bomb implies that you have recently witnessed enough disturbances around you to last you a lifetime! You appear to be in a "no-win" situation with some people you know. If others around you choose to make blunders along their road in life, then they will simply have to contend with their own mistakes. Remember, not everyone you know is about to listen or adhere to your sound logic. Perhaps some people must learn the hard way in life.

**BONNET**

You are a very independent, mature, and compassionate individual. Being kind and talented as well certainly makes you a very remarkable person to know; and those who do know you well sense that they are in the presence of a very wise soul!

**BOOK** (e.g., a literary or scientific work, poetry book, novel, text book, pamphlet, notebook) (see *also* **AUTOBIOGRAPHY**, **BIBLE**, **BIBLIOGRAPHY**, **BIOGRAPHY**, **BOOKLET**, **CLASS BOOK**, **COMIC BOOK**, **DICTIONARY**, **LIBRARY**, or **TELEPHONE BOOK**)

Basically, reading or seeing a book within a dream is a very promising revelation. You will not only succeed in your chosen profession, but you also have the potential to eventually be noted for some outstanding achievement or contribution to your society or to the world!

## BOOKEND

Your impartial feelings towards life in general will not bring you happiness. As long as you continue to pout over some past or present turmoil, you can hardly expect a bed of roses to fall on your lap. When you decide to utilize your better judgment and compromise in matters pertaining to the core of your problem(s), you will then commence to be more caring and comfortable with your life.

## BOOK JACKET (i.e., a dust jacket of a book)

You will gain and prosper through your own labour, initiative, and enterprising spirit in life. You keep your promises, social commitments, and loyalties with people whom you like and admire. You have a keen sense of responsibility and expect the same from others, as well. You will rise above your fondest hopes in life as an intelligent, dedicated, and inspiring human being.

## BOOKMARK (e.g., a brochure or pamphlet)

Do not tell all your trade secrets to anyone unless you are absolutely certain about the person's honesty and integrity. You never know how far and how fast these so-called secrets can ricochet right back to you, leaving you deeply disappointed and humiliated. If you must share a secret with anyone, then share it with a loved one whom you know and trust. Better still, if the secret is too personal and intimate, keep quiet.

## BOOK REVIEW

Reading or writing a book review strongly implies that you are a very knowledgeable person who has a deep concern for the destiny of man. You are slated to be in the limelight in some way (e.g., radio, television, theatre, motion pictures, syndicated newspaper columnist). Whatever you choose to become, or whoever you may be, you certainly do have a magnetic personality and an unyielding desire to improve this world. You are ahead of your time!

## BOOKSTORE

An emotional difficulty you are presently experiencing will soon dissipate. Before this happens, however, you must be more tolerant with your inner needs and demands as well as be willing to accept, with an open mind and heart, an apology from someone special. When you honestly wish to belong to someone, then you must be prepared to make a few sacrifices in your life (i.e., shedding bad habits, temper, and one-sided opinions, etc.).

## BOOMERANG

You appear to be vexed over a series of incidents involving one to three people. This dream symbolism advises you NOT to retaliate in any way. In simple terms, forgive and forget your enemies!

## BOREDOM (see *also* APATHY)

Being bored within a dream state actually infers that you find life rather uninteresting and unvarying. It seems that much of your time is wasted on boring, monotonous activities. In fact, you have never really given yourself a chance to explore or expand your way of thinking (e.g., taking a course on self-improvement, joining a club, being an uncle or aunt to a young person who has no father or mother). Keep yourself busy with constructive measures in mind, and never be afraid to learn and to grow inwardly. Life, as we know it to be, stops for no one. Sooner or later, we must all move on to a greater awareness of learning. A tip: the more you learn now, the better off you will be later!

## BORROWER

You will gain financial stability through your own efforts or through sheer determination to do something that will get you out of the financial slump in which you appear to be. Taking a lethargic attitude in these matters will get you absolutely nowhere in life. There is a way for you, but you must seek and find this way, until you feel your monetary needs and wants have been replenished.

## BOTTLE (see *also* DECANTER or FLASK)

An empty bottle or one filled with liquid and so on suggests that you do not appear to have a great tolerance level for people of different races. In spite of your thoughts or actions, we earthlings share a basic need for one another (regardless of race, creed or colour); and that is, unequivocally, the need to love and understand one another in good fellowship. Many people do share their love and understanding with their fellow man, but many people refuse to accept this simple road to heaven. When you look into the mirror, try to see what makes you any different, any better, or any wiser than a person of another race. Think about this for a while: a soul has no colour!

A broken bottle indicates that some decisive action on your part will bring you closer to fulfilling a hope or aspiration (e.g., falling in love with the right person, building a new home, being promoted, moving to another country). Whatever your good wish may be, it is hoped that you will be happy beyond your greatest dreams!

**BOULDER** (see **ROCK**)

**BOUQUET** (see **FLOWER**)

**BOUTIQUE** (see **STORE**)

**BOWL** (see **BASIN** or **BATHROOM**)

**BOWLING** (i.e., a game played at a bowling alley, or lawn bowling)

You will discover shortly that a member of your family appears to be in some emotional, physical, or financial difficulty. This problem can be solved, providing logical decisions are made not only from your point of view, but from your family member's as well.

**BOWMAN** (i.e., an archer)

Do not shun the talent that is within you. There are times when you feel your lifework is a waste of time; but this is not so at all. You are being overtaxed with so many other activities or obligations that you fail to realize the importance of your purpose on earth. You are very perceptive, determined, and honest in your dealings with others; you must utilize these positive forces with yourself as well. At this time, more introspection concerning your thoughts and actions is the key remedy to your state of being.

**BOX** (see *also* **KIT**)

A sealed box or an intact one intimates that you may betray a closely guarded secret of a friend, business organization, or scientific project of national or international importance. Since this betrayal has not yet taken place, do everything humanly possible to avoid this happening! Bear in mind that the stigma of being labeled a traitor by others may take months or even years to remove.

A box that is torn or one with its top open reveals that you will have a heated exchange of words with a spouse, friend, relative, employer, or employee before too long. After this takes place, you will begin to show more consideration and respect towards that individual who you thought might back down from your intellectual prowess.

## BOXCAR (see **RAILROAD**)

## BOXING (see *also* **COMPETITION**, **CONTEST**, or **EXERCISE**)

Someone you know will survive a personal ordeal and slowly awaken to a better sense of reality. This person is confused, unreliable, and perhaps footloose and fancy-free in some actions of his or her life, at this time. You will be very relieved to know that your prayers are being answered!

## BOYFRIEND

Will your future be happier than your past? The answer to this question is an emphatic yes, providing you dream about a boyfriend whom you like and respect. Be very patient and obedient to your better instincts in life, and you will experience the satisfaction you were always meant to have.

Dreaming about a boyfriend from your past or present whom you do not necessarily like or respect implies that you will commence to make some sound changes within your life. These changes will give you the mental stability and freedom you seem to be seeking. You certainly are levelheaded enough to know exactly where you are going and what you want with your life. More power to you!

## BRACELET

Wearing a bracelet is a direct sign that a token or gift will be presented to you. This could be for some past kindnesses you have shown a spouse or friend or for simply being very special to someone who cares.

A broken bracelet implies that certain fears and tensions sometimes usurp your better judgment of people, places, and things. By using more willpower and faith in this entire matter, you will master the transition you are presently undergoing.

## BRAGGART (see *also* **CONCEIT**)

Your present or past anxieties appear to be self-inflicted. Sometimes you are your own worst enemy, simply because you fail to harmonize with the positive influences around you. You are basically a very good person; however, you must learn to disband some of your critical, cynical attitudes in life. Try to be more optimistic and caring as you go into the future.

## BRAID (see HAIR)

## BRAILLE
Your unselfish and compassionate individualism will lead you towards higher realms on this earth plane. Your expressions of love and kindness are dedicated measures of a very special soul! Even though you may suffer and struggle from time to time, it is with your binding humanitarian feelings and actions that you will be ultimately victorious!

## BRAIN
Seeing the brain tissue of a human being or animal advises you to be more considerate and understanding towards the needs of your family. Any form of unreasonableness on your part will simply create more anguish and hard feelings. There are times when your family members are correct in their wants and needs in life. Do not hinder the progress of a soul for, in so doing, you will automatically hinder yourself in ways you did not anticipate. Let go of your self-righteous and unchangeable habits; you will gain by this wise choice of self-improvement.

## BRAKE
Using the brakes of a motorbike or other form of vehicle implies that you have the ability to be decisive and forceful in most everything that you do. However, there are occasions when certain tensions from family members, friends, work, and so on build up within you. This symbolism advises you to stop, look, and listen to your inner needs at this time. You are burning the candle at both ends; this will simply not do! More rest or simply getting away from it all for a while should give you the time and space to sort things out both within and around you.

## BRASSIERE
You are a highly organized individual! You take life rather seriously, and you have the capability of plunging into a problem headfirst and still come out smelling like a rose. Your leadership capabilities, combined with your sharp-witted mentality, are true gifts that can be utilized for the betterment of your community, state, or country.

## BRAVERY (see HEROISM)

## BREAD

A parent may be experiencing some mental, physical, spiritual, or financial anguish at this time (e.g., exhaustion or over-work, sadness about being alone, misunderstanding with someone). Whatever the problem may be, this parent could certainly use the encouragement, the hope, and any other type of support system that may be applicable at this time. And what person could possibly do this better than you!

Bread crumbs in a dream reveal sickness or injury to the beholder. Be careful; look after yourself in the best way possible so that this ill-omen may pass you by without a hitch.

## BREADBOX

Good news from a distance, as well as good news closer to home, will make the next month or so very rewarding for you. Pending changes in the immediate horizon will give you an opportunity to alter the course of your life's events into something more worthwhile and beneficial to your well-being.

## BREAKFAST (see FOOD or MEAL)

## BREAST

A female dreaming about another female's breast implies a complete disinterest in a task you have been asked to perform. Acceptance or refusal of this task is entirely a matter of honesty and good judgment.

If you are a male dreaming about a woman's breast, then you are either infatuated by the opposite sex, and/or you are far too extravagant in life. Perhaps you are trying to impress the opposite sex with your prowess and macho outlook, or you are spending more than you make. In either case, you are advised to be more rational and clear-sighted in your wants and needs in life.

A male dreaming about a male's breast suggests some emotional and sexual confusion about one's personality (e.g., inhibited or uninhibited sexual desires, inability to communicate well with the opposite sex). You are obviously going through some phase of personal learning or development in your life with some emotional misgivings. There are literally hundreds of authoritative books on sexual matters. You could read one or two of these books; they would perhaps indicate to you that you were very adequately sane in your present thoughts. Or, you could seek some help through a parent, doctor, teacher, good friend, and so on.

**BRIBERY** (i.e., money given or promised to induce a person to do something wrong or illegal)

To witness any form of bribery within a dream intimates that you generally fail to complete what you start. The goals you strive towards are within the bounds of reality only if you allow this to happen. The things you do for yourself and others are those special signs of responsibility to yourself and respect for others. By ignoring your God-given talents and goals in life, you are merely standing in one spot where no one hears you. Failing to accept life's challenges can, and will, bring you unsatisfied heartaches, both now and into the future. Lesson one: finish what you start. Do not be a quitter. Lesson two: do not be afraid of succeeding in life, nor be afraid of losing once in a while. Lesson three: stop feeling so sorry for yourself, and commence to realize the miracle you really are and the miraculous potential you possess with your mind, heart, and soul. Lesson four: believe in yourself, and never forget to believe in God, no matter what trials or tribulations you may encounter.

**BRIDE**

If you are a female and dream of a bride dressed in white, then you can look forward to admiration, love, and contentment within your life. You will never be surrounded or hounded by difficulties which you could not surmount.

If you are a female and dream of a bride dressed in black, then you will not find the immediate happiness you seek. The tide of events will eventually change for you, but not necessarily before you realize your own mistakes and obstinacies in life.

If you are a male dreaming about a bride dressed in white, then you are advised not to become so stressful at the slightest provocation around you. You are looking at life as though it were closing in on you, whereas a vast, beautiful future yet awaits you. Be at peace with yourself and the world, and you will find the inner strength you seek.

If you are a male dreaming about a bride dressed in black, it symbolizes an overall slump in your daily activities. Recently, things have not been going too well for you. The advice this dream gives you is to replace your feelings of despair and defeat with confidence and limit-less faith. You will rise over and above this depressive time with gutsy determination and foresight.

## BRIDEGROOM

If you are a female dreaming of a bridegroom, then you can look forward to a positive order of events that will lead you directly to the goal you wish to attain. Will you be successful in life? Predominately, yes.

If you are a male dreaming of a bridegroom, then beware of some past careless habits which may deter your present progress (e.g., gambling, drinking). Hopefully, you will keep your head above water in this matter, and everything should turn out all right.

## BRIDESMAID

A female dreaming about a bridesmaid is a warning not to be mis-guided or mismanaged by a male or female friend. This may involve romance, a financial loan, or some other business venture. Be wary about being deceived and thus avoid the emotional hurt that could follow.

Self-worship and conceit are glaring characteristics of a male who dreams of a bridesmaid. Trying to acquire the virtues of humility and thankfulness may be a lifetime chore, but this is by no means an impossibility for you. Good reading habits, meditation, prayer, and perhaps a desire to help the underprivileged people in your society could very well awaken the positive forces within you.

## BRIDGE

To see, walk, or ride across a bridge implies that your future will be upheld with loyalty, security, and many outstanding experiences that will comfort you. You are obviously a very dedicated person who shows much love and attention to those who need your comfort and guidance. Has anyone ever told you that you have the heart of an angel? Well, you certainly do!

Seeing a bridge collapse signifies that you will be greatly distressed by one of the following: marital or romantic conflict(s); educational problems; a business contract not being fulfilled; a minor vehicle breakdown or accident; an unlucky move to another residence or city; a loss of revenue through bad investment; or illness. These events are not permanent, so your disappointment will dissipate with time.

**BRIDLE** (i.e., a head harness for guiding a horse)

At this moment it appears as though you were in a spider's web, unable to escape. Some pressing difficulty or emotional conflict with self or with someone else is creating havoc within your mind and spirit. The remedy here is for you to be logical instead of emotional in this matter; then you will come out of this depressive state with excellent results!

**BRIEFCASE**

You must weather a few personal struggles before you see better changes around you (e.g., domestic strife, career dissatisfaction). By getting a grip on yourself and your life's problems, you will commence to slowly find the fulfillment and satisfaction you seek.

**BRIGADE** (i.e., a large unit of soldiers) (see *also* **BATTALION**)

You may be interested in community, state, national, or international organizations who serve your fellow man through good fellowship. In time, it appears that you will belong to a wholesome organization whose service will awaken your scope of knowledge, inventive ideas, and interests in improving the society in which you live.

**BROADCAST** (see **ANNOUNCEMENT, NETWORK, PROGRAM, RADIO, STUDIO,** or **TELEVISION**)

**BROOK** (see **WATER**)

**BROOM**

You have created your own little world of daydreams and wishes that never really become fulfilled. Life, with all its highs and lows, is really not that difficult to face; however, you must buckle down a little harder in order to see some of your better hopes and dreams come to fruition. Happiness and achievement should be an integral part of everyone's life style. You can make it, but you must face the reality of "sweat and toil" that comes with the package of success.

**BROTHEL** (i.e., a house of prostitution)

Essentially, you are a well liked, mature, and industrious individual. However, you believe that everyone must work just as hard and diligently as you in order to see any possibility of achievement in their lives. In some cases this may apply; but in other cases this may not. Success comes to people in a variety of ways. Some people succeed by the sweat of their brow, like you; others become successful with an inspirational thought or dream. This symbolism advises you to be more tolerant and less demanding with people whom you deal with or know.

## BROTHER

A brother who greets or meets you in a pleasant manner or who perhaps saves you from some disaster within your dream is a sign that you will be enriched and prosperous by the changes and struggles in your life.

Seeing a brother who is greedy, unpleasant, or wicked reveals that you are often misunderstood by others simply because you cannot verify or justify some of the comments you make. Know the facts before you attempt to convince others with your information.

A brother who appears suddenly within your dream and shows a great sadness by waving "good-bye" to you is a direct warning that he may have a sudden accident or illness. This accident or illness may have dire consequences! You, the dreamer, may assist your brother by urging him to be explicitly careful for the next month or so. A prayer for his guidance and safety at this time would certainly be wise and helpful.

Seeing a brother who has already passed away reveals that your brother is requesting a prayer from you. Say a prayer for his "guidance and protection within the Light of God", and be assured that he will be most profoundly grateful to you. Did you know that when you say a prayer for the dearly departed, they say a prayer for you as well? Why not! The heavenly states are a beautiful place to abide; whereas we on earth could use all the prayers we can get!

## BROTHER-IN-LAW

A brother-in-law who appears happy and content or who saves you from some disaster within a dream foretells fulfillment and victory in your lifelong undertakings.

A brother-in-law who is saddened for some reason reveals that you should show greater consideration and harmony towards your in-laws. This may be trying for you to do; but, in doing your best in this matter, you may be surprised by what a little bit of love and attention can do for you.

## BRUISE

Seeing a bruise or to self-inflict a bruise is an unlucky sign. Do not expect personal matters around you to change too quickly. A downward trend in most matters of your life is strongly indicated here; a bad storm is brewing. However, in maintaining your unbending courage and confidence, you will rise beyond one of the lowest ebbs of your life.

## BRUSH (e.g., cleaning brush, polishing brush, painting brush, hair brush)

After careful deliberation and much want, you will commence to make in your life a profitable change you were half convinced would never work! So many difficulties and other shortcomings have held you back in life that, at times, you felt there was absolutely no hope or road ahead for you. Nothing is impossible for you, providing it is of good order and that you show humble gratitude for what you want and receive. Look hard into your soul with understanding and with a determined outlook to find your "planned" direction in life. Now and then, try to be more decisive in your daily affairs, and everything else will take care of itself. Be at peace, continue to work as diligently as before, and—very soon—you will commence to see the rewards of your thoughts, actions, and deeds.

## BUBBLE (e.g., underwater air bubble, soap bubble, plastic or glass bubble)

This pleasant dream symbolism signifies good health and good wealth are in store for you. For the time being, however, feel strengthened and secure by the mere prospect of this good vision being directed to you.

## BUCKET (see PAIL)

## BUCKLE (i.e., belt buckle; shoe buckle)

A sudden appearance of a buckle within a dream shows that a great interest or hobby of yours can completely change your life around. By putting your interest to some practical use, or by showing your hobby to others, you may well be on a road to fortune and fame! Why, some of the smallest ideas of inspiration have become the greatest inventions of all time (e.g., bobby pin, nail file, button).

**BUG** (e.g., bedbug, cockroach, gnat)

You believe in the removal of political or social abuses within your society. Your guiding light should be reflected to many people of every race, colour, and creed! Honour and distinction are in store for you, in time to come.

**BUGGY** (i.e., a one-horse carriage usually with four wheels and one seat) (see *also* **SURREY**)

If the horse-drawn buggy appears not to be impeded in any way, then you can expect a happy family reunion. However, if the buggy appears to be hindered by anyone or anything, then the family gathering will be shadowed with jealousy and perhaps sadness.

**BUGLE** (i.e., an instrument used chiefly for military calls and signals)

You will gain by giving more of yourself to those who love you as well as to your community at large. Sometimes, you fail to see or hear a plea for help when it is staring right at you (e.g., charitable work, ignoring the good wishes of a loved one, doing someone a favor). This is not to say that you are totally selfish; however, you do harbour an attitude of indifference, thinking why should you help anyone when nobody helped you in life, and so on. Changing your attitude in life could make a world of a difference for you. Try it, and see for yourself!

**BULB**

You possess psychic talent; this is a gift that should always be used wisely. Neither overestimate nor underestimate the importance of your keen senses, visions, or ability to do good on earth. The biggest mistake psychics can make is to use their innate talent(s) before they are totally prepared to do so and when they are lacking the inner attunement to God. A true psychic is a direct channel to the Cosmic Masters. Do not let anyone tell you differently.

**BULL**

A calm bull advises you to show more consideration towards people's feelings. Your blunt, straightforward remarks can be both shocking and devastating to those around you. A little bit of foresight, kindness, and compassion are endearing practices you should adopt.

A ferocious bull advises you to heed your unpredictable temper.

These unwarranted rages, tantrums, or moods can and will ostracize you from people who do have your best interests at heart. Loving others can only bring you love; whereas showing bitterness can only bring you inner loneliness and false self-esteem.

Seeing a bull chasing or about to chase you or someone else within a dream signifies that you will be assisting someone who is very low in spirits at this time. Do not take this matter lightly! This person will admit that they have made some terribly wrong mistakes in their life style. In spite of your possible annoyance or hurt in this matter, do not forsake this soul; your comfort and guidance is needed more than you know! Remember, we never really miss someone until it is too late!

**BULLET** (see **MISSILE**)

**BULLETIN** (see **LIST**, **NEWSLETTER**, or **PROGRAM**)

**BULLETIN BOARD**

You are beating your head against the wall with a particular sentimental problem to which you already know the answer, but in which you fail to follow your own good advice. This symbolism shows that you are prolonging your agony by waiting and hoping that everything will be as it used to be, whereas this possibility becomes more remote with each passing minute. Some of your intimate friends have already told you to face this problem head-on by going forward in life, without ever looking back. The sooner you resign yourself to this fact, the better off you will be!

**BULLFIGHT**

You will be conscience-stricken over some neglected duty you failed to perform at work or over some negative action you created at home. These matters will settle. However, since you feel the brunt of your actions so strongly, try to do your utmost not to repeat these actions. Remember, history can repeat itself!

**BULLY**

You will eventually recognize that a major decision you had to make now was not only timely, but will have proved to be successful, as well. Through your own confidence, efforts, and gutsy get-up-and-go mentality, you will prosper in life!

## BURGLARY

Repel negative temptations like you would a plague! Anger, revenge, violence, or pride are those evil displays which have far-reaching effects upon the heart, mind, and soul of a person. Even though a person may not think so at first, there is a time and a place where all thoughts and actions have their day of reckoning. Strive to be good, honest, and sincere, no matter what negative influences come your way. In so doing, you will be wise beyond your years.

## BURIAL (see *also* CATACOMB, CENOTAPH, CHURCHYARD, COFFIN, CREMATION, DEATH, FUNERAL, GRAVE, GRAVEDIGGER, GRAVESTONE, GRAVEYARD, MAUSOLEUM, MONUMENT, MORGUE, or URN)

To see yourself or someone else being buried indicates that either you or a member of your family will be sickly for a brief period of time. Nonetheless, great care should be taken in this matter to avoid any future complications.

To see yourself or someone else being buried alive reveals that you will undergo a future operation, which will be successful. It appears that you will be very doubtful about having this operation; however, you will also realize that it is quite necessary for your benefit and well-being.

Seeing the burial of a family member who has already passed away or someone else whom you know who has already passed away indicates that you are a very devoted, compassionate, and unselfish human being. You walk in the footsteps of angels and saints before you! Never look back at all your suffering in life, for you and God alone know what you have been through. Instead, be joyous in knowing that the cross you carry will not be forgotten or unacknowledged. Pray for those who have already passed on in your life. They may come to you in a variety of ways within your dream. Do not be alarmed by this occurrence; rather, be content and elated to know that they chose you specifically for your prayers.

## BURLESQUE

You are destined for great success, in whatever career or lifework you choose. But, be wary of people who will try to dissuade you from achieving your chosen goals. Be wise, courageous, and loyal to your wants and needs in life, and you will soar above and beyond your antagonists like an eagle!

**BURN** (see **FIRE** or **INJURY**)

**BURNOOSE** (i.e., a long cloak with a hood as worn by Arabs or Moors)

Be prepared for busy times ahead! Your intellectual and spiritual maturing will allow you to utilize your humanitarian talents in greater ways. You have a job to do here on earth; that job is to uplift people around you. In touching the soul of another person you will, in effect, perceive the true meaning of love and self-sacrifice. There can be no greater accomplishment on this earth than to save a lost or fallen soul.

**BURNT OFFERING** (i.e., an animal, food, etc., burned at an altar as an offering or sacrifice to a god)

Ominous events may deprive you of better health, happiness, and prosperity should you happen to dream of a burnt offering. Although this dream has many negative connotations, your own strong faith and belief should give you the strength to weather this would-be storm.

**BURP**

Burping in a dream suggests you will no longer tolerate any one or two of the following: an old habit you wish to give up, a place of residence you despise, a job that offers no advancement, or a person who continually offends and humiliates you. The positive changes you make in your life will inevitably give you the peace of mind you seek.

**BUS**

This is a good-omen dream! You will advance threefold in your present undertakings. By keeping up the good work you are presently doing, you will begin to see the deserved rewards of your labour. Never underestimate your potential, as you tend to do from time to time. You are a perfectionist in what you enjoy doing the most, but not necessarily in boring day-to-day chores. Confusion with self and with others may take hold on occasion, but you always find a way to undo hasty miscalculations with inner ease and intellectual understanding. Basically, you seek inner peace and harmony with self and others, but you have very little patience for man's misjudgments, follies, and stupidities in life. Your sound character will bring you much good luck, success, and friendships, as you commence to enter a cycle of soul development, supernaturalism, and a sharing of your inner gifts with others.

## BUSH (see FOREST, SHRUB, or PLANT)

## BUSINESS (see EMPLOYMENT or OWNERSHIP)

## BUTCHER
Sometimes your priorities are off base in life (e.g., failing to look after yourself properly, not listening to good advice). Your excessive indulgence in other matters, however, needs to be corrected. The wearisome chore to change may seem impossible to you at this time. However, this is a complete fallacy on your part. A person is never too young or too old to make positive alterations within, if they honestly want to feel better about themselves. That vital choice is up to you.

## BUTLER
According to this symbolism, you should heed your intuitive feelings more often than you have done in the past. So often, you have made simple or major blunders in life only to realize that your instincts were correct in the first place. Heed your instincts; you will certainly be better off for using this form of mind-soul communication!

## BUTTERFLY
You are a well-admired individual! Your mere presence at a function, gathering, or simply anywhere draws people's attention to your poise, dignity, and overall magnetic personality. Obviously, you are a very special, unique, and talented individual. Your future offers you more achievements, travel, and good will wherever you may go.

(*Note*: You may have the pleasure of knowing that if, for example, you are experiencing a very negative dream but at the very end of your dream sequence or anywhere during your dream sequence you happen to see a butterfly, then this butterfly symbolism takes precedence over your entire negative dream. Consequently, you have nothing to worry about simply because the butterfly acts as a "buffer zone" to anything negative within a dream.)

## BUTTOCK
You are revealing a certain amount of indecisiveness about some pressing problems. You will solve some of these problems; however, do not expect too much encouragement from several members of your

family. It appears that your past attitudes, actions, and mistakes are being reflected on these family members with mistrust. They do not necessarily believe that you have turned over a new leaf or improved your ways. You can, however, prove otherwise. Today can be the beginning of a more enriched tomorrow, if you honestly and faithfully want this to become a reality.

**BUTTON**
You have the capability and initiative of putting your ideas forth into action. When you want something done, you simply immerse yourself in the task and get it done! Your high-powered spirit will carry you far in life, with many accomplishments and noteworthy innovations created by your own ingenious thoughts and actions.

**BUZZARD** (see **BIRD**)

**BUZZER**
Seeing or pressing a buzzer denotes that you will be receiving both good and bad news from a distance. It seems that you have recently been experiencing a depressive, heavy, or ominous feeling, but you simply cannot put your finger on the matter. Whatever the news may be, you will display a great amount of courage, strength, and comfort to all concerned.

**BYWAY** (see **PASSAGEWAY**)

**CABARET**
You appear to be at a complete standstill in your life. However, when you only put half an effort into your work, you can hardly expect wondrous results! Too much idleness in one's life merely breeds unrest, discontentment, and some likelihood of trouble. There are no shortcuts to happiness or any type of success here on earth. Hard work and being content in what you do are the two key elements that will fulfill your inner hopes and aspirations.

**CABIN** (i.e., a hut or cottage built of logs or a small room on a ship)
At some future time you will succeed not only through your sincerity, diligence, and hard work, but from some lucky breaks that will firmly place you at the top of your chosen profession or field. Keep up

the good work now, and you will be very thankful for the opportunities and blessings yet to come.

## CABIN BOY

Tempers will fly and foolish disagreements will upset you today. You will be thankful when this day is over! If at all possible, use plenty of self-control in your dealings with others around you; then, perhaps, this onslaught will pass you by.

## CABINET (e.g., a china cabinet, medicine cabinet)

You will lose, misplace, or have something of value stolen (legal papers, credit cards, watch, ring). Being as meticulous as you are, this entire matter will come as a shock to you. If you are planning a trip or holiday before too long, be extremely careful about your personal possessions.

## CABLE (i.e., a thick, heavy rope)

Lacking faith in your own efforts and beliefs has hindered you considerably up to now. A need for self-assertion, spiritual uplifting, and discovering your true purpose and inner worth should allow you to forge into the future with great ease. Remember: through the compassion of your own heart, you can surmount all things!

## CABOOSE (see RAILROAD)

## CACTUS

You are on the verge of expanding your educational and intellectual pursuits. You appear to be harmoniously guided by the compass of your mind with a great amount of calmness and responsibility. Eventually, you will be led towards the prosperity and wisdom you seek. Your personal world is not a dream world, but a striving reality towards happiness and security!

## CAD (i.e., a man or boy whose behaviour is not gentlemanly) (see *also* DISOBEDIENCE, MISBEHAVIOUR, or MISCHIEF)

You fear many things: life, death, growing old, being sick, feeling pain, and so on. Your many experiences, such as your joys, hopes, dreams, sorrows, and anguishes can be like a beautiful rainbow, like the mighty roar of a storm, or like a tear that falls gently to earth and is no more. We must all learn to cope with and accept what life brings us, no matter how difficult our journey may seem. We are all passengers on this spaceship Earth. And, at the end of our journey, when that heavenly train arrives, we must get on board, waving goodbye (if there's time), making our peace (if there's time), and then intelligently accepting the Eternal Frontiers that await us.

**CADAVER** (see **CORPSE**)

**CADET** (i.e., a student at a military school)
You are heavy-hearted over some oppressive matter concerning one to two people who continually insult your better intelligence. Do not fight back per se, nor take a defeatist attitude. Call upon your inner forces with strength and courage; and then, gently, make your feelings known to those involved. Stick to your feelings; do not back down! You will either receive a sincere apology or a feeble excuse. If the latter happens, then realize that your antagonist or antagonists are merely using you as a scapegoat for their own emotional insecurities.

**CAESAREAN SECTION**
If you are a female dreaming of a caesarean section, then be prepared for some verbal discord or physical abuses from a spouse or friend. If you and the other person involved in this matter prevent yourselves from pointing an accusing finger at one another, then there will be peace. In situations of this nature, there really is no winner in an argument or fight; there are only two losers who want to believe that there is.

If you are a male and dream of this method of delivering a baby, then be prepared for an upward trend, both socially and economically. Bear in mind, as well, that this dream only shows promise and reward to a male who is mature, enterprising, and considerate. Failing this criteria, you can look forward to some more anxieties and struggles in your life unless, of course, you decide to change.

**CAFE** (see *also* **CABARET**)
You lack self-reliance! Far too often, you envy other people, hoping to be exactly what they purport to be, but not really taking into account that they may be worse off than you. Envy no one, nor try to live in the shadow of someone else's importance or expertise in life. In all matters of self-reliance, you must painstakingly forge ahead—seeing,

doing, and accomplishing your own goals, in your own time. You can do it! You can reach this personal achievement when you decide to disperse that inactive spirit in you with faith, vitality, and courage.

## CAFETERIA

Deciding to buy something or to eat in a cafeteria signifies that you are attempting to avoid an issue with another person. You may discover that what you really have to say to this person may not be taken as an insult, but more so as a solution to an intimate problem.

Carrying a tray of food in a cafeteria intimates that your character, honour, or repute may be at stake because of someone's senseless, narrow-minded gossip. You will wade through the surmounting embarrassment and humiliation with a great amount of spirit and courage, and you will come out of this entire matter smelling like a rose!

Going back for more food indicates that you will attempt to help two people who are about to make one of the biggest mistakes of their lives. The roots of their problem appear to be money, foolish pride, and some uncompromising matters of sex. Your counseling will be invaluable to them. Hence, their reconciliation will prove both fulfilling and rewarding to everyone concerned.

Dropping a tray or a dish in a cafeteria implies that before you can like and love someone else, you must first learn to like and love yourself. A conceited, high-strung individual stands little chance of measuring up to a happy individual who has found the true pathway of goodwill and joy. In order to elevate your thoughts, actions, and deeds in life, you must strive very hard to know yourself, to correct yourself, and to inspire yourself and others through experience, learning, and wisdom.

## CAGE

Show more concern for your life: who you are, where you are going, what you wish to attain, the good you can do for others, and so forth. Begin to actually see yourself achieving your innermost wishes in life. Have faith, and pray for these good wishes, sincerely and humbly. Do not give up at any time but, rather, go from day to day with the assurance that your calm, inner voice will be heard. It will be heard, as you will eventually see; remember, however, that in reaching out into the Cosmic Forces of Life through prayer and visualization, it will be your patience, love, and thoughtfulness that will ultimately bring you the gifts and joys you seek.

## CAKE

To see or to bake a cake suggests that you will be making greater strides to improve your personality (e.g., attitudes, appearance, mannerisms). This dream does not in any way imply that you are a person with great problems, but rather a person who wants to make positive strides towards self-improvement. As long as you keep thinking and acting in this manner, you will inspire others around you with your sensibility, integrity, and maturity.

If the cake you see or bake is burnt or unpleasant to look at, then beware of other people's premeditated attempts to put you down. Unfortunately, you appear to be a victim of circumstances in this matter. So, when someone does put you down again, simply "agree" with them wholeheartedly; nothing irks a person more! They will back off so fast, you will be amazed by the humour of it all! Do not be hurt by their ignorance; realize they need to be taught a lesson in good fellowship and understanding.

## CALCULATING MACHINE (i.e., a calculator)

Seeing or using this device symbolizes that you are backlogged with work (e.g., homework, unsigned contracts, unfilled orders, repairs). Whatever your backlog may be, you are advised not to leave such an overload of yesterday's work for today or tomorrow. Of course, this is up to you.

## CALCULUS (see MATHEMATICS)

## CALENDAR (see *also* MONTH)

A calendar with the days, weeks, months, and year written on it reveals that you will be motivated and encouraged to use your God-given talent(s) with respect, dignity, and greater purpose. Up to now, it appears that you were beset by many earthly limitations (e.g., not enough money, lack of education, too much education without any practical experience). Happy tidings are forthcoming through some good event or circumstance. From this vantage point, your future will have greater significance to you than your past.

Dreaming about a specific day of a month (e.g., Thursday, June 3rd) reveals that something rather special could happen to you on that day, such as a surprise party, a winning, buying or selling something rather special, or some other event that will affect you in a meaningful and helpful way.

## CALF

This symbolism forewarns you of some pending illness or health problem that will manifest itself quickly but will not be long-lasting. Faith, strength, and possibly medical assistance will see you through this trying time.

A disfigured, diseased, or slaughtered calf, however, warns that a communicable disease or some other sickness will assail a younger family member. This matter will not be long-lasting either.

## CALL

To call or shout in your dream intimates that you will have to wait eight months to a year before you see a certain project or event become a reality for you (e.g., travel, promotion, graduation, engagement, marriage). Hold on to your good wishes; you have much to look forward to, as your future gently unfolds.

## CALLING (i.e., having an inner urge towards some occupation, vocation, or work)

It is quite obvious that you have overcome much struggle, sadness, and sorrow in your life. You are like a wandering traveler who, upon occasion, gets lost in a forest but realizes that eventually there will be an opening or a clearing to help you gain your bearing. Once you have gained your bearing or position, the return journey home becomes relatively simple. Your many experiences and lessons in life have also taught you that the storms you encounter on earth (e.g., mental, physical, or spiritual) will pass you by, sooner or later. You will go far in life, with your uplifting and encouraging, self-reliant spirit!

## CALVARY (i.e., an outdoor portrayal about Jesus' crucifixion)

Dreaming about Calvary denotes that you are a child of destiny! Whatever gift(s) or talent(s) you possess, you can be sure that you will share these with your fellow man (e.g., acting, music, writing, inventing, healing, prophecy). You were born to be special here on earth; you will lead a very high and honourable existence!

## CAMEL

Your forceful mind, self-determination, and decisiveness are continuously applied and utilized simply because you know yourself very well, and you certainly seem to know where you are headed. It would take more than an army to destroy your wholesome attitude about life, the universe, and all created things hidden from your senses. Limitless doors will commence to open for you as time goes on; your purpose, goodness, and knowledge will be like a guiding light for others to follow and embrace.

**CAMEO** (i.e., an engraved gem or shell)

Your consideration towards others less fortunate than you is a high reflection of your good upbringing. You have a great peace of mind when you assist others—realizing, as well, that there never seems to be enough help to go around. You are a respectable, dependable, and devoted individual with a great desire to make your little corner of the world a better place in which to live. You are, indeed, accomplishing that goal with limitless blessings!

**CAMERA** (i.e., motion picture camera, television camera, home movie camera, flash camera, still camera, box camera, zoom lens camera, micro-camera, etc.)

You will gain by finishing what you start (e.g., rather than being lazy at home, school, work). Learning to show greater concern and incentive towards life in general will give you much more peace of mind. No one can expect to receive splendid rewards for services not rendered. Doing more for yourself today will ultimately bring you greater harvests for tomorrow.

A broken camera suggests that you should cease any further arguments or embarrassing conflicts with a younger or older person. This distressing symbol reveals future trouble and difficulties are forthcoming unless more human love, understanding, and compromises are made in this matter.

**CAMP** (i.e., temporary quarters for travelers, hunters, fishermen, and others)

Observing a camp or setting up camp advises you to avoid any acts of violence as you would a plague. In times of stress, always remember to control your bitterness with common sense and foresight. A disturbing incident could have some dreadful consequences for you, if you are not prudent and wise!

Playing games at a camp or breaking up camp implies that you are faced with a personal problem (e.g., alcoholism, drugs, gambling, financial or marital or romantic difficulties, some sexual hang-up). The solution in this entire situation requires explicit honesty, faith, and courage on your part. Your lifestyle and happiness will improve upon this earth plane, providing you seek the help and guidance you need.

**CAMPAIGN** (i.e., a series of planned actions for electing a political candidate)

You appear to be financially restricted or broke at this time. Your past spending activities are the cause of your present strife. Consider your present experience as though you were being taught a very special lesson on earth, such as complete honesty and loyalty to self and others, tolerance with self and others, and the courage and patience to forge ahead when all doors are closed to you. Through your perseverance, trials, and tribulations, you will slowly commence to perceive the truth and wisdom to your existence.

**CAMPUS**

Your dedicated and sincere desires to succeed in life are worthy thoughts to nourish and uphold. You are unique and cultured and possess a dynamic personality capable of making you rich, famous, and widely respected.

**CAN** (e.g., a container such as a milk can, a garbage can, a soup can, a coffee can)

You are a talented person who is not as disorganized or incompetent as some people think you are. Within you lies the most important key to your future, where personal hopes, success, and happiness are concerned. By simply commanding your soul to guide you with courage, you will soon discover that your pathway in life will begin to be more meaningful and pleasantly productive. Never give up! Keep asking and commanding your inner spirit (force, drive, impetus) until your cup overflows with good results!

**CANAL**

You will prosper by your farsighted and levelheaded thinking and overall performance. Some forthcoming events will place you at the forefront of your innermost hopes. Today you are merely wishing for better things to happen; but, as your future progresses, you will see the reality of your good wishes bear fruit.

A canal that appears to be obstructed in some way signifies that you have been rather apathetic recently. You will come out of this state soon but, in the interim, strive to be very patient with yourself and others around you, have less doubt about your inner worth and potential, and try a little harder to know and understand your true purpose for being here on earth.

## CANCER

Dreaming about cancer does not necessarily imply that you have this dreaded disease. On the contrary! It merely suggests that you are consciously or subconsciously frightened of it. If you are haunted by the fear of this disease during your wake state as well, then you must begin to condition or harness your mind to stop this mental harassment. Before you go to sleep at night, simply think or command your mind that you are "well" and "active" and do not wish to be bothered any longer by thoughts of cancer—or any other disease, for that matter. Continue to do this every night until these thoughts leave you alone. Before you know it, you will be at peace—quite alive, active, and well.

(*Note*: If your fear in this matter becomes phobic or goes beyond the point of being levelheaded with yourself, then by all means seek some medical advice, for your own peace of mind.)

## CANDLE

To dream of wholesome-looking candles or beautifully lit candles acknowledges the fact that you are slowly beginning to take stock of the metaphysical or psychic world around you. There are occasions when worthy men and women on this planet receive inspired thoughts or flashes of wisdom. Where do these great thoughts of wisdom come from? Perhaps they emanate from the denizens of a Universal Cosmic Force somewhere in time and space. The people chosen are mentally and spiritually prepared to accept and share their gifts with mankind. The world is in need of this special breed of people who are not only attuned to the Universal Cosmic Force, but who also edify wholesome thoughts through philosophical books and mystical awareness. You will gradually merit some of this Cosmic awareness by your willingness to perceive the other side of life through meditation and prayer. You will be likened unto an astronaut in space who discovers another world impressively resounding with enduring life.

Broken candles, black candles, or candles that are lit but tend to go out within a dream imply that you can unburden your conscience by exercising greater truth and honesty. Now, whether you have created falsehoods, myths, defamation, perjury, forgery, or anything else of a dishonest nature, there is still hope for you to rectify the wrong committed. Even as a tree is given new vitality in the spring of its life, so you, too, can be blessed with new hope, faith, and peace if you admit to yourself and to your God the wrongs of your ways. Speak to your God as though you were actually talking to your closest friend. Pour your heart out to God about many different things: your troubles, sorrows, joys, ambitions, and so on. When you have temporarily exhausted your state of mind in prayer, let go of yourself for a moment or two and begin to feel the embracing warmth and understanding that will enshroud you. Do not ponder nor wonder what you have said to God; instead, be thankful and grateful that He took the time to listen to your wants and needs in life. Just as you drink a glass of water to quench your thirst, so you must believe without any doubt whatsoever that you were heard and that your prayers will be answered. Seeing the results of your prayers may take time—or may happen instantly. Remember, however, that you must begin to prove to yourself and to God that you are changing for the better.

## CANDLEHOLDER

You are not necessarily practicing what you preach, nor are you putting your best efforts into your livelihood. A good piece of advice would be for you to apply more positive thinking in your daily affairs. You will slowly commence to see improvements within your life when you learn to treat others equally, honestly, and respectfully.

A candleholder that appears badly stained, is broken, or falls to the floor suggests that you are knocking yourself out concerning the welfare and happiness of another person and/or a career position you are hoping to attain. Do not stop fighting for the causes you believe to be correct and just. Sooner or later, you will get through to the person whom you are hoping to help or career position you are hoping to attain. Be patient. As long as you maintain your sound philosophy about giving more than you receive in life, then you can be sure that your future's blessings will far exceed your past discouragements.

## CANDY

This dream symbolism cautions the dreamer not to go overboard where sweet foods are concerned. Whether you do have a sweet tooth or not, you are strongly advised to keep away from negative foods that do absolutely nothing for you. Remember, you have only one physical body here on earth; what you do to keep yourself fit and healthy is entirely up to you.

**CANE** (i.e., walking stick)

A white cane implies that your organized life is a measure of your good upbringing. You are best suited to help younger, less fortunate people than yourself. Whoever you may be or whatever you do in life, you will always be sincere, productive, independent, and resourceful in all you undertake.

A black cane implies that you tend to exaggerate, much to the annoyance of others around you. This tendency should be curbed with common sense, respect, and more appreciation and love for self and for life around you.

A cane of any other colour reveals that a culmination of disturbing events has taught you to intensify your search for spiritual faith, joy, and rest. In light of the many problems you have to manage, you are certainly on the right pathway in life. Your inspiring motivations will bring you the freedom to achieve your earthly goals and the wisdom to teach others courage, loyalty, and unending hope.

**CANNIBALISM**

You have affected someone through your thoughts or actions (e.g., spending more than you make, gambling, drinking, taking advantage of someone's good friendship). In order to rectify this particular situation you must courageously make amends now, otherwise you may lose someone very near and dear to you.

**CANNING** (i.e., putting foods in cans or jars for future use)

There does not appear to be much love, union, or harmony in your household. This problem could relate to someone's bad habits, such as alcoholism, unfaithfulness, indifferent views or opinions, physical or mental violence, and so forth. All you want in life is some understanding, peace, and contentment. Unfortunately, you appear to be dealing with a very stubborn individual. Seek help for this person, but if they absolutely refuse to be helped—which is often the case—then do not blame yourself for trying. Sometimes, we simply have to hope and pray for people who refuse to improve, hoping that somewhere and somehow the school of hard knocks will teach them a valuable lesson. Some people learn quickly through bad experiences in life; however, some people continue to make the same mistakes over and over again.

## CANNON

Showing more patience and being more careful in your activities may save you some future anguish or injury. Your adventurous spirit may lead you to strange places no average individual would dare enter. Strive to use more discretion in your thoughts and actions by thinking twice before you leap headfirst into some foolish situation.

## CANOE (see BOAT)

## CANOPY (see AWNING)

## CANTEEN (i.e., a place where food is served to people in times of distress)

Seeing people entering or leaving a canteen indicates an imminent, drastic change is in store for you (e.g., sudden move to another town, city, or country; losing your job; dropping out of school, walking out of a home environment you can no longer tolerate). Perhaps this change must take place in order for you to know and feel that somewhere on this planet there is a place for you. Let us hope that you will find the calmness and truth your heart, mind, and soul appear to be seeking.

## CANVASSER (i.e., one who goes among people to estimate the outcome of an election, opinion poll, orders, sales campaign)

Do not let one personal defeat upset you so much! There is no excuse for you to quit your intended goal or project at this stage of the game. You have not failed! You have, in reality, risen a step higher towards the true goal that yet awaits you. Carry on!

## CAP

You are anxiously waiting for some good event to materialize soon. Do not be too disappointed if the outcome is not exactly to your liking (e.g., promotion, scholarship, travel). This letdown or setback will actually be a blessing in disguise for you, as you will eventually see. You will not fail or falter in life; rather, you will forge ahead towards a great destiny.

**CAPE** (i.e., mantle or cloak)

You are a shy, retiring person. Your alienation from people appears to be more from some past events rather than by choice. As long as you are personally happy in your present state, then you need not concern yourself any further. However, if you are discouraged and sad with your present state, then you and you alone should make the effort to change things around for yourself. You must, of course, give yourself half a chance to meet and greet people. Slowly, you will discover that most people are very warm and friendly when you at least meet and greet them half way.

**CAPSULE** (i.e., a small gelatin case for enclosing medicine, or a time capsule)

You cannot see yourself the way other people actually see you. Since you are a very emotional person, it would be wise at this time of your life to control your "ups" and "downs" or "fanciful whims" with a certain amount of reality and maturity. By discarding your petty contradictions and bringing forth the knowledge and understanding of your experiences thus far, you can become a winning personality!

**CAPTAIN**

You may be in for a long, hard struggle ahead. However, your good common sense and hard work, combined with a mixture of good luck, are the moving forces that will assist you in this matter. You will triumph over all your obstacles!

**CAR** (see *also* **DASHBOARD**, **FRAMEWORK**, or **HUBCAP**)

Taking a ride in a car at a moderate pace suggests that you are a philosophical, poised, and coolheaded individual. Your ideas are basically formulated from a good, solid foundation, slowly working its way upwards towards a spire. With your levelheaded thinking and competence, you are bound to gain honour and success in your lifetime!

Riding in a car or hot rod and so on at a reckless pace and conceivably having an accident or seeing this happen to someone else suggests you are unreasonable and faultfinding at times. Your hot-tempered, moody, and wayward nature nowadays is quite inconsistent with your past behaviour. This dream symbolism advises you to pull yourself together, make better plans for your future, and commence to treat your loved ones with more consideration and respect.

Dreaming about purchasing a new or used car could mean precisely what you are dreaming. If this is not applicable to you at this time, then this symbolism implies that you are an alert, thorough, and farsighted individual. You will reap more profit and happiness in time to come.

Dreaming of riding in a car that stalls implies that if you do own a car, it may fail or break down within a day or two. Should this not apply in your case, then this dream reveals that you outwardly offer too much flattery to some people, when inwardly you actually feel a great dislike towards them. This attitude cannot possibly bring you much peace of mind and happiness in life. Begin to love and appreciate your fellow man through acts of humility and good fellowship.

Repairing a car intimates that if you do own a car, you may have to repair it within a week or two of this dream. Should this not apply in your case, then this dream means that you are a warmhearted, charitable individual who places the needs of others ahead of your own. You are a shining example of a fine person who truly knows and understands what life is all about!

Having a dream whereby you lose your car indicates that you have led a very difficult life and that, even though you may be financially established, you are still mentally and spiritually in turmoil. It appears as though you are haunted and harassed by unseen forces within and around you, which give you little or no peace here on earth. This crisis can slowly be corrected through prayer, medical counseling or medication, reading positive books, seeking spiritual advice, and by adopting a clearer state of mind about your past, yourself, and others around you.

To have your car stolen within a dream is a forewarning that this act can actually take place or that you may be involved in a minor accident. Be watchful and careful, where this matter is concerned. Hopefully, this entire negative revelation may be averted. If the aforementioned does not apply to you, then this dream signifies that you tend to be ungenerous and miserly. Your materialistic ideas and habits need to change; the sooner you realize this fact, the better off you will be.

To be thrown out of a car forcibly or accidentally, or to jump out of a car for some reason, or to see this happen to someone else signifies that you very often have to overcome your doubts through persuasive arguments. You tend to live in the past, far too frequently reflecting upon your hardships and sorrows and upon the love and happiness you did not receive in life. This dream also reveals that you are attempting to completely dominate a younger person in your life (i.e., young adult). This could be because you are a parent or because you feel older and wiser. You will gain absolutely nothing by assuming control over this young man or woman in your life. For your own peace of mind, you should stop smothering this young soul with your dominant love, fears, and weaknesses. There is betterment ahead for you—but you must learn to control your thoughts and actions, be more humble and grateful for your blessings, and pray for spiritual and moral strength.

If a car is stuck in the mud, rain, snow, and so on, then you simply abhor the thought of doing some work and not being able to finish what you start. This feeling could be because you are constantly interrupted by the needs of the people around you or because you feel there just is not enough time in a day to complete your task. Patience, self-discipline, and a good sense of humour are the sensible requirements which will allow you to work with more ease and less frustration.

To merely see a parked car or to be sitting in a parked car that gets rammed by another car, etc., denotes a sense of insecurity, doubt, and depression you are experiencing at this time. Your future is a lot brighter than you could remotely imagine! There is much happiness, prosperity, and good work ahead for you. As a matter of fact, your sensibility and good intentions towards all living things will be your passport to a rich and rewarding future.

## CARAVAN

The frustration in your life will soon dissipate, and the focus of attention will be towards establishing new hopes and ideals for a better tomorrow. As you slowly come out of your doldrums and depressive state, the visibility of your life's path will become more clear and meaningful to you. Your future reveals that your ability, action, and courage will at last allow you to forge ahead with peace and prosperity.

## CARCASS (i.e., a slaughtered animal dressed as meat)

To see the entire carcass of a dead animal indicates a period of stress, sadness, and the possibility of mourning. You will come out of this mental and physical state with a new perspective about yourself and about life in general. Greater attention should be placed on the importance of one's soul rather than on materialistic gains. Greater attention should also be placed in treating your loved ones with more respect and attention while they are still with you on this earth plane. Much too often, people tend to neglect their loved ones, always putting aside their communication for another day (e.g., a visit, letter, telephone call). Unfortunately, another day may be too late!

Seeing half or a portion of the carcass advises you to follow good food habits and to learn to control or avoid any negative cravings you may have (e.g., liquor, drugs). This dream is trying to guide you away from the possibility of some physical burden that could one day be your own undoing. That choice, of course, is entirely up to you.

**CARD** (e.g., cheque cashing card, credit card, fortunetelling or tarot cards, greeting card, identification card, playing cards, police card, show card, social security card, or window card)

Your foresight, maturity, and positive influence with people are praiseworthy beginnings to a bright future! You have a magnetic, showmanship personality that will inevitably enhance your opportunities and prospects in due time. Prosperity, respect within your society, and happiness are slated ahead for you. Realize, as well, that these praises and good tidings are the result of your hard work, perseverance, and positive beliefs.

**CAREER**

Dreaming about your present career or one you anticipate signifies that you are presently going through a maze of spiritual, mental, and physical changes. Be at peace! When you finally stabilize this condition through prayer, meditation, exercise, and possibly some form of medication, a transformation within you will take place. A more understanding, patient, responsible <u>you</u> will emerge—giving you a mature insight about life and a greater purpose to pursue your role on this planet.

**CARESS** (i.e., an endearing touch or embrace)

You have an affinity for being easily hurt or upset by situations that appear quite innocent to another person. You are a serious, sensitive person who cannot be bothered by childish pranks, jokes, or sarcasm. Although you are forgiving, you definitely avoid people who have upset you in some way. You will endure in life, simply because you have an unyielding faith and an inner belief to succeed in your own time and in your own way.

**CARELESSNESS** (see **NEGLECTFULNESS**)

**CARETAKER**

A series of wholesome events will finally allow you to advance your position on earth. Within a short period of time, you are destined to make a long journey to be with some special relatives or friends whom you have not seen for quite some time. Cheer up! A decent break is in the horizon for you, with a promise of good luck and rejoicing.

## CARGO

Your hard-working attitude and rugged energy are guiding factors that will ultimately lead you closer to financial security and providential circumstances. Others may sit and hope for good things to happen; whereas you endure, suffer, and experience the road of life with an air of sensibility. Keep up the good work! Your good spirit is destined to guide you towards lasting fulfillment and well-being wherever you go.

## CARHOP (i.e., a waiter or waitress who serve customers at a drive-in restaurant)

To see or to be a carhop within a dream intimates that you are somewhat restless at home, school, or work. You should begin to ask some serious soul-searching questions about yourself.

What do you really want to do in life? What inner potential or talent do you possess now that could possibly lead you closer to your chosen goal(s)? What inner weaknesses do you possess now that could hinder your progression in the future? Are you a poor loser? Do you accept some form of failure or hindrances in your life as total defeat within yourself? Do you care about others as much as you care about yourself? These are but a few of the questions you should begin to ask yourself. Perhaps, somewhere in the maze of everyday living, you will commence to find your niche with the prospects of becoming more farsighted, responsible, and productive in your ways.

## CARIBOU (see DEER)

## CARNIVAL (i.e., a small fair with sideshows, rides)

Better tidings are ahead for you with regards to travel, spiritual growth, and finally being able to pursue some field of interest that has always intrigued you. Your life has not been easy, but you have always managed to climb out of your depressed tempests with stronger determination, courage, and faith.

## CAROLLER

You will alienate yourself from a situation or problem involving a loved one. Since your sensitivity is greater than your willpower at this time, it would be an opportune moment for you to think about changing the course of events facing you. Simply begin by being honest to your loved one by explaining what is troubling you. Silence is not the answer! Some measure of compromise and lasting peace can be achieved, providing you commence to unravel your pent-up anxieties and feelings about your present situation.

## CARPENTER

You are behaving in a shortsighted manner! By being too critical of others, by acting in an anti-social manner, and by allowing false pride to guide your judgments, you are creating havoc within your life. The antidote here is to simply be more thoughtful and kindhearted with your thoughts, desires, and actions in life. Be more realistic. You are never too young or too old to change!

## CARPET

A multi-coloured carpet or any other coloured carpet except black suggests that you are a creative, productive individual. Your ideas show good foresight, originality, and inventiveness. The interest you have in the mysteries, philosophies, and theories of life appear to be endless! Whatever it is that you do in life or aspire toward, this dream symbolism reveals that—in some small or large way—you will fulfill your hopes and wishes.

A black carpet reveals that you will undergo a temporary illness. Carelessness or inattention to this illness could create unpleasant complications. Be prudent in this matter.

## CARPET SWEEPER

This device implies that you are overburdened with domestic or office work. You do not seem to have the leisure time to pursue some of your creative or social interests. However, if you are determined enough to reshuffle your work load to suit your other needs, then your so-called impossibilities will become realities.

**CARRIAGE** (see **BABY CARRIAGE** or **CHARIOT**)

**CARROUSEL** (see **MERRY-GO-ROUND**)

**CARSICKNESS** (see **NAUSEOUSNESS**)

**CART** (i.e., a two-wheeled vehicle drawn by a horse or a two-wheeled vehicle drawn or pushed by hand)

It is not enough to merely be intelligent in life. If this intelligence is not used in a mature manner through acts of honesty, self-discipline, confidence, and unselfishness, then it can be considered ineffective and unproductive. Sometimes you lack these positive qualities; acts of humility and obedience would be auspicious beginnings for you. These acts would begin to bring you more calmness, peace of mind, and soul-satisfying achievements.

**CARTOGRAPHY** (i.e., the practice of making maps or charts)

You are subject to spells of exaggeration. Consequently, you may have some explaining to do when you are approached by people who do happen to know the truth. To be foolish in life, all a person has to do is reveal their negative habits with senseless pride and complacency. To be wise in life, always strive to be honest and loyal, and make every effort to correct the wrongs of your ways.

**CARTOON**

Within several days of this dream, an event will transpire that will literally send you reeling over with laughter! Whatever this occurrence may be, it will have a pleasing effect on you for a long time to come. This dream also suggests that your lifestyle, unlike the average person's, is filled with drama and a high content of humour. Being quick-witted should allow you to handle situations of uncertainty, unusualness, or amusement with the greatest amount of ease and pleasure!

**CAR WASH**

To merely speak of or to compare yourself to others who have succeeded is not enough for you to succeed. Hard work and determination are the realistic ingredients necessary to elevate you to the top of your chosen field. Do not expect too much on a silver platter in life; rather, realize that your greatest desires can be fulfilled through initiative, faith, courage, and strength.

**CASH** (see **MONEY**)

**CASHIER**

You are preoccupied with improving your financial status and will eventually do so. In the meantime, you should also acknowledge the fact that money, although necessary, is not the only means of happiness on earth. You are not in a state of being totally destitute yet, so consider yourself very fortunate up to now. Maintain an optimistic outlook, cast off negative thoughts about being in a future poorhouse, and you just might surprise yourself by becoming very wealthy in more ways than you know.

## CASH REGISTER
Some confusing and embarrassing moments may befall you if you persist in delving any deeper into the private or personal affairs of people around you. The most important key to your happiness is to reflect more upon ways to improve yourself, rather than ponder about the weaknesses and anguish of other people.

## CASSETTE (see CAMERA or TAPE RECORDER)

## CASINO (i.e., a gambling place)
Your aims in life should be oriented more towards spiritual values of the soul rather than towards earthly prestige, riches, and gain. The peace, humility, and understanding you require can be fulfilled for you and can bring you greater prosperity than you have thus far experienced. However, before any improvements can come your way in life, you must permanently let go of your selfishness and pride.

## CASTANETS
Seeing, playing, or hearing castanets within a dream implies that you will be tempted to reveal a personal or business secret to another person. This private or confidential matter should be told to no one. The possible cause and effect may unwittingly bring you future trouble. This entire matter rests squarely on your honesty and integrity; use your good judgment here and keep quiet!

## CASTAWAY (i.e., a shipwrecked person)
You are a very serious-minded and communicative individual. Nonetheless, you are worried or uneasy about a very personal matter that appears to torment your heart, mind, and soul. The ravages of time, people, places, and events have created a sorrowful impact on your emotional harmony. You have obviously been used and abused by others who have shown very little consideration for your true feelings, hopes, and desires. The past scars of your traumatic experiences may

never heal permanently; but, despite all the unfavourable happenings in your life, there is hope for a better tomorrow. You and you alone hold the key to this hope. An improved life awaits you as you gather inner strength, courage, and confidence through prayer and faith. Let your past go by the wayside; look more towards the future where dreams—your dreams—can come true!

**CASTLE**

This symbolism suggests that you are burning the candle at two ends; you are overworked! You appear to be working on nerves alone. This fact will not bring you healthier times. Plenty of rest and a temporary cessation of your busy schedule should be in order.

**CASTRATION**

For the next several weeks, exercise extreme caution where any type of travel is concerned. This is an accident symbolism. Allow this dream to be your guiding light; please consider seriously the unpleasant consequences of not being prudent!

**CAT**

Seeing any coloured cat (other than black) denotes your lack of concentration from time to time. Your mind wandering or state of exhaustion often leaves one with the impression that you are listening with one ear and letting it go just as fast out the other. Who knows? Perhaps your mind wandering is simply a blessing in disguise for you, considering that you are not a scatterbrain but a highly intelligent individual.

Seeing a black cat indicates a minor or major vehicle accident and/or a slipping or falling accident which could result in having to wear a cast. This foreboding revelation can apply for one week's duration. Carelessness or ignorance on your part could result in some serious physical and financial ramifications. Please note: this serious matter can be avoided if you stop, look, and listen!

**CATACOMB** (i.e., vaults or galleries in an underground burial place)

You are a very domineering individual. By being so insensitive to other people's needs and wants in life, you have created a mental and emotional division with those who want to know and understand you better. Your out-of-date attitudes and underestimation of people's intelligence is far too unbecoming a person like you. Strive to be a better listener, show more humility and thankfulness for what you already have, show more respect and consideration for others, and be guided by the wisdom of your experiences rather than compelling others to live by your hardheaded attitudes in life.

## CATALOGUE (see *also* LIST)

According to this symbolism, you are a peace-loving individual who shares harmonious feelings and understandings with your fellow man. You truly are a remarkable person, simply because no matter how hard you have to struggle in life you still see a ray of hope and love. Others may fall by the wayside because of their lack of determination, but you admirably plough forth like a conquering hero! You are on the right road in life, and you will continue to illuminate and inspire others when all else appears hopeless and ending. You are veritably an architect of your own future!

## CATAPULT (i.e., in ancient times, a military device for throwing stones, spears, etc. and/or a contrivance for launching a rocket missile, airplane, etc.)

You are beginning to make some fine changes in your life! For example, your temperament has cooled down, your objectives are now in perspective, and you are slowly beginning to realize that life is not one big, careless and carefree jungle. Settling down in life is a wondrous joy, providing you can accept the responsibilities that go with it. This dream reveals that you have finally ripened to a state of maturity, with significant and concrete reality. Selfless concern and gracious feelings towards your fellow man is one of the main routes you should constantly follow. Keeping this is mind, other situations and problems will commence to fade away like clouds in the morning sky.

## CATCALL (i.e., a whistle or shrill noise used to express disapproval of a speaker, actor, etc.)

To deride someone with catcalls or being subjected to catcalls personally reveals that you should show more consideration and kindness towards someone whom you have misjudged. An apology appears to be in order. Do not judge a person through hearsay or from some gossip column. Even if the rumour is correct you, as a member of the human race, should not jump on the bandwagon or be a member of a lynch mob simply because "everyone else" feels this is correct. As a matter of fact, those who cast stones are more guilty than the victims themselves!

**CATECHISM** (i.e., questions and answers in a handbook for teaching the principles of a religion)

Seeing or reading a catechism handbook stresses a need for you to concentrate on some domestic project or upon some educational or business commitment. Although the results of your labour may appear unrewarding at first, the end results will prove to be beneficial and profitable for you.

**CATERPILLAR** (i.e., a wormlike larva of various insects, such as a butterfly, moth)

Basically you have a very strong mind and will, but recent events have made you rather sad, uneasy, and irritable. Being a bit of a perfectionist does not help much either! Looking at your stresses from an optimistic point of view reveals that you can regain your composure and stamina by not being so demanding on your time, labor, and pleasure. Strive to be more calm, cool, and collected in times of stress. Then you will certainly be more willing to enjoy life's pleasures around you.

(*Note*: If the above entry does not apply to you in any way, then this entry implies that you have a fear or hatred towards this tiny grub.)

**CATHEDRAL** (see **CHURCH**)

**CATTLE** (e.g., cows, steers, or oxen) (see *also* **BULL**)

Seeing undisturbed cattle perhaps grazing or drinking water and so on suggests you are undergoing some family strife at this time. These problems are fleeting ones. More compromises, forgiveness, and inner gratitude should be adhered to by all concerned. Peace of mind and more harmony are the peace-loving rewards of this dream!

Should the cattle be stampeding, chasing someone, or surrounding someone, then there is a person very dear and near to you who needs help. The problem is not financial, nor is it an illness. It appears that this individual is very lonely, despondent, and depressed beyond words! You will be directly instrumental in assisting this person (e.g., family member, friend, acquaintance) through your generous encouragement and direction.

Slaughtered cattle is an augur of possible sad times. The illness, accident, or death of a family member is shown here. Pray now like you have never prayed before for the safekeeping and well-being of your entire family! A prayer from the heart, as you know, is the best means of asking for your Creator's intercession to guide and protect your loved ones. With God all things are surmountable!

Sick or crippled cattle indicate a loss of revenue and social prestige for you. What a mess unhappiness, money, ownership, wealth, or vices can bring if one's time is not disciplined or used wisely for the benefit of all concerned. This symbolism advises you to change some of your ways and habits for the good of yourself and your family—and for the overall betterment of your shaky future.

Seeing a snake, lizard, worm, or insect go through the hoof of a cow signifies that someone you know may attempt or actually commit suicide. Once again, a prayer for the safety and guidance of all your loved ones is advised at this time! Hopefully, this unfortunate being will be saved from the terrible torment of being so alone and lost in this life.

**CATWALK** (i.e., a narrow walk or platform especially along the edge of a bridge, over the engine room of a ship or diesel locomotive)

This world is constantly progressing towards inner space and outer space. This is wholesome and comforting! Your mind is the greatest warehouse of knowledge; however, it requires some prodding and direction. Through meditation, through prayer, and by simply acknowledging the fact that you are an integral part of the entire universe, you will literally begin to understand and utilize what lies beyond time and space. Your Creator's Gifts to you are your gifts to see beyond the conscious mind with cosmic thoughts and adventurous faith.

**CAUTION** (see *also* **RELUCTANCE**)

Being cautious in any situation within a dream reveals a down-to-earth realization that you are in complete control of your life, no matter how "testy" situations may appear to be around or within you. The world must go on, and so must you! People tend to frighten themselves to death by harbouring simple, foolish imaginings that are totally alien to their well-being. Not you! Being both creative and logical allows you to utilize your reasoning powers with great foresight and common sense thinking. Your sure-footed attributes as a human being obviously give you the freedom in choosing your objectives in life with greater love and appreciation.

# CAVALIER (See **KNIGHT**)

**CAVE** (e.g., a rock shelter, cavern, or grotto)

To see a cave or to walk into a cave without any fear indicates that you are a motivational and inspirational type of person. You practice honesty, modesty, and other moral principles which, by virtue of your understanding and undertakings in life, make you a shining example of good character and heart. Your awakened spirit still sees the break of day as being worthwhile and purposeful. From time to time, mankind is endowed with someone like you who can teach and instill in others the need to find their purpose and worth on this earth plane.

To see a cave or to walk into a cave in fear suggests you have some misgivings about a decision you made during the last week or so. Did you make the right decision? The answer, according to this symbolism, is both yes and no. You made the right decision as far as your sensitivity and tied-down feelings in life are concerned. You made the wrong decision where your lack of interest is concerned and where your stubbornness is concerned. Remember, no matter where you go or what you decide to do with your life, you should not run away from logical truths. Rather, face these truths head-on until you are masterfully triumphant and inwardly happy.

Being trapped/lost in a cave or being in a cave-in suggests a mental, physical, spiritual, or financial setback within the next several months. You will survive this tense period through your mature, composed nature. For the moment, however, consider the voice of your dream as being a guide, preparing you to strengthen your inner forces. When you are prepared, you will be able to withstand and defeat the unwholesome event(s) yet to come. Be at peace!

Dreaming of actually living in a cave signifies that you are bored, vexed, and dissatisfied with life around you. The proud and the mighty on earth are often weighed down with mental and spiritual darkness because they have acted unwisely and have taken upon themselves more than they can handle. Exaltation of one's self or expressed pompous airs are useless, destructive attitudes to the soul! The peerless choice of a wise man is not to flaunt his wares, but rather to find a resting place to grasp, to share, and to love this life. There is a splendid niche for you on this earth; first, however, you must begin each day of your life with vision, understanding, and humility. One day, you may find what you are seeking; but, above all, you may finally discover the joy of knowing yourself and appreciating life around you.

**CAVE MAN** (see **NEANDERTHAL** or **PRIMITIVISM**)

**CELEBRATION** (i.e., holiday, anniversary, coronation, presentation, remembrance, Mardi Gras, birthday, etc.) (Also see **APPLAUSE**, **BANQUET**, **CHRISTMASTIDE**, **CHURCH**, **EASTER**, **FAME**, **FIREWORKS**, **HARVEST**, **MARRIAGE**, **ORDAINMENT**, **PASSOVER**, **PRAYER**, or **RELIGION**)

If the celebration is happy and gratifying, then you will break down and confess some wrong you have done in your past to a loved one or close friend. This will take great courage on your part, but you will feel much better for doing so. Fear of being misunderstood, criticized, or condemned has stopped you from revealing some of your past secrets. The most important lesson of this dream is that you will finally rekindle your trust and belief in others around you.

An unhappy or unsatisfying celebration foretells personal strife ahead for you unless you get rid of your depressive, pessimistic views in life. You are creating your own stresses by your own thoughts, actions, and deeds. Have you forgotten how to laugh and be happy? Laughter, alone, is the cure for many stresses. Don't be afraid to let your hair down once in a while, cut loose, and be as funny as a mad hatter. This, too, is good for the mind, body, and soul.

**CELEBRITY** (see **FAME**)

**CELESTIAL** (i.e., a heavenly being or someone who lives in the heavens; a god-like being) (see *also* **SPACEMAN**)

Seeing a divine celestial within your dream indicates that your perception or intuition about life will be greater, your well-being will be more gratifying, and your success will be more assured in the not-too-distant future. You are a very mature, staid person who constantly strives to enlighten others through good, sound judgment.

In the event that the celestial scolds or broaches you about something that you supposedly did or said, then be prepared for an onslaught of verbal criticism from others around you. These verbal lashes may or may not be justified; you will know. If these verbal attacks are justified, then make amends to those unduly affected by your actions. If the attacks are not justified, then battle this trying time with inner peace, justice, and sincerity. Sometimes we are being tested by heavenly beings who appear to us only in dreams, guiding and helping us in ways we cannot even remotely fathom.

(*Note*: You may also have the pleasure of knowing that if, for example, you are experiencing a very negative dream, but at the very end of your dream sequence or anywhere during your dream sequence you happen to see a celestial, then this celestial symbolism takes precedence over your entire negative dream. Consequently, you have nothing to worry about simply because the celestial acts as a "buffer zone" to anything negative within a dream.)

**CELESTIAL NAVIGATION** (e.g., observing the sun, moon, stars, or planets to ascertain one's location)

You have been set back emotionally and physically by some traumatic experience quite recently. Some positive opportunity will fall on your lap very soon, thus giving you a chance to reestablish your courage and confidence once more. The darkest hours of your life may appear hopeless for a brief period of time, but your strength and purpose will awaken your spiritual, moral, and mental motivations with new vigour and new hope. Be optimistic!

**CELLAR** (i.e., a storeroom usually below ground level)

Entering a cellar without fear signifies a lack of communication with a family member, relative, friend, or acquaintance. If you are to blame, then make your peace by apologizing. Forget your hurt or angered pride! If you are not to blame, then wait for an opportune moment to communicate with this person. Peace can only be attained through love, understanding, and a great willingness to make compromises.

Hiding from someone/something in a cellar or being afraid to go into a cellar suggests that you are not striving hard enough to become more worthy and useful to self and others around you. Your energies and knowledge should be utilized with inspirational zest, rather than lethargic indifference towards life in general. Nothing can or will be handed to you freely on earth unless you make some sound efforts to change your depressed, uncaring attitudes. Do not neglect your talents while you are on this earth plane. If you could realize your worth and usefulness for only a moment or two, you would be awestruck by the attainable possibilities within your grasp. Only you can make this possible!

Falling into a cellar indicates that someone will attempt to trick or dishonour you. Although you will be affected by this act of disloyalty, you must realize that it will be the other person who has a problem—not you. Two wrongs, as they say, do not make a right; it is so true! Be foresighted, and show a complete lack of concern for any wrongs another person may do to you. In reality, the wrongdoer creates more harm to himself or herself, in the end, than he or she could ever have foreseen.

**CEMENT** (see **CONCRETE**)

**CEMETERY** (see **GRAVEYARD**)

**CENOTAPH** (i.e., an empty tomb or monument respecting a deceased person whose body is someplace else)

Seeing a cenotaph without fear or prejudice suggests that you show an ample amount of stability and moral strength in life. In times of difficulty, you are capable of displaying complete control with love, logic, and mettle. You are a person who cares for, and about, people—no matter what race, colour, or creed they may be. In dollars and cents, you may not necessarily be one of the richest people, but you certainly are one of the luckiest people on earth! Why? Simply because you are a person who has found faith and happiness in what you think, feel, and do. Like the beacon of a lighthouse, so you, too, bring illumination, courage, and hope to those lost, abandoned beings whose call for help seems unending.

Seeing a cenotaph with fear or prejudice suggests that you possess cynical views on human nature and human affairs. Nonetheless, you would be wise to listen to your complaints, once in a while. If what you do in life is dull and uninteresting, then what have you done to make things better for yourself and for others around you? You are wasting some of your most valuable time on irrelevant matters of interest, whereas you could be devoting far more of your constructive energies towards unselfish progress and good fellowship. You certainly have the brain power to be successful in what you want to do; all you need now is the willpower to refine and strengthen your character.

**CERAMIC** (see **EARTHENWARE** or **POTTERY**)

**CERTIFICATE** (i.e., a written or printed statement declaring that one has met specified requirements to become a doctor, lawyer, teacher, tradesman, etc., or a document certifying birth, marriage, death, ownership)

A certificate for acceptance in some profession implies that you will prosper by continuing in your present line of work. Be patient. Do not try to get to the top of your profession too quickly, for if you do, you could dissolve your chances of attaining that goal! Continue to work hard and to be kind and honest in all your dealings with others. Before you know it, some happy event will place you squarely at the forefront of your work.

Seeing a birth/marriage/death certificate or a document of ownership and so on implies that you will be given many opportunities to fulfill your ambitions and wants in life. However, be wary about being too neglectful or apathetic in fulfilling your deepest aspirations. Opportunities can fall by the wayside with this attitude! Assuming that you will adhere to the positive aspects of your life, then you can be quite content in knowing that your future will be blessed with good health, wealth, and happiness.

**CHAIN** (i.e., joined, flexible metal links)

You are advised not to act in an impulsive manner by word or deed for the next several months. This caution on your part could save you much future conflict, uncertainty, and regret. At this stage of your life, it appears as though you are flirting with fate, or you are doing something that is not in harmony with your destiny or the life forces around you. You cannot come out of your state without placing your entire trust in the Almighty God!

**CHAIN STORE** (see **STORE**)

**CHAIR**

Once in a while, sit down in silence to reflect upon your life, as though you were reading a book. You will discover that some chapters of your life are rather pleasing to read, and some may bring a bit of discomfort to the mind. In this world, you will discover that greed and hate are the two most vicious words that anyone can employ; love and hope are the two most inspiring words that everyone should live by; and truth in all things is what we should all seek. So you, too, must apply your past and present experiences with that love, hope, and truth in advancing your mind and character. Remember, you can only find true wealth and prosperity within the Temple of your mind, body, and soul!

Seeing a broken chair, breaking a chair, being hit by a chair, or hitting someone or something with a chair in a dream advises you to know and acknowledge your mental and physical limits. You are striving to accomplish too many goals or projects at once without much consideration of what this strain is actually doing to your system. Slow down! Being healthy is far better than being sick.

Falling off a chair or being pushed off a chair intimates that you are becoming too bold in your actions and somewhat snobbish where personal achievements are concerned. No person is born on earth to be a snob! You are such a fine individual that it is such a pity that you would allow yourself to be subject to this state. You were always meant to awaken the world with your inner light, goodness, and deeds, rather than dim your light with top-lofty ideals and personal prestige.

## CHAMBERMAID

You are a very fickle person. Just when you are about to make some positive headway with your life, you suddenly change your mind by doing something else or nothing at all! To receive greater respect and response out of your existence, you must commence to show more fixity of purpose. In other words, carry out your thoughts and deeds without being so fearful and doubtful! So what if you make a mistake or two along the way? A person simply tries to do their best; and if they err along the way—well, then that is what makes life so challenging and meaningful. You struggled very hard to be born; why stop now?

## CHANDELIER

A lighted chandelier augurs long-lasting happiness and social popularity. It appears that you have been somewhat of a recluse, but you will commence to regain your self-confidence and socialize more before too long.

An unlighted chandelier reveals that a sequence of events may offer you contentment. The end results, however, are not too gratifying! One bad mistake at this point in time could cost you plenty at a later date. Do not be mentally or sexually dazzled by the appearance of another person whose sole aim may be to harm, misuse, or abuse you. Do not be lured by the luxury of instant wealth through some business transaction for this, too, could be a total letdown. You will be thankful for your sagacity and prudence in these matters. Better opportunities will present themselves to you at a later time.

## CHANNEL (see CANAL, HARBOR, PASSAGEWAY, RADIO, or TELEVISION)

**CHAPEL** (i.e., a small place of worship such as in a hospital, school, army post, prison)

You could be described as a person whose inner qualities project moral strength, self-discipline, and determination. Being as responsible as you were always meant to be, you can rest assured that this dream symbolism promises fulfillment in your present and future ambitions.

**CHAPLAIN** (i.e., a minister, rabbi, or priest serving in a religious way in a hospital, school, army post, prison)

To see or to be a chaplain in a dream signifies that some absurd, almost freakish accident or situation may befall you (e.g., slipping on a banana peel, a toy; falling off a chair that suddenly breaks; some object falls on you). Be very cautious and wary for the next week or so!

**CHARIOT**

At long last, some explosive turn of events will bring you some measureless gain and happiness (e.g., a promotion, change of residence, winning a lottery ticket, a trip to another land, buying a business, receiving honour and prestige through your career). Whatever this change may be, you are bound to maintain an unselfish attitude and cheerful disposition throughout your entire lifetime.

**CHARITY** (see **ASSISTANCE**, **COMPASSION**, **GIFT**, **POORHOUSE**, or **POVERTY**)

**CHARLATAN** (i.e., a "quack")

Your tolerance level towards any authority is very minimal. You also hate criticism or nagging to any degree. Furthermore, you are not the greatest compromiser. There is nothing wrong with your mind, but you lack the direction and reassuring initiative to get ahead. By sharing your energies in a positive way, you will slowly commence to escape your impatience and hardheaded attitudes. Begin to reveal the positive courage that you truly possess by being an honourable and joyful human being. Did you know that your potential and opportunities in life are limitless, providing you open the joys and gifts that lie dormant within your being? Only you can tap that reservoir of wealth and knowledge; only you can change your future.

**CHARM** (see **TALISMAN**)

**CHASE** (see **PURSUIT**)

**CHASSIS** (see **FRAMEWORK**)

**CHAUFFEUR**
This symbolism encourages you to fulfill all your contracts and promises, at all times. Your conscience will be at peace, and you will feel much better for being a wiser, more responsible person.

**CHAUVINIST** (i.e., a person who shows excessive pride about one's own sex, such as a male; female chauvinism)
Acts of chauvinism within a dream strongly indicate that your lack of modesty, taste, or propriety is not conducive to your future's well-being. Throw away your self-pity and hopeless thoughts about tomorrow never becoming better. Tomorrow will become better— with or without you. If you desire to be so demonstrative, different, and "far-out" in life, then your message is quite clear: you have a love-hate relationship with life and self.

**CHEATING**
This action within a dream advises you to tread lightly! You may be tempted to cheat someone; or, someone may be tempted to cheat you. Cheating is always a no-win situation in life. The Universal Law is that if you cheat someone, you will be cheated; if someone cheats you, they will be cheated.
Refusing to cheat within a dream merely reveals your honesty and integrity during your wake state. Remember, cheating is a very strong emotional scheme perpetuated by dishonest people. Normally, when a person is honest during their wake state, they will be as honest in their sleep state—unless they are victimized or traumatized into doing something against their will in the dream.

**CHECKPOINT** (i.e., a highway border crossing where traffic is stopped for inspection)
Someone will attempt to lead you away from some goal or venture you had originally set out to do. Do not be swayed or cajoled by any-one who might lure you away from your good intentions; you may be the victim of a practical joker or of an overly obstinate person who

might be envious of your abilities and strong determination to do better things in life.

**CHECKROOM** (i.e., parcels, baggage, hats, coats, etc., are kept here for safekeeping until called for)
You will hear some terrifying or shocking news about someone whom you know. The ominous news could pertain to an accident, sickness, divorce, or even death. This person appears to be rather close to you and your family. All you can do here is to pray and hope that everyone you know is safe and happy.

**CHEERLEADER**
Be wary of any verbal or written commitments you cannot keep. You may be bogged down with a work load you had never bargained for or anticipated. Do only those things you know you can handle; otherwise, you could be walking on thin ice, where other people are concerned.

**CHEESE** (see **FOOD**)

**CHEF** (see **COOK**)

**CHEMICAL WARFARE**
You appear to be searching for knowledge outside the normal boundaries of sight, sound, and time. Through your willingness, determination, prayers, and meditation, you can perhaps find that proof which you are seeking. Nothing is impossible to the inner mind of your soul (e.g., levitation, astral projection). Your mystical potential could master or harness those mighty, inner forces. Remember to always use those forces for the betterment of mankind.

**CHEMIST** (see *also* **DRUGGIST**)
You can be a very prideful, stubborn person—especially when you want to teach someone a lesson or prove a point. The most important factor here to remember is that you are not always correct! But, will you admit this fact to yourself? Sometimes you do; yet, sometimes you simply carry on without pacifying the person whom you affected. Learn to be more appreciative inwardly by sharing your views with others—instead of forcing your views upon others. This positive action can bring you the peace and appreciation you seem to be lacking.

**CHEST** (i.e., part of the body between the neck and abdomen)

A female dreaming of a male chest or a male dreaming of a female chest signifies that your conscience is bothering you over some past, remorseful event. With your basic sensibility and mature attitude, you are bound to come out of this state with a new outlook on yourself and on people, places, and things.

A female dreaming of a female chest or a male dreaming of male chest alludes to a variety of inner frustrations. This could involve some personal failure; an inability to forge a satisfying relationship with someone; some family or spiritual matters that appear confusing or unsolvable to you, and so on. This symbolism advises you to be more patient, giving, and open-minded, rather than clinging to your actions with bitterness.

## CHEST OF DRAWERS

There are times when you get carried away with your own suspicions and mistrust. It is wholesome and wise to be a skeptic, once in a while; but to adopt this attitude beyond common sense could leave you in a very confused state. Not everything you read, see, or hear may be believable to you. However, remember that there are "unbelievable" events occurring on earth each moment of our lives—maybe not to you precisely, but to other people who happen to be experiencing something traumatic, phenomenal, or inspiring, such as a freak accident where no one gets hurt, seeing a flying saucer, or someone seeing the Virgin Mary. You are, in fact, a tunnel vision thinker who should strive to be more open-minded. In viewing life with greater perception, you may commence to admit the possibility that there is, indeed, more to this earthly life than meets the eye.

## CHEWING GUM

Although you may try to run away from everything else on earth, you cannot run away from yourself. The grass is not so green on the other side of the fence. Think about your future for a moment or two, especially about your uncaring attitudes at this time of your life. Being rash, hasty, or foolish now could bring you great hardships in time to come. On the other hand, being level-headed now would have a positive and pleasing effect upon your life—that is, if you have the patience to see this truth become a reality.

**CHICK** (i.e., a young chicken)

You or someone very close and dear to you should exercise extreme caution where anxieties, fears, and worries are concerned. Too many stresses of the mind can produce stresses on the body. Heart attacks have been caused by less than this! Remember that your mind is very powerful. When you think in positive ways, then positive situations normally commence to happen, both within and around you. A mental and physical rest is recommended with this dream, in the hopes that you or your loved one will finally learn to adopt a more relaxed, peaceful attitude in life.

**CHICKEN** (i.e., a hen or rooster)

You should be proud of your work performance, skill, and adaptability in conforming to sudden changes within your life. However, there are occasions when you are beset by uncomfortable apprehensions or unwarranted, depressing fears. These mind upheavals or horrible thoughts are basically created by your harbouring personal doubts, by your being overanxious about something, or by your being too prideful. The solution here is to pray and meditate, be more humble and thankful for all your blessings, and be truthful with self and others.

Cooking, beheading, or seeing the innards of a chicken denotes a lack of initiative or willpower on your part. You are not really a quitter in what you do; however, you are not endowed with a lot of ambition, either. Your biggest challenge in life is yourself and the hosts of fears you tend to harbour (i.e., fear of failing, fear of being a disappointment to someone, fear of not being able to comprehend something, fear of taking chances). Your fears are basically groundless and worthless; but, until you commence to realize this fact for yourself, you will continue to thwart your mental, emotional, and physical capabilities.

**CHILD** (see **ADOLESCENT**, **BABY**, **CHILDHOOD**, or **ORPHAN**)

**CHILDHOOD**

A happy childhood advises you to live a peaceful life, to mind your own affairs, and to always strive to be constructive in your thoughts and deeds. For your sake, do not let your life pass by in bitterness, shame, insecurities, and selfishness. Even if you live to be one hundred years old, this life is far too short to waste on personal ignorance or on misinformed intentions.

Seeing an unhappy childhood suggests that there is plenty of difficulty and sadness in your life right now. Although you are trying desperately to find the love and contentment you so earnestly desire, there just does not appear to be any letup on your personal hardships. It will not always be this way! There is happiness and prosperity ahead for you. Understand that in all your present anxieties and anguish, some vital lessons are being learned: inner strength, patience, and wisdom.

## CHIMNEY

You possess a restless desire to accomplish something within your life, but there appears to be some verbal opposition standing in your way. It is your own fortitude and willingness to carry on that will see you through this trying time. Eventually, you will attain the success, prosperity, and harmony from the harvests of your labour.

## CHIMNEY SWEEP

Sudden plans, changes, or moves within your life at this time could bring you eventual frustrations and hardships! Curb your impulsive thinking, cease your unrealistic schemes and fancies, and begin to settle down with a realistic sense of accomplishment and happiness. When you learn to give and to appreciate the love and kindness that is both within and around you, some of your most heart-felt hopes will be fulfilled.

## CHIMPANZEE (see APE)

## CHOICE (see OPTION)

## CHOIR

You are concerned about someone's assumed and overbearing authority over you. As well, you are concerned about some inheritance or property rights. Personal happiness and financial gains appear to be some distance away. Be very patient, keep busy, and never let go of your hope and faith during these trying times. One day you will awaken to the joy, freedom, and peace of mind you desperately seem to be seeking.

## CHOIRBOY

Your thoughts shift or veer like the wind! Barring all intrusions, you should learn to concentrate on single ideas and problems with more sureness and fixity of purpose. Be more firm with yourself! By being more steadfast in life, you can achieve your fondest ambitions.

## CHOIRMASTER

You have all the endowments to think and act for yourself. However, somewhere down the road of life, you have adopted some illusive philosophic teaching or dogma which appears to dispirit the mind and soul. Remember that in life you become the teacher, and your day-to-day experiences become the school. Always strive to discern the rights and wrongs you feel until your mind and spirit are once more attuned and gratified. Use your better judgment in all things! In time, you may discover that the greatest knowledge of all is the love you have within your soul.

## CHOKE (i.e., strangle or suffocate)

You appear to be having a very difficult time in making a decision that could affect your home life or career. Persistent doubts about something could well imply that you should not commit yourself to anyone or anything at this time, no matter how alluring the prospects sound. That inner warning or inner hunch is a sign to heed! However, if you are happy, thrilled, and totally prepared to handle concessions and changes in your life, then by all means accept those vital challenges that do come your way.

## CHOPSTICKS

You are somewhat lazy and reckless! Strive to be more systematic and neat in life; be more honest and sincere; be a good listener; and be less manipulating. These practices will collectively create and motivate a new style of living for you. To simply allow life to pass you by in an uncaring or indifferent manner is to do the greatest disservice to yourself. Unshackle the confusion of your past with strong determination, and bravely commence to live with dedicated purpose, dignity, and satisfaction.

## CHRIST (see JESUS)

## CHRISTENING (see BAPTISM)

## CHRISTMASTIDE (i.e., Christmas time) (see *also* NEW YEAR'S DAY)

The year ahead will bring you much happiness, prosperity, and travel if you dream of Christmastide as a very joyous event. You are headed towards positive changes and domestic progress. Well deserved business and career opportunities are also high on the scale of this dream symbolism.

Dreaming of Christmastide as a very sad event predicts the year ahead will not be as comforting or profitable as you would like it to be. Personal strife and diverse influences will disturb your better judgment, causing you to fall behind in domestic bliss and in business or educational pursuits. Nonetheless, if you are strong-minded, logical, and tolerant, then you will survive these luckless signs with ease.

**CHRONICLE** (i.e., register of facts or historical record)
You appear to be intensifying your personal problems by trying to be infallible in what you say or do. Try to hear and see yourself as others do, from time to time. In order to achieve soul-winning graces, you will have to become less self-centered and more giving, loving, trusting, forgiving, and humble. Instead of expecting praises and plaudits for your work, centre your thoughts and actions on the good you can do for others.

**CHUCK WAGON**
This symbolism denotes that you have been rather unsettled and unsure about so many things for quite some time. Just when situations appear to be bright and shining for you, something happens to hinder your progress and happiness. Well, this dream may very well be the turning point in your life! You will soon be asked by someone who appears to be in difficulty to do a small task or favor. Trustingly, you will assist this person. Shortly after this event takes place, you will begin to feel and experience a higher level of conscious thought, action, and love within your being. You will also know that your future will be filled with accomplishment, happiness, and prosperity.

Then when at last your soul is at last totally awakened to the truth, wisdom, and love you so desperately seek, come forth and teach us what you know.

**CHURCH** (see *also* **ALTAR, ALTAR BOY, BURIAL, CHAPEL, CLERGYMAN, CONVENT, GRAVE, MAUSOLEUM, MONASTERY, MOSQUE, REFUGE, RELIGION,** or **RETREAT**)
You have recently become lethargic and despondent because of another person's notions, habits, or actions. Neglecting your well-being because of someone's ignorance or foolishness is neither wise nor wholesome. Look around you, and commence to see that your life,

with all its trials and tribulations, has a greater substance and purpose than to merely pine for or coax a person to change. Do not go wild because this individual refuses to listen to your good, sound advice; some people will never change on this earth plane. Regretfully, they must learn the hard way. Vanquish your morbidity by becoming more self-reliant; regain your spiritual calmness through prayer; and, with courageous inspiration, realize that we are all God's children.

Sitting on a pew with an offspring or two indicates that you are having some discipline problems with your children. You are a good parent, but you must recognize this fact without condemning yourself for feeling so helpless when they refuse to listen. They will grow up, but this will take time and plenty of love, patience, and understanding on your part. Some parents forget about their own struggles and pain while they were growing up and now assume that their children should be perfect angels. Not so! Everyone goes through some growing pains—even the parents themselves! Whether you are a parent or an offspring, just remember that no one promised you a rose garden on this planet. Cooperation, compromises, and love are the key elements all parents and children should learn to cherish and recognize.

**CHURCHYARD**

Seeing a churchyard implies hardship, sickness, or even death for someone whom you know. This does not necessarily imply your immediate family, but it does reveal that you will be unduly affected. You can only pray and hope that this ill omen will pass by without too much pain or sadness.

**CIGAR** (see **SMOKER**)

**CIGARETTE** (see **SMOKER**)

**CINDER**

You are boring people with personal, mundane problems that hold no interest for them. Next time you converse with someone, strive a little harder to be a good listener, instead of a complainer. By doing so, you may discover that you are not the only person on earth with a problem or two. Bear in mind, as well, that you cannot solve a problem merely by thinking about it or by telling everyone about it. You must actually do something about it!

## CINNAMON (see **SPICE**)

## CIRCUMCISION

You are advised to suppress your aggressive and quarrelsome habits. Health problems affecting your mental and physical state will ensue unless you learn to be more calm and sensible with yourself and with others around you. Free your spirit of these undisciplined, emotional outbursts, and begin to recognize your inner being with honour, courage, and truthfulness. When you honestly begin to see how fortunate you have been in life thus far, then maybe you will begin to appreciate the peace and happiness staring right at you.

## CIRCUS

Financial and other personal difficulties are foreseen unless you pay more heed to your better instincts and judgment. Being skillful and shrewd in your dealings with others will not guarantee you great profits or admiration in life. Strive more to improve yourself through honesty, integrity, and self-reliance, rather than believing that great wealth and total freedom to do what you want to do will bring you all the happiness in this world. Think about this for a while; perhaps then you will see your joys magnified and multiplied beyond your wildest dreams!

## CITIZEN'S ARREST (see **ARREST**)

## CITIZENSHIP PAPERS

If you are, in fact, anticipating becoming a citizen of a country and dream about receiving citizenship papers, then this act merely intensifies your conscious and subconscious feelings towards this fulfillment. In other words, you will eventually receive your citizenship papers! However, if this is not the case, and you have no sound reason for dreaming about citizenship papers, then be prepared for some pending economic changes within your life. Tighten your money belt! Eventually, when prosperous times do return, you will reflect back and realize that some of the greatest pleasures in life are actually free.

## CITY

If the city you see is relatively peaceful and natural looking, it indicates that you show an ample amount of friendliness, affection, and dependability. You are a strong-willed individual who detests boasting or speaking falsehoods about other people. There were times when sadness and failure knocked unmercifully at your doorstep! Today, you have reached a certain plateau of achievement and success and realize that some of your personal hardships and disappointments were all guided steps towards a greater tomorrow.

If the city you see is destroyed, desolate, or unnatural looking, then it is time for you to take stock of your thoughts and actions in life. By mentally placing a steel wall around your heart and affections, you have cast yourself adrift. You seem to be living in a private world of bitterness, hopelessness, and fear! This symbolism advises you to return your complete trust into the Hands of your Creator through human love, kindness, and hope. There can be nothing in your past, present, or future that cannot be mended, providing you are willing to let go of your doubts and affected feelings in life. It is you who must go forward in life, not your past!

**CIVILIZATION** (see *also* **HUMANITY**)

Dreaming about a past civilization signifies that you are experiencing some emotional trials and tribulations involving a spouse or a very close friend. This dream symbolism reveals the possibility of a loved one parting company with you (e.g., divorce, separation, moving away). If this parting is merely a threat, then do your utmost to patch things up between you. On the other hand, if this so-called threat is now a reality, then you must face this fact head-on. You cannot spend the rest of your life dwelling on this situation. Rebuild your life with greater discipline, responsibility, and spiritual strength.

Dreaming about a futuristic civilization shows that you are keenly aware and concerned about the needs of others, far beyond your own needs and wants. From the bottom of your heart there reigns a gift of compassion, gentleness, and truth which literally compels you to help others out of the darkness into the light! You care about today and tomorrow and thoroughly understand that God's Love is everywhere. You will rightfully reap your rewards of praise and distinction upon heaven and earth for your dynamic, humanitarian spirit. Indeed, you are a guiding star!

**CLAIRVOYANCE** (i.e., the ability to see things not present to the senses)

Some recent changes and occurrences which have affected you will prove to be of invaluable importance to you in time to come. Try not to feel too vexed or perplexed by these recent happenings; rather, face these changing times with new hope, vitality, and good common sense. As you go on in life, some inspiring and measureless gifts await you.

**CLAM** (see **MOLLUSK**)

**CLARINET** (see **INSTRUMENT**)

**CLASS BOOK** (i.e., a book, published by members of a school or college class)

You are harboring certain ill-feelings towards a person who embarrassed you. Whatever the circumstances may be, you are strongly urged to consider this matter finished; let bygones be bygones. This dream advises you to concentrate more on your talents and leadership potential in assisting this world on which you live. Many fine surprises and honours yet await you, but you must always be true to yourself and others, no matter how difficult life's road may be. Remember that some of the greatest souls on earth walked the saddest mile of their lives, feeling unaccomplished and unfulfilled—only to realize that the fruits of their labour were truly in God's Hands! And, God in turn showered their love and glory beyond the fringes of this planet with resounding joy!

**CLASSMATE** (see **SCHOOLMATE**)

**CLASSROOM** (see **SCHOOLROOM**)

**CLAUSTROPHOBIA** (i.e., an unnatural fear of being in a confined place)

If you do, in fact, suffer from claustrophobia, then this dream is merely personifying the dread or terror you feel about confined areas. However, if you do not suffer from claustrophobia, yet you have a dream about being in an enclosed area with great anguish and dread, then this dream signifies that added commitments and responsibilities are forthcoming. Contracts, negotiations, and agreements in various matters look very promising and beneficial for you. In essence, you appear to be headed towards financial security and social prestige.

**CLAY**

Your present expectations may not necessarily be met at this time. Nonetheless, your dream reveals that, eventually, you will move on to bigger and better plateaus of achievement. In matters concerning self, always strive to be patient, firm, confident, and loyal to your hopes and goals. By doing this, you will discover that all worthy things can come your way.

## CLEANLINESS
Keeping yourself or anything else clean within a dream intimates that your worrisome nature, combined with an over-imaginative mind, often leaves you in a perplexed, stressful state. Most of your worries are unwarranted simply because they are mere figments of your imagination. Do not be so fearful of life and the possible storms it may bring you. Not everything is peaceful on planet Earth, and we must all learn to cope with our problems in a disciplined, mature manner. Today we live, tomorrow we die; these facts of life must be faced head-on. However, while we are alive on this planet, we must do our very best to plough onwards with strength, courage, faith, and dignity. It is very true that some people suffer more than others! Yet, their suffering will pass by, one way or another, too. You are urged to accept and face your existence in a realistic manner, rather than play "hide-and-seek" with unpleasant events and tribulations.

## CLERGYMAN (e.g., a minister, priest, rabbi) (see *also* BISHOP, CHAPLAIN, CHURCH, DEACON, MONK, ORDAINMENT, or POPE)
You seem to be restricted in what you can or cannot do in life, yet these so-called guidelines are basically positive, and they do make sense. Would you sooner follow someone's fanatical rules (e.g., cults, self-proclaimed dictators, tyranny) against the true worldly and spiritual concepts of life? The total "feeling" of being good is "doing" good in all that you do, no matter what people say. One's life may sometimes be cloudy, stormy, and unclear; but many chances are given to recognize, repair, and ultimately rectify wrongdoings into blessings. There isn't one person on this planet who does not have some cross to bear, in some way. However, when they apply their nobler thoughts, actions, and deeds in the best way possible, then truly they stand among the greatest heroes in the Kingdom of Life. The greatest church and all its teachings is <u>within</u> you; what you do with this knowledge should be served with holy honesty, human love, and self-sacrifice. There are many obligations to fulfill on earth. When you are ready, willing, and able to understand the inner concepts of Universal Truths,

Commands, and Obedience, then you will be ready, capable, and free to inspire your fellow man and all life that is.

Having an argument with a clergyman within a dream presages a day of bitterness, distress, irritability, and vexation. Do not let anyone make you angry this day. If you can, be calm, cool, and collected throughout its duration; then you will disperse the negative vibrations within and around you with productive results.

**CLERK** (i.e., office worker, official clerk of a school board, court, town, etc., hotel clerk, salesclerk at a store, teller at a bank, etc.)

Shy away from negative or pessimistic people who may try to lead you away from your better judgment or direction in life. Follow the road that you know is right and important to you. No one can walk in your shoes but you alone! Direct your actions with truth and reason; and someday you will reflect back upon this dream with thankfulness.

**CLIFF**

Seeing a cliff, hanging onto the edge of a cliff, or falling off the edge of a cliff indicates that you are very restless and anxious to have all your worldly problems disappear. Everyone's worldly problems will disappear in time! In the interim, however, you must strive to conquer your immediate problems with logic and wholesome determination. In order to achieve your present wishes and aims, you should strive to be more independent minded, instead of complaining or feeling sorry for yourself. You can surmount anything in life as long as you have the inner conviction that you can master the so-called impossibilities. When people place impossibilities in front of themselves, they are merely deluding themselves. A rich man can become poor; a poor man can become rich. Why? Simply because the rich man allowed his impossible circumstances to become a reality, whereas the poor man allowed his inner dreams and hopes to become a reality, even under odds. So you, too, like the poor man, can make your hopes come true!

To see anything unusual near or on a cliff, being pushed off a cliff, or to see a vehicle go over a cliff intimates that you are seeking fame and fortune in the wrong places and with the wrong people. Too many "good times" can lead to "bad times"! Careless attitudes, irresponsibility, and bold dealings with unethical people can bring nothing but grief to someone's life. This dream counsels you to gain command of your life with constructive reflections and directions, instead of destructive reflections and directions. Someday soon you may realize that by wanting less, you will receive much more; namely, your peace of mind and human dignity.

**CLIMBER** (see *also* **MOUNTAINEER**)

Climbing a building, hill, fence, and so on implies that you possess an ample amount of compassion, confidence, energy, and initiative to see you through some of the most difficult times of your life. This dream reveals material and financial gains and soul-winning triumphs! Your ability to plan, create, and lead others towards innovative changes within their lives are but a few of your dedicated actions in life. You will not rest until the world you love and cherish commences to improve.

**CLINGER** (i.e., a person who shows a great amount of attachment to another person)

Some people affect you deeply and intimately because of your sensitivity and lack of willpower. People often say things at the top of their heads, without honestly realizing the negative effect of their words or statements. No one expects you to be thick-skinned in this matter; however, there are occasions when you should simply ignore those offenses you happen to hear or see. Sensitive people normally compound their hurt feelings by listing and compiling them in the recesses of their mind. In due time, they simply expel their stresses and pent-up anger by overreacting, exaggeration, and traumatic behaviour. It is not wise to bottle up anger! Perhaps, with the graces of time, experience, knowledge, and understanding, you will begin to perceive and control your touchy feelings.

**CLINIC** (e.g., a place where physicians treat patients, a health clinic)

Overtly, you are a self-styled individual who detests assistance or advice from anyone. This form of independence is fine as long as you do not go to extremes in your chosen lifestyle. Total isolation from others could lead to mental breakdown, frustrations, and so on. Having one or two friends to rely on in life is not only wholesome, but essential as well. Also, bear in mind why you have come to planet Earth: to learn, to share, to love, and to live your life with mental, physical, and spiritual satisfaction. We all learn from each other; no man is wise unto himself.

## CLOAKROOM

Through luck, fate, or whatever you wish to call it, your financial insecurities will be alleviated. Approximately four months from the time of this dream, you will begin to see a marked improvement in your financial standing. Have you forgotten? In your life, you have always had to accept humility, in the truest sense of the word, before any form of progress came your way. This soul-cycle pattern has not changed. Be at peace, still your restless mind and soul, and await your pending good fortune!

## CLOCK

A variety of problems and disappointments will beset you this month. Take note, however, that what you experience during this trying time will weigh heavily on your future happiness. You can come out of this shaky period by being steadfast, unselfish, and patient; or you can falter and fail by being impatient, haughty, and over-confident.

## CLOCKWORK (i.e., the innards of a clock, watch, mechanical toy) (see *also* PENDULUM)

There is no one in our lives that can do us more harm than we do to ourselves. Always strive to be calm, honest, and gentle in your dealings with people. Far too often, people become angry or vexed over mundane matters; this simply reveals the immaturity of their ways and habits. If some people could see themselves or hear a playback of their day-to-day activities, they would probably hide in shame! This dream counsels you to go forth in life with dignity and understanding. Do not be taken in by pride, temptations, or sudden rages which could ultimately upset or destroy your inner peace.

## CLOISTER (see CONVENT or MONASTERY)

## CLOSET

An empty closet or one filled with clothes, linen, and so on signifies that you are subject to harassment and criticism from your relatives and/or in-laws. It will take a great amount of tact and perseverance on your part to continue your link with some of these people. It is possible that nothing you do or say will make them change or be happy with you as a person. Should this situation go from bad to worse, then you will more than likely estrange yourself from their binding hold and clutches.

To be locked in a closet or to hide in a closet from some impending danger intimates that you are or were misunderstood and taken for granted by a parent. This dream shows a strong love for one parent, but a wall of indifference is now consciously and subconsciously related to the other parent. The mental anguish and cruelty you have experienced thus far is an unfortunate tragedy! Let us hope that history does not repeat itself with you being a parent or potential parent. Many times a person's deprived upbringing is foisted upon their children, and the whole vicious cycle is repeated. It is believed, however, that you would never allow your offspring to suffer the way you did. By being emotionally strong, by placing your past behind you, and by bringing forth all the love and inspiration you can humanly muster, you will survive this life quite admirably.

To approach a closet with fear or to open the door of a closet and see a skeleton, dead body, animal, or anything unusual in it signifies that you are trying very hard to influence or impress people. In reality, not too many people are visibly impressed with your attitudes or personal hang-ups. What is most important here is that you should try to be your natural self at all times. You have some fine talent that should be applied wholeheartedly, not halfheartedly. This world can offer you many opportunities for fame, fortune, and success; but you must work very hard towards that goal. Remember that actions speak louder than words! Just how much sweat, toil, and tears are you honestly willing to endure in order to attain your goals or aims on earth? Maybe someday you will reach that ladder of success through experience, knowledge, and perseverance. Oddly enough, it could be at that plateau that people will begin to listen to you; and you, in turn, will be in a better position to influence and impress others.

**CLOTH** (see **MATERIAL** or **RAG**)

**CLOTHES** (i.e., wearing apparel or bed clothes) (see *also* **BLANKET, BONNET, BRASSIERE, BURNOOSE, CAP, CAPE, GLOVE, HANDKERCHIEF, HAT, HELMET, RAINCOAT,** or **TURBAN**)

If the clothes you see are clean and neat, it signifies that you are striving very hard to improve your home life conditions. Oftentimes, you feel guilty and responsible for certain negative events at home, so you bend backwards in order to keep everyone happy and content. In essence, you are not the happiest person in life; however, you do have a tremendous will to persevere and accept life without too much anguish, fear, or hostility. Your basic self-control and self-confidence are truly fine and admirable attributes. You will prosper through your determination, skills, and eventual good fortune.

Seeing clothes that are soiled or torn advises you not to tamper with or interfere in other people's lives. Even though you may be clever and know many worthwhile shortcuts to save a person a lot of time and energy, most people want to learn about life for themselves. Surely by now you must realize that some people whom you know will not heed your advice, even if you stood on your head. Why give yourself a mental ulcer simply because a loved one, for instance, wants to think and act independently? This dream strongly urges you to be less possessive in your thoughts and actions towards others around you. Those who know you, by the way, realize that you know better but that you fail to use sound logic, trust, faith, and understanding in your dealings with them.

## CLOTHESLINE

Seeing a clothesline with or without clothes implies that you should be extremely careful at this time where health problems are concerned (e.g., pregnancy, diabetes, heart, lung or throat problems). Extra care, common sense, and perhaps following some good medical advice could help you avoid some untimely physical difficulties or complications.

## CLOTHESPIN

Learn to be more appreciative for all your blessings and for the important things that really matter. When was the last time you took a good, long walk to observe nature around you? How long has it been since you took the time to honestly hear the needs and wants of your loved ones? When was the last time you prayed for the innermost purification of your soul? Treasure your gift of life as you would a beautiful flower; and, perhaps, everything else that appears out of sorts in your life will simply fall into its rightful, perspective place.

## CLOUD

White, peaceful looking clouds intimate that some of your annoying problems will clear up very soon. There is also a great amount of luck ahead for you; it will enable you to fulfill some of your travel dreams.

Dark, foreboding clouds, on the other hand, suggest you often vent your frustrations and suspicions on others because of your own insecurities, hang-ups, and probable self-doubts. Take a long journey into your heart, mind, and soul; and commence to ask yourself why you have allowed yourself to become this way. Look at life around you, and realize that people have enough of their own problems, without having to cope with your frustrations and suspicions, as well. Life is far too short to spend your wholesome energies on unfounded, frivolous mistrusts and doubts about people, places, and things. If you honestly want to be more successful and satisfied in your life, then let each moment come and go with calmness, freedom from base desires, and a willingness to give more than you receive.

**CLOVE** (see **SPICE**)

**CLOWN**

Acting like a clown or merely seeing a clown alone within a dream reveals that you are very vexed and worried about some bad decision or investment you or a member of your family made recently. By keeping your wits about you, situations may not be as bad as they appear. First, realize that you or your family member cannot come out of this situation overnight. There may be some legal involvement, financial loss, and perhaps some humiliation before you see this matter completely closed. Second, be strong. Realize that most human misjudgments or oversights today can bring about wiser decisions tomorrow.

**CLUB** (see **CROWD, ORGANIZATION, PUNISHMENT,** or **STICK**)

**COACH** (i.e., an instructor or trainer in athletics, acting, dancing, singing)

You are trying to be too assertive and demanding with people who already know exactly what to do. Take stock of your actions and words, before you become a tyrant in the eyes of others. By showing more compassion, respect, and understanding towards the needs of others, you will be amazed at the response you will receive in return. A smile and plenty of kindness from you will normally draw the same attitude from other people!

## COAST GUARD

When progress, change, improvements, or reforms within your society take place, you tend to show a very nonchalant attitude. Since caring individuals take the time to make your village, town, or city more livable, then you should take the time to respect the reforms that are taking place. This is not to imply that you have to agree with everything that is taking place in the world today; but surely there must be some civilized and beneficial improvements around you worth beaming about. Did you know that you have the capacity to become a more active member of your society in order to help mold and shape the direction in which this world is headed (e.g., civic government, charitable work)? What you do for your country now will surely have a good effect on your country later.

## COAT (see CLOTHES)

## COAT OF ARMS (i.e., a combination of emblems and figures
which serve as the distinctive insignia of some person, family, institution)

All people are supposed to be born equal on this planet. This sound idea, however, has never been well upheld by mankind. Greed, anger, hatred, discrimination, and all types of corruption have swayed man away from his true destiny on Cosmic Earth! Imagine a world without money, corruption, and wars! Each person would consequently have to work equally and share equally. Maybe one day this meant-to-be paradise will actually become one, and man will begin to realize how utterly important it is to treat all people fairly and equitably. A message to you personally: never forget to extend your love and warmth towards your fellow man for, in so doing, you are creating a foundation of earthly friendship and heavenly brotherhood.

## COBRA (see SNAKE)

## COBWEB (i.e., a spider's web or net)

To see a spider's web or to be ensnarled in one signifies that you are finally beginning to find some direction in your life. In the past, you have spread your wings or talents in far too many directions to honestly make you happy. Now, it appears you will begin to concentrate on that one goal that interests you the most. Day by day your hopes and aspirations will lead you closer to your fulfillment because of your committed determination and worthy actions. What could be a greater event than you discovering your worth and purpose on earth? Truly, even the angels sing for you!

**COCKFIGHT** (i.e., a fight between two gamecocks)
   The pathway to self-destruction is already in motion when inner hatred, skepticism, and a frightful disgust for life exists within the portals of your heart, mind, and soul! Personal ruination is strongly indicated here unless you are willing to compromise and show more enthusiastic interest in living. Your attitude is working against the basic grain of life. Unless you free yourself from such outrageous thinking, then torturous discontent and offensive harassment of the conscience and soul are indicated. Obey only the positive impulses or instincts that are within you, and begin to fulfill your worthiness in life with constructive thought and purpose. You have wallowed in self-pity much too long; now it is time to put your nightmarish thinking to rest! Be strong, dispose of some unworthy habits, and—at long last— let the sun shine over the shadows of your past and your present.

**COFFEEPOT**
   Your symbolic dream is desperately trying to tell you to ignore some of your childhood fears. A typical fear could be, for example, that if you do not put your shoes away exactly in the same spot as before, something terrible will happen to you or to your loved ones. These fears are totally unfounded and unrealistic. You should know that by now! How can you dispose of these unwarranted, slave-oriented ideas that simply wish to rule your life? Commence to realize that anything can happen to you or to your loved ones no matter what you do, think, or ritualize. We know that there is no escape from death; we know that life has its good and bad moments; and we know that we should strive to improve our ways. These three simple facts should allow you to reflect upon, and ultimately disband, some of your far-fetched fears and perfectionisms. Strive for simplicity, independence, good will, and trust. By so doing, you will commence to face your life with a sense of freedom and reality.

**COFFEE TABLE**
   This dream indicates some family disharmony due to emotional unreasonableness, financial disappointments, or illness. This situation may not necessarily last long, but it is very difficult for you to accept or digest this particular earthly crisis. Most people tend to become stronger

during a crisis; however, some people merely throw in the towel and give up. You are urged to elevate your thoughts through prayer, hope, and patience, rather than immerse your thoughts in negative failings and temporal weaknesses that merely come and go like a storm.

## COFFIN

Dreaming about a coffin with or without a body in it emphatically denotes that you tend to feel abandoned or neglected by your family. These strong feelings have developed over a period of time. Your family does care about you and does have your best interests at heart, but you cannot expect to be pampered or served hand and foot simply because you feel your needs are more important than anyone else's. It is most unreasonable to expect a sympathetic ear to your "ills and pills" when you make very few attempts to help yourself or rectify your own problems. You must learn to give all family members their own space to think, to act, and to accomplish what they want in life. You can hardly expect each family member to think and act exactly like you do! Everybody on this planet has a soul which should be nourished with faith, love, and understanding; everybody on this planet has a mind which should be nourished with self-reliance, experience, and good common sense. In summation, your impatience and self-regard are two major factors that have created your self-imposed problem. The sooner you admit this fact, the sooner you will commence to feel the emotional security and comfort you rightfully deserve.

(*Note*: A repetitive dream about a coffin with or without anyone in it denotes stress, strife, or sadness to the dreamer: for example, emotional or physical stress; financial, marital, or romantic strife; sadness involving injury, sickness, or death.)

## COIL (see SPRING)

## COINAGE (see MONEY)

## COLD (i.e., an illness of the throat, nose)

Dreaming of having a cold or catching one could, in fact, imply that you presently have a cold or you are about to catch one. Should this not be applicable to you at this time, then this symbolism implies that you are working too hard, exercising too hard, or doing both beyond the levels of human endurance. In any case, you are advised to set time limits on these strenuous factors, otherwise you just may become ill.

**COLISEUM**
Seeing an empty coliseum advises you to plan ahead, to create new interests, and to try to circulate with people who share common interests. Of recent, you have been in a depressive rut, so to speak, simply because you seldom make time for yourself. Well, this dream is trying to tell you what others have been telling you for quite some time. For a change, do something just for yourself (e.g., take a trip, be daring and buy yourself something special, take a course, join a club or organization).

Seeing a coliseum with some form of activity present suggests that you are somewhat chatty and highly persuasive in your conversation with people. Nonetheless, you seem to have an inner fear about being accepted or rejected by people whom you know or meet. You appear to be very self-conscious about your appearance and basic personality. Strive for self-improvement wherever possible; and, from time to time, visualize how others tend to see you. Are you a clean, well-groomed individual? Are you all-knowing when a conversation takes place? Do you blame others for your mistakes? Do you have a fear of being dependent upon others? Do you make or lose friends very quickly? Do you make any efforts to rekindle friendships when they have gone sour? Do you resent others for their stunning appearance or special abilities? Do you inwardly hate yourself for many reasons? Do you distrust most people? Are your feelings of inferiority really substitute fears about the possibility of failing or being unhappy in life? Are you afraid of being alone in life? Is it difficult for you to swallow your pride and admit your mistakes to yourself and to others, as well? Recognizing your weaknesses within some of these questions should give you the opportunity to rehabilitate yourself.

**COLLECTOR** (i.e., tax collector or a collector of stamps, books, coins, flags)
Sometimes you are exceedingly happy with the direction your life has taken; yet, there are times you wish you were never born. These extreme feelings are quite common with many people but seem to have their roots based on a love-hate relationship with self, life, and everything else that goes with it. When there is sunshine "outside", you may be sunny inside; but when it is dull and dismal "outside", you may be depressed inside. Such is life! You are strongly urged to do

some serious introspection or soul-searching until you can inwardly recognize the prime reasons for your high-low scenarios in life. You just may discover that your upbringing and childhood days hold the key to your feelings (e.g., love-hate relationship with a parent, brother, sister, friend, school). Once you discover this prime fact for yourself, a great weight will lift from your mind, and you will be free at long last to be a happier person.

**COLLEGE** (e.g., secretarial college, business college)

This auspicious dream advises you to forge ahead with your present goals. Often, life's illusions may stir, toss, or twist the hopes of some people, but you appear to possess that strange calling for outstanding accomplishments within your lifetime. Your motivating spirit and leadership potential are to be admired! Someday, when you do reach that pinnacle of success, do not change or become too complacent in your ways; rather, open your mind and heart to others who may require the same encouragement you once received.

**COLLISION**

To be in a collision or to see a collision implies that you are easily provoked by others; you are far too impulsive and petty at times; and your unending hassles with people, places, and things are the direct results of your stubbornness. You are not the happiest person in life, but you could be happier if you decided to rise above your "old" ways. You are not as crude as you appear to be simply because you are hiding behind a shield of deep hurt, vexation, rejection, confusion, and perhaps a host of other fears. Change your present mode of living and thinking by simply appreciating your existence on earth. The gift of life is precious and should always be humbly and unselfishly utilized, in the best way possible. Do not waste your life on personal doubts, selfishness, and unnecessary tension when, in fact, you could be a worthy contributor to the well-being of life around you. Look more deeply within yourself until you commence to see one of God's greatest creations; namely, you!

(*Note*: Having a repetitive dream about a collision could very well imply that what you are seeing or experiencing within your dream state can actually happen! This is very often called a warning, "prophetic" dream. The best advice that can be given here is that when you do have a recurring dream of this nature which could relate to self, a loved one, a friend, etc., then share this warning with those who may be affected. Pray for everyone's well-being and safekeeping, be careful or simply avoid travel for a while, and sincerely hope that your dream's vision will not come to pass.)

**COLOGNE** (see **PERFUME**)

**COLUMNIST**
You are very altruistic and levelheaded in your dealings with people. Your friendliness and diplomatic know-how are excellent qualities in a human being. Your interchange of thoughts, ideas, and actions with others is often quite open and frank, and the end results are always harmonious and effectual. Futuristically speaking, you should be in the public eye! Your humane, intelligent style of living is a commendable virtue that should allow you to elevate to a very prestigious position on earth.

**COMB**
Deep within the portals of your mind are resentments towards several people who have affected your peace and courage to carry on. Your complaints are distress signals that you, and you alone, can answer. Do not ignore the fact that you have affected some people down the road of life as well! Nothing in life is totally one-sided; you will simply have to admit that some of the barriers placed in front of you were self-imposed. In essence, you appear to be harboring and creating negative factors within your mind that should have been forgotten long ago. There are people who are a lot worse off than you will ever be—people who, with courage and self-determination, recaptured their purpose and passion for living. You can do so, too!

**COMEDIAN**
Being very impulsive, you often say or do things that could make one literally reel over with laughter or sit back in anger. You also demonstrate a fair amount of temper and stubbornness, which merely adds flavour to some of your mind-boggling episodes in life. You are destined for a very successful life with ample happiness, interests, and travel. You would like to see more people laugh their troubles away. Perhaps someday you may play an ambitious role in making this possible (e.g., writing about or displaying your keen sense of humour and comical experiences to others).

**COMEDY** (i.e., a play or motion picture with humorous situations, characters, and happy endings)

Your strictness with self can at times be overpowering and somewhat suffocating to the mind and spirit. Disagreeable and worrisome thoughts often beset you while you struggle for total perfection. You have, in fact, become a slave to your perfectionist mind much too long! This dream symbolism is desperately trying to tell you that as when you relax to enjoy a comedy from time to time, so you, too, must learn to relax and enjoy your life, as well. Whoever gave you the idea that your life had to be so stressful, trying, and exacting?

**COMET**

Seeing this heavenly body streak across the sky infers that a culmination of events will suddenly surface to reality, thus elevating you to the rank or position you rightfully deserve! Sometimes your intuition is stronger than your intellect; this allows you to simply plunge into a serious situation without too much time to reflect or ponder over the circumstances involved. Many great souls on this planet often employ this technique; and it works! Now, with your expertise and unresisting spirit, you will follow your intuitive feelings towards even better things.

**COMIC BOOK**

Reading or seeing a comic book within a dream denotes a lack of self-confidence, compounded with strong feelings of inadequacy and guilt. The roots of your dissatisfaction appear to originate from your home life or basic life style. Your mind is capable of accepting hearty challenges and intellectual pursuits, but someone or something is holding you back. It may not always be this way, however. This dream advises you to be very patient and to think positive. In the not too distant future, you will be in a better position to rise above your present circumstances with impressive results!

**COMIC STRIP** (i.e., a series of cartoons as seen in a newspaper)

You are seeking attention in the wrong manner! Those sudden, explosive outbursts of anger you display are not only shocking, but downright frightening! You seem to be emotionally unpredictable. This often leaves others around you in a state of bewilderment. You may be leaving yourself wide open for unnecessary confrontations and hard feelings that will ultimately bring you future strife and unhappiness. Stop, look, and listen to yourself once in a while, especially during one of your traumatic sessions. It's amazing what a little bit of mirrored feedback can do for you. At first you may not like what you see and hear; however, you have a free will to change now or suffer later.

**COMMANDO** (i.e., a unit of specially trained troops who operate inside a territory held by the enemy)

Many times, your earthly suffering or discomforts are difficult to bear (e.g., poverty, mental or physical pain, loss of a family member, unhappy marriage). Whatever your struggles may be, this dream urges you to continue to be courageous, humble, and spiritually confident that you are a step closer to the joy and freedom that yet await you. Eventually, the darkness of your life will be transformed into earthly satisfaction and eternal thankfulness.

**COMMERCIAL** (see **ADVERTISEMENT** or **ANNOUNCEMENT**)

**COMMUNE**

If you truly want to destroy some of your old ways and bad habits, then listen to your conscience with love and wisdom. You have been wanting improvement or correction in your life for quite some time; however, you never really buckle down to face your problems head-on. There are no miracles here unless you disband your fears with inner trust and good judgment. To improve your life, be more honest and determined; stop procrastinating.

**COMPACT** (i.e., a small cosmetic case)

This dream advises you to think twice before you decide to become involved in some dim-sighted love affair or in sexual promiscuity. Your unhappiness basically stems from your own lethargic views in making your present life more meaningful and purposeful. Did you know that your responsibilities, abilities, and suffering all belong to you? It is unfortunate that so many people go out of their way to make trouble for themselves when deep down they know the difference between right and wrong. This dream counsels you to stay out of trouble by listening to your supposed logical mind, instead of your emotional heart.

**COMPASS**

You have great urges to see happy people around you. If you had your way, your world would be one big garden of bliss and peace—a true Garden of Eden. Your thoughts and intentions are very honourable and sincere. However, it would take more than a wish to hope to eradicate conflict, hardship, ignorance, and despair on the face of this globe. The truth of the matter is that today it takes people like you, who harbour a calling, to change things around. Perhaps you are one of those dedicated, goodwill ambassadors whose work will not slacken or fail until some of those obstacles in your part of the world disappear. This revelation is wholesome, but only you and God hold the key to your futuristic endeavours.

**COMPASSION** (i.e., forgiveness, pity, or showing sorrow with urges to help)

The urges of sympathizing with and helping others is so strong within your being that to differentiate these human qualities between your wake state and sleep state would be an impossibility. In other words, you are simply carrying your wake state feelings and activity into your dream state, with obvious good fellowship and inner satisfaction! The strength of this dream shows that you are exact and methodical in your thinking and that your general responsibilities and relationships with people are positive. Your good upbringing and the proof of your sincere, persevering individualism are all triumphant qualities of a very good soul!

**COMPENSATION** (i.e., anything given as an equivalent such as for a loss, damage, unemployment)

To compensate someone or to be compensated within a dream suggests that you are not too settled within your being. Inwardly, you appear to be somewhat confused and impatient, and you lack foresight in some of your decision-making schemes. You cannot expect to be happy and successful in life if you fail to learn from your mistakes, or if you repeatedly make hasty decisions without some forethought. Basically, you mean well; however, you are failing to apply your inner strength with greater concentration and systematic effort in order to complete a task. You cannot do ten things at one time and hope to do a good job. Do one task at a time; finish it; then go on to your next task, and finish it. Strive to know your real purpose or duty on earth, and calm your inner spirit and sensibility.

**COMPETITION**

This dream advises you to be more assertive, especially where certain circumstances compel you to say yes when, in fact, your mind is saying no. The word no can be one of the most beautiful words on earth, when used properly and diplomatically! That so-called tug of war with yes and no answers should always be dealt with truthfully.

**COMPLAINER** (see *also* **DISSATISFACTION, FUSSINESS, KILL-JOY,** or **MUMBLER**)
Your whining and fussy habits are sometimes just too much for others to bear. Some serious emotional trouble may be brewing ahead for you unless you start curbing some of those hard-to-please attitudes now. Normally, when a person is very young, their complaints are tolerated—but only up to a certain degree. You know better! In fact, you have enough stubbornness in you to actually turn over a new leaf with positive results.

**COMPLETION**
Completing something within a dream signifies approval and praise in your recent endeavours. It appears you have taken some very positive steps in combating your personal indecisions through gutsy trust and determination. So you see, your feelings about being imperfect actually gave you the incentive to prove something to yourself; and you did! You have discovered a new masterpiece in life, a friend whom you can rely on forever; namely, you!

**COMPLIMENT** (see *also* **ADULATION** or **CONGRATULATION**)
This dream symbolizes a conscious or subconscious desire to walk away from your present surroundings or home life situation. Who told you life would be easy? You are far too quick to blame the next person for some matters you are partially responsible for as well. The sooner you begin to compromise and appreciate those who have been bridled to your dogmatic ways, the sooner happiness will be yours. Unfortunately, your pompous and demanding attitudes have created some distance between you and those who honestly want to like and appreciate you. This dream counsels you to stop complaining; rather, show more courtesy, respect, admiration, and praise for those around you.

**COMPOSER**
You live a life of independence, trust, self-sacrifice, affection, and understanding. Those all-too-soon forgotten kindnesses of others such as a smile, a compliment, a friendly handshake, or some other gesture

of unselfishness are actions you do not forget. No matter how upsetting or unhappy your life may appear, it seems that your philosophic thoughts and wisdom always allow you to come out on top. Indeed, your pleasing and mature personality is an inspiration for all to see, to know, and to emulate.

## COMPROMISE

To settle a problem by mutual agreement signifies that a move or sudden change at home may appear to be alluring, but the end results will not be inwardly satisfying. The future promises you a more reliable change that will not only make you proud and happy, but successful, as well! Silence your pride and impatience for a while; sit tight, and anticipate happier events yet to come.

## COMPUTER

Seeing a computer or working with one intimates that you have very original ideas, designs, or plans that could be put to practical use (e.g., inventions, science, music, writing, new business concepts). Some of the concepts you seem to be harboring at this time could conceivably alter the course of your destiny, if placed in the right hands. What you do with your ideas, however, is entirely up to you. You can keep them; or you can share them! When you commence to realize that many people would benefit from your concepts and sense of imagination, then maybe you will commence to realize that they were not so farfetched, after all. Bear in mind, as well, that all great ideas and thoughts originate with sudden inspiration from the denizens of the mind and soul. One could imply that these sudden inspirations emanate from the God Source within each and every one of us. Since many great ideas and thoughts have their time, day, and glory on earth, perhaps your great ideas and thoughts will be next.

## CONCEALMENT (see HIDING, INVISIBILITY, MASK, or MYSTERY)

## CONCEIT (see *also* BRAGGART or SNOBBERY)

One of the highest goals to pursue in life is to know yourself; one of the hardest lessons to learn in life is the truth about yourself. You basically know yourself rather well, but the essential lesson here is that you are conceited! Did you know that you are more important to the world just being your natural self, rather than being foolish and ego-tistical? It is true! In facing your detrimental weakness with honesty, emotional self-control, and spiritual self-awareness, you will slowly begin to like what you see.

## CONCENTRATION CAMP

You are uneasy or anxious to succeed in some personal matter of importance. Be at peace; you will! This dream also reveals that you have a great aversion against anyone or anything that causes despair and misfortune towards any race, colour, or creed. Unfortunately, not all people think this way; therefore, the sadness and sorrows of this world still continue. But, it is very gratifying that there are people like you whose lofty thoughts and ideals still shine above anguished earth!

## CONCERT

There are times when you express needless anxieties over minor, trivial matters. Your nit-picking habits have almost become an obsession with you! In fact, you seem to be a walking bundle of nerves because of your strange need to know every little detail that comes your way. Be careful! This habit can lead you to some form of mental difficulties, as the future progresses (e.g., phobias, fears, depression, breakdown). Accept life with its many faults and pleasures, for nothing is perfect. Ignore your many doubts about matters that are not worth the time, effort, or light of day; you have much more important things to do!

## CONCRETE (i.e., cement)

Unfortunately, you tend to close the doors of your mind too quickly, concerning the thoughts and actions of others. There are always two sides to a story in most matters. Being too judgmental, hardheaded, and temperamental very often places others in an awkward position with you. Your final words in any matter seem to become an unwritten law, which automatically creates friction and misunderstandings with those around you. In essence, you are out of touch with people's thoughts and feelings. When was the last time you praised someone? When was the last time someone praised you? Never fail to project kindness wherever you go, for this action alone will give you the satisfaction and understanding you require.

**CONDOLENCE** (see **CONSOLATION**)

**CONDUCTOR** (i.e., a music conductor or train conductor, etc.)
You are a very strong-minded, self-confident, and self-sufficient individual. Although you may be misunderstood for some of your forceful ways, your mature sense of direction and expertise are to be respected. You are slated for wholesome success and happiness, both in your profession and in private matters.

**CONE** (i.e., the fruit of a pine, spruce, or fir tree)
To dream about the cone of a tree signifies that your authenticity and wisdom about some of the secrets of life and the universe are awe-inspiring! You may be one in a million with this inner gift to perceive and instantly know the truths to the mysteries of man and life. Perhaps you are a miracle worker! Even in the occasional bitterness of your daily life, you never allow yourself to be spiritually downcast; rather, you maintain a fearless and assured attitude about all things. You are meant to be famous! One day, past the pages of your life, your name may be spoken by generations yet unborn!

(*Note*: You may also have the pleasure of knowing that if, for example, you are experiencing a very negative dream but at the very end of your dream sequence or anywhere during your dream sequence you happen to see a cone, then this cone symbolism takes precedence over your entire bad dream. Consequently, you have nothing to worry about simply because the cone acts as a "buffer zone" to anything negative within a dream.)

**CONFECTIONARY** (i.e., candy store, etc.)
You have very little money sense! You either spend more than you make, or you buy foolish, nonessential items through force of habit. Strive to curb your desires in wanting items beyond your financial reach. In fact, a lot of your worries may vanish if you use more foresight and self-control. Money, as you know, is the root of many evils, when used improperly; but, it can also be the root of much good, if used wisely.

**CONFERENCE**
It is regrettable that you, with so many virtuous characteristics, should fall behind in human understanding. You are allowing your pride and your position in life far too much freedom to overrule the

good thoughts and actions of people around you. You are the boss and master, and that's the end of the conversation?! The secret of true success, in any language, is to love many things but, above all, to treasure those beings whom fate brings to you. A successful person never works alone! Good teamwork, comradeship, honesty, compassion, and kindness are essential to give any boss success in life. Nothing less and nothing more will do! If you truly want merit, honour, and prosperity in life, then overrule your sense of self-importance with inspired trust and common sense.

**CONFESSION** (i.e., confessing a crime or wrongdoing to another person or confessing one's sins to a priest)

Confessing some wrongdoing to another person within a dream intimates that you are being dishonest with yourself and with some people whom you know. You are hiding behind a mask of false intentions and actions that can only bring you future embarrassment, trouble, and pain. Nevertheless, somewhere in the faint recesses of your mind and soul, there is hope! This, of course, depends on your willingness to detach yourself from your old ways and habits. You can start by being honest in all things that you do, no matter how painful that truth may be. Then, have more confidence and faith in your own personality and abilities. Stop reaching for instant wealth, prideful pursuits, and other schemes that are cunning and deceitful. Let your world, instead, become a better place, with purpose and hope. Be wary; do not succumb to self-flattery or false excuses—these could inevitably lead you down a sorrowful pathway in life.

**CONFETTI** (i.e., small pieces of paper or candies scattered at various celebrations)

You seem to express more honour and affection towards strangers than you do towards your own kinfolk. Perhaps your reasons are just; or perhaps they are irresponsible. Only you have the answer to this entire situation. With your intelligence, there is bound to be some future introspection concerning your feelings in this matter. In time, you may find that your heritage is far more important to you than you are now willing to admit!

**CONFIDENCE** (i.e., self-confidence)

You are a decisive, courageous, happy, and emotionally secure individual. These admirable characteristics are just a few of your fine attributes as a human being. You say what you mean and expect others to show you the same regard. They generally do. You will master the road ahead of you with duty, knowledge, and inspiring confidence.

## CONFUSION

You are highly suspicious about people's thoughts, actions, and deeds. Somehow you feel that there are some underlying, negative motives or reasons for things people do. Not so! People are very different in their habits and actions, but you will discover that most people are very honest and trustworthy. Some people whom you know or meet may exaggerate the truth a little bit, but you should at least give them a chance to prove themselves. In essence, you do not admire or like deceitful people. Most people will concur with your feelings! Bear in mind that the people who tend to continually lie to you have a serious problem, not you! If fate should reward you with two or three good, sincere friends in life, then be thankful for your blessings, and rest your case. If you are dissatisfied with some unwholesome people around you, then it is up to you to move beyond their thoughts and actions in life.

## CONGRATULATION

Congratulating someone or being congratulated within a dream suggests you have a tendency to contradict other people much too often. You are bound to receive some feedback from others because of your critical views and careless expectations of what you feel people should be like (e.g., physical appearance, behaviour, habits, dress apparel). You dwell with pleasure upon a person's unhappiness and misfortune, rather than wishing and expressing happiness for another person's good fortune and success. It is never too late to change, though! Begin by being more sincere and loyal to those around you. Love and understand people's feelings as you would your own, and show more gratitude for the joys and happiness this life has already brought you. Reflect upon your own fears and weaknesses, from time to time, so that you will never lose sight of your own imperfections. As well, be more encouraging to others through your work and spirit of giving. Continue to prevail in this manner until, beyond any shadow of a doubt, you have proven your worthiness—not only to yourself and to others, but to God as well.

## CONGRESS (see GOVERNMENT or LAW)

# CONQUER

To be victorious over someone or something implies that you are attempting to reform your feelings, habits, and manners when you are around people. It seems that you were always seeking attention from others because of your emotional, physical, and financial insecurities. The special aspect about this dream symbolism is that now you are really trying to improve your shortcomings with positive ideas and aspirations (e.g., reading good books, listening to other people's thoughts and ideas, educational pursuits). Your own confidence, determination, and good fellowship are the keys to self- improvement.

# CONSCIENCE (see *also* GUILT or REGRET)

Wrestling with your conscience while you are asleep simply is an indication of your inward sadness, disharmony, or confusion involving a person, a group of people, or some other matter of vital importance to you. If you know you are to blame about something, then make every effort to correct the matter.

However, if you are too late in making amends or restitution in any matter, then you will simply have to resign yourself with courage, peace, and hope. If you are innocent of any wrongdoing and have made every effort to maintain your innocence in the entire situation, then the only recourse you have is to sit tight and hope that justice will prevail. Normally, justice does prevail, sooner or later! Whether you are right or wrong in anything, you cannot escape a truth or yourself forever. Cherish and always respect your life; and the truths of many things will follow you wherever you go.

# CONSERVATIONIST (i.e., a person who cares for and protects natural resources)

Believing in or swaying towards any negative or illegal facet of life can only bring you misfortune and shame. Do not allow anyone to tell you otherwise! This dream symbolism indicates negative irregularities around you which could conceivably victimize you into doing something you may later regret. You have a choice in life: 1) to become an impoverished human being through wrongful acts and deeds, or 2) to become a content human being through honest acts and deeds. Temptations may be difficult to surmount; however, if you truly believe and care about your life, then you will take the right road without ever looking back.

**CONSERVATORY** (i.e., a school of music, art)

A few minor changes are looming in the horizon for you, but these changes will not deter you from forging ahead with your plans or ambitions in life. You possess enough self-confidence to carry you through the mightiest storms! Blessed with hosts of creative and innovative thoughts and ideas, you are bound to make all your wishes and aspirations come true! You are a very special, caring, dignified human being who assuredly intends to serve others with loving truth and compassion.

**CONSOLATION**

A plan or expectation you have been banking on may be disrupted by one, two, or three people who do not necessarily admire your good intentions or courage. Single-handedly, you must defend yourself against any intruder(s) who wishes to hinder your progress. You will walk out of this situation victoriously, providing you maintain your mental strength and fixity of purpose. Perhaps, someday, your opponent or opponents will see the folly of their ways.

**CONSTABLE** (see **PEACE OFFICER**)

**CONSTELLATION**

You are a very respected, mature, and hard-working individual. In fact, all the things you ever strived for thus far have been created by your own diligence and skill. Even now, nothing comes too easily for you, yet you still have the satisfaction in knowing that you are capable of ploughing forward without any past regrets. You have lived long enough to know the things you do for yourself are those things that will bring you the greatest pleasure in life. This world would be so much better off if more people followed your good judgment and foresight!

**CONSTIPATION**

Your inquisitiveness regarding the personal faults and failings of people whom you know or meet is neither wholesome nor wise. Those "juicy tidbits" you hear about people could not possibly help you in life. Besides, some of those rumors are probably no more than tall tales concocted by gossips who have nothing better to do with their valuable time. For your own well-being, you are advised to take a serious look at your own life, and see how you would feel if someone discovered and revealed a certain secret in your closet. Well, other people feel the same way when certain matters about their lives become public and known.

## CONSTRICTOR (see SNAKE)

## CONTACT LENS

Seeing or wearing contact lens within a dream suggests that you are basically friendly with most people whom you know. Your emotional upsets are generally subdued by self-analysis and sound logic. You are bound to be happy and successful in life, but not without some sweat and toil on your part.

Expressing a fear about losing your contact lens or actually losing them within a dream denotes that should you ever hold a high position in life, you may lose sight of yourself by becoming impatient, proud, and much too intolerable for your own good. This dream urges you to become more diplomatic and generous in your everyday affairs. Getting along with people today should automatically allow you to get along with others tomorrow, thus alleviating any future possibility that a high-ranking position might "go to your head".

## CONTEMPT

Feeling contempt within a dream state implies that you also harbour this feeling while you are awake. You obviously are annoyed with someone or something in your life, so it is basically up to you to solve your problem in a sensible way. Understand that harbouring this feeling for too long can bring about greater stresses to the mind and body. This is not wise! The sooner you alleviate the bitterness within your life (e.g., become peaceful with the person who seems to annoy you, strive to make your home or work conditions more harmonious, do not be too annoyed if your plans or actions fail from time to time), the better off you will be.

## CONTENTMENT (see HAPPINESS)

## CONTEST

The constant routine of your life is truly enough to make you want to abandon your present surroundings. In so many words, you seem to be in an emotional and environmental rut! This situation will not improve without some tangible action on your part. Delaying or procrastinating in something you wish to do or improve in your life merely augments the boredom and unhappiness. Do not expect any magic wand to make things better for you; rather, commence to solve or improve those routine matters which vex you so much. Actions speak louder than complaints!

**CONTESTANT** (see **CONTEST**)

**CONTRABAND** (see **SMUGGLER**)

**CONTRACEPTIVE**

Using or seeing a contraceptive device or agent signifies that you are governed by strong emotional and sexual impulses during your dream state. Those sexual matters you tend to suppress during your wake state are subconsciously expressed quite freely during your sleep state. These human feelings are fairly common; you are neither alone nor unique in your thoughts and actions. There are many variable factors that will either direct you towards, or restrain you from, sexual matters. You are the best judge of your own sexual and emotional happiness and weaknesses, so what you do to effectively regulate a more or less pleasant standard in this regard is left entirely up to you. The point is to always be mature and stable in your sexual wants and needs in life.

**CONTRACT**

Seeing or signing a contract suggests that you are consistent in thought and action. You have a fine reputation for being a doer instead of a quitter. You certainly seem to have the upper reins in knowing yourself and what you want to achieve in your life. Rest assured that your knowledge, skills, abilities, or gifts are all commanding factors which will bring you future peace and prosperity!

**CONTRADICTION**

You would like to contradict someone who appears to know all! However, you are not about to create any waves, now or later, due to this person's age or rank. Well, there may come a time when you will be compelled to say what you feel and to contradict this person. No one becomes all-wise simply because of age or rank. There are many youthful people today who could put some people with age and rank to shame. People can make a fool of themselves at any age!

## CONTROL TOWER

In times of depression and uncertainty, do not vent your frustrations on anyone. When you do feel hopeless or inadequate, from time to time, always strive to solve your own problems unselfishly and maturely. Unfortunately, many unhappy people have the habit of making others feel just as miserable as they are. These unhappy people are often selfish, impatient, and insecure. Their hang-ups are self-inflicted simply because they fail to cope with or solve their problems in a sensible manner. They could be happier if they learned the art of serving others with kindness, instead of serving themselves with self-pity.

## CONVENT

The complex nature of your perfectionist mind very often brings you doubts about life and death itself. Sometimes you feel that you are living in some illusion, or that what you feel, see, or experience are not realistic events at all. Unfortunately, all types of anguish and suffering on earth upset your good intentions, peace, and serenity to the point where you begin to harbour doubts about many things. Life on this planet is very real, and death is a fact of life; however, it is not an end to life! Your soul —the real you—continues to eternal life! Occasionally, people are confronted with mind and soul battles, which are common (e.g., doubts about God, life, death, oneself, one's family). By praying and meditating and by simply ignoring or rebuking the negative forces around you, you will find the peace and serenity you are attempting to resurrect in your life. Nothing is hopeless as long as you maintain even a thread of hope in your life. Why, even when you were born, you were a tiny bundle of hope yourself!

## CONVENTION (see *also* CONFERENCE)

You are experiencing some mental or physical strain due to some personal urgency to complete a task or job on time. For your own sake, do not create an ulcer over this situation. You will fulfill this task or job with admirable results and worthy praise, even if you are a day or two early—or a day or two late.

## CONVERT

If you succeed in converting someone against their will or someone succeeds in converting you against your will, then be prepared for some unexpected difficulties as the days or weeks go by. You will eventually come out of this depressed time with more initiative, vigor, and hope.

If you fail to convert someone against their will or someone fails to convert you against your will, then some personal or depressing matters will be solved before too long. The days to follow will be cheerful, satisfying, and productive.

## CONVICT (see INMATE)

## CONVOY

Seeing a convoy of ships, troops, cars, airplanes, and so on signifies that a project you think is completed is, in fact, not completely finished or perfected (e.g., a music score, book manuscript, invention, building design). Whatever this project may be, it appears that more time and labour is required before you will actually see this worthy undertaking become a reality.

## CONVULSION (see EPILEPSY or FIT)

## COOK (see *also* BAKER)

Cooking food implies that you like to associate with good, friendly, wholesome people (e.g., loyal friends). In spite of your many positive wants and needs in life, your past losses, money problems, sadness, and indifferences with various members of your family have created great anguish within your mind and soul. You have survived these ordeals with faith, calmness, and courage; and perhaps with small miracles that have often saved your day. In the most loving sense of the word, you are a very remarkable person!

Seeing yourself or someone else as a chef of a restaurant, etc., intimates that you will be receiving some unwelcome company. You will do your best to make these people as comfortable as possible; but, deep within your mind, you will not be able to forget the past difficulties they have caused you. It takes a great amount of willpower and diplomacy to handle these types of people; so, for your own sake, grit your teeth, and be strong in this entire matter. Their attitude about life and about you will not change overnight. Maybe one day they will see the truth about themselves and then realize that you and your family were sadly misjudged.

## COOPERATION

You are a very self-reliant person. It is your nature to affect and strengthen those around you because of your noble character and ability to bring about sudden and purposeful changes and results! In essence, your presence is like a warm breeze to those who require your particular comfort, assurance, and guidance. To know you is to like you; to know you is to have a true friend in life!

**COPIER** (see **PHOTOCOPY**)

**CORD** (see **ROPE**)

**CORONER**

Being or seeing a coroner indicates your deep regrets for not having changed for someone special when you had the chance. This special person could very well have passed away, moved away, or simply walked out of your life through divorce, separation, and so on. What can one say when it is too late to make amends on this earth plane? Well, you simply have to go on with your life in the hopes that you are forgiven. It is never too late to say you are sorry to God. Try your very best not to repeat past, foolish mistakes; and the future that awaits you will give you the comfort and love you sorrowfully miss now.

**CORPSE**

This symbolic dream merely relates to your fears about dead bodies or about death itself. This is not a death omen dream but rather a symbolic sign to bring you closer to the realization that life is what it is. There is birth on this planet; and eventually there is death on this planet—no more and no less. How you wish to cope with this fact of life is entirely up to you. For your own sake, however, why not read a few of the hundreds of books written about various aspects of life after death? This could well help allay some of your superficial fears and bring you closer to understanding the bonds between heaven and earth.

**CORRIDOR** (see **PASSAGEWAY**)

**CORROSION** (see **RUST**)

**COSMETIC**

You often go through the motions of trying to be a happy person; but, deep within your being, you are actually very insecure and unhappy. Before you go looking for your happiness in different places, you would be wise to know yourself a little better. This dream strongly reveals that you are guided more frequently by sudden impulses, rather than by reason or logic. Using good common sense, once in a while, would certainly do no harm in improving situations. Sometimes people have happiness staring right at them, but they fail to accept the simple, pleasant, and peaceful way of existence. They keep searching for something unique, different, or nebulous until, at long last, they discover that truth and happiness come from within the mind and heart, not outside the mind and heart. The entire essence of this dream highly recommends that you learn to cope, adjust, and solve your problems with sensible thinking. Remember that the love and understanding you project to others will be the love and understanding you receive in return.

## COSTUME (see CLOTHES)

## COUCH (e.g., a sofa or divan)

There are pending problems involving money or property matters. You may be asked to read the fine print of a contract a family member, in-law, friend, or acquaintance failed to understand. You may also be asked to intervene or settle some unfortunate misunderstanding, where this contract is concerned. Hopefully this problem can be solved in a pleasant manner; otherwise, the law may have to settle this embarrassing reality of life.

## COUNTERFEIT (see CHEATING, DECEPTION, FORGERY, or THIEVERY)

## COURSE (see CAREER, LEARNING, SCHOOL, PASSAGEWAY, or RACE TRACK)

## COURT (see *also* ADJUDICATION, JUDGE, JURY, LAW, LAWSUIT, or LAWYER)

There are no shortcuts to achievement. If you have enough willpower to get down to the basics in what you want to do and accomplish in life, then you will commence to see some of your wonderful expectations come true. Do not expect life to serve you in any way unless you make great efforts to serve life. You cannot expect to reap the harvest of a garden if you fail to plant the seeds. Stop wasting valuable time, stop procrastinating, and stop stalling; do what you have to do in this life!

**COURTYARD** (see **PATIO**)

**COUSIN**

Dreaming about a cousin who appears relatively happy or content implies that this cousin is thinking about you, that you may be meeting within a week or two, or that this cousin may be experiencing some financial or emotional difficulties at this time.

Seeing a cousin in some type of pain or torturous situation could very well imply that you will hear about some tragic, sad, or unfortunate circumstances involving this family member (e.g., accident, death, sickness). A prayer, or even contacting your cousin at this time, may help in averting some difficulty or sadness.

**COVER** (see **LID**)

**COW** (see **CATTLE**)

**COWARD**

You are striving very hard to handle your personal problems with mature responsibility and plenty of self-control. You are a proud person who literally fears any form of self-doubt or mental and physical stresses which could alter or paralyze your way of living. With your fortitude, pioneer attitude, endurance, and positive actions, you are bound to have the satisfaction of doing the right and honourable things in life. Nothing brings more peace to the soul than to know that one's life on earth was well spent!

**COWBOY**

You are advised to be more attentive to other people's experiences and knowledge in life. Sometimes your attitude is a bit conceited and overbearing, thus placing you apart from people who could teach you things you should know. Be more open-minded towards all people, even if they do not have your so-called intellect. They could surpass you with raw experience and wisdom. Your inexperience in life could certainly use some positive direction.

**CREMATION** (see *also* **URN**)

This dream warns you not to take unnecessary risks or chances with just about anything for a month or two. Serious consequences could result from impulsive, careless, or hotheaded actions (e.g., arguments, physical violence, careless driving, mixing with bad company, walking alone in a dangerous section of a city or town). Think very carefully before you attempt to do anything too unusual or foolish; your future may weigh heavily on your actions at this time.

## CRIB

You appear to be plagued by many irritations at this time (i.e., unreasonable or groundless fears, misunderstanding among friends, negative outlook on life, etc.). Be at peace! How does a person cure a tired mind and body? Well, you could take a good, hard look at your busy schedule and see what this is doing to you. Heed your body's cry for rest! Your restless and sometimes sleepless nights are all signs of inner fatigue. Ask yourself whether you want to help yourself now or suffer the consequences later.

## CRIMINAL (see *also* CANNIBALISM, EVILDOER, HEAD-HUNTER, INMATE, MAFIA, or PRISON)

Several of the following interpretations may be applicable: A) that you are, in fact, a criminal and merely dreamt about your present state of being; or B) that you know of a person or several people who are criminals; or C) that you are presently working with these individuals in order to rehabilitate them; or D) that you were a criminal long ago, but not any longer; or E) that you have fears about being apprehended by the law for some wrongdoing; or F) that you have no thoughts of remorse or shame for any wrongdoing in life; or G) that your irresponsible, perverse, and impatient ways are unhealthy for you, as well as for those around you; or H) that some of your personality and physical defects need professional attention in order for you to gain true peace and self-control within your life; or I) that your doubts about self and others are very critical and farfetched; or J) that due to your sad upbringing, such as being unloved, abandoned, or rejected, you do not care one way or another in what direction your life may lead you; or K) that you are seeking some form of revenge towards something or towards someone who misjudged you; or L) that you simply despise this world and everything on it, in spite of the help you are presently receiving; or M) that you know there would be less crime in this day and age if more people would learn to encourage, understand, and love one another on earth; or N) that you feel God loves the criminal, but the criminal must love and respect God before becoming truly free and being forgiven; or O) that until mankind is unshackled from sin and temptation—perhaps through divine intervention—there is no possibility of eradicating crime: or P) that this dream has little or no significance for you at all at this time.

## CRITICISM

Criticism towards someone or something within a dream merely personifies your anger or hostilities displayed or hidden during your wake state. Sometimes you are overly dramatic, too quick-tempered, and too demanding for your own good! There is a right way, and there is a wrong way in dealing with people and other factors of life around you. Whatever happened to kindness, politeness, common sense, and understanding? You will certainly have to accept the ups and downs in your life with greater affection, truth, and love before you see better days ahead.

## CROCHET (see LACEWORK)

## CROCODILE

You are failing to compromise with a loved one, or you are in anguish about some past event or careless incident which seems to haunt you. Being such a fine individual in so many different ways, it is certain that you will solve your emotional state before too long. For example, if you are failing to compromise with a loved one, then simply get rid of your pride and stubbornness and make peace! Or, if something from your past haunts you, continue to pray for inner peace, keep busy, and—if necessary—rebuke your mind until this so-called obsession leaves you.

## CROP (see FOOD, GRAIN, or HARVEST)

## CROSS (see *also* CRUCIFIX)

The cross represents hope and betterment for the dreamer. It seems that you have been so alone in your worrisome thoughts and actions that you simply forgot about the possibility of a better future ever coming your way. That time has now arrived! Some of your heavy problems will soon be resolved, thus giving you a better awareness about life, love, and friendships. You rightfully deserve much happiness; you have earned it!

Seeing a cross thrown, broken, or destroyed in any manner signifies that you are frequently being verbally attacked by family members and friends. Lack of understanding, differences of opinion, and stubbornness from you and others involved appear to be at the crux of this unhappy situation. Although most of your ideas are positive and constructive, you must learn to back down once in a while, especially when someone offers new plans or ideas that could be as valid and effective as yours. Be more open-minded, patient, and fair in all your dealings with others around you. By doing this, you will be treated as kindly as the next person. Then there should be no room for anyone to criticize you or for you to criticize them!

**CROSSBONES** (see **SKULL** and **CROSSBONES**)

**CROSS-EXAMINATION** (see **INQUIRY**)

**CROSSROAD**

To be at a crossroad, not knowing which way to go, infers that far too many people around you are giving you advice. This merely adds to your confusion and lack of self-confidence. Begin to think for yourself! As long as you continue to fear making your own decisions or to rely on other people's good or bad advice, you will continue to be at a crossroad in your life. Do not allow any past errors or humiliation to rule your present life. You have the ability to do great things for yourself and others, but first you must let go of your inhibitions with courage and common sense. You were born with good thoughts and ideas; use these gifts wisely.

**CROWD**

Whatever your reasons or desires may be for wanting to do or achieve something in life, you must have the willpower to make this possible. A hope or dream that may appear impossible to you now may certainly become feasible and attainable later on. Far too often, people give up with the first signs of any obstacle or rejection coming their way. They simply do not try hard enough. Never give up if you honestly feel and believe that you can attain something good or great in your life. Never underestimate or overestimate your potential or talents in life either. You never know when you will have to move a barrier or two in front of you. The ultimate key to success and inner fulfillment is persistence and levelheadedness!

**CROWN** (i.e., the headdress worn by a king, queen, etc.)

You have a great tendency to be outspoken; at times,this can be intolerable. Not all people accept your views or thoughts as willingly as you might want this to be. You are not always correct in all that you say or do. Sometimes, it is a very good idea to try to listen more and speak less! This course of action will give you the respect and dignity you rightfully deserve.

**CRUCIFIX**

After having this dream, you will gather your strength and courage, and will triumphantly remove the negative barriers that seem to hinder you. The good that is within you and the love and faith that you so often project to others will bring you closer to the true awareness of God, of your soul, and to many other beautiful hopes that will yet come true! And who said faith could not move a mountain?!

(*Note*: You may also have the pleasure of knowing that if, for example, you are experiencing a very negative dream, but at the very end of your dream sequence or anywhere during your dream sequence you happen to see a crucifix, then this crucifix symbolism takes precedence over your entire bad dream. Consequently, you have nothing to worry about simply because the crucifix acts as a "buffer zone" to anything negative within a dream.)

**CRUELTY**

Any one or two of the following definitions may apply: A) that you are, in fact, a very cruel person who relishes the idea of hurting people or animals; or B) that you are basically a peaceful person, but when someone bothers you the wrong way, you lose your self-control and literally become vicious; or C) that you harbour some thoughts about hurting some people, but something deep within your being warns you not to tread that road in life; or D) that you become very easily upset, no matter how big or small the problem may be; E) that you had much cruelty inflicted upon you while you were young, and now you inflict the same on your loved ones; or F) that you will have nothing to do with anyone who behaves in a brutish, cruel manner; or G) that you are helping, or have already helped, someone who has experienced mental and physical anguish from a spouse, parent, friend, etc.; or H) that this dream has little or no significance to you at all at this time.

## CRY

Crying in one's dream is always a favourable sign! Did you ever wake up on the right side of the bed? Well, today you have! For the next week or so, you will be experiencing your daily activities with harmony, laughter, and a sense of accomplishment. Your future? With your courage and independent outlook, you are bound to see your greatest aspirations fulfilled.

(*Note*: You may also have the pleasure of knowing that if, for example, you are experiencing a very negative dream, but at the very end of your dream sequence or anywhere during your dream sequence you happen to cry, then this crying symbolism takes precedence over your entire bad dream. Consequently, you have nothing to worry about simply because crying acts as a "buffer zone" to anything negative within a dream.)

## CUCUMBER (see FRUIT)

## CUP (see DINNERWARE)

## CUPBOARD

A cupboard filled with food suggests that there is a great amount of unrest or unhappiness where you work or reside. These stresses appear to be emanating from one or two people who appear to be very oppressive and difficult to get along with, no matter how hard you or anyone else tries. At this point, there is very little you can do other than face this problem head-on. Speak to the person(s) involved and try your very best to settle this matter with down-to-earth logic. If this fails, then the only other recourse is to seek outside help or simply wait, hope, and pray for some miraculous changes to take place. Should this fail, then you may have to seek your happiness somewhere else or, at best, sadly remain where you are until you have the courage to see beyond your despair.

An empty cupboard implies that someone's shrewd thinking or cunning may leave you penniless, if you are not careful. If you happen to be loaning a person a great deal of money, be sure to route this transaction through legal channels rather than by word-of-mouth promise. As this dream warning involves many different types of situations pertaining to money or other transactions involving personal security, you are strongly advised to be very prudent in your dealings with people at this time. The possibility of deception or fraud could affect you financially for years to come!

**CUPOLA** (see **DOME**)

**CURE** (see **ANTIDOTE, MEDICATION, PRESCRIPTION,** or **RECOVERY**)

**CURIOUSNESS**
Dreaming about being curious for the sake of knowledge or wisdom is commendable. This implies that you are in complete control of your life. You are secure, happy, and very productive in your daily affairs. However, dreaming about being curious for the sake of being a snoop implies that you wish to know more about a certain person's past (e.g., spouse, parent, relative, friend, acquaintance, stranger). Now, if this party is unwilling to divulge any more information than they already have, then there is very little you can do. Should this person be already dead, then you may have to rely on second-hand information. Should your inquiries be for some selfish, personal gain or your wants and needs in this matter for prying only, then this dream logically advises you to stop while you are ahead. Curiosity used in a negative way can only produce negative results!

**CURLING** (see **GAME**)

**CURSE**
You should begin to disband some of your hostilities and suspicions about some people whom you know. No one is trying to harm you or your family in any way. Your mind, unfortunately, is playing all kinds of tricks upon your better judgment. Simply ignore your mind's harassing thoughts and accusations, which seem to trouble you so much. Be at peace! The fact of being cursed or cursing someone within a dream simply reveals that some maturing on your part is in order. Remember that sometimes people curse themselves in believing that something bad was done to them by someone else when, in fact, nothing was done at all! Therefore, the possible hardships they experience are either circumstantial or self-inflicted.

**CURTAIN**
Seeing curtains that are in good shape and order infers that you will be entertaining unexpected company before too long. Maybe this is commonplace with you; maybe it is not. In any event, pleasant com-

munication and laughter will be shared, and youthful episodes will be reflected upon during this brief visit.

Seeing curtains that are not in good shape and order suggests that sleep is your only escape from the realities of your life. Your struggles, strife, sadness, and losses are sometimes too hard to bear. However, no one's life on earth is totally trouble free! The ache you feel within your heart and mind will cease when you honestly believe that one day your losses and sadness will turn into overflowing Cosmic truths, understanding, and angelical peace. The self-sacrifices you make in your life now are truly "flowers" you place in God's Hands.

**CUSHION** (see **PILLOW**)

**CUT** (see **DISSECTION**, **INJURY**, **KNIFE**, or **SURGERY**)

**CUTLERY** (see **KNIFE**, **SCISSORS**, **SILVERWARE**, or **TOOL**)

**CYCLONE** (see **TORNADO**)

**CYMBAL** (see **INSTRUMENT**)

**CYST** (see **LUMP**)

**DAGGER** (see **KNIFE**)

**DAIRY**

You have great doubts and strong reservations about your abilities and worth in life. Apparently, you would like to do many things on earth, but hosts of inner fears often beset you (e.g., fears about being rejected by others, about failing in something, about fearing to travel alone). These fears are basically self-inflicted; they can only bring burdensome quarrels to your mind. When you decide to replace your pessimistic thoughts with optimistic intentions and purposes, you will commence to see the positive fighting spirit you honestly do possess. When was the last time you gave yourself a pat on the back for doing something rather special? If you haven't, it's about time you did! You must like yourself before you can like anything else on earth. By realizing that you are as important as the next person, you may realize that your doubts and self-hate are nothing more than harsh, foolish values you place upon yourself. Don't waste an hour of your life feeling sorry for yourself or for your past mistakes. Instead, see what measure of good you can do upon this planet—not only for yourself, but for others, as well.

## DAIS (see PODIUM or STAGE)

## DAM

You are a very emotional individual who generally does not like sudden changes, variations, or new rules to take place in your life. Even minor changes at home, at work, and so on bring you great disappointment and annoyance. There are no major setbacks foreseen with this dream. Nonetheless, you should strive to be more compromising with any changes that do take place in your life. With progress, one must maturely accept new concepts, ideas, plans, actions, systems, and so on in life. This world cannot, and will not, stand still for you or for anyone else.

Seeing a dam that breaks cautions you not to become involved with someone whose fly-by-night schemes could bring you legal trouble and shame. Use your good judgment in such matters, and always remember your fine heritage with dignity and thankfulness.

## DAMAGE (see DESTRUCTION or MISCHIEF)

## DANCE (see *also* BALLET, CELEBRATION, JUMP, MEDICINE DANCE, MUSIC, REHEARSAL, STUDIO, or THEATRE)

Seeing a dance or dancing with relatives, friends, acquaintances, or strangers signifies that you are being unduly criticized (from a distance) by people whom you know and admire. Pay no mind to others' unjust opinion about you, and continue to carry on your good, wholesome work. There appears to be no justification for this criticism other than the fact that you are no ordinary individual. You appear to be gifted and talented in creative areas that could make less knowledgeable people envious and condemning. You were born with a God-given purpose; with dignity and perseverance, you will attain your most cherished wants in life.

If the dance you attend is excessively unhappy, then be prepared for some somber news concerning an elderly person who may be a family member or a very dear friend. This is a direct death dream that appears to be inevitable, as the cycle of life goes on. Hopefully, this dream will not frighten you, but rather prepare you for the ultimate outcome of this vision. If you truly believe in your Creator and in the promise of a greater hereafter, then you will not plunge yourself into some deep depression with this foreknowledge. However, if you have doubts about life or your Creator and disbelieve that the hereafter exists, then yon must bear the consequences of your narrow spiritual upbringing. Are you aware that many souls who pass from this life to the next literally weep for us left behind? They are happier than we are!

## DANDRUFF

You are too possessive and demanding. Is it any wonder that some people fear your presence? With one mighty sweep of your mind and mouth, you strike down your prey with spirited vigour and anger! Full stop! Your violent temper and impetuous moods achieve absolutely nothing. Mind you, you can remain this way until the rivers run dry; just do not expect too much in return.

## DANGER

To be in danger or to see someone else in danger intimates that you will be experiencing some type of mental, emotional, or physical difficulties for a brief period of time. Sometimes there must be an inner battle before there is inner peace. Do not panic, but maintain your ground; with a little bit of perseverance, you can once more assume your normal activities.

## DAREDEVIL

Being risky, not cautious, and downright fearless within a dream implies that you are, in fact, the complete opposite during your wake state. You are a bit forgetful and, at times, untidy and somewhat disorganized. In some ways you could be referred to as a scatterbrain or an absent-minded professor. These quirks you possess may be a blessing to you in some ways, a disappointment to you in other ways. In spite of all your unique characteristics, you are a serious-minded individual who does complete a task with foresight, plenty of self-confidence, and a knack for being eccentric—in a likeable manner!

## DARKNESS (see CLOUD, ECLIPSE, NIGHT, SHADOW, or SORROW)

**DARKROOM** (i.e., a place where photographs are developed)

A suggestion or idea that you will present to your family, friends, or employer will be received enthusiastically. With your innovative thoughts and actions, your honesty, and your keen sense of fair play towards others, you are bound to see many accomplishments within your lifetime. And, remember: there are no struggles in your pathway that you cannot surmount with good, sound thinking!

**DARNING**

You will be both surprised and annoyed at someone's impulsive decision or action (e.g., marriage, divorce, move, pregnancy). Whatever this may be, you will simply have to admit that some people, including loved ones, must learn the hard way when they fail to reason with facts and logic. Maybe some people need to struggle before they can truly understand their irrational thinking and unreasonable conduct. Who really knows? They must inevitably find out for themselves!

**DASHBOARD**

Try not to impress others with self-importance or greatness. Instead, display gratitude, kindness, and humility. People who are truly great and outstanding on this planet never need to flaunt, brag, or boast about their accomplishments. Greatness is not always based on what a person does in life; it can be measured in the way a person thinks, acts, feels, and so forth. Not all scientists, musicians, movie stars, singers, and so on are notable. Why, you can have a conversation with a total stranger sometimes, only to later discover that you were talking to someone very outstanding! That same person may think the same of you. The truth is that everyone has some greatness within them; however, they can destroy this complimentary fact through pride and negative actions.

**DATE** (see **CALENDAR** or **MONTH**)

**DAUGHTER**

If the daughter you dream about is relatively happy and content, then you can be sure that her life appears in order. In other words, she is not only productive with her time, but she should also enjoy a sense of accomplishment with her efforts and work.

Seeing a daughter who is unhappy reveals that she is experiencing some emotional or physical stresses at this time. Even though this difficult time is temporary, it would be advisable to pray for her guidance and protection. As well, offer her all the positive encouragement you can at this time.

A forewarning is given to your daughter if you see her wave good-bye to you within a dream. Sad or serious ramifications can result where the following matters are concerned: driving a vehicle carelessly, experiencing persistent physical pain without seeking some medical attention, or going to unwholesome places where shady characters can actually harm her. These warning signs are very serious and could be the beginning to an end if proper guidance in these matters is ignored. Hopefully, this advice will be heeded!

Dreaming about a deceased daughter indicates that you should say a prayer for her. She entered your dream state for a reason. Saying a prayer for her now will assist her on the other side of life. Remember that when you pray for your loved ones on the other side of life, they pray for you, as well. Say a prayer from your heart, and ask that her journey into the heavenly mansions be peaceful, comforting, and filled with exploring goodness, knowledge, and love. Tell her to "ask for the Light"!

## DAUGHTER-IN-LAW

The meaning of this dream is dependent upon your feelings towards your daughter-in-law during your wake state. If you honestly love her and have accepted her as your daughter in many ways, then you can be sure that contentment in family matters is well-deserved and forthcoming. On the other hand, if you do not get along with your daughter-in-law for some reason, then you can also be assured that your family circle will not be as close or united as you would want it to be. Pride, selfishness, and hate are all the negative ingredients which work to alienate any family member from your mind. Holding resentments towards your daughter-in-law, consciously or subconsciously, could cause you to lose your son's love and respect. Reflect upon these thoughts gently; and maybe tomorrow you will realize that your daughter-in-law may not be as horrid as you possibly make her out to be. Do you really want peace and harmony within your family? Then, be more loving and respectful.

Dreaming about another person's daughter-in-law who is alive and well intimates that you will be seeing her shortly, or you will hear some good news about her in the very near future.

Dreaming about a deceased daughter-in-law intimates that she wants a prayer from you. She comes to you for a reason. You can be sure that when you pray for her, she will be praying for you as well. From the outpourings of your mind and soul, also tell her to "ask for the Light"!

## DAYBREAK (see SUNRISE)

## DEACON

With your basic honesty and stubbornness, you can ward off most trouble in your life. At times, you do encounter would-be troublemakers, but your tact, determination, and moral integrity give them very little room to haggle or hassle. Nonetheless, be cautious with your sometimes bold and daring attitudes! When you least expect it, someone may create great unrest and turmoil in your mind and soul which you may not be able to handle or solve. Know your limits with anything in life, and you will prosper and flourish.

## DEAD END

Seeing or reaching a blind alley, passage, street, and so on or some sort of a deadlock in thought or action implies that you are often misunderstood, ridiculed, and rejected by others. Some people may even look upon you as a total failure. So what! Let them say what they want to; the truth of your place and purpose upon this earth is greater than they can possibly envision. This dream reveals that you were almost ready to accept their feelings about you. Look at yourself. What do you see? Is there anything about you that is so unusual that time cannot solve or heal? Don't worry about what others say, feel, or do. They will have to contend with their own lives. What is important here is that you can achieve anything your heart desires, providing you have the belief, willpower, and gutsy character to make this happen. All great people think this way; and so must you. Remember that you only reach a dead end in your life when you allow it to happen. Bear in mind also that a dead end in one's life can also be a major turning point from rags to riches. This fact can be as true and real to you as the tears within your eyes or the smile upon your face. Use your gifts wisely, and you will see that the person least likely to succeed can be first, and the person most likely to succeed can come last.

## DEAFNESS

If you are deaf and dream about being so, then this dream merely reflects your present state of being. This does not imply that because you are deaf, you do not understand life or are less important as a human being. As a matter of fact, you probably understand life much better and are more appreciative than many who can hear!

If you are not deaf and dream of being so, then this symbolism is trying to tell you to be more mutually understanding and harmonious with people around you. You tend to hold grudges with pent-up feelings until all hell breaks loose within your being! You would be well advised to be more open with your views and opinions. Of course, be diplomatic in these matters. You have been moody and stressful much too long!

**DEAN** (see **LEADERSHIP** or **PRINCIPAL**)

**DEATH**

No matter who we are upon this earth, death is a fact of life we must all face. Like the joy of birth, death should be an even greater awareness to happiness and joy. Yet the word death is so final and base sounding that most people are afraid or worried about dying. Attuning yourself to God's Eternal Breath of Life through prayer, meditation, good deeds, and expressed love towards your fellow man will certainly give you an inkling that life continues beyond this planet. There are many "mansions" on the other side in life. In very simple terms, your goodness on Mansion Earth will determine your mansion or rightful place in Heaven. The many states of Heaven are very, very busy! Each soul strives to uplift their awareness and love towards God, until eventually they earn their passage through "the eye of the needle" with Christ's Love! There is no end to life, just bold beginnings; death merely opens the door to them.

Dreaming about your own death indicates your preoccupation with living and with dying. Acceptance of life's rewards and struggles is essential for your soul's growth upon the planet. There are good times and there are bad times you experience on earth; this dream is simply trying to direct your thoughts to a better understanding and awareness of self, life, and death. This is not to imply that you are about to leave this planet today or tomorrow. On the contrary. Just be good, natural, and logical wherever your road may lead, and your soul will be most content and secure.

(*Note*: A repetitive dream about one's demise combined with an unhealthy body and other death symbolisms could reveal the actual death of a dreamer through natural causes. Various accident symbolisms could reveal the same outcome. Prayers for God's intercession in these matters is always wise. With God, prayer, and faith, many things can be overcome.)

Dreaming about a loved one's demise reveals your fears and nervousness about this event happening. In other words, you love your family and friends so much that you never want to see them die. When you learn to think less of your own needs in these matters, your unwieldy fears will diminish and, once more, you will begin to live in harmony and peace. God has the final word regarding anyone's length of time upon this planet. When you learn to accept this fact, then your quarrelsome and possessive struggles and your wants and needs will wash away.

(*Note*: A repetitive dream about a loved one's death could actually happen, provided other death symbolisms are revealed. Again, a prayer for God's assistance, guidance, and protection is advisable. An intercession could take place, for the happiness of all concerned.)

Dreaming about many people dying suggests that your overall unhappy outlook on life has given you no personal or spiritual satisfaction. Your solitude—combined with gloom and doom attitudes—are basically self-inflicted. It's time you altered your thinking! With unselfish patience, hope, trust, determination, and maturity, above all, you can unshackle your needless fears and dreary outlook regarding yourself and life. Do not forget, as well, that good friendships, laughter, and love are wholesome matters that should not be ignored or taken for granted.

## DEBT
Seeing a debt or bill reveals that you will be attending a happy celebration before too long. This occasion will bring you momentary joy and reflections about your past and about your present state of being, as well. Within about a year of this dream, you will travel a great distance within your country, or you will visit a foreign country.

## DEBUTANTE
Along with your tendencies to worry, your own imagination can ensnarl you away from the real truth about yourself and about others. Sometimes, you are so worried about what people think and say about

you that you simply become inhibited and mistrusting. Did you ever stop to think that people have more to do than just think and muse about you? You are basically a well thought of individual; accept this fact! Return the courtesy, trust, and respect others show you, and you will commence to be much happier than you are now.

## DECANTER

You will be surrounded by a bit of controversy before too long. This controversy seems to have its roots based in a personal relationship you have with another person or in your attitudes regarding several other people. This entire episode will interrupt your orderly course of activities and could very well cause you to become a recluse for a brief period of time. The blessing in disguise here is that everyone involved will have an ample opportunity to see themselves with greater understanding, forgiveness, and self-control.

## DECAY (see ROTTENNESS)

## DECEPTION (see *also* AMBUSH, BETRAYER, BLACKMAIL, BRIBERY, CHARLATAN, CHEATING, DECOY, FORGERY, IMPERSONATION, LIAR, MARE'S-NEST, MASK, MIRAGE, MOUSETRAP, PHANTOM, QUICKSAND, or THIEVERY)

The action of deception within a dream could imply that you harbour deceptions during your wake state. In spite of your cleverness, originality, and resourcefulness, the harmful effects of any type of deception within your life can dampen your better hopes and aspirations. To eradicate deceptive thoughts and actions, a person must become humble and must be willing to serve others with truth, honour, and respect. A good, healthy mind can be attained with positive thinking and action. An unhealthy mind merely serves to enslave its owner with negative thoughts and actions. Being honest and good are by far the greatest treasures you can bestow upon your soul!

## DECODER (i.e., one who decodes messages)

You are a very determined individual who literally despises half-answers or half-truths. It seems that you will go to limitless ends to seek total answers and total truths. This is good and wholesome! Seek the truth, and the truth will find you. Never give up on anything until you have at least satisfied your mind, heart, and soul—beyond any shadow of a doubt. This is what knowledge and wisdom are all about.

**DECOMPOSITION** (see **ROTTENNESS**)

**DECORATION**
Seeing body ornaments or Christmas, birthday, or other decorations within a dream indicates that you are looking forward to some special event within the very near future (e.g., going on a long journey, buying a new automobile or home, getting married). Whatever this special event may be, it is revealed that you will be very pleased with the outcome. You are a good person; this happiness is very deserved!

**DECORATOR** (see **INTERIOR DECORATOR**)

**DECOY**
You are a wishful thinker. Regretfully, you are not turning those sound, "wishful" thoughts into reality. Do not be afraid to forge ahead with your daydream thinking; some of the greatest ideas, inventions, and talents emanate from this realm of thought. What may appear to be far-fetched and mere wishful thinking on your part could conceivably be futuristic possibilities and probabilities. Do not be afraid to share a good, wholesome idea with the right people; you never know where this idea will lead you.

**DECREASE** (see **REDUCTION**)

**DEED** (see **DOCUMENT**)

**DEER**
Seeing this animal suggests a nagging physical problem may require some medical attention. You will recuperate, but not without some inner qualms about your over-zealous attitudes and sureness in life. Nothing is certain here on earth; and as long as we hold the breath of life within us, we must all be thankful for each second, minute, and hour given to us. Do not take your existence for granted at any time. With sound mind and body, and without procrastination or poor excuses, do the things you have to do (e.g., making a will, seeking medical attention when required, fulfilling a life-long wish).

**DEFEATIST**
This attitude within a dream suggests that you fail to commit yourself to straightforward answers or actions in life. In so many words, your

yes answers could mean maybe; your maybe answers could be yes or no; and your no answers could mean yes. Your superficial attitudes and half-hearted attempts are selfish, immature, and unrealistic. Are you ready, willing, and able to make some positive changes in your life? Then read on. First, ask yourself who you really are and what you want to do with your life. Do you wish to continually hedge with your thoughts and actions, or do you honestly wish to forge ahead with your thoughts and actions? Second, do not be afraid to speak and live the truth, no matter how inwardly painful this may appear to you. If there are some personal matters about your life you do not wish to discuss with anyone, then keep your secrets to yourself and God. Third, begin to share your time with people you want to be with, rather than with people you wish to impress. A true friend will see you through your darkest hours, whereas some other people will simply ignore your call for help. The fourth measure advises you to have more faith and courage in yourself. The positive things you do for yourself are your rewards in life; the positive things you fail to do for yourself are like opportunities lost forever in the wind. For a moment, ask yourself why you have failed to pursue some of those positive things. Is it too late to recapture some of those past opportunities and transform them to joys and happiness? Your fifth directive is to get down on your knees and begin to pray for love, stability, and loyalty in your life. This is within you now, but you must put your thoughts and feelings into action. Mean what you say, and fulfill what you say; but only if it is of good order. Then, when your life begins to improve—and it will—be humbly grateful that you are alive and well.

**DEFECATION** (i.e., removing waste matter from the bowels)

You are obviously a person with many insecurities who must be reasoned with, encouraged, and often told what to do. In spite of your high intelligence and talents in life, you still persist in dabbling in unrealistic ventures or investments. Those who love you try very hard to reason with your impatience and stubbornness, but this sometimes seems hopeless. In order to improve, you should be more positively decisive in your own affairs; show more faith and courage in what you believe in and do; do not harp on your past glories or mistakes so much, but rather see what you can do to improve your life, here and now; do not be afraid to listen to and follow good advice; and remove your other self-doubts with logic and foresight. Remember that you can do yourself more harm through irrational or thoughtless thinking than by using down-to-earth common sense in your daily affairs.

**DEFECTOR**

You are very annoyed over some mistake you or someone else made recently. Why all the fuss? This error can be corrected! Strive to be more forgiving, inspiring, and understanding when situations around you fail to meet your high standards or expectations.

**DEFORMITY**

To see yourself or anyone else in a deformed manner intimates that, at times, you are a cruel, pitiless person, or you are having difficulties with a person who is, in fact, cruel and pitiless. Now, assuming you are the enemy within this revealing vision, then you are advised to get your act together for the sake of your future well-being and for the betterment of your soul. Unless you commence to be more logical, kind, and trusting with yourself and others, you will continue to be confused, unhappy, hated, and isolated. You have a choice in life—to be happy or to be miserable. If you decide on the latter, then rest assured your misery will catch up to you, sooner or later! Now, if someone else is a troublemaker around you, try to reason with this individual. Should this fail, then do not hesitate to seek outside help. Should this fail as well, then walk away from this foolish association and suffering. Do not be mesmerized into thinking that a cruel and pitiless person will change by themselves. They need all the inspiration and courage they can get, but if they refuse this help, then common sense will show that they are deceiving no one but themselves! There is, indeed, no fool like an uncaring fool!

The act of disfiguring someone or something within a dream indicates your unwillingness to correct some of your immature ways and habits. The hate actions in your life appear to be stronger than your love actions. You are failing to seek those nobler thoughts and actions that lie dormant within your being. Through prayer, meditation, and good deeds, you can come closer to knowing yourself better. But the big question is this: will you comply with your dream symbolism's good wishes for you? You fought so hard to be born; yet now you fail to understand your true worth and purpose on earth. You are here to progress, not regress! Do not let past circumstances or present difficulties dissuade you from finding yourself or from seeking those nobler opportunities that yet await you. Who you are today will have an effect on who you become tomorrow.

**DEGREE** (i.e., a title conferred by a college or university or an honour given to a person)

Although opportunities for success appear endless, there is a restless urge within you to achieve some lasting goal that would perhaps be widely known. If you honestly have that gift, talent, or spark to become famous or known, then rest assured you will follow that route! Who knows? You just could be that outstanding genius or great personality whose finest hour has not yet arrived. Be patient; everything has its time and place.

**DELINQUENCY** (see **JUVENILE DELINQUENCY**)

**DELIRIUM** (i.e., mental turmoil such as restlessness, mumbled speech, and unreality)

Get a firm grip on your mind today and, for the love of life, do not do anything hasty or absurd on land, air, or water! One thoughtless moment could usher you from this world very quickly. Think about this: it could be your own life that you save today! By being careful and wise, this symbolic accident dream can pass you by without a scratch or a dent.

**DELIVERY** (i.e., goods being transferred from one person to another)

Your present difficulties and troublesome worries seem endless, but these will disappear from your life. It seems that good people sometimes suffer more than bad people. Maybe so! This could be perhaps because good people are more willing to face their problems head-on instead of hiding behind deceit and shame. A good person's conscience will always reveal a rainbow of peace at the end of a storm within their life. They appreciate and know the true value of life. So, in your life too, realize that in spite of your ups and downs, there are worthy treasures awaiting you. Those mighty storms may come and go; but each time they do go, you should become infinitely wiser than before!

**DEMAGOGUE** (see **DEMONSTRATOR, DISOBEDIENCE**, or **DISSATISFACTION**)

**DEMAND** (see **REQUIREMENT**)

**DEMOLITION** (see **DESTRUCTION**)

**DEMON** (i.e., an evil spirit, person, or thing)

Whether you are willing or unwilling to be confronted by a demon within a dream reveals that a wave of personal disappointments are in the immediate horizon for you. These disappointments may vary in intensity. This depends upon your inner capacity to persevere and ignore or rebuke those obstacles or barriers that happen to be in front of you. Above anything else, be on a friendly footing with yourself and others when those dark clouds commence to descend upon your pathway. Bear in mind, as well, that this entire experience can be one of the greatest rewards of your life, if you can inwardly perceive these disappointments as being heavenly lessons, instead of earthly trouble.

**DEMONSTRATOR**

Someone whom you know is in dire need of help; this person has a problem (e.g., alcoholism, drugs, compulsive gambler, suicidal, is cruel and insensitive towards others). Whatever the problem may be, you could perhaps try to assist this person. Medical, psychological, and spiritual assistance should be suggested. If they ignore this advice, they will have to stand on their own two feet to fight their problem, or they will slowly succumb to their weaknesses. You can at least rest assured that you did your best in the matter. No more and no less can be done in matters of this nature.

**DEMOTION** (see *also* **DISQUALIFICATION**)

You do not always finish what you start; hence, you often have great remorse for being a so-called quitter. This lack of self-confidence certainly seems to stem from the background of your life (i.e., childhood abuse, feeling loveless, being a "black sheep" within the family, etc.). Only you and God know what troubles you. Nobody's existence on this planet is totally perfect or peaceful, no matter who they are, yet somehow we must all face those sad and happy realities with an open door to God, prayer, and service to our fellow man, one way or another. This dream is throwing you a lifeline of hope. Expel your betrayals, abandonment, and disappointments to the wind, and begin to look deeper into your character. Can you see the realities of happiness and goodness within your being? You are not bad; you are simply sad. The anguish you feel will disappear when you honestly begin to believe that you are more worthy and needed than you know. God loves you; this dream cares about you. But above anything else, you must learn to love yourself, as well. The lowness, ignorance, or disgrace which your past has revealed to you is not worth dwelling upon or keeping.

## DENTIST

If you are, in fact, a dentist who dreams about dentistry, then your dream state is a mere reflection of the work that you do. If you are not a dentist, but you dream about seeing or being one, then this signifies that you are dealing with some very stubborn, uncompromising people (i.e., parent/parents, offspring, brother, sister, relative, friend, employee, employer, etc.). Unfortunately, it is very difficult to compromise with anyone who is generally indifferent to good ideas and suggestions, who is too self-centered and demanding for their own good, and who fails to see the love and compassion you try so hard to project to them. Time will heal your emotional pain in this matter, just as time will give those beings a chance to mature with awe-inspiring truth, introspection, and humility.

## DENTURE (see TEETH)

## DEODORANT (i.e., a salve or liquid used on the body)

So often you come out of situations literally smelling like a rose, yet you walk away feeling hopeless and inadequate. There is nothing wrong with you except your self-appraisal. Is it so hard to accept praise and success? You have a choice: you can wallow in your self-inflicted insecurities from here to eternity, or you can fly like an eagle with determination, logic, and positive courage. If you really want to be satisfied with yourself, then take hold of your emotional fears and phobias and toss them away; they are totally useless to you. Don't you think you have suffered enough already?

## DEODORIZER (i.e., a spray or device used to remove odors from a room, etc.)

You are a clever, persuasive person who often succeeds in getting what you want in life. However, to what degree of dishonesty are you willing to descend to achieve your goals in life? You may be clever, but you are also shortsighted! Just as a deodorizer attempts to mask some smell within a room, you are attempting to mask some wrongdoing within your heart, mind, and soul. Do not forget the mighty force of your conscience in any negative matter you happen to undertake! It would be much better to account for your actions upon this earth plane now rather than wait for future trouble. That decision is totally up to you.

**DEPARTMENT STORE** (see **STORE**)

**DEPENDABILITY** (see **RESPONSIBILITY**)

**DEPORTEE** (see **BANISHMENT**)

**DEPOSITORY** (see **SHED**)

**DEPRESSION** (i.e., being very sad or low in spirit, or a time or place with far-flung unemployment and depressed prosperity, etc.)
Along your many experienced stages of life, you must never ignore someone's plea for help, nor should you frown or scoff at anyone who may appear to be in a lower state than you. Life has its many twists and turns, so you never really know whether or not you will be in the same predicament yourself. Being compassionate and giving in life is a wholesome, spiritual attitude to always maintain. Realize that you are better off and more privileged than some people you hear about or know.

**DEPUTY**
This dream reveals that you are a person who cares about the future of your society, state, or country. It just takes one person out of so many thousands to stand up for what is just and fair. With your persistence, reasoning power, and honest-to-goodness logic, you are bound to create some positive changes around you. The world and its many laws may not change overnight, but it is people like you who can initiate better laws, views, or attitudes for this modern day and age or who have the innate ability to fight corruption.

**DERRICK** (i.e., a tall framework such as over an oil well)
There are occasions when you would sooner believe your own imaginative thoughts about someone than listen to someone's honest-to-goodness truth about themselves! Your imagination can play hosts of tricks on you, so be careful whom you judge or misjudge in life. You may find yourself very isolated and feel extremely foolish due to this type of behaviour. Trust beyond any shadow of a doubt people who love and care about you. Unless you have some concrete proof to back up your claims of mistrust and so on, then you would be advised to keep quiet and learn to trust yourself more. Very often, when people mistrust or foist their problems upon others, it is because they fail to

believe in themselves. They essentially feel that because they have some inner weakness, everyone else has the same weakness (i.e., infidelity, dishonesty, etc.). This belief is a fallacy and is not worth the anguish or depression it creates! There is so much good to do upon this planet that it simply boggles the mind why people create such mischief for themselves!

## DESERT

This dry, forlorn, barren place is like the doldrums and unhappiness of your daily existence. You are a secretive, inward type of individual who finds it very difficult to socialize, to travel, or to simply change your life style around. You are on the inside looking out, hoping—somewhere, somehow—life would begin to change for you. Well, this dream symbolism reveals that certain events and circumstances will yet allow you to move gently towards creative, social, and educational programs. No one on earth is ever too young or too old to improve their status in life. Your thirst for better things to happen will soon be quenched with a spirit of adventure, maturity, and respect.

## DESERTION (See ABANDONMENT)

## DESK

You are trying very hard to impress someone (e.g., employer, business associate, parent, teacher, friend), but you are being far too bold, rash, or anxious in this matter. Slow down, be natural; before you know it, your worthy and deserving efforts will be noticed and appreciated. All good things that are meant to happen will happen (e.g., promotion, friendship, love, affection, praise).

## DESPAIR (see HOPELESSNESS)

## DESSERT (see CAKE, CANDY, FOOD, or FRUIT)

## DESTINY (see FUTURE)

## DESTRUCTION

This dream encourages you to do something very special today. You could perhaps consider any of the following suggestions: be kind and thoughtful towards your family; help an elderly person across the street; visit an orphanage and, if possible, bring the children a treat;

visit a shut-in at an institution or hospital; be sociable and kind to your fellow employees and employer; be willing to help a young teenager who needs some form of guidance and direction; be helpful to your neighbours and friends; be willing to forgive your enemy; be mature and responsible for all your actions this day; be courageous and optimistic, no matter how difficult this day may be; be a friend to someone, and let someone be a friend to you, as well; break a bad habit, and see how you feel; put aside your greed, lust, or other temptations with a spirit of hope that you will honestly try to change; be at total peace with yourself and God; and, if you are sad this day, then sing or whistle a song for just being alive. These are a mere fraction of the small miracles that can take place today, if you allow them to happen. And, since miracles do happen, this could be one of the happiest days of your life!

## DETECTIVE

There are times when you handle your problems with strong, gutsy determination; but there are times when you simply become laid back and could not care less what happens. There is a certain amount of confusion, disappointment, and doubt within you at this time. It seems that you are searching or probing for some answer or truth which haunts you from time to time. First, get a clearer picture about yourself and about your wants and needs in life. These answers or truths you seek should be more from within yourself, rather than from outside the portals of your being. Your suspicions and mistrust can become an obsession with you. Be more reasonable with yourself, and be prepared to accept unusual circumstances, alibis, or excuses from others with more trust. Your many questions about certain matters is questionable itself!

## DETERGENT

You appear to be plagued by some people's unfair discrimination towards you. Whatever it is that these people seek from you, one thing is known for sure: they are displaying an unholy violation of human rights! Their ruthless, hounding persecution is nothing more than medieval madness! Overwhelmed by their own hate, jealousy, misunderstanding, ignorance, stupidity, and spiritual waste, these persecutors are on a one-way trip towards being judged themselves. Let the Heavenly Courts decide their fate! For your part in this unbearable activity, you are advised to pray, meditate, and—if possible—consider moving away from your immediate surroundings. Do not consider moving away from a bad situation a cowardly or weak act. On the contrary! This simply reveals that you care enough about your life to look elsewhere for peace and happiness. What a shame that a person like you has to fight for freedom and justice because a pitiful group of people choose to follow evil thoughts and actions instead of God's Thoughts and Actions!

## DETERMINATION

Being determined within a dream state reveals that you are determined within your wake state as well. No matter what detours you have to make, you finish what you start! You have a powerful outlook about your life, aims, ambitions, and so on; or, to put it in simpler terms, the oceans would have to dry out before you changed one iota in your convictions and determined outlook. Without a doubt, you have enough self-esteem and self-assertiveness to carry you through the gamut of life.

## DETOUR

You may be asked to take a pleasure trip with someone whom you know quite well. Think twice before you decide, for it is true that you may never really know someone until you go on a trip with them. Many friends have become lifelong enemies after their trip together. Say no if you have any qualms or doubts; say yes if your inner intuition and better judgment approve.

## DEVIL (see DEMON)

## DEVOTION (see PRAYER)

## DEW

Be it friend or foe, you do not wish to offend anyone. However, there is someone who appears to be taking advantage of your good company and hospitality. Some people simply fail to realize that their free time may not necessarily be your free time. They fail to realize that their constant intrusions and visits may be a bit interfering. This is not to imply that you do not like guests to visit; you enjoy company very much! But when someone continually pops in without any concern for your valuable time, then it could be time to draw the line. Do not bottle your feelings in this matter, but clear the air with kindness and

195        *dice*

logic. A false friend may inwardly disagree with you; a true friend will understand and respect your feelings.

## DIAMOND

You may be asked to be a peacemaker in a marital or family dispute. You will do your very best to patch things up; but you will be amazed at the childish behaviour some adults employ to win their side of a battle. This dispute can be settled, providing the people involved use foresight instead of hindsight! No one ever wins in an argument unless they are willing to be compromising and sensible.

## DIAPER

You may have to postpone your immediate plans because of some unforeseen domestic problem. Understanding, patience, and plain good common sense should be at the forefront of your mind at this time. These essential conditions will give you recognition for being devoted or for simply being there when you are needed most! You will come out of this domestic strife with admiration and respect.

(*Note*: A new parent often dreams about diapers. This reveals a physical tiredness, especially with the mother who appears to be doing all the household and diaper work, as well. This may leave her with a subconscious hatred or misunderstanding towards her husband [e.g., why doesn't he change the baby's diaper once in a while; why doesn't he take care of the baby more often]. So, these pent-up feelings could readily force a parent, especially the mother, to be sensibly demanding until the matter of parenthood becomes a more loving, sharing experience.)

## DIARY

There are a few emotional surprises and disappointments ahead for you. You will especially note that the intensity or character of these disappointments will require more logical thinking, rather than sentimental thinking. Let your mind rule this time, instead of your heart! Chin up, cheer up, smile; and you will make it!

## DICE

Dice within a dream implies that you may be breaking an oath or a promise. The outcome, of course, depends upon your conscience and attitude about yourself and about anyone else involved in this matter. The aftereffects of any wrongdoing can be devastating! Think twice before you decide to act in haste. However, if breaking this oath or promise means saving a person's life, your country, and so on, then do what you must do.

## DICTATOR

Being or seeing a dictator indicates your refusal to listen to reason where money matters are concerned (e.g., poor budgeting, spending too freely, bad investments, being too miserly, gambling). Whatever it is, you are advised to look at your situation with down-to-earth practicality before untimely losses come your way. You have a one-track mind! Do not forget that no matter how hard you wish to prove your point in theory to yourself and others, there may come a time when you will simply have to heed the advice of those who honestly care about you.

## DICTIONARY

This auspicious dream points to family harmony, spiritual betterment, and economic advancement. The absence of certain stresses and obstacles will certainly have a great effect upon you and your general outlook in life. You deserve this forthcoming happiness and much more!

## DIE (see DEATH)

## DIET (see FAST, FOOD, MALNUTRITION, or PREVENTION)

## DIFFICULTY (see PREDICAMENT)

## DIKE (see DAM)

## DINNER (see FOOD or MEAL)

## DINNERWARE (e.g., dishes, cups, saucers)

You appear to be materialistically minded. Those earthly treasures you possess and cherish are fine, providing you never lose sight of your true inner needs as well (i.e., love, affection, friendships). Happiness may, at times, be based on what you own or wear, but true and lasting happiness is based within the denizens of a person's soul! As in setting a table with fine dinnerware, you must also set your life's wants and needs in order. God should come first in your life, then you (even if you choose to be last on this list), your loved ones, your wants and needs, and, last but certainly not least, your love and help towards your fellow man. Remember that your soul should be more important to you than all the treasures in the world! Each person is on a one-to-one basis with God; even though you may care about your loved ones perhaps more than yourself, this does not change the fact that each person must account for their own soul. When you meet God, He will question you about yourself only. He does not want excuses or alibis from anyone! If a person knows better, they should act better! No ands, ifs, or buts will do! The good things you do on earth will certainly open doors for you in Heaven!

## DINOSAUR

Seeing this ancient lizard signifies that you need to curb your impatience. Your unreasonable demands and extreme short-comings can only bring you needless stresses and disappointments. The good news in this dream is that you can, and apparently will, balance your immature thoughts and actions with time and experience. You are bound to excel in life simply because your intelligence and courageous outlook would have it no other way!

## DIPLOMA (see DOCUMENT)

## DIPLOMAT (see MESSENGER or POLITICIAN)

## DIPPER (i.e., a long-handled cup for drinking water)

Sometimes you are in such a hurry to go someplace that you literally end up going nowhere. What's your rush? To be first in anything could mean that you could eventually be last in everything. Do not ignore the calm state of life around you, such as nature, sitting on a bench to think or read, gazing up at the stars, meditating on life and its wonders. Did you know that some people who drive a vehicle cannot tolerate having another vehicle in front of them? They simply must pass all cars, no matter what happens! But, sadly, things do happen in these cases. Slow down; enjoy your life.

## DIRECTORY (see TELEPHONE BOOK)

## DIRIGIBLE

This rare airship denotes that you have a great understanding and control over your destined purpose upon this earth state. These attributes are not mere transitory words but honest-to-goodness powerful and courageous blessings! You are a person with strong direction and conviction, as time will prophetically prove. Your words and deeds are bound to have a positive effect upon many people. Why not! You were always special and will continue to be so.

## DIRT (see *also* MUD)

There are times when you feel totally inadequate or believe that you are a nobody in the eyes of your loved ones due to some minor failings in your life. This low self-esteem you harbour is not justified. The only person who thinks less of you is you! Practice more self-control where your mind's nonsensical chatter is concerned. Then proceed to overcome your strained feelings of abandonment or self-pity with the responsibility and enthusiasm you always upheld. Your fighting spirit has never yet betrayed you; and it is not about to do so now. You will come out of this mind state with renewed hope and vigor!

## DISAGREEMENT (see QUARREL)

## DISAPPEARANCE

Seeing someone or something literally disappear in front of you suggests that you are withholding some fact or truth about yourself from a loved one. You must have a very sound reason for doing this, or else you are a very insecure, secretive person. The question here is, are you being unduly affected in keeping this secret, or would you feel better revealing it? If you are troubled about this matter, speak and then forever hold your peace. If you are not troubled, then carry on without a qualm.

## DISAPPOINTMENT

Being disappointed or disappointing someone within a dream intimates that some family members, friends, or people at work expect far too much from you. Now, in most cases they may be eternally grateful for the work that you do; but in some cases, you know that you are being used or taken for granted. You are very fast and efficient, whereas many people are not. Even though you may get tired of being asked to bale people out of certain workload situations, be proud of the fact that you are so special! Overlooking your disappointments with inner peace, self-reliance, and enthusiasm will always bring you the acknowledgement you desire.

**DISAPPROVAL** (see *also* **CRITICISM**)

You are finding it very difficult to express your feelings to someone who has some inner hang-up about themselves or about life in general (e.g., spouse, offspring, parent, friends). It appears that you do not wish to hurt anyone's feelings simply because you feel they should change. In most cases, people do not see themselves the way another person might see them; for example, displaying a bad habit during a meal or out in the open for that matter (i.e., nose picking, nail clipping, creating a scene, etc.). Do not be afraid to speak in confidence and truth to those whom you love and respect. An understanding person will always listen and be willing to more or less change, even though a difficult person will not be so receptive. You can only do your best, and hope for the best in these matters.

**DISASTER** (see *also* **MISFORTUNE**)

Economic, business, and domestic disturbances around you may discourage you from finishing a task or project, at least for a certain length of time. Keep your wits about you; adopt a greater sense of responsibility, self-control, and determination; and you will come out of this hostile state of affairs triumphantly. This experience should give you an inkling of your own mental strength and courage.

**DISBELIEVER** (see **AGNOSTIC** or **ATHEIST**)

**DISCIPLE** (i.e., a follower of any teacher, school, or religious learning, etc., or any one of the Apostles of Jesus)

Seeing or being a disciple within a dream intimates that you are a very brave, thoughtful, and inspiring individual. People are automatically attracted to you because of your knowledge, attitudes, words, and acts in life. Whatever your calling may be in life, you are certainly attuned to the creative forces around you and to the Light of Creation within you. Just knowing that people like you exist on this planet today gives hope for a brighter Cosmic Future tomorrow.

**DISCIPLINE** (see **PUNISHMENT**)

**DISC JOCKEY** (see **ANNOUNCER** or **RADIO**)

**DISCOLORATION** (see **STAIN**)

## DISCOURAGEMENT

To give discouragement or to receive discouragement in a dream intimates that you will suddenly become frightened or unsure about your marital or romantic status, or you will have great doubts about your career prospects. At times, you seem to be living in a nightmare of thought, not really knowing which way to turn or where to go for help. Much too often, you have immersed yourself in an earthly mode of life without even assuming that God's Love could give you the inner support and happiness you need. You can whine, pine, and look all over the world for true happiness and success, but you will not find this until you absorb the infinite trust, faith, and truth that your Creator wishes to bestow upon you. Pray for your peace of mind, and meditate for the world's well-being; you will then see your fears transformed into happiness and success. You are one of God's finest created miracles. Why would He deny you a miracle or two within your life?

**DISCRIMINATION** (see **GHETTO, HATRED, PERSECUTION,** or **PREJUDICE**)

**DISEASE** (see **SICKNESS**)

**DISFIGUREMENT** (see **DEFORMITY**)

**DISGUISE** (see **DECEPTION** or **MASK**)

**DISGUST** (see **CONTEMPT, HATRED,** or **NAUSEOUSNESS**)

**DISH** (see **DINNERWARE** or **POTTERY**)

## DISHCLOTH

Poor eating habits or simply being too busy to take the time to eat properly can create minor or major health problems. A good, healthy body generally harbours a good, healthy mind. Remember that you only have one physical body here on earth. You can either respect and nourish it, or you can ignore and destroy it. That choice is up to you!

**DISHONESTY** (see **CHEATING, DECEPTION, LIAR,** or **THIEVERY**)

**DISHWASHER** (see **APPLIANCE**)

**DISHWATER** (see **WATER**)

**DISMISSAL**

To dismiss someone from a job, room, building, and so on reveals that you are fed up with your life style, with someone else, or with some other matters of concern around you. These anxieties or irksome demands you seem to be receiving from others will dissipate before too long. In fact, you need not lose the battle or the war if you maintain a clearheaded, optimistic outlook in this entire situation. Bear in mind that everyone gets fed up once in a while, but after some serious introspection we commence to see the folly of our overanxious attitudes! Can you believe that patience is one of man's best virtues?

To personally be dismissed by someone from a job, room, building, and so on reveals that you feel neglected or rejected by someone, or you feel insecure and unqualified to achieve some special goal you have in mind. In order to solve a problem, you must go to the source of your problem. If someone has offended you in some way, then it is up to you to go that individual for some logical explanation. Their explanation, however truthful, may not be exactly to your liking, but you will have at least solved that problem. As well, if you feel insecure and unqualified to achieve some goal, then you always have a choice to either go for that goal in spite of your fears or to substitute that goal for another. You would be amazed at how many people feared what they wanted the most in life, yet when they accepted and faced the difficult challenge ahead of them, they ultimately prospered!

**DISOBEDIENCE**

Refusing to obey someone's demands or orders within a dream merely signifies that you have a good mind of your own and that you will not be pushed or cajoled into doing something you do not wish to do. You are a fighter for justice, truth, and loyalty, and anyone who does not adhere to your high standard of thought and action may be sorely disappointed. You have shocked and even offended more than one person because of your high expectations of them. Perhaps rightfully so! In any event, many people are impressed by your courage and determination. You would make an excellent politician!

**DISORDER** (see **CONFUSION**, **DISOBEDIENCE**, **DISSATISFACTION**, or **NEGLECTFULNESS**)

**DISPUTE** (see **CONTRADICTION** or **QUARREL**)

**DISQUALIFICATION**
Being disqualified from some act or event within your dream actually reveals your fear about being rejected or failing in some manner during your wake state. The sooner you dispel your doubts and uncertainties about yourself and your true capabilities, the better off you will be. Do not be afraid to accept a few pitfalls along your road in life. Strive to always do your very best, but be sensible when uncertainties, obstacles, or even failure comes your way. Life is like a baseball game sometimes. You have two teams; both teams would like to win; yet only one team is allowed to do so. A good loser, in many respects, can be a good winner next time; a good winner can also be a good loser next time. We do not always win in matters of the heart, mind, and soul either, but we do not always lose either.

**DISROBE** (see **CLOTHES**, **BURLESQUE**, or **NAKEDNESS**)

**DISSATISFACTION**
Any form of dissatisfaction within a dream symbolizes your basic ability or inability to cope with the strain or stresses that are presently within or around you. Being able to cope with your many trials and tribulations reveals that you are not one to whine or pine about useless thoughts, actions, and deeds. When something has to be done, you do it. Being unable to cope with your present strain and stresses suggests that self-sacrifice, love, praise, and humility are the strong elements that will lead you towards a truthful life and ultimate understanding of self. Do not lose your courage or hope when tempests come your way; battle on until you are appeased. Out of the mire of your dissatisfaction can come joy, happiness, and appeasement, providing you have the willpower to make things right.

**DISSECTION**
The dissection of a plant or animal portends sickness to the dreamer. The length of this sickness will depend upon your state of mind. If you are basically optimistic, calm, and happy, then rest

assured your illness will not last long. If you are doubtful, impatient, and depressive, your illness will hang on for a while.

## DISTANCE

Being at a distance from a person, place, or thing or being unable to reach a person, place, or thing because of distance implies that you have some conflicting and confusing thoughts about your family, friends, acquaintances, and life in general. No one is out to get you, and no one is working against you, except your own fabricated apprehensions and imagination. Now is the time for you to get a better grip on your mental, sexual, and spiritual thoughts and feelings. You have placed some distance between yourself and reality; this is not at all wholesome! Seek some outside help if you must (e.g., medical assistance, psychological help). If, however, you do master this problem alone, be aware that unrealistic views, now or later, can spell serious trouble.

## DITCH

Seeing, digging, or falling into a ditch signifies that you are going to extremes to make your existence supposedly more meaningful and purposeful. By forcing yourself to do something you do not necessarily like to do or by associating with people whom you do not necessarily enjoy being with is not exactly a wholesome way to live. Rushing, pushing, and forcing your way into business situations or people situations just for the sake of being someone or belonging will not bring you peace of mind. Why don't you take your time in these matters? Wait for better, more opportune moments for good friendships and success, instead of wasting your energies on false promises and hopes.

## DIVER (e.g., deep-sea diver, frogman, skin-diver, pearl diver, diving board, high-diving board) (see *also* PLUNGE, SWIMMING, or WATER)

Seeing or being a diver who is already immersed in calm, clear water or is about to plunge into this water reveals that you are a very well-informed, honest, forthright individual. You make no bones about who you are or what you intend to do in life. Whether it be through hell or high water, you believe in getting things done quickly and efficiently.

Seeing or being a diver who is already immersed in choppy, turbulent, unclear water or who is about to plunge into this water suggests that you are vexed about someone's feelings towards you, you are staying or living in a very uncomfortable place, or you are presently experiencing some financial setbacks. Your predicaments will eventually be surmounted, but not necessarily without some wear and tear on your mind and soul.

Seeing or being a diver on dry land or air (not water) reveals that you are breaking away from old haunts and habits in order to settle down and find your happiness or niche in life. This action on your part is not only timely, but wise as well! One day, you will reflect back upon your life with happiness, fulfillment, and no regrets.

**DIVING BOARD** (see **DIVER**, **SWIMMING**, or **WATER**)

**DIVINING ROD**
You appear to be receiving a certain amount of disrespect from a loved one or two or from some business associates. It appears you are being condemned for some past endeavour or scheme which did not turn out to anyone's satisfaction. Their attitude towards you may be hard to bear; but, in the interim, do your best to maintain your composure. In some respects you are a visionary—and visionaries, as you may already know, are not too easily understood on planet Earth. Someday, though, your fondest hopes and desires may be realized.

**DIVORCE**
You just may be one of the world's greatest procrastinators! This dream advises you to stop whining and feeling so sorry for yourself. The more you preoccupy yourself with things you love to do, the better off you will be. Did you know that your rainbow is right at your doorstep? If you strived harder to make your living more worthwhile and meaningful to yourself and to others around you, you might discover that the gift of life is not so bad after all. Remember what you put into your life is more or less what you will receive in return. This dream cautions you to try a little harder, mean what you say, and do what you say with meaningful dedication and self-sacrifice.

**DOCK** (see **PIER**)

**DOCTOR** (see *also* **DENTIST** or **OPTOMETRIST**)
Get a grip on your better judgment and true feelings, and begin to perceive your life in a more positive, realistic manner. Your many

fears are not only groundless, but naïve, to a certain point. Tell your mind to keep quiet when unwarranted fears, phobias, and visions upset you. Do some serious introspection in every matter of your life, and then begin to realize that to know yourself is to believe yourself, as well. Facing your obligations and responsibilities must be sanely and maturely fulfilled, otherwise you will continue to flounder with your worries and other senseless obstructions. Maybe this dream will open that door of understanding to you; maybe today you will commence to realize that your life can be enriched through foresight and effort— or it can be impoverished through hindsight and indifference.

**DOCTRINE** (i.e., a belief, rule, or theory in religion, politics)
Do not try to outsmart your opponents in life through false patronization or information. This can work for you some of the time, but not necessarily all of the time. This action can bring you future trouble! Deceptions are evils of the mind and heart; they have a way of bouncing right back to the perpetrator. Nothing is foolproof on earth, especially man-made laws and intrigue.

**DOCUMENT** (e.g., a deed, patent, license) (see *also*
**CERTIFICATE, CONTRACT,** or **DEGREE**)
This dream reveals that there is some mental, physical, or financial barrier standing between you and what you would like to do in life. For instance, you may have the courage and knowledge to want a higher education, but you lack the resources to make this possible; or you may want to be a commercial pilot, but your height and eyesight have held you back, and so forth. Whatever your barrier happens to be, remember that nothing is impossible to anyone who has enough willpower to see the probabilities or options open to them. If people want something bad enough, they will find a way to see their dreams fulfilled.

**DOG**
A dog is not only one of man's best friends during his wake state but can truly be considered an ally to man during his sleep state! This auspicious dream reveals that any difficulties you may be experiencing at this time will be handled or solved in an amicable manner. It appears that you have been at a complete standstill or crossroads where personal happiness, prosperity, or personal achievement is concerned. Busy times lie ahead for you, as well as certain events,

happenings, or introductions to make your life more meaningful and prosperous.

(*Note*: You may also have the pleasure of knowing that if, for example, you are experiencing a very negative dream but at the very end of your dream sequence or anywhere during your dream sequence you happen to see a dog, then this dog symbolism takes precedence over your entire bad dream. Consequently, you have nothing to worry about simply because the dog acts as a "buffer zone" to anything negative within a dream.)

## DOGFIGHT (see DOG or FIGHT)

## DOGHOUSE

Some personal difficulties will befall you unless you begin to compromise in some matters close to home (e.g., respect, love, loyalty, finances). You have already affected some people by your uncaring behaviour. This attitude cannot continue, otherwise you will be playing a one-string guitar all by yourself. Everyone has their limits, as you may soon discover.

## DOLL (see TOY)

## DOLLAR (see MONEY)

## DOLPHIN

Dreaming about a dolphin is a direct call for help. Someone you know, be it a family member or a close friend, will be asking for your assistance and guidance before too long. Your advice will be sound and to the point. In fact, you are a character builder! With your knowledge and experience, you are bound to share your goodness with many people as time goes on. This world is very fortunate to have you around!

## DOME

Seeing a dome by itself reveals giving something and receiving something in return (e.g., present, package, letter, card). There should be happiness and good fellowship in this mutual exchange. As well, a recent request or suggestion you made to someone will be gratified within a day or so.

## DONATION (see GIFT)

**DONKEY**

Seeing a donkey is actually a feather in your cap! You are basically a calm, cool, and collected individual who always strives to think twice before you rush into something you may later regret. Your maturity and stubbornness are both wholesome and wise! You are not a leader or a follower; you are a thinker. By virtue of your cordial and pleasing personality, you are a bit wiser. The donkey has a mind of its own; so do you!

**DOOMSDAY** (see **JUDGMENT DAY**)

**DOOR**

An open door reveals that an outpouring of favourable surprises are in store for you. You will be blessed with good luck and a lifetime of friends who will always stand by you in your hour of need. If you have any qualms whatsoever about traveling, advancing your education, buying or selling something, and so on, then you can be at total peace. The time is ripe to do those special things you always wanted to do! Your endeavours will be recognized, appreciated, and enriched because of your willingness to make things happen.

A closed door signifies that some immediate plan or wish may be a lot harder to achieve than you realize. Concentration, determination, and hard work are the key factors in fulfilling your aspirations in this regard. If you go on with your plan or wish, you should basically have no regrets. Should you decide to call it quits at this stage of the game, you may have nagging thoughts about it at a later date. The overall decision, however, must be yours alone to make.

A damaged door suggests that you can be very frustrated and insecure from time to time. When things do not go your way, it appears that you harbour all types of depressed, morbid thoughts; these merely add to the confusion you are already feeling. Your problem seems to be rooted in fears about being neglected or rejected by someone or about failing in some other vital matters of your life. Take stock of your mental, physical, sexual, and spiritual wants and needs in life. Begin to understand that not everything will go your way in life, no matter how insecure or frustrated you choose to be. There is really nothing wrong with you except your sensitive feelings about yourself and your supposed inability to cope with trying situations. In difficult times, use your mind instead of your heart, and you will be amazed at the results. You have utilized this method many times before, and it worked for you. Why stop now?

## DOORBELL

You seem to be undecided about a major decision in your life. Weigh this situation very carefully. If you know that the negative aspects of your decision are stronger than the positive aspects, then simply do nothing at this time. However, if the positive aspects of this decision far outweigh the negative, then you know you are making the right choice or move. If there is a fifty-fifty chance either way, you are advised to wait for a certain length of time until the odds are more in your favour. Or, you can take a chance and go for it; it is up to you.

## DOORKEEPER (see PORTER)

## DOORKNOB (see LATCH or LEVER)

## DOORMAT (see MAT)

## DORMITORY (see LODGING)

## DOUBLE-DECKER (see BUS)

## DOUBTFULNESS

This dream advises you to put your own house in order before you attempt to cast doubts and suspicions on people and other matters of truth. You seem to be having a difficult time believing things you see, hear, or read. In some cases you may be justified—but certainly not in all cases. Would you believe that some of the most far-fetched sounding stories you hear about can actually be true, yet some of the seemingly straight-laced stories could be fabricated? Anything is possible! Seeing or hearing is believing; yet, is it possible to believe what you cannot see or hear? That is the question! There are moments when we must learn to accept the things we cannot totally explain or understand. (e.g., ghosts, phantoms, time travel, flying saucers, prophecy). In retrospect, be more reasonable and flexible in your thinking instead of being a doubtful, tunnel-vision thinker.

## DOUGH (i.e., a mixture to make bread, pasta, and other foods)

Constructive changes within your home environment and lifestyle are foreseen for you. By uplifting your thoughts and actions with practical visions and plans, you are certainly headed in the right direction.

Now, stay with some of those better visions and plans until they are carried out. In building a better foundation for yourself, you must always be sensible, mature, and determined; and, surprisingly, all things thereafter will be mastered.

**DOWN'S SYNDROME** (see **MENTAL RETARDATION**)

**DRAFTEE** (i.e., a person drafted into the armed forces)
Going through the motions of being drafted expresses nervous panic or depression over someone's dictatorial behaviour towards you, and/or you are in anguish about being accused of something you did not do. Thoughts of leaving or moving away from your present surroundings are rampant within your mind. Hold on! In a very short period of time, the tension and stresses around you will ease up. Your good judgment and hope will eventually set you free.

Going through the motions of being a draft dodger implies that you are very worried about some embarrassing problem (e.g., legal, financial, marital, romantic, educational). Facing this problem head-on would be the most sensible route to follow. Do not, however, foist your responsibility upon someone else. You can master this state of affairs by being firm and completely honest with yourself.

**DRAFTSMAN** (i.e., a person who makes plans of buildings or machinery)
Some unusual circumstances at home or at work have beset you recently. Normally, you are very easy to get along with, but due to some unwarranted pressures, demands, or complaints from people around you, the burden of all these actions has left you bewildered and depressed. Just about everyone experiences those so-called "brick wall" days! No matter what you say or do, there is someone or something out there bound to spoil your good intentions or ruin your day. Be at peace. This disagreeable period will settle, and harmony and order will reign once more within and around you.

**DRAGON** (i.e., a mythical winged reptile that breathes out fire)
Seeing a dragon, often represented in Oriental festivals, intimates that you are harbouring some anger or hatred towards another person. To put it bluntly, you are becoming obsessed with the idea of actually seeking revenge. Do not go this route—under any circumstances! If you cannot compromise or settle this matter peacefully, then simply go

about your daily activities with good desires and constructive efforts. You have a good mind; use it wisely!

**DRAMA** (see **THEATRE**)

**DRAWBRIDGE** (see **BRIDGE**)

**DREAM**

Having a dream within a dream reveals that a respite or lull is in store for you. Regrettably, it appears that your workhorse attitudes, stresses, fears, and immediate wants and needs play havoc with your peace of mind. Hence, you have forgotten how to rest properly, think clearly, and act calmly. In essence, you are presently defeating your own purpose! Modify your work habits, slow down, and begin to get a grip on yourself; you are not a robot or machine. For your own good, do not forsake those leisure moments your mind and body require.

**DRESS** (see **CLOTHES**)

**DRESSER** (i.e., a mirrored chest of drawers)

Although you are very perceptive about people, places, and things, you do tend to argue or debate these thoughts or feelings with yourself. Psychic awareness is wholesome and good, providing the knowledge given is utilized in a positive manner. Many people ignore or fear their awareness or premonitions simply because they do not know how to handle or master what they see or hear. First of all, a good psychic never gets carried away in these matters but realizes that simple common sense is the ruling factor in dealing with the unknown. The gifts of the soul can be infinite, and the knowledge, wisdom, or warnings that do come through from time to time should be used courageously, truthfully, and compassionately.

**DRESSMAKER**

You are often misquoted or misrepresented in the things you say or do. You cannot understand why people are so demeaning and hurtful, especially when your intentions have always been of good order. There is very little you can do to change the attitude or actions of jealous or ignorant people who simply refuse to mind their own business. The advice this dream gives you is to always be your good self and to simply ignore those beings who fail to understand your good mind and spirit. Besides, you are far better off than they will ever be; your conscience is clear and peaceful.

**DRILL** (see **TOOL**)

**DRINK** (see *also* **BEER, DRUNKENNESS, FOUNTAIN, LIQUOR,** or **WATER**)

Drinking water or something pleasant within a dream could very well imply that you are actually thirsty. Whether you wake up to satisfy your craving or not is up to you.

Drinking something rancid, on the other hand, signifies that bad habits are hard to eradicate, but good habits are even harder to adopt. It seems that you have some bad habit you are not willing to give up. No one can force you to change. Hopefully, when you are ready, willing, and able to let go of this habit, you will commence to realize the folly of having been so complacent and stubborn.

**DRINKING FOUNTAIN** (see **FOUNTAIN**)

**DRIVEWAY** (see **PASSAGEWAY**)

**DROPOUT** (i.e., a student who leaves school before graduating)

Your boredom and impatience with self, others, career, and so on could be because you are not given the encouragement or recognition that you feel you rightfully deserve or because you find it more expedient to complain about your life style than cope with it. You should adopt a more firm, self-helping, self-assured attitude about yourself. Doing so would give you the opportunity to see life in a more patient, sensible manner instead of in a taking, selfish manner.

**DROUGHT** (see **MISFORTUNE**)

**DROWNING**

To see yourself drown intimates that you will be busy and prosperous in life. In the midst of your many successes, your status, rank, or life style will be enhanced by good luck in a variety of ways.

Seeing someone else drown suggests that a loved one or someone very near and dear to you must exercise extreme caution for the next several weeks or so. This warning sign is pertaining to a person whose job may be hazardous or who has a habit of driving recklessly. A strong word from you to this person could, perhaps, save much future trouble and anguish.

## DRUG ADDICT

Seeing yourself or someone else in this degraded state signifies that you are a very lonely, misunderstood individual. Very often you are confronted by individuals who go out of their way to make you feel uneasy and unwanted. The humiliations inflicted upon you are about the lowest measures of behaviour anyone could tolerate! It just seems like a dark cloud has attached itself to you, and that is that! This, of course, is not so. Avoid these negative people, if you can; they are more troubled than you will ever be. Think positive in all that you do, and you will overcome your anxieties and anguish in this entire matter. Just be grateful and happy to be who you are. Don't look back at the sorrows in your life—look forward to a rich, enduring future.

(*Note*: If you are, in fact, a drug addict and dream of being one, then your dream is a reflection of you and your bad habit. You will "lose" more than you will "gain" by pursuing this course in life. Unless you bring God and some stability back into your life, there can be nothing ahead but sadness, shame, and trouble.)

## DRUGGIST

You are a highly intelligent individual who takes a very realistic approach to life. In most areas of your life, everything seems all right except, on occasion, in matters of the heart (e.g., marital or romantic bliss, wanting to love in a sensitive, caring way). It is very difficult for you to express your feelings with great emotion or overt affection. This inability to express your feelings through love and warm embraces probably stems from childhood days. Maybe you were subjected to having your hands slapped by a parent who didn't want you to touch something or who wanted to teach you a lesson; maybe you did not get along with a parent; or maybe you simply felt unloved. Whatever your reasons may be, this dream symbolism urges you to not be afraid of holding, touching, or embracing your loved ones, at any time. If your fears or phobias in this matter are greater than your willingness to change, then you are strongly urged to seek some professional counseling.

**DRUM**

Some recognition or award of honour will be bestowed upon you in time to come (e.g., personal achievement, good work performance). You have made great progress in your life thus far, and you have also proved to yourself that, no matter how disappointed or depressed you were at times, your struggles were all worthwhile. Indeed, you stand tall and dignified among your fellow men and deserve that recognition which yet awaits you.

**DRUNKENNESS**

One or two of the following definitions may be applicable: A) that you are an alcoholic but do not wish to admit this fact to yourself or to others around you; or B) that you know of someone who has a tendency to drink too much on occasion, but you do not feel that this person is an alcoholic; or C) that you are an abstainer where alcoholic beverages are concerned and wish that others around you would follow your example; or D) that you cannot tolerate anyone who acts poorly or immaturely when they do consume alcohol; or E) that you enjoy having a sociable drink from time to time but have no intentions of getting drunk, now or in the future; or F) that you know alcoholics are "running away" from some truth about themselves and that unless they give up this habit entirely, they will waste their lives on self-pity and self-hate; or G) that alcoholics must seek God's help and professional counseling otherwise they rarely, if ever, can help or better themselves; or H) that this dream has little or no relevance for you at this time.

**DUCK** (see **BIRD** or **POULTRY**)

**DUGOUT** (i.e., a crude dwelling or shelter dug in the ground or on a hillside)

At times you display a pompous attitude; this is not a good thing to do. Strive harder to be your natural self, instead of going out of your way to impress others. Those who know you like you the way you are and—surprisingly—are impressed with you already. You are a very fine person with many good attributes. Be humble, and you will prosper in life.

**DUMP** (i.e., a place for depositing rubbish) (see *also* **GARBAGE** or **JUNK**)

You have recently been in the dumps, so to speak. Your depressive anxieties will clear up soon; but, in the interim, stop blaming yourself so heartlessly for things you could have or should have done. Accept your present situation for what it is now. Today you may be sad or mad with yourself; tomorrow you may be the happiest person around. Remember that those golden opportunities you supposedly fail to see in life now can quite easily become a reality another time.

**DUNG** (i.e., manure or animal excrement)

Try not to be too critical in things you see or do. You may be striving much too hard to see things your way only and fail to realize that not everything in life can be as perfect as you might want it to be. Instead of complaining or belittling what you see or do, learn to be more praising. You are not perfect, nor is anyone or anything else, for that matter. When you are casting stones at anyone or anything in life, you are in effect casting stones at yourself, as well.

**DUNGEON** (see **PRISON**)

**DUPLICATOR** (see **PHOTOCOPY**)

**DUSK** (see **SUNSET**)

**DUSTER** (see **BRUSH** or **RAG**)

**DUSTPAN**

You will meet and greet someone from a distance before too long. This meeting of the ways will be a happy, surprise-filled event and could involve some regional travel. This dream also reveals that a contract you signed or a promise you made recently will need your attention before too long.

**DUTY** (see **RESPONSIBILITY**)

**DYE** (i.e., a colouring agent used to colour hair, clothes)

You are not only a good thinker, but you are a good worker, as well. Your dynamic personality is something to behold! People can only deduce that you are special when they meet or work with you. The love, happiness, and kindness you so often radiate towards people is a mere reflection of your wisdom and "old" soul. You are indeed born under a lucky star, for your future will be filled with successes you never deemed possible.

## DYNAMITE

Much too often you give up in hopeless agony because of your inhibitions and foolish fears. Your problems are not as serious as you make them out to be. Building mountains out of molehills or being melodramatic over mundane matters are unworthy measures, on your part. You can be an inspiration to self and others if you really want to be, but first you must believe in yourself and in your abilities. In spite of some of your weaknesses, you are still a very good person. You can become a greater person within yourself when you commence to understand and acknowledge your worth upon this planet. Do not hold back your good wishes or intentions; rather, fulfill your good wishes and intentions with a new-found and gutsy determination. You came to earth to learn, to share, and to achieve good things; don't stop now!

## EAGLE (see BIRD)

## EAR

When you are bored and lonely, you fail to heed some good advice from caring people around you. The trouble here is that you expect to be pampered, served, or catered to whenever something goes wrong in your life. Those around you will listen and sympathize with you, but they also recognize the fact that you are not helping yourself in these matters. Keep yourself pleasantly busy in times of boredom and loneliness, and you will discover further unselfish ways to conquer your basic insecurities.

## EARACHE

Someone close to you is not treating you right! What remote chance do you have of bettering your life? First, stop being a defeatist. Forget those good old days, for you cannot bring them back. Second, get a firm grip on your present status. If what you are going through is love, then what is your definition of hate?! Third, do not linger in situations that could become more serious and intense as time goes on. Seek professional help (e.g., clergy, marriage counseling) if you must, but do something to change the present upheaval you seem to be experiencing . Life is far too short for you to endure such pain within your soul. And, if you must, move on to better things.

## EARPHONE

This dream urges you to stand firm on a positive decision or contemplated move. Do not let anyone change your mind! The direction you are about to take will finally bring you the peace and prosperity you have always visualized. Do not look back; just peacefully do what you have to do.

## EARRING

Very often your eagerness, confusion, depression, and flightiness leave you in a state of euphoria. Your priorities in life are a bit off base. Find some isolated place for relaxation, and commence to seriously find and know yourself better. Somewhere in the denizens of your troubled mind and heart there lingers a very sensible person who simply yearns to come out. That sensible person is you! Take a long, hard look at yourself. Know your wants and needs, and know that you can bring peace of mind and understanding into your life if you sincerely make an effort to do so. Face all your realities with unquestionable truths, for these truths will lead you to greener pastures, still waters, and peace. It is these things your mind and soul need.

## EARTH

Viewing Earth as though you were seeing it from outer space or inner space reveals that profound and significant events during the past several months have unfolded many truths about your purpose in life. You are very special! Being gifted or talented in your own right should eventually give you the recognition you rightfully deserve. Isn't it amazing what you can learn by just being "alone" for a while?

Seeing a globe or a model of Earth reveals that you are naturally curious about planets, stars, outer space, and time itself. It seems that you would enjoy the privilege of traveling in time and space. Who knows? Maybe you will! But if this is not possible in your lifetime, you can be sure that man will eventually travel from planet to planet as fast as the twinkling of an eye. He will explore and colonize other planets as the "gods" of old before him. Man will eventually find his great plan and purpose within the Cosmic Heavens; for he, too, will become as the "gods" of old.

## EARTHENWARE

Dreaming of earthenware implies that you are attempting to monopolize someone's way of life. Recognize that you are treading dangerous territory. Your attempts will eventually fail! Everyone has a right to learn and progress in their own way. No one, not even God Himself, has given you the authority to take over in the manner you seem to be employing. If you truly want to be needed and respected by someone, then treat that person with kindness and understanding. Teach others the good things you know, but listen to what others can teach you, as well.

## EARTHQUAKE

Your sarcasm and pompous attitude can bring you future anguish, if you are not careful. The two enemies you seem to be harbouring are pride and self-centeredness. This is likened unto walking on a tightrope without a net. Tread gently or you will be profoundly affected! The three qualities you should adopt in your life are "humility" for kindness and gentleness; "honesty" for truth and valor; and "patience" for self-control and inner quietude.

(*Note*: A repetitive dream about an earthquake could, in fact, be prophetic. In other words, having this dream nonstop for a week or two could indicate that an earthquake or something just as devastating could happen where you live or could happen in some other familiar location. A prayer for guidance and protection would certainly help at this time.)

## EARTHWORM (see WORM)

## EASTER (see *also* PASSION PLAY)

Dreaming about this Christian celebration reveals that you are about to embark upon a greater concept of knowledge within your life. In other words, the "new birth" within your mind and soul will compel you to improve your thoughts and actions through higher education, reading books on philosophy or wisdom, or traveling abroad to expand your spiritual and earthly awareness. You are destined for many fine, unique experiences within your lifetime. Like the joy of a mystical song that could be heard by those who truly want to hear, so your life will be awakened with unseen force and vitality!

## EASTER EGG

You can be very insistent and overprotective towards those whom you love. At times, these qualities are both wholesome and beneficial.

There are times, however, when you become stubbornly naive or foolish in your thinking. When situations appear perfectly safe and sound where your loved ones' requests are concerned, you still refuse to let them explore or learn matters on their own. Sometimes you harbour great remorse for your refusals; at other times you feel that you are totally justified. This, too, is a learning process. Realize that no matter who your loved ones may be, whether young or old, they will eventually seek their independence with a long breath of fresh air. They will like this independence, and they will want more—perhaps more than you can bear later on? For your own sake, handle present situations wisely now.

## EATING (see FOOD)

## EAVESDROPPER

You are presently experiencing some personality or sexual frustrations. Some self-hatred could be at play here, so be vitally careful not to accept your frustrations as the gospel truth. Educate yourself with wholesome books and literature about your problem(s); perhaps then you will realize that you are not as out of control or confused as you thought you were. If necessary, seek some professional guidance to completely alleviate your mind in this matter.

## ECCENTRIC (i.e., a person who does not conform to customary standards, habits, etc.)

Perhaps you are an eccentric who has simply dreamt about your state of affairs. However, if this is not the case, then this dream symbolism infers that some of your motives, actions, and wants in life are sensibly oriented, whereas some of them are so far advanced or seemingly stranger than fiction that they would be impossible to fulfill in this lifetime! You are ahead of your time; you belong to the future. The things you know, comprehend, or feel seem to be vital, practical areas awaiting mankind in the future. It falls squarely on the mind of a genius or visionary like you to try to create the changes yet to come. Who knows? Maybe you will go down in history as another Leonardo da Vinci.

(*Note*: There are many occasions when a person may act eccentric for a moment or two within a dream. These moments of eccentricity would infer that you are farsighted, but not necessarily to the degree of becoming renowned. The above-mentioned entry primarily refers to a person who actually has full or complete dreams about being eccentric. This, by the way, is rare simply because most people strive very hard within their dream state to create some logic or common sense in what they see, hear, or do.)

## ECHO
Hearing an echo strongly urges you to complete some unfinished business or other matters of concern. Further delays could cost you valuable time, money, or more frustration!

## ECLIPSE
Seeing a solar or lunar eclipse alludes to some unusual annoyances or hardships at home or at work. These annoyances or hardships seem to be human-related problems such as greed, jealousy, spite, money matters, and so on. This matter may last for about a month or so. Be patient and understanding during this uncertain time, and you will see much better days ahead.

## ECONOMY
Difficult times are in store for you and your country if you see the economic situation as being exceedingly prosperous. Hardship, famine, and strife are but a few of the warnings foreseen. On the other hand, better times are in store for you and your country if you see economic situations as being very poor and wanting. Prosperity, better weather conditions, more employment, and so on will be at an all-time high. At this point in time, the world will show greater harmony, good diplomatic relationships, and an eager desire for peace.

## ECSTASY (see HAPPINESS)

## ECTOPLASM (i.e., a luminous substance that is occasionally brought forth by a medium in a trance state)
Slowly you are coming towards a plateau in your life whereby you are beginning to perceive and comprehend your soul's obligations. This new dawning will come through your insight in knowing or feeling God's true Love for you; in believing and loving all life that is and all life yet to come; and in serving others less fortunate than you. Your spiritual reawakening will inspire others, and you will fearlessly continue to soar to immeasurable heights in human love. You are special and, in many degrees, saintly.

## ECZEMA

Dreaming of seeing or having this uncomfortable disease merely personifies your hate for this type of disorder or your fears about contacting other forms of communicable diseases. This dream does not in any way imply that you will be infected with any type of disease. However, on this planet anything is possible. We must all truthfully face those possibilities simply because they are realities. This dream indicates that you do look after yourself very well; no more and no less can be expected of anyone. Remember that a healthy mind and a healthy body should create a healthy outlook, too.

## EDELWEISS (see FLOWER)

## EDGE (see CLIFF)

## EDITOR

Seeing yourself or someone else as an editor of a newspaper, magazine, or publishing company implies that your decisive manner and intellectual stimulus will allow you to achieve your innermost desires in life. Your high-spirited, serious nature is a true asset which will give you the recognition, fame, and understanding you seek. You are constantly looking for better change and quality, both within and around you. This planet is truly enriched by your presence, teachings, and awareness. Your soul, without a doubt, is like a light or cresset, guiding others towards an understanding about themselves and about life in general.

## EDUCATION (see FACULTY, LEARNING, PRINCIPAL, SCHOOL, or TEACHER)

## EEL (see FISH)

## EFFIGY

To see, burn, or hang an effigy reveals that several people are opposed to you in a tasteless, vulgar way. This serious problem can only lead to personal stress or fear if something is not done to clear the air. You seem to hold the vital key in bringing about peace. You are the "cause" and they are the "affected" people in this entire matter. Any illogical arguments or actions on your part could be your untimely downfall! The outcry of people should not go unheeded. If there is something you said or did that makes others very unhappy or troubled, then gather around the conference table and compromise until the matter is solved. Nothing is impossible!

**EGG** (see *also* **EASTER EGG**)

Never flinch from the highest thoughts of your mind, nor be too discouraged by the thoughts or actions of others, especially your loved ones. Accept each challenge with a touch of learning here and a touch of wisdom there. Believe in yourself, but do not forget to believe in others, as well. Their life and thoughts could be more wholesome than your own. Listen to the truth of your heart and mind when you want inner peace. And when you want truth in your life, bow low to that inner peace so that God may enter your inner Kingdom.

Seeing broken, rotten, or misshaped eggs suggests that some of your selfish attitudes and habits have created untimely difficulties for you. Why? Simply because you have failed to see yourself the way you should. There are literally hundreds of ways to deceive yourself and others if you want to; but this, in effect, can only create havoc within yourself. This dream counsels you not to be afraid to admit that you are wrong, confused, or misguided once in a while. Not everyone has your best interests at heart, so be aware of those beings (bad company) who may encourage you to do something you may later regret. As well, never feel that good, sound advice is useless. It is people who have suffered and struggled in life who can, indeed, give the best practical advice. Respect your life, and respect those around you, at all times.

**EGGBEATER**

This kitchen device suggests that you have two decisions to make. One is quite wholesome and positive and very much to your liking; the other is somewhat challenging and leaves you a bit perplexed and jittery. Either situation can turn out favourably for you. However, be sure that you let your mind rather than your emotions guide you at this time.

**EJACULATE** (see **INTERCOURSE, MASTURBATION,** or **SEX**)

**ELBOW** (i.e., a part of the body between the upper and lower arm)

Much too often you skirt around a problem rather than face it headstrong. In many respects, you do not practice what you preach. You have the intelligence to advise and guide others towards a better change within their lives, yet you have failed to listen to your own good advice. This dream counsels you to face your problems head-on and with honesty. Know yourself better, and commence to ask yourself what you intend to do with your life. Do not just sit back and hope for things to happen. Nothing will happen unless you stop running away from yourself and from the truths around you.

## ELECTION (see CAMPAIGN, CANVASSER, NOMINATION, OPTION, or VOTE)

## ELECTRIC CHAIR

You have an enemy! Your enemy is very easily swayed and often rushes through some task with inaccuracies or sloppiness. This person has very little patience and somehow does not seem to learn too much from past mistakes. This person is also disorganized, seems to have little respect for elderly people, and tends to harbour some prejudices towards certain nationalities. At times this individual feels that life is totally meaningless and senseless. Your enemy can also be bitter and unhappy and certainly lacks good fortune and peace. In addition to all this, this person tends to blame others and God whenever things go sour. Is this all true? Could this be you?

## ELECTRICIAN

You have recently been lacking interest in what you say or do. You are emotionally confused and discouraged about some change or event created by one or two people. This heartbreaking situation may necessitate a change of residence for you; it may compel you to move far away or change your job; or it could force you to stick it out and see what happens next. You are at an impasse in this entire matter! Be at peace; for, very soon, this mind-boggling situation will settle. However, even after it does, you will continue to hold great reservations and regrets about some people's honesty and integrity.

## ELEMENTARY SCHOOL (see SCHOOL)

## ELEPHANT (see *also* MAMMOTH)

There are so many things you would like to achieve on this earth plane that it becomes difficult at times to focus on the routine chores of your life. There is something very special in the back of your mind that you would like to accomplish, but you often wonder whether this plan or project is a mere pipe dream or a figment of your wild imagination. With your intelligence, enterprising efforts, and inner stability you are destined to do great things! Some people have fulfilled their wildest fantasies simply because they believed in themselves and in their purpose or God-given mission. They may have been assisted in many ways (e.g., financially, emotionally, or spiritually), but they did get the job done. So can you!

**ELEVATOR** (i.e., a caged car that raises and lowers people or things, or a grain elevator)

Going up in an elevator suggests that you will be given some moral support from an outside source. It appears that you have been experiencing some difficulties for quite some time now; if ever you needed a word of encouragement or at least a word of hope, it couldn't be more timely! Here it is! The outlook ahead for you is both wholesome and promising. You will master your problems realistically and successfully.

Going down in an elevator cautions you to watch how you spend your hard-earned money. In fact, if you are about to invest in some business transactions, you would be wise to analyze all aspects of this arrangement before you sign on the dotted line. Some financial losses are foreseen ahead for you unless you think twice in matters pertaining to money (e.g., investments, selling something).

Seeing a grain elevator suggests that you are not handling some matter of importance in a logical manner. In other words, you are foisting a matter of importance on to someone else so that if anything goes wrong, you will not be the one to take the blame. This act may be shrewd thinking on your part, and perhaps you can get away with these things from time to time, but not every time! Face all your responsibilities wisely and honestly. Do not expect immediate rewards for being just and fair. It is far better to live peacefully in knowing you have done some good than to be guilt-ridden and shameful, knowing you have done wrong.

**ELF** (i.e., a small, mischievous fairy)

Your keen awareness about worldly affairs is not enough to enlighten you; nor can you hide behind a panacea of elaborately written philosophies that assume to hold all knowledge of life. The true knowledge of your life is within you. You can look hither and yon for the rhymes, reasons, questions, or answers about this life only to discover that what you have been looking for was in you already. The things you feel, say, or do in your daily activities are generally progressive attempts to better yourself, to expect another tomorrow, and to generally try to improve life around you. Some things you learn upon this planet are wholesome, some wise, and some sheer nonsense. When you have an experience of some type, you know beyond any shadow of a doubt that your experience was real and genuine. You walked that road—that mile—and no one can tell you otherwise. It is this inner, experienced philosophy that really matters for your soul's progression upon this earth plane. No one else's adventure in life can be yours; you must experience life and truth for yourself.

## ELIXIR (see ALCHEMY or MEDICATION)

## ELOPEMENT

This dream advises you to be more direct and sincere with the people you know. Sometimes, you want to please a person so you simply agree with their not-so-wise plan or decision. You do not wish to hurt anyone's feelings, especially when they have set their mind on something. If you honestly feel that something is amiss with someone's plan or decision, do not fail to say what you feel. You may not necessarily stop them from doing what they want to do, but you certainly would be giving them some food for thought. Who knows? Maybe your good advice could, the odd time, save someone a lot of trouble.

## EMBALMMENT (see *also* BURIAL or FUNERAL HOME)

You can be overly pessimistic about yourself and about life in general. Do you really know how lucky you are just to be alive and well? The many things you take for granted are the same things many less fortunate people pray to have and to cherish, such as good health, intelligence, and opportunities. Be very grateful that your life has already given you hope, happiness, pleasure, pain, and friendships. There is still so much more to experience and learn, but you must be clearheaded and brave as your future progresses. Carry on without bitterness or complaints and, in your darkest moments of despair, seek the teachings of old prophets and wise men, for it is there that your mind will find its sanctuary and peace.

## EMBANKMENT (see DAM)

## EMBARRASSMENT (see CONFUSION)

**EMBASSY** (see **MESSENGER** or **POLITICIAN**)

**EMBEZZLEMENT** (See **THIEVERY**)

**EMBLEM** (see **BADGE, COAT OF ARMS**, or **SYMBOL**)

**EMBROIDERY**
Essentially, you are a very fine person; however, you have a habit of being blunt and hurtful to some people from time to time. This habit of embarrassing others should be curbed. If you place yourself in their position, you would be as offended as they. Be more polite, and things around you will turn out rather nicely.

**EMERALD** (see **JEWELLERY**)

**EMIGRATION** (see **MIGRATION**)

**EMPLOYEE**
If you are an employee and dream of being or seeing one, then your dream is a mere reflection of your state of being, your ability or inability to get along with others at work, and the happy or sad atmosphere of your place of employment. On the other hand, assuming you are not an employee but still dream about being or seeing one, then this symbolism suggests that you would like to take a course, travel, or do something more constructive with your life. Perhaps all these things, and more, are available to you. You must not merely hope for these possibilities; you must actually allow your good wishes to become realities. How? Do some inquiring, get your facts and figures straight, and then commence to see whether or not your wishes are feasible at this time. If not, wait for another time. A negative answer today could become a positive answer a month or two down the road. Do not give up; be patient.

**EMPLOYER**
You often maintain a low profile; but, deep within you, a host of sound character qualities gives you the strength to carry you through difficult periods of your life. You accept life for what it is without too much worry or fear. Out of this combined positive living you can honestly state that your love for life is the greatest factor that restores your faith in yourself. No more and no less could be asked of anyone.

**EMPLOYMENT** (see *also* **EMPLOYEE** or **EMPLOYER**)

Dreaming about one's place of employment has two basic connotations: you either like your profession, or you do not like your profession. If you happen to appreciate the work that you do, then more power to you! There is nothing more satisfying than to see someone happy and progressive in their line of employment. If, however, you do not like your line of work, then you would be wise to do some serious soul-searching, where this matter is concerned. Perhaps considering the possibilities of working elsewhere or simply doing something else could be a solution to your problem. As well, never assume that you are over the hill or not qualified to look elsewhere. The only element that can hinder or stop you from really finding some happiness on the job is you.

**EMPORIUM** (see **MARKETPLACE**)

**EMPTY-HANDED**

Seeing yourself or someone else in this state signifies that some form of humiliation or put-down is in store for you. This is not to imply that you necessarily deserve this treatment. However, events and circumstances, being what they are, will unfortunately place you in this awkward position. Be strong, deflect these base matters when they occur, and you will be on top of the whole situation.

**ENCAMPMENT** (see **CAMP**)

**ENCHAINMENT** (i.e., condition of being chained)

You are overwrought with work and other anxieties that literally bend your mind, body, and spirit with frustration and hate. In some manner, you could almost say that you were in shackles and that it is very difficult for you to come out of this bitter state. The good news here is that you can come out of this self-inflicted bondage providing you dispel your self-pity and animosities right out of your system. You are mentally shouting for help, but no one seems to hear you simply because you refuse to say what you feel. Your loved ones do care about you, even though you think that they are indifferent to your needs or wants. The root of your inner trouble is your sensitive nature. Perhaps this cannot be helped. However, it would not hurt to speak your mind from time to time in order to clear the air. You will feel much better for doing this. Try it and see for yourself.

## ENCHANTRESS (see **WITCHCRAFT**)

## ENCLOSURE (e.g., fence, wall)

Seeing a fence or some other type of barrier used to enclose and protect property suggests you have great reservations about a neighbour or about another person whom you know. Whatever your reasons may be, there appears to be some justification for your thinking. You are a very private, analytical type of individual who would not harbour suspicions or any type of animosity without some good, sound reasons. In fact, you could be considered a very lucid thinker. Hopefully, this matter will be solved, and you will be at peace once more.

Seeing a wall or some other type of barrier which seems to hinder you within a dream suggests that someone or something is obstructing your road to betterment. You appear to be confined to a certain area of work without any possibilities of advancement, promotion, self-improvement through educational courses, and so on. The first thing you can do here is to adopt a more serene, patient attitude about yourself and others around you. For quite some time now, you have been rather edgy and impatient, tending to complain too much. These attitudes cannot help you one bit. Second, stop harbouring all the wrongs or injustices that have supposedly been done to you. Disband your pessimistic views about your past and think about your present and future with an optimistic outlook. Third, show more initiative, and be willing to compromise in certain situations around you. If, for example, there is no promotion available to you at this time, who is to say that next time might not be your turn? Every good thing that could happen to you has its time and day. And, last, say a prayer or two asking God to uplift your life. Ask Him to open those locked doors to your wants and needs. Then, carry on humbly, and await your results.

## ENCOURAGEMENT

If you encourage someone to do good within your dream, then you will have to wait for something you want or wish to do. In all likelihood, you will have your better wishes fulfilled. On the other hand, to encourage someone to do something bad or evil forewarns of marital, romantic, emotional, physical, or financial difficulties. Be strong, be absolutely fair and just in your thinking, and you will survive this pending ordeal with greater ease.

## ENDORSEMENT (see **ADVERTISEMENT**)

## ENEMA

This dream has three meanings: you may require this medical treatment before too long; you may have already had this treatment during the last little while; or you are afraid of having an enema or simply loathe the idea of having one. That is all.

## ENEMY

Any of the following definitions may be applicable: A) that you are an enemy to someone; or B) that someone is an enemy to you; or C) that you do not wish to be an enemy to anyone, nor do you wish anyone to be an enemy to you; or D) that you are a peacemaker at heart who has, on occasion, brought peace between enemies; or E) that your enemy could very well be your own government, country, state, city, town, or village; or F) that your enemy could be the government and people of another country; or G) that your enemy is someone in authority over you who has a tendency to belittle your good intentions; or H) that your enemy is a fear or phobia, perhaps created or inflicted upon you during your childhood years; or I) that your enemy could be anyone who has wronged you, either willingly or unwillingly; or J) that your enemy is basically yourself, but you do not wish to face up to this fact of life; or K) that you are a very mature individual who has enough sense to stay away from an enemy but also have enough compassion to pray for their spiritual uplifting; or L) that this dream has no significance to you at this time.

## ENGAGEMENT

If an unmarried woman dreams about getting engaged, then she can look forward to many years of happiness, peace, and fulfillment. Her husband yet-to-be should treat her lovingly and fairly; her children should bring her honour.

If an unmarried man dreams about getting engaged, then he can look forward to a life filled with good expectations, love, and success. He must, however, accept his responsibilities in a mature, sensible manner at all times.

Should a married man or woman dream about getting engaged to a friend or stranger, then it can be deduced that there are some emotional, sexual, physical, or spiritual impediments or hang-ups in their marriage. Resolving this matter should be of prime importance to them, otherwise they could drift away from each other as time goes on.

Should a divorced man or woman dream about getting engaged to a friend or stranger, then it can be deduced that they are presently engaged, that they want to be engaged, that they are looking for some companionship or are displeased with the person they are presently seeing, or last, that they have no intention of ever settling down or getting married again.

If you happen to be a celibate and dream about being engaged to a friend or stranger, then this dream is merely a reflection of your innate curiosity about being engaged, getting married, or having children. This is not implying that you will go this route; you are merely wondering what it would be like if you happened to have chosen another direction in your life (e.g., marriage).

**ENGINE** (see **MACHINERY**)

**ENGINEER**
You are fast, efficient, and enjoy your chosen profession or line of work. The efforts of your own labour will bring you the success and happiness you rightfully deserve. It seems that you will choose to go "first class" in what you do or accomplish in life; nothing less will do. You can look forward to an ample amount of good luck, travel, and wise investments as your future progresses.

**ENGRAVING**
This form of artistry depicts the dreamer as being a faithful, loving individual who is guided by earthly and spiritual goals. The magnitude, force, or distinction of this individual depends entirely on the willingness to become an achiever. If success comes, the dreamer could become a well-known personality in his or her chosen work. Should success be moderate or minimal, then the dreamer must accept these hard realities of life, too. Obviously, in this latter case, the dreamer would have chosen to be a follower.

**ENJOYMENT** (see **HAPPINESS**)

**ENLISTMENT** (see **DRAFTEE**)

**ENROLLMENT** (see **REGISTRATION**)

**ENSEMBLE** (see **ACTOR, DANCE,** or **CHOIR**)

**ENTERTAINER** (see **ACTOR, COMEDIAN,** or **MUSICIAN**)

**ENTOMBMENT** (see **BURIAL** or **GRAVE**)

**ENTREPRENEUR** (see **DETERMINATION**)

**ENVELOPE**

You are about to embark upon a new field of endeavour, and/or you are looking forward to receiving a contract or letter of vital importance to you. Allay your fears! With your leadership qualities, expertise, and determination, you are bound to achieve your most precious goals in life.

**ENVOY** (see **DEPUTY** or **MESSENGER**)

**EPIDEMIC**

This dream cautions you not to be so hardheaded, agitated, and sometimes prejudiced towards people who do not necessarily agree with you. Being a poor loser with selfish, biased attitudes can only bring you frustration. Look around you. Many people still find time to get along with others, in spite of their troubles and woes. Why can't you? The fact is you can, but you insist on being disgruntled and blameless whenever situations turn unpleasant or not to your liking. Be more loving, caring, and understanding with yourself and others. This course of action should give you the peace of mind you require.

**EPILEPSY**

Seeing or having this disease within a dream suggests: you already have this disease and merely dreamt about your state of being; you are assisting someone who has epilepsy; you know someone who has this disease; or, last, you fear the thought of becoming epileptic. The message here is that you must always show spiritual gratitude, patience, and recognition for God's special Love towards you, whether you are sick or well. Appreciate your life, no matter what trials and tribulations you may be experiencing. Nothing is easy, but not everything is hopeless, either.

**EPISTLE** (see **BIBLE**)

**EPITAPH** (see **GRAVESTONE**)

**EQUATOR** (see **EARTH** or **PLANET**)

**ERASER**

Hiding behind some falsehoods or trying to mask some wrongdoing cannot bring you inner happiness or joy. The Jeckyll and Hyde routine many people adopt within their lives can only bring about nightmarish discomforts and guilt. Being true to yourself at all times is the simplest method to liberate the conscience. There can be no inner peace to your life unless you are ready, willing, and able to make this happen. Hopefully, you will!

**ERECTION** (see **INTERCOURSE, GENITALS, MASTURBATION,** or **SEX**)

**EROTICISM** (see **SEX**)

**ERRAND** (see **MESSENGER**)

**ERROR**

Making a mistake or error within a dream state is no different from making a mistake or error during your wake state. However, within a dream state the mistake or error could be more strange, bizarre, or totally out of the ordinary. This is not to say that people have not made unusual or freakish mistakes while they are awake. They have, and they probably always will! What this dream symbolism is primarily trying to reveal to you is that you are creating some inner fears about making mistakes or about coping with your mistakes, flaws, or weaknesses in life. This is normal and very common with most people on this planet. You obviously care about yourself, and want to make things better. To make things better you must ignore or conquer your fears with determination and courage. For your own peace of mind, do not seek infallibility on this planet; it simply does not exist!

**ERUPTION** (see **VOLCANO**)

**ESCALATOR**

To merely see an escalator, or to go up on one, intimates that you are on the right road in your thoughts, actions, and deeds. Sometimes you have personal doubts as to whether or not you are going places in your profession or doing the right things in life to get ahead. According to this dream, you are headed in the right direction. But perhaps your hopes, wishes, and successes are not materializing as fast as you would like. Be patient; nothing happens overnight in these matters. Just keep up the good work you are presently doing, and you will eventually see the rewards of your labour come to pass.

Going down on an escalator intimates that some personal difficulties or stresses will beset you before too long (e.g., marriage, romance, finances, employment, vehicle). Whatever your problem(s) may be, you should be able to handle this matter quickly and efficiently.

## ESCAPE

Escaping someone or any situation within a dream signifies that you are a responsible, courageous, and independent individual. You face reality squarely and honestly. These are all admirable traits you possess. However, there are times when you simply must shrug your shoulders and walk away from or escape people or situations not to your liking. You are not a troublemaker, so your positive thinking in these matters is very justified. You are a credit to yourself and to your fellow man!

## ESCORT

Escorting someone or being escorted by someone infers that a sudden change or challenge is in the horizon for you. Whether or not you accept this opportunity to better yourself remains to be seen. If you reflect upon this sudden change or challenge with sensibility, assurance, and trust, then it is quite conceivable that you will gladly go for it. However, if you look upon this change or challenge with self-pity, fear, and downcast courage, then you would be wise to forget it.

## ESPIONAGE

Sometimes a person has to go through strange highways and byways in life before they honestly learn to appreciate what they already have. There are difficulties pending which could bring you to one of the lowest ebbs in your life. Keep your wits about you at all times; and, out of the shadow of disappointment, you will have learned many things about life that you would not have otherwise. Such is the value of this life: to recognize that suffering is but a brief shadow of one's inner light and that from this suffering we emerge more joyous and wise.

**ESTATE** (i.e., the gains or losses of someone who has passed away, or the gains or losses of a bankrupt individual)

You seem to be attracted to money and other materialistic gains. It seems that having everything you could possibly need now is really not enough to satisfy you. It is perfectly all right to be or to want to be wealthy. Used wisely, wealth can do wonderful things for you and for the world around you. However, if being wealthy implies being miserly, greedy, and selfish, then no amount of words can describe the sad and slow downfall of a soul. If you truly wish to better your life no matter how poor or rich you may happen to be, then commence to thirst for spiritual truth, gratitude, and compassion. These virtuous thoughts can be a lifeline to anyone who has a misdirected obsession in life.

**ETCHING** (see **ENGRAVING**)

**ETERNITY** (see **AFTERLIFE**, **HEAVEN**, **HELL**, or **IMMORTALIZATION**)

**EULOGY**

You have a great imagination and possess a restless desire for knowledge about the mysteries of life, the universe, the soul, God, the afterlife, and so on. You are willing to plod uncharted territories of the mind and spirit where others would dare not tread. Your pioneer spirit is wholesome simply because it is people like you who see the truth in seeking the truth. If everyone had your mind, this world would be more heavenly than earthly.

**EUNUCH** (see **CASTRATION**)

**EVACUATION**

To be evacuated from some danger or from a city, town, village, and so on infers that you are failing to treat some people around you equally or fairly. You seem to be pushing or "evacuating" certain individuals right out of your life.

Regardless of what motivates you to act this way, you would be wise to look further into the depths of your thoughts, actions, and overall character behaviour. In all likelihood, your depression—coupled with some of your egocentric tendencies—has created a barrier between you and those who truly like you. Being aloof, vain, and complacent with people's feelings cannot, and will not, bring you happiness. To find yourself and to be content with yourself, you must share the wealth of good that lies within your heart, mind, and soul. Pray for this, wish for this, and act on this until you are inwardly satisfied to be who you are. By the way, no one really knows oneself completely until faced with some flaw of character within one's being.

**EVICTION** (i.e., to be removed from a place for failing to pay rent)
Seeing yourself or someone else in this exasperating situation reveals that you will meet or greet someone from your past, and/or some hidden secret from your past will be revealed by another person to some people whom you know. These seen or unforeseen events may be more than you bargained for; simply handle them with diplomacy and sensibility.

**EVILDOER**
To see an evildoer cautions you to be aware of false friends, commonly referred to as bad company. These people may say the nicest things to you but not really mean them, or they may lure you into doing something wrong, immoral, or illegal. If you want order and peace in your life, then have the common sense to stay away from would-be mischief or trouble.
To be an evildoer, on the other hand, cautions you not to seek revenge or not to be tempted to do something foolish or on a dare; this you may later regret. This world is full of false temptations! Do not be another victim to their evil-based snares and clutches. Your life is far too important to waste on wrongful matters.

**EVIL EYE** (see **EVILDOER**)

**EXAMINATION** (see **TEST**)

**EXCAVATION**
There will be some trying moments and minor setbacks for you during the month to follow. If you are flighty and emotional, you may experience a more difficult time than if you were stable and perceptive. In any event, use your highest sense of logic and discretion in matters that tend to obstruct or hold you back in life. This pending ordeal may be an excellent character builder or will certainly give you some food for thought about your disappointments or progress. Only time will tell.

**EXCREMENT** (see **DEFECATION** or **DUNG**)

**EXCUSE** (see **ALIBI**)

**EXECUTION** (see **ELECTRIC CHAIR, GAS CHAMBER, GUILLOTINE, HANGING, KILL,** or **MURDER**)

**EXERCISE**
    You basically have the force, drive, or impetus to carry out a plan or idea. A challenge to you is like facing a very dear old friend in the mirror and, happily, you like what you see. Your future, like your past and present, will be fulfilling to you simply because you accept the highs and lows of life with equanimity. Without a doubt, you are a comfort to others because of your more or less relaxed attitude and sureness that things will be better. And, you know what? You are absolutely right! Things do get better.

**EXHIBITION** (i.e., public exposition, fair, or pageant)
    There are many things in your life that you would like to do. Unfortunately, you seem to be stuck in a situation or mode of life that makes your better wishes seem futile. A lack of money and initiative and many other disappointments seem to rule your life. Sometimes, when situations are very despairing, there is very little one can do but hope, wait, and see what the future brings. Sadly, this dream brings you little or no comfort except to advise you to change your attitude around a little bit, pray a little harder, and really begin to see what other alternatives you may have to improve your present state of being. Bear in mind, as well, that if a person tries hard enough in any-thing, he or she is bound to see some progress or clearing ahead of them.

**EXHIBITIONISM**
    Seeing or being an exhibitionist within a dream implies any of the following: A) that you are, in fact, an exhibitionist; or B) that you are inwardly reserved and shy and would not, in any way, reveal your body to anyone; or C) that you are inwardly sensuous and do not mind if others see your body; or D) that you are a rational individual who realizes that from time to time your body will be exposed to oth-ers (e.g., swimming pool, sauna, medical examination). If you truly know and understand your intimate feelings, then you should not

have a problem in categorizing yourself in one of the above-mentioned definitions.

**EXHUME** (see **GRAVE** or **GRAVEDIGGER**)

**EXILE** (see **BANISHMENT**)

**EXIT**

You have recently been in a temporary state of extreme mental agitation. However, with determination and concentration, you have demonstrated a great amount of mastery over self. In some strange way, it appears as though you have fulfilled some unforeseen or immediate need to understand yourself and life around you a bit better. You could almost say that you have commenced to liberate yourself from old ways and ideals for new and better ones. A pervading spirit of courage, skill, and knowledge is shown for your immediate future.

**EXORCISM**

This dream reminds you not to overlook or shrug off other probabilities, realities, or truths in life which you hear about from time to time but which you feel do not concern you. In so many words, do not debunk those strange facets of life that you cannot perceive, believe, or understand. On earth, the so-called "unknown" is often ignored, feared, and grossly misunderstood. Some cases involving the unknown forces have been solved; many have not and probably never will be. If mankind could attune its mind to the unseen positive forces of the Cosmic Universe, those so-called "unknown forces" would be no different than seeing a negative earthly human being (a troubled soul) versus a positive earthly human being (a non-troubled soul). Man's "psychic" mind, eyes, and ears are not yet open, except for the handful of beings on earth who can truly understand, see, and hear the Psychic Realm. The big question here is whether or not you wish to adopt a more open-minded attitude towards things you cannot presently see or hear.

**EXPEDITION**

It appears that you are striving very diligently to help another person. A change of environment, more stress on individuality such as self-expression and self-realization, and more tolerance in distressing situations would be some of the advice this person needs. There will be improvement in this individual providing he or she is prepared to listen and follow your good, wholesome guidance.

## EXPERIMENT
Discovering something new or something unique within a dream reveals that you have brave ideas and high ideals. Regretfully, you do not always carry out your better plans or wishes. Your fears, inhibitions, and insecurities all play a negative role in your judgments and actions. To put it bluntly, these negative hang-ups are holding you back in life. This is not to imply that you should in any way do foolish or silly things in order to act upon your brave ideas and high ideals. On the contrary! You should begin to understand that possibilities can only become realities when you begin to utilize your brilliant and exploring mind to its fullest capacity. What good are your needless setbacks when you have the fullest capabilities of being triumphant in almost everything you do? Wise people will always seek beyond their limits until they are consumed with the answers they seek.

## EXPLORER (see EXPEDITION)

## EXPLOSION
Your journey in life may not always be pleasant or comforting, but one thing is known for sure: you are equipped mentally and spiritually to handle most situations with sure-fire success! You are a very special and talented person who knows the intrinsic value of spending your time doing good upon earth. As you go down that beautiful roadway into your future, you will prosper, succeed, and—above all—continue to share your inner honesty, joys, and peace with others.

## EXPRESSWAY (see HIGHWAY or PASSAGEWAY)

## EXTORTION (see BLACKMAIL or THIEVERY)

## EXTRAVAGANCE (see ABUNDANCE)

## EYE
Step one: Look at yourself and ask yourself what right you have to lower your standard of thinking or actions simply because some foolish person made you feel inferior? Step two: What have you honestly

done to vanquish your inferiority feelings? Step three: What steps have you taken to bring forth your gifts or talents, in spite of past disappointments and failures? Step four: Are you your best ally in times of great trials and tribulations? Step five: What innermost feelings do you have towards God, prayer, hope, and faith? Step six: Do you pray and then wonder and doubt whether God and His Angels will answer you? Step seven: Are you blaming other people and situations around you for your dilemmas in life? Step eight: Are you harboring hate towards yourself and life? Step nine: Are you willing to bring peace, harmony, and betterment into your life, or do you expect someone else to do this for you? Step ten: Are you prepared and willing to make small sacrifices for yourself and others in order to improve your life? By repairing each negative step written above with a positive step within your mind and heart, you may be on the road to unraveling your own flaws or weaknesses. The eyes you saw within your dream state are, in fact, the reflections of your soul and conscience.

## EYEBROW

This dream advises you to speak freely; however, if you have nothing nice to say about others, then keep quiet. Some people do not know what you will say next, so they have no recourse other than to be defensive when they meet or greet you. A little bit of finesse and diplomacy goes a long way. If you peacefully follow this advice, then you, too, will go a long way in being wiser and happier.

## EYEGLASS (see *also* MONOCLE)

You are not going backwards in life; you are going forward. But, can you actually believe this fact? It is true that you have been experiencing some disappointments and various problems, here and there. However, these are all daily factors that everyone faces from time to time; and don't forget you have always managed to rise above your inner frustrations and discouragements. It is no different now. You will continue to forge ahead. You always do!

## EYELASH

You are a very conscientious, compassionate, and adaptable human being! Your mature and directed outlook is one to be admired, along with your vigorous desires to achieve betterment and justice for all. The mighty strength and force within your mind and soul will carry you to many distinguished achievements.

**EYEPIECE** (see **MICROSCOPE** or **TELESCOPE**)

**EYEWINK** (see **WINK**)

**FACE** (see **HEAD**)

**FACTORY**
   Perhaps you do work at a factory. If so, then your dream is merely reflecting your likes or dislikes pertaining to your specific line of work. If you do not work in a factory but dream of seeing one, then this dream intimates that you are experiencing some confusion or bitterness brought about by a group of people (e.g., relatives, schoolmates, an organization you belong to). This disorder may very well pertain to false promises, money matters, property, or some foolish suggestion or proposal. There may be some haggling in this entire situation before common sense prevails!

**FACULTY** (i.e., staff members collectively of a school, college, university)
   Seeing a faculty of a school denotes that you are a very dedicated person. No matter what you do or where you go, you always share your knowledge with others. Your innate ability to solve difficult or even unusual problems stems from your high intelligence and analytical mind. You are destined for success, happiness, and many special rewards in life simply because you know who you are, and you know exactly what you are capable of achieving. No one deserves honour and prestige unless they warrant it. You certainly do!

**FAD** (i.e., a short-lived fashion or craze)
   You appear to be running away from a personal problem which should be faced head-on. Your overly imaginative mind has certainly not helped you in this matter. Your situation is not as bad as you think it is; stop tormenting yourself so needlessly! Be strong, adopt a positive outlook, and handle this matter of concern realistically and intelligently.

**FAILURE**
   You are so motivated in outdoing or outshining the next person that you fail to see the logistics of the rights or wrongs of your actions. On one hand, you have an obsession about winning; on the other hand, you

have a great fear about losing. There should be no shame whatsoever in being defeated in something or failing in something. In fact, there should be honour and dignity in losing once in a while simply because this should motivate a person to try again except with perhaps more caution and wisdom. Most people fail many times until they learn to surmount their obstacles with glowing satisfaction and success. Learn to accept what comes your way! You will not always succeed, nor will you always fail, either. Life is only as complex as you want it to be.

## FAINT

This dream cautions you to be very careful for the next week or two. It appears you might be accident-prone or simply careless around sharp objects, great heights, heat, or water. Take care!

## FAIR (see EXHIBITION)

## FAIRYLAND

Seeing a rare spectacle such as a fairyland within a dream indicates that you are rather special, yourself. You are a very creative, productive, and well-adjusted person whose intellect appears to go beyond the bounds of simple, average thinking. Being an eccentric to some degree, your philosophy or gifts are a rarity in themselves. Do not rule out the possibilities of becoming famous on this earth plane; this is very possible! Has anyone ever told you that you have a great mind and soul? If not, you read it here first!

## FAITH (see CONFIDENCE, DOCTRINE, LOYALTY, or RELIGION)

## FAITHLESSNESS (i.e., having no faith in God or some close friend) (see *also* ADULTERY, AGNOSTIC, ANTI-CHRIST, ATHEIST, or CHEATING)

This act within a dream state infers that you either do or you do not believe in God, and/or you have great doubts about your own existence and about the people whom you know. If, for example, you fail to believe in God, then it can be assumed that someone or something within your life made you feel this way. This can be deduced, as well, if you fail to have faith in a friend. When you were a baby, you were quite innocent where matters of belief or disbelief were concerned. You are who you are today, except with adopted ideas and opinions of your past or present experiences. You have a right not to believe in anything, if that's what you want; however, this mode of thinking certainly cannot bring you much happiness or peace of mind. People very often blame God for their disappointments, struggles, and hang-ups, assuming He does not care or that He has not heard their prayer for help. God hears everyone loud and clear, all the time! Maybe too often! The big question is this: should God serve and respect mankind, or should mankind serve and respect God, the Father of All Things? Those who do serve and respect Him in a loving way are deserving; and, sooner or later, He grants their wishes and desires through their prayer, hard work, and perseverance. Note, however, that they serve and respect Him as their True Father of Life, not as a God who merely grants favors or wishes. The lesson here is simple. They worked hand in hand with God in their wants and needs and strangely discovered that their load was lessened by the mere fact of their faith in Him. Far too often, people want something for nothing. God does not work this way at all. Loving your God with all your heart and soul is the Universal Key to having a direct line between Him and you. The life you own belongs to God! If you respect your earthly parents, why can't you respect your Heavenly Parent as well?

**FAKIR** (i.e., a Moslem or Hindu beggar who claims to perform miracles)

You have a very searching and inquisitive mind. Some people know and respect you for who you are; some people merely take you for granted or constantly challenge your ideals, plans, or actions in life. What is important is that you have enough belief and courage to make your life move productive and worthwhile. This dream encourages you to forge ahead with your sound concepts and not to submit to anyone's negative feelings or attitudes towards you. Be happy that you are a bit different or unique!

**FALCON** (see **BIRD**)

**FALL** (i.e., to drop down)

To fall down a short distance, such as in tripping oneself, reveals that you will be doing something rather tedious and uninteresting for the next month or so. The end results of your labour, however, will be most rewarding and fulfilling to you. You will prosper in time; but, for now, do not put the cart in front of the horse, so to speak. Be patient; many of your lifelong dreams will come true!

If you are an adult and dream about having an endless fall, then this signifies that you are growing in a spiritual manner. You are beginning to focus your attention upon the inner values of your being (e.g., prayer, meditation, reading good inspirational books, charitable work).

If you are an adult who dreams about falling a great distance and suddenly hitting rock bottom, then be aware of the fact that you need a new outlook with regard to yourself and where your lifestyle is leading you. Are you going nowhere fast? Well, actually you are going somewhere, but you must realize that not everything you hope for will be realized (e.g., romance, career, education, travel). Some of your expectations can go sour on you because of your depressed, pessimistic attitudes. As a matter of fact, you have disappointed yourself on more than one occasion due to your stubbornness and hard outlook where people, places, and things are concerned. You are very hard to please! If you truly want to be more content with yourself and with others, then stop being so dogmatic in your ways. A little bit of kindness goes a long way. Try it once in a while; you could amaze yourself!

If a youthful person or juvenile dreams about having an endless fall or hits rock bottom after a deep fall, then this person is not only growing physically, but is also showing a pronounced growth mentally and spiritually. The so-called growing pains are still there, but some maturity is slowly beginning to take shape within this individual. This fact, alone, should give a momentary reprieve to any parent!

**FALLING STAR** (see **METEOR**)

**FALSEHOOD** (see **DECEPTION**)

**FALSE TEETH** (see **TEETH**)

**FAME** (see *also* **IMMORTALIZATION**, **PUBLICITY**, or **REPUTATION**)
Seeking fame and finding it within a dream could very well imply that you are already famous. You may have extravagant tastes and wants in life from time to time, but deep down you are a natural, fun-loving, hospitable individual. Your fame will continue to grow and prosper as long as you never lose sight of your gifted mind and soul. Pride, laziness, and indifference can be your worst enemy! So be very careful about these things, and everything else should work out just right for you and your place in history!

Becoming famous within a dream state, but not actually being famous in life, implies that you would like to be someone very special on earth. Perhaps you will, but you must realize that a lot of sweat, toil, and tears go with the package. If you are honestly headed in this direction now, then may God speed your journey and grant you the wisdom and comfort you may need. If you are honestly contemplating this direction in time to come and know that your gifts or talents are special, then—with hard work and gutsy determination—you can become famous. Why not? Others had the same inkling or calling, just as you are having now!

To dream of becoming famous and not achieving this goal within a dream state suggests that you are on the right track in doing something of special interest or great importance to your fellow man. Whatever your gifts may be, it appears that you are a person who certainly knows what you want and where you are headed in life. There are quantum levels of success ahead for you, as your future will reveal. And rightfully so! You are a child of destiny.

## FAMILY

Seeing a family unit as a whole showing great indifference to joy, pleasure, grief, or pain reveals that some health or financial burden will beset you before too long. This may not be long-lasting, but you can be sure this brief episode will be a tremendous test of character for you. Courage, humility, compassion, and understanding are the key elements that will bring you out of this trying time. After it is over, be a true fisherman of souls; teach others what you know and what you have learned from your deep experience.

Seeing a family unit as a whole dancing, showing great remorse, or behaving in a frantic, confused manner reveals that some sad, traumatic event is in the wind. A family member, relative, friend, or someone whom you once knew may be extremely sick, have a terrible accident, or—sadly—may pass on. Pray for those you know. Hopefully, your prayer will be the answer needed, and perhaps this dark cloud will blow away. If not, accept life for what it brings. You can do no more, no less.

## FAMILY TREE

You obviously are interested in your family roots. Who knows, maybe you will search further into your family history and discover greater things about yourself. In any event, your thoughts and ideas are basically laudatory. Through your efforts and methodical endeavours, you will find lasting satisfaction and gratitude in all that you do.

**FAMINE** (i.e., shortage of food)

Seeing this grave need within your dream state forewarns of troubled and needy days to come! Drought conditions, diseases, spiritual upheavals, and money shortages are but a few of the problems that will affect many people in the months to come. Traumatic changes on the face of this globe are taking place! Your dream is primarily calling for help! In other words, pray for and help your fellow man, if at all possible. If you are presently doing so, then your dream merely affirms the fact that your help is needed, wanted, and appreciated. This, by the way, could be another way God thanks you for the good work you are presently doing!

**FAN** (i.e., an electric fan or a folding device for cooling oneself)

A dominant personality appears to have a grip on you. This dominant person seems to be a demanding perfectionist who needs someone for an audience. You, obviously, are that audience! Be firm; do not give in to this person's whims or notions. If this fails, suggest professional counseling. Failing this, then you should commence to seriously think about freeing yourself from this person's confusion, bitterness, and super-inflated ego. This, of course, is entirely up to you.

**FANG** (see **TEETH**)

**FARMING** (i.e., operating a farm such as in agriculture, cattle raising, etc.) (see *also* **COMMUNE**, **KIBBUTZ**, or **PEASANTRY**)

There are times when you are exceedingly happy; yet, there are times when depression goes beyond its limits with you. This happy/sad state of affairs you have been experiencing is enough to make you want to throw your hands in the air and give up. The truth of the matter is that you are basically content with yourself and with others around you, but there is a part of you that yearns for something better. Yet, sadly, you know that what you have in life is more or less what you are fated to have and nothing more. What you really seem to be asking for is more communication, affection, appreciation, and understanding for simply being a good, hard-working individual. You feel suppressed so many times by others around you that you cannot help feeling indifferent to their many demands and needs. Unless you start talking to those who affect you and unless you at least make a few demands for yourself, their one-sided attitudes will not change. Be more assertive, and life within and around you may present a new beginning for you.

**FARMSTEAD** (i.e., land and buildings of a farm) (see *also* **BARN** or **BARNYARD**)
    Like millions of others on this planet, you often desire to be free of all earthly cares and woes. That is a good desire, but it just can't be. There are some things we have to experience, whether good or bad. This should not deter you from trying to do your very best or to smile from time to time, knowing that life has its good moments too. This dream counsels you to rise above your impatience, boredom, and work habits by thinking more about your blessings than about your hardships. Improvements are foreseen for your future; but, before you see this happen, you must ascend to a more hopeful, optimistic outlook about yourself, about your loved ones, and about life in general. Things may seem bad now, but they are not as bad as they seem to be. Only your courage and time can prove this to you.

**FAST** (i.e., to abstain from food)
    With your keen sense of perception, intelligence, sincerity, and ambition, you are bound to rise above any situation that happens to come your way. Your gains in life will be from your own labour, self-assertiveness and, last, from your many experiences. There is a long road ahead of you; and down this road you will share your labour of love and dedication with others. Those who choose to listen to your wise counsel will strive harder to bring peace into their own lives.

**FATHER**
    Dreaming about a father whom you like or dislike simply reveals your emotional love or hate towards this parent while you are awake. If you love and respect your father, then you certainly must feel good about yourself and about life in general. Obviously, your upbringing is something to be proud of, in many ways. However, should you harbour hate and disrespect for your father, then there have to be some reasons behind your attitude. Perhaps your father is cruel, unloving, unforgiving, blaming, or irresponsible? Who knows?! Only you have the prime answer to your inner turmoil, where this matter is concerned. Realize, as well, that your father may have experienced a very

bad childhood. His reflection on you could be the way his parent(s) treated him. Of course this is no prime excuse for his doing the same things to you; but these facts of life do exist. Sadly, instead of seeking help to refine his thinking and attitudes about himself and about life, he is bitterly foisting his confusion on those whom he should love and cherish. Time, experience, and maturity can heal all inner wounds. Maybe this is the route you will have to take before you can even remotely forgive your father.

If you dream about a father who has passed on, then your dream is counseling you to say a prayer for him. He has come back to you for a reason. He loves you and is now asking for one simple request from you. When you pray for him, do not forget to tell him to "ask for the Light!"

## FATHER-IN-LAW

Dreaming about a father-in-law whom you respect or disrespect simply reveals your emotional love or hate towards him while you are awake. If you respect your father-in-law, then you are to be commended for your maturity and fine sense of judgment. However, if you disrespect your father-in-law, then there obviously is some reason within you or within him that makes you feel this way. Time could heal those inner hurts or wounds both you and your father-in-law seem to be expressing or sharing. He has his reasons for being the way he is; you have your reasons for being the way you are, as well. Locking horns is not the answer! A little bit of compromising just might settle matters here. The big question is, are both of you willing to try to get along or to at least meet each other half way?

Dreaming about a father-in-law who has passed away infers that he wants a prayer from you. He comes to you specifically for this one simple request. When you do pray for him, be sure to tell him to "ask for the Light"!

## FAUCET

A faucet denotes that a misunderstanding or argument may ensue between you and a parent, spouse, or friend because of someone's misguided information about you. Be frank and levelheaded in this matter. Clear the air once and for all. The truth in all things will bring you the freedom and peace you so rightfully deserve.

## FAULTFINDER (see COMPLAINER or MUMBLER)

**FAUN** (see **SATYR**)

**FAVORITISM** (i.e., showing more kindness or attention to some people rather than others)
You are at times very uneasy and insecure with some family members, friends, or fellow workers. It seems that you would like to blend more with these people, but inwardly you know that their thoughts and actions are far more practical than your own. This is not to imply that you hate or envy these people in any way. As a matter of fact, you often wonder what makes them behave the way they do or why they do not reach out further, where their lives are concerned. Well, as you know, no two people are alike. What is important is that you be your natural self at all times. Obviously, you are destined to think and do things your way, whereas they are destined to think and do things their way. You never know—the thoughts and feelings you harbour about others could be the very same thoughts they harbour about you. You fear them; they fear you. You would be amazed at what you could learn by mingling with a cross section of people! A little effort on your part could make a world of a difference for you.

**FEAR** (see **ACROPHOBIA, AGORAPHOBIA, CLAUSTROPHOBIA, COWARD, DANGER, EVILDOER, HYSTERIA, STARTLE,** or **SUPERSTITION**)

**FEAST** (see **BANQUET** or **CELEBRATION**)

**FEATHER**
In this life, there are so many things you would like to do and accomplish; unfortunately, it always seems like someone or something gets in your way. This dream reveals that there are pending changes ahead for you that will finally give you more than one opportunity to fulfill some of your almost forgotten wishes. Could this be a long trip, a marriage, or the start of a new business? Whatever it is, you will follow your better instincts this time!

**FEE** (see **MONEY**)

**FEEDER** (i.e., a device used to supply food for animals or birds)
In some respects you could quite easily become a hermit, living high on a mountain and feeling as much at home there as anywhere

else. Due to the lack of attention that has bothered you lately, the thought of isolating yourself somewhere far away is not such a bad idea. Of course, this is not your way of doing things. You are not begging for attention or feeling sorry for yourself. All you want is some endorsement from those whom you know and love that you are a human being with a mind, feelings, and wants, just like the next person. The solution here is for you to change your attitude towards these people—even for a brief period of time—until they begin to understand what they are doing to you. Be more assertive and less giving, and commence to do more for yourself rather than be subservient to their wants and needs. Your absence in thought and action will slowly make them think about you, respect you, and once more be grateful that you are alive. Go "on strike" until they change their selfish tune!

**FEET**

Healthy looking feet reveal your natural tendency to be surefooted, supportive, and optimistic in life. You have a magnetic personality which automatically radiates comfort and assurance to those around you. Your friendships are lasting simply because you know how to treat friends equally and maturely. There are many pleasant surprises for you as you go on in life. But, then again, you are always surprising others with your good intentions, gifts, and love. Yes, it is better to give than to receive.

Unhealthy looking feet symbolize personal defeat in something and/or the possibility of a prolonged illness (e.g., bankruptcy, divorce, emotional or physical strain, operation). This dream advises you to pray, think positive, keep yourself pleasantly busy, but know your emotional and physical limits. It also advises you to be more willing to listen to good, sound advice. The above-mentioned forewarning is primarily applicable to anyone who actually goes the limits with their mind and body or with their possessive or negative actions in life. Regretfully, these people do not know when to stop—until it is too late!

Seeing anything unusual (e.g., a snake, frog, toad, lizard, animal) actually go through your feet or those of someone else intimates that you or someone whom you know has a very low opinion of themselves. Your depression appears to be at an all-time low! Do not do anything foolish or unwise now, later, or at any time. You are more worthy than you know! You cannot think that your life is not of any value or importance to anyone. It is and will always be! Talk to someone about what troubles you, or seek some professional assistance, if you must; but, for all that is good and glorious, think about your life as being hopeful, not hopeless. Today you may be unhappy; but tomorrow can give you the brightest ray of hope ever. If you could only see how bright your future really is, you would be clicking your heels. This dream urges you to pray for inner peace of mind and to really talk to God as you would talk to a parent or a friend. Communicate!

## FEMININITY

If you are a female, then there is no need at all to be concerned about this quality or state. You are merely projecting a part of your personality and actions; that is totally normal and natural. After all, you do belong to one of God's most cherished of all creatures—womankind!

If you are male and dream about personally displaying this quality or state, then you can be sure that you have some bizarre or mixed feelings about your sexual needs and preferences. This is not to say that you are not masculine during your wake state; you probably are. What your dream is trying to tell you, in blunt terms, is that you have some type of fetish or neurosis which can be directly or indirectly related to sexual matters. You may come out of this hang-up through strong determination; if this fails, seek some professional assistance until this matter is solved.

## FENCE (see ENCLOSURE)

## FENCING (see FIGHT, GAME, or SWORD)

## FENDER (see BUS, CAR, or TRUCK)

## FERRY

Your ambitions vary from moderate to great. Your dream is encouraging you to go after that one main goal in life that you are best qualified to do. Do not go beyond your reach unless you know, beyond a shadow of a doubt, that you have the knowledge, integrity, determination, and willingness to persevere. Finish what you start. One other thing: do not go looking for riches unless you are prepared to wear rags first.

## FERTILIZER

You may encounter some opposition from family members or close friends because of something you are presently doing or intend to do. At this juncture of your life, bear in mind that your family and friends have your best interests at heart, and they do not wish to see you disappointed or hurt in any way. Right now, it appears that you are intolerably indifferent to any good advice that happens to come your way. Before you trip and fall on your own steam, you would be advised to carefully study the pros and cons of your lifestyle or intended plans. If you can, put aside your emotional state for a moment or two and begin to see this entire matter in a more realistic, harmonious sense. Hopefully, the impact of your introspection will begin to calm you down and perhaps stop you from making what could be a big mistake!

## FESTIVAL (see CELEBRATION)

## FETUS

You feel downcast and uninspired because you have made very few attempts to really discover yourself and your potential in life. You simply go with the flow. First of all, you could compliment yourself once in a while; begin to like who you are. Appreciate all life around you, and try your best to uplift your mind through inspirational books, courses, lectures, and so on. No one is ever too old or too young to better themselves. Your purpose on earth is to grow with your experiences, to be able to think and do things for yourself, and to recognize that your weaknesses and doubts can be conquered, if you try hard enough.

## FEVER (see SICKNESS)

## FIANCÉ (i.e., the man engaged to be married)

Seeing your fiancé or fiancée smiling or content within a dream state reveals you should have a happily married life (e.g., children, good health, and prosperity). On the other hand, seeing your fiancé or fiancée appear angry or disappointed reveals that there is something amiss in your relationship with this person. Some serious evaluation about each other's wants and needs, habits, ideals, goals, preferences, and so on should be looked into now, not later; later may be too late. Do not be duped into feeling that you can change someone after you get married. This is a fallacy. Nothing really changes then; except, perhaps, situations may get progressively worse. Know the person you want to marry very well before settling down on a permanent basis!

**FIANCÉE** (see **FIANCÉ**)

**FIDDLE** (see **INSTRUMENT**)

**FIELD** (see *also* **MEADOW** or **PASTURE**)
An open field without obstruction or danger present signifies that you need time to think and reflect about your life. No matter whether you are satisfied or not with your lifestyle, there are moments you need to be alone in order to sort things out. You would be amazed by what you can actually learn by going for a nice, long walk in an open field or merely sitting peacefully on a bench. Just to see a leaf gently fall to earth or to listen to the wind wail through tree branches should give you enough inspiration to find yourself.
An open field with obstructions or danger present intimates that you are afraid to face some realities about yourself or about some matter of concern around you. Showing closed-mindedness or deferring or neglecting some truth merely prolongs your agony or guilt. It is your life; what you do to make things better or worse for yourself is entirely up to you.

**FIESTA** (see **CELEBRATION**)

**FIGHT** (see *also* **BATTLE** or **QUARREL**)
To have a fight in your dream signifies that a host of incidental disturbances or annoyances will manifest themselves within the next week or two. Some of these illogical, thoughtless, irresponsible, and foolish situations may be created by you; some by others. Perhaps when this is all over, you will have some interesting stories to tell; or, sadly, you may reflect upon the effect this trying experience had on you.

**FIGURINE** (see **STATUETTE**)

**FILMSTRIP**
Recently, you have been harbouring your worrisome thoughts to yourself (e.g., heartache, sadness, regret, financial trouble, some nagging affliction of the mind or body). This low profile is fine, up to a

point, but sooner or later you may have to discuss this matter with someone. Two, three, or four heads together in any vital matter always helps. Allay your inner disputes or arguments. Peace will come.

**FIN** (see **FISH**)

**FINE** (i.e., a sum of money to be paid for breaking a law)
There appears to be a mountain between you and what you want in life. Maybe someday your better wishes will be realized, but for now you must learn to accept facts as they stand. Realize, as well, that not everything you hope for will come to pass. Be thankful for the things you have now. As frustrating as this may sound to you today, there will be other times and other moments when your greatest wishes will be realized. How can you possibly believe that your song will not be heard?

**FINGER** (see **HAND**)

**FINGERNAIL** (see **HAND**)

**FINGERPRINT**
You are a very critical and demanding individual. You are not very easy to live with, to know, or to tolerate, for that matter. Your tyrannical ways could be your undoing unless you commence to show more order and discipline within your life. Your super-ego, pride, and selfish attitudes simply must go! Do not abuse your life in any manner; rather, use your time and efforts to create a better being within yourself.

**FIRE** (see *also* **KINDLER**)
Seeing a fire within a dream counsels you to curb your temper for emotional and physical reasons. Do not continue to harbour animosities toward others you fail to trust or like. This would then suggest that you fail to trust or like yourself, as well. You are in charge of your life. This is not the time, place, or hour to play mysterious games, act dumb, or be ignorant about yourself, about your stresses, and about other people, as well. Your dream cautions you to change for your own good, thus avoiding any future embarrassment, grief, or hardships that could befall you.

(*Note*: A repetitive dream about a fire could, in fact, be a direct warning about some disaster or loss that could involve you, your family, or someone you know—such as a fire, accident, sickness, financial ruination. Pray for your loved ones, for yourself, and for all people you know. One can only hope that this dire warning may be heeded and disaster or loss perhaps averted in time.)

## FIRE ALARM

Symbolically, this dream infers that you are a very nervous, high-strung individual. Having a highly imaginative mind often leads others to believe that you tend to exaggerate or stretch the truth a little bit too far. Basically, you are a peaceful person, but you seem to crave attention by being a know-it-all. This domineering personality trait can alienate you from your friends and associates unless you learn to be quiet, rational, and more compromising.

## FIREBOAT

Have you ever wondered why people come to you with their problems? It's as though they were magnetized to you! It is probably because you have an innate understanding about life, about being honest, and—above all—knowing that one ray of hope or one word of encouragement can lead others on the right track. You certainly are a remarkable, loving person. This world needs more people like you!

## FIREBUG (see ARSONIST)

## FIRECRACKER (see FIREWORKS)

## FIRE-EATER (i.e., a person who goes through the motions of eating fire)

It seems that you are far too sensitive to continue your dealings with some people whom you know. Did you ever have the impression that you just do not belong with a certain group? What is the use in trying to be helpful and levelheaded when, in the end, you know that you are going to be put down one way or another? Can you win this losing battle? Unlikely! Deactivate your feelings here, and—with discretion—gently pull out of this thankless situation.

## FIRE ENGINE

You cannot expect to have happiness and success in one part of your life and create havoc and disorder in another part of your life. For example, you may be the nicest person in the office, but when you get home you could perhaps be a dictator, or vice versa. Maintaining two personalities can be a chore and a pain; above all, it can give you need-less moments of guilt, shame, and despair. If you are unhappy with one part of your life, then you should begin to ask yourself why and what you can do to make things better. Failing to patch things up or to make some improvements or sensible compromises where your unhappiness lies can ultimately find you very much isolated and alone in the future. Right now, you seem to be headed on a collision course with yourself!

**FIRE ESCAPE**

Isn't it about time you took credit for your own mistakes? Stop looking for "outside" answers and excuses when all your "inside" answers are right in front of you. Face yourself and your problems with foresight, maturity, courage, and determination. And, if you truly want to surprise yourself, add some faith in the package. You can never escape the fact of being who you are; however, you can improve your state of being to the point of liking yourself a lot better.

**FIRE EXTINGUISHER**

You will either quell a disagreement between two people, and/or you will do something very noble and admirable for someone in dis-tress. Your dream commends you for your general thoughtfulness and concern where others are concerned. You are a well-admired, respected, and courageous human being!

**FIREFIGHTER** (see **FIREMAN**)

**FIREFLY** (see **BEETLE**)

**FIRE HYDRANT**

There are enough plans and activities ahead of you to keep you busy for the next month or so. A move or some positive investment in the not-too-distant future is strongly revealed in this dream. With your belief, expertise, and willingness to make things happen, you are bound for bigger and greater things in life.

**FIREMAN**

If you are, in fact, a fireman and dream of being or seeing one, then you are in effect merely reflecting upon the work that you do.

However, if you are not, then your dream is trying to tell you not to be in such a hurry to get somewhere or to be a somebody in life. So, where's the fire? By being confident, patient, skillful, and inwardly satisfied with each stepping stone along your way, some of your fondest goals will be achieved. However, remember that nothing happens overnight. This will take time.

**FIREPLACE**

It seems that some excessive and perhaps annoying demands have been placed upon you within the last month or two. You are the type of person who wants to get everything done quickly and effectively. However, there are times when certain matters at work or at home cannot be done on the spot. Be a bit more reasonable with yourself. Do what you can one day and, if you must, continue where you left off the next day. Do not push yourself to extremes even though a rest, once in a while, may be frustrating to you. Even a machine can break down. Be careful; you can too!

**FIRE STATION**

Through travel, through study, or in making personal contact with the right people at the right time, you will commence to see some of your good hopes and dreams come true. A talent shines through your soul like a beam of light that is both worthy and outstanding. You are a very special person! Success, prosperity, and happiness are yours for the asking, providing you continue to maintain your powerful views, theories, philosophy, and understanding about the world in which you live. You will utilize this knowledge in time to come.

**FIRE TOWER** (e.g., a lookout tower in a forest for spotting fires)

Sometimes people upset you to the point where you are tempted to use some form of violence. And perhaps, at times, you do. This solves nothing for you or for them. You may say you feel much better after you release your tension or violence on someone else. How can this possibly be? After a conflict you still suffer stressfully; the person you harm or injure suffers stressfully and possibly physically. So what is gained? Your dream counsels you to think twice before you vent your hatred, anger, or frustrations on others. You certainly will be wiser for being calm, cool, and collected in such matters.

## FIREWORKS

As you allow your good mind and heart to guide you through life, you will see the intrinsic value in knowing that the best things in life are indeed free. People often go from day to day failing to see life's love around them. They are simply too busy to care or too preoccupied with matters of self-importance to see the sun shining, or to see a cloud disappear from view, or to see the majesty of stars at night, and so on. This dream advises you to look around you from time to time; be more observant. And, who knows? Maybe the star or two you actually see traveling across the night sky could be a UFO! And, no doubt, it probably is just that—and perhaps more than meets the eye.

## FISH

Dreaming about active, wholesome-looking fish reveals that your financial status will improve before too long (e.g., winning some money, inheritance, selling something at a profit) In whatever manner your gains may come, they will be higher than your losses. And thankfully so!

Dreaming about dead fish reveals that a brief illness may beset you, and/or you or some other family member will experience some losses of revenue or income. Allay your fears. This entire matter will be mastered with logical thinking and actions.

Cleaning or scaling fish intimates that you are concerned about some mental anguish or fear that haunts you from time to time, and/or you are worried about some physical problems which you do not wish to discuss with anyone. These problems will not disappear overnight, unless you at least seek some sound, professional advice. The end results should be both assuring and gratifying to you.

## FISHBOWL (see AQUARIUM or FISH)

## FISHERMAN

Dreaming of seeing or being a fisherman always alludes to a closeness you have with your family, friends, and to nature itself. Lately, you may have experienced a bit of emotional, financial, or physical discomforts. Your spirits may be down at this time, but help is on its way! Several people will be instrumental in assisting you, where your problems are concerned.

**FISHERY**

You are a very hard worker, but it seems the harder you work, the faster the money goes. It just seems so very hard to make ends meet and to survive. You would like to give everything up, move away, and start all over again. Yet, you somehow know this is not the answer— stay with this feeling, if you can! In due time, you will come out of this state not only a wiser person, but with a profit in your pocket as well.

**FISH HOOK** (see **FISHING TACKLE**)

**FISHING TACKLE** (i.e., hooks, lines, rods, reels, etc. for fishing)

You are worried about some job opportunity or employment prospect that may not turn out in your favour. The fact remains that you know you would be much better off being your own boss rather than having someone be a boss to you. With your expertise, experience, and insight into your profession, you should have very little difficulty in setting up your own business. If not now, then perhaps at a later date you will do precisely that and more!

**FIT** (i.e., a seizure whereby a person may become unconscious and convulse) (see *also* **EPILEPSY**)

Maybe you or someone you know has fits. If so, then your dream is merely reflecting your knowledge or experiences about such matters. Assuming you do not have fits but dream of seeing yourself or someone else have one, then your dream is trying to tell you that you are seeking sympathy, affection, communication, or some form of understanding from someone you know. It appears that you are being ignored or taken for granted by someone who has other interests or who cannot be bothered by your wants or needs. Face facts! If someone chooses to turn their back on you, there is very little you can do about it. Realize that some serious bond of friendship has been broken. Normally, it takes two people to break a friendship, but not always. If the person you deal with has a wanderlust or is simply uncaring, then accept what life brings you. If you are somehow responsible for this scenario taking place, then realize you may have gone just a bit too far. Maybe this person will forgive your actions; maybe not. You can only hope, wait, and see what transpires. Sometimes life's lessons can be devastating!

## FLAG

This auspicious dream gives hope that one day you will be in a better financial position to travel or to do something special with your time and talents. It seems so unfair that a person of your caliber and understanding should be held back because of money hardships. But these are facts of life you must face today. One day you will reflect back on your hardships, only to realize that they were a blessing in disguise, in many ways. Appreciate what you have now. When your prosperous tomorrows come, you will be more equipped in terms of experience to fulfill your good hopes and wishes.

## FLASHBULB

You are a very mature, compassionate person. You especially feel the needs of people who have suffered at the hands of war or who have experienced political or religious persecution. The pain and suffering on this planet is shocking beyond all words! Your dream affirms that you are already assisting or contributing towards worthy causes of peace and freedom. Whoever you may be, your understanding and sympathy towards others is poignant and inspiring.

## FLASHLIGHT

Someone may intend to harass, intimidate, or humiliate you in front of a group of people. This person doubts many things, so be sure you can back up your theories, arguments, or statements when the time is appropriate. Be calm and clearheaded, and strive your best to maintain a logical line of communication with this individual. You can master this situation rather well if you honestly keep your wits about you!

**FLASK** (i.e., a narrow neck, bottle-shaped container often used in hospitals, laboratories, schools)

To see a flask filled with something indicates that you have the potential to influence people (e.g., politics, business, religion, entertainment, writing). The possibilities seem endless. If your ambitions are positive and honourable, then you are bound to make your world a better place in which to live. However, if you are dishonourable with your actions and intentions, then what you sow now is exactly what you will reap further down the road.

Seeing an empty or broken flask suggests you are wanting more out of life than you are willing to give. You cannot expect something for nothing. It seems that your plans or actions are a bit premature, at this time. Perhaps later on, when you are more experienced and realistically inclined, you will then see the foolish attitudes you once held. For the moment, though, your dream advises you not to become involved in matters beyond your present capabilities.

**FLATTERY** (see **ADULATION**)

**FLATUS** (i.e., stomach or intestinal gases)
    You are not paying enough attention to your own well-being or that of someone else. If you know this to be true, then your dream is simply advising you to be more mindful and caring in the future. Failure to do so could have some unexpected and unpleasant ramifications.

**FLEA** (see **LICE**)

**FLIRTATION** (see **AFFAIR** or **LOVE**)

**FLOAT**
    To float on land, air, or water suggests you are a very resourceful, independent, and steadfast individual. Your work load may be overbearing at times, but you always manage to complete your tasks with overwhelming sureness and success. Do not worry about some recent, pressing, and bothersome matter. This, too, will be handled smoothly and efficiently!

**FLOOD**
    You can be quite stubborn in certain matters, but your dream also admits that you can back away from situations which appear to be a waste of your valuable time. To argue for the sake of proving a point or a principle seems foolish if the next person is unwilling to at least be reasonable. Do not let other people's ignorance, confusion, or illogical thinking get you down. Your understanding, self-disciplined nature will be a true asset to you and perhaps to others who wish to follow your good example.

(*Note*: A repetitive dream about a flood with muddy, dirty-looking water reveals that situations around you can go from bad to worse. Be prudent and levelheaded during these trying times; they, too, will pass.)

## FLOORING (see *also* CARPET)

Your fears, inhibitions, and misunderstandings all take their toll on you. As well, your daily stresses are compounded by the fact that you seem to harbour a very low opinion of yourself. Sometimes, you think you are a so-called "doormat" for other people. Maybe you are, but only if you allow this to happen. Be more assertive, say what you feel, and—above all—have more faith and belief in yourself. You are a very deserving person, but unless you honestly feel and believe this fact, do not expect immediate miracles in your life. No one can help you unless you are willing to help yourself. Your dream has thrown you a lifeline; think about it, and grab it.

## FLORIST (see FLOWER or SALESMAN)

## FLOUR

There is no dark cloud hovering over you except scattered thoughts, attitudes, and actions of other people who have upset you. Will you ever find comfort and enjoyment on this earth plane? Yes, you will! But first you must learn not to be so quick-tempered, accusing, or demanding, where others are concerned. No one is perfect here, nor will they ever be. You have been striving much too hard to find your peace "outside" your being, whereas peace can only come from "inside" your being. Isolate yourself from time to time. Begin to read good inspirational books; listen to good, inspiring music; take a long walk; pray; meditate; and begin to see how you can change things around for yourself, instead of others having to change for you. When you do these things, you will then find the comfort and enjoyment you seek.

## FLOWER

Seeing healthy looking flowers indicates that matters of the heart, mind, or body will commence to improve for you. For example, receiving more love and affection from your loved ones, settling some argument between yourself and another person, or beginning to improve health-wise are but a few of the possibilities open to you, where this dream is concerned. Be grateful for small miracles; some are coming your way now!

Seeing flowers that are decayed, withered, or perhaps diseased indicates that you or someone whom you know may be in a totally uncompromising situation (e.g., marital dispute, divorce, engagement breakup, business or personal bankruptcy). There will be no winners here—just anguish, tears, and bitterness for those involved.

**FLOWER GIRL** (see **ADOLESCENT** or **FLOWER**)

**FLUTE** (see **INSTRUMENT**)

**FLY** (see **INSECT**)

**FLYING** (see *also* **FLOAT**)

To fly by your own accord without using any form of conventional transportation (e.g., airplane, glider) is a very great sign. This dream reveals that you will be honoured and praised for some outstanding deed, task, or lifework in time, such as a rescue mission, signing a major transaction that will affect many people in a good way, an invention, composition, or a literary work). Whatever your gifts or talents may be, the outcome of your efforts and labour may be felt by hundreds or perhaps millions of people. Time will tell.

(*Note*: You may also have the pleasure of knowing that if, for example, you are experiencing a very negative dream but at the very end of your dream sequence or anywhere during your dream sequence you happen to be flying, then this flying "symbolism" takes precedence over your entire bad dream. Consequently, you have nothing to worry about simply because flying acts as a "buffer zone" to anything negative within a dream.)

**FLYING SAUCER**

You have a great desire to communicate with the "angels" from space, or you would like to see these Cosmic Beings come down to earth to help mankind in quantum ways (e.g., eradicating all wars forever; teaching every nation on earth true friendship and brotherhood; curing all sicknesses; prolonging life on earth; acquainting this planet with other worlds beyond this solar system; and teaching us our destiny and our duty to obey and respect God). Someday, there will be mighty changes on this planet; and then all weapons, famine, and strife will cease to exist. There will at last be brotherhood on earth as there is in space.

(*Note*: You may also have the pleasure of knowing that if, for example, you are experiencing a very negative dream but at the very end of your dream sequence or anywhere during your dream sequence you happen to see a flying saucer, then this flying saucer "symbolism" takes precedence over your entire bad dream. Consequently, you have nothing to worry about simply because the flying saucer acts as a "buffer zone" to anything negative within a dream.)

## FOG

To see a fog or to be lost in one denotes emotional, sexual, or spiritual confusion and depression. These ravages of the mind and body may be very trying for you, but with a bit of courage, hope, and logic, little by little things will get better. If you must, do not hesitate to seek professional guidance.

## FOGHORN (see HORN or SOUND)

## FOLIAGE (see FLOWER, LEAF, PLANT, or WREATH)

## FOOD (see *also* BACON, BANQUET, BREAD, COKE, CANDY, CARCASS, CHICK, CHICKEN, EGG, FISH, FRUIT, MEAL, MEAT, MOUTH, PICNIC, PLANT, POULTRY, or PREY)

Any one of the following definitions may be applicable to you: A) that you were, in fact, hungry at the time of your dream; or B) that you are on a diet but do crave some other types of food; or C) that you may be a compulsive eater and a highly depressed person who simply cannot get food out of your mind, day or night; or D) that you are obese but do your best to control your diet, or you are quite content to be who you are; or E) that, because you went to bed hungry, it seems only natural that you would have dreamt about food; or F) that this dream has little or no relevance to you at this time.

## FOOLISHNESS (see ABSURDITY)

## FOOT (see FEET)

## FOOTBALL (see GAME)

## FOOTPRINT

If the footprints you see are more or less sensibly proportioned in size and distance, then your immediate plans will materialize with comfort and ease. You are on the right road in life.

Should the footprints you see be totally out of proportion in size and distance between them, then some of your immediate and long-range plans will flounder and fail. Although you are on the right road in life, your timing appears to be wrong where some of your plans and actions are concerned.

## FOOTSTOOL

You are a workaholic. That is all right providing you do not affect those who care about and love you. If you do, then you had better reconsider your working habits, otherwise they can be your own undoing. Learn to enjoy life by doing your best at work and your best at home. You will feel much better for this compromising measure.

## FOOTWEAR (see *also* MOCCASIN or SNOWSHOE)

Seeing matching or neatly arranged footwear indicates that you are taking a very mature, stable direction in life. You know exactly where you are headed and exactly what you have to do in order to make your good wishes come true. Rarely are you disappointed with this attitude!

Seeing different sizes and shapes of footwear or footwear that is scattered here and there indicates that your thoughts and actions are also scattered and unfocused. There is no system or planned thought to your actions. Doing ten things at a time will get you no further ahead than if you were to do five things at a time. Do one thing at a time, and do it well; then go on to your next project. Be more systematic in your thinking and actions; and you will be wiser for doing so. At least, you will get more things done in half the time!

## FORCEPS

You get very upset when you are wrong and, at times, appear very incapable of coping with this fact. You do not traumatize the situation; you merely go inside yourself and continue to be stressful and anguished. Two wrongs do not make a right here! If you honestly made a mistake or you were wrong in something, simply admit it and then let it go sailing in the wind. That is, of course, providing this mistake or wrong action is not something evil, wicked, or lawbreaking. If it is, then your stress or anguish appears justified until you can honestly see the wrongs committed, and you will not repeat your actions again. When you have broken any law, only time can correct the problems within you.

## FORECLOSURE

Perhaps you are in the throes of being foreclosed. If so, then your dream is merely reflecting upon a situation that seems inevitable. Should this not be applicable to you, then your dream infers that you are holding back some facts or truths from a loved one. A troubled conscience cannot bring you peace or freedom. As well, your fears may be totally unfounded in this matter. Your loved one may be more sympathetic and understanding than you realize! You have a simple choice: say what you want to say, and get it out of your system; or say nothing, but be prepared to linger with your mind's burden.

## FOREFATHER (see FAMILY TREE)

## FOREHEAD

An unwrinkled forehead reveals that you have a long road to follow and much to learn and experience. As you do, a greater philosophy of life, death, time, and space will be revealed to you. Your thinking is brilliant! Combining this fact with your determination, abilities, and sound beliefs should give you an inkling that you are destined for great achievements within your lifetime.

A wrinkled forehead reveals that you are very worried, disappointed, or disgusted with yourself for something you said or did recently. The bleak world outlook makes you terribly depressed. Who needs more depression? This dream shows that you will find a way to solve your problems. However, do not expect immediate results unless you are honest, humble, and sincere in your attempts.

## FOREIGNER

This dream advises you to adjust to your present circumstances with down-to-earth logic and courage. Your losses in life are trying experiences, but you must learn to face your heartaches with continued hope and understanding. You are not alone! There are inner struggles, battles, and wars people master on a daily basis. This dream advises you to isolate yourself for a while. Sit down, relax, and meditate. Slowly, let there be stillness within you. Smile, make a wish, say a prayer, and your sorrows will commence to disappear from view. You will have in effect opened the door for God to help you, and He will carry you past your sorrows and your strife.

**FOREMAN**

You have a one-track mind! You do not give many people a chance to explain themselves, to defend themselves, or to offer you some good, wholesome opinion or advice about certain vital matters of concern. Nothing is gained by this attitude. Your dream advises you to show greater respect for the wisdom and sensitivity of the human mind! Show more fairness and sensibility in dealing with others; and you will find that others will begin to look up to you, not away from you.

**FOREPLAY** (see **INTERCOURSE**)

**FORESKIN** (see **GENITALS**)

**FOREST**

Seeing a lush green forest indicates that matters within and around you are relatively all right. What could be more comforting than to have a dream knowing that situations will continue to get better? Well, your dream happily confirms this revelation to you. Many of your fondest wishes will be realized during the days or months to follow.

Seeing a forest that is destroyed, decayed, or uninhabitable suggests that some of your past difficulties, phobias, or fears still linger within you. These difficulties cannot simply disappear overnight unless you make some serious attempts to solve or settle whatever it is that bothers you. If, for example, someone else is handling some matter of importance for you, and somehow you feel that this person is not working hard enough for you, then look elsewhere. This dream is trying to advise you to "clean your past slate" so that you can forge ahead with greater peace and comfort.

**FORESTRY** (see **CONSERVATIONIST** or **FOREST**)

**FOREWARD** (see **BOOK** or **INTRODUCTION**)

**FOREWARNING** (i.e., premonition) (see *also* **CAUTION**)

Seeing or experiencing a forewarning within a dream state merely advises you to be more aware of any danger and/or unnecessary upheavals within your wake state. Many people experience some type of forewarning while asleep or awake; but still they fail to use common sense and inner wisdom and heed those foreboding signs. They follow, instead, that old adage that "it can never happen to me". Anything can happen to anyone if they are not careful; yes, including you! Any forewarning, whether revealed to you or unwittingly imagined by you, should at least be seriously reflected upon, sifted, and weighed as to the possibility or impossibility of it actually happening. Sometimes, what we feel is impossible can be possible, or vice versa. Note, as well, that to see a forewarning continually for about a week or two within your dream state can be prophetic (e.g., car accident, sickness, death). In other words, what you see is what will happen, unless you somehow heed the warning or, if possible, forewarn those involved.

## FORGERY

There is no greater sadness in life than to see some people's stupidity, folly, or vices being foisted upon other people (e.g., drugs, prostitution). You see this hopeless situation from time to time, but there is very little you can do to help. These wrongdoers are lost, imprisoned souls who can never really know hope or happiness unless they vanquish their misconceptions and dishonesties about themselves. When they finally eradicate the pain, shame, or guilt of their past, they will be on the road to recovery. This road to recovery may not be easy but, in the long run, it is far worth their efforts. It is far better to save one's soul, than to ignore one's soul. Perhaps in time, you will find a way to assist these lost souls; but if not, say a prayer for their "conversion to God".

## FORGETFULNESS (see AMNESIA or NEGLECTFULNESS)

## FORGIVENESS

One or several of the following definitions may be applicable: A) that you can forgive a person, and you can forget the trespasses done against you; or B) that you can forgive a person, but you cannot forget the wrongs committed against you; or C) that you cannot forgive anyone or forget anything done against you; or D) that no one treats you "fair and square so why should I treat them otherwise?"; or E) that you do not always believe some people when they apologize or when they ask for forgiveness; or F) that you recently apologized to someone; but, deep down, you did not mean what you said; or G) that this dream has little or no significance to you at all at this time.

## FORK (see SILVERWARE or TOOL)

**FORMULA**
Seeing or creating a formula or a recipe reveals that you will have a sudden change of mind about something you have been planning to do, purchase, and so on. Your intuition will be correct in this matter! You will not only be saving yourself a lot of wear and tear, but you could be saving yourself some money, as well.

**FORNICATION** (see **ADULTERY**)

**FORT**
Some pressing matter may force you to borrow money from a bank, loan institution, friend, relative, or acquaintance. This recourse could perhaps alleviate some of the financial tensions and uncertainties that you have been experiencing lately. This dream also reveals that sometimes your extravagant spending habits go beyond the bounds of logic. A good policy to employ would be to hold back on great luxuries until you can absolutely afford them or until you feel financially secure enough to afford them. Remember: not having something today does not imply that you cannot have these same things in the future. Be patient. When times are hard, learn from this experience; when times are good, enjoy this experience.

**FORTRESS** (see **FORT**)

**FORTUNE**
To seek a fortune or to amass a fortune advises you to be very careful about some business proposition, some personal investments, or signing some contract that promises you more than it can deliver. Your losses in these matters can be far greater than your gains! If nothing else, be prudent; otherwise you may be paying a fortune for legal fees to get you out of what could be a crooked mess!

**FORTUNETELLER** (e.g., palm reader, card reader)
Do not be afraid to tap or to explore for more potentials or talents within your being. Keep searching, analyzing, and perceiving, and honestly believe that there is more within your being than you have thus far thought possible. There truly is more, but you must stop being so routine oriented or complacent with what you have now. There is a vast universe within your being which can be explored through silence, meditation, and good thoughts. These states of purification can bring

forth those latent potentials or talents sitting dormant within your being. Remember: you are the key, and your soul has a hidden door which can be opened. Find that door, open it, and then see what rightfully belongs to you.

## FOSSIL
Along your destination in life you should be able to plod onwards rather comfortably, accepting your responsibilities and challenges with reassuring dependability, maturity, and pleasure. You will excel in whatever line of work you choose. Water, great heights, and scenic places all fascinate you. This affirms that you are attracted to the finer things of life and/or to the beauties of nature and life itself.

## FOUNDATION (i.e., the base of a building generally made of concrete, etc.)
You are not too easily convinced when someone gives you good advice or when someone tells you the truth about something. Regretfully, you keep seeing flaws in just about everything you read, see, or hear. Perhaps you are masking your own fears, inhibitions, or mistrust of self? Only you can answer that question. This dream advises you to build all your good thoughts from a foundation to a spire, realizing that as you go upwards there will be flaws and truths here and there. Even if you have to go downwards once in a while, you will also experience flaws and truths here and there, as well. Do not be too harsh on these realities of life, for even within a flaw there lies some truth; or within a truth, there can also be a flaw or two. Be more open-minded, and the world you presently see and understand will expand around you.

## FOUNTAIN (i.e., drinking fountain, soda fountain, bar fountain)
Unfortunately, you seem to have a great talent for creating more incidental problems for yourself than you can honestly handle or solve. Making promises you cannot keep, taking on more work than you can handle, procrastinating, and being late for appointments are but a few of the incidental troubles you cause yourself. The bottom line is that although you are highly intelligent, you are just as highly unorganized. Can you visualize your mind as having dozens of rooms? What you are in effect doing is trying to be in every room at once. This you cannot do. Naturally, you should go to one room at a time, do what you have to do there, then proceed on to the next room, and so forth. Know

your limits; be slow and efficient, if you must; and, above all, have the patience to see things through. No job is worth doing unless you do it right!

**FOUNTAIN PEN** (See **PEN**)

**FOWL** (see **CHICK, CHICKEN, BIRD**, or **POULTRY**)

**FOX**

Beware of being robbed or cheated by some unscrupulous individual. Although this dream warning is only for a week's duration, it always pays to be observant and alert where any type of thievery is involved. On the other side of the coin, this dream also reveals that you will be receiving a gift of love and appreciation from someone before too long.

**FRAMEWORK**

Seeing the framework of a building implies that you would very much like to start all over again to make things right, just, and wholesome in your life. There is so much in life that has upset and disturbed your inner peace that you cannot possibly fathom how you survived up to this point. You can surmount your present disillusionments but not without prayer, hope, and determination. If you maintain a hopeless, spiritless attitude, then do not expect too much change in your present situation.

Seeing the framework of a vehicle, airplane, ship, or other water vehicle suggests that you are going through a trying, transitional period. At this time, you are a very moody, difficult person to know and understand (e.g., growing pains, change of life, having a stroke of bad luck). Whatever your problems may be, this dream advises you to do your very best not to be so hard on yourself and on others around you. There are some people who are a lot worse off than you will ever be. You have a support system of loving people around you. Cherish what you have now, and do not say things you may later regret.

**FRATERNITY** (see **ORGANIZATION**)

**FRAUD** (see **CHEATING, DECEPTION, IMPERSONATION**, or **THIEVERY**)

## FREAK

Life is filled with sorrows; not only during your wake state, but during your sleep state as well. This vision encourages you to be more understanding, compassionate, and helpful to those unfortunate beings who suffer daily because of some physical or mental impediment. Do volunteer work at a hospital, mental institution, and so on. Sometimes, there are not enough hands to go around to somehow tell these people that someone cares.

## FREEDOM (see LIBERATION)

## FREEWAY (see HIGHWAY or PASSAGEWAY)

## FREEZER (e.g., refrigerator, deep freezer, icebox, ice chest)

This dream advises you to cool or freeze your present plans or inclinations. Otherwise, you may be disappointed! Sometimes people reach out for something they think they must have or they must do, yet much later they realize that the grass was not so green on the other side of the fence. Sadly, human nature being what it is, you may have to find that out for yourself.

## FREIGHTER (see SHIP)

## FREIGHT TRAIN (see RAILROAD)

## FRESHMAN (i.e., a first year college student, or a first year student of a high school, or a person involved in any undertaking or venture for the first year)

Never let go of your high aspirations, worthy thoughts, and actions! You have much to offer this world; and, by the stars above, you will. In many respects, it is people like you who are the foundation for a better tomorrow. The poet, philosopher, composer, artist, scientist, and hosts of other talents on this planet have contributed towards Earth's betterment. So you, too, will enter a new space age with remarkable insight, truth, and giving.

## FRIAR (see MONK)

## FRIEND

Seeing a friend or acquaintance friend within a dream state

implies that this person may be thinking about you, that you will see this friend before too long, or that they are in some type of mental, physical, or spiritual difficulty. It is also quite conceivable that you will have some hand in advising or assisting your friend in some manner before too long.

Dreaming about a friend who has passed away implies that this person comes into your dream state for a reason. A prayer is requested from you specifically. Say a prayer for your friend, and do not forget to tell them to "ask for the Light"!

**FRIGIDITY** (i.e., habitual failure of a woman to become sexually aroused, or abnormal repulsion by sexual activity)

Having a dream of this nature could imply that you are, in fact, frigid. If so, some medical or psychological advice or assistance could be in order. If the above is not applicable to you, then this dream infers that you are treating your spouse indifferently instead of as a loving human being. Perhaps you have your prime reasons. Maybe your spouse is not a kindly human being, and you have no recourse but to reject your spouse's immature and irresponsible behaviour. Who knows! Only you have the answer. This problem can only be solved if two people are working in harmony with each other, rather than against each other. Unfortunately, some people simply refuse to change!

**FROG**

You will be disappointed with someone or something before too long. In some respects, this situation will be like having the rug pulled from right under you! You are strongly urged not to retaliate; rather, keep a calm, cool, and collected head on your shoulders. By doing so, you will come out of this quandary a little wiser and far more discerning should this type of circumstance ever repeat itself.

**FROGMAN** (see **DIVER**)

**FROST**

There are thousands of people who do not necessarily relish the thought of going to work every day or becoming totally immersed in domestic chores and activities. What you need is some diversion from your regular work activities (e.g., hobbies, night courses, dancing, sports). You need to balance your life in a fair and equitable manner.

Simply get out of the rut you are in with a wholesome attitude! The good things you do for yourself are for your benefit, well-being, and happiness. No one can give you peace of mind unless you make some attempts to make this realistically possible yourself.

**FROSTING** (e.g., icing on a cake) (see *also* **FOOD**)

Do not be deceived by the frosting you see within your dream. It may be enticing and edible, but not necessarily nutritious to the mind and body. Be careful! Some action or plan which you, a loved one, or a friend may have could backfire, resulting in emotional anguish. Perhaps you fail to realize just how well off you are now! Remember, if your high expectations do not pan out, you will only have yourself to blame. Such is life with its many hard-learned lessons!

**FRUIT**

You are a very adaptable, likeable person. Having a keen sense of judgment and being sensible and headstrong allows you to be more adventurous and daring than most people. You are not afraid to suffer or to forge ahead through any type of difficulty. As well, you are not afraid of anyone or practically anything that tends to impede your progress in life. Your shrewd thinking, common sense, and "gift of the mouth" are all that you will ever need!

**FRYING PAN** (see **UTENSIL**)

**FUEL** (e.g., coal, gas, kerosene, oil, wax, wood)

You are presently satiated, bored, and unhappy with your present circumstances and environment. This could refer to home or work conditions, surrounding neighbourhood, your city, your town, province, state, and so on. It seems that the more you reflect upon dissatisfactions, the greater your urges are to move. Maybe you will; maybe you will not. This entire matter will rest squarely on your mind. Are you making the right or wrong decision? A right decision can only be made with a clear, uncluttered mind. No one thinks clearly if angry, vexed, or impatient. Give yourself a bit more time in this matter. In about a week or two, see how you feel. If situations have improved, maybe you will stay. If not, then maybe you will move.

**FULFILLMENT** (see **COMPLETION**)

## FUMIGATOR

Seeing or being a fumigator within a dream intimates that you are very sensitive to chemical smells, allergies, certain types of water, insects, and so on. Since you already know this, your dream is merely reaffirming your state of being in such matters. Some people happen to be more sensitive to certain things in life; you just happen to be one of them.

## FUNERAL (see *also* BURIAL)

This dream does not imply that there will be a funeral or a loss to you at all. Actually, this dream wants you to be more willing to accept life's challenges in a more sensible manner and to be willing to grasp and understand the implications of life after death. For those who believe that death is a final act to life—well, that's their loss and ignorance. But for those who know and believe that death is no more than a new beginning, a new road to life, then truly they are guided by inner wisdom. There are many Mansions on the other side of life. Believe it! What you learn now and the good things you do now all have a bearing upon which Mansion you will enter. It is that simple.

## FUNERAL HOME

Many people shudder at the fact of seeing a funeral home during their wake state. Seeing one or entering one within a dream state may be just as frightening. This dream symbolism indicates that you have some doubts about life and many doubts about death; these bother you, from time to time. Allay your fears! The body, as you know, can die—but not the soul. The soul lives forever! In time, some personal experiences may prove this truth to you.

## FUNNEL (i.e., a cone with a tube ending for pouring liquids into bottles, containers)

What is life without some struggle? It would be a rather sad state of affairs not to be able to think and do things for yourself. Laziness breeds inner discontent, so life without some struggle would simply never do. There are no real shortcuts in ploughing a field or in clearing the land. What has to be done, has to be done. The same is applicable to every living being on this planet. When you are facing some minor or major trials and tribulations, you have to face your problems head-on, solve them, and keep moving onwards. Those who seek shortcuts in matters that they should face up to will find out, sooner or later, that their attempts were merely detours—merely half-hearted victories! They may have to confront their problems again and again until they learn to deal with their struggles, piece by piece. Mastery of one's struggles brings forth maturity, courage, and appreciation. Who could possibly ask for more?

**FURNACE**
You will be or are presently repairing or painting your premises or something on your premises. As mundane as this definition may sound to you, it is good to know that your dream state is in harmony with what you are doing or intend to do.

**FURNITURE (see BED, CABINET, CHAIR, CHEST OF DRAWERS, COFFEE TABLE, COUCH, CRIB, CUPBOARD, DESK, DRESSER, FOOTSTOOL, HIGHCHAIR, HOPE CHEST, LOVE SEAT, RECORD PLAYER, ROCKING CHAIR, SPINNING WHEEL, TABLE, or TELEVISION)**
When things tend to go your way, you are secure and ecstatic; however, when things do not go your way, you are overcome with depression and panic. It is not unusual or unnatural for anyone to feel like this; try, if you will though, not to feel so terribly isolated and alone when unpredictable and unforeseen events occur in your life. Your faith and courage alone could move a mountain or two, so never let go of that inner strength, not even for a moment. This inner strength should be your lifetime companion!

**FURROW (see RUT)**

**FUSELAGE (see AIRPLANE)**

**FUSSINESS**
Fussiness within a dream state implies that you or someone within your household is fussy or hard to please. Most households have one or two characters who behave like this, so you are not alone. Realize that being fussy with anyone, anywhere, anytime is a habit that can be mastered. The fussy person should simply settle their mind; count to ten; and then admit that their behaviour is inappropriate.

**FUTURE** (see *also* **AFTERLIFE, JUDGMENT DAY,** or **PROPHECY**)

Seeing a futuristic scene or event could be a prophetic dream. In other words, what you are seeing will eventually take place. People who experience consistent futuristic dreams should always attempt to guide or advise people whom they recognize within their dream state. But they must always be certain that their perceptions are accurate, honest, and sincere. The future is important to all of us. We all stand to gain from a God-given foreknowledge of events released through a prophetic dream. Many people have been guided this way in life.

**GALAXY** (i.e., often referred to as the Milky Way; a galaxy is composed of millions or billions of stars)

Experience will always be your teacher, and the joy of being self-reliant and appreciative will carry you through some of your darkest and brightest hours. You seem to be somewhat concerned about your future. However, your dream assures you that, as time goes on, you will ascend to illuminable heights of prominence and leadership in your chosen work. You have come to earth to seek knowledge and truth, but you also have an extraordinary capacity to lift the foundation of your spirit beyond this world with your perceptive mind. You return home with a host of knowledge and wisdom, only to discover that, in all reality, most things in life are not only free, but soul-rewarding as well!

**GALE** (see **STORM**)

**GALLEON** (see **SHIP**)

**GALLERY** (i.e., a display room of a museum or an art gallery)

You have two choices to make on this planet Earth: a) to find your way to a better future through prayer, encouragement, and strength; or b) to remain aloof, proud, and lonely. The blessings that come with the first choice are infinite; the lessons that come with the second are vain, contemptuous wounds to the soul. When you honestly begin to practice humility and thankfulness in your life, and when you commence to see equality in others, you will then know your true purpose on earth. You have a brilliant mind; do not flaunt it—simply use it wisely.

**GALLEY** (see **SHIP**)

**GALLOWS** (see **HANGING** or **KILL**)

**GAMBLE** (see *also* **BET** or **CASINO**)

The act of gambling within a dream infers that laziness and both lack of determination and consistency at home and at work are your weaker points in life. It seems that you are looking for more leisure time in your life rather than responsible time. This attitude cannot bring you happiness forever! Sooner or later, you will have to face yourself head-on in a more realistic manner. Do you wish to progress in life or regress in life? That will be your prime, haunting question. Less wishful thinking and more determined thinking on your part could make your tomorrows more worthy, productive, and successful.

**GAME** (see *also* **ATHLETE, BILLIARDS, BOWLING, CARD, DIVER, GAMBLE, JUMP, SKATE, SKI, SLEDDING, SWIMMING,** or **TOY**)

You always strive to be fair-minded in things that you do; and rarely, if ever, are you a poor loser in the eyes of others. It appears that you know exactly what to do in difficult times. You may occasionally fumble and fall, but you quickly pick yourself up and simply start again. Only this time, you utilize greater foresight and skill! You will always be a winner because of your positive determination, sense of humor, and all-round sincerity.

**GANG** (see **CRIMINAL** or **JUVENILE DELINQUENCY**)

**GANGSTER** (see **CRIMINAL**)

**GARAGE**

Some people in your past have taken advantage of your nature, hospitality, and money. Your prime fear is that someone will take advantage of you again. This is possible. However, since you learned a very hard lesson in your past already, it is unlikely that you would ever allow this to happen again. Allay your fears and be kindly; but also be more discerning in the company you keep.

## GARBAGE

Sometimes you feel totally useless and hopeless. This low opinion of yourself will prevail unless you act upon the positive aspects of your life. Absolutely nothing is useless or hopeless, especially you! There is very little progress in your existence now simply because you continue to live in the past. You are not letting go of your past's irritations and cheerless times. You cannot continually have one foot somewhere back in time and another foot somewhere in the present. You will not be able to go forward this way. Today counts; yesterday is gone! Your road to recovery and happiness is quite simple: pray; accept yourself totally for being a person with a heart, mind, and soul like everyone else; do not hate so many things; and appreciate the faith and hope that is still within you. You are a child of God! Since He looks after the smallest seeds on earth, how could you possibly think that He would ignore you? Why, you are one of His Greatest Creations! To feel good about yourself means that you will feel good about all things. Love your fellow man, be good and inspiring, and you will then be happy with yourself.

## GARDEN

Seeing a garden or working in one with a happy frame of mind signifies that you are a very strong-willed person who works very hard. You heed advise only when it is absolutely necessary; otherwise, you prefer to think and do things your way. In time, there will be more leisure periods for you; but, in the interim, you prefer to keep busy, active, and productive. Besides, you are more "relaxed" when you are working.

To work in or to see a garden with a sad, dejected frame of mind indicates financial struggles, sickness, or the slandering of your good name by someone. These unhappy, worrisome times show no letup for quite some time to come. Be strong, though; for from all this experience you will amass a fortune of insight and knowledge.

**GARDENER** (see **GARDENER**)

**GARLIC** (see **FOOD** or **PLANT**)

**GARMENT** (see **CLOTHES**)

**GARRISON** (see **FORT**)

## GAS (see FLATUS or FUEL)

## GAS CHAMBER

Adverse times lie ahead for you or for some member of your family if you see a gas chamber by itself or if you see yourself or someone else being led into a gas chamber. It appears that you or some family member is pursuing life in a rather reckless, uncaring, and short-sighted manner (e.g., drugs, alcoholism, prostitution, thievery). Whatever the wrongdoing may be, this dream counsels you or the family member to disband all negative attitudes and actions before great trouble and difficulties arise.

## GAS MASK (see MASK)

## GAS PUMP (see PUMP)

## GAS STATION

You often give good advice to people, yet you are failing to follow this wholesome advice yourself. Many people do this to themselves. Perhaps it is easier to help others than it is to help oneself in the same predicament. When you are faced with some hard reality about life or yourself, the best policy is to heed your positive intuition or instincts. Nine times out of ten, you will be correct in your feelings. If you ponder too much about your problems, you can become confused, panic-stricken, and—ultimately—you can make wrong decisions or do the wrong thing for yourself. Since you have the innate ability to think for others, you should have the same ability to think for yourself.

## GATE

Seeing or using a gate intimates that some of your immediate plans or wishes will come true (e.g., travel, new home, becoming pregnant). The pending improvements in your life will bring happiness, peace of mind, and an ample amount of financial security.

Seeing a gate that cannot be opened, no matter how hard you try, suggests that some turmoil and restlessness may assail you and your family (e.g., loss of revenue, losing a job, sickness, emotional hardships). You are advised to be very logical and mature during this trying time. Doing so will make matters so much easier to handle; and, before you know it, better times will come your way.

## GAYNESS (see HOMOSEXUALITY)

**GEAR** (i.e., a train of toothed wheels and pinions for transmitting motion)

Your suspicions and hostilities can create many hardships for you in the not too distant future. For the sake of your peace of mind and happiness, you are strongly urged to reconsider and rectify some of your one-sided and narrow-minded views and actions. You have affected some people already. Be careful; those people you see, know, and perhaps love today may not be there for you tomorrow.

**GEARSHIFT** (see **GEAR**)

**GEESE** (see **BIRD** or **POULTRY**)

**GEISHA**

You display a great amount of loyalty towards others, self-reliance in your actions, and philosophic comprehension within your thoughts and feelings. Magnetism, charm, and wit are all added graces bestowed upon your good personality. You are an inspiration to many and will continue to be so throughout your life. Your future holds progress, good fortune, and happiness for you. Indeed, you are a very special and fortunate human being!

**GEM** (see **JEWELLERY**)

**GENESIS** (see *also* **BIBLE** or **UNIVERSE**)

This dream, although rare, wishes to state that man should not destroy life in any way; rather, man should reach out to all nations with peace, harmony, and giving. Unfortunately, the forces of good and evil reign supreme on this earth, thus placing man at a crossroads where total peace is concerned, but it will not always be this way. When God's Heavenly Light descends upon planet Earth, man will then see a new order—a new time. You might even say man will eventually be experiencing a new genesis of awareness and love on a universal scale. This may not be too far off, either.

**GENITALS**

You have a healthy or unhealthy attitude about sex should you dream about sexual organs. If you are a levelheaded and mature person, then a dream of this nature should not disturb you at all. You accept sexual matters for what they are instead of going to emotional extremes or creating problems for yourself. However, if you are not sensible and mature in matters of sex, then a dream of this nature could arouse or incite your problems (e.g., sexual fetishes, rape, lust). People with sexual problems should always seek professional help and guidance. They should also know that time, honesty, introspection, and determination are key factors that can assist them in facing their problem(s).

## GENIUS

If you are in fact a genius and dream about seeing or being one, then your dream is simply reflecting upon your special gifts or talents in some way. Should you not be a genius but dream of seeing or being one, then this implies that you would like to play some prominent role within your society, state, country, or the world at large. Are these delusions of grandeur? No, not necessarily so. Many outstanding people who are not in the genius category have contributed immeasurably to the world and continue to do so. The point is that individuals who apply themselves with great spirit (force, drive, impetus) can make a tremendous mark upon this planet. You do not have to be a genius to be great or immortal; you just have to be determined!

## GENOCIDE (i.e., an action or program intended to destroy a race of people or ethnic group)

It is bad enough to dream about genocide let alone know that this action has already been perpetrated upon innocent people on earth. This dream is of a world order and specifically forewarns of earthquakes, fire, flood, famine, pestilence, war, and other unimaginable calamities that will beset life upon this planet. Man's so-called progress can be a very difficult experience; but time has a way of healing all worldly problems.

## GEOMETRY (see MATHEMATICS)

## GEYSER

You may be inviting some trouble into your life. Whether this stems from jealousy, greed, hate, lust, or another type of negativity within your being, you are strongly urged to reconsider your stand in this matter. Do not do something you may regret later on. Life is far too precious to waste on evil or wicked actions. Think carefully upon these words!

**GHETTO** (i.e., an area of a city where a minority group of people live because of economic reasons or discrimination)

One or several of the following definitions may be applicable: A) that you are already living in a ghetto and see no hope of, or encouragement to, ever coming out of this state; or B) that you once lived in a ghetto and vow that you would never live under those conditions again; or C) that you are opposed to any society which would allow its people to live under such dire conditions; or D) that you are bitter about greedy and narrow-minded governments of the world who make little attempt to wipe out poverty and racial discrimination; or E) that you are blaming God for man's greed and lack of concern for poor people; or F) that your society is doing its best to assist people in ghettos or abject poverty; or G) that someday you know you will leave your ghetto; or H) that this dream has little or no meaning for you at this time.

**GHOST**

The appearance of a ghost within a dream is rarely clear and distinct, as opposed to a deceased family member, friend, and so on who appears totally real and natural-looking within a sleep state. First, ghosts are earth-bound souls who have passed away with "something" troubling them. While alive, they could have committed suicide unbeknownst to anyone, or could have committed a so-called perfect crime, or could have been involved in some undetected corruption, and so forth. In other words, their "perfectly" executed foul deeds went with them to the grave. These ghost beings now desperately wish to communicate with someone in order to reveal their wrongdoings to them or wish to reveal something they stored away in secrecy. Once earth-bound soul beings reveal their wrongdoings or secret to a receptive individual on earth, they are free to progress onwards to their proper mansion. However, until such a time, they are locked in some vortex between this side of life and the other side of life. If the ghost you happen to see in your dream fails to reveal anything to you, then simply let your dream go by as being tension oriented. In other words, you may have talked about ghosts recently, or you may have read something about them recently, causing their image to be subconsciously presented to you within your dream state.

**GHOUL** (see **DEMON**)

## GIANT

Seeing a giant person or animal within a dream state infers that you should concentrate more on your talents and skills. It appears that recently you have been a bit uncaring or discouraged about your career, work habits, other work disparities, and so on. Allay your fears! You will be happy and successful in life. Why not? You certainly have the intelligence, maturity, and determination to make your wish and dreams come true. If John Doe down the street can make it in life, then by all that is true and just, so can you!

Giants (human or animal) battling within a dream reveals that you have a very changeable and unpredictable nature. You can be your own worst enemy at times. For your own good, settle down within yourself. If you honestly want to, you can help yourself in this matter. When you intend to do something good and honourable, do not hold yourself back from this action; just do it! When you speak with others and they make some plans with you, do not back down at the last minute. This action disappoints everyone! You are only as honourable and as just as the things you say or do in life.

## GIBBON (see APE)

## GIFT

To receive a gift indicates that you will be giving a gift to someone before too long. On the other hand, to give a gift to someone within a dream indicates that you will be receiving a gift before too long. That is all.

## GIGGLE (see LAUGHTER)

## GIGOLO (i.e., a paid escort or male prostitute)

Symbolically, you may be a gigolo in real life and your dream is merely reflecting your way of life; you either envy or abhor the lifestyle of a gigolo; or, last, you are an unfaithful person not only to yourself, but to your loved ones as well. Only you know who you are or whether your actions in life are honourable or deceitful; only you can make things right or wrong for yourself. In the end, it is you who must live with yourself.

## GINGER (see SPICE)

## GIRAFFE

There is no necessity to rebel or to be angered at good thoughts and actions that are directed towards you by family members, friends, acquaintances, and so on. No one wishes you any harm whatsoever! Most people enjoy your company. The situation shown here is that, often, you wish to be left alone for a time without interference from anyone. However, that is not always the way things are around your home, work, or school. Do not be vexed; rather, consider it to be a privilege and an honour that you are so well-admired and highly thought of—and in such a loving, caring manner. And, yes, you are entitled to some privacy from time to time; this should be understood by those who know you.

## GIRDLE (see CLOTHES)

## GIRLFRIEND

Will your future bring you more happiness than your past? Someday, love and happiness will shine upon you more than you could possibly envision if you dream about a girlfriend whom you like, admire, and respect. By being very patient and obedient to your better instincts, there will be much rejoicing in your lifetime.

Dreaming about a girlfriend whom you do not necessarily like, admire, or respect reveals that you are far too impatient with yourself and with others to actually know what you want in life at this time. There are one-sided elements here which reveal that you would like someone to bring you happiness, but you are not willing to give them happiness. Life just does not work this way! If love or respect is not reciprocated between two people then, realistically, there can be no love or respect between these two people. It is that simple. People in this situation often deceive themselves into believing there is love—only to admit, years later, that they were afraid to face the truth about a no-win situation.

## GLACIER

Is there anything on this planet that will make you happy? Whether situations are good or bad, you always find time to bicker and complain. The positive and negative aspects in life come in cycles or spurts. You must learn to cope with both situations through understanding, determination, and belief in yourself and in others. Be more grateful for being as lucky and fortunate as you have been thus far. There are some people who would love to be in your shoes!

## GLADIATOR

Seeing a gladiator or being one suggests that sexual matters of concern often dominate your mind. This could very well be because you are oversexed, or you are undersexed. Whatever your problems may be in this regard, you would be advised to seek some professional guidance to stabilize your thoughts and actions in this intimate and personal subject area.

## GLASSWARE

Seeing glassware intact and perhaps beautifully designed signifies the wholesome attention and care you devote towards your loved ones. Your presence is like a breath of fresh air. You possess many fine qualities which simply bring out the good in other people. You are living proof that there is abundant hope for mankind, simply because people like you honestly and sincerely care!

Seeing broken or disfigured glassware intimates that someone is not treating you fairly or properly. If you know this to be true and continue to live with this situation, then do not complain. However, if you know beyond any shadow of a doubt that you cannot live under these circumstances, then surrender yourself to better pursuits in life. A move may be in store for you.

## GLIDER (see AIRPLANE)

## GLOBE (see EARTH or PLANET)

## GLOVE

This wearing apparel for the hands indicates that you will be assisted in some manner, within a day or two, from an unknown source or that you will assist someone who requires spiritual, moral, or financial help (e.g., family member, friend, neighbour, stranger). There is a feeling of good will in the air, and you will be a part of it.

## GLUE

You are either glued to a boring or to a happy situation within your life. If you are bored with something, do your best to maintain other interests as well. Your life can only be as dull or as interesting as you want it to be. Being in a happy situation, on the other hand, is certainly very gratifying. People strive harder and work harder in happy environments. Happiness, though, is not given to anyone on a silver platter; it must be earned.

## GOAT

Seeing a goat grazing or resting peacefully suggests that you are very content with your life. You are quite adept at handling almost any type of situation that comes your way. You are not afraid to forge ahead under difficult circumstances, nor are you afraid of working hard for some belief, cause, or principle. Your courage and stamina are to be admired. Look forward to many forthcoming successes!

Seeing a goat that is lost, agitated, or hurt signifies that you are impatient, confused, and somewhat stifled by certain recent events. It appears that these events could have been avoided, but someone decided to stir up trouble. This will settle in time; relax. Keep yourself busy, and try to find a few more interests in your life. Remember: a busy person very often forgets to worry!

## GOD (see *also* JESUS)

To dream about seeing God Himself would be such a rich, rewarding, and historical event that the dreamer would be "blinded" with sheer ecstasy and awe! A few privileged beings on earth may have experienced this very rare, gifted vision. This dream of dreams implies that something very special is about to happen to the dreamer. In effect, this could pertain to a miracle healing, transformation, second sight, prophecy, new abilities or talents, or whatever joys or blessings God wishes to bestow upon one so privileged to see Him. The Pure Light of God is billions of times brighter than our sun. Can you imagine the joy in just seeing a fraction of that Light? Can you imagine the inner bliss in just feeling a fraction of that Light?

(*Note*: You may also have the pleasure of knowing that if, for example, you are experiencing a very negative dream but at the very end of your dream sequence or anywhere during your dream sequence you happen to see God, then this symbolism of God takes precedence over your entire bad dream. Consequently, you have nothing to worry about simply because God acts as a "buffer zone" to anything negative within a dream.)

## GODCHILD

Dreaming about a godchild intimates that this person may need your advice or guidance before too long, or you will be seeing the godchild's parents, along with the goddaughter or godson, in the very near future. The overall picture to the above-mentioned definitions reveals mutual understanding and contentment.

## GODPARENT

Dreaming about your godparents symbolizes a need for you to reevaluate your ideals, beliefs, and social standards in life. It appears that far too much emphasis is placed upon materialistic gains rather than spiritual gains in your life. Do not lose sight of what prayer can do for you or how you can refine your mind and soul with Christ-like thoughts and feelings through positive actions and deeds. Do not just sit back, complacently thinking that you have it all when in fact your spiritual necessities go unattended. True prosperity is knowing you belong to Earth, and you belong to God; do not ignore His Great Love for you.

## GOGGLES (see EYEGLASS)

## GOLD

Dreaming about gold itself or gold coloured objects (not jewelry) is an ill-omened sign. Sadly, this dream symbolism signifies untimely events could transpire either to the dreamer, to a loved one, or to very close friend (e.g., heart attack, accident). Be especially alert for any unusual health problems at this time for yourself or for anyone else concerned. Be also extremely cautious when traveling in a vehicle. A prayer from the depths of your soul is very essential at this time. Perhaps, with your earnest prayer, this heaviness and foreboding will pass by, leaving everyone safe and sound.

## GOLF (see GAME)

## GONDOLA

This dream reveals that you appear to be overworked, underpaid, and unappreciated for all your good efforts. Obviously, you feel some resentments for what is transpiring, but there is very little you can do about this matter, at this time. There will be an opportunity in the very near future which will allow you to stress some demands for your worth or talents. Be patient. Surprisingly, what you thought was a hopeless situation will now turn out to be a prosperous situation!

## GONORRHEA (see INTERCOURSE, SEX, or SICKNESS)

## GORILLA (see APE)

## GOSPEL (see BIBLE)

## GOSSIP

This dream shows that you are, in fact, a gossipy person or that you abhor this type of activity. The gossip normally looks for flaws in people, places, or things. However, they cannot see the same flaws or weaknesses within themselves. They are casting stones upon others with their actions and deeds. If you are a gossip, it would be a good idea to look at yourself in the mirror and see whether you are perfect or imperfect.

## GOVERNMENT

To dream about a government that appears relatively active, peaceful-looking, or more or less in order reveals that you are a very patriotic person. You are proud and happy to be living in a country where freedom and peace reign, side by side.

Seeing a corrupt, spiteful, hateful government, on the other hand, reveals that you are saddened for the many people who are suppressed, threatened, or tortured by false or dictatorial governments. There can be no joy in knowing there are people in some countries who experience countless hardships, limited freedom, and unbearable anguish because their government chooses to be vile and corrupt. Nothing is gained; those people responsible for any injustices to man will have a great debt to pay one day.

## GOVERNOR

If you are, in fact, a governor of a state, then your dream merely reflects your present position. If you are not a governor, then to see or be a governor within a dream intimates that you are concerned about a regional, national, or international situation. Perhaps, this is your cue to write to your governor or other government representative with your viewpoint(s) and concern over the matter that is bothering you. You will then have at least appeased your conscience.

## GOWN (see **CLOTHES**)

## GRADUATION

Your dream is like a diploma in that it is revealing the great strides you are making to become more responsible, respectable, and distinguished in your own right. It is quite obvious that you are maturing beyond your years in many ways. Your attitude and actions are very commendable and praiseworthy!

# GRAIN

Ripe, healthy-looking grain denotes busy times, good health, and prosperity to the dreamer. You can look forward to many rewarding achievements in the future because of your diligent and sincere work efforts.

Grain that is decayed, diseased, or destroyed foretells of privation and strife to you and to some areas of your country. These terrible tribulations will be very trying. Hence, hope, confidence, prayer, and determination are vital measures to uphold.

# GRANARY

To see a granary filled with ripened grain suggests that you will share some of your good tidings, expertise, or wealth with some other people (e.g., family members, friends, charity). You will then agree that it is far better to give than to receive. Sometimes, when people share what they have, they also receive greater blessings—in another way, from another source.

# GRANDCHILD

If the grandchild appears happy and content within your dream, then you can be assured that all is well where this person is concerned. You will probably be communicating or seeing your grandchild before too long.

If the grandchild is unhappy or in some sort of difficulty and anguish within your dream state, then you can be sure that something is wrong where your grandchild is concerned. It seems that your grandchild is desperately trying to communicate with you. Hopefully, this matter is not too serious. To allay your fears, though, it might be a good idea to communicate with your grandchild, just in case.

Seeing a grandchild who has already passed away suggests you say a prayer for him or her; your grandchild comes to you specifically for this reason. When you do say this prayer, please do not forget to tell your grandchild to "ask for the Light"!

# GRANDPARENT

Seeing a grandparent suggests that you should take stock of where you are going in life. In other words, are you happy with yourself, with what you are doing, with where you are headed, and so forth? If you are basically content with your lifestyle, then simply continue to forge ahead. If, however, you are not content with yourself or with the lifestyle you keep, then it is time to make some serious changes within yourself. In some respects, it is as though your grandparents were scolding you through your dream state. No one can lead you by the hand in these matters of personal change; you must do this alone. You will also feel much better for doing things your way—only this time, you will be doing things the right way.

To dream about a grandparent who has already passed away infers that this specific grandparent wants a prayer from you. Say a prayer, and when you do, please do not forget to tell your grandparent to "ask for the Light"!

**GRANT** (see **PRIZE**)

**GRAPE** (see **FRUIT**)

**GRAPHOLOGY** (i.e., handwriting analysis)
Perhaps you are a graphologist? If so, then your dream is merely reflecting the work that you do. If you are not, then this dream indicates that you have a very inquisitive and analytical mind. There is something you wish to know about yourself, either through therapy or perhaps through a psychic. Something puzzles you. You are also interested about someone else and about a vital matter that troubles you. You will eventually find your answers.

**GRASS** (see **FIELD, LAWN, MEADOW, PARK**, or **PASTURE**)

**GRASSHOPPER** (see **INSECT**)

**GRAVE** (i.e., a hole to bury a dead body) (see *also* **GRAVEYARD**)
Some people frighten themselves sick after seeing a grave in a dream. Their fear is totally groundless. This dream symbolism merely reminds the dreamer not to be too complacent with their truths, knowledge, and wisdom about matters of life, death, the universe, God, and so on. The grave symbolism is a reminder to fulfill your destined duties, obligations, aims, wishes, and the many other things you wish to do in your life. This is not a death dream; it is merely trying to tell you to accomplish some of those things you may have longed to do. Even if you live to be one hundred ten years old, this life is still so very short. So live your life to the fullest, in the best way possible—and never look back as you plough that field. How sad to know that

one has wasted time and efforts on nonsensical actions, only to pass away feeling dejected, unaccomplished, and unfulfilled.

(*Note*: Having a repetitive dream about a grave whereby you see a person hovering above or near the grave could mean that an accident, sickness, or death might befall that person. You may or may not know the person you see. If you do know this person, then do your best to forewarn them or, at best, tell them to be extremely careful at this time. Bear in mind that a dream of this nature must be seen practically on a daily basis for one to two weeks before this forewarning becomes prophetic.)

## GRAVEDIGGER

Any of the following definitions may be applicable to you: A) that you are, in fact, a gravedigger; or B) that you are afraid of death but often visualize your demise; or C) that you do or do not believe in a life hereafter; or D) that you wish you were never born but realize that you must go on, no matter what happens now or later; or E) that you may have suicidal tendencies because of some traumatic experiences in your life; or F) that this dream has little or no relevance to you at this time.

## GRAVESTONE

Seeing a gravestone with your name on it, that of someone else, or no name on it indicates that you are very unhappy about some of life's realities. You often wonder why people must suffer so bitterly on this planet. First, there is birth. Then there is some pain and anguish between birth and growing up. Finally a person supposedly grows up to maturity, and their struggles still persist! Yes, there is a minimal amount of happiness, but that is all. And to top things off, a person grows old and suffers some more! Is there no end to this strife? The cycle of life can he so bitter and unrewarding at times! We must all face these facts about this existence. Sometimes life is easy; sometimes it can be unbearable. But people still continue to weather their storms with their unshakable survival instincts. No one promised us a bed of roses here, and slowly—whether happy or sad—we must continue to move forward.

## GRAVEYARD

Someone whom you know is sick, is troubled, or appears to be making a wrong decision in their life. Inner faith, common sense, and determination could help him or her.

To defile a graveyard within a dream state reveals hardships to the dreamer. This could involve loss of a job or income, bankruptcy, severed family ties, divorce, romantic disappointments, mental breakdown, and so forth. Whatever the difficulties may be, you are advised to keep your head above water, to be logical in your thinking, and—above all—to try to rectify any problems which you know are brewing. If you can correct any matters that involve stubbornness or pride, then this dream's foreboding may be conquered. Don't just let things happen. Destiny can be altered to certain degrees, providing a person makes serious attempts to make things right in their life. You can if you really want to!

**GREASE** (See **LARD** or **LUBRICANT**)

**GREENHOUSE**

Apparently, you are adopting a more sane and calm perspective about yourself, about people around you, and about life in general. You are not as stressful, demanding, and temperamental anymore. You seem to have graduated to another school of thought and action; this is good news! Stay with this refinement of attitude and learning. As you will eventually see, this stepping stone in your life will bring you a great amount of happiness, learning, and prosperity!

**GRENADE** (see **BOMB**)

**GRIEF** (see **SORROW**)

**GROCERY** (see **FOOD** or **STORE**)

**GROOM** (see **BRIDEGROOM**)

**GROOVE** (see **RUT**)

**GROTTO** (see **CAVE**)

**GUARD** (see *also* **AIR FORCE, ARMY, BODYGUARD, COAST GUARD, CONVOY, ESCORT, FORT, GUARDHOUSE, NAVY, NIGHT WATCHMAN, PATROL, POLICE OFFICER, PRISON,** or **WARDEN**)

There are better times awaiting you down the road of life. This may not come to pass, however, unless you change your pessimistic and depressing concepts about yourself, your work, and your general outlook on life. Utilize your talents in the best way possible; do not shrug your duties on to someone else; be more sincere and self-reliant; learn to like yourself more. There are many fine qualities within you that you should accentuate. Strive to think more optimistically about things which inwardly or outwardly appear hopeless to you; you would be amazed at what a little bit of hope can do for you. As well, think more futuristically; see yourself today and where you would like to be ten years down the road. Visualize yourself as being alive, well, and prosperous ten years from now. Read good inspirational books about people who were lost in themselves but then discovered the truth, talents, and gifts within themselves. And, last, say a prayer, from time to time, to give a richer meaning and a greater purpose to your life.

**GUARDHOUSE** (i.e., a place where a person is confined for some minor or major military offence)

Although many people are free to walk and do as they please, they sometimes become imprisoned victims of their own thoughts, actions, and deeds. Fear of some kind is the reason! Their insecurities grow like weeds; and, eventually, it becomes difficult for these individuals to cope with themselves and with the outside world. Communicate with someone who understands, or seek help in a professional way. Remember: bottled problems can create greater problems.

**GUIDED MISSILE** (see **MISSILE**)

**GUIDEPOST** (see **SIGNPOST**)

**GUILLOTINE**

Some trying times are foreseen ahead for you in the not too distant future. You will handle and master these difficult times admirably. And, when this is all over, you will commence to rebuild your life with greater peace, discipline, and activity.

**GUILT**

Several of the following definitions may be applicable: A) that you are, in fact, guilty of something and wish to correct this matter before too long; or B) that you are guilty of something but have no intention of correcting this matter now or later; or C) that you may be partially guilty of something but feel that the other person involved made you react the way you did; or D) that you may feel guilty for not standing up for your honour and rights; or E) that someone made you feel guilty because of their personal hang-ups (e.g., alcoholism, drugs, physical abuse); or F) that you have been accused of being guilty of something but, in truth, you are innocent but have no way to prove otherwise; or, G) that you feel so hopelessly lost with guilt feelings about your past and your present that you honestly do not know which way to turn; or H) that you feel guilty for not making changes in your life when you had the chance to do so; or I) that you feel guilty for being some kind of burden on your family or someone else; or J) that you have quite recently helped someone with a guilt problem; or K) that you feel a person will harbour guilt until they finally decide to be self-forgiving; or L) that this dream has little or no relevance to you at this time.

**GUITAR** (see **INSTRUMENT**)

**GULL** (see **BIRD**)

**GUM** (see **CHEWING GUM**)

**GUN**

This dream presages spiritual peace, harmony, and better earthly conditions ahead for you. The more positive you are, the greater your rewards will be. But, assuming you are somewhat negative, then this dream would imply that you have to work much harder for your joys, peace, and earthly improvements.

**GUNNYSACK** (see **SACK**)

**GURU** (i.e., a spiritual Hindu teacher or adviser)

If the guru gives you some good advice within your dream, then you are making the right choices and plans in your life. You are headed for bigger and greater things (e.g., promotion, more travel, settling down to marry). Good fortune and good luck are on the horizon for you.

If the guru is giving you bad or false information, then you are advised to think about your thoughts, actions, and plans for a while. Do not rush into anything nor sign any contracts that you may regret much later. Do not be gullible at this time—be cautious and extremely logical!

**GUT** (see **INTESTINE**)

**GYMNASTICS** (see **ACROBAT**, **EXERCISE**, or **GAME**)

**GYPSY** (see *also* **NOMAD**)
   It appears that you must settle some fact or argument with your-self before you decide to forge ahead. Use clear deliberation and foresight to stay ahead of your past doubts and insecurities. Just how important are you to yourself? Sometimes people have to disregard sentimental views in favour of realistic views and actions. Do not frighten yourself into believing that you cannot succeed or cannot handle matters of great importance. You can do these things, and more! And, you probably will!

**HABIT** (i.e., an acquired, repeated action that is difficult to break)
   Performing a bad habit implies that your dream is giving you a taste of your own medicine. In other words, you are seeing yourself like other people see you when you display your habit. Not a pleasant sight, right? Your dream is trying to tell you that repulsive practices are neither polite nor edifying. You may not realize the effect these habits have on others. Many people are "dazed" when they see someone go through their habitual routine but are too polite to tell that person to stop doing what they are doing. They merely cringe and turn away. For your own sake, let go of some of your ingrained habits. It may not be easy at first, but try!

**HADES** (see **HELL**)

**HAG** (see **WITCHCRAFT**)

**HAGGIS** (see **FOOD**)

**HAIL**
   With all the extra worries upon you now (e.g., business, financial, physical, spiritual), it appears that someone very close and dear to you is creating a new series of negative waves; this is just about the last straw, in your view! You will survive this traumatic experience with some misgivings about yourself and about those whom you respect and trust. Your faith is being tested at this time; hence, try to be more forgiving to those who trespass against you.

## HAIR (see *also* BEARD or WIG)

You go into a project wholeheartedly, but you are often thwarted by the limitations and crudeness of others around you. Some people do not have your mature judgment and desires to forge ahead. This dream advises you to use your talents the best way possible; and if others around you refuse to better themselves in some manner, then that is their loss, not yours. Do not let people's limited views, plans, and actions hinder you; simply do what is best for you!

## HAIRBRUSH (see BRUSH)

## HAIRCUT

You are not giving too many people a chance to come closer to you because of your stubbornness and inferior attitudes about yourself. You cannot profit from these attitudes. Look for more inner peace, order, and purpose within your life. Be more open to your wants and needs rather than hiding behind some defense system which you feel is working for you. Realistically, your attitudes are not working for you! This dream counsels you to be more concerned about your todays and tomorrows, with a more caring and giving attitude. Use your God-given intelligence at all times. Keep busy, be happy to be alive and well, and you will soon forget about your personal, self-inflicted hang-ups.

## HAIRDRESSER

You will be seeking some personal advice and/or some financial aid from a known source before too long. This assistance will allow you to carry on during these trying times. As well, there are many wholesome opportunities awaiting you in the not too distant future. With your good mind and with your determination, you are bound to accept some of these challenging occasions with resounding success!

## HAIRNET

This dream reveals that you are not being treated fairly for your efforts (e.g., home, school, work). You would be wise to get some reasonable explanation from those beings who are affecting you this way. Some workable or effective agreement can be reached between you and those involved, but this cannot happen unless you make your feelings more known and pronounced. With sensibility and reasonable attitudes, you will triumph over such matters quite effectively.

**HAIRPIECE** (see **WIG**)

**HAIRPIN** (see **BOBBY PIN**)

**HALF BROTHER** (see **BROTHER**)

**HALF-MAST** (see **FLAG**)

**HALF SISTER** (see **SISTER**)

**HALL** (see **AUDITORIUM**)

**HALLOWEEN**

You may be masquerading as a friend to someone, or someone is doing so with you. Finding a soul brother or soul sister on this earth plane can be one of the most rewarding of all experiences! When two people have something in common, share some spiritual bond between them, and like each other in spite of their minor weaknesses or flaws, then truly they have discovered a good friendship—one which should grow and last a lifetime. In your case or that of your so-called friend, there is a cat and mouse attitude at play here which will not last much longer. The friendship is over; perhaps there was never one there in the first place.

**HALLUCINATION** (see **DECEPTION**, **DELIRIUM**, or **MIRAGE**)

**HALLWAY** (see **PASSAGEWAY**)

**HALO** (see **AUREOLE**)

**HAM** (see **FOOD** or **MEAT**)

**HAMLET** (see **VILLAGE**)

**HAMMER** (see **TOOL**)

**HAMMOCK**

To a total stranger you appear to be kind, understanding, and very communicative, but with some of your loved ones, you are displaying a great amount of mental silence and distance. This is neither wholesome nor wise! Unless you are willing to behave in a more loving, caring, understanding, and communicative manner, you may find yourself quite alone in time to come. Be more forgiving and let go of your pride; above all, pray for your peace of mind. Then, peace will come.

## HAMPER

You are very easily impressed, and somewhere down the road of life you have acquired a host of anxieties and doubts that haunt and control your life. Being nervous and agitated does not help matters much either. Begin to eradicate your fears one at a time. Think very positively about yourself and others, and strive to keep yourself occupied with new and interesting activities (e.g., hobbies, sports, books, music). These suggestions should help you to some degree; if necessary, however, seek professional assistance. Do not let your life go by with needless fears and panic. You deserve more happiness!

## HAND (i.e., fingers, palm, and thumb)

It seems that no matter what you undertake in your life, the workload seems endless. Consequently, you have very little time for anything else. Even though you may have the ability to cope with your busy schedule, what are materialistic gains if you have to lose your health or the respect of those who care? There is time for work, and there is always time for pleasure. Tailor your life in a more equitable manner; you will be happier for having done so.

## HANDBAG (see PURSE)

## HANDBALL (see GAME)

## HANDBILL (see ADVERTISEMENT)

## HANDBOOK (see BOOK)

## HANDCUFF

If you are a positive, self-respecting, and self-satisfied individual, then you are "handcuffed" to the better joys of life. More power to you! However, if you are a negative, defiant, and uncaring individual, then you are presently "handcuffed" to the aimless absurdities of life. Doing wrongs for yourself and others is a very sad state of existence. The stresses and anguish you can create for yourself are needless, senseless, and shameful. Forget about your vengeance, hatred, and anger. Do good things for yourself and others. Pray and be patient and kindly; and the magnitude of your actions will bring you immeasurable victories and successes!

**HANDICRAFT** (e.g., weaving, pottery making) (see *also* **HOBBY** or **LACEWORK**)

A sudden turn of events will give you a splendid opportunity to head towards a more definite direction in your life. You may be a breath away from realizing a lifelong goal, or perhaps you will be meeting someone who will assist you in making your wishes come true, and so forth. Whatever it may be, you can be sure that something very special awaits you in the not too distant future. You will have earned this, and much more!

**HANDKERCHIEF**

Do not be afraid to stand alone for something you believe to be just and honourable. Although there are many people who might try to dissuade you from your beliefs, it does not imply that you are wrong. The only time a person can be wrong is when their beliefs project harmful acts towards their fellow man. Good visualizations and actions will prosper; negative ones will eventually crumble and fall.

**HANDRAIL**

You will apologize to someone before too long, or someone will apologize to you. Your honesty and integrity in matters such as this is highly commendable. If more people would make greater strides for peace and compromise, this planet might not be such a stressful place in which to live.

**HANDSAW** (see **TOOL**)

**HANDSET** (see **TELEPHONE**)

**HANDSHAKE**

This act within a dream will not necessarily bring you the response or appreciation you so desperately seek in life; at least, not at this time. You have a habit of believing that you are always left out of certain situations around you, or that people are merely taking you for granted. Perhaps, to some degree, this is true. However, you cannot please everyone; nor can everyone please you. Appreciate those times when people want your company; but, by the same token, respect those times when you are not invited. Understand as well those times when some people simply refuse to be your friend at all. Accept these realistic facts of life graciously and humbly.

**HANDWRITING** (see *also* **GRAPHOLOGY, LEFT-HANDED-NESS, OVERWRITE, RIGHT-HANDEDNESS,** or **SIGNATURE**)
You are basically an intelligent, responsible, and down-to-earth individual who simply desires a good, untangled, and successful life. Yet, so many times, you were thwarted by greedy or unscrupulous individuals who did not care whom they hurt or cheated. Your emotional pain in this matter is profound. However, you are now entering a new cycle in your life whereby more determination, courage, and consistency will at last bring you the happiness you rightfully deserve. You will not plummet to earth on a collision course this time! No, this time you will liberate yourself from the discomforting and troublesome ways of others; and, like the "faith that moves mountains", you will peacefully remove those mountains by merely walking around them.

**HANGAR** (i.e., a shelter or repair place for aircraft)
At last, you are adopting some complimentary orderliness and rules in your life. Being more mindful of what you say to others, watching your buying and spending habits, putting your mind to work where studies are concerned, and so forth are but a few of the good intentions you have set out to achieve. You obviously mean business this time—and, in all likelihood, you will succeed! It is truly revitalizing to know that, on this earth plane, we are all given many chances to better our concepts and actions. We are indeed fortunate!

**HANGER** (i.e., a metal or plastic frame upon which garments are hung)
You are a bit of a nonconformist. However, in spite of your unique views and attitudes, you are not that difficult to understand. Some of your thoughts and ideas are futuristic, but not everyone you meet takes the time to review what you say. You are unique in many ways simply because you choose to be so. This is all right, for you are true to yourself. You are not sophisticated or outspoken, so you are not merely trying to bring attention to yourself, as some nonconformists

do. On the contrary! You are just finding your niche and awareness in life in poetic thoughts, feelings, and actions.

**HANGING** (i.e., to be put to death by hanging)

As sordid as this dream may appear, it is a simple reminder that life for each one of us is not a forever thing on this planet. When you do something marvelous or achieve something special, you obviously feel ecstatic about it. However, are you giving credit where credit is due? In other words, are you thanking God for your many blessings, or are you simply taking them for granted? This dream counsels you to look after your earthly needs at all times, but to look after your heavenly needs as well. Your soul is far more important than all the wealth on this planet and more. If you fail to look after your soul's well-being, who will? You are responsible—it is up to you. You have much to be grateful for, so do not forget to thank God once in a while. This is not too much to ask of any man, woman, or child on this planet.

**HANGMAN** (see **HANGING**)

**HAPPINESS** (e.g., contentment, ecstasy, enjoyment, jubilation, pleasure, rapture, or satisfaction)

This strong, emotional feeling within a dream often reveals over-confidence in one's attitude or abilities. You are very good at what you do. However, you must not flaunt yourself too openly, otherwise those around you may be slighted or, at least, may feel inferior and resentful towards your behaviour. You will be much happier by sharing your knowledge and talents with calmness and peace rather than by surveying, comparing, or ridiculing others' attitudes and abilities. Remember that being gifted or talented in some things does not mean that you are all wise in everything.

**HARASSMENT** (see **ANNOYANCE** or **PERSECUTION**)

**HARBOUR**

You are attempting to over-praise or over-please someone you know (e.g., parent, spouse, friend). Most people do not mind some attention or catering to, but when this act is overdone, you will discover that they become edgy and hostile. Bluntly, enough is enough. People will resent too much adulation and attention simply because they are independent-minded, not dependent-minded. As well, they do not feel comfortable being served hand and foot or being praised beyond their expectations or beliefs. This dream counsels you to know your limitations in these matters so that you may avoid some embarrassing episodes of displeasure in the future.

## HARDSHIP (see MISFORTUNE)

## HARDWARE (see STORE, TOOL, or UTENSIL)

## HAREM

If a female dreams about a harem, this implies that she will not be chained down to any man's whims or notions. In other words, she has a head on her shoulders, and she will stand up for her rights, ambitions, wants, needs, and so forth. She cannot tolerate any type of male chauvinism! Equality in all things is her motto—and rightfully so!

If a male dreams about a harem, however, it implies that he does not necessarily believe that women have the same rights as men. He may or he may not be chauvinistic in his actions. In either case, it is the "dominance" factor of a male that makes him think the way he does. This is not to imply that he is correct in his thinking. Under the Laws of Life, we are all equal, and that is the way it should be! Any person who disagrees will discover this vital truth eventually.

## HARM (see MISCHIEF)

## HARMONICA

Thoughts of anger, pride, discouragement, or shame may enter your mind because of some recent episode in life. This dream advises you to disband your negative feelings and to finally recognize the fact that you are capable of making mistakes and blunders like anyone else. Do not be so hard on yourself. Your objectives and responsibilities will be respected in due time; in the interim, learn to be more inwardly satisfied that you are on the right road in life. Be more self-forgiving, as well.

## HARNESS (see *also* BRIDLE)

You have a tendency to be somewhat domineering over others. You may feel it is important and necessary to be domineering. However, your attitude is very demeaning to the individual(s) involved. Think twice before you foist your demands on others.

Remember, also, that in shaming and humiliating someone with your actions, you invariably shame and humiliate yourself as well.

## HARP (see INSTRUMENT)

## HARPOON
Sometimes tender, loving help is but a breath away. But, too willingly, you accept the bleak outlook of your mind. You were never meant to stagnate with pessimistic views and hopes. Bear in mind that a bleak outlook can bring you bleak results! Always think positively about matters in your life; and—with good direction, authority, and management—you will commence to see glowing results from your efforts. Greater opportunities await you in your future. For your own sake, do not thwart these occasions by thinking pessimistically.

## HARPSICHORD (see INSTRUMENT)

## HARVEST
This dream expresses an upward climb in your life. Negotiations and dealings with others will be at an all-time high, along with any other activities you may be planning. The possibilities of travel, job promotion, other financial improvements, moving, or anything else that could possibly improve your state of being are strongly indicated here. A dream of this nature is like receiving special treatment wherever you go or whatever you do.

## HASSOCK (see FOOTSTOOL)

## HAT (see *also* BONNET, CAP, HELMET, or TURBAN)
Be careful! This day can bring you trouble and plenty of guilt. A sudden impulse or momentary whim may induce you to act in a very hurtful manner towards someone very special in your life. Do your best to be good-natured and helpful to everyone around you today. You will gain by being so.

## HATCHET
You are trying too hard to change someone to fit into your thoughts and actions. Although you may have some very admirable qualities you wish to impart, you cannot expect a person to act and do precisely what you feel, think, or do in life. No two people are alike;

everyone must be given a chance to explore and to think for themselves. The more you harp on this person's weaknesses and failings, the more distant this person will be to you. In fact, if this action persists, you may not have anyone to control in the future. Tread lightly! Most people change for the better, but this does take time. Give this person a chance to grow and learn, and he or she will eventually discover love, compassion, self-reliance, and many other truths about the rights and wrongs of life. A good piece of advice is for you to take a bit of fresh air and to consider how much of your inner self needs correcting. No one—not even you—can be perfect.

## HATRED

This attitude within a dream reveals that you are retaining some latent hostility towards someone or something (e.g., spouse, parents, relative, friend, education, career, religion). Do not hide behind a mask, where this matter is concerned. Open up, and begin to talk to the sources of your anguish or hate. You may discover that your lowest feelings towards someone or something were no more than premature conclusions on your part.

## HAUNT (see GHOST or PHANTOM)

## HAWK (see BIRD)

## HAY (see GRAIN)

## HAZING (see INITIATION)

## HEAD

To see a head with a kind-looking, pleasant face signifies that you have a natural tendency to trust and believe in people. You always strive to better your lifestyle in many ways and, even though your work may be tedious and mundane, you maintain a hopeful outlook in all things. Your thoughts and actions are sincere and admirable!

Seeing a head with a wicked, ugly, or distorted face implies that someone is out to cause you repeated trouble. There is an enemy in your midst who is unpleasant and burdensome to your better judgment and general progress. Indifference and rebuke are two stern measures to employ where this troublemaker is concerned. Should this fail, for some reason, then you may have no other recourse but to have absolutely nothing to do with this person. This decision, however, should not deter you from praying for your enemy. Anyone so troubled needs all the help they can get.

Seeing the side, back, or top of a head signifies that you have been ignoring or criticizing someone you know or else someone is doing this to you. Kindness, respect, and cooperation are the key qualities that can bring about harmony and peace in this matter. The initiative and willingness must be there, however, before unwholesome attitudes change. Sadly, sometimes attitudes never do change.

## HEADACHE

Experiencing a headache within a dream state may indicate that you do, in fact, have a headache. This could be created by the way you are sleeping on your pillow, or by the hardness or softness of your pillow, or by some mental or physical tension you are presently experiencing. Dispelling one's trouble or anguish can ultimately dispel a headache. If the headaches persist, however, seek medical assistance.

## HEADBAND

You may be striving too hard to be somebody you were never really meant to be. For example, you may be trying too diligently to become popular and outgoing with others when you know you are not comfortable with this attitude, or you may be striving too hard to impress someone with a macho-type personality when, in fact, you have a very inward personality. Whatever it is that you are trying to change within yourself, you are strongly advised to be yourself at all times. No one is really impressed with any kind of false front people may try to create for themselves. If nothing else, a person merely ends up appearing foolish. Many people like you the way you are already. Be true unto yourself!

## HEADHUNTING (i.e., the primitive practice of collecting human heads as a memorial of victory)

This dream symbolizes a fear of someone in authority over you (e.g., a manager, foreman, supervisor, instructor). Basically, you have been treated fairly well by this individual; but, due to some nervous tensions within yourself, you seem to "fall to pieces" whenever this person is near you or approaches you for something. Even though this person in authority has a more prestigious position than you do, he or she is basically no different than anyone else. Relax your mind in these matters. Your nervousness can be conquered by being more confident and assertive within yourself. As well, do not forget to honestly accept the fact that you are a good worker and that you are respected for your conscientious efforts.

**HEADLINE** (see **NEWSPAPER**)

**HEADPHONE** (i.e., telephone or radio receiver that fits over the head)

Any one of the following definitions may be applicable to you: A) that you are in the communications business, and your dream merely reflects the work that you presently do; or B) that you are very depressed and restless about someone in your town or city or someone living far away from you; or C) that you are very disappointed with yourself regarding some matter or decision that did not turn out well; or D) that some compromising and rewarding news from a loved one or a friend has made you very happy; or E) that this dream has little or no relevance to you at this time.

**HEARING AID**

Any one of the following definitions may be applicable: A) that you do, in fact, use a hearing aid, and your dream merely reflects your need for this device; or B) that you are unable to communicate with a youthful person simply because he or she appears to give you the "deaf ear" to anything you have to say; or C) that you feel somewhat justified and relieved over a decision you made quite recently, even though there was some misunderstanding at first; or D) that you feel handicapped sometimes because of a personal problem, but you know that you can surmount this difficulty if you put your mind to it; or E) that you feel neglected by some members of your family; or F) that this dream has little or no relevance to you at this time.

**HEARSE**

Your mind has been preoccupied recently with sad, morbid thoughts about life, death, tragedies, and so on. You even think about your own demise or that of another person. These thoughts you harbour place you in a depressive, self-pitying state. Why pine or become worn out over personal events that have not even happened yet? Who knows, maybe you will live to be one hundred years old; and, by that time, you just might welcome leaving this planet behind for something much better. This dream counsels you to cultivate each day with constructive thoughts and actions (e.g., pray, read wholesome books, go for long walks, exercise). Do not be afraid to live your best upon this world or to accept the realities of eternal life when it is time to bid farewell to this world. What is truly important here is that you lead a good, wholesome life.

## HEARTACHE (see SORROW)

## HEART ATTACK

To see yourself or someone else have a heart attack within a dream state implies that you may have already experienced a heart attack, or you are worried about the possibility of having one. Your fatigue, depression, and mental anguish can be dispelled from your being once you come to terms with your present situation. It appears that you are masking a certain problem or bad habit which is making your daily burdens heavier. Sooner or later, you will have to make some concessions and changes with regard to your personal hang-ups; otherwise, some of your present fears may be justified. Remember: you benefit from the good things you do for yourself. Your verbal promises should be accompanied with positive action.

## HEAVEN (i.e., a Paradise where God and good souls abide or a place of great peace and comfort) (see *also* GOD, HOLY MOTHER, or JESUS)

What a privilege and honour to be able to have a true glimpse of this Divine State! This is very rare, yet a few beings on earth have experienced their great vision of Heaven. A dream of this nature is attempting to encourage the dreamer to become better, truer, and nobler in their thoughts, actions, and deeds in life. In other words, do not be too complacent in what you have done thus far; rather, always strive for constant improvement within your being. For example, if you are good, you can become much better; if you are bad, you can become good. The constant upward climb for betterment within oneself takes time, but a person must at least strive towards this end on earth. You may not necessarily reach the state of purity within your lifetime, but there will come a time and a place when you will. There are many Mansions on the other side of life prepared for each one of us, but Heaven itself is a very special Pure State of existence. We all must work our way towards Heaven.

(*Note*: You may also have the pleasure of knowing that if, for example, you are experiencing a very negative dream but at the very end of your dream sequence or anywhere during your dream sequence you happen to see Heaven, then the "symbolism" of Heaven takes precedence over your entire bad dream. Consequently, you have nothing to worry about simply because Heaven acts as a "buffer zone" to anything negative within a dream.)

**HEIFER** (see **CATTLE**)

**HEIR** (see **INHERITANCE**)

**HEIRLOOM** (i.e., a special possession handed down, perhaps through generations)

You are very sentimental about the things you own, the people you meet, and the places you have journeyed to thus far. This is all right simply because you feel the peace and tranquility you desire in life. The inner quietude of your thoughts and feelings is wholesome! There were times, however, when you were called upon to be a peacemaker between several people. Your sense of humour and your sane perspective on things have given you the ability to make people think twice about their actions. You have brought hope to many people and will continue to do so for many wholesome, rich, and rewarding years to come.

**HELICOPTER**

You behave very impulsively. There are times when you say things "at the top of your head" without realizing the effect your words have upon people. Much later, when you are alone and relaxed, the impact of your words and actions hits home, so to speak. You may not necessarily wish to offend anyone; yet, some people have been affected by you. This dream counsels you to be more careful and farsighted regarding people's feelings.

**HELIPORT** (see **AIRPORT** or **FIELD**)

**HELL** (i.e., a place of punishment where negative souls dwell) (see *also* **DEMON**)

Seeing a state of hell within a dream should jolt the dreamer into realizing the terrible consequences a person must face if one fails to lead a good, decent life. If the dreamer is a good person, then there is no cause for worry. However, if the dreamer is evil or wicked, then this dream should hit home; hell is not a pretty sight! It may be a lot colder than you could ever imagine—no light, no warmth, but all the anguish you could possibly imagine. The "play now, pay later" attitude so many people on this planet show is tragic. The message this dream brings is for good people to always pray for the conversion of sinners to God. This prayer throws a lifeline to the wrongdoers on Earth and to those beings in the nether regions of hell.

**HELMET** (e.g., an armored headpiece, army helmet, football helmet, a fencing head mask)

Your own fears, worries, and stresses will make you ill if you do not curb them. This dream symbolism is desperately trying to tell you to allay all those unnecessary, worrisome thoughts you tend to rehash over and over again. Think about more pleasant things and situations; pray; meditate; mingle with good, happy people; exercise. Positive ventures can lead you away from unwholesome, troublesome thoughts. Simply clear your mind, and allow this day to be a new beginning for better days ahead.

**HELPING** (see **ASSISTANCE**)

**HELPLESSNESS**

You are striving to assert your position or stand with someone or something, and/or you are attempting to come out of a certain dilemma or serious situation within your life. Whether you win or lose, in either case, remains to be seen. If you have the positive mettle to conquer the trouble within or around you, then indeed you stand an excellent chance of rising above your despair. If, however, you feel defeated before you even begin, then your chances of winning in these matters are basically nil.

**HEN** (see **CHICKEN**)

**HENHOUSE**

Symbolically, this dream indicates that you will be visiting someone in a hospital before too long. That person should recover rapidly—to everyone's happiness and satisfaction!

## HERBALIST

If you are, in fact, a herbalist, then your dream is merely reflecting upon the wholesome work that you do. If you are not, then your dream (with the greatest concern for your well-being) admonishes you over your bleak attitude, behaviour, and vain promises. Will you ever change on this earth plane? That's entirely up to you. Start with doing some serious introspection and housecleaning within your mind and soul. Weed bad habits; reseed good habits. And, with the Grace of God, you should be able to slowly climb out of the mire you have created for yourself. Do not let the false judgments of your mind overrule the needs of your soul.

## HERDSMAN

You care about the needs and wants of other people. In fact, you would not think twice about helping a person or animal in distress. This deep compassion and love you hold within your being is a true example of an admirable and praise-worthy human spirit. As you continue your silent vigil and help, your future will unfold bringing many rich and rewarding events. Are you aware that angels sing for people like you?

## HEREAFTER (see AFTERLIFE, HEAVEN, or HELL)

## HEROISM

What a pleasure to know that you are striving to improve yourself in so many different ways. You are beginning to put two and two together within your life, and now it is all making more sense to you. You are becoming a more mature, caring individual; this is the right attitude to uphold and cherish. There can be no greater joy than to know that someone, such as you, has finally decided to grow inwardly and to be pleased with what you see and do. Welcome home!

## HESITATION (see DOUBTFULNESS or RELUCTANCE)

## HIDE (see PELT)

## HIDE-AND-SEEK (see GAME or HIDING)

## HIDING (i.e., the act or state of being concealed)

To hide someplace or to conceal something from someone implies that you are perplexed about certain aspects of your life. These matters of confusion could pertain to sex, physical or emotional matters, or anything else that seems to trouble you. The only logical explanation is for you to seek assistance from someone more knowledgeable than you or to commence to read informative books that could answer your vital questions. The information you want is out there somewhere; search a little harder, and you will be pacified.

**HIEROGLYPHICS** (i.e., an ancient writing using symbols or pictures to represent a word)

This dream reveals two possibilities: you are very happy and productive with your life, or you are unhappy because most things you have done up to now have been a complete disappointment or failure to you. If the first definition is applicable to you, then you are to be commended for your sensible initiatives and logical thinking. If the latter definition applies, then you would be advised to think twice before jumping into uncertain situations. Before happiness and success become a reality for you, you must be willing to be more determined and persevering than you have been thus far. Unfortunately, you always quit when matters became too hard to handle. Know what you are capable of doing or achieving; then, with common sense, do your job well. Also know your limitations. If you know that a task or a job is much too big for you to handle, then accept this fact within yourself and with anyone else involved. Honesty in all things is your vital key to a better tomorrow.

**HIGHCHAIR**

There are some present matters of importance surrounding you that will take time to settle. With your elevated thoughts and actions, you are very capable of handling most trying situations. You will succeed again. However, do not forget the power of prayer and positive visualization which have helped you on previous occasions. You may be up against a brick wall for the moment, but this wall will crumble—providing you utilize your inner energies in a positive way.

**HIGH SCHOOL** (see **SCHOOL**)

**HIGHWAY**

Seeing an unobstructed highway reveals that some of your present plans and wishes can be fulfilled. However, nothing will be given to you on a silver platter. You will have to work very diligently towards making these plans and wishes come true. Also, be alert! Some pending opportunities can assist you in your endeavours, but be wary lest you forsake these good opportunities for something else.

Seeing a highway that is obstructed in some manner reveals that some of your immediate plans and wishes can be fulfilled; however, you must be prepared for an arduous struggle. The obstacles in your life may be self-created or may be created by someone or something else. In either case, there is much hope ahead for you, providing you are ready, willing, and able to remove those challenging barriers from within or around you.

Seeing a highway that simply goes around in circles, or one that goes over many hills or mountains, or any other highway situation that appears somewhat ludicrous within a dream implies that you are presently too mixed up to make any sound or far-reaching plans; your life is presently too hectic and scattered to do anything too profound. The outlook is rather bleak here unless you "pull up your socks" and seriously consider what you intend to do with your time and actions on earth. Your habits and basic lifestyle appear to be holding you back from the progression you rightfully deserve. As long as you maintain a self-pitying, unwholesome attitude about yourself and about your basic worth in general, then—sadly—you will continue to flounder, somewhat foolishly and aimlessly. But it is never too late to change or improve; if you do, your world will change for you, too. Then perhaps the sky can be your limit!

(*Note*: If the highway you see is very long, then the possibilities of your pending trials and tribulations can be long-lasting as well. However, if the highway is relatively short in appearance, then your trials and tribulations may be short in duration.)

**HIJACK** (see **THIEVERY**)

**HINGE** (i.e., a hook or joint which enables a lid, door, gate, or other structure to turn or swing)

This dream advises you to concentrate on the positive aspects of facing up to your moral duties and financial obligations. Careless attitudes and bad investments at this time can bring you profound and unexpected difficulties. Show more self-control and foresight in all that you do—and, happily, there will be peace and prosperity ahead for you.

## HIPPOPOTAMUS

You may have to account for some past mistakes to a group of people. If you can justify your actions and convictions with courage, truth, and sensibility, then you stand an excellent chance of being exonerated. However, should tempers fly and accounts of your actions seem gravely doubtful and deceptive, then you may be strongly criticized or ostracized by these people.

## HISS

Beware of some imminent danger if someone or something hisses at you or you at them in a dream. Whatever this danger may be (e.g., falling off a ladder, tripping, cutting yourself), you are advised to use your highest intuitive feelings and guidance at this time. Do not underestimate the seriousness of this dream; do your very best to avoid the unparalleled anguish and pain strongly revealed here!

## HISTORIAN (see AUTHOR)

## HITCHHIKER

You may want the best of everything right now, but unless you are willing to put more effort and determination into your life, there will come a time when your losses will exceed your gains. So far, you have been relatively lucky. However, your restlessness, discontent, boredom, and fickle ways all reveal the necessity for you to settle down to some position or task that will at least give you the comfort and security you need. Do not waste your wholesome talents by merely sitting and waiting for something great and glorious to transpire within your life. You must make things happen through your own initiative, courage, and fixity of purpose. If you really want to, you can do this—and more!

## HITTING (see PUNISHMENT)

## HOAX (see DECEPTION, MISCHIEF, or MARE'S-NEST)

## HOBBY

Seeing yourself or another person at some hobby reveals that your skillful inventiveness and creativity will bring you closer to the professional success and happiness you desire in life. Keep following your good thoughts and hunches and, without a doubt, you will succeed beyond your wildest imagination!

**HOBO** (i.e., a vagrant)

This dream counsels you to think about the following. When all else appears to have failed for you, let there still be room for a prayer, a wish, a dream. When pride and indifference begin to control your conscious thoughts, let visions and acts of humility be your guide. When money, power, and greed attempt to dictate to and enslave your mind and soul, think about the less fortunate people on this planet and what you can do to help. When worrisome thoughts, hate, and revenge enshroud your delicate pathway in life, consider the total futility of such emotional negativity. When unholy thoughts and actions come upon you like a thief in the night, look upwards and begin to perceive the hope and peace that rightfully belongs to you. When laughter, happiness, and good fellowship appear to be with you no more, think about your patience, love, and courage which still lie dormant within your being. And when you awaken to find yourself very much alive and well, be happy and grateful to be a part of God's Universal Light!

**HOCKEY** (see **GAME**)

**HOE**

Do not seek revenge on someone who has done you wrong. If what you say to others is true—that you are honest, sincere, and forgiving—then you must practice what you preach. Love and forgive your enemy! And, with wisdom, stay away from your enemy until some form of rationality and compromise is achieved. You would be totally amazed by the awesome results that can be achieved by merely sending good thoughts towards your enemy. Far too often, people send out negative thoughts towards their enemy, thus prolonging the agony between the two or more opposing forces. If it is peace you really want to achieve, then it is your inner actions that will create peace.

**HOG** (i.e., a pig)

Sometimes, in making a decision that is vital to our earthly progress, we may create a sadness or confrontation with those directly involved (e.g., family members, friends). It appears that you may be making such a decision before too long. This may involve your home life, career, education, a move, or whatever you deem necessary to fulfill your better hopes and wishes. This may not be easy, but nothing is too easy on this earth plane. You will no doubt be making the right decision; however, be prepared for some criticism from those who temporarily place sentimentality ahead of reality.

A slaughtered hog reveals that a sickness, an accident, or other dreadful possibilities can occur if the dreamer tends to be overly careless and foolish in thoughts and actions. Be exceedingly careful when driving a vehicle, handling or spraying chemicals, becoming too stressful with problems, and so forth. The life you save could be your own! Remember, this dream is not intending to frighten you in any way; it is desperately trying to guide you away from negative actions which can harm you!

## HOLE

To merely see a hole signifies that you may be tempted to do something you may later regret. A sudden whim or notion could lead you astray, and/or someone may convince you to commit an illegal or spiteful act. This entire forewarning may be nullified, providing you are mindful of your actions and more cautious with the company you keep.

Falling into a hole signifies that you appear to be at a crossroads in your life. It is as though the four winds—from the north, south, east and west—are blowing upon you, and you simply do not know which road to take. You fear taking the wrong road. Be at peace! A big clue is given to you within your dream. Several people have already forewarned you about a certain person or matter which they sense could bring you unhappiness and possibly suffering down the road. These same people have given you some encouragement about another person or matter that seems much better. Weigh these situations very carefully, and look deep within yourself for the right answer. Another clue: God very often gives us messages through the mind and eyes of other people. Unfortunately, in matters of great importance, far too many people disregard their realistic views for emotional views.

To be trapped or stuck within a hole signifies that you may be in a quandary about any one of the following definitions: A) that you have an emotional, sexual hang-up with self or with someone else; or B) that a romantic situation may be broken because of your high expectations of someone or someone's great expectations of you; or C) that a marital problem has left you very bitter and uncaring; or D) that a financial burden created by you or someone else has affected your state of mind and bodily health; or E) that you are in a business that is constantly losing profits, which could quite conceivably force you to quit, or to lose your job, or—if you own the business—ultimately sell at a loss; or F) that this dream has little or no relevance to you at this time.

## HOLIDAY (see CELEBRATION or VACATION)

## HOLOCAUST (see BURNT OFFERING, FIRE, GENOCIDE, KILL, or MURDER)

## HOLY BIBLE (see BIBLE)

## HOLY MOTHER

To actually see, hear, or talk to the Virgin Mary within a dream state is one of the most rewarding of all dreams! Whether she counsels you on earthly or spiritual affairs, Her Message must be adhered to for, in essence, She has come to you for a very important reason. To be counseled by Her Holy Presence is an honour beyond any comprehension; consider yourself very fortunate and privileged to have had such a visitation. Perhaps you or someone close to you needs help, or the world at large may require Her Message at this time. Whatever the Virgin Mary's Blessings to you may be, you can be sure that the days to follow will be highly significant to you and thought provoking to anyone else involved. This dream also advises you to be wary lest you feel this dream visitation is not important. The task, mission, or good advice that may be given to you is far too important to ignore! Sometimes it takes a Holy Personage like the Virgin Mary to appear to a few chosen beings on earth to "rattle" or "jolt" the mind of someone in desperate need of help or to impact mankind as a whole. And, speaking about mankind; be prepared, for all "unholy" things will yet disappear from the face of this planet. God's Laws will survive; man's injustices will crumble!

(*Note*: You may also have the pleasure of knowing that if, for example, you are experiencing a very negative dream but at the very end of your dream sequence or anywhere during your dream sequence you happen to see the Holy Mother, then the "symbolism" of the Holy Mother takes precedence over your entire bad dream. Consequently, you have nothing to worry about simply because the Holy Mother acts as a "buffer zone" to anything negative within a dream.)

**HOME** (e.g., one's own residence, village, town, city, state, or country) (see *also* **HOUSE**)

This auspicious dream reveals your inner desires to make life around you more pleasing and livable. Sometimes that chore can be trying and exasperating; nonetheless, do your very best to maintain peace and happiness in whatever you do and wherever you go. Just seeing your home within a dream state should give you the encouragement to carry on or the impetus to fulfill some of your immediate plans or wishes. You will do these things; but, even more so, you will continue to be an inspiring individual to those who know and love you.

**HOMELAND** (see **BIRTHPLACE** or **HOME**)

**HOMESICKNESS** (see *also* **BIRTHPLACE**, **HOME**, or **SADNESS**)

What you need is a good month's rest from the storms which appear to be bombarding your good intentions. There comes a time when you must bypass the needs of others in order to regain your own peace of mind and strength of body. If at all possible, a retreat, vacation, or some other type of release from your hectic schedule is in order here. You need a reprieve from the stresses, strains, and cluttered demands placed upon you.

**HOMESTEAD** (see **BIRTHPLACE** or **HOME**)

**HOMEWORK**

Why not give yourself a pat on the back, once in a while, for the good things you have already accomplished? As well, do not forget to smile for the good things you are planning ahead. If you have managed to come this far with your gifts and tokens, why would you have any doubts or uneasiness about your future? Your future will be greater than your past! Carry on, and see these truths for yourself!

**HOMICIDE** (see **KILL** or **MURDER**)

**HOMOSEXUALITY**

Any one of the following definitions may be applicable to you: A) that you are, in fact, a homosexual who has little or no qualms about the lifestyle you lead; or B) that you are a homosexual who has great qualms, doubts, and guilt about the lifestyle you lead; or C) that you think you have latent homosexual tendencies; or D) that you know of someone who is a homosexual; or E) that you personally oppose and fear any type of homosexual lifestyle; or F) that this dream has little or no significance to you.

**HONEY** (see **FOOD**)

**HONEYCOMB** (see **BEE** or **FOOD**)

**HONEYMOON**

A honeymoon indicates that your emotional, sexual, and spiritual needs are compatible with someone who is mature, loving, and communicative. Whether you are presently in a good relationship remains to be seen. If you are not, then this dream urges you to work harder towards the happiness you wish to achieve. Having a true "soul mate" in life is like looking into a pool of water and seeing your reflection within that person at all times. Soul mates work together, harmonize together, and learn to accept their trials and tribulations with a great amount of understanding. Their love has lasting attunement simply because their thoughts and actions are headed into the same stream of life.

**HOODOO** (see **VOODOO**)

**HOPE CHEST**

You have close-knit family ties that appear at times to be a blessing, at other times a bitter and tearful burden to you. As you already know, some relatives can be your worst enemies, whereas a total stranger can treat you with human respect and kindness. You are neither jinxed nor star-crossed; there are simply some people on earth whom you will never satisfy, no matter how hard you try. Relatives are no exception to this rule. This fact of life is older than the Sphinx itself! The important thing is that you have done your best. If someone does not like or appreciate you for the good that is already within you, then just wisely continue to be your natural self.

**HOPEFULNESS**

Being hopeful within a dream state merely reveals the optimistic spirit within your being. Nothing will shake you from your loyalty, belief, or faith on earth simply because all your joys and blessings have been fulfilled in this manner of thought and action. Without that inner hope, you know that you would be left in an abyss of confusion, hate, and profound sadness. Your hopeful outlook is like a bright light which ultimately gives you the courage to accept another day with inner peace and patience.

## HOPELESSNESS

Feeling hopelessness within a dream state reveals your pessimistic attitudes and feelings in life. This does not imply that you are always this way. It just seems that quite recently you have been experiencing some mental, physical, and spiritual stresses. In fact, you feel like you are in a "no-win" situation! First, realize that God is on your side. Pray to Him, be determined, and maintain a strong belief that things will get better. They will—that is, if you have the time and patience to see this happen. If you must, seek some professional guidance; it should give you additional encouragement to forge ahead.

## HOPSCOTCH (see GAME)

**HORN** (i.e., the hard, bony protrusion from the head of an animal, or a vehicle horn, foghorn) (see *also* **SOUND**)

The antler or horn of an animal implies that you basically do not like anyone to tell you what to say, how to act, or what to do with your life. This sense of independence and stubbornness is good and wholesome, providing your conduct and character are positive in nature. If your conduct and character are negatively oriented, then you should utilize all the good advice you can humanly muster. Failing to lead a good existence can only bring you heartbreaking results! It is so sad to see people go the wrong way in life. They think they know it all now; in the end, they discover how very little they really knew.

Seeing or hearing a foghorn, vehicle horn, or other kind of horn could very well imply that you are, in fact, hearing that precise sound while you are asleep. In other words, hearing a sound while you are asleep allows you to "symbolize" what you hear. However, if this is not the case, then this symbolism indicates that your recent complaints concerning a family member, a financial loss, or some other personal matter may be well-founded. However, do not expect miraculous results overnight. Right now it appears as though you are a "voice in the wilderness"; nobody seems to be listening to your sound logic! These issues of importance will eventually be mastered; in the interim, maintain patience and sensibility.

## HOROSCOPE

You are so anxious to know what the future will bring you that you fail to realize what your duties and obligations are today. Tomorrow will come; in its wake, you will discover some joys and disappointments which you can accept or reject. Realize that your anxious, worrisome ways can hinder your progress in life. Live each day as it comes. Your positive endeavours today should certainly have a positive affect upon you tomorrow. It is what you do for yourself and others—now, here, at this moment—that truly foretells the truth about your future. When you decide to get rid of your impatience, needless worries, and fears—and when you begin to believe more in your own efforts each moment of each hour of each day of each year—then, and only then, will you begin to see the futuristic purpose to your existence. A new dawn will always be there for you, but will you be willing to create a better world for yourself?

## HORSE

Seeing a horse or group of horses in a peaceful manner, such as grazing in a pasture, reveals that some of your inner conflicts, confusion, and sexual tensions will be dissolved before too long. Be strong and courageous during these troubled times. Better times are revealed ahead.

To see many horses walk or gallop past you in a more or less friendly manner reveals that you are blessed with true, soul mate friends. People far and near will always believe in your God given truth and wisdom! You are special in many ways; and, gladly, you will continue to serve your fellow man for many years to come.

To see a stampede of horses acting in a confused, troubled manner signifies emotional stresses and physical hardships may be bothering you or someone you know at this time. These problems may be conquered, but not necessarily alone. If deemed necessary, seek professional or medical assistance.

To see a slaughtered horse foretells of a possible illness or accident that could perhaps be averted. Be very careful in what you eat for the next several days or so. This predicted illness appears to be more like food poisoning than anything else. Also, be cautious in your driving habits; do not take unnecessary risk on any highways or byways. Hopefully, these measures will assist you in avoiding anything unpleasant or unwanted in your life.

To see a snake, a worm, a bug, or anything else that might be creepy and crawly go through the hoof of a horse implies that you may hear of someone who will try to commit suicide, but luckily they fail. Or, you will hear of someone who has actually succeeded in their attempts to commit suicide. Perhaps you suspect someone you know of being capable of planning such a deed; if so, do not hesitate to offer some good advice to this person and, by all that is good and glorious, literally take this individual by the hand to a professional counselor for further assistance. One good word of inspiration, one good thought, can save a person's life!

Seeing a horseman or horsewoman dressed in casual clothes suggests that you have an above average desire to travel, to explore, and to be creative in some artistic field. You will probably do this and more; remember, however, that you will have to work very hard to become successful in what you wish to do.

Seeing a horseman or horsewoman dressed in black riding on a black horse signifies that you are very interested in the Cosmic, mystical, positive forces of life around you. You are a very perceptive person! Someday you may write about or talk about a Universal Love and Wisdom which appears to emanate from the "temple" within your soul. Your inspiring mind will help many people in time to come.

## HORSESHOE

There is good luck ahead for you! This could involve a windfall of some nature; it could imply a move that will bring you greater prosperity and happiness; it could be some business venture that will he exceedingly successful; it could also be a great composition that will be published, or anything else that might elevate you to a higher position in life. And who could be more deserving than you? Always remember, however, to be thankful and humble for all your good tidings and blessings.

## HOSE (i.e., a flexible tube or pipe for transporting water or liquids)

You would like to be relatively free and independent in life. Perhaps you are fed up with the daily routine of your home life and desire a new career outside the home which would be harmonious to you and to your loved ones. Or, perhaps you plan to retire early from your career or job so that you can advance yourself in other ways, and so forth. Your better wishes will no doubt come true. Understand that if they do, it is because you had the determination and courage to make them happen.

**HOSPITAL** (see *also* **CLINIC** or **NURSING HOME**)
This dream is trying to tell you to accept your responsibilities maturely and to face your troubles head-on instead of hedging or blaming other people for your problems. Do not expect too much of something for nothing on this planet. You must earn your way in order to survive and prosper. Your outlook, both within and around you, will commence to change when you decide to accept your load of the work in an honourable and sensible manner.

**HOST** (see **HOSTESS**)

**HOSTAGE**
This dream could imply any of the following definitions: A) that you were once a hostage; or B) that you know of someone who was a hostage; or C) that you are experiencing some marital disharmony because of some mental, physical, or spiritual abuses being foisted upon you; or D) that you are very proud of yourself and of the many great things you can supposedly do; or E) that you are very easily influenced by the actions and attitudes of other people; or F) that you are very stable in your thoughts and actions, but you tend to be very possessive towards people you know; or G) that this dream has little or no significance to you at this time.

**HOSTEL** (i.e., a youth hostel)
You seem to be searching for some inner truths or happiness "here and there"; however, you are sometimes failing to realize that what you seek is already within your being. All you have to do is be a bit more communicative instead of so mysteriously silent; then you will commence to see the outpourings of your mind come through. Sharing what you know and what you have learned thus far will certainly give others around you a better concept about your philosophy and wisdom. If you must, continue your journey to find your worth; but, along your way, do not be afraid to make your spiritual and cosmic awareness known. You never know—somewhere out there, you may be helping a soul in dire need of your great insight.

## HOSTESS

This dream advises you to always be kind, good, and just in all that you do. Above all, remember to use your discretion with people who tend to lean too heavily upon your words, judgment, and wisdom. It is true that you may have a sound, logical answer for some of these people; however, there are those certain, vital occasions when they must begin to think and act for themselves. Sometimes people have to actually go through a hardship or two in order to appreciate their capabilities and their life. A few "hard knocks" here and there, and a person soon wakes up to reality! That is why we are here in the first place— to learn! It is fine to share some things with those you know, but there are times when a vital lesson or two must be learned on a personal, individual basis.

## HOTEL

You have some latent aims that you have never really put to practice yet. What you really need to do is have a face to face confrontation with yourself sometimes. Look into a mirror and, with deep reflection, think about those several items you have always wanted to do but— somehow—something or someone got in your way. Do you think you might be able to carry out one or two of those wholesome plans now?

## HOTELIER (see HOTEL, MANAGER, or OWNERSHIP)

## HOT ROD (see CAR)

## HOT SPRING

If the hot spring has clear water, then emotional harmony, good luck, and positive decision making await you. As well, a greater sense of responsibility towards your wants and needs will allow you to think more logically instead of sentimentally (e.g., letting go of the past for a brighter future).

A hot spring that has murky, filthy-looking water signifies that your enthusiasm and courage appear to be at an all-time low because of some personal problem. You will solve your problem soon, but not without learning some valuable lesson about your self-doubt. Faith can move your mountain—but you must be ready, willing, and able to crawl, walk, or run around that mountain.

## HOURGLASS

To really advance or improve yourself, you must be willing to forfeit some of your mundane activities for something more educational and purposeful. You can waste all the time you want on this planet; however, later in life, you may have great regrets, guilt, and even anguish for all the wonderful things you could have done but failed to do. There is so much to learn on this planet that it is incredible why so many people choose to close their "books" to knowledge and understanding. This dream is simply reminding you that what you do with your free time now may have a vital effect on your limited, valuable time later on.

## HOUR HAND (see CLOCK)

## HOUSE (see *also* HOME)

To see a house, but not your own home, within a dream state reveals the following definitions: A) that you would like to buy a house someday; or B) that you hope a family member or friend will be able to afford to buy a house before too long; or C) that you know of someone who must give up their house because of careless financial planning; or D) that you would like to live in a very big house one day, but right now that wish is a mere pipe dream; or E) that you may be having some legal or financial trouble buying a house; or F) that you wish you could move away from your neighbourhood; or G) that you are presently renting a house which either pleases or displeases you; or H) that you are presently being forced to vacate a house for a sound or unsound reason; or I) that this dream has little or no relevance to you at this time.

## HOUSECLEANING

One or several of the following definitions may apply directly to you: A) that you enjoy housecleaning; or B) that you detest housecleaning, even at the best of times; or C) that you are a professional housecleaner, and this dream merely reflects your day to day work activities; or D) that you wish to finalize some vital papers in order to pacify yourself, a family member, or a friend; or E) that you are presently experiencing some business or property management difficulties that could ultimately bring about great financial losses to you; or F) that you recently had to postpone a trip or plan because you were short of funds; or G) that you are presently experiencing some depression because someone broke a vital promise to you; or H) that this dream has little or no relevance to you at this time.

## HOVERCRAFT

You are very futuristic-minded! This should give you an opportunity, from time to time, to use your wildest imagination about what Earth might be like three hundred or a thousand years from now. Can you imagine the astounding inventions and progress that lie ahead for mankind? Traveling to outer space would perhaps be no different than taking a flight from Vancouver to New York City or wherever you wish to go. These ideas have been planned or visualized by many great minds already. Even some of the movies and comic books nowadays reveal what the future will hold—but not everything! The future ahead will be more peaceful and more loving than the past. Our world now may be chaotic, but the world yet to come will be inspired and guided towards other worlds, newer concepts about the correct "highways" in space, and time travel. As well, man's brain will finally be fully utilized. Man has been "programmed" to use only a portion of his brain thus far; there will come a time, however, when a generation yet to be born will be blessed with god-like gifts, intelligence, and miracles.

## HUBCAP

This dream reveals that somewhere in your past you may have been swindled, cheated, robbed, or mistreated; to this very day, this leaves your mind ill at ease where certain people are concerned. You no longer take anything for granted! Continue to be levelheaded and prudent. This will at least allay your inner fears about being deceived or traumatized again.

## HUMANITY

To see mankind in peaceful or cataclysmic times within a dream reveals that you have an inner concern and need to assist your fellow man in some big or small way. All good thoughts, ideas, and actions have a tremendous bearing upon the balance within the wheel or cycle of life. Even if you help someone cross the street or pick up a piece of paper for someone, these minute actions still bring harmony, love, and understanding towards mankind. Any peaceful thought or action that you carry out on earth links you towards the Christ Consciousness or Christ Harmony that is within you. We all bear this Light. Sadly, however, we fail to strive harder to attune ourselves to its immeasurable joys and gifts. Three vital keys are important for this attunement: praying, meditating, and loving your fellow man with all your soul!

## HUMANOID (see HUMANITY)

## HUMILITY

This dream has two meanings: a) you are humble, or b) you are not humble. Take your pick! If you are humble, then truly you have found some inner joy and peace that most people might envy. However, if you are not humble, then it is time to do some serious soul searching, be more honest with yourself and others, and do not let selfish motives and self-righteous attitudes blur your scope or vision in life. Pride, if allowed full rein, can destroy a soul!

## HUNGER

Experiencing hunger pangs could mean that you are hungry at the time of your dream. However, assuming this is not so, then this dream symbolism infers that you place the needs of others above your own. Imagine if everyone thought the way you do: this world of plenty would probably wipe out starvation. Sadly, however, this is not yet the case. Still, it is very comforting and rewarding to know that there are people like you who truly reach out to others with a loving, caring mind and soul!

## HUNTING (see *also* POACHER)

This dream advises you not to neglect your duties and obligations. It is by far easier to dwell upon other interests and activities than it is to buckle down to some chore or task. Life is not all work and no play. But, you must also realize that neither is life all play and no work. By adopting good working habits, you should be able to do the same with your leisure habits, as well.

## HURRICANE

It seems that you depend on what other people say or do before you make a prime decision for yourself. God gave you a good, wholesome mind. Why do you hesitate to use it? Your fears about being criticized or ostracized for doing something on your own appear to have their roots in your upbringing. Lift this terrible burden from your mind and begin to think and do more for yourself. Just let go! You would be amazed at all the new decisions you could make on your own if you began to believe and trust yourself as much as you do other people. Do not be afraid to falter, sway, cry, or fall when you have made a wrong decision. Everyone on this planet makes mistakes. As well, do not be afraid to accomplish something which requires some struggle and disappointment along the way. Accept your life for all its good offerings; but also accept life's bitterness with a strong mind and with a persevering and self-reliant attitude.

## HUSBAND

Any of the following definitions may be applicable to you: A) that you have a good, loving husband who basically shares your interests at heart; or B:) that you have tried very hard to have a good, lasting relationship with your spouse, but there are personal difficulties standing in your way; or C) that you often feel left out because of your husband's or children's attitudes towards you; or D) that you are very optimistic that your relationship with your spouse and family will eventually improve; or E) that you realize your mate is not quite the "Prince Charming" he once pretended to be; or F) that if improvements concerning your spouse are not forthcoming, you realize that you cannot maintain this relationship any longer; or G) that your spouse's trust, faith, and hope are simply lost in the void somewhere; or H) that you dreamt about a husband who has passed away. If this is the case, say a prayer for him from the denizens of your soul, and be sure to tell him to "ask for the Light"!; or I) that this dream has little or no significance to you at all at this time.

## HYDROGEN BOMB

Your sudden emotional changes and moods can draw you away from your intended progress and happiness in life. By learning to cope with your anxieties and frustrations on a more sure-footed basis, however, you would still be on track with things. Flying off the handle for minor reasons or displaying your confusion and depression for other reasons can only bring you heartache and disappointments. No one gets a promotion this way! Be more realistic in these matters. If something is troubling you so profoundly, then it is time to seek some type of professional guidance. On the other hand, if you feel you can handle this matter alone, then as a member of humanity, you are advised to use your sense of judgment and wisdom with down-to-earth sensibility, forgiveness, and self-restraint.

## HYDROPLANE (see BOAT)

## HYMN

A hymn sung, played, or composed within a dream is truly of good order. You have already embarked upon or are about to embark upon some new venture in life that will literally shower you with praises and success. Obviously, you know who and what you want in life; and as luck would have it, you just happen to be at the right place of your destiny path, at the right time. This dream is attempting to reinforce your good wishes and hopes and to assure you that now you are the captain of your ship. Full steam ahead!

## HYPNOTISM

This dream cautions you not to trifle with other people's emotions and feelings. Whether you consider the trifling serious or not remains to be seen. However, you are strongly advised to consider the hurt, sadness, or havoc you may be creating. Do good unto others, and others will do good unto you. That is the rule to follow; there is no other rule!

## HYSTERIA (see *also* CRY, FIT, or LAUGHTER)

This dream cautions you to be wary of someone's apathetic and demeaning views about life; these may influence you to do something you may later regret. Do not take any chances at this time by doing something foolish or mindless that could result in some great sadness or tragedy. Stop, look, and listen to your inner self before you believe that nothing could happen to you or someone else on a simple "dare". Many people before you have made terrible mistakes by believing that nothing could happen to them—only to realize how badly mistaken they had been (i.e., careless driving accident, drowning, etc.). This warning is clear! The rest is up to you and to your better judgment.

## ICE (see *also* GLACIER)

It would be nice, from time to time, if you were a bit more reciprocating where others are concerned. You seem to hold a one-sided view in this matter. Bluntly, you like to be catered to; but when someone asks you for help, you create excuses. You cannot hope to gain friendships in this manner. Without a doubt, it is far better to give than it is to receive! Let your selfish motives go by the wayside, and—with goodness in your mind—think of the needs of others as being far greater than your own. You will progress with immeasurable satisfaction this way!

## ICE BAG

Some people are beginning to get on your nerves (e.g., business associates, relatives, friends, acquaintances). Perhaps these people do not treat you fairly, or perhaps their views are totally alien to your own, or maybe you need a change of scenery. Basically, when people do annoy you it is because you are already "nerved up" and upset with yourself for some reason or because their bothersome attitudes and actions simply get the better of you after a period of time. This dream advises you to be more inwardly tolerant; above all, learn to rise above your doldrums with greater thoughts and pursuits. Consider that sometimes it is more advantageous to simply ignore your inflicted stresses or annoyances. They are far too petty to even think about or harbour.

**ICEBERG** (see **ICE**)

**ICEBOAT** (see **BOAT**)

**ICEBREAKER** (see **BOAT**)

**ICE CREAM** (see **FOOD**)

**ICE CREAM PARLOUR** (see **PARLOUR**)

**ICE SKATE** (see **SKATE**)

**ICICLE** (see **ICE**)

**IDOLATRY** (i.e., the practice of worshiping an idol or idols)

You are not a very organized individual. Pronounced scattered ideas and actions have already created problems for you. This dream advises you to sit down once in a while, and do some serious introspection. Look deeper into yourself, and really begin to know who you are, what you want to do, and exactly where you want to go in life. Plan the work ahead of you. As a matter of fact, you could have more time for leisure if you were to map out a strategy or two, where your work load is concerned. Do not just do things in a careless manner and expect praises for doing nothing. Try not to begin a major project that could be too big for you to handle; this could lead to a big, disastrous mess! Sensibly, get help when required. As well, try to be a bit more neat and tidy; this will have a positive effect upon your well-being.

### IGLOO

Sometimes, when people have just about everything in life, they still want more; enough is simply not enough for them! This dream advises you to think twice before you go overboard in your wants and needs. There are limits to everything, so do your utmost to be more satisfied, knowing your cup already runs over. Do not succumb to greed or selfishness; otherwise, your cup of plenty could run dry!

### IGNITE (see FIRE or KINDLER)

### ILLEGITIMACY

Dreaming about illegitimacy could entail any of following definitions: A) that the person you dreamt about could, in fact, be illegitimate; or B) that you know someone who is illegitimate; or C) that you may have a subconscious fear about having a child out of wedlock; or D) that you have had a child out of wedlock; or E) that you know a baby, no matter how he or she arrives to this planet, is still and will always be a God-given gift of life to Humanity. All labels are man-made; all souls are God-made; or F) that this dream has little or no significance to you at this time.

### ILL FORTUNE (see MISFORTUNE)

### ILLITERACY

If you are indeed illiterate, then you are merely dreaming about your state of being. Your dream counsels you to look further into the possibilities of learning to read or write. Do not try to convince yourself that you are too young or too old to learn. Where there is a will, there certainly will be a way for you—that is, if you really want something special in life. If you are not illiterate but have a dream of seeing yourself or someone else in this state, then you show great empathy towards people who cannot read or write.

### ILL-MANNERED (see RUDENESS)

### ILLNESS (see SICKNESS)

### ILLUSIONIST (i.e., a person who performs tricks by sleight-of-hand)

Dreaming of being an illusionist or seeing one suggests that you usually enjoy the company of many people. You obviously enjoy being the center of attention as well. A very deep thinker, you often analyze situations until there is no more to analyze. You are also fascinated by the mysteries of life, and being secretive is one of your prime attributes. You are headed towards bigger and greater events as your future progresses.

**ILLUSTRATOR** (e.g., a person who illustrates for books, magazines)
This dream advises you to show more respect and consideration towards other people. This does not imply that you are inconsiderate all the time. Rather, you tend to go on your moody, unfriendly binges every so often; these literally baffle those around you. There are some people you know or work with who are still very reticent about getting to know you better. They appreciate and admire you from a distance. To them, it is at least much more comfortable and less hurtful this way. Consider these thoughts for a while; perhaps you will emerge a bit more humble and wiser for having done so.

**IMITATOR** (see **IMPERSONATION**)

**IMMIGRATION** (see **MIGRATION**)

**IMMORALIST** (i.e., a person who practices sexual vices or other unchaste practices)
Any one or several of the following definitions may be applicable: A) that you are immoral and have no desires to change your lifestyle; or B) that you are immoral and would very much like to change your style of living; or C) that even though you outwardly oppose this behaviour where people are concerned, you inwardly envy or fantasize about the lifestyle they keep; or D) that you know of someone who is immoral, yet this factor does not bother you in any way; or E) that you are tempted to become immoral, but your better instincts tell you to stay away from this sordid existence; or F) that this dream has little or no meaning to you at this time.

**IMMORTALIZATION** (i.e., to be given lasting fame on earth)
Perhaps you would like to be immortalized on earth? Who knows, maybe you will be! But if this prospect seems unlikely to you, then this dream is simply trying to tell you not to give up on a plan or project which, in the end, may prove to be very fulfilling and rewarding for you. You have the capability of accomplishing many fine things on this

earth plane. Never look back; just move forward with some of your far-ranged plans. The plaudits that await you will be yours to uphold and cherish.

**IMPERSONATION** (i.e., to mimic another person for entertainment purposes, or to pretend to be another person for fraudulent purposes)
You very often foist your insecurities and phobias on other people. Not all people, however, are taken in by your repetitious sorrows and pains. You can hardly expect a sympathetic ear if you fail to do anything about your problem(s). When you honestly decide to become more self-assertive and make greater efforts to detach yourself from those "ills and pills" harboured within your mind, you will then commence to perceive vast improvements within your life. Remember: self-pity is no more and no less than one's refusal to face reality.

**IMPOLITENESS** (see **RUDENESS**)

**IMPOSTER** (see **IMPERSONATION**)

**IMPOTENCE**
Any one or several of the following definitions may be applicable: A) that you are, in fact, presently impotent; or B) that you were impotent quite some time ago, but not any more; or C) that you inwardly fear this problem; or D) that you know of someone with this problem, but this person refuses to seek professional help; or E) that your sexual needs are not being fulfilled with a marriage partner or personal friend; or F) that you are undersexed and happy or unhappy with your situation; or G) that you are oversexed and happy or unhappy with your situation; or H) that this dream has little or no relevance to you at this time.

**IMPOVERISHMENT** (see **POVERTY**)

**IMPRISONMENT** (see **PRISON**)

**IMPULSE** (see **NOTION**)

**INCEST** (i.e., sexual intercourse with a close family member)
One or several of the following definitions may be applicable: A) that you have committed incest; or B) that you may have been a

victim of incest; or C) that you are vehemently opposed to this type of action by anyone or by any society or culture who endorses this type of relationship; or D) that you know of someone who has committed or is presently committing incest; or E) that a person subjected to incest should not hesitate for a moment to report this matter to the proper authorities; or F) that this dream has little or no relevance to you at this time.

**INCINERATOR** (see *also* **CREMATION, FIRE,** or **FURNACE**)
Do not let others who are less experienced sway or dissuade you from making the right choices or decisions. Be aboveboard in all family or business matters at this time. This wise action on your part will pay off later on, as you will eventually see.

**INCISION** (see **DISSECTION** or **SURGERY**)

**INCOME**
Any one or several of the following definitions may be applicable: A) that your income is fairly adequate, and you are grateful for this fact; or B) that your income is well below the standard of living, but you hope and pray for better days ahead; or C) that you do not manage money too well, and that is why you seem to spend more than you earn; or D) that you tend to be somewhat boastful about how much you earn, but you know these boasts are not true; or E) that you are frugal or miserly in your ways; or F) that your creditors take most of your earnings; or G) that you maintain a very sensible budget which allows you to be relatively secure; or H) that this dream has little bearing or significance to you at this time.

**INCUBATOR**
It is inner peace that will make you wholesome and well. A troubled mind can only bring you added stresses and fears. Your sensitive mind is like a sponge; sometimes, when you are feeling out of sorts, you tend to absorb in your mind all types of horrendous sicknesses which you occasionally read about and constantly fear. Later on, when you have recuperated, you realize that your groundless worries of the mind were no more than doubts and exhaustion. Your dream counsels you to think more positively when you are not up to par. Do not be afraid to laugh or smile during these times, either; laughter itself is one of the keys to better health.

## INDEPENDENCE

Any one or several of the following definitions may be applicable: A) that you have always strived for independence and appreciate being able to continue in this manner; or B) that you have very little confidence within yourself and always seem to need a great amount of encouragement to do something; or C) that you are overconfident in what you do, which can inevitably have its setbacks; or D) that some individuals tend to belittle your thoughts and ideas, which gives you very little incentive to move forward; or E) that you are a scheming individual who could not care less whom you stepped over in order to serve your own interests; or F) that you realize that even though a person may be mature and independent in their own right, we are all still dependent upon one another for something in life; or G) that this dream has little or no relevance to you at this time.

## INDIFFERENCE (see APATHY)

## INDIGESTION

To see this state within a dream could imply any of the following definitions: A) that you were, in fact, experiencing indigestion at the time of your dream state; or B) that you tend to have a very squeamish stomach, and just about anything not to your liking will give you indigestion; or C) that you have experienced some past stomach difficulties and simply dread the thought of this traumatic experience occurring again; or D) that you have recently been eating far too much junk foods; or E) that you are nervous about someone or something, which literally makes your sick to your stomach; or F) that you are not being too realistic about certain health problems; or G) that you maintain a very healthful outlook in life and hope to continue in this manner for many years to come; or H) that this dream has little or no significance to you at this time.

## INEBRIATION (see DRUNKENNESS)

## INFANT (see BABY)

## INFECTION (i.e., the state of being infected by a virus or bacteria) (see *also* PUS or RASH)

To dream about an infection could imply any one of the following meanings: A) that you presently have some type of infection that bothers you; or B) that you fear any type of infectious disease; or C) that you have had an infectious disease quite some time ago and simply dread the thought of this happening to you again; or D) that you have recently recuperated from some type of infectious disease; or E) that this dream has little or no relevance to you at this time.

**INFERNO** (see **FIRE** or **HELL**)

**INFIDELITY** (see **ADULTERY, AFFAIR,** or **SEX**)

**INFLATOR**

To inflate something within a dream state (e.g., a balloon, tire) reveals that you will be tested or admonished by someone who basically has your good interests at heart. This person does not wish to offend you, by any means. This person wholesomely wishes to teach you some valuable lessons about things you take for granted or about some other vital matters of life you tend to ignore or fail to comprehend. Be thankful that someone cares enough to show you a better way.

**INHERITANCE** (i.e., a legacy or heritage)

When someone has a stroke of good luck or a big windfall, do you wish them ten times more, or do you wish them ten times less? When you see poor people, do you wish them well, or do you simply ignore their plight with indifference? When a person is in some sort of difficulty, do you go out of your way to help, or do you simply feel that you have enough of your own problems, let alone help anyone else with theirs? When someone offends you, are you forgiving, or do you retaliate? When you are with a parent, a spouse, or a friend, are you ashamed to be with that individual, or are you content to love and appreciate that individual? When you are unhappy and relatively depressed, do you become temperamental and unforgiving, or do you try to solve your own problems in a calm, sensible manner? When you feel alone and forgotten from time to time, do you panic, or do you get down on your knees for some true assurances and comfort? If you can honestly say yes to the positive answers to these questions, then truly your outlook in life is far greater than all the wealth in the world. If, on the other hand, most of your answers are negative, then your outlook in life requires some deep soul-searching and rectifying.

## INITIAL (see *also* MONOGRAM)

Writing, printing, or merely seeing initials within a dream state reveals that you have a dynamic, aspiring personality. You are not one to sit back on your laurels! It would take a mighty force to even remotely hinder you on your profound journey in life. With your knowledge, sensible outlook, and gutsy character, you are bound to be successful and well known for your outstanding efforts and brilliant work!

## INITIATION

To be initiated or to see someone being a part of an initiation reveals that you have a very perceptive, curious mind. You would love to explore all the wonders of this world, or you would love to achieve some outstanding goals within your lifetime. Everyone, from time to time, has great and glorious ambitions; unfortunately, not everyone is equipped or capable of carrying out their lofty wishes, ideas, or concepts. This does not imply that you will not be successful in life. You can—and you probably will—be successful, but not necessarily on a worldly scale. Then again, you can be, providing you have an unshakable, determined quality of greatness about you. Only you would be able to determine that possibility.

## INJURY (see *also* BRUISE)

You may, in fact, have injured yourself recently and your dream is merely projecting a similar incident to you. However, if this is not the case, then this dream forewarns you of some lurking danger. There could be many possibilities, such as slipping on a sidewalk, falling down some stairs, falling off a ladder or roof, or cutting yourself. Just be careful!

## INK

Your desire to complete or finalize something seems so close, yet so far away. This dream reveals that you will complete this very important task, and you will prosper by the fruits of your labour, as well. Your destiny lies in assisting and serving others; yet, in many strange ways, you will also be served.

## INKBLOT

You are making your life far more complex, difficult, and confusing than is deemed necessary. What will you gain by harbouring horrendous visions of your past or present, or by blaming someone for their stupidities, or by seeking revenge upon those who trespass against you? Your mind is quite capable of moving onwards—that is, if you really try hard enough to make this happen. Right now, it appears that you are merely standing in one spot, going around in circles, and shouting for some understanding as to why you were ever born or why "this" or why "that" was inflicted upon you. This dream counsels you to get a complete grip of your mind with a positive visualization of yourself, instead of constantly negating and fighting yourself and your good intentions. Your past is behind you now; it will not return! Do not be afraid to move forward in life with good faith and actions. When you do, you will finally begin to know that there is a purpose to your mind, body, and soul being upon this planet.

**INKWELL** (see **BOTTLE** or **INK**)

**INMATE**

Your sense of bitterness, unhappiness, lack of progress, or isolation in life is totally self-inflicted. In other words, you have a choice to improve your attitudes and actions if you honestly and sincerely strive towards this end, or else you can continue to feel sorry for yourself in a needless, futile way. Thus far, you seem to be waiting for some miraculous event to carry you across a bridge where better things might await you. Not so! What you put into life will be exactly what you get out of life, not only on earth but in the hereafter, as well. Think about what you can do for yourself now instead of five years down the road. Remember: God will help you, but first you must be willing to help yourself. Just make an effort; you will find the way.

**INN** (see **HOTEL, LODGING,** or **MOTEL**)

**INNKEEPER** (see **HOTEL, LODGING, MANAGER, MOTEL,** or **OWNERSHIP**)

**INOCULATION** (see *also* **SYRINGE**)

You have been through many bitter times and have survived your ordeals with remarkable insight and fortitude! Recently, you have been despondent, sad, and somewhat hopeless, feeling that things within and around you will not get better. They will; but you must not lose your hope and faith during these troublesome times. This dream, in fact, is like a shot in the arm in that it is trying to tell you to fight onward with peace, conviction, and courage. You will win both the battle and the war! Be strong, be logical, and live your life to the fullest capacity. You will prosper and be happier this way.

**INQUIRY** (see *also* **CATECHISM, CURIOUSNESS, DOUBT-FULNESS, EAVESDROPPER, EXPEDITION, EXPERIMENT, LABORATORY, PURSUIT,** or **TEST**)

Whether your inquiry happens to be an investigation, interrogation, questionnaire, research, interview, or some other type of inquiry, this dream advises you to heed your intuition, instincts, or hunches in life. So often, you fail to act on your inner thoughts only to later regret losing out on something worthwhile and beneficial to you. People tend to ignore their better instincts because they feel that their imagination is working overtime or playing tricks on them. Actually, they were tuned in to the right source of information and knowledge. So, in the future, try to heed that inner voice when good, sound hunches come along or when warnings are suddenly felt.

**INSANITY**

Dreaming about insanity could imply any of the following definitions: A) that you know of someone who is presently insane; or B) that you fear this condition yourself, for some reason; or C) that you are so nervous, confused, and exhausted that you fear having a nervous breakdown; or D) that you have a great amount of empathy and understanding for anyone in this state; or E) that you know great strides and improvements have been made where mental illness is concerned and hope that one day this sickness can be eradicated from the face of this planet; or F) that this dream has little or no significance to you at this time.

**INSECT** (see *also* **ANT, BEE, BEETLE, BUG, BUTTERFLY, CATERPILLAR, LICE, MAGGOT, MOTH, SCORPION, SPIDER,** or **WORM**)

To merely see insects within a dream state infers that you are presently coping very well. Upon occasion you go overboard with your spending habits, but this seems to be a luxury you seem to enjoy even if you have to scrimp and save later on to make up for your losses. There is a fair amount of prosperity, travel, educational pursuits, and leisurely times ahead for you.

Killing insects, on the other hand, signifies that you are trying to solve, settle, or correct a problem or two within your life. Obviously you will succeed. Eradicating a "pesky" problem within your dream state reveals that you will eradicate a "testy" problem within your wake state. That is all!

**INSECTICIDE** (see **POISON** or **SPRAY**)

**INSPECTION** (e.g., serious examination of something, or surveying)

Some people are endowed with very special talents; but, due to financial reasons or other sound reasons, they are profoundly discouraged and sadly turn away from their life's goal. This dream encourages you to go on with your aims, ideals, and notions. There will be a "once-in-a-lifetime break" for you before too long. Hopefully, the lucky star that shines on you will grant you all your innermost wishes, now and always!

**INSTIGATOR** (see **DEMONSTRATOR, DISOBEDIENCE, DISSATISFACTION,** or **ENCOURAGEMENT**)

**INSTRUCTOR** (see **COACH, GURU, MAHARISHI,** or **TEACHER**)

**INSTRUMENT** (see *also* **BAGPIPE, BANJO, BELL, BUGLE, DRUM, HARMONICA,** or **ORCHESTRA**)

You try to do your very best in life; but, like many other people, you certainly have your minor faults and failings. However, you also make sincere efforts to correct the wrongs both within and around you. In many respects, you are a realist; you see things as they are. As well, you cannot tolerate leaving things undone. When there is something to do, you do it! You are highly respected for your intelligence, common sense, and ability to create improvements—not only for yourself, but for others, as well. In many respects, your life is like an instrument; whether you play a high note or a low note, the sound that fills the air is still very pleasant to the mind and ears of those willing to listen.

**INSULT** (see **ANGER, HATRED, MOCKERY,** or **RUDENESS**)

**INSURANCE** (e.g., an insurance policy for car insurance, life insurance)

Any one or several of the following definitions may be applicable: A) that your dream merely reflects the work that you do because you are in the insurance business; or B) that you are quite pleased with the insurance policies you presently hold; or C) that you are not content with the insurance policies you now hold, and perhaps you will be looking into this matter more seriously before too long; or D) that you do not own any type of policy and could not care less; or E) that you would like to purchase an insurance policy before too long; or F) that you are encouraging someone to purchase a policy or to give up a policy; or G) that this dream has little or no relevance to you at this time.

**INTERCOM** (i.e., a radio or telephone communication system in a home, office, plane, ship)
No one wishes you any harm! However, you can concoct more mischief for yourself if you persist in nourishing wrongful thoughts and actions against those who upset you. This dream counsels you to be more tolerant of minor, incidental, foolish, or nonsensical situations. It is not worth it to create stomach ulcers, pains, and stresses for anyone when, in fact, you have better things to do. Change your tune, and commence to live your life in peace and harmony.

**INTERCOURSE**
Any one or several of the following definitions may be applicable: A) that your sexual attitude is wholesome, sound, mature, and gratifying; or B) that your sexual appetite is not being appeased or gratified at all; or C) that you have a frustrated, unwholesome attitude about sexual intercourse or perhaps anything else pertaining to sex; or D) that you fantasize about sexual matters quite frequently, which does seem to bother you; or E) that you have been embittered, confused, and misled by someone's ignorance about the facts of life; or F) that you feel if more people were properly educated about sexual matters, their anxieties and frustrations would disappear; or G) that you are a basic abstainer where sex is concerned; or H) that this dream has little or no relevance to you.

**INTERIOR DECORATOR**
This dream suggests you may be powerfully attracted to someone who is out of bounds to you, and/or you possess a personal, inner weakness which tends to overcome your better judgment. Lacking self-confidence, feeling pity for oneself, as well as harbouring some silly notions or phobias about life will hold you back from a better future. Rushing blindly into situations could ultimately bring you offensive

accusations or could leave a lasting scar upon your well-being and reputation. This dream urges you to think carefully before letting yourself get carried away with some impulsive mental, physical, or sexual hangup. Use your better judgment in all things, at all times! By doing so, you could save yourself great battles of the mind and conscience.

**INTERMARRIAGE** (i.e., marriages between persons of different tribes, races, religions; or between closely related people)

Seeing this type of marriage within a dream state signifies that you either endorse intermarriage or that you do not endorse intermarriage. Whether you are for or against this type of marriage, only you know why you feel the way you do.

**INTERMENT** (see **BURIAL**)

**INTERMISSION**

To witness an intermission within your dream state infers that you possess introvert qualities. Sometimes you try to fight your shyness or inward ways, but to no avail. Be very patient with yourself, and begin to realize that your introvert endowments are a great virtue, instead of a hindrance. Maybe you are not as outgoing as other people around you, but you do have the satisfaction of appreciating more those wholesome moments of the heart, mind, and soul that an extrovert might ignore. Whether you know this or not, you are well-admired and pleasing to the mind and eyes of others, even if they fail to tell you so once in a while. Accept who you are; be proud to be who you are; and, above all, be thankful to be who you are.

**INTERPRETER** (i.e., a person who verbally interprets a foreign language)

This dream predicts extensive travel for you as well as meeting and greeting very influential people on your journey in life. Needless to say, you will be known in many high circles of society. Being admired and appreciated will be but a fraction of the many plaudits that yet await you. As a precautionary note, however, you are advised to always remain humble and to never forget to utilize your humanitarian gifts and qualities, wherever you go. Peacefully, you can make all your tomorrows become richer and better by reaching out to the needs of others you meet and greet.

**INTERROGATION** (see **INQUIRY**)

**INTERSECTION** (see **CROSSROAD** or **PASSAGEWAY**)

**INTERVIEW** (see **INQUIRY**)

**INTESTINE**
Seeing the intestines of a person or animal cautions you to not overindulge in certain foods (e.g., junk food, sweets) or drink (e.g., liquor, pop) or exercise (e.g., running, jogging) that may be harmful to you. Most times, people crave what they cannot eat or crave what they supposedly cannot have, so be wary about any desires that could give you premature troubles.

**INTOXICATION** (see **DRUNKENNESS**)

**INTRODUCTION** (i.e., foreword, preamble, or preface of a book; or the presentation of one person to another)
If there ever was a time to sketch out some future plans (e.g., travel, education, marriage, romance, career, move), now is the time to contemplate this with ease and anticipation. With a sure-fire tug of the heart, mind, and soul, your profound wishes and visualizations will one day be fulfilled. The blueprint of your life is relatively clear; you are a go-getter who intends to go forward with significant clarity and purpose. So be it! You are the architect of your own life, which will be both rewarding and successful.

**INTROSPECTION** (i.e., looking into one's thoughts, feelings, actions; self-examination or soul-searching)
Everyone does a little bit of soul-searching within their dream state simply because a dream can be the "eyes and ears" of the soul. What you do right or wrong in life can be ignored by you whenever you wish; however, your dreams can quite easily remind you of these rights and wrongs whenever the need arises. Your dreams, like your conscience, can quite easily haunt you when you have done something terribly wrong. Introspection is wholesome and good. In a dream, it allows you to be your own psychiatrist, so to speak, so that you can actually observe and analyze the rights and wrongs within your being. Upon waking up, many people actually reform and transform into better, more wholesome, and productive beings.

**INTUITION** (see **CLAIRVOYANCE** or **PERCEPTION**)

**INVASION**

Seeing an invasion of a village, town, city, state, or country by some military force or any other kind of group or force suggests that you are concerned about the well-being of the world and its peoples at large. Your caring personality is one to be admired and emulated, simply because it is people like you who show others the need to love, understand, and respect all races, colours, and creeds on this planet. Keep hoping and praying, and certainly continue your good efforts for peace; one day, when the world least expects it, a mighty Heavenly Force will make efforts like yours more worthy, profound, and lasting!

**INVENTION**

Some great inventors of the past prophetically foresaw some of their finest inventions-to-be within a dream state. Even today some great inventors have this perception! Not everyone, however, has this unique talent and foresight. If you are not an inventor but dream of inventing something or seeing a novel invention that appears workable, then you will be commencing a higher soul cycle within your life. In other words, the decisions and plans you will be making before too long should carry you into a brighter, greater, more rewarding future. Someone will assist you, and some opportunity will allow you to forge ahead as though you were on a flying carpet. Be patient, and be alert concerning your betterment. All good things happen, when the time is ripe.

**INVESTIGATION** (see **INQUIRY**)

**INVESTMENT**

To make a "good" investment within your dream means that you generally think seriously and cautiously before you buy, spend, or invest your money. Although you are not a Scrooge, by any means, you certainly will not throw your hard-earned money around, either. You are to be commended for your wise thinking and foresight!

To make a "bad" investment within a dream warns you against boasting, bragging, or putting on a false front where your supposed wealth is concerned. Do not try to impress or to manipulate others into believing you are greater, better, or richer than you are presently capable of being. Honesty and humility are the best investments anyone can make within themselves. You are no exception to the rule. Be true unto yourself, and your earthly wealth will grow!

## INVISIBILITY

To turn invisible or to sense an invisible presence or being within your dream state implies that you are seeking a niche, a reason, or a purpose for simply being here on earth. The so-called unknown facets of life such as miracles, extraterrestrial life, or ancient cultures, interest you. With your better judgment, intuitive mind, and psychological know-how, you will master some of your innermost goals and wishes. With each prayer you make and with each meditative step you take, you will eventually discover that the mind and soul have no limitations for betterment and attunement. But be wary lest you place mundane barriers in front of your pathway; these could ultimately set you back a peg or two. And bear in mind as well that in order to unveil the mystical knowledge that lies hidden within and around you, you must be as free and innocent as a child.

## INVITATION

Receiving or sending an invitation to do something worthy and constructive signifies that you are a mature, trusting, and loyal human being. You show compassion towards people by going out of your way to guide and assist them whenever the need arises. In other words, your actions do speak louder than words!

Receiving or sending an invitation to do something unworthy and unsound suggests that you sometimes use people for your own advantage. This shallow thinking is not wise, nor will it get you very far! Some people are not as dumb as you think they might be. Do not take advantage of anyone; you never know when you will meet someone with the same scheme in mind. This dream counsels you to be fair and just towards everyone you know; that is the only way you will truly prosper both inwardly and outwardly in life.

## INVOICE (see DEBT)

## IRON (see APPLIANCE)

## IRRIGATION (see *also* SPRINKLER)

If the irrigated area you see is rich with nature's growth and abundance, then you can be sure you are on the right track in life. Your life should be pleasantly comforting, open to communication, and filled with an abundance of pleasing surprises and happenings. All is well with you!

Should the irrigated area you see be barren, diseased, or laid waste for some reason, then your needs or wants or that of someone you know may be at an all-time high. A state of depression, anguish, loneliness, or impoverishment could very well be what is being experienced at this time. Situations will improve, but you must be willing to forego your present annoyances and disappointments for something more substantial within your life. In other words, you must believe that you can not only cope with your problem(s), but that you can conquer your problem(s), as well. And, by all that is good and glorious, you will! Judging by your dream, you are just about as gutsy as they come; you can do just about anything you set out to do!

## ISLAND

Seeing an island or being lost or stranded on one reveals that you sometimes feel forsaken by others around you. Being ignored, not complimented enough, taken for granted, being used or abused by someone, or perhaps just having the inner feeling that you are unwanted for some reason are but a few of the possibilities for your depressed, insecure, lonely feelings. There was more than one occasion when you felt that you would be much better off being away from people who merely seem to "see" you but don't "know" you exist. You would not mind being on an island, alone, forlorn, and forgotten! Truthfully, this is not the answer for you. On the contrary! What you must do is try a little harder to feel wanted and needed rather than fantasize about how people think and react when you are present. Basically, most people you know are not even aware that you feel the way you do. Be a good listener, but commence to be a better communicator, as well. Many people would be delighted to hear some of your intelligent views and insights, if you gave them half a chance. Do not feel out of place, either, when there is a group of people conversing about something unfamiliar to you. Just be content and listen. No problem! Sooner or later another topic of conversation will arise, and then perhaps you can join forces with them. No one—absolutely no one—has abandoned you! You are doing this to yourself. You can snap out of this state as soon as you come to grips with the reality of controlling your sensitive attitudes.

## ITINERARY (see AIM, JOURNEY, or VACATION)

**JACK** (i.e., a machine used for lifting or hoisting something such as a hydraulic jack, automobile jack)

Using or seeing this device within a dream cautions you to not be so overly confident in everything you do. Untimely accidents of various sorts can happen if you persist in maintaining this attitude. By being careless or risky, you are leaving yourself wide open for something to eventually happen. Always use your discretion and better judgment, no matter what you do in life. It is far better to be safe now than sorry later.

**JACKASS** (see **DONKEY**)

**JACK-IN-THE-BOX** (see **TOY**)

**JACK-O'-LANTERN**

Recently, you have been pondering about some worthy matter or plan of action which could, in the end, bring you much happiness and joy. Your inner feelings seem to be telling you to go ahead, whereas your practical thinking appears to be telling you to wait for another time. You would like to forge ahead but, from a logical point of view, the prospects at this time appear to be somewhat unpromising. Clear your mind and begin to visualize the positive aspects ahead *for* you, rather than ponder over the negative possibilities, which you could, in effect, surmount. If you can disband your fears and doubts about this entire situation, then you will be headed in the right direction.

**JACKPOT** (see **FORTUNE**, **GAMBLE**, or **LOTTERY**)

**JACKS** (see **GAME**)

**JAIL** (see **PRISON**)

**JAM** (see **FOOD**)

**JAMBOREE** (see **CELEBRATION**)

**JANITOR**

Perhaps you are a janitor? If so, then your dream is merely reflecting the work that you do. If you are not but dream about being or seeing one, then your dream reveals that you can anticipate better times ahead, but not without first making some important strides in improving your concepts, habits, and goals. Be more humble, compassionate, and understanding in everything you do; treat everyone with respect; do not try to be a know-it-all because, in the end, you may discover just how little you do know; strengthen your spirit and basic concepts of life with truth and much more thankfulness; be more determined; and always strive to carry out your goals and aims to the best of your ability. As you strive to improve your ways on a daily basis, you will slowly commence to see your true God-given qualities and capabilities reach out beyond your fondest expectations.

## JAR (see GLASSWARE)

## JAYWALKER

This action within a dream state reveals that there are some laws within your society which you feel are antiquated and ludicrous. Even so, these laws must be obeyed until they are changed. Perhaps it would take a person like you to lobby for a law change—that is, if you feel your actions would benefit many people.

## JEHOVAH (see GOD)

## JESUS

To have the honour and privilege of a dream visitation of Master Jesus within a dream is so overwhelmingly inspiring and fulfilling that even these words cannot do justice to the love, harmony, and friendship He has for you and all your loved ones. He has come to you for a very special reason: He does not want you to be disappointed or discouraged in life. If your life is full of burdens, sadness, or anguish, He wants you to know that He is beside you all the way and for you not to lose your hope, faith, and love in Him, yourself, nor in others, as well. He also wants you to know that your many sacrifices in life are all recorded, and one day the shadows of your past and present will disappear. Your dream of Jesus, the Christ Messiah, is in fact encouraging you to go forward in life, always seeking heavenly ways to assist your fellow man! Be good and love your fellow man—and truly your light, your pathway, your destiny will be attuned to Him forever!

(*Note*: You may also have the pleasure of knowing that if, for example, you are experiencing a very negative dream but at the very end of your dream sequence or anywhere during your dream sequence you happen to see Jesus, then the "symbolism" of Jesus takes precedence over your entire bad dream. Consequently, you have nothing to worry about simply because Jesus acts as a "buffer zone" to anything negative within a dream.)

## JETLINER (see AIRPLANE)

## JEWELLER

If you are a jeweler, then your dream merely reflects upon the work that you do. Assuming this is not your case, then this dream implies that you are a cautious, logical thinker. In fact, you are a survivor of sorts in that you have mastered many trials and tribulations, thus far. As you go on in life, your sincere, steadfast, and determined actions and outlook will at last bring you the prosperity and comfort you so wholesomely merit.

## JEWELLERY (see *also* BRACELET, BIRTHSTONE, CAMEO, DIAMOND, EARRING, or LOCKET)

Being cynical and suspicious of others are negative thought processes that will only lead you towards greater anguish and insecurities in your own personal life. You are far too hasty in condemning others and just as hasty in sweeping your own problems under the rug. Stop looking for flaws, weaknesses, and failings in other people, for everyone has these qualities, including you. You are advised to be more compassionate and spiritual-minded towards all people whom you meet and greet. Do your utmost to always accentuate the positive characteristics within yourself and within others. By doing this, you will draw more admiration and respect.

## JIGSAW PUZZLE

You are trying much too hard to impress others around you. Is it so difficult to be your natural, contented self? If the people you deal with are sincere and loyal, then they are very pleased to accept you for the true person you are, not for the person you are pretending to be or trying to project. Do not envy anyone, do not feel bad if someone has more than you have, and do not feel less fortunate if your heritage seems less rich than that of someone else. If you truly desire to be someone very special in life, then be your natural self at all times. You do not have to be a raving beauty to be beautiful; nor do you have to be a dashing prince to be handsome. God gave you a good mind, plenty of capabilities, and enough foresight to fulfill your daily activities with constructive thoughts and actions. Do so wisely!

**JOB** (See **CALLING, CAREER, EMPLOYMENT, LIFEWORK,** or **OWNERSHIP**)

**JOBLESS** (see **UNEMPLOYMENT**)

**JOCKEY** (i.e., a professional racehorse rider)
Perhaps you are, in fact, a jockey. If this is the case, then your dream merely reflects the state of your work either in a pleasant or unpleasant manner. If you are not, then your dream cautions you not to be so impatient and irritable towards people who are less knowledgeable than you. Not everyone has your intelligence, so be a bit more patient with those who fail to be as quick-minded as you. Besides, isn't it a great compliment to know that you have the insight and expertise to teach others what they do not know?

**JOCKSTRAP** (see **CLOTHES**)

**JOGGER**
Any one or several of the following definitions may be applicable: A) that you are a jogger and enjoy this particular type of exercise; or B) that you were a jogger at one time, but not any more; or C) that you would not consider jogging simply because this form of exercise can be harmful to your back, legs, or feet; or D) that you envy others who do jog but, due to some physical impediment, you cannot consider the prospects of this exercise at this time; or E) that you know of someone who was injured by jogging; or F) that because of your size or physique, you feel much too insecure to run, jog, or do some type of exercise outside; or G) that this dream has little or no relevance to you at this time.

**JOURNAL** (see **CHRONICLE, DIARY, MAGAZINE,** or **NEWSPAPER**)

**JOURNALIST** (i.e., a news editor or reporter)
You utilize your mind and talents to the best of your God-given abilities. These fine attributes as a human being can be very rewarding;

you are always searching, analyzing, and ultimately finding the answers you want in life. Keeping busy and being productive and constructive in all that you do are the right concepts to uphold! Who knows, maybe someday the world will know of your good work and actions. This would depend entirely upon the ambition you harbour within yourself. But, for the moment, do not rule out any possibilities where your life is concerned. You are certainly headed towards greater things and higher plateaus—to what degree remains to be seen.

## JOURNEY

Any one or several of the following definitions may be applicable: A) that you will be making a journey before too long; or B) that you have just returned from a journey; or C) that you wish to embark on some trip before too long but have second thoughts about leaving; or E) that you are worried about someone who is either planning a trip or who has already set out on a trip; or F) that you are a bit of a high-strung individual who becomes upset or fearful when embarking upon a journey; or G) that your journey within your dream state was so realistic that you honestly feel you actually did take a trip; or H) that this dream has little or no relevance to you at this time.

## JUBILATION (see HAPPINESS)

## JUDAS (see BETRAYER or DISCIPLE)

## JUDGE (i.e., a person appointed or elected to settle cases within a court of law, a person so appointed to settle a dispute of some nature, or a person so appointed to pick a winner in some pageant or contest) (see *also* ADJUDICATION)

Never depart from your high ideals and hopes in life. It is when you literally throw your hands in the air as though you were about to give up that things can commence to become worse for you. Yet, inwardly you know that you can never give up on anyone or anything. Even though your struggles are sometimes far greater than the next person's, you still manage to carry on with deep conviction, sincerity, and a willingness to serve the needs of others. This may not always be reciprocated with kindness, love, or appreciation by others, but somehow you have that innate wisdom to forge ahead. You are not only a survivor of many things; in many ways, you are also a leader!

**JUDGMENT DAY** (i.e., man's final judgment at the end of the world)

There are two choices for people on this planet. Choice one: be good and live a clean, positive, productive life. If you disobey God's Laws on occasion, then pray for forgiveness, count your blessings that He does forgive you, and then try not to deviate from the positive road you are upholding. Choice two: be corrupt and live an unclean, unwholesome life and just see where this action will get you. It will get you nowhere! There are no shortcuts to heaven, so do not feel for a moment that you can get away with sinning or other wrongdoing without repentance. The highest Laws of Life are God's Laws; without His Love within your soul, you have absolutely nothing. What will you say to Him on your judgment day?

**JUDO**

You have already learned some invaluable lessons in life by doing or saying the wrong things. Rarely do you make the same mistake again; once is enough! This dream advises you to carry on with your wholesome concepts, attitudes, and work habits. Someday, you will prosper beyond your fondest wishes!

**JUG** (see *also* **EARTHENWARE** or **GLASSWARE**)

Most people who maintain an "easy come, easy go" attitude in life are certainly headed for a collision course—not only with themselves, but with their destiny, as well. This dream advises you to accept your responsibilities at all times. Refusing to do so can only lead to emotional turmoil and a host of financial insecurities down the road. Isn't it better to build your life in a sensible manner than to ruin your life in a careless manner? What you do today, you may regret tomorrow. Think ahead, and maybe then you will commence to perceive the message this dream has brought you.

**JUGGLER**

You seem to juggle your ideas and plans so frequently that sometimes it becomes impossible to know just what you want or where you are going in life. Hold on! Utilize more forethought in your mind and actions. The difficulties shown here is that you plan something which seems relatively wholesome and good, but this never appears to satisfy you. You always strive to supercede your plans with some greater ideas which, when put to practice, never seem to turn out in your favor. In other words, you find it very difficult to please yourself, no matter what you do! This dream advises you to do the very best you can when you are doing something, and then, as a matter of good common sense, let matters rest there. The less hassling you do with yourself, the better off you will be!

## JUKEBOX (see RECORD PLAYER)

## JUMP

To jump up (e.g., to the top of a mountain, building) implies that some of your immediate, pressing problems and worries will be solved. Do not panic; situations will start improving within a day or two of this dream!

To jump down (e.g., from the top of a mountain, building) implies that you may be creating more worries and problems for yourself because of your attitude or unwillingness to listen to common sense. If you know that what you are doing is wrong or that your actions can bring you unnecessary difficulties, then heed the good advice you have already received. Trouble is where you find it; it appears to be lurking just around the corner, if you are not more mindful.

Jumping up and down within a dream state reveals you seem to have the better of two worlds. Some things are going well for you; some things are not going so well. Nonetheless, you should be able to master your present difficulties rather admirably before too long. Be patient, for someone will assist you shortly. This should give you more peace of mind, as well.

## JUNCTION (see CROSSROAD or PASSAGEWAY)

## JUNGLE

Sometimes you feel as though you live in a jungle! By the time you come out of your maze of detours and difficulties, there is always something else happening. A person feels like laughing and crying at the same time! What next? Well, this dream foretells that you will come out of the darkness into the light; and, when you do, your inner blessings will be far greater than your disappointments. You will rise above your despair in a very short order of time. Be still; pray, keep your faith, and—above all—maintain a hopeful outlook regarding all those trying events surrounding you. Better days are but an arm's length away from you.

## JUNIOR HIGH SCHOOL (see SCHOOL)

## JUNK

This dream implies that you have a low regard for yourself. Begin to unravel the reasons why you feel this way. There is really nothing the matter with you except your negative feelings about your personality, appearance, and so on. What makes you any worse than the next person? You are just as good, if not better than, many people around you. The sooner you decide to snap out of the terrible feelings you have about yourself, the better off you will be. Do not hesitate to seek professional advice if you find your problem too complex to handle.

## JUNKYARD (see JUNK)

## JURY

You are a very determined individual who is not afraid to battle uphill all the way until you have accomplished your set goal(s). You are highly admired for your fortitude and determination! Being slightly eccentric adds to your already gifted and highly creative individualism. You are indeed a very special person to many people. Those who truly know you truly love you for just being you.

## JUVENILE (see ADOLESCENT)

## JUVENILE DELINQUENCY

Any one or several of the following definitions may be applicable: A) that you are a juvenile delinquent who is being reminded through your dream about the wrongs you have created; or B) that you were a delinquent many years ago but not any more; or C) that you know of someone who is a delinquent, but there is very little you can do to help this person at this time; or D) that you have been robbed, raped, or manhandled by several delinquents; or E) that you feel society is much too lenient with this type of individual; or F) that you abhor this type of behaviour in anyone and can only hope that all children of the world would grow up to be more responsible and caring citizens; or G) that you blame the parents directly for their children's wayward thinking and habits; or H) that you blame society as a whole for the way young people behave; or I) that you blame the young people themselves for their own wayward behaviour—since they obviously know the difference between right and wrong; or J) that this dream has little or no relevance to you at this time.

**KALEIDOSCOPE** (i.e., a tube-like, rotating instrument used for seeing a variety of symmetrical patterns, or anything that repeatedly changes in pattern and colour)
You are a very hard worker. There are times, though, when you feel that your work is all in vain. Not so, according to your dream; you cannot possibly make a better world for yourself without trying! Your dream, in fact, is patting you on the back for your sincere, diligent efforts. Be happy to be who you are, for in due time the measure of your insight and understanding will ultimately bring you the prosperity and leisure moments which you so honourably deserve!

**KANGAROO**
This animal signifies that your recent action or decision concerning home, business, or career matters was totally in order. There are times when people must embark upon greater avenues within their lives, otherwise they get caught up in their own emotional, confused rut. Never look back at any minor or major positive changes within your life. You have come to earth to progress, not regress; so have no remission about going forward with your thoughts, attitudes, and actions. The biggest traumatic setback you could possibly encounter is to allow your own fears, inhibitions, and outside interferences to prevent you from progressing in life. You have that God-given right to forge ahead; no one and nothing should ever stop you!

**KARATE**
The emotional order and materialistic sights you seek within your life are well founded. However, it would not hurt to become more consistent and determined with the positive goals you have laid out for yourself. In many respects you have already "turned over a new leaf"; this is very commendable. These positive intentions can be the beginnings of a very promising future, but you must be inwardly patient, and you must be prepared to work very hard for what you desire in life. If you keep up the good work, you will eventually reap the harvest of your labours with happiness, peace, and prosperity!

**KARMA** (i.e., a belief that one's past existence on this planet will determine the state of being or destiny of one's future existence on this planet)
Any one or several of the following definitions may be applicable: A) that you believe in the principle of karma; or B) that you do not

believe in the principle of karma; or C) that you are confused about the man-made philosophy of reincarnation and karma; or D) that you have gained a clearer perspective of life over the years and realize that we have to account for our one and only chance on earth now, not later, no matter what the popular books profess or what ancient myths and philosophies are in vogue today; or E) that you do not believe in karma, reincarnation, or the hereafter, for that matter; or F) that you have read some stories about reincarnation and karma and merely accept this theory at face value by simply going along with this flow of thought like "the blind leading the blind", so to speak; or G) that you could never understand why God, who is truly loving and forgiving, would keep sending His children back to earth to be punished for something they did a century or two ago; or H) that this dream has little or no relevance to you at this time.

**KAYAK** (see **BOAT**)

**KEEPSAKE** (see **SOUVENIR**)

**KEG** (see **BARREL**)

**KENNEL**
You are a kind, considerate, and conscientious individual who rarely, if ever, would hurt or abuse another person's feelings. Your fondness for life and for people themselves is a sheer joy to behold! With your humanitarian and creative endowments, you are bound to share your truth, considerations, and inner strength for many years to come. In many ways, you are a like a person whose light illuminates the way for those without hope, without meaning, or without love. Indeed, you are a very special human being!

**KERCHIEF** (see **HANDKERCHIEF**)

**KERNEL** (i.e., the inner part of a nut or a fruit pit, etc.)
You are a broad-minded, generous, and independent individual. The weight of your problems is very often made lighter because of your great sense of humour and overall pleasing characteristics. What really annoys you in life is seeing or hearing about people who go out of their way to hurt, cheat, or rob innocent victims, or people who misuse their God-given talents in an underhanded manner under the

guise of innocence or indifference. True to life, you are a very productive, talented individual; you are very willing to share the seeds of your
experience and knowledge with others around you. In many respects,
you are the master of your own destiny; and, so far, you are doing quite
an admirable job!

**KETTLE**
Essentially, you are a very pleasant, witty person—except when
you are confronted with situations not to your liking or when someone disagrees with you. Raising your temper or blood pressure in
disappointing matters or problems will not accomplish anything for
you. This dream advises you to calm down, be more willing to give
and take in any conversation or heated discussion, and to finally stabilize your maturity with more sensibility and self-control. Since
you are intelligent enough to know better, then it only stands to
reason that you should act better; do so at all times. Be at peace!
There are other mountains to cross, with many successes ahead for
you.

**KEY** (i.e., a metal instrument for moving the bolt of a lock and locking or unlocking something)
To see a key intact suggests that you are on the forefront of doing
something rather special. This could perhaps imply a marriage, a long-
awaited trip, writing a novel, or anything else that would appear to be
stimulating and rewarding to you at this time.
A key that is broken, bent, or lost within a dream state implies that
you are searching for some happiness, satisfaction, or progress within
your life but fail to realize that all this is attainable when you learn to
let go of your dissatisfied attitudes. How can you possibly be happy
and content with anyone or anything on this earth plane if you refuse
to see and feel the positive side of people, places, and things? You hold
that key to your happiness and progress on earth; no one else does. If
you choose to be bitter, critical, and disappointed with most things
you do and see, then it is your outlook that needs an overhauling, and
only you can do it. A little clue: where's your sense of humour? Why
don't you entertain yourself with some hilarious books or fun-filled
activities and have yourself a good, laughter-filled day! This will help
you. Laughter can re-channel your thoughts to more pleasing visualizations and concepts within your life. Do not ignore this vital factor;
you need it!

**KEYBOARD** (see **COMPUTER, INSTRUMENT**, or **TYPEWRITER**)

**KEYHOLE**

To see a keyhole reveals that you are insecure or frightened where you live or work. This could very well imply that someone may be bothering, harassing, or threatening you for some reason, or there could be other circumstance that would make you fearful about your safety or well-being in life. Your living nightmare will end when you commence to take some positive steps to defend your rights and to secure a safer place of refuge for your peace of mind and betterment.

**KIBBUTZ** (i.e., a collective settlement or farm, especially in Israel)

A talent or gift of any nature is based upon reasonable intelligence, hard work, and a fighting, determined spirit to carry on, no matter what impediments lie between you and that once-in-a-lifetime goal. Using excuses or being uncaring, lazy, proud, and self-centered, or allowing others to impede your progress in a variety of ways is indeed a crime upon the soul. Note, as well, that any regrets you may experience at a later date will be but a mere reflection upon a wasted life. There still remains a hope and a prayer that you will commence to acknowledge your inner worth with triumphant inspiration and responsibility.

**KICK**

Kicking someone or something within a dream state (with the exception of participating in some type of game or sport activity) reveals that you have been straddled with a variety of personal fears and hang-ups over the years; only you know what they are. Now is the time to take stock of these negative elements and to try to dispose of them one by one. Do not be afraid to smile when you are happy or to shed a tear when you are sad, for these are true emotional expressions that are wholesome and compensating to the body, mind, and soul. Do not be afraid to live a good life or to express your thoughts to those who feign greatness or importance; their lives, on many occasions, are shallow and meaningless. Do not be afraid to be humble and thankful for all your spiritual and earthly possessions, for these, too, are enlightened measures to make your road in life a little easier to bear. Do not be afraid to face your tomorrows but, in truth, live each moment, each hour, each day as though tomorrow might not come. Do not be afraid to grow and prosper inwardly, and always remember to not become greedy, mercenary, or prideful. Do not be afraid of yourself or to know more about yourself and your many weaknesses and misgivings, for it is in these soul-searching measures that you will commence to repair your flaws with impressive results. And, last, do not be afraid to be an understanding, helpful, and obedient soul to those who care and love you the most.

**KID** (see **GOAT**)

**KIDNAPPING** (see *also* **HOSTAGE** or **RANSOM**)
   Any one or several of the following definitions may be applicable: A) that you were a kidnap victim at one time; or B) that you know of someone who was kidnapped; or C) that you have, in fact, taken part in a kidnapping and are now being haunted by this act; or D) that you feel anyone who kidnaps another person should be dealt with severely by the law; or E) that you sometimes fear for the safety of your loved ones where kidnappers are concerned, but you have taken all necessary precautions to this effect; or F) that you never really paid too much attention to this matter of kidnapping simply because you feel a kidnapper would not gain anything from seizing you or your family; or G) that a kidnapper is no more and no less than a depraved, sick human being; or H) that this dream has little or no relevance to you at this time.

**KILL** (see *also* **MURDER**)
   To kill someone or to kill something within a dream state but to not consider this act a murder indicates that you are a very temperamental individual who can either think and act positively when the mood strikes you or think and act very negatively when the mood strikes you. On the negative side, you have the capabilities of being easily provoked; this could create mental and physical havoc not only for yourself but for the next person, as well. Curb your temper. While you are at it, learn to forgive and forget any wrongs that have befallen you thus far. Revenge, hate, and any passion for mischief and misconduct on your part could lead to very serious ramifications from here to eternity. Respect all life around you; and you, too, will be respected.

**KILLER** (see **CRIMINAL**, **KILL**, or **MURDER**)

## KILL-JOY

Being or seeing a spoilsport within the dream world implies that you or someone you know tends to behave this way. If you do behave this way, then you obviously have great difficulties in accepting any form of rejection that happens to come your way. This inability to accept rejection may be created in a child who is overly protected and stifled by one or both parents, or in a child who is overly neglected, abused, or reprimanded. They seek attention; they also need love, respect, and trust. If they fail to receive these, then they ultimately carry their spoilsport attitude with them into adulthood. So, in effect, spoilsports should begin to acknowledge their misguided past with honesty, common sense, and—above all—maturity. You may never know the many whys and wherefores of your past or even remember the fine details of your upbringing, but you certainly can account for your actions of today and tomorrow.

**KILN** (see **OVEN**)

**KILT** (see **CLOTHES**)

**KINDERGARTEN** (see **SCHOOL**)

**KINDLER** (i.e., a person who starts or ignites a fire)

Kindling a fire pertains to one's physical and emotional state of being. You have recently been under a depressive spell that appears to be somewhat self-inflicted. While you are harbouring inner thoughts of hurt, resentment, jealousies, and hatred, your imagination is working overtime to compound your feelings and bitter state. At this time you are only seeing your side of the story; but, if you are sincere and honest, you will find the real truth behind your gloom. Think less of self in these lowly times, and you will soon discover that your problems are but a mere raindrop when compared to another person's downpour. Count your blessings, look up, be grateful, and plod on like a valiant soldier who has conquered an enemy. That enemy, of course, is within you.

**KING** (see **ROYALTY**)

**KING COBRA** (see **SNAKE**)

## KISS

Kissing someone reveals that you will never be lonely or lack a friend or two to help you through your most trying hours of life. You are very fortunate to be blessed with such loyal and true friendships. A true friendship is like a beautiful star or a beautiful flower—precious to behold and inspiring to know.

## KIT (e.g., tool kit, first aid kit, salesman's kit, sport kit)

If the kit you see is open, then you have a good conceptual view of yourself and where you are headed in life. You know the difference between a dollar bill and a loaf of bread and that if you spend your money unwisely, there will be no bread on the table. It is quite obvious that you would never allow this to happen. Your future will be most rewarding to you simply because, with sensibility and money in your pocket, there will be many opportunities to gain the wealth, leisure, and freedom you so desire.

If the kit you see happens to be closed, then be prepared for some discouraging and disappointing events to follow. Some financial and emotional struggles are foretold by this dream. However, you can surmount these difficulties with common sense and plenty of inner courage. Facing this storm head-on will bring you immeasurable rewards and comfort. If, however, you decide to run away from your responsibilities or realistic views in this matter, then your struggles will continue to grow.

## KITCHEN

A neat, orderly kitchen infers that everything should be going relatively smoothly for you at this time. This dream suggests harmony with self and others, financial improvements, and possible travel abroad. All is well and will continue to be so for quite some time ahead.

A disorderly kitchen infers that all is not well with you or your loved ones. The problems may involve money, liquor, drugs, unfaithfulness, greed, hate, jealousies, or just about anything that might stifle your present progress. If these matters can be changed in any way, then you should commence to see some progress within a month or two of this dream. If no attempts are made to correct what appears to be stressful and wrong in your situation, then sadness and anguish will prevail.

**KITCHENMAID** (see **MAID**)

**KITCHENWARE** (see **UTENSIL**)

**KITE**

Seeing a kite sail peacefully in the air indicates that you are trying to help someone or uplift someone because of their mental or physical state of being. It appears that you will be very successful in this matter; and, before too long, you will receive the praises you rightfully deserve! There are not enough people like you on earth; you are like an angel in disguise!

Seeing a kite fall heavily to earth intimates that unless you change some of your wayward and slothful attitudes someone may tell you to go fly a kite! Do not take advantage of anyone for your own underhanded reasons. You will lose more than you will gain by manipulating or cajoling someone to do your work for you. Accept what lies ahead of you by being more responsible. There will come a time when you will simply have to change; the sooner you do this, the better off you will be. You can hardly expect any rewards in life if you fail to earn them.

**KITTEN** (see **CAT**)

**KLEPTOMANIA** (i.e., a constant, abnormal desire to steal)

Any one or several of the following definitions may be applicable: A) that you suffer from kleptomania and would like to be helped or would not like to be helped with your problem; or B) that after proper treatment and counseling, your desires to steal left you; or C) that you deal with maintaining the law and your dream merely reflected the kleptomaniac-type individual(s) that you apprehend from time to time; or D) that you know of someone who steals quite constantly but seem helpless in doing anything about this action; or E) that you feel stealing is more like a daring hobby or the next best thing to working for a living; or F) that you feel stealing even a penny is totally wrong; or G) that this dream has little or no relevance to you at this time.

**KNAPSACK** (see **PACKSACK**)

**KNEE** (see **LEG**)

## KNEEL

Today, your faith may be stronger, and your needs may be greater. Your better instincts tell you that you will not only conquer your problems, but inspire others to do the same. Life may not always be easy, but simply knowing that things can and will get better is the simplest key in making things better. Your thoughts can be more powerful than your words. Your thoughts can inspire and, at times, can create all kinds of wholesome changes within and around you (e.g., a silent prayer that is answered, a wish that comes true, a deep desire that is fulfilled).

## KNEEPAD

You seem to be going through extremes with respect to a certain matter that will eventually solve itself anyway. Your fussing and fretting in this entire affair will have been all in vain! Settle down, compose yourself, and relax. Why don't you give more credence to what your tomorrows might bring you? Oh, you of little faith. Your tomorrows bear gifts!

## KNIFE

The symbolism of a knife often frightens people. However, a knife—no matter how it is seen in a dream state—always refers to a spiritual and mental uplifting and betterment within one's life. If you are presently experiencing something traumatic, then this dream assures you that the pending improvements will be both wholesome and deserving. Hopefully, you will have become wiser from your trials and tribulations.

(*Note*: You may also have the pleasure of knowing that if, for example, you are experiencing a very negative dream but at the very end of your dream sequence or anywhere during your dream sequence you happen to see a knife, then this knife "symbolism" takes precedence over your entire bad dream. Consequently, you have nothing to worry about simply because the knife acts as a "buffer zone" to anything negative within a dream.)

## KNIGHT

Do not be too complacent or smug in life; there is always room for improvement, no matter who or what you are. Sometimes, when you think you have the whole world at your beck and call, something happens that disappoints you. What this dream is trying to tell you is to always appreciate those better days wholesomely and wisely because you never know when you might be set back a step or two. A knight in shining armour represents inner peace and joy; but his armour advises you to be prepared for anything unusual or anything else that might beset you when you least expect it to happen.

## KNITTING

There are some people who are very willing to be helped or assisted on this earth plane; but there are others who simply refuse to listen to common sense. Do not feel defeated if your attempts fail to help someone in need or if you counsel someone and they fail to heed your sound, logical advice. This world is full of hard knocks for both ignorant or intelligent stubborn people! Sooner or later, they learn.

## KNOCK

To hear a knock within a dream or to knock on someone's door implies two things: A) that someone is calling for help and needs a prayer from you; or B) that you will be called upon to settle a dispute between two people or help these two people out financially. Either case can be handled logically and amiably. You can consider yourself very fortunate to be able to use your sound judgment in order to help others. You are very stimulating, generous, and assertive in most things that you do.

## KNOT

Making a knot or seeing a knot implies that you are creating more problems for yourself, and perhaps for someone else, than is deemed necessary. You must realize that there are some things you may never achieve in life, but the vast majority of projects you set out to do will probably be accomplished. What you do not achieve today, you can always try again to achieve tomorrow. Your demanding ways can make you miserable at times! You want things to happen right now, or not at all! You know this is not feasible all the time, even if you are deserving. Why, some of the greatest people today had to wait years before their accomplishments were even known to mankind. You are no exception to that rule. Be grateful for events that happen now, and be just as patient for events that will take time to materialize. Be at peace, for your life is likened unto an open book whose many chapters have yet to be written, experienced, and fulfilled.

**KOSHER FOOD** (see **FOOD**)

**KU KLUX KLAN** (i.e., a society of white men who strive to uphold white supremacy such as being anti-Negro, anti-Semitic, anti-Catholic)
   Any one or two of the following definitions may be applicable: A) that you are a member of the Ku Klux Klan; or B) that you are not a member of this society; or C) that you are not a member yet, but hope to be one in the very near future; or D) that you were once a member of this society; or E) that you oppose their terrorist tactics; or F) that you know of someone who is a member of this society; G) that you feel this society has its roots based on demon knowledge and actions; or H) that, quite frankly, you believe those who play with fire will eventually be consumed by fire; or I) that their behaviour on earth is a great disgrace to white people who desire peace and good fellowship with all mankind; or J) that this dream has little or no significance to you at this time.

**KUNG FU** (see **KARATE**)

**LABEL** (e.g., a sticker)
   Some hostilities and hate have been created towards you because of your strict and unbending rules and regulations (e.g., at home, work). You obviously run a very tight ship, so to speak, and do not wish to see anyone fall or fail in your midst. However, you must realize that not everyone thinks or acts as you do, nor are they as dynamic as you are. Some people will probably never have your mettle and stamina, no matter how hard you try to instill your will upon them. Be fair, and be more willing to give them their freedom of mind and deed in order to prove their worth and stamina to you. Of course, you may not see immediate results where these matters are concerned; but, then again, you never became "all-wise" in a day, either.

**LABORATORY**
   You are very logical and level-headed, always looking for the right answers here and there. Sometimes you think so deeply about the whys and wherefores of life and its wonders, joys, and mysteries that you fail to see the possibilities that not all things emanate from logical concepts. You seem to be looking for concrete answers wherever you go;

yet, so many things that are not as yet discovered, invented, created, and so on will actually emanate from thoughts and ideas which at first seem unrealistic, far-fetched, and totally illogical until they are put to practical use. In essence, this dream is trying to tell you to go a step further with your sensible thoughts when you are probing, analyzing, or trying to figure out something that appears totally bizarre and puzzling to you. Other concepts and possibilities do exist on this planet. However, they do not always stem from "a, b, c" thoughts—but rather from "z, y, x" thoughts.

## LACEWORK (see *also* DECORATION, EMBROIDERY, or KNITTING)

Life is only as pleasant or as sad as you make it out to be, for—in truth—there appears to be a cause and effect with everything you do. For example, if you are unpleasant to someone during the day, you can be sure that someone else will do the same thing to you before too long. Or, if you gossip about a person, you can be sure someone is gossiping about you, as well. What is important here is that you should always strive to minimize your flaws and inner weaknesses instead of allowing them to grow on a daily basis. Each time you improve in life, you literally climb a step closer to your enriched self; and, by the same token, climb a step away from your bitter, troublesome self. What would you prefer to be in life, happy or bitter? Some people are gluttons for punishment, so they simply refuse to better themselves; some people peacefully realize that the miracle of change cannot come unless they do something to bring it about. Which one would you prefer to be in life?

## LACROSSE (see GAME)

## LADDER

Merely seeing a ladder by itself within a dream state reveals that situations within and around you are somewhat stable and not too electrifying, either here or there. In other words: no news is good news! This is an ideal time to get caught up on all your unfinished business, or—if possible—make some attempts to break away from your busy schedules and chores.

A broken ladder intimates that someone will break their promise to you. Do not become emotionally upset or disappointed in this matter at all. If you are strong and sensible, you will adhere to this advice.

However, should you become emotionally upset over this matter, you will be creating quite a bit of unnecessary anguish for yourself.

To climb up a ladder intimates that you are either climbing out of an earthly rut, or you are climbing out of a situation that has troubled you for quite some time. Be happy; better times are foreseen ahead for you, with greater prospects towards achievements, happiness, and financial prosperity.

Climbing down from a ladder suggests that you are refusing to let go of some matter that is bothersome to you, or you are reverting back to some old haunts or habits which may be unpleasing or unwholesome to your better personality. It is your willpower alone that will conquer these weaknesses. Maybe this time, you will listen!

**LADLE** (see **UTENSIL**)

**LADYBUG** (see **BEETLE**)

**LAGOON** (see **WATER**)

**LAKE** (see **WATER**)

**LAMA** (see **CLERGYMAN** or **MONK**)

**LAMB**

Seeing a lamb or a flock of lambs graze, rest, or sleep within a dream state intimates that you can be very easily hurt or deceived by others around you. You are likened unto an innocent lamb who can be overtaken by an enemy when you least suspect it. Begin to recognize your own God-given capabilities in dealing with situations not to your liking, but remember that "an eye for an eye and a tooth for a tooth" is not the answer. In fact, it is far better to be meek than to be cruel, wicked, or evil in life. This dream suggests you use your intelligence, discretion, and diplomacy whenever someone offends your good character.

Seeing a lamb who is lost or who appears to be in some type of difficulty signifies that you are that symbolic lamb. There is no need to fret, fumble, weep, or panic in your present anxieties or hardships simply because, with a little bit of foresight and encouragement, you will come out of your situation triumphant. Do you recall that whenever you were weary, forlorn, or in some kind of anguish there was always that inner feeling that guided you towards calm waters and greener pastures? Well, it is no different today. You may think you are lost in some deep valley of life or that your difficulties are just too much to bear, but—with prayer, patience, and logic—you will find the peace you rightfully seek.

## LAMENESS (see PARALYSIS)

## LAMP

You are overestimating your own abilities in trying to cope with anything that happens to come your way. Be careful lest someone more disagreeable and more challenging attempts to lock horns with you. Know when to back off if situations beyond your control are too much to handle. Disagreements and dissensions of a minor sort could lead to a bigger sport not to your liking!

## LAMPPOST (see LAMP)

## LANDING FIELD (see AIRPORT)

## LANDLADY (see LANDLORD)

## LANDLORD

If the landlord (or landlady) you see appears to be content and peaceful, then your place of lodging should be secure and blessed with comfort and goodness. You will always have good friends and plenty of outstanding times with those around you. Travel, new acquisitions, and financial improvements are foreseen in the very near future for you.

Seeing a landlord (or landlady) in a vexed, disappointed mood suggests that you will be deceived and mocked by someone whom you have trusted. The big question here is will you be strong enough to forgive that person, or will you seek some form of retaliation? This dream strongly urges you to simply ignore this entire affair, if you can. You may have lost a supposed friend in the process, but in the long run you will have maintained your sanity and avoided needless wear and tear. Should you decide to retaliate, however, then be prepared for one of the biggest, longest hassles of your life! Tears, anguish, and restless nights are foretold here. For your own sake, think twice about your intentions.

## LANDSLIDE

In one way, you can be very charitable and kind; but, in another way, you can be very impatient and caustic. The next time you talk to someone, listen to your words very closely. If the urge comes to fault or humiliate someone, then you would be advised to say nothing. Do not lose your respect over some habit(s) that can be controlled and curbed.

## LANGUAGE

In general terms, any language known or spoken within a dream state intimates that more communication and togetherness is required within your family circle (e.g., mother, father, brother, sister). People very often distance themselves from their family because of their independence or career, or whatever the case may be. This is all right up to a point. However, the greatest measure we have on earth is the family bonded together in love, compassion, and communication towards one another; and, to some degree, still being dependent upon one another. Independence is fine providing you do not give up or abandon your family for whatever reasons you might deem necessary. Truly the most profound language we have on this planet is the communicative, close-knit, unselfish, trusting, believing, responsible, law-abiding, appreciative, charitable, prayerful, and loyal unit known as the family. Parents should always love, teach, honour, and respect their children, from the time of conception. And children should always love, honour, and respect their parents. These truths are not always adhered to because of certain circumstances or events within the family circle (e.g., abuse, hatred, divorce, money problems, death). There are thousands of reasons why people do not get along or try to get along on this plane of life. In essence, this dream advises you to love and forgive one another here, for in the afterlife you will have to adhere to this Universal Principle, one way or another.

(*Note*: The prime reason to include this encompassing, universal dream symbolism of language was to broaden the dreamer's scope about themselves and to further emphasize the importance of one's family. The word "language" itself cannot be cross-referenced simply because most dreams are composed of some type of language which is silently thought of, spoken, or written. So the word "language" would have to be cross-referenced in every entry. This was deemed impractical. It is hoped, however, that as you flip through the pages of this book, you will come across the general meaning of this word, and perhaps you will then find some truth about the soul of your family and yourself.)

## LANTERN (see LAMP)

## LARD

Seeing or using this product in a dream intimates that you are experiencing some emotional or bodily discomforts. The longevity of your problem depends upon your basic attitude and outlook in life. If you think in a depressive, negative manner, then obviously you will be prolonging your problems. However, if you harbour a healthy and positive outlook, then your present state of affairs can change drastically for you. Prayer, rest, patience, confidence, and hope are all wholesome inner ingredients that can assist you to become better. If you feel your problem is too severe, then do not hesitate to seek professional counseling or medical assistance.

## LASER (i.e., a device used to emit laser beams)

You act quickly, emphatically, and sometimes angrily when someone close to you fails to heed your realistic advice. It just annoys you to know that the answers are right in front of them, but they refuse to face the truth about themselves or about their life in general. In matters of this nature, there is very little you can do but to continue to be your pleasant self and to never close the doors of love to those same people who might heed your advice later on down the road. Do not let people's thoughts and actions frustrate you so much; everyone is different, and most everyone has their day or hour to change. Just be your pleasant self, be more open-minded, and continue to help or guide others whenever you can. Your good work is still greatly appreciated!

## LASSO (see NOOSE)

## LAST JUDGMENT (see JUDGMENT DAY)

## LAST RITES (i.e., special sacraments said upon a dying person, or prayers and rites said upon a dead person)

Any one or several of the following definitions may be applicable: A) that you believe in the last rites being said upon a dying or dead person; or B) that you do not believe that saying the last rites over anyone will or can save their soul; or C) that you have witnessed the last rites being said over a dying or dead person; or D) that you feel the last rites said upon a dying person can and does ease the mind of the family involved; or E) that you would like to have more tangible proof that the soul exists beyond the last rites and the grave; or F) that you fear sickness or death, so the mere thought about last rites is very disturbing to you; or G) that you feel the spiritual tradition where last rites are concerned can certainly do no harm to anyone; or H) that this dream has little or no relevance to you at this time.

**LAST SUPPER** (i.e., the Lord's Supper before His Crucifixion)

This dream, though very rare, symbolizes your inner quest to find the solace, peace of mind, wisdom, and truth to living a better, Christ-minded life. You couldn't be in better, safer Hands than Christ Himself, no matter what direction you turn to on earth. And, remember: by your virtues and through your obedience to His Teachings, you will conquer your human distractions and fears. To be Christ-minded, you must truly love God, Jesus, and the Holy Mother from the depths of your soul, and you must lead a good, honest, loving life. Be helpful to everyone, and love and respect your fellow man at all times.

**LATCH** (i.e., a fastening for a window, gate, or door)

You are advised to seal your mind tight with regard to the actions or affairs of another person. If you do know something about this individual, then it is extremely wise to not make matters any worse than what he or she is presently experiencing. What you know may be a truth, a half-truth, or an unsound fallacy; revealing what you think you know could have serious consequences. Instead of reflecting upon someone else, why don't you look at the other side of the coin and see whether or not there is room for self-improvement within your own life?

**LAUGHTER**

If you laugh within a dream, then you can expect some sarcasm, mockery, and indifference from practically anyone during the next three days. Some people may act snobbish towards you, and someone may even provoke you into an argument. This is the type of dream that would almost compel people to isolate themselves for the next three days!

To see someone else laugh within your dream suggests that you will be the instigator for the next several days. You will be edgy, domineering, and argumentative with practically anyone you meet. The only advice this dream can give you is for you to test your self-control. If you can do this and succeed in not offending anyone during the next several days, then indeed you know more about the internal and external forces around you than the average individual.

**LAUNCH PAD** (i.e., a platform from which rockets, missiles, and other devices are launched)

You are about to embark on some impressive, constructive turnabout changes within your life. New horizons, challenges, and long-awaited realizations lie ahead of you. It is amazing what a little bit of hope and faith can do, especially when you believe in yourself and when your friends encourage you to go ahead with your formulated ideas and plans. Life can be rich, rewarding, and beautiful to those who are willing to let go of old ways for greater, "believe it or not" realities! You certainly fit this category rather admirably.

**LAUNDRY**

Clean-looking laundry reveals that you are a well-adjusted, well-admired individual. You have a great sense of humour and are blessed with enough sensitivity to respect the rights of others around you. This dream also reveals that you would literally take the shirt off your back for a friend in need. This type of loyalty is innate. You can be sure that, as you go on in life, there are some extraordinary surprises, rewards, and plenty of luck to carry you beyond your fondest dreams!

Seeing soiled, dirty-looking laundry reveals that you are being just a bit too inquisitive where other people's private lives are concerned. The intimate details of another person's life should not concern you at all. What you should be doing, instead, is investing more time in rectifying your own weaknesses and failings. You may be proud to know that your motivations and actions are considered bold, daring, and brave; however, your inner fears, frustrations, and jealousies are just as consuming. Be good and respectful; others will reciprocate.

**LAUNDRYMAN** (see **LAUNDRY**)

**LAUNDRYWOMAN** (see **LAUNDRY**)

**LAVA** (see **VOLCANO**)

**LAVATORY** (see **BATHROOM**)

**LAW** (i.e., all rules of action established by authority, legislation, community, state, or other recognizable assembly of persons)
If the laws you see are sensibly created and administered, then you a law-abiding person. Seeing good laws and order within a dream state implies that there are good laws and order within your being.
Seeing laws that are disorganized, mishandled, and administered in some foolish manner intimates that you have some distorted views about the law, or you are disrespectful where some laws are concerned. Seeing bad laws and disorder within a dream state implies that there is some type of confusion and disorder within your own being.

**LAWN**
A lawn that is neatly mowed and landscaped reveals that you have a close bond towards your family, friends, workplace, work associates, and others. You take pride in your life's role as a breadwinner, house-wife, mother, and so on. You would not change your place of happiness for anything else in the world!
A lawn that is unkempt, with little or no landscaping, however, reveals that you are not a content person and that you certainly are not satisfied with your home life, work life, friends, and so on. Your feelings in all these matters may be temporal; on the other hand, they may be pent-up feelings which you have harboured for years. What is important here is that you are unhappy and disinterested with your life the way it is. Now, what have you done to try to solve your problem(s)? You cannot hope for better things unless you are ready, willing, and able to do some-thing to improve your own state of affairs. If you truly want to be a happier person, then you must stop complaining and bickering about your difficulties. Show more love, kindness, compassion, charity, and sin-cere attention towards others. Forget about your needs for a moment or two, and begin to ask yourself how much have you contributed towards making your life more meaningful and purposeful. Do not expect some-one to make your life happier or better for you; you must do this yourself.

**LAWN BOWLING** (see **BOWLING** or **GAME**)

**LAWN MOWER**
There are several opportunities ahead for you which you may decide to accept or reject (e.g., new job offer, a move, educational

course to advance yourself). Whatever they may be, the challenges seem worthy and beneficial to you. It's strange, isn't it? Sometimes people hope and yearn for better improvements, but when opportunities knock at their door, they suddenly have inhibitions and qualms about making those quantum leaps within their lives. Do not be afraid to move forward on this earth plane. We are not here to obstruct our destiny; we are here to fulfill it!

## LAWSUIT

This dream reveals that you have placed several people through some embarrassing, humiliating, and uncompromising situations. You may feel that you have the sanction to walk over or threaten those less privileged than you. In truth, you do not have the sanction to mistreat anyone, not even yourself. What will you gain from your rules, ideas, and tactics when suddenly your life takes a turn for the worse? So far, so good; but are you prepared to deal with your conscience now or later? This dream encourages you to consider all this and to correct the many flaws you need to correct before you begin to see the better part of a peaceful day.

## LAWYER

To be or to see an honest, just lawyer advises you to rest your mind about the days to follow. Your depression and indifferent attitudes will begin to change and, once more, you will become active and begin to feel needed and wanted. There were moments when you were about to give up; luckily, your strong intuitive feelings and pioneer-type outlook prevented you from doing so. Your future will be brighter; and with each passing day from here to there, you will too!

To see a lawyer who is dishonest and unjust reveals that some traumatic losses may befall you (e.g., money loss, bad investments, bankruptcy, losing a job, demotion). These losses seem to emanate from your own negligence, carefree ideas, and attitudes in life. If you think you can repair or rectify any problem(s) which you feel you are headed towards, then do not hesitate to at least try to make things better for yourself. In some respects, it may not to be too late; yet, in other respects, the wheels of motion appear to be against you.

## LAXATIVE (see ENEMA or MEDICATION)

## LAYOFF (see UNEMPLOYMENT)

**LEADERSHIP**

Seeing peaceful leadership qualities within yourself or someone else reveals that you are basically satisfied with the way your life has treated you thus far. There may have been a few complaints and regrets here and there, but, in general, you have been relatively happy, healthy, and somewhat successful in your own right. In many respects, you are like a leader; you valiantly move on in life with a clear, open mind and with a few inspirational plans yet to be fulfilled.

Seeing ruthless or troublesome leadership qualities reveals that there are many things not in order in your life. Hardships of various sorts still plague you, as well as some disturbances from several people who simply refuse to act maturely and sensibly. Not everything will correct itself overnight. It appears that little by little, and piece by piece, you will commence to place your life in its proper perspective. Keep hoping for better things, and keep striving to make things right; and with prayer, things will slowly but surely commence to improve for you.

**LEAF**

A healthy-looking leaf or leafage within a dream state indicates that there may be a waiting period involved for something you wish to presently do or achieve. Within a very short period of time, you will be able to carry out your plan of action with outstanding success. By the way, there are many rewarding accomplishments ahead for you in life!

An unhealthy looking, shriveled up leaf or leafage denotes that an aspiration or plan you have been talking about will not be fulfilled, simply because someone will dissuade you, or you will change your mind for personal reasons. "Nothing ventured, nothing lost, and nothing gained" could pretty well sum up this dream's definition. However, another similar aspiration or plan may be consummated by you in time to come; only this time, you will be ready, willing, and able to forge ahead.

**LEAKAGE**

Seeing a leakage such as water, air, light, radiation, chemical, and so on denotes your basic concern for the food you eat, the water you drink, and the air you breathe. There is enough pollution on this planet to justify your basic concerns. As well, perhaps you are living near a dam, a chemical plant, or a nuclear plant that does trouble you and your family members. The solution here is to reflect upon these matters, try to do something about these matters, and—if you fail— then consider the remote possibilities of moving elsewhere so that you can at least gain some peace of mind and assurance that you are living under safer conditions. One other possibility is presented by this dream, however: you may have had some water or some chemical leakage within your place of dwelling. If this is so, then your dream has merely reminded you of this fact.

**LEAN-TO** (see **SHED**)

**LEAPFROG** (see **GAME**)

**LEARNING**

If you happen to dream about learning something exceptionally special from some type of higher being or from some strange place of wisdom, then you can consider yourself highly perceptive, intelligent, and inspirational. It appears that you are attuning yourself to the Great Cosmic Forces around you with spectacular results! Now, the biggest challenge of all is what are you going to do with the knowledge or wisdom you have learned? Will you share what you know, or will you bottle what you know for another time? Many men and women have been inspired through their dreams to become great beings on this planet. They slept, they saw, they acted upon, and ultimately they achieved their highest aims in life. Perhaps your destiny will be as great; only time will tell.

**LEATHER**

It appears that you are dealing with a very thick-skinned, bull-headed individual. Whoever this person might be, you should begin to realize that there is very little, if anything, that you can do to make things different or more livable. This person is already molded and couldn't care less, one way or another, what people think, say, or do; what you see, is what you get! Tolerance, patience, and employing a deaf-ear attitude towards this individual once in a while might assist you in keeping your sanity intact. Do not fret about this person so much. Just be a bit selfish from time to time, and begin to uplift yourself for a change.

**LEASE** (see **RENT**)

**LEAVE** (see **ABANDONMENT**, **BEQUEST**, or **EVACUATION**)

**LEAVEN** (see **DOUGH**)

**LECTURE** (see *also* **MONOLOGUE**)

Giving or hearing a lecture in a calm and peaceful way suggests that you should strive harder to strengthen your views and actions with more belief and conviction. It is not enough to do something in a half-hearted manner or to pretend something is right when, in fact, it is wrong. Do not be afraid of people's criticisms, scorn, or judgments upon you when you stand alone with your nobler thoughts and wisdom. Use your precious time on earth to learn as much as you can, teach others as much as you can, and appreciate your experienced truths as being invaluable earthly lessons to carry you further. And, as you go further in life, be prepared to do bigger and greater things.

Giving or hearing a lecture in a scornful or scolding manner implies that you are alienating yourself and your talents from your true destiny in life. You can isolate yourself from anyone and anything you want in life; but, remember, you cannot be isolated from yourself, no matter how hard you try. Giving excuses and placing all other types of obstructions in front of you cannot change the fact that you could be doing more with your mind, your time, and your talents. Thus far, you should consider yourself very fortunate. You know your purpose on earth; many do not.

**LECTURER** (see **LECTURE** or **ORATOR**)

**LEFT-HANDEDNESS** (see *also* **RIGHT-HANDEDNESS**)

If you are, in fact, left-handed in life and dream about using your hand that way, then this action merely reflects your personal preference in being left-handed. However, if you are right-handed and dream about being left-handed, then you are trying to be noticed by someone, or else you are trying very hard to bring some attention upon yourself by what you wear or by what you say. If you truly want to impress someone very special in your life, then do not hesitate to impress yourself into being normal and natural at all times. You will be admired and appreciated more this way than any other way; your experiences alone will verify this truth to you. And remember this: you are "somebody" already; you do not have to demonstrate this fact to anyone.

## LEG

Seeing legs within a dream state denotes sexual desires that are normally or abnormally satisfied or repressed. One's sexual life can be rational, uplifting, and pleasurable, or it can be totally irrational, inhibited, and unbalanced. Take your pick. If you happen to be in the latter category and do harbour sexual hang-ups, then it might be a good idea to seek some professional advice regarding this matter.

Seeing legs that are sickly-looking in appearance denotes that you are seeking more appreciation and affection from your spouse, lover, friend, etc. Whatever your prime reasons may be, you will surmount this problem or need in due time.

## LEGALIZATION (see LAW)

## LEGEND (see *also* SATYR, TROLL, or UNICORN)

You are creative and talented in many respects; yet, you do not focus your mind long enough in these matters to actually accomplish something. Perhaps it is your boredom, or perhaps you feel too insecure and fearful that you will not succeed. Only you hold the answer to this area of your life. Nonetheless, it would be nice if you could only prove to yourself how truly unique and special you are! You can, if you replace your fears and inhibitions with unselfish loyalty towards your beliefs and efforts. No one can make you do something you do not wish to do, but you can impel yourself to do something very special that you were always meant to fulfill. Don't just sit on your potential; harness it towards unlimited success!

## LEGION (see ARMY)

## LEGISLATURE (see GOVERNMENT or LAW)

## LEMON (see FRUIT)

## LENS (see BINOCULAR, CONTACT LENS, EYEGLASS, MAGNIFYING GLASS, MICROSCOPE, MONOCLE, PERISCOPE, or TELESCOPE)

## LENT

Being highly rational, analytical, independent, and courageous allows you to conquer many of your earthly temptations and spiritual obstacles in a rather winning sort of way. These positive attributes also give you a perceptive understanding about the self-sacrifices people have to make in order to improve their lives. You not only feel the needs of others; you also help them in their needs! What could be more profound on this earth plane than to extend your hand to a troubled soul? You know—simply because someone once extended their hand to you.

**LENTIL** (see **FOOD** or **PLANT**)

**LEPROSY**
Something is seriously amiss here! In order to gain more peace of mind, physical well-being, and a greater certainty about your future, you will have to change some of your character habits and outlook in life. It is pride, fear, self-deception, impatience, wasted energies, and worthless thoughts that have limited your earthly progress. Through prayer and humility, you can conquer your problems. Or else you can continue to lead a confused, reckless existence. It would be so very sad to see a person like you limiting your thoughts and actions towards dubious ideals and concepts. Seek the truths within yourself; then, with hope and peace, go forward.

**LESBIANISM** (see **HOMOSEXUALITY**)

**LESSON** (see *also* **LEARNING, LECTURE,** or **FOREWARNING**)
If the lesson appears to be sensible and justifiable within the dream state, then you can be sure that your present turmoil and confusion will clear up very soon. Apologies are in order either from you to someone or from someone to you. This will take place so that peace and harmony will prevail.

If the lesson is senseless and unjustifiable, then someone will attempt to embarrass or humiliate you within the week. This could take place at home, in the work place, or almost anywhere you happen to be at the time. If at all possible, say nothing and then politely walk away from this base person. Several people will be there to come to your defense. Although you will appreciate their support, you will also realize that this personal matter can only be handled your way.

**LETDOWN** (see **DISAPPOINTMENT**)

**LETTER**

To see, to write, or to receive a letter in a down-to-earth sort of way is basically a harbinger of good tidings. This could involve travel, meeting someone special after a long absence, finding more peace of mind and happiness, financial prosperity, receiving good news via letter, and so forth. This sudden turn of events is very timely! Enjoy this well-deserved reprieve; you have earned it!

If a letter is torn or damaged for any reason, then you are advised to settle some matter of importance. This could involve a friendship, a home or business matter, or some other unfinished business which appears to be affecting you. Do not dally too long; sometimes an opportune moment can pass you by and then, sadly, it may be too late to make amends at a later time.

**LETTER BOX** (see **MAILBOX**)

**LETTER CARRIER** (see **MAILMAN**)

**LETTUCE** (see **FOOD** or **PLANT**)

**LEUKEMIA** (see **CANCER** or **SICKNESS**)

**LEVEL** (i.e., an instrument used to determine the horizontal plane of a surface)

At long last you are beginning to place your life in order! Everything just seems to be so clear and sanely oriented to you now, whereas in the past you gave in to your excuses and failings. No matter! What is important today is that you are finally beginning to think and visualize in a horizontal manner instead of in a parallel manner. It is far greater to think, to feel, and to broaden your concepts by actually thinking in an expanded way instead of thinking in a limited way. To be more precise, a horizontal thinker sees life with an open mind; the parallel thinker sees life with a closed mind, as though wearing blinkers like those given to a horse. They can only see what is in front of them and fail to see the things beside them or around them. Indeed, your yesterdays are all gone, but you now have the inner satisfaction of accepting your todays and tomorrows with a greater awareness, not only of yourself and others whom you know but of all aspects of life around you.

**LEVER** (i.e., a bar used to pry something)

Seeing or using this device within a dream state signifies that you will prosper through your own ingenuity and efforts. You do not need to depend upon others too much simply because you are quite capable and independent enough to do many things for yourself. This dream wishes to impart this to you: never forget to keep your spiritual values in close harmony with your earthly values as you plod onwards in building your earthly prosperity. Many times when people become prosperous in life, they forget to thank God for all their "borrowed" wealth! Do not neglect to thank God.

**LEVITATION**

No matter how unbearable life may appear to you during these troublesome times, this dream will always see you through your most difficult and horrible moments. Be at peace. Help, comfort, consolation, and "rescue" forces in a variety of ways are on their way to guide and assist you. This assistance could perhaps be from your family members or friends, or it could very well be a source of good news via telephone, telegram, letter, or any other means and ways that are deemed possible. Remember: God does work through people in order to assist you, and He also works through you in order to assist other people; it is that factual and that simple. That is why you should be more grateful when someone, out of the blue, comes forward to help or guide you; this source of help is directed by God.

(*Note*: You may also have the pleasure of knowing that if, for example, you are experiencing a very negative dream but at the very end of your dream sequence or anywhere during your dream sequence you happen to experience levitation, then this levitation "symbolism" takes precedence over your entire bad dream. Consequently, you have nothing to worry about simply because levitation acts as a "buffer zone" to anything negative within a dream.)

**LEXICOGRAPHY** (see **DICTIONARY**)

**LIAR**

According to this symbolism, either you or someone whom you know lies. If you, in fact, have this tendency, then it is time to look within yourself and begin to find out why you fail to speak the truth. There could, perhaps, be many reasons why you speak falsely; but this does not solve your problem(s), nor does it make matters any better for you or anyone else who believes you. It would be much better to say nothing at all than to tell a lie. Sooner or later, people who lie become entrapped through their own behaviour. Why? Simply because liars cannot remember every little lie they tell; they forget what they say and to whom they say it. Before you know it, they are detected and ultimately confronted, as well. Always tell the truth, no matter how painful this truth may be. In the long run, you will be wiser and more conscience-free to progress further and more peacefully in life.

**LIBEL** (i.e., a defamatory statement, portrait, sign, or effigy that tends to injure or ruin a person's reputation)

Your free will gives you the option of leading a good life or a not-so-good life. A wise person will always seek the better virtues and graces of life because the need, knowledge, and patience required to deal with self and life on this planet is totally adhered to and understood. An unwise person, however, can be very deceptive and tends to seek glorification over others through power, greed, or wealth. This person fails to realize that earthly power and glory is only a temporal state; he or she cannot take this power and glory to the other side of life. So, no matter how intellectually superior or gifted you happen to be, never use these blessings in a proud, boastful, or ruthless manner. Instead, use your mind and time in totally constructive endeavours. This could save you the needless suffering and disgrace that unwise people often have to bear.

**LIBERATION** (see *also* **PASSOVER** or **RESCUE**)

Very often your desires to do something special are stifled by the negative actions of others around you. Hence, over the years, you have created an image of being a defeatist or else you have created a bit of an inferiority complex for yourself. So what if you are not a raving beauty or a handsome model or that you have not been blessed with a perfect upbringing? Do not allow anyone (including yourself) or anything to hold you back from your rightful progress on earth. Pay no heed to the cruelty of others towards you, for very often it is these cruel, cynical people who are aimless and lost in life. They will have to deal with their own problems. Never forget the fact that you are a child of God. You have as many restrictions, rights, and privileges as anyone else. As a matter of fact, you may be more gifted than the next person.

Even if you are not, however, this does not mean that you are any less important. You are very, very special simply because you are here. Do not let your self-inflicted weaknesses rule your destiny; conquer them with faith—not with doubts and insecurities. Believe in your goodness no matter what anyone else has told you thus far, and project this inner goodness beyond yourself by being helpful, caring, and loving. Then, in time, you may look back to see what a small ray of hope has done for you.

**LIBERATOR** (see **LIBERATION**)

**LIBERTY** (see **INDEPENDENCE** or **LIBERATION**)

**LIBRARIAN** (see **LIBRARY**)

**LIBRARY**

Your emotional and financial difficulties will be settled shortly; however, these could have been averted in the first place had you listened to someone's wise counsel and direction. Since you are so highly independent, it may be difficult for you to actually heed someone's good logic and advice—you want to do things and prove matters for yourself. This dream strongly advises you to not be ashamed, humiliated, or too proud to accept common sense advice or help when the need arises. Remember, people lean heavily upon your help and advice too, and they are just as independent as you are. You do not seem to mind this too much, do you? There are those times when you simply cannot always be in the driver's seat. Sometimes you have to take the back seat in life and allow someone else to guide and direct you; not always, but just those rare times when things happen to go sour for you.

**LICE**

Someone or something is bothering you in life; this literally makes you cringe with disappointment and despair. Whoever or whatever this may be, you had best gather your courage and thoughts together in order to combat this problem. Curb your stresses, otherwise you may create a bigger problem for yourself. It appears as though you cannot handle this matter alone so, for your benefit, seek some professional help or advice. Another opinion or two is better than trying to handle an almost impossible situation alone.

**LICENSE** (e.g., marriage license, medical license, teaching license, driving license)

Very often you get geared up to do something, but when the time arrives, you are either sleeping, daydreaming, or wasting your time on other matters of low interest. This dream advises you to carry out your plans with a more determined outlook, otherwise you will continue to go around in circles hoping, wishing, and longing for something to happen—but it never will. So many things are possible to you in life; sadly, they will not transpire unless you commence to expend your time and energy with responsible foresight. Negligence and oversight on your part are totally inexcusable!

**LICENSE PLATE**

This dream advises you to avoid making comparisons between yourself and someone else. In other words, if someone happens to be more proficient at something than you are, do not be offended. You have other talents that could far outweigh the next person's. Be your natural self at all times, and strive to accentuate your positive talent(s) and goals. There is not a person on earth who does not have some kind of talent. Your own may be different from someone else's, but then this is what makes the world so interesting and challenging.

**LICKING** (e.g., a person licking a fork; a dog or other animal licking a paw or a bone or other food)

This action within a dream state indicates a deep desire to be appreciated. Perhaps you feel neglected by a parent, brother, sister, relative, friend, or someone else whom you admire? It is vitally important that you be willing to at least meet a person halfway in order to be wanted, needed, or appreciated. Some of your loneliness is self-inflicted; and unless you are ready, willing, and able to come out of your shell, do not expect immediate and profound results. If you choose to stay home feeling sad, lonely, and dejected, it is because you have made no efforts to change matters around for yourself. Stop complaining, and stop feeling so sorry for yourself. There are many people who are a lot worse off than you are. Show more appreciation for all life around you, no matter what trials and tribulations you may be experiencing. Then you will see a transformation, a miracle of love, take place within the very essence of your being.

**LID** (e.g., a cover for a jar, pot, box, trunk, garbage can)

As long as you persist in dipping into your past for some minor incident or traumatic happening that affected you, you can hardly expect to progress on a sure-footed basis now. What took place yesterday need not take place today or tomorrow. Let go of your hurt feelings or fearful thoughts that some past chapters of your life will repeat themselves. Nothing need repeat itself again as long as you forge ahead with new ideas, concepts, and actions in mind. If you want to get ahead in life, then look ahead, not behind you!

**LIE DETECTOR** (see **POLYGRAPH**)

**LIFE BELT** (see **SAFETY BELT**)

**LIFEBOAT** (see **BOAT**)

**LIFE BUOY** (see **LIFE PRESERVER**)

**LIFEGUARD**

Seeing yourself or someone else as a lifeguard reveals that you have a genuine concern for the welfare of your immediate family, relatives, and friends. This enlightened attitude should be adopted and practiced by more people around the world. If it were, we would all experience closer family ties, warmer friendships, and more Universal Love towards our fellow man. Your philosophical and spiritual outlook is genuine and sincere. As long as you walk upon the face of this globe, have absolutely no qualms about your wholesome actions, deeds, and concepts.

**LIFE JACKET** (see **LIFE PRESERVER**)

**LIFELINE** (e.g., a line or rope thrown into the water to save a life, or a rope used by sailors in very dangerous situations)

Seeing a lifeline thrown to you or to someone else indicates that you will come out of a very gripping situation with the help of another person. This could involve marital difficulties, romantic indifferences, financial embarrassments, being stranded somewhere, and so on. Be very mindful of your present situation, and be very careful about taking unnecessary risks or chances at this time.

**LIFE NET** (e.g., a net used by firemen to catch people from a burning building)

Give yourself a generous gift today: be helpful to others, but do not ask for anything in return. Do not complain, and try your very best not to harbour any animosities, petty jealousies, or other negative feelings. Try your best to adopt a complete, positive outlook, no matter how grim situations may appear. Later, when you go to bed at night, think about the good things you may be able to do tomorrow and the day after tomorrow. Then, gently, as you fall asleep, realize you have reached the end of a perfect day.

**LIFE PRESERVER**

It seems as though you are more capable of handling a major crisis than those small, mundane, daily problems. Sometimes you become very upset over incidental matters which are more laughable than serious. This is a part of your nature, which you have accepted without any thought of changing. No one can force you to change; however, you realize that your overall daily stress factors can bring you future problems. Simply ask yourself: How many times during the day do I get upset? This, alone, will tell you whether or not you are too stressful for your own good. It might be far better for you to adopt a more passive or indifferent attitude when things get you down. Be calm; do not waste your valuable time and energies on useless, irrelevant matters. You may thus live longer; you will certainly begin to enjoy life a lot more!

**LIFE RAFT** (see **BOAT** or **RAFT**)

**LIFEWORK**

Seeing your lifework with a positive frame of mind denotes your willingness and optimistic determination to fulfill a present task, no matter how long it may take. Since your work gives you so much satisfaction, you are bound to complete this task a lot sooner than you think. However, there are other duties ahead of you which you will quite aptly perform and accomplish. You future will be very successful and outstanding, simply because you would not have it any other way!

Seeing your lifework with a negative frame of mind intimates that you may have second thoughts about your work, or else someone is making your life more difficult than you deserve. If you do have some great doubts about your work, then be sure to consider every possible reason why you feel this way. Do not make any drastic decision(s), moves, or changes you may later regret. However, if you know beyond a shadow of a doubt that what you are doing is absolutely not for you, then by all means look elsewhere for your happiness and success. You will find it. Now, if someone is giving you more trouble than you deserve, then it is high time to get a grip on this situation. Do not play the martyr—filled with anguish, pain, and sorrow—so that other people might feel sorry for you. In fact, stop feeling sorry for yourself. If you truly want to correct some matter within or around you, then stop giving excuses. Face the truth the way it is, not the way you imagine it should be. No one will change for you; only you can change for yourself. Be strong, seek other opinions from good people whom you know, and then, wisely, save your own mind and soul. Your future looks much brighter without the hassles!

## LIGHT BULB

There are some pending improvements (e.g., promotion, better understanding between you and your spouse, meeting someone to assist you with your career) which will give you some opportunities to forge ahead. Whatever they may be, you can be sure that you will be entering a new soul cycle which will allow you to fulfill some of your innermost wishes. This will take time—it will not happen overnight. However, you are presently headed in the right direction, as you will eventually see.

## LIGHTER (e.g., cigarette lighter)

There appears to be something you have to do, but you are continually dodging your responsibilities where this matter is concerned. This dream advises you to complete the neglected task, and be relieved in knowing that your contribution will still be worthy, accepted, and praised.

## LIGHTHOUSE

To see a clear-looking lighthouse within a dream state intimates that you are a mature, highly organized, and very private, shy individual. Your good attributes far outnumber your weaknesses, and you are appreciated and admired by those with whom you deal and know. Your success in life man be moderate to great—this, of course, depends upon your actions and deeds and the opportunities that happen to come your way. Whether you are rich or poor, you will always strive to be happy and constructive, in your own way.

Seeing a lighthouse that is obscure, abandoned, or destroyed suggests that you are a very ambitious and demanding individual. You probably will be very successful in life; however, it certainly would not hurt to be more kind to, and cooperative with, people you know. Do your very best to eradicate some of your cynical, bullheaded, and indifferent views; otherwise, it might be very difficult for others to deal with you later in life. As a matter of fact, you might find yourself rather intolerable, as well! Think about it—then see what you are willing to do now in order to vastly improve your future.

## LIGHTNING

This dream forewarns you about living in the fast lane of life and/or flirting with some type of dangerous activity or anything else that may be considered foolish and reckless. Life is far too important to gamble away on some foolhardy act; do not harbour the foolish thought that you are infallible and that absolutely nothing can happen to you. Understand that being careful is not good enough! What is important here is that you show more respect and consideration for your existence on this planet, rather than playing a kind of Russian roulette with yourself, with your life, and with your fate.

## LIGHTNING ROD

This dream forewarns you that someone or a group of people may intend to defraud, cheat, or rob you. Be careful where money matters are concerned; do not sign any contract unless you are absolutely sure it is valid; and be careful when buying, selling, or trading something. Do not be a loser in this situation. Be very prudent and discerning for the next month or so, and you just may come out of this situation unscathed.

**LIGHTSHIP** (see **SHIP**)

**LILAC** (see **FLOWER** or **PLANT**)

**LILY** (see **FLOWER** or **PLANT**)

**LILY PAD** (see **LEAF** or **PLANT**)

**LIMOUSINE** (see **CAR**)

**LINEAGE** (see **BIRTH, FAMILY, FAMILY TREE**, or **RELATIVE**)

**LINEMAN** (i.e., a person who repairs telephone or electric power lines)

If you are in fact a lineman and dream about seeing or being one, then your dream merely reflects the work that you do. However, if you are not a lineman but have a dream about seeing or being one, then this symbolism reveals that you are not on speaking terms with another person (e.g., spouse, offspring, relative, friend, co-worker). This silence may not last long, and the cooling off process will certainly assist you and the other person involved. Apologies will be made, and the bonds of friendship will become stronger.

**LION**

A peaceful-looking lion shows courage, determination, and much success for you in life. A major purchase or two is foreseen in the not-too-distant future, as well as a certain amount of travel that will keep you busy and happy.

Seeing a lion that is ferocious, wounded, or about to attack you or someone else shows domestic strife involving arguments and mistrust. There will be no peace here until the people involved learn to compromise, learn to show more respect and loyalty towards one another, and finally learn to use more common sense instead of complaining about each other's faults and imperfections.

**LIP** (see **MOUTH**)

**LIPSTICK** (see **COSMETIC**)

**LIQUOR** (see *also* **BEER**)

You tend to be very unpredictable and temperamental. You also show great signs of vexation when things do not go your way. Maturity is a quality that must be earned and will draw respect, when the person acts accordingly. If you wish to remain a spoiled child in an adult's body, there will be a rude awakening ahead for you. If you have the courage to listen, then cleanse your mind of the temper and flightiness you harbour, and begin to see the brighter side of life, for your future's sake.

**LIST** (e.g., a grocery shopping list, price list, attendance list, roster) (see *also* **ATLAS, BOOK, CALENDAR, CATALOGUE, DICTIONARY, MANUSCRIPT, PROGRAM, TELEPHONE BOOK,** or **VOTE**)

As the old saying goes, you appear to be overworked and underpaid! Life has not been easy for you, and being a perfectionist in these difficult times certainly does not help matters much. You are quite ambitious; but, due to your financial status and/or someone's mental abuses towards you, you seem to be pushed back into a corner. You have given up in so many areas of your life that you are not necessarily the same person you were several years ago. Yes, you do deserve much better than what you have now or where you perhaps live at this time. Be patient; times will be better for you! As you plod on, you will prosper with earthly and spiritual satisfaction.

**LITANY** (i.e., a form of prayer in which the clergy and congregation participate)

You are trying very hard to maintain your hope and courage during these trying times of your life. Nothing comes very easily for you except the assurance of an inner type of spiritual love, warmth, and peace that seems to draw you closer to God. This is so wholesomely comforting to know. Before long, you will rise above your problems. When you do, you will assist some needy people who need your love, friendship, and spiritual understanding.

**LITERATURE** (see **AUTHOR, BOOK, LEARNING, POET,** or **READING**)

**LITIGATION** (see **LAWSUIT**)

**LITTLE DIPPER** (see **CONSTELLATION**)

**LIVELIHOOD** (see **CALLING, CAREER, EMPLOYMENT, LIFEWORK,** or **OWNERSHIP**)

**LIVERY STABLE** (see **BARN**)

**LIVESTOCK** (see **ANIMAL**)

## LIVING ROOM

If you feel comfortable in the living room you happen to see, then be assured that a decision you are about to make will be good and profitable for you. Some good luck from another source awaits you in the very near future, as well.

Feeling uneasy, worried, or just plain unwanted in the living room forewarns you about someone who may be taking advantage of your kindness and hospitality. This does not imply that you should be unkind or unfair to anyone who thinks this way; simply to be aware that you are being treated on a one-sided basis. You will have to weigh this matter more carefully within yourself. Perhaps a more amicable agreement can be reached between you and the other person involved.

## LIZARD

Do not strike down another personality unless you are prepared to receive the same treatment. People do not always cast stones at one another; they throw boulders instead! This dream advises you to always use your best diplomacy and discretion, where other people are concerned. Stay away from gossip as you would a plague! You do not belong in that league of tongue waggers, and you should certainly not allow anyone to sway you towards it. Mockery and bitter sarcasm are so wide-spread on this planet; avoid this ugliness.

## LLAMA (i.e., a South American animal related to the camel)

You do not desire honour and prestige in life. As a matter of fact, you would rather seek virtuous pleasures through living a good, clean, simple life. You would prefer to work hard and to continue to make self-sacrifices where you can for the betterment of self and others around you. Indeed, your humble acts of kindness and thankfulness will lead you to quieter, happier pastures. You are a very rare and wonderful human being!

To harm a llama or to see this animal hurt or wounded suggests that your life is not in order. You seem to be biting more than you can chew—such as through acts of greed, jealousy, and disloyalties. By harming the feelings and needs of others, you automatically harm your own being in ways you never dreamed possible. Time—and perhaps a guilt-ridden conscience—will snap you back to the realities of life, love, and respect.

**LOAN** (see **BORROWER**)

**LOBBY** (see **PASSAGEWAY**)

**LOBSTER**

Some things in life are just not worth pursuing; for example, over-confidence, evil ideas and intentions, faultfinding, impulsive judgments, foolish pride, self-deception, vanity, impatience, disobedi-ence—not to mention a hundred or two more. This dream advises you to always pursue the most positive, virtuous feelings and actions you can humanly muster, for in so doing you will find your true purpose for being on earth. When you adopt good habits and understanding and fulfill your daily obligations, you stand a much better chance of satisfying the needs of your heart, mind, and soul. What could be greater on this earth plane than to know that you have the ability to transform your daily battles into daily love. You have a good mind and a free will; use them wisely!

**LOCK**

This dream advises you to not lock yourself out of someone's life; by the same token, someone should not lock themselves out of your life. It is quite simple: make amends, compromise, and let there be peace for all times! This is a never-ending story; a person becomes angry at another person for some reason, then the lines of commu-nication and friendship are broken. Eventually, one of these two people gets sick and dies. The person left behind then suffers anguish because no attempts were made to bring peace. The roots of the problem were stubbornness and pride—do not let this happen to you!

**LOCKER** (e.g., school lockers, gym locker)

Some of your present actions seem somewhat aimless; but, with time and patience, you are bound to straighten everything out for yourself. Right now you want to be in control of all things within your life. Perhaps you simply have to go through some of those vain, blind, senseless, temporal shortcomings in order to learn some valuable les-sons about yourself and about life, in general. Everyone goes through some wise or foolish phase within their lives in order to learn and mature. Be patient; know your limitations; and you will begin to see things more clearly in due time.

**LOCKET**

This symbolism indicates that you are a very sentimental person. As you reflect upon the very good times in your life, your inner force, drive, and impetus move you forward. Your sorrows or regrets are now behind you. Those rainbows you follow or lucky stars you latch on to are inner wishes or hopes that you will attain your happiness and goals in life. And why not? You can attain anything your heart desires, providing you have the determination to do so. You have some fine attributes to help you along in that direction.

**LOCKSMITH** (i.e., a person who repairs locks and keys)

You have been thwarted in life so many times that it is as though your soul were marooned on an island with pain, sorrow, and tears! Yet, out of this gamut of despair, a mind blessing comes through, when you least expect it to happen: wisdom and knowledge that, no matter what difficulties you have had to surmount up to now, you survived and conquered your problems boldly and efficiently! You are dearly loved in Heaven. One day you will understand that your earthly trials and tribulations were gifts of faith, truth, love, kindness, knowledge, and understanding. Let today be the best day of your life, knowing that in time there is a higher purpose in store for you—beyond the veil and sadness of earth.

**LOCOMOTIVE** (see **RAILROAD**)

**LOCUST** (see **INSECT**)

**LODGING** (i.e., temporary quarters for sleeping and eating)

You may learn many things alone, but you also can learn many wholesome things from the thoughts and actions of others around you. Basically, you do. You are so fortunate and privileged to have people around you who honestly and sincerely love you so much! True friendships on earth deserve the highest respect, honour, and unselfish reflections of the heart, mind, and soul. True friends are like guiding stars—they are there when you need them the most. Soon, someone will call out to you for help; please be there.

**LOG** (i.e., a section from a felled tree used in building a structure or used for firewood)

You certainly do not have to travel the world over in order to fulfill your dreams, wishes, and hopes. Your sentiments are basically home-based; you find peace and contentment in what you have and where you live. The simple life is by far the best way to live; you have the freedom to be yourself and to be less troubled, where money matters are concerned. As a matter of fact, you have the advantage over many other people in that you are happier and closer to nature's wisdom. You are truly a natural, wholesome being who has found a treasure in being true unto yourself.

**LOGGER** (see **LUMBERJACK**)

**LOINCLOTH** (see **CLOTHES**)

**LOLLIPOP** (see **CANDY**)

**LONESOMENESS**

This emotional state within a dream is very often reflected while you are awake, as well. Never bottle your loneliness; rather, tell someone how you feel. By sharing your thoughts in this matter, you will commence to feel better, knowing that someone has taken the time to listen and to possibly advise you when you needed advice. This dream advises you to cope with each moment of your life with more realistic views, instead of fantasizing about how you think your life should be or how you want your life to be. You cannot have everything in life; some things will be granted to you, and some things will not. Be grateful for what you have—be even more grateful for the things you should not have. There are people who are tempted to go after the wrong things in life. Sadly, they learn a vital lesson about themselves—but often too late. Do not pine, whine, or complain about your life. Be happy that you are here. Greater things await you, providing you have the stamina and patience to wait, to see, and to ultimately appreciate.

**LONGBOAT** (see **BOAT**)

**LONGSHOREMAN** (i.e., a person who loads and unloads cargo aboard ships)

If you happen to be a longshoreman and dream about being or seeing one, then your dream is merely reflecting the work that you do. If you are not, then this dream indicates that some awaited prosperity and travel are in store for you. You have struggled for practically everything you have on earth—nothing in your life has come easily. Well, times can change, and they will for you! God be with you, good luck, and bon voyage!

**LOOSE-LEAF** (i.e., a loose-leaf notebook used in schools, an album, etc.)

You have lost something, but you will find something far more valuable in its place: for example, losing your self-respect but becoming wiser from your experience; breaking a friendship but finding a new one that supersedes the first; losing a quarter but finding ten dollars; losing your patience but finding greater self-control; losing your job but finding a better one; losing yourself to pride but later finding humility. There are many "lost and found" situations in life. It is hoped that what you find will carry you through endless routes of satisfaction and peace.

**LORD'S PRAYER** (see **PRAYER**)

**LORD'S SUPPER** (see **LAST SUPPER**)

**LOST** (see *also* **MISPLACEMENT**)

To lose someone or something within a dream or to be lost yourself intimates that you harbour some inner fears about actually losing someone or something very close to you (e.g., parent, spouse, offspring, pet, family treasure). Your fears are quite groundless, for we do not own anyone or anything: everything belongs to God. Accept it or not—that is the way it is and will always be! Many people become too possessive of what they have and never wish to let go of things that are "loaned" to them. According to this dream symbolism, you will not lose anyone or anything, except your unwarranted and somewhat nonsensical fear. Be at peace!

**LOTION** (see **COSMETIC**)

**LOTTERY**

To dream of winning or losing in a lottery game, to buy or to sell lottery tickets, to see a possible winning number, or to see a lottery being played by other people suggests that you are too preoccupied with thoughts of becoming a big lottery winner. This is not to say that you will never win; if you play the game, then your chances are as good as anyone else's. This dream is simply advising you to ease your mind about winning a fortune—at least for a while. Who knows, when you least expect it, your lucky number just may be drawn!

**LOUDSPEAKER** (i.e., a public address system)

Any one or two of the following definitions may be applicable: A) that you do own a public address system; or B) that you do not own a public address system; or C) that you sell loudspeakers; or D) that you will be needing a loudspeaker system before too long; or E) that you loaned your workable loudspeaker to a friend, but when the friend returned it, it was not working properly anymore; or F) that someone you know is very loud, vexatious, and somewhat of a bore; or G) that you would like to be in the public eye someday; or H) that this dream has little or no relevance to you at this time.

**LOUNGE** (e.g., a theatre, hotel, or office lounge)

For your own sake, end your fantasies of wealth and illusions of grandeur, and begin to be yourself! You would be amazed by the powerful potential within your being, if you gave yourself half a chance to prove it. You were never short-changed in any way in life—except in your ability to face a few truths about yourself and other matters around you. Hiding behind a facade of self-contradictions and deceptions will get you absolutely nowhere. If you are as bright and talented as this dream is projecting, then—without a doubt—you will aspire to become a better person; but, if you are not as bright and talented as this dream is projecting, then—without a doubt—you will continue to be sad, dejected, and aimless in life.

**LOUSE** (see **LICE**)

**LOVE**

Love expressions within a dream state are your conscious or subconscious reflections about your "need for love" or your "lack of love" in life. The greatest misused and abused word in all history is the word love! To truly love someone in life means to not hurt, maim, accuse, abuse, cheat, lie, steal, destroy, or desecrate anything, in any way. Yet, these negative actions are performed in the name of love continually! Love dies when it is not nourished; that is why so many people on this planet today appear to be undernourished for affection. Before you can love anything in life, you must learn to like yourself; then, slowly, you will begin to like other people, places, and things. Eventually, as you mature and begin to understand the true concepts of life, you will begin to elevate your "liking" habits into "loving" habits. But be careful—the word love must be used honestly and sincerely, at all times! It is so easy to say you love someone, when, in fact, you also love the sun, the moon, the trees, and so on. Ask yourself: are you placing your mind-love towards someone, or are you placing your soul-love towards someone? Express your love from the denizens of your soul and really mean it, rather than from the top of your head with arguments and doubts. Remember, the heart and mind can be deceptive, but the soul is the purest tree of life, directly connected to God. So when a person misuses the word love through a negative habit or action, they are automatically offending God with their mind, heart, and soul. To love someone on earth, such as a wife or a husband, means to honestly and sincerely work side by side in oneness, with great loving feelings, and with sweet attunement—the total impact of which they may not even fathom until they reach the other side of life.

**LOVE AFFAIR** (see **AFFAIR**)

**LOVEMAKING** (see **INTERCOURSE, KISS, LOVE,** or **SEX**)

**LOVE POTION** (i.e., a drink generally concocted by a very negative person, said to arouse passion in the innocent recipient)
      Seeing a love potion in your dream warns you that someone whom you know quite well is exceedingly jealous and spiteful of your happiness and prosperity in life, or this dream is advising you to cool your heels where the happiness of someone else is concerned. Do not have any dealings at all with anyone who is jealous or spiteful. Perhaps someday they will come to their better senses. If the culprit creating havoc for someone in life is you, then you are strongly urged to control your mind and actions before very unpleasant troubles beset you. Let people live their own lives; leave them in peace. You have enough of your own problems to handle, let alone being bothersome to someone else. Settle down and be good in life; you will prosper in life by doing so.

**LOVE SEAT**
      You are more appreciated than you know, and—regardless of how you think and feel—there are some people who would really like to

know you better. You may be shy and somewhat introverted; however, the spirit within you is honourable, kind, generous, and loyal. Let this fact give you the inspiration to finally step out of your inner shell. When you are with mature, understanding people, you will discover that your loneliness and inhibitions will simply wash away. It really is not so difficult to have a good friend or two in life, you know; nor is it so difficult to gain another very special friend, either. Simply put your mind to it, and make your presence felt; and a simple "hi" might be the beginning of a very wonderful friendship.

**LOVESICKNESS** (see **LOVE**)

**LOWLINESS** (see **HUMILITY**)

**LOW-MINDEDNESS** (i.e., a person who has a vulgar, coarse, or indecent mind)

Someone or something in life has made you a very bitter person! The act of being low-minded within a dream state is very often a carry-over from your wake-state thoughts and activities. You are adding more pressure to your system through your grievances, frustrations, and unforgiving attitudes than you remotely realize! Take it easy, and strive to be more forgiving towards those who have trespassed against you in life. You are wasting more good energy on verbal abuses than you are on wholesome activities. Getting back at everyone and everything in life is not your answer. Be levelheaded and thankful that you have been given so many chances to put your act together. Use your mind and actions productively on earth; and you will begin to see how much more you can accomplish. If you are truly a wise person, you will shut the door and throw away the key—now and forever more—to any form of low-mindedness you possess.

**LOYALTY** (e.g., being faithful to a friend, belief, cause, a duty or job) (see *also* **FRIEND, IDOLATRY, PRAYER, PROMISE, OBEDIENCE,** or **PATRIOTISM**)

If you dream of being loyal to someone or something to which you are, in fact, loyal in your wake state, then this dream merely acknowledges the honesty, integrity, and sincerity in your daily thoughts and actions. Your lifestyle is basically beyond reproach!

If you dream about being loyal to someone or something to whom or to which you are not loyal during your wake state, do not be alarmed. Sometimes your dreams may have you displaying loyalty towards things you actually abhor in life! Simply recognize that your thoughts and actions would never stoop low, as your dream portrayed. You know that you would not behave that way towards yourself or towards anyone else. Some dreams can project horror, bizarre behaviour and situations, and urgings completely unrelated and alien to the dreamer's good lifestyle, habits, beliefs, loyalty, and farsightedness in life. These dreams may carry scary overtones and affect the dreamer profoundly. Do not let dreams of this nature frighten you; let them, instead, strengthen your wholesome beliefs, courage, and perseverance.

**LUBRICANT** (e.g., oil or grease)

Seeing or using this substance for whatever reason indicates that you are attempting to ignore, cover up, or nullify some wrong that was committed either by you or by someone whom you know. One, two or a million wrongs on earth do not make a right for you or for anyone else. Every good thought, action, or deed that you carry out makes life a little better and less complex for others; and it certainly gives you the priceless benefit of a clear conscience. A wrongdoing, however, is like giving a bit of yourself each time to the negative forces of life: there are no benefits—just guilt, regret, and shame.

**LUCIFER** (see **DEMON**)

**LUCK** (see **BET**, **FORTUNE**, **GAMBLE**, or **LOTTERY**)

**LUGGAGE** (see **BAGGAGE**)

**LULLABY** (see **MUSIC** or **SINGER**)

**LUMBER** (e.g., beams, planks, boards made from timber)

Wherever the lumber appears to be in your dream, the symbolism reveals that you would like to make some constructive changes within your life but are not willing to make a few small sacrifices to consummate that wish. How lucky you are to be given a chance to improve! Never stop striving to become attuned to the highest ideals, thoughts, and actions upon this world, no matter what sacrifices you have to make! Those so-called sacrifices are of no comparison to the benefits you will reap by putting your best wishes and desires into action.

**LUMBERING** (see **LUMBER**)

**LUMBERJACK**

The majority of your fears and anxieties are unfounded and self-inflicted (i.e., fears of being hurt, fears of flying, fears of being inadequate in many things, fears that someone will leave you, and so forth). These insecurities, in addition to an over-active imagination, will not bring you peace; stop believing in them and harping on them. You are wallowing in self-pity and displaying a conscious desire for attention. Place your feet firmly on the ground, walk around, and start living! Don't you think you deserve some happiness in life? If you feel you do, then discard your make-believe attitudes in life, and share the light with the rest of us, with whom you rightfully belong. You fought so very hard to be born to this planet; now you must fight equally hard to accept the realities of this planet. Do so with all your heart, mind, and soul.

**LUMBERYARD** (see **LUMBER**)

**LUMP** (i.e., a swelling on the body caused by either a cyst or a tumour)

Seeing a lump on your body or someone else's body infers that you are very self-conscious about your body. You appear to be harbouring some mental, physical, and sexual inhibitions and hang-ups. Did you know that your past holds the key to your inner confusion and frustrations? Nonetheless, you—and you alone—can unmask and unravel the hopelessness, harm, and perhaps brutal displays of emotions you received earlier in life. You have to trust someone besides yourself in this matter; your dream strongly urges you to seek professional counseling, to pray to God for His Wisdom for you, and to commence to change your cynical and sometimes cruel attitudes towards people, places, and things.

**LUNACY** (see **INSANITY**)

**LUNAR ECLIPSE** (see **ECLIPSE**)

**LUNCH** (see **FOOD** or **MEAL**)

**LUST** (see **SEX**)

**LUXURY** (see **ABUNDANCE** or **MONEY**)

**LYNCHING** (see **HANGING, KILL,** or **MURDER**)

**LYRICIST** (see **COMPOSER** or **POET**)

**MACARONI** (see **DOUGH** or **FOOD**)

**MACE** (i.e., a rod, wand, or staff used as a symbol of authority)
   For the sake of peace and harmony, curb those inner tendencies to show off, brag, or be prideful when things go well in your life. Most people have enough of their own problems; they have neither the time nor patience to hear your know-it-all, top-of-the-world attitudes. This is not to imply that others are not happy for you; they probably are. However, they cannot always listen to your so-called remedies when their aims, struggles, and problems are so different from your own. When life is good to you, just be grateful that something you are doing is working for you. You certainly may suggest your step-by-step remedies to others, but do not emphatically guarantee that what you know will work for them. Sadly, your means of good fortune or success will not always apply to everyone you know or meet.

**MACHETE** (see **KNIFE**)

**MACHINE** (see **MACHINERY**)

**MACHINE GUN** (see **GUN**)

**MACHINERY** (see *also* **DERRICK, FACTORY, MILL,** or **STEAMROLLER**)
   If you tried harder to be more understanding and less practical, your life might be happier and more meaningful to you than it has been up to now. You are much too rigid and regimental in your ways. Consequently, your daily routines can sometimes become a struggle— a battle of wits. Be more lenient with yourself; you are not a work horse, nor do you always have to prove you can do something to the limits of endurance. Do not forget how to smile and laugh sometimes, for this, too, is good for your well-being. Be less selfish, secretive, and inhibited when occasions call for your help and cooperation. There is a time and a place for everything, but to be stubborn for the sake of

stubbornness is not a good policy. As well, be more open-minded and flexible in weighing another person's point of view. Two heads are better than one; and you never know when another person's good opinion or advice may come in handy for you.

**MADHOUSE** (see **INSANITY**)

**MADMAN** (see **INSANITY**)

**MADNESS** (see **INSANITY**)

**MADWOMAN** (see **INSANITY**)

**MAFIA**

If you are not a member of this criminal society but dream of being one, then your dream is reflecting your opposition or hatreds towards someone or something. This does not imply that you are criminally minded; on the contrary, all this dream means is that you are vexed and confused about someone's attitudes or actions against you. This situation will change before too long—be at peace!

Dreaming about the mafia and actually being a member of this society indicates that you are disregarding the nature of your thoughts and actions on earth, with a great deal of indifference. You do not appear to be very concerned about what your fate may bring you. Note this: nothing, absolutely nothing, is overlooked in your thoughts, actions, and deeds upon this planet. Unfortunately, if you persist in disbelieving in, and disregarding, life's good and positive goals, then, in time, you will learn the truth. The Higher Powers of God will have the final word.

**MAGAZINE**

There is an ample amount of prosperity and success ahead for you, providing you do not allow anyone or anything to hinder your intended progress. As you already know, there are some people who gloat over the failures and hard times of other people; it is as though they want everyone else to fail. Do not let anyone upset you this way! Follow your greatest instincts, where your fondest wishes and aspirations are concerned. To some people you may be the last person on earth to succeed; but you can proudly prove otherwise. Let the struggles of yesterday be your fulfilled tomorrows and—with a ray of hope—go forth into the world to reveal what you can do.

**MAGGOT** (i.e., a wormlike larvae often found in decayed matter and filth)

This dream forewarns the dreamer not to become run-down, otherwise a variety of stresses and sicknesses may be the outcome. Do your work; however, do not burn the candle at both ends. Know your limitations, and almost everything else will turn out in your favour!

**MAGI** (i.e., an ancient priestly caste of wise men who had mystic talents)

To be so privileged to see the Magi within a dream state is not by chance or by any kind of luck; it was actually meant to be! You are about to be rewarded for something special you have accomplished or for some good work you are presently undertaking. Your uncommon talents or gifts are special! This very rare dream is granted to very few people on this earth plane. You, however, seem to be under the Universal Light of Angels, Masters, and Philosophers who peacefully entered this earth plane to enlighten your fellow man towards greater visions and plateaus of life. Such is the wisdom of your great soul and the majesty of God's Blessings ahead of you, as assigned to the Magi within your dream state.

(*Note*: You will also have the pleasure of knowing that if, for example, you are experiencing a very negative dream, but at the very end of your dream sequence or anywhere during your dream sequence you happen to see a Magus or the Magi, then the "symbolism" of the Magi takes precedence over your entire bad dream. Consequently, you have nothing to worry about simply because the Magi act as a "buffer zone" to anything negative within a dream.)

**MAGIC** (see **BLACK MAGIC, ILLUSIONIST, EVILDOER**, or **WITCHCRAFT**)

**MAGICIAN** (see **ILLUSIONIST**)

**MAGISTRATE** (see **JUDGE**)

**MAGNET** (see **MAGNETISM**)

**MAGNETISM** (i.e., magnets and magnetic phenomena)

This dream indicates that, when you think negatively, all hell seems to break loose within your mind. This is totally uncalled for and unnecessary! Be aware that you have already left a trail of hard feelings, despair, and fear in the minds of some people around you. This simply will not do—certainly not if you want to be happy on this earth plane. Use more self-control in your thoughts and actions, and strive very hard to harness the love, peace, joy, and understanding that lie dormant within your being. Become a new person with inspiring trust but without complaints, hatreds, and revenge. And, if you must teach others anything, teach them about the spirit of giving, sharing, caring, and hope. You personally have so much to offer; do not forsake your better worth and purpose upon this planet for ephemeral pursuits.

## MAGNIFYING GLASS

You have a very good imagination, but sometimes you get carried away by blending your imaginative thoughts with factual information when speaking to others. By doing this you may misguide or mislead others into believing that your fabricated ideas are truthful. Be careful! Slow down, calm down, and speak cautiously and honestly at all times. If you are not sure about something, it would be far better to say nothing than to expound half-truths.

## MAGPIE (see BIRD)

## MAHARAJAH (i.e., a prince from India who ruled a major state or two)

Do not just touch the surface of things to be learned and accomplished in life, and do not merely sift through certain information that could be helpful to you. Anyone who makes half-hearted attempts in anything cannot expect to know it all! You are no exception to this rule. Your destiny is vitally important, but it is only as far-reaching as you wish it to be. Do not just sit idly by nor be afraid to forge ahead with wholesome views, theories, and inspirational duties that could touch the hearts of many around you. When you are ready, willing, and able to accept your naturally endowed leadership potential, you will commence to see some of your fondest hopes and wishes come true. Do not dally; the time is ripe now!

## MAHARISHI (i.e., a Hindu teacher or master of mysticism and transcendental meditation)

Your ideals are likened unto a person looking at a beautiful mountain, wanting desperately to climb to its peak with surefooted accuracy.

So, with your sincere efforts, time, and patience, you are not only trying to better yourself in many different ways, but you are striving to help others, as well. This world could use more such elevated and humanitarian souls. And why not? It is people like you who make this world a more profound, thought-provoking, elevated, and inspiring place in which to live.

**MAHATMA** (i.e., in Buddhism: a high-soul person held in high esteem or veneration)
Seeing or being one of these holy men of wisdom within a dream state reveals the great love, respect, and duty you hold towards all life. In your own way, you radiate hope when situations may appear dark and dismal to others; you offer kindness when tears and sadness beset someone; you bring joy to others in times of loneliness; and you are thankful for being given the strength and courage to simply lend a helping hand whenever the need arises. Such is the finery of your soul, your thoughts, your actions, and your deeds upon this earth plane. In many respects, you are like an angel of mercy whose love and work will go on and on.

**MAID**
Do not be too pushy or demanding in life. There are some things you can still do for yourself, no matter how intelligent you happen to be or what position or rank you hold in life. No one has the right to ever treat another person as a slave. In order to receive respect from others, you must show respect to others. Always be fair and sensible in all your earthly wants and needs; never for a moment think that all your whims or notions should be served by others around you. God gave you a mind and a body; use them diligently and intelligently.

**MAIDEN** (i.e., a girl or young woman who is not married)
Any one or several of the following definitions may be applicable: A) that you are a maiden and that you would, in fact, like to be married; or B) that you are a maiden but have no desire to marry at all; or C) that you are very undecided as to whether or not you wish to settle down now or later in life; or D) that you are presently married but often reflect upon your youth with fond memories of better times, hopes, and dreams; or E) that when you were single you always wished for a perfect marriage—but today you are hoping for more love, understanding, and communication within your marriage; or F) that

you are happily married, have fond memories about your youth, and certainly look forward to an even brighter future; or G) that this dream has little or no relevance to you at this time.

**MAIDEN NAME** (i.e., a woman's surname before marriage)

Flashes of your surname, or someone else's, appearing in a dream state could mean any one or several of the following definitions: A) that as a married person you feel very content with your life up to now; or B) that you feel resentful about doing most of the work at home—work which does not seem to be shared by your marriage partner; or C) that you have some doubts about your marriage, but your instinct tells you to hold on for the children's sake or for some other reason; or D) that although you strive for more affection and understanding within your marriage, you simply realize that you cannot change a person to your way of thinking simply because you are married to that person; or E) that something you did in your past, not related to your marriage partner, now causes you to have great fears that someone will reveal the truth to your spouse; or F) that you are a very inhibited person, both emotionally and sexually, and often wish that you were single again, because you somehow feel that you are incapable of making your marriage partner happy; or G) that you were happier as a single person than as a married person; or H) that you would like to add your surname before your married name, feeling no one should give up their family name when they get married; or I) that you were widowed and are possibly pondering upon the idea of reverting back to your maiden name; or J) that you merely dreamt about your present surname; or K) that this dream has little or no relevance to you at this time.

**MAID OF HONOR**

Modify your thinking habits, otherwise your impatience, nervousness, frustrations, and boredom can lead you down a pathway of problems you never expected. So life is not exactly what you had hoped it might be for you—so what? You can certainly make it better! Everyone would like to go on a magic carpet to some Shangri-La, but that is not the way life on earth happens to be. Never mind your past, or your present bitter moments, or what someone has done to supposedly ruin your life. You have plenty of energy and potential to carry on with your life, providing you do not give in to your sorrows and self-pity. Your future is filled with betterment; but, before this can be possible, you must commence to revamp your negative uncertainties into positive thinking and achievements.

## MAIL

Seeing mail is always an auspicious sign for the dreamer. For example, you may be receiving a promotion in your career; receiving a new job offer; making a major purchase such as a house, car, boat, or other item; traveling abroad; receiving some long-awaited news from a distance concerning a contract or some other business proposition; doing some creative work that might be known to many people in time, or attaining anything else that you are desperately trying to attain. It is sincerely hoped that you will be happy and content, whatever your good news.

## MAILBOX

Life could be a lot simpler for you if you did not switch your feelings so abruptly and irrationally. One minute you are optimistic, pleasing, and ambitious; the next you seem to be depressed, angered, and rude. Your unpredictable behavior can create much anguish for you down the road, if you do not seriously look into this matter now. What appears to be happening is that some argumentative thoughts come into your mind very suddenly and simply alter your attitudes and moods. Strive for more self-control over your thoughts. Do not get so upset when unwarranted or bad thoughts happen to wander through your mind. As long as you have done nothing wrong, then be at peace, for no sin was committed. Simply ignore those unwholesome thoughts; they obviously do not belong to you! Now, on the brighter side of things, it appears that you will have to make a major decision within your life before too long. This decision, by the way, will be lucky and positive for you!

## MAILMAN

Any one or several of the following definitions may be applicable: A) that you are a mailman who enjoys or dislikes the work that you do; or B) that you are worrying about some news from a distance; or C) that you find your life boring and mundane because of the daily routine of your home or work activities; or D) that you admire people who are very happy simply because you cannot seem to find the key to happiness within your own life; or E) that you are pessimistically stubborn with most people whom you know or with anything you seem to do in life; or F) that you are confused about a personal relationship with one or more individuals; or G) that the only bearing this dream has to you is that you saw or talked to the mailman lately; or H) that this dream has little or no relevance to you at this time.

## MAKE-BELIEVE

The world of make-believe is synonymous with dreaming in that a dream is like a stage in which we, the dreamers, play a part, be it logical, illogical, humourous, sad, or tragic. Some dreams could, perhaps, win grand awards for their realism, projected truths, and universal symbolisms, whereas others are forgotten or put aside because of their "mumbo jumbo" effect upon the dreamer. Everyone, in a sense, is creative; and while we dream, we are creating images and scenes at various intervals during sleep. Bear in mind as well that the world of make-believe can be just as emphatically gripping within your sleep state as it is during your wake state when you go to the movies, the theatre, and so on. In many ways, whether you are wide awake or dreaming, the world of make-believe helps each one of us to either escape from some realities within and around us or to find some truths and realities within and around us. Sooner or later, most people come to grips with their limited realities and simply carry on from there. Yet, it is always comforting to know that we all have the ability to "fly away" to a place with limitless visions, concepts, ideas, and actions by simply falling asleep and finding ourselves within a dream.

## MAKEUP (see COSMETIC)

## MALADY (see SICKNESS)

## MALARIA

Dreaming about this tropical disease, whether it is just the name itself that flashes by you and/or the disease itself, reflects upon your personal hygiene and general attitude about looking after yourself. As touchy as this topic may be, your dream is making you aware that sometimes your haste or laziness can create an embarrassing problem for you. It is kindly advising you to take pride in your mind, body, and soul at all times. Cleanliness and good grooming are natural and normal daily habits everyone should adopt, no matter how busy you happen to be or where you happen to live.

**MALL** (i.e., an indoor or outdoor shopping centre)

This dream symbolizes either the joys and happiness or the basic humdrum existence one chooses to maintain in life. This, of course, depends upon you and the degree to which you want to improve, repair, or refine your style of living. Some people do not care what comforts they possess; whereas the vast majority of people do have a great concern to live as comfortably as possible on this earth plane. Basically, there is nothing wrong with either choice, providing people are happy, well-adjusted, and productive with their lives. The bottom line is to always strive to do your very best in life and, like a rising soul who gleans knowledge here and there, you will prosper over and above your greatest expectations. Always remember, however, that you do not have to live in a castle in order to be happy and productive!

**MALLARD** (see **DUCK**)

**MALLET** (i.e., a short handled wooden hammer or a long-handled hammer used for playing croquet or polo)

This dream cautions you not to be so prideful, bullheaded, and overly sure of yourself. The illusion that everything will always go your way is sheer folly; nothing is absolutely sure on this earthly plane, and we must all be prepared to take a fall or two once in a while. Absolutely no one is immune to this truth here! Try to gain a better perspective about yourself and about life in general. Perhaps in due time you will learn to master some of those unforeseen challenges yet awaiting you. Then you will see, and you will know that there are many thorns amongst the roses along your highways and byways of life.

**MALNUTRITION**

Any one or several of the following definitions may be applicable: A) that you are suffering from poor nourishment; or B) that you know of someone who is suffering from inadequate nutrition; or C) that you are aware that many people in poor countries suffer in this manner, and you at least contribute to their needs in some manner; or D) that you feel all governments of the earth should concentrate upon the needs of people instead of wasting their time and energy on other matters; or E) that you may be on a diet and went to bed hungry, which automatically produced symbolic visions of malnutrition within your dream state; or F) that you simply went to bed hungry which, in turn, produced symbolic visions of malnutrition within your dream state; or

G) that you often think about your responsibility as a human being for the many people on this planet who do go to bed hungry and crying and who are tormented with a bleak future outlook; or H) that you always seem to think about food when you are lonely and stressful; or I) that you often wonder why this world cannot shed its ignorance and greed in order to reach out to all its planetary citizens with peace, sharing, and love; or J) that when a child is born it cries for comfort and food, but how could anyone on this God-given planet of plenty ignore the tears of a child, of a mother, and a father who have nothing to give?; or K) that this dream has little or no relevance to you at this time.

**MALPRACTICE** (i.e., professional misconduct)

Any one or several of the following definitions may be applicable to you: A) that you are a professional individual who fully understands and adheres to proper conduct at all times; or B) that you are a professional person who fully understands the nature of malpractice but, from time to time, you become overzealous, which could place you in jeopardy with your peers and others whom you represent; or C) that you know of someone who has been charged with malpractice; or D) that you are a very intelligent and cautious individual who prefers a second or third opinion where any profession is concerned; or E) that you have been deceived by all types of people (including professionals), and these lessons have taught you to be more wise and prudent in all your activities; or F) that you have complete trust in all professional people; or G) that this dream has little or no significance to you at this time.

**MAMBA** (see **SNAKE**)

**MAMBO** (see **DANCE**)

**MAMMAL** (see **ANIMAL, DOLPHIN, SEAL, WALRUS,** or **WHALE**)

**MAMMOTH**

Dreaming of this extinct elephant-like animal reveals that you are searching for some answers in your life which appear to be hidden from you. There appears to be some mystery or missing link to your past which you simply cannot comprehend, nor does anyone who might know wish to assist you in this matter. Your dream reveals various situations that you might perhaps be looking into: being adopted and wanting to know more about your biological parents; losing a parent when you were very young and wanting to know more about this parent; losing a twin brother or sister at birth and wanting to know what happened; believing that some tragedy struck your family when you were young and wanting to know exactly what the circumstances might have been; being attacked mentally, physically, or sexually when you were very young, and now you want to know whether this is true or a mere figment of your imagination; having certain fears that seem totally unnatural to you, and all you want to know is whether something traumatic happened to you when you were very young; or, last, searching for anything else that seems to haunt or puzzle you. Whatever you are searching for, it is hoped that, with time, you will find the answers which you rightfully deserve to know. However, if you do not find what you are seeking, then simply carry on with inner strength, peace, and acceptance.

## MANAGER

If you happen to be a manager and have a dream of being one, then your dream is merely reflecting your status or position in life. Sometimes you stand and smile all alone in your position simply because of the friction you receive from others under your authority. This, unfortunately, goes with the position of being a manager; but, then again, you would not be there if you were incapable of handling matters around you. On the other hand, dreaming about seeing or being a manager but not actually holding this position in life implies that you would like to be "a somebody" rather than a "mere nobody" on this earth plane. The simple fact is that you are important, whether you wish to believe this or not. It does not matter whether you are rich, famous, or poor—you are still a vital link to the Universal Order of Life. Many rich men were once poor, and many poor men were once rich; both were given a chance to display their importance and charitable deeds. Should they fail in some manner, then there are those mighty lessons for anyone who becomes too smug, prideful, ruthless, or greedy. The greatest, most important lesson of all in life is to learn humility and thankfulness and to love your fellow man. These virtuous actions are those memories of earth you take with you; by the same token, these are the same joys of love you leave behind.

**MANDATE** (see **LAW**)

**MANDOLIN** (see **INSTRUMENT**)

**MAN-EATER** (see **CANNIBALISM, LION,** or **TIGER**)

**MANGER** (e.g., a trough or box which holds food for cattle, horses, and other animals)

Seeing a manger signifies that you are seeking refuge from a specific person who wishes you harm and/or from some other dangerous situations around you. There are only two logical answers here: overcome your problem by seeking some outside guidance and help, or move entirely away from your surroundings. If the latter does not appear feasible to you, then you will simply have to bear the consequent uncertainties that go with your problem(s). You have a God given right to be happy and free, but unless you pull yourself together in this matter, there is much loneliness and heartache ahead for you. The choice to find inner peace is entirely up to you. Decide quickly!

**MANGO** (see **FRUIT**)

**MANHOOD** (see **MASCULINITY**)

**MANIAC** (see **INSANITY**)

**MANIC-DEPRESSIVE** (i.e., a person who displays great exuberance and fits of exaggerated fancy to great depths of depression)

Seeing yourself or someone else with a manic-depressive condition signifies that you are a very stubborn individual who seldom seeks, finds, or understands the pleasures and simple joys of life. You have built a cold barrier around yourself due to your tragic past which, in part, did not give you the opportunity to be loved, needed, and wanted. However, if you have had enough of your past memories and trauma, then simply toss those old thoughts away from your mind, and begin anew today. You have paid your dues! Throw away your bitterness by thinking kindly of others—even those who harmed you—and begin to pray very hard for God's Blessings upon you. Fight hard like a true soldier in battle until you have vanquished every morsel of hate within your entire being! Then, when you have arrived at the plateau of ageless love and understanding, you will then know why your life is not over, but miraculously just beginning. Go forward with your life, and share your love and joys with others, who literally weep for help. And—as you look here and there—be a servant of God and of all good things.

## MANICURE
You are longing for more kindness and communication with a loved one (i.e., spouse, child, relative, friend, etc.). It seems that you have bent backwards to try to please and appease this person. Time, endurance, patience, understanding, love, and spiritual health are all necessary ingredients to bind the minds and souls of any two people who are experiencing some form of distance from one another. Bear in mind, as well, that everyone has limitations and shortcomings, and we must all learn to correct ourselves before we make quantum leaps to correct others. Be silent with your anguish, for soon there will be peace and love where you know there was misunderstanding.

## MANIFESTO (see LAW)

## MANIKIN (i.e., an anatomical model of a human body with detachable parts such as those used in medical schools, art classes, window displays)
You were recently embarrassed over a situation that should not have even taken place. Your humiliation in this matter, however justified, should be forgotten. No one is blameless on this planet for something said or done in an unthinking manner; and to err truly is human! Keep yourself busy, realize that one lesson is quite enough, and that this will never happen to you again—not if you can help it.

## MANKIND (see HUMANITY)

## MANNA (see FOOD)

## MANOR (see MANSION)

## MANSION
You are either looking for or scheming to find shortcuts and loopholes that would supposedly bring you instant wealth and success. No!

It will not happen this way for you at all! Like most people on this planet, you must start from the bottom and slowly work your way up that so-called ladder of success. Be prepared to work very hard towards your goals, for what you sow is exactly what you will reap in life. This dream advises you to let go of your shortsighted, self-centered attitudes. If you truly want to be a success at anything, then be sensible and determined enough to proceed in the right direction.

**MANSLAUGHTER** (see **KILL** or **MURDER**)

**MANTELPIECE**
Financial, emotional, and some physical troubles could very well be upsetting you at this time. Life is like that sometimes; when it rains, it pours. Try your very best not to be disappointed or discouraged with what befalls you from time to time, but rather carry on with patience and courage. This earthly life, with all its goodness and shortcomings, teaches us many lessons of "how, when, where, why, because, although, since, when, as, if" and so on until we learn to grasp some inner truths about ourselves and about our flaws and weaknesses. You just happen to be in the midst of such a lesson; somehow, you will master it quite admirably.

**MANTIS** (see **INSECT**)

**MANUAL** (see **BOOK**)

**MANUFACTURE** (see **FACTORY** or **MILL**)

**MANURE** (see **DUNG**)

**MANUSCRIPT**
This auspicious dream infers that something you are doing now, and/or something you hope to achieve in time will be fulfilled! The scientific, inventive, and creative forces within you are constantly at work, always rising over and above the nadir of despair and reflective anguish you often harbor. You will make it; do not give up. You are headed in the right direction! Can you accept some good news? Well, a realization, a hope, and a very great wish is coming true for you! Even the angels sing because they know that in the morning's glory they have a "new star" in their midst.

**MAP** (see *also* **ATLAS, BLUEPRINT,** or **CARTOGRAPHY**)

Beware of something underhanded being plotted against you by a jealous person and/or by a group of people who appear to be using quite a bit of ignorance lately. You seem to be the center of attention where their gossip, envy, and ridicule is concerned. Hold your ground! With your sound judgment, diplomacy, fairness, and tolerance you should be able to master this situation quite well.

**MARATHON** (i.e., a foot race)

You are trying much too hard to prove yourself to others. Yes, you have impressed some people, but what about yourself? How long can you continue your so-called supernatural feats and activities without falling down or collapsing? For your sake, tune in to your natural energy level and speed rather than going beyond common sense and human endurance. Simply do your own very best instead of trying to do more than you are capable of doing.

**MARBLE** (see **GAME** or **SCULPTURE**)

**MARCH** (i.e., the act of marching in a military, grave or resolute manner; quickstep; promenade)

Seeing yourself or anyone else march forward within a dream state indicates that you are striving for a higher level of awareness and understanding in life. You may be reading great philosophical books, self-awareness books, religious books, and so on, or you may be attending some school, university, or educational program in order to enhance your thinking capabilities, as well as planning your future actions and deeds. "Seek and you will find" is basically what this dream symbolism is all about. You will ultimately discover many truths and gain much awareness in due time.

Seeing yourself or anyone else march backward indicates that some recent event or circumstance have created a hopeless outlook where you are concerned. It appears as though you are carrying the weight of the world on your shoulders, when in fact you should be counting your blessings. The situation is not as bad as it appears to be, but you seem to be blinded by the fact that things should have turned out differently for you. It is much too late to correct any past mistakes now, but you certainly can reflect upon a better future, if you gave yourself half a chance to do so. Success and happiness lie ahead of you. First, however, you must close a door or two within your mind so that you can reach out to other avenues and prospects which will ultimately fulfill your fondest wishes and hopes.

**MARE'S-NEST** (i.e., something thought to be a marvelous discovery only to be recognized as a hoax or a misconception)
No one really wants to purposely make mistakes or wrong decisions in their life. Yet, one's entire life's journey can be fraught with the unknown possibilities or probabilities of disappointments and failures. Sometimes we slip, fall, and fail; sometimes we slip, fall, and succeed. Such is the state of this earthly life and its many trials and tribulations and its love for you. This dream only wishes to remind you that, no matter who you are or what you do in life, there are no guarantees that what you yearn for will bring you end-of-the-rainbow happiness or anything else which you may desire. If you are basically ready, willing, and able to take a chance at something, then you must hope for the best. That is all anyone can do.

**MARGIN** (i.e., a blank space around a page or sheet of paper)
Seeing a margin indicates that you take unnecessary risks or chances with some things you do (e.g., using a broken ladder, jaywalking on a busy street, careless driving). Stop, look, and listen before you do something you may regret. For your sake and for the sake of those who truly love and care about you, use more foresight and logic in everything you do. Life is far too valuable to waste on some careless, unreasonable judgment.

**MARIMBA** (see **INSTRUMENT**)

**MARIONETTE** (see **PUPPETRY**)

**MARK** (see **STAIN**)

**MARKER** (i.e., a person who marks the score at games, or a device for keeping score)
You seem to be overly preoccupied with some activity, action, or thought that could eventually lead you towards anxieties and stresses you never anticipated. What you need is a reprieve so that you can at least gain control of yourself in a reasonable, sane manner. Put your feet back on the ground, grit your teeth, and commence to face your realities just like you used to do. Doing so could prevent mental and physical hardships for you in the future.

## MARKETPLACE

A busy marketplace advises you not to be so dramatic, extreme, and shortsighted when something not to your liking takes place. Be respectful of people's feelings; sometimes you can be very offensive, not realizing that your cutting remarks affect those around you. Once in a while, take the trouble to listen to your words and see whether or not most of your complaints are justifiable. You may surprise yourself into realizing that most of your complaints are merely petty indifferences you harbour towards people, places, and things.

A deserted or not-so-busy marketplace indicates a possible change of residence, school, employment, city, state, or country. This change or move appears to be all right providing you are basically content with what you are planning to do. If you have great doubts, then seriously think twice before leaping into a situation you may later regret.

A messy, disorganized, or ravaged marketplace reveals that you have had enough of some situation that has affected you for quite some time. Face this matter with down-to-earth maturity. Do not be irrational, otherwise you will be the loser, in the long run. The choice of a better future rests with you; hopefully, you will find your way towards the love, peace, and comfort you so rightfully deserve.

## MARMALADE (see FOOD)

## MAROON (see ABANDONMENT)

## MARRIAGE (see *also* BIGAMY, ELOPEMENT, INTERMARRIAGE, or POLYGAMY)

Any one or several of the following definitions may be applicable: A) that you are happily married; or B) that you are partially happy with your marriage for a variety of reasons; or C) that your marriage will break up unless some drastic changes are forthcoming; or D) that you are presently separated and divorced but look forward to a possible future marriage with greater luck and happiness; or E) that you anticipate marriage in the future; or F) that you are in the process of getting married, but now you are not sure whether you made the right decision; or G) that you feel your past mistakes are a great detriment to finding a marriage partner; or H) that you feel your age is a great barrier to finding a marriage partner; or I) that you have resigned yourself to a solitary life because you were too picky or too slow in choosing a mate; or J) that, due to the words and actions of other people who seem to have a bad marriage, you make yourself quite unavailable for relationships and courtships; or K) that because your parents' marriage was not the best one to behold, you have an inner fear that this could also happen to you; or L) that because of some mental or physical disability or some other sickness, marriage for you is out of the question; or M) that you are homosexual and marriage in a heterosexual way does not seem logical or feasible to you now or possibly at any time of your life; or N) that this dream has little or no significance to you at this time.

**MARS** (see **PLANET**)

**MARSH** (see **SWAMP**)

**MARSHMALLOW** (see **FOOD**)

**MARTYR** (i.e., a person who chooses to suffer or die rather than give up their belief or faith)

You are a very strong-willed individual who literally hates any type of social injustices targeting any minority group or race of people. In your own small way, it appears that you are either helping the needy in your society, or you are very financially charitable towards those needy and trustworthy organizations who do require your help. In truth, we are all our brother's keeper in many ways on this earth plane. You are to be commended for your positive beliefs and for your determination to never turn your back when someone is in great need or calls out in anguish.

**MASCARA** (see **COSMETIC**)

**MASCULINITY**

If you are a male and dream of being masculine, then all is in order, for you are merely reflecting upon a natural and normal attitude of the male species.

If you are a female and dream about being masculine, then there may be some identity crisis about your feminine role in life. Inhibitions, phobias, and a variety of neurotic feelings and beliefs may plague or sway you into believing that you are not the person you were born to be. Acceptance of self is vital here; however, if this matter is impossible to handle alone, then of course you should seek professional psychological and spiritual guidance.

**MASK** (i.e., a disguise) (see *also* **MASQUERADE**)

This dream reveals that you are not facing up to some basic reality about yourself, and/or you are not admitting a truth to another person for some reason. If this is your choice, there is very little anyone can do to prompt you to change your mind. Let your conscience be your guiding light in this entire matter.

**MASOCHISM** (i.e., receiving sexual pleasure by being dominated or mistreated in a physical and mental manner by one's partner, or receiving the same pleasure through one's own actions) (Also see **HATRED**)

Any one or several of the following definitions may be applicable: A) that you are a masochist; or B) that you are not a masochist; or C) that from time to time you tend to desire this type of treatment but do not consider yourself masochistic; or D) that you know of someone who does behave in this strange manner; or E) that you know this type of behaviour is demoralizing and extremely painful to the mind, body, and soul; or F) that anyone who does behave in this manner must have suffered some terrible abuses when they were young; or G) that this dream has little or no relevance to you at this time.

**MASQUERADE** (i.e., costume party)

You seem to be hiding behind a facade of unrealities which could very well involve your lifestyle, financial status, home surroundings, and so on. You are trying to believe that your life is marvelous and super when, in fact, everything is not this way at all. There is no need to pretend when situations not to your liking happen to come your way. Face your todays squarely, and maybe your tomorrows will commence to improve for you. Wanting others to believe that you are sitting on top of the world is false when, in fact, you seem to be in a very low valley working your way up. Times will change for you. But, for your greater peace of mind, accept the realities of yourself, your family, and your life style; accept what is now.

**MASS**

Seeing a Mass within a dream suggests that you tend to be a bit too critical, analytical, and doubtful for your own good. Sometimes in life you have to take a few things here and there for granted rather than concentrate on the minute trivia and unnecessary facts that are of no consequence to your earthly and spiritual growth. This dream is trying to tell you not to be so picky. You have been given a very precious gift in life—your mind. Use it and guide it well.

Seeing a Black Mass within a dream forewarns you not to get carried away with any type of superstitions and false philosophies that tend to be base and highly deceptive. Do not let anyone convince you otherwise. Be more discerning in what you read or hear for, at times, you may come across some false dogma, beliefs, literature, and so on that are not in keeping with God's Laws. Seek your wisdom, gratitude, self-control, and peace with positive efforts, and begin to realize that the truest religion you can uphold on this planet is the purity and goodness within your own heart, mind, and soul.

**MASSACRE** (see **GENOCIDE, KILL,** or **MURDER**)

**MASSAGE**
This dream reveals that you are concerned and somewhat uncertain about some health problem, family ties, and about your job or career. You are strongly advised to persevere with a positive outlook, but also be willing to make certain concessions and compromises in order to make situations within and around you a little better. Very soon, those earthly matters which trouble you will dissipate; then you can continue to be your natural, wholesome self once more.

**MASSAGE PARLOUR** (see **MASSAGE** or **PARLOUR**)

**MASSEUR** (see **MASSAGE**)

**MASSEUSE** (see **MASSAGE**)

**MASTER OF CEREMONIES**
Something is troubling you but, sadly, you are maintaining a silence towards someone who does not have the foggiest idea why you are so cool and aloof. Now, unless this person is a mind reader, you can hardly expect to get ahead in this matter unless you commence to reveal your inner anguish and silent mind arguments. When something troubles you, do not "bottle and cork it"; rather, express your views and opinions until some self-satisfying compromises are made.

## MASTERPIECE

Seeing or creating a masterpiece within a dream state advises you not to hurry through situations or tasks just to be first in everything you do. Granted, you are intelligent and basically a very quick thinker; however, it pays sometimes to go a little slower in order to ensure more quality in your work.

Destroying a masterpiece, on the other hand, reveals that you inwardly want to break away from old ties, influences, or habits; otherwise, you cannot see improvements forthcoming. If you know that someone or something is hindering or troubling you to the point where you cannot progress, then by all means make those long-over-due changes. This may not be too easy to do. However, if you honestly intend to move on with no remorse, then you can be sure you are on the right track to self-improvement and happiness.

## MASTURBATION

One or several of the following definitions may be applicable: A) that you do, in fact, masturbate and accept this act as being whole-some and natural rather than sinful; or B) that you experience a high sense of remorse and guilt after you masturbate; or C) that you do not masturbate; or D) that because of your high moralistic beliefs and religious upbringing, masturbation is considered wrong; or E) that even though you are married, you still masturbate when the need is there; or F) that you are unhappily married or single and you would sooner masturbate than have sex indiscriminately; or G) that you are a celibate by word only, but in act and deed you are not practicing what you preach; or H) that you are sexually abusive and/or neurotic—not only to yourself, but to others, as well; or I) that you have strong sexual inclinations or weak sexual inclinations; or J) that you seem to have mixed feelings whether masturbation is normal, abnormal, or sinful; or K) that you are incapable of this act or any other sexual act because of some physical or mental impediment; or L) that this dream has lit-tle or no significance to you at this time.

## MAT (e.g., doormat, bathmat, car mat)

Sometimes you feel like you were being used as a doormat, in the way others treat you. It seems like you never stop satisfying the needs and wants of people around you; but who, in turn, listens to your needs and wants? Well, no one seems to be, that's certain! This dream counsels you to turn over a new leaf by simply making a few demands here and there. You are not a slave to anyone's whims and notions, and you certainly have a God-given right to be heard and to be satisfied, just like the next person. Do not be afraid to be a little bit self-centered and firm, from time to time, if this is what it takes to teach a person or two a vital lesson in life. This may be drastic; but, by the same token, you may win the ongoing war and be free to bask in the harmony you rightfully deserve.

**MATADOR** (see **BULLFIGHT**)

**MATCH** (i.e., a small piece of wood, cardboard, or waxed cord tipped with an ignited material)
It seems as though you are going to light up someone's day! A person with a problem or two will approach you; you, in turn, will give them some down-to-earth advice that will not be forgotten. Shortly thereafter, a gift will be presented to you.

**MATCHBOOK** (see **MATCH**)

**MATCHBOX** (see **MATCH**)

**MATCHMAKING** (e.g., the act of arranging marriages for people, or arranging a boxing match, tug of war)
This dream indicates that you are being too dictatorial where someone is concerned, and/or someone is doing the same thing to you. This action towards anyone is both futile and senseless. A person may try to control the spirit of another, but nothing is gained here except anguish and deep hatreds between two people. Tread lightly, for the person whom you abuse or accuse could very well be an angel or even a Cosmic Master whose love for you is far greater than you could ever hope to imagine. You do not own anyone, nor does anyone own you. We are all here on borrowed time. Treat everyone with all the kindness and respect you could humanly gather, for you never know what your tomorrows may bring. Never forget, as well, that the person whom you mistreat can wander out of your life in many different ways. Then what would you do?

**MATERIAL** (e.g., cloth, fabric)
You would like everything in life to go smoothly for you; unfortunately, this is not always the case. It seems that when you do one thing

right, there are always three things you do wrong in the eyes of others. This dream counsels you to make your decisions and plans with deeper convictions; do not change your mind so frequently. When you plan to do something with a person or two, do not put a damper or crease on these plans unless you have a very sincere reason to back you up. As well, you tend to be a bit forgetful. You preoccupy yourself so deeply with one task that you simply become oblivious to another task that needs your immediate attention. Do your very best to place your thoughts and actions in order; this will assist you further down the road in life. Consider, as well, that you are a marvelous person except that, from time to time, you seem to get yourself into some needless quandaries which could have been avoided.

**MATHEMATICS** (e.g., arithmetic, geometry, algebra, calculus)
    Solving a mathematical problem within a dream state implies that you are a very intelligent, industrious person. You are bound to be highly successful in your own way as you plod down the highways and byways of your life. However, there appears to be one small piece of advice this dream wishes to impart to you: be more lenient with yourself when you make a mistake or two. It seems that when this happens you cannot believe that you, of all people, could make a blunder! Do not suppress your fine mind with depressive thoughts when you do; just carry on. Even if you happen to be in the genius category, you will discover that this is quite normal and natural. At present, you just happen to be too much of a perfectionist for your own good. As your experiences grow, this attitude will eventually dissipate.
    Being unable to solve a mathematical problem within a dream suggests that you may have some past or present hang-ups about school, which seem to haunt you. Do not let anything upset you in this matter because you are, in so many ways, a highly learned and gifted soul! There is fame ahead for you, as you slowly reach out to offer your services to the world!

**MATRIMONY** (see **MARRIAGE**)

**MATRON** (i.e., a female superintendent of a hospital, prison, or other institution)
    You cannot hope to gain any happiness if you tend to hide your good intentions and feelings from others. For some reason or other, you appear to be very aloof or reticent towards anyone who wishes to

know more about your thoughts, aspirations, or yearnings in life. Do not be afraid to share a little bit of this or a little bit of that about yourself with someone who happens to find you intelligent and interesting. Many friendships are formed this way. Furthermore, you can be a very good friend to yourself by not being so overly secretive and private.

**MATRON OF HONOR** (see **MAID OF HONOR**)

**MATTRESS**

Whether you are at home, at school, or at work, it appears that you are not being praised, rewarded, or promoted for your diligent and praiseworthy efforts. It seems as though you want to go on strike or simply lay down your efforts until you are properly compensated or at least treated as fairly as the next person. This dream reveals that, before too long, this entire matter will straighten itself out, much to your satisfaction.

**MAUL** (see **BRUISE** or **INJURY**)

**MAUSOLEUM**

Whenever you are disappointed, everything appears depressive, morbid, and boring to you. It thus becomes very difficult for you to come out of your deep, dark moods unless something drastic happens to change your mind. You tend to harbour uneventful memories much too long; whereas you should strive harder to think about positive thoughts and actions, instead. As you go on in life, there will be many struggles and disappointments you will experience; realize that the sooner you master your problems, the better off you will be. You create far too many unwholesome stresses and strains within your mind and body (e.g., headaches, inability to eat, sleep, or think properly) when something not to your liking happens to cross your pathway. Be more courageous, confident, and clearheaded when minor or major difficulties beset you. These guiding tools can carry you through the darkest valleys of your life.

**MAYDAY** (i.e., a signal for help used by aircraft and ships)

A mayday signal or call for help intimates that something is dreadfully wrong at this time. It may involve you, a loved one, or someone else whom you know. Be very careful for the next week or two where any form of land, air, or water travel is concerned. Also, the possibility of nature itself creating some devastating havoc within or around your territory is feasible! With this dream, there is confusion, pain, and anguish which can perhaps be avoided; praying for everyone's guidance and protection is highly advised. Hopefully, this critical period will pass you by, leaving you unscathed.

**MAYHEM** (see **DESTRUCTION** or **INJURY**)

**MAYONNAISE** (see **FOOD**)

**MAYOR**

Recently, you may be ignoring or procrastinating about certain matters or promises that need your undivided attention. Failure to fulfill these business or personal commitments can have some serious setbacks for you. Your dream only wishes to remind you that loyalty to self and to others is the true nature of a reliable person, which you still happen to be. Do not spoil your unbroken record, where truth and honesty are concerned!

**MAZE** (see **CONFUSION**)

**MEADOW**

To be "happy" in or near a meadow indicates that you are breaking away from some old habits and customs. Good for you! Better times are certainly foreseen ahead of you because of the diligent strides you are making towards self-improvement. Look ahead; you will never regret it!

To be "confused" in or near a meadow advises you to not stretch the truth beyond repair. If you have something to say, tell it the way it is, not the way you think it should or could be. You will feel much better about yourself for having done so.

To be "indifferent" in or near a meadow infers that you are presently coping with your daily activities in a tolerable sort of way. Your life may not necessarily be very exciting or exhilarating at this time, but you do have a wholesome "do your best and let it be" attitude. In due time, some lucky event will bring you added prosperity and happiness.

To be "shocked, depressed, or injured" in or near a meadow indicates that your stubbornness and wayward thinking is holding you back in life. Unless you commence to alter some of your illogical and uncompromising attitudes, do not expect too much of anything. You have created your own barriers, and it is only you who can lift these barriers which form a yoke around your mind, heart, and soul.

## MEAL (see *also* FOOD)

Having a meal with loved ones or strangers who appear relatively pleasing and happy indicates improvements in health and money matters. This transitional change is long overdue and should be very welcome!

Having a meal with loved ones or strangers who appear sad or mournful suggests you will be attending a funeral. This funeral may not necessarily relate to you or to your immediate family directly, although the possibilities are there. As well, an educational program which could broaden your sense of awareness and responsibility seems to be in the horizon for you.

## MEASLES (see SICKNESS)

## MEASUREMENT (see *also* BAROMETER, CARTOGRAPHY, CLOCK, COMPASS, HOURGLASS, MATHEMATICS, METER, PEDOMETER, SCALE, SEXTANT, SUNDIAL, THERMOMETER, or THERMOSTAT)

Taking a measurement of someone or something advises you not to be envious of, or begrudge, another person's worth, acts, or talents. Everyone has their own inner gifts. Some people choose to share their special talents with others; some do not. Some choose to become leaders in their rightful fields; yet, many do not. Some choose to be confident and satisfied with their lives; many do not. Some choose to utilize their expertise wisely and avoid infamy, ruthlessness, and greed; many do not. Some choose to help their fellow man; many do not. There are no two people alike on this planet. Even though there may be similarities, each person has their own distinct mind, soul, wants, and needs, which only they can account for and satisfy, in the end. Envy no one on this planet nor lust after those things which another person may have. Count your own blessings, and tend to your own flowers, for God has given you more than your share already.

## MEASURING CUP (see MEASUREMENT)

## MEAT (see *also* BACON or CARCASS)

Seeing fresh meat advises the dreamer not to be so inconsiderate, inhospitable, or intolerant when someone else happens to complain or have some kind of problem. This does not imply that you always do this; however, from time to time, you get fed up with repeated complainers or anyone who complains but refuses to do anything about it. Be patient with everyone around you; others have to be patient with you sometimes, too. Even though some people make little or no efforts to help themselves, they are still our brothers and sisters on this planet. Sooner or later, they mend their ways. It just could be that some people whom you know need you as a kind of "leaning post" once in a while in order to feel momentarily better within themselves. Be more tolerant of others around you, be a bit more sympathetic, and somehow place yourself in their frustrated, shortsighted mind for a moment or two. It's not such a pretty picture. Nonetheless, just consider how often God forgives and helps each and every one of us. That's mindboggling too!

Seeing meat that is dry, moldy, smelly, or infested with some type of disease advises you and/or your loved ones to be wary of negative places, situations, health problems, or any type of careless activities that may be dangerous and outright foolish. This type of dream urges caution all around you. Do not take chances on anything at all; for, if you do, anything can happen!

## MEATBALL (see FOOD or MEAT)

## MECHANIC

Seeing or being a mechanic forewarns the dreamer to neither make any drastic changes at this time nor to go overboard with major buying sprees. You may be sorely disappointed! This dream advises you to wait at least a month or two until the dark clouds passing by completely disappear from view. Later on, you will feel much more secure, and you certainly will get a better bargain for your money—that is, if you decide to stop, look, and listen to what this dream is trying to tell you.

## MEDAL (see *also* MEDALIST)

You are a very sensitive individual. It seems hectic enough for you when you deal with major problems, let alone having to deal with your delicate feelings as well. Many times you feel as though you were carrying two crosses, not one. You are such a fine, intelligent, and capable person that to meet you is to instantly like you. It is vitally important that you commence to like yourself completely, inside and out, with no exceptions. Right now you are likened unto a person who is in a room full of people; yet, nobody knows you are there! Well, it's about time they did! Begin to communicate, praise, and share your thoughts and feelings with others around you. Do not be afraid to say what you feel, for this is as normal as drinking a cool, clear glass of water. Make your presence known and felt wherever you go in a thoughtful, kindly way. You have so much to offer your fellow man; it would be a great pity to simply keep your great thoughts to yourself.

## MEDALIST

Someone is giving you the runaround, especially with promises that are not kept. You are deeply affected, and you certainly feel that you do not deserve this treatment from anyone. Honesty and sincerity are and will always be your best policy; that is why this present situation seems totally unbearable. Today may bring you uncertainties, but very soon the truth to this entire matter will be revealed to you; and, once more, you will go on to yet another chapter of your life—coping, probing, and ultimately conquering.

## MEDALLION (see MEDAL)

## MEDICAL EXAMINER (see CORONER)

## MEDICATION (i.e., a medicine)

Any one or several of the following definitions may be applicable: A) that you are presently taking some type of medication, or B) that you are not taking any type of medication at this time; or C) that you are allergic to some medicines; or D) that you would sooner take some type of vitamin than a medicine; or E) that you do not believe in taking any type of medication, at the best of times; or F) that only under great duress, pain, or stress would you consider taking medicine; or G) that this dream has little or no relevance to you at this time.

## MEDICINE DANCE

Although you basically mean well in the things you say and do, there is always someone around to criticize or reject your good intentions. Some people are just too difficult to get along with, let alone please! This dream counsels you to be diplomatic and sensible in this matter; that, alone, will speak for itself. You are sincere, and you try to do your very best, at all times; this places you in a first-class rating with some other people you know. Accentuate your good friendships; ignore the bad ones.

**MEDICINE MAN** (i.e., among the North American Indians, a man who cures disease and controls spirits; shaman)

Be more realistic and forthright in your dealings with others, for this will give you a greater measure of self-determination. Do not be afraid to say no to anyone who happens to make a request which you know, beyond any shadow of a doubt, that you cannot fulfill. The word no can be one of the most beautiful words on this earth plane when used with kindness and sincerity. Be more firm in your convictions; as this, too, will discourage others from trying to take advantage of your good, wholesome nature.

**MEDICINE SHOW** (i.e., a group of people who once went from town to town selling cure-alls and quack medicines)

A surprise in the form of a package, a cheque, a letter, a telephone call, or a winning of some kind is in store for you. Which one will it be? Whatever you receive, may you prosper and be happy in the promising and rewarding days ahead!

**MEDIEVALISM** (see **MIDDLE AGES**)

**MEDITATION**

Whether you meditate during a dream or when awake, this wholesome act uplifts the soul. You obviously are aware of the positive results both prayer and meditation can create. True meditation is a giving prayer; whereas prayer is both asking and giving. The real heroes of our world are the givers who unselfishly share their truest emotions, spirit, and soul with the needs and wants of others. When you meditate, you send your wholesome thoughts to the God-Head Plateau where your thoughts are sifted, "weighed", and then returned to the source you wish to help. In many respects, your mind is like a radio transmitter, and your soul is like an antenna. Together, and in harmony, they reach God. When you pray and meditate, you ultimately commence to work on a mighty powerful frequency which knows no limits!

**MEDIUM** (i.e., a person who has the ability to see, hear, and talk to departed souls; psychic) (Also see **ECTOPLASM** or **SÉANCE**)

Any one or several of the following definitions may be applicable: A) that you are a true medium whose God-given work is both praised and endorsed by many people; or B) that you have some mediumistic talent; or C) that you have put some of your mediumistic talent to use but often worry about people's reactions towards you; or D) that you are hoodwinking people through your actions and false statements and your supposed communication with someone from the other side of life; or E) that you do believe there are talented and gifted mediums on earth; or F) that you have had some unusual experiences which leave no doubt in your mind that the soul lives on; or G) that you are an agnostic, atheist, or a Doubting Thomas who finds it difficult to believe anything supernatural unless you see it with your own eyes or hear it with your own ears; or H) that you have recently read books about mediums; or I) that you are far too busy in life to be bothered with anything involving mediums and psychics; or J) that you have had several "out of body" experiences which you will never forget; or K) that this dream has little or no significance to you at this time.

**MEETING** (i.e., an assembly of people or things; rendezvous) (see *also* **CONFERENCE**)

Are you aware just how unique you are on this earth plane? Although there may be similarities between you and other people, you are still unlike anyone else. Celebrate who you are! If you will be so kind today, look within yourself and gently begin to probe for the highest virtues within your being. Then, with gratitude and a peaceful mind, go help someone who is far less fortunate than you. Bear in mind, however, that you must be totally attuned to your innermost, pure, spiritual, clearheaded self before you do this task. Later, when you have accomplished your good deed of the day, close your eyes for a moment or two; and, with reflective meditation, ponder over your spirit and the joys you can create for others. Realize that one good deed, one good word, can quite easily change a person's entire life. Today, the angels sing for you because in some strange, unique way, you laid a handpicked rose at God's feet.

**MEGAPHONE** (i.e., a device for magnifying the volume of a voice)

You apparently are dealing with a very thick-skinned individual who does not care to listen and learn, and/or you are in a delicate situation which appears totally hopeless and pointless to pursue. Even though you are calling out for help in a loud and clear voice, you appear to be gearing up for an alternative plan deemed necessary to handle the problem(s) at hand. The symbolic clue within this dream is that you should commence to look inward with peace; then you will be able to leave this matter far behind you.

**MELODY** (see **MUSIC**)

**MELON** (see FRUIT)

**MELTAGE** (i.e., melting something, or the thing or quantity resulting from the melting process)

Seeing ice, snow, or anything else being melted down signifies that you are trying very hard to prove your worth to someone whom you consider rather special (e.g., a parent, spouse, friend, acquaintance, employer). Realize that there are some people who are very difficult to reach simply because they are bitter, frustrated, sad beings. Such is life with or without happiness. Realize that nothing will grow unless it is nourished in a loving, caring manner. Perhaps this person you seek did not receive that nourishment, thus making it very difficult for them to reciprocate in a friendly, caring manner. Sometimes in life, we have to finally let go of heartbreaking situations with inner foresight and courage. As sad as it may seem to be, this could be the route you may have to take.

**MEMBERSHIP**

Any one or several of the following definitions may be applicable: A) that you are presently an active member of an organization, group, society, etc.; or B) that you are not a member of any organization, group, or society—or of anything else, for that matter; or C) that you intend to join a club, group, or organization but wonder whether or not you should; or D) that you recently left an organization simply because you felt the members were too self-centered; or E) that in spite of the fact that your organization or society has a very bad reputation, you have no qualms about being a member; or F) that a friend of yours wants you to join a club, league, etc.; or G) that in the past you have had some very bad experiences with a group of people who were more money-minded than humanitarian-minded; or H) that this dream has little or no relevance to you at this time.

**MEMENTO** (see **SOUVENIR**)

**MEMOIR** (see **AUTOBIOGRAPHY** or **BIOGRAPHY**)

**MEMORANDUM**
Do not let people pull you down simply because they lack inner concord and the ambition to get ahead. This memorandum from your dream state advises you to go forward with dedication and unreserved confidence, for no one else can fulfill your good intentions better than you can!

**MEMORIZATION**
You may be creating some difficulties for yourself by being too exacting, petty, and picky. People do appreciate and admire you; but, when it comes to trivial matters that could or should be cast aside, your actions in this regard annoy them tremendously. You know yourself better than anyone else; so, if you can, try to alter your attitudes or habits, in a minor sort of way. By doing so, you may be avoiding some minor or major confrontations down the road.

**MEMORY** (see **AMNESIA, ABSENT-MINDEDNESS, AUTOBIOGRAPHY, BIOGRAPHY, MEMORANDUM, MEMORIZATION, REMEMBRANCE,** or **SOUVENIR**)

**MENACE** (see **BLACKMAIL, BULLY, DANGER, EVILDOER, FEAR,** or **FOREWARNING**)

**MENAGERIE** (see **ZOO**)

**MENDING** (see **DARNING, REPAIR,** or **SEWING**)

**MENOPAUSE** (i.e., change of life)
Any one or several of the following definitions may be applicable: A) that you are presently undergoing some mental and physical changes due to menopause; or B) that you anticipate, accept, or reject the thought of menopause within your life; or C) that you have heard some horrifying stories about women who go through menopause, and now you really do not know what or whom to believe in this matter; or D) that you are either sexually inhibited or over-sexed and often wonder if menopause will change your outlook on such matters; or

E) that you would be foolish to worry about menopause now or later—when it comes, it comes, and that is all there is to it; or F) that this dream has little or no relevance to you at this time.

## MENSTRUATION
Any one or several of the following definitions may be applicable: A) that you are in the puberty stage of your life and seem to either accept or traumatize this course of events; or B) that you are exceedingly uncomfortable when your menstruation period occurs; or C) that you have a very irregular menstruation cycle, which makes it very difficult to plan for a family; or D) that your menstrual cycle is presently late, and this worries you; or E) that because of some physical impediment or mental stress, your monthly periods have ceased entirely; or F) that you find this topic much too personal to discuss with anyone; or G) that this dream has little or no significance to you at this time.

## MEN'S WEAR (see CLOTHES)

## MENTALIST (i.e., a person who professes to read minds or tell fortunes) (see *also* FORTUNETELLER)
It appears that you would like to be more successful than you have been up to now; and, you probably will be—but not in the very immediate future. Success in any field of life is not without struggle; however, if you have what it takes to forge ahead, then rest assured that you probably will amass a fortune, as time goes by. Be wary, however, for not all rags to riches stories have happy endings. Some do; some do not. A truly happy, successful story is when a person learns to appreciate success with humility and never forgets the past struggles that made everything possible.

## MENTAL RETARDATION
Any one or several of the following definitions may be applicable: A) that you or someone in your family is mentally retarded; or B) that you know of someone outside your family who is mentally retarded; or C) that you are afraid to be near anyone who is mentally retarded; or D) that you are in the process of learning more about mentally handicapped people; or E) that you feel your society is not doing enough to help these people lead normal, productive lives; or F) that you hope there will be a total cure for mentally retardation because, in

truth, the people who have this condition are very loving, beautiful, gifted people; or G) that you or someone whom you know has been labeled as being retarded, yet this label has not deterred you from forging ahead in life; or H) that this dream has little or no relevance to you at this time.

## MENTOR (see COACH, GURU, MAHARISHI, or TEACHER)

## MENU

This dream indicates that you will have to make up your mind about something which seems to only require a yes or no answer. In all likelihood, you will choose the right answer with the help of one or two friends. Be at peace; everything will turn out in your favor!

## MERCENARY (i.e., a person or soldier who will do anything for money)

Any one or several of the following definitions may be applicable: A) that you are a mercenary who has very few scruples about the things you do; or B) that you are not a mercenary nor would you ever be one; or C) that you abhor anyone who would harm another human being for the sake of money; or D) that you know someone who is a mercenary; or E) that you recently read an article or two about mercenary activities; or F) that you feel the mercenary's role can be exceedingly beneficial in times of war or other situations that appear extremely dangerous for the average individual to tread in or solve; or G) that this dream has little or no significance to you at all at this time.

## MERCHANDISE (see STORE)

## MERCHANT (e.g., storekeeper, shopkeeper)

If you are, in fact, a merchant, then your dream is merely relating to your position and the type of work that you do. However, if this is not the case, then your dream intimates that you are overburdened with unwholesome, worrisome thoughts. Perhaps your mind worries are centered upon losing a loved one (when everything appears to be all right), or fearing some type of accident (that will not happen), or fearing any other type of negative thoughts unrelated to your normal, wholesome activities. Ignore and rebuke these base mind thoughts! Say to yourself: "Begone, you foul thoughts. Leave me in peace! Who have I to fear with God and Jesus by my side? I will not listen to your foul whispers and suggestions even unto my death; and even then I will fight you for the sake of the Cross and the salvation of other souls. You will not tempt me to believe in any false thoughts and actions, for I know what is true, just, and honourable. Begone from the temple of my mind's soul, and never return!" Read and reread this guidance until you are free of your fears and phobias—until there is peace within the temple of your heart, mind, and soul.

## MERCURY (see PLANET)

## MERCY (see COMPASSION or FORGIVENESS)

## MERMAID

This symbolism indicates that there are some matters in your life which couldn't be better; but, on the other hand, there are some other painful matters you wouldn't wish on an enemy. Perhaps you are financially stable but lack love and affection; perhaps you have some love and affection but lack financial stability; perhaps you are blessed with love, affection, communication, and financial security, but some habit or activity has made you very fearful and sad. Whatever it may be, you are advised to seriously get a grip on your problem(s), and begin to see what you can do to finally make your existence more wholesome, rewarding, and meaningful. Do not just sit back on your laurels or feel that you have done everything humanly possible, when in fact there could be several other avenues not yet explored. Remember that struggles are stepping stones towards peace and happiness. Do your part; and you, too, will be rewarded!

## MERMAN (see MERMAID)

## MERRY-GO-ROUND

If the merry-go-round is not moving, it implies that you are not moving, so to speak. You are either refusing to do something which could be beneficial to your well-being, or you are maintaining a lazy, uncaring attitude about getting ahead in life. There is no magic wand here. When you decide to uplift your attitudes and concepts about your daily life, then you will commence to see greater rewards and improvements.

If the merry-go-round is moving at a moderate, natural pace, then you are a sure-footed, logical, and self-assured individual. You will be successful and happy in life simply because you face your todays and tomorrows with optimism and down-to-earth determination.

To see a merry-go-round moving at a very fast pace intimates that you are excessively busy, sometimes too busy to care about yourself or about people, places, and things that should also be of importance to you. Slow down, go for a long walk, and begin to find yourself. You were born on earth to learn, explore, and to ultimately accomplish many things. You were certainly not meant to ignore or forget the true values of life. Find your niche in life, be a great success, but, in the process, do not forget to be your natural, God-given self. You are not a machine—you are a human being!

**MESH** (see **COBWEB**, **LACEWORK**, **MATERIAL**, or **NET**)

**MESMERISM** (see **HYPNOTISM**)

**MESSAGE** (see **LETTER**, **MEMORANDUM**, or **MESSENGER**)

**MESSENGER**

With your constructive thinking, knowledge, and creative mind, there is no limit to the degree of good that you can accomplish on this earth plane. Just be confident in all that you do, and slowly you will commence to see some of your fondest dreams and wishes come true. In the interim, however, do not forget to seek your innermost desires with truth, honour, and dignity; for, in many ways, these will unlock hidden doors and treasures for you.

**MESSIAH** (see **JESUS**)

**METALWARE** (see **UTENSIL**)

**METALWORKING**

Do not offend others by being excessively thick-skinned or loud-mouthed just to bring a point across or to try to prove that you are always correct. You are not always correct. Be logical, fair, and just in whatever you do and wherever you go, for these are matter of fact concepts that will allow you to progress on this planet and in the next world. Old habits may be hard to eradicate, and better habits are even harder to adopt and uphold; so, in finding yourself, be prepared to climb uphill all the way. Do not look down nor descend as you are climbing that so-called hill of understanding and wisdom. Bear in mind, as well, that as you improve your ways, habits, and feelings, you are also gaining a greater conceptual view of life around you.

**METAMORPHOSIS** (i.e., a transformation: change of form, shape, structure, appearance, or character)

If the person or animal you see transforms from a loving, kindly nature to something unbearable and gruesome, it implies that you are dissatisfied with your progress or present state of being. Actions do, indeed, speak louder than words. There are a lot of words floating around, but where is your action?

To see a frightful, unbearable person or animal transform into a loving, kindly nature implies that you wish to keep your distance from anyone who has tendencies towards being gossipy and two-faced or who is outright deceptive. Your views are entirely correct! Continue to carry on exactly as you are; your future holds much luck, happiness, and prosperity for you.

Seeing inanimate objects change from one thing into another implies that you base too much credence on the things you own, do not own, or wish to own. In essence, you are not an easy person to satisfy. It seems the more you have, the more you want; or the less you have, the more you want which, in turn, becomes a vicious battle within your life. Greed, selfish motives, and materialistic gains can be one's downfall! You are directing all your energies towards earthly prosperity, without stopping to realize that your soul is not based on dollars and cents or what your financial assets happen to be. You cannot buy your way to heaven, nor can you take your so-called earthly wealth with you when you pass over. Use more insight where your temporal, earthly wants and needs are concerned. Above all, do not forget your eternal, spiritual wants and needs.

**METEOR** (i.e., a shooting or falling star)

Sooner or later, some good must fall into everyone's life. Well, it is not sooner or later, but now! This auspicious dream denotes all-round peace, improvement, happiness, and prosperity for the dreamer. Before too long, some unexpected and rewarding event will take place in your life, and/or someone whom you know or do not know will be highly instrumental in assisting you. This new-found prosperity could not be more timely nor could someone like you be more deserving!

**METEORITE** (see **METEOR**)

**METEOROID** (see **METEOR**)

**METEOROLOGY** (i.e., study of weather, making forecasts of weather)

This dream implies that you are planning to do something very special before too long, but you are hoping that you will not be deterred by bad weather conditions or anything else, for that matter. Your wish will be fulfilled to you; all your expectations should be met with flying colours! Better times, lasting affection, and greater concepts lie ahead for you. Keep up your good work because, in time, you will see the dividends of your wholesome efforts pay off beyond your fondest dreams.

**METEOR SHOWER** (see **METEOR**)

**METER** (e.g., gas meter, electricity meter, water meter, parking meter, postage meter) (see *also* **PEDOMETER**)

This symbolism advises you to put some money aside for a rainy day. You are not exactly the most frugal person on earth, and you never know when some unpredictable financial needs may arise.

**METER MAID** (i.e., a woman hired by the police department to hand out tickets for jaywalking, illegal parking)

Seeing or being a meter maid indicates that you may be having some difficulties with a family member, friend, or employee. The solution here is to compromise, not hassle. Swallow your pride, if you must; but, for the sake of future peace and harmony, do your very best to maintain good relationships with this person.

**METRONOME** (i.e., an instrument for measuring musical time or tempo)

You are very good at what you do, but you must learn to accept a little bit of constructive criticism from time to time in order to develop your craft or work in a masterful way. Even though you get fed up, want to quit, or become so tired you honestly do not care one way or another, you know deep down that your determination is far greater than your momentary weaknesses of self-pity. You are not a quitter, where challenges are concerned—you are a fighter! One word of caution, however: do not be so temperamental and impetuous when difficult times beset you. Instead, strive to be more calm, patient, and understanding, for these qualities alone will make your road to success far more satisfying and certainly less selfish.

## MICROPHONE

The changes you wish to make in your life should not be verbally advertised here and there; instead, they should be accomplished with practical actions! You *talk* more than you *do!* This, in effect, leaves you miles behind, where personal accomplishments are concerned. Time waits for no one, and you are no exception to that rule. This dream strongly urges you to stop procrastinating, let go of your personal hang-ups which consistently seem to chain you down, and finally begin to believe in your potential and worth. Right now, you could have been at the top of the mountain looking down—instead of being at the bottom of the mountain looking up. Think on this for a while. Then perhaps you will begin to put your intelligent mind and actions into motion.

## MICROSCOPE

This dream intimates that you are trying to sort out a matter of concern which involves you and a person very close to your mind and heart (e.g., spouse, offspring, parent, friend). Your humble, forgiving, peacemaking efforts are both praiseworthy and wise! Do not worry; the problem, in fact, will solve itself.

## MIDDLE AGES (i.e., a period of European history: culture, costumes, law, chivalry)

Dreaming about the Middle Ages intimates that sometimes you feel you should be living in another time era. This does not necessarily imply that you are unhappy in this time period every day. But it is those moments when you feel like a failure or have feelings of being unwanted and unloved that spur you towards your mind-boggling thoughts. Do not panic. Most people think of faraway places when they are unhappy, too. Sooner or later, the fantasy ends, and they must return to face their realities on earth; and so must you. Everyone on earth suffers or struggles from time to time; but, with foresight and courage, people seem to have a special kind of willpower that places them back on track again. You are an individual who also has this ability. Use it sincerely and wisely, and you will calm the waters both within and around you.

## MIDGET

If you are in fact a midget, then your dream is merely reflecting upon your present state of being. However, if you are not a midget but dream of being one or seeing one, then your dream advises you to be your natural self at all times. Do not pretend to be someone you are not or dupe people into believing you are very wealthy when you are not, and so forth. If you truly want to impress someone within your lifetime, then impress God by being humbly thankful for your life and for all its blessings. Speak the truth, and prosperity will surely follow you always.

## MIDNIGHT

If the midnight hour happens to be a peaceful or happy event, then you can expect to be busy, productive, and financially secure for a long time to come. Travel, social and business events, lectures, and seminars are on the immediate horizon for you.

Dreaming about the midnight hour being a sad, unhappy time indicates that you recently failed to act on an opportunity which could have improved your lifestyle (e.g., refusing a good job offer, rejecting a contract, refusing to go back to school when you had the chance). Whatever it may be, it is certainly hoped that you will be given another chance or two in the very near future. Opportunities, you must understand, do not come knocking at your door every day. But when you actually miss one or mess one up, the possible impact and inner remorse can be felt later on. Be wiser and perhaps more open-minded in these matters; your future may depend upon it.

## MIDWAY (see EXHIBITION)

## MIDWIFE

It seems that a series of untimely events and circumstances have held you back from doing the things you wanted to do most in life. Unfortunately, this happens to many people around this planet, practically on a daily basis. There are just those unforeseen times when you must weigh the importance of your needs with those of someone or something else. It is regrettable and quite obvious that your anguish in not fulfilling your needs and wants in life will haunt you for a long time to come. This dream advises you to carry on, to be strong, and to do your utmost to create new endeavours and interests. You certainly cannot bring back your past, but what on earth can stop you from creating a better future for yourself?

**MIGRATION** (see *also* **FOREIGNER**)

To see the migration of people, birds, or animals intimates that you feel isolated and alone at times simply because you choose to be this way. You have other alternatives, but you refuse to accept them. In life, you can be as happy as you want to be or as sad as you choose to be; that is up to you. However, to truly be happy on this earth plane, you must forget your ego and pride, and begin to share your joys and talents with others. This is for you to see and master for yourself.

**MILDEW**

Never mock, ridicule, or condemn another person, for in so doing, you could very well become your own worst enemy! Also, you never know when hardship and strife may befall you. To hurt another person in any way reveals an outright disregard for the Laws of Justice within the Universe. It is far better to conquer your own weaknesses than to harp or muse upon those of someone else. Showing more thoughtfulness and feeling towards others and their basic rights to be human will place you in a more compassionate, forgiving, and understanding mode of existence. The golden rule is not to degrade your fellow man; it is to love your fellow man!

**MILK** (see **DRINK**)

**MILKMAN**

This dream advises you to shoulder your own responsibilities and to try to be a bit more sincere in overcoming a bad habit or two. You seem to have a tendency to blame others before accepting the realities of your own faults and weaknesses. You cannot account for anyone else on this planet but yourself; the sooner you begin to face the truth about your behaviour and actions, the better off you will be. Harness the loyalty, sincerity, and logic within your being; and you will gain three-fold through this important action. If you think it is too late to change, you are merely playing mind-games with yourself. It is never too late to change!

**MILKSHAKE** (see **DRINK**)

**MILKY WAY** (see **GALAXY**)

**MILL** (e.g., flour mill, textile mill, coffee mill, cider mill, sawmill or other mill)

Your life is a mixture of many joys and hardships, yet you know that everything you went through was not entirely in vain. As a matter of fact, you have much more for which to be grateful than to be sad. The greatest measure to this dream is that you have learned the true value of living. Whenever there was a struggle, you faced it; whenever there was happiness, you accepted it—no fuss, no muss, and no superficial whining or pining about what was or could have been. That simple logic is the heart of a dedicated, wholesome, loving, and natural human being. When you reflect back once in a while on your life, can you believe how far you have come with your confidence and hopes? Carry on, for it is people like you who truly experience and master this life wisely and faithfully.

**MILLET** (see **GRAIN**)

**MILLING** (see **MILL**)

**MILLIONAIRE**

Any one or several of the following definitions may be applicable: A) that you are a millionaire and are quite happy to be one; or B) that you would like to become a millionaire one day; or C) that you do not envy wealthy people; or D) that you handle your money very unwisely but intend to correct this matter before too long; or E) that you wish to assist someone in a financial way, but (due to other obligations and burdens) this is simply not feasible at this time; or F) that even though you are poor, you are quite happy in life; or G) that you wish money were non-existent on this planet and that everyone would share their efforts, blessings, and resources to help one another; or H) that this dream has little or no relevance to you at this time.

**MIMIC** (see **IMPERSONATION**)

**MIND READER** (see **FORTUNETELLER** or **MENTALIST**)

**MINE** (e.g., coal mine, salt mine)

This symbolism shows that you need more time to yourself. It seems as though you are constantly giving to and serving other people but getting very little in return. For a change of pace, try a little harder to express your own feelings and actions with more conviction rather than giving in to the wayward, stubborn demands made upon you. Sometimes it becomes essential to deal with your logical mind rather than with your emotional heart, especially when others around you tend to take you for granted.

**MINE DETECTOR** (i.e., a device used to detect mine fields)

Dreaming about one of these devices suggests that you are harbouring some latent or active suspicions about a family member or a very close friend. Basically, it is not too healthy to imagine or fantasize about this unclear matter. If this individual told you the absolute truth, would you believe what you heard, or would you continue to be suspicious? Bear in mind, as well, that you are not a judge or jury, nor can you account for anyone's deeds but your own. If someone has done you wrong—be it mentally, physically, or spiritually—then God will eventually look after this situation. However, if someone has not done you any wrong but you still suspect or wrongfully accuse this individual of wrongdoing, then you will have to account for your shortsighted behaviour. In essence, this dream is telling you to disband your suspicions about this individual, for in many ways your negative imagination has made you more guilty than the so-called accused.

**MINE FIELD**

Seeing a mine field or being in a mine field intimates that someone or something is making your life almost unbearable. Anguish, pain, and suffering seem to be predominantly what you are experiencing; and unless you rectify, modify, or seek some help in this matter, there does not appear to be any breakthrough. For the sake of your sanity and peace of mind, do not contend with this torturous, unpredictable, and unbelievable manner of living. Be strong, listen to your conscience, and be prepared to make greater sacrifices and changes within your life. No one can help you unless you honestly, willingly, and truthfully begin to reach out and help yourself!

**MINER** (see **MINE**)

**MINERAL** (see **ORE**)

**MINE SWEEPER** (see **SHIP**)

**MINING** (see **MINE**)

**MINISTER** (see **CLERGYMAN, DEPUTY, GOVERNOR, POLITICIAN**, or **PRIME MINISTER**)

**MINK**

This animal symbolism reveals that you will be disappointed over someone's attitudes and actions. It is strange, but sometimes you can know someone for years and not really know them as well as you think you do. People change over the years; this is something you must learn to accept. Do not, however, panic over this forthcoming situation. A person may act moody, difficult, or wayward one day, only to come to their better senses the next day. There is no parting of the ways shown here at all—just some differences of opinion and actions between you and another person.

**MINOR** (see **ADOLESCENT**)

**MINSTREL** (see **MINSTREL SHOW, MUSICIAN, POET**, or **SINGER**)

**MINSTREL SHOW**

Seeing or being a member of a minstrel show reveals that you are overly opinionated, biased, and critical of people, places, and things. In many respects, you are a cynic who tends to harbour hurt feelings and deep resentments from your past. Furthermore, you are very defensive and very quick in offending others even before they have a chance to defend themselves! This may surprise you, but there are quite a few people who would like to be your friend if you gave them half a chance. Let your old past go, and commence to show more consideration, respect, and inner peace towards your fellow man. You certainly will be happier when you decide to get rid of your bitterness and distrust. Why don't you do so today?

**MINUTE HAND** (see **CLOCK**)

**MIRACLE**

Life in itself is a miracle, and many things we say or do can be considered personal miracles, either knowingly or unknowingly. In dreams we often create our own miracles simply because we search and somehow find that precious supernatural moment to make things turn out favorably when things appear dangerous or hopeless. So, what your dream is trying to tell you is that you do have the capability of making things turn out right in your daily life, providing you believe in yourself and in the Powers of Christ within you. Love, faith, belief, humility, charity, and wholesome Christ-like desires can create many miracles upon this planet. Can you recall a time when matters within and around you seemed totally hopeless, but—out of the blue—something happened to completely change everything around for you? That, in essence, was a miracle! Many people unfortunately fail to believe that miracles do take place within their lives. They are misinformed! If you truly want to see something awesome and very special, then take a look in a mirror; there you will see—a miracle!

## MIRAGE

There is a multitude of images and scenes within a dream state that could very well be classified as a mirage. They appear, disappear, and reappear again, if the mind so wishes. Failing to reach a mirage within your dream signifies that something you want or hope for will take time. Actually reaching a mirage signifies that your inner wish or desire will come true, providing it is of good order.

## MIRROR

You are either a deep thinking individual with great ideals or visions, or you are an average thinking individual with good desires and actions. It really does not matter which category you belong to because both are just as purposeful and outstanding, in their own right. Your outlook, purpose, and strength is what angels are made of—those souls who dared to venture where others feared to tread. As you move onwards in life, you can move mountains along your pathway by simply holding on to your rightful actions and unselfish aims. Very soon, someone will encourage you to do something rather special; and you, in turn, will inspire another person in the same way.

A broken mirror intimates that you are standing in someone's pathway for happiness or someone is standing in your way, for some reason. Are you meddlesome, selfish, and discouraging, or do you simply wish to make someone's life miserable for some other underlying reasons or motives? If so, then you are advised to stop while you are still ahead of the game. Sooner or later, the person to whom you are unpleasant will walk away from you; then, sadly, you might find yourself quite isolated and alone.

## MISBEHAVIOR (see *also* DISOBEDIENCE or MISCHIEF)

You are dealing with someone who has a discipline problem, if you see an adult or a young person misbehave within a dream. Unnecessary put-downs or sudden punishments can aggravate this problem beyond repair, so be careful! Talk to this person and suggest some form of compromise or a peace plan that can be formulated and upheld. Do not give up if this matter fails at first. Learn to praise one another, for—as you already know—a little bit of love and understanding can go a long way. The outcome here appears to be very favorable; this individual will eventually mature and adopt a calm, intelligent outlook.

## MISCARRIAGE (i.e., premature ejection of the fetus from the womb)

Any one or several of the following definitions may be applicable: A) that you recently had a miscarriage; or B) that you fear the possibility of having a miscarriage; or C) that you know of someone who recently had a miscarriage; or D) that you are inhibited sexually and/or refuse to have any children for a variety of personal reasons; or E) that you presently feel incapable of coping with situations around you and would like a change of pace or scenery; or F) that you are contemplating a separation or divorce from a spouse; or G) that you have severed ties with a friend for no particular reason, or a friend has done this to you; or H) that you envy people who can have children because, for some reason or other, you cannot; or I) that this dream has little or no relevance for you at this time.

## MISCHIEF (e.g., prank, damage, or harm)

A great amount of confusion, bitterness, and shame may be associated with your actions or those of your spouse, an offspring, or someone whom you know rather well. Troubled minds and misguided souls are all at the root of this problem. It is true that sometimes situations can become worse before getting better, but who knows what is worth fighting for or upholding when matters appear hopeless. Unless there are some solid, logical compromises forthcoming, there is very little you can do but hope and pray for better times.

## MISER

A miserly action suggests that you will be unable to claim or receive something that rightfully belongs to you. Perhaps you loaned something to a neighbour who refuses to give it back, or maybe you loaned some money to a person who now denies this fact, and so forth. Should the law be brought into this matter, then it is revealed that someone's false testimony will rule against your better judgment and honesty. This appears to be a no-win situation, no matter how you look at it! Perhaps the only logical thing to do would be to chalk this up to experience and hope that this type of situation never repeats itself.

## MISFORTUNE (e.g., ill fortune, bad luck, hardship) (see *also* COLLISION, CONFUSION, CRUELTY, CURSE, DEPRESSION, DESTRUCTION, DISASTER, ENEMY, EPIDEMIC, EVILDOER, FAILURE, FALL, FAMINE, FOREWARNING, GUILT, INJURY, MISCHIEF, PREDICAMENT, or SICKNESS)

A minor-looking misfortune implies that you are a very sensitive, cautious individual. You want things to go relatively smoothly and peacefully at all times. Should there ever be a great misfortune within your life, you just might not be able to handle the matter rationally. Hopefully, this will never happen to you; but, life being what it is, you never know when an unpredictable event might happen.

Seeing a major-looking misfortune indicates that you have been through some mighty heavy hardships within your life thus far and have learned over the years not to rule out any possibilities of something happening to you or to anyone else, for that matter. Anything can happen to anyone, anytime, and anywhere! The one thing you have learned, as well, is that prayer, caution, instinct, or intuition are all major actions that can guide you away from some possible misfortune(s).

## MISGIVING (see DOUBTFULNESS)

## MISHAP (see COLLISION or INJURY)

## MISJUDGMENT

To misjudge yourself, someone, or something within a dream state implies that you have doubts about yourself, someone, or something during your wake state. The entire object here is to try to settle or solve this matter once and for all time. When you bottle doubts, you harbour anxieties which may not even be justified. Talking to someone about your personal uncertainties will help you beyond words! As well, if someone or something is affecting you, then go to the source of the problem and settle it. This dream advises you to reveal your point of view with honesty and dignity so that you will be relieved and appeased and not ashamed, in any manner, for clearing the air.

**MISLEAD** (see **DECEPTION**)

**MISPLACEMENT** (i.e., putting someone or something in a wrong place)

To misplace someone or something implies that you are a bit absent-minded, you appear to have a few fears here and there which you seem to be able to handle at most times, you can be overly excited, and you tend to build mountains out of molehills on occasion; but, in general, you are doing rather well in life. A person's dreams may present the most outlandish and sometimes hilarious situations of misplacement one could possibly envision. For example, dreaming of misplacing a broom within a fridge may indicate that your home needs cleaning up; misplacing a clean cup within a toilet bowl may indicate that something you frequently drink may not be wholesome for you; misplacing an employer, employee, or loved one on a window sill suggests there is a strong personality clash between you and this person, and so forth. The whole point of this dream is for you to try to understand yourself, your habits, and your life a little bit better.

**MISSILE** (e.g., spear, bullet, rocket, guided missile)

Dreaming of a missile reveals your general dissatisfaction with home and work. This situation will not clear up until you are willing to unshackle the routine of your life with courage and plenty of common sense. Begin to create more happiness for yourself by doing some of the things you always wanted to do (e.g., take a course, learn a hobby, travel). However, be cautious. This dream does not advise you to act in an irrational or irresponsible manner; doing so could very well bring you more unhappiness, besides personal defeat and shame. Always seek ways to solve a problem, not ways to create a problem. Furthermore, do not just sit on a worrisome matter—do something about it!

**MISSION** (i.e., an establishment of missionaries, or charitable organizations who help the needy both at home or abroad)

There are times when a person must go through the darkest valley or through a bottomless pit before life begins to change for the better. Nothing comes easily in this life, and it is useless to complain about this fact! Until a person learns to throw out a lifeline to someone in need from time to time, then that person has not lived! We are all fortunate on this planet to have so many brothers and sisters. But, do we look after our brothers and sisters? Be it in a big or a small way, this dream counsels you to strive a little harder to make life a little better for those around you. And, when the occasion arises and you are there to throw a lifeline to someone calling for help, you will have built a bridge of infinite caring, sharing, and gratitude towards all living things from that time forward.

**MISSIONARY** (see **MISSION**)

**MISSPELLING**

By verbalizing all the time, you have placed yourself in some embarrassing situations (i.e., saying the wrong things at the wrong time or saying too much). You seem to have a communication problem with others; you often interfere when someone talks, you fail to hear what is said, and you do say things at the top of your head without realizing the implications of your words. Be a good listener! You would be amazed at what others can teach you. Silence can, in many ways, be your greatest ally when used wisely.

**MISTAKE** (see **ERROR**)

**MISTLETOE** (see **DECORATION** or **PLANT**)

**MISTREAT** (see **BLASPHEMY, CRUELTY, CURSE, DISAPPROVAL, FIGLHT, MISCHIEF, MOCKERY, PERSECUTION,** or **PUNISHMENT**)

**MISTRESS** (i.e., a woman who is having sexual intercourse for a period of time with a man she is not married to)

Any one or several of the following definitions may be applicable: A) that you are a married man who does have a mistress; or B) that you were a married man who once had a wife and a mistress; or C) that you have some doubts about your present relationship with a mistress; or D) that you somehow think that by having a mistress all your family troubles will vanish into thin air; or E) that you are ashamed and very sorry for your past actions where adultery is concerned, and now you would do practically anything to make things right for your family; or F) that you not only lost your family, but practically all your worldly possessions because of your wanton ways with other women; or G) that you have no remorse for any acts of infidelity you may have committed towards your spouse; or H) that you are, in fact, a mistress who is happy or unhappy with your state of being; or I) that you feel very secure with the man you know and strongly believe his many promises to you; or J) that you do not believe in this type of relationship, under any circumstances; or K) that you are a mistress who has been jilted many times before, but somehow these lessons in life have not taught you much; or L) that this dream has little or no significance for you at this time.

**MISTRUST** (see **DOUBTFULNESS**)

**MITTEN** (see **GLOVE**)

**MIXER** (see **APPLIANCE**)

**MIX-UP** (see **CONFUSION**)

**MOAN**

Moaning signifies that you are experiencing some type of pain or sorrow within a dream, or you are having some reflective thoughts or visions about your past, present, or future within a dream. You tend to be a bit excitable at times, and you also tend to over-worry. So, what you see or hear within your dream may not necessarily be as bad as it sounds. Sometimes life makes no sense at all to you because of the suffering, greed, and wickedness that take place on this planet. Why, just reading a newspaper can give a person a nightmare! However, your inner voice, instinct, intuition (or whatever you wish to call it) will continue to remind you to cast your fears and worries to the wind, for life in all its glory and pitfalls is but one step closer to understanding and peace. We are but mere children upon this planet who must seek, fall, climb, and discover new and better horizons within our world and within ourselves.

**MOAT** (see **DITCH** or **PASSAGEWAY**)

**MOB** (see **CROWD**)

**MOBILE HOME** (see **TRAILER**)

**MOCCASIN**

Seeing or wearing a pair of moccasins intimates that a certain amount of emotional setbacks, physical discomforts, and financial hardships are forthcoming. If you normally feel depressed and pessimistic, then try to visualize better times ahead instead of negative times ahead. It appears as though you are bringing this strife upon yourself! Do your very best to change your attitude and outlook; and maybe the cold, ill winds will pass you by.

**MOCKERY** (see *also* **CATCALL**)

You are harbouring some hatred, a grudge, or a vendetta towards another person (e.g., a spouse, offspring, parent, friend). This shortsighted thinking will get you nowhere in life! You may claim to be right in your thoughts and feelings, but your dream begs to differ with you. So maybe your pride was hurt; by the same token, can you honestly say that you never offended another person? Do not be so stubborn and wayward; be open-minded and forgiving. You know, it would be such a pity for you to create a needless ulcer over this entire affair. Let it go!

**MOCKINGBIRD** (see **BIRD**)

**MOCK-UP** (i.e., generally, a full-sized scale model of something)

Seeing or constructing a mock-up suggests that, currently, you are not being too realistic about a personal decision or problem. Do not avoid this matter or contradict others when good information is being offered to you. Get a grip on yourself, and begin to perceive the truth in a head-on manner. The flesh is not stronger than the soul; nor is the mind weaker than the heart. You, as a mature human being, should be so grateful to be given so many opportunities to make things right. Do so with foresight and wisdom.

**MODEL** (i.e., a small scale model of an airplane, ship, building; a person so employed to wear and display clothes)

A scale model of something intimates that you feel life has not treated you fairly up to now. Maybe so, but what have you done to

deserve otherwise? You can sit on a rock and be sorry for yourself forever, but this attitude will not be of benefit to you at all. You know this
already. What you need to do is find your peace of mind. You are a
child of God, you are loved by God, and you belong to God! Use your
good, wholesome, mature mind without self-pity, and begin to live.
Find your peace of mind by forgiving, loving, and sharing the good
that is within you. You do, indeed, have better tomorrows awaiting
you; but first you must face the stark realities of your life now. If you
continually place barriers in front of yourself, how on earth can you go
forward?

Dreaming about being a fashion model intimates that you are
worried about financial security, investments, or personal financial
losses. Materialistic gains or losses are basically matters that go with the
territory of life. A gain will bring you happiness; a loss will bring you
depression. Most times, however, people create their own downfall
where money matters are concerned. Spend foolishly now; cry later.
They never stop to think about what happens should they go broke! If
you truly desire security in this life, then love each day more than the
last. You know, as well, that to like and to love someone special is by
far the greatest guarantee of well-being you could possibly hope to
experience. Love, itself, cannot put bread and butter on your table, but
love can instill hope, determination, and courage for you to go forth
to amass a fortune, if your heart so desires! God wants you to be prosperous until your cup runs totally over; but, in the process, use your
common sense, and keep your priorities in order.

## MODESTY (see BLUSH or HUMILITY)

## MOISTURE (see DEW)

## MOLD (see MILDEW)

## MOLDING (i.e., a decorative strip of wood commonly used for ceilings, furniture)

To be "far away" from yourself implies being just as far away from
other people. You can be stubborn, critical, and indifferent for months
on end, but this will merely give you the displeasures and resentments
you ask for. Nothing can come from unhappiness, if you are not ready
to do something about it. What this dream is trying to tell you is for
you to create more interests in your life instead of swimming around

aimlessly within your heart and mind. Come out of your inner shell, begin to appreciate yourself more, and begin to anticipate those wonderful joys and challenges which lie ahead of you. Don't waste your life; fulfill your life!

## MOLE

A vital part of a recent problem has been solved, but there is a remaining half yet to be resolved. Do not give up nor be impatient, otherwise your inner wish will be swept away by the wind. Be it today, tomorrow, or the day after, your problem will be untangled, clarified, and answered.

## MOLLUSK (e.g., clams, mussels, octopuses, shellfish, slugs, squids)

Determination, confidence, and self-control are all vital keys in allowing you to come out of your possessive, controlling nature. Did you realize that when you place shackles on another person you are, in effect, placing shackles on yourself? You are chaining yourself down with your own illogical reasons and stern judgments upon other people. Whatever gave you the idea that people must think, act, and do exactly what you wish of them? This is just another way to start a major conflict, especially with those beings who are independent minded. You may have a very good, sound mind, but you must remember there are many others around you who do as well. Do not under any circumstances push or force your will upon anyone. If a person wishes to listen to, sift through, and adhere to your reasoning, then this is fine; but, if this person does not, then this is fine, too. You are not always correct in your earthly values, so be careful. People can, and do, think for themselves.

## MONARCH (see ROYALTY)

## MONASTERY

It appears that you are trying too hard to satisfy the needs of others. In the process, you are forgetting about your own well-being. It truly is a wonderful virtue to help others—but, for your own sake, leave some room for yourself. This is vitally important because you are important to others. Without some type of rest or rejuvenation, you would not be able to carry on in a sensible, healthy state. You may think you have some super strength and stamina, but the fact is that you are working on nerves alone.

**MONEY** (e.g., coins; paper money) (see *also* **ABUNDANCE, INCOME,** or **TREASURE**)

Any one or several of the following definitions may be applicable: A) that you are very materialistic, and money has become somewhat of a fetish to you, whether you have it or not; or B) that you are very wealthy in life; or C) that you have more money than you know what to do with, but you are miserly; or D) that no matter how hard you try to budget your money, there never seems to be enough to buy the basic necessities; or E) that you recently lost a sum of money for some reason; or F) that you would like just enough money in life to do some of the things wishes and dreams are built on; or G) that you are a very logical person who knows how to save and invest money wisely; or H) that you have no money sense at all; or I) that you have no great desires for wealth—that as long as you have your good health and happiness, that is all that matters; or J) that this dream has little or no significance to you at this time.

**MONEYBAG** (i.e., bag for holding money)

If the moneybag you see is full, then this dream cautions you to be wary about loose spending and buying. This may not affect you now, but in time you may realize that some of your purchases can be useless. Be a wise shopper, not a careless spender.

Seeing an empty moneybag advises you to buy what you can afford, not what you cannot afford. Going beyond your means at this time can place you in a terrible financial bind. Logically speaking, what good is a new, expensive-looking car to anyone if there is no money to put food on the table? Think twice before going overboard where money matters are concerned; you will be thankful you did.

**MONEY BELT**

Be wary of someone trying to sweet-talk you into buying something worthless, signing a false contract, or doing just about anything that may be considered underhanded. Do not assume or take anything for granted during this trying period. The wheels are in motion, so be very careful. Otherwise, some unscrupulous person will "take you for a ride"!

**MONEY-CHANGING** (i.e., generally, a foreign place of business where a person's money or travelers cheques are exchanged to that country's currency)

Finding yourself or seeing someone else at a money-changing centre denotes your desire to be more financially independent and to be able to do the many things you have always hoped to accomplish. Whoever told you that this would never happen? Be patient! Very soon an opportunity will arise which will allow you to join forces with another person to market a certain product, and/or you will be given a chance to invest a minimal amount of money into some venture that looks both highly promising and rewarding. You are now entering a high cycle of good luck and good fortune. May all your dreams and wishes finally come true!

## MONEY ORDER

There appears to be some sort of conflict of interest between you and another person, and/or someone has accused you of not paying for something for which you know you did. In either case, both situations will be settled in a short period of time. In the future, however, be more discerning where people are concerned, and do your utmost to keep your records and files in order. Failing to keep a bill or receipt can make it very difficult to prove payment on anything later on.

## MONGOLISM (see MENTAL RETARDATION)

## MONGOOSE

This animal symbolizes that you are quite opposed to new concepts, ideas, and changes within your life. When you set up a routine for yourself, it becomes very trying to alter or change it to any degree. In many respects, you simply are not as versatile or open-minded as some other people around you. This is not a crime; however, there will be occasions in your life when you will have to adjust your thinking or change your attitudes where speed, efficiency, and progress are concerned. Space-age technology is here, and there is far more to come!

## MONITOR (i.e., a device or instrument for monitoring something such as airwaves, communication, radar)

In many respects, you seem to be monitoring yourself. It appears that some guilt feelings concerning something you did in your past or present are holding you back from progressing. Perhaps you fear you will be discovered, or perhaps you are too ashamed to admit what you did. Only you have the answer to this. Your dream is trying to tell you to free yourself from this troubled state of mind. Talk to someone you can trust; but, for your sake, get it out of your system now and forevermore. Live your life in peace. Remember, as well, that in rehashing old wounds and actions, you must be prepared to totally forgive yourself. Without self-forgiveness, you cannot be free.

## MONK

To find faith and hope in self is to truly find faith and hope in others, as well. You seldom waste your time on unimportant, mundane matters; instead, you preoccupy your mind and actions with ways to make others around you more happy, comfortable, and productive. "Neatness is next to godliness" seems to be your motto, and it is indeed a very good motto to uphold! But what is so enchantingly appealing about you is that your good soul and good spirit serve with the virtues of patience, silence, and obedience. No conflicts can be seen, nor can complaints be heard, when a man or woman unselfishly surrenders vain pride and fear for faith, hope, and other Heavenly desires.

## MONKEY (see APE)

## MONOCLE (i.e., an eyeglass used for one eye)

You lead a somewhat secretive, inhibited life which, at times, can either be a blessing or a pain. If you are happy the way you are, then by all means continue to be your natural, normal self. However, if you are not happy with this arrangement which you have created for yourself, then you should do your very best to acquire a friend or two, go out once in a while, and certainly join a group or club that will allow you to mix and mingle with others more frequently. You have a pleasing personality, a good mind, and a very worthy outlook in life. Don't hide your fine attributes; accentuate them and share them!

## MONOGRAM (i.e., initials of a name generally placed on clothing, ornaments, stationary)

Seeing your monogram or that of another person intimates that you will follow your inner feelings and plans until you succeed. With this attitude, you will not only succeed, but you will rise above and beyond your fondest expectations. Travel, creative activities, teaching, lecturing, writing, singing, and inventing are but a few of the possibilities open to you. Whatever it is that you intend to do in life, you can be sure that you are headed towards a very rich, rewarding, and purposeful future.

**MONOLITH** (i.e., enormous pieces of stone blocks used in sculpture or architecture) (see *also* **OBELISK**)

If you happen to be optimistic, then this symbolism reveals that your present difficulties will dissipate very shortly. By projecting a positive attitude and outlook towards your immediate future, you stand a greater chance of coping and mastering your problems in a sane, perceptive manner. On the other hand, if you are pessimistic, then you can be sure that some of your immediate problems or setbacks will continue to linger for quite some time. You are curtailing your own progress in countless ways! You are essentially harbouring doubts, hopelessness, and fear without any justification whatsoever. Maybe you feel your way of thinking will give you the so-called shelter you need just in case you actually do fail? If so, then ask yourself why success and happiness seem to be so hard to come by? Why? Simply because you are projecting negativity both within and around you. What you project is basically what you get. You could learn a vital lesson or two from an optimist you happen to know. Change your tune; then see what a little bit of hope can do for you!

**MONOLOGUE** (i.e., a long speech by a person who generally monopolizes a conversation, or a play spoken by one actor only)

There will be greater peace and understanding ahead for you when you learn to control your temper, curb your impatience, and nullify your highly opinionated thoughts and feelings about others. The setbacks you have recently experienced are bitter reminders of your egotistical attitudes and one-track mind in life. By being more self-analytical, you can solve your personal hang-ups and problems. Do not just think about it; do something about it!

**MONOMANIA** (i.e., an irrational preoccupation with one subject)

Having a dream whereby you just seem to be obsessed with one topic or thing implies that you do have some kind of unusual fixation during your wake state. Only you know what it is. This dream is trying to tell you to totally ignore this habit if it is mentally and physically straining. Doing the same thing over and over again does not prove anything except that you may be harbouring some guilt or fear within your mind. If you somehow cannot handle your problem alone, then do not hesitate to seek some professional assistance.

**MONOPLANE** (see **AIRPLANE**)

**MONOPOLY** (i.e., an exclusive possession or control of something)

You are a very ambitious person who may, from time to time, be mistakenly accused of being self-centered and greedy. You may be impulsive and quick-tempered, but you certainly do have a sharing and giving mind. Your logical, communicative, and explorative nature will eventually bring you to the heights of prosperity and happiness; for, in so many ways, you would not settle for anything less!

**MONORAIL** (see **RAILROAD**)

**MONSOON** (i.e., heavy winds with rain)

This dream intimates that you are trying to eradicate those inner and outer storms in your life. You know that sometimes you are the cause of your problems; yet, on the other hand, you also know that someone else can create just as much trouble and mischief for you as you can for yourself. This dream places you at a crossroads wherein you are seriously contemplating changing your entire outlook about yourself, people, places, and things. This is good and wholesome! You are trying; that speaks for itself. Remember, a new outlook can create whole new horizons in your life!

**MONSTER**

Be it in human form, animal form, or a combination of both, a monster within a dream state is the monster you perceive within yourself, someone else, or something else in your life. You can be your worst enemy, but someone else or something else can be your worst enemy, as well. The symbolic vision of a monster reveals fears, phobias, insecurities, hang-ups, failings, difficulties, and so on which you mentally harbour about yourself, someone else, or something else. In other words, you may be the monster, another person may be the monster, or something else in your life may be the monster. So, when you do have a dream of this nature, try to figure out who or what is causing you difficulties at this time. Then, with a prayer, a clear mind, and some gutsy determination, begin to solve that problem!

**MONTH**

Dreaming about a month under any circumstances reveals that you are expecting someone or something before too long, and/or you are making some arrangements to do something rather exciting in the very near future. The days ahead certainly look promising and fulfilling for you! Be happy; a more worthy soul could not ask for anything better.

**MONUMENT** (e.g., tablet, statue, pillar) (see *also* **BURIAL, CENOTAPH, GRAVESTONE, MASTERPIECE,** or **OBELISK**)
Life does not turn back for anyone on this planet, so—in many ways—you must constantly move forward with a spirit of new revitalization, greater awareness, and adventure. Do not be afraid to express your views and actions, even if they appear to be odd or unusual at times. The greatest writers, painters, and other artists all had unique and sometimes bizarre ideas and concepts, only to realize much later that they were ahead of their time. Let go of your inhibitions, give the very best of what is within you, and you just may discover that you are on a new-found, monumental road in life.

**MOON** (see *also* **MOONSCAPE** or **MOONWALK**)
Seeing the moon at a distance implies that you are striving to reach out or grasp new avenues, ideals, concepts, or plans which could improve your daily living. Perhaps you want to go back to school; perhaps you are starting to do some creative work which could eventually be your lifework; perhaps you want to become a missionary. Whatever it is that you are seeking, you can be sure that you will not only find it, but you will also set an example for others with your aspirations, hopes, and inner strength. In many respects, this dream likens you unto astronauts or explorers who venture far or near for hidden mysteries and truths. Upon returning home, they begin to unravel and comprehend the things they brought back with them. They have, in effect, become wiser. You will, too!

**MOONSCAPE** (i.e., surface of the moon)
Seeing the surface of the moon at close range suggests that you are not looking at your earthly problems in a realistic manner; you do not seem to have your feet planted firmly on the ground, at this time. You seem to know precisely what you want to do or what you have to do but, sadly, you are reticent in moving forward. Look up instead of down, and call upon the Mighty Forces of God to help you. Visualize yourself going through a tunnel and that you are finally coming out of this tunnel with earthly peace and serenity. Reach out until your inner soul is consummated with courage and understanding which you, and

you alone, can awaken, feel, and comprehend. Then, weighing all matters for what they are, trust your good, positive instincts, and be thankful for finally making a quantum leap in your life.

## MOONSHINE (see LIQUOR)

## MOONWALK

Seeing yourself or someone else walk on the surface of the moon indicates that you are enjoying the better of two worlds! For example, you may be happy with your home life and with your job or career, or you may be happy to be at school and happy to be doing something else out of school. Whatever it may be, it is comforting to know that you are at peace with yourself and with your life in general. Not too many people can honestly say that their existence is totally harmonious. You can!

## MOOR (see SHORE or SWAMP)

## MOOSE

Your introverted and isolationist thoughts and actions can be a blessing in disguise; yet, there are times when you feel very indisposed with, and upset at, the way you are. Since you cannot be someone else, no matter how hard you try, it would be most advisable to accept the fact that you are quiet and shy. There is certainly nothing wrong with you except perhaps your tendency to envy others who are more loud and outgoing. You are not any less a person for being who you are—nor will you ever be! You have some remarkable talents, including a fantastic ability to write, to compose, or to fill the air with music. You are blessed in so many ways. Use your gifts wisely, and go forth into the world in your silent, dynamic way. Did you know that some of the greatest people of this day and age are just like you?

## MOP

Seeing or using a mop, for whatever reason, suggests that you feel like a slave to someone's whims and notions, and/or you feel like you are being chained down by someone's practicality, stubbornness, and blindness. This dream advises you to seriously reconsider your position in this matter and to see whether or not you can be more confident and assertive in your ways. Do your very best to identify with your own abilities and worth but, if for some reason or other this cannot be accomplished at this time, then be prepared to do so in the very near future. Times are beginning to change; and, happily, so will you!

**MORALIST** (i.e., a person who conforms to accepted standards of righteousness in character, conduct)

To dream of being a moralist reveals that you are a moralist during your wake state, as well. You are often misunderstood and stigmatized by others because of your high integrity and obvious inner foresight and knowledge. Carry on as you are, and do your best to pay no mind to those beings who tend to scoff at the truth. Should someone refuse your help, do not fret or fuss. Instead, realize that everyone has a God-given right to choose and to find their pathway in life in the manner which they deem necessary. There are many roads leading to Heaven; and this is also applicable to people finding their way on earth. Sooner or later, they do.

**MORGUE**

This inauspicious dream can be a harbinger of sad times and events unless matters within or around you are properly looked into and resolved (e.g., sickness, accident, financial collapse). If you or a loved member of your family is sick, be sure to not overlook this matter, otherwise things can get profoundly worse. Or, if you or a family member tends to be rather reckless when driving a vehicle, motor bike, motor boat, or other vehicle, then stop, look, and listen; and, above all, slow down. No one wants an accident, so do your best to avoid one! And, if there appears to be anything else that you are uneasy about or anything in your home that needs repairing or checking into (especially electrical wires, etc.), do not hesitate to act on your intuitive, inner feelings. It is far better to be safe than to be sorry.

(*Note*: Having a repetitive dream about a morgue simply adds more fuel to the fire. Be careful; something is terribly wrong or about to happen! Please heed this dream's warning, and everything may turn out all right. Pray for everyone's well-being and safekeeping. Above all, be prudent and watchful during this trying time.)

**MORSE CODE**

Seeing or using the Morse code infers that you are a very private, secretive, and sometimes mistrusting individual. You obviously would like to improve your ways, but so often you tend to delay this move by being too busy or uncaring. This will never do simply because you have created your own isolation and problems, which only you can rectify. You are not as complex or mysterious as you want people to believe you are. In fact, you are very intelligent—but also stubborn and insecure. This truth should not deter you from making a few positive changes within your life—that is, if you truly want to.

## MORTGAGE

Any one or several of the following definitions may be applicable: A) that you have mortgage payments to make, but everything so far seems to be okay in this department; or B) that you are worried about not having enough money to make your next mortgage payment; or C) that you refuse to make your mortgage payments from now on; or D) that you are remorseful for not having tried harder to keep up the mortgage payments, because now you have lost practically everything you owned; or E) that you know of someone who has lost their home or business because of financial reasons; or F) that you are assisting a family member or friend who is in some kind of financial bind at this time; or G) that you would like to purchase a home or business very soon, but you are very worried about the high mortgage payments; or H) that this dream has little or no significance to you at this time.

## MORTUARY (see FUNERAL HOME or MORGUE)

## MOSAIC

Seeing or creating a mosaic picture or design implies that you have already overreacted or you will overreact to some particular incident or matter that needs correcting. However, you are sensible and logical, so you should come out of this very brief, minor storm quite admirably.

## MOSES (see *also* MESSENGER)

Having the rare honour of seeing Moses in a dream reveals that you are about to make some very drastic, positive changes within your life. Obviously, something is very amiss with you and your lifestyle. A letter, a telephone call, or talking to someone very special before too long will commence to change your entire concept about yourself and about many other things. This dream is likened unto a person being lost in life and being found again through unusual, almost mystifying ways. Great peace, fulfillment, and spiritual satisfaction are ahead for you. As you accept this remarkable change within you, you will eventually teach others good things about their spirit and soul.

(*Note*: You may also have the pleasure of knowing that if, for example, you are experiencing a very negative dream but at the very end of your dream sequence or anywhere during your dream sequence you happen to see Moses, then this "symbolism" of Moses takes precedence over your entire bad dream. Consequently, you have nothing to worry about simply because Moses acts as a "buffer zone" to anything negative within a dream.)

**MOSQUE** (i.e., a Moslem temple of worship)
This dream symbolism means that you are overly opinionated and much too harsh on yourself and others where emotional, physical, spiritual, social, or political issues are concerned. You may be knowledgeable and convinced in your ways, but you must realize that you cannot always convince or force others to accept your views and theories. Some people accept what you say; some do not and perhaps never will. Respect all people upon this planet, be more open-minded, and learn to compromise with yourself and with the needs and wants of others around you. Be fair and patient with everyone, and be less desirous to promote any philosophy that is not in keeping with your inner soul and the Universal Mind of God. Humility is your key to betterment; and silence is your door to more worthy, inner perceptions.

**MOSQUITO** (see **INSECT**)

**MOSS** (i.e., plant often seen growing on rocks, trees, moist ground)
Life is only as complex as you wish it to be. At this time, you are strongly urged not to isolate yourself from your family and friends; rather, seek their counsel and wisdom whenever the need arises. Use your insight and talents to the best of your ability, and you will soon discover that your existence is far more meaningful and purposeful than you had previously imagined it to be.

**MOTEL**
You would like to run away from, or escape from, some minor or major situation or involvement within your life. Not everything will go your way, so do not expect a bed of roses when, in fact, you are des-

tined to face the music when the time comes. You are strongly urged to do some serious introspection where your true motives, feelings, and activities are concerned. As well, strive very hard not to be so emotionally impetuous, at this juncture. This can lead you down a garden path where trouble and stresses abound!

## MOTH

There is a troublemaker around; be careful. But also be very wary that this troublemaker is not you. If it is someone else, then you will be able to handle this matter sensibly and diplomatically. However, if it is you, then you are strongly urged to back down while you still have the chance. Failing to do so will cause you grief, anguish, and insurmountable hardships you never deemed possible! Vengeance does not belong to you; it belongs to God. He will be the Judge and Jury of what ails you. Think twice before you leap backwards in life!

(*Note*: A repetitive dream about a moth is neither wholesome nor good. It reaffirms the above entry but also forewarns the dreamer to be very careful because trouble is brewing right around the corner. Be guided by this thought and certainly by the dream's symbolic warning to you.)

## MOTHBALL

You have been appeased or pacified about a recent misunderstanding you had with someone and/or about a misunderstanding involving a money transaction. At the moment everything appears to be working relatively smoothly for you, and you certainly wish to keep it that way. No doubt, you will!

## MOTHER

Dreaming about your mother in a peaceful, pleasant way suggests that there are good, harmonious feelings between you and your mother. Your inner feelings towards your mother show love, respect, and gratitude, which is certainly the right attitude to uphold!

Dreaming about your mother in a bitter, disrespectful way, suggests disharmony, anger, or hatred towards your mother. Whatever it is that is troubling you, it certainly would be advisable not to hold grudges or vendettas towards someone who is older, and perhaps wiser. Respect your parent(s). Far too often, people fail to do so, only to weep, wail, and feel sorry for themselves when a parent passes over. Do not let this happen to you.

Seeing your mother in a sickly state or some other painful predicament implies that your mother may be sick, or else she could be experiencing some type of trauma at this time. Pray for your parent(s), and communicate with them, as well. Hopefully, everything will correct itself before too long.

If your mother gives you a lecture or scolds you within a dream, then you are strongly urged to correct some attitude, outlook, or problem within your life. You are doing something that is not in order! For your sake, find out what it is, settle it, and—with courage and peace— forge ahead.

Seeing a mother who has already passed away indicates that she wants a prayer from you. Say a prayer for your mother from the denizens of your heart, mind, and soul. In many respects, your mother wishes to help you in some manner; and she will! In your prayer, do not forget to tell her to "ask for the Light"!

## MOTHER-IN-LAW

Any one or several of the following definitions may be applicable: A) that you respect and harmonize with your mother-in-law; or B) that you cannot get along with your mother-in-law, for some reason or other; or C) that your mother-in-law lives in another city or state, and you couldn't be more grateful for this fact; or D) that you find your mother-in-law is very hospitable but far too inquisitive; or E) that your mother-in-law will be visiting you shortly; or F) that you find your mother-in-law far too possessive, where your spouse is concerned; or G) that there is harmony between you and your mother-in-law because of the lifestyles you both lead; or H) that you feel anyone who does complain about their mother-in-law is either exaggerating or simply fabricating horror stories about her; or I) that you are about to be married and feel sometimes respectful, sometimes angered, towards your future mother-in-law; or J) that you are divorced but still think highly about your former mother-in-law or you feel relieved to be out of her life; or K) that you have had several confrontations with your mother-in-law already, but apparently the last battle should have settled matters, once and for all time; or L) that you are about to become a mother-in-law, and you have made a vow to yourself that you will not interfere with your children's marriage and happiness; or M) that this dream has little or no significance to you at this time.

**MOTHERLAND** (see **BIRTHPLACE** or **HOME**)

**MOTION PICTURE** (see *also* **STUDIO**)

If you happen to be in the motion picture business and dream about seeing or producing one, then this symbolic action reveals your concern, interest, or involvement in the kind of work that you do. However, if this does not apply to you, then this dream suggests all-round improvements are in store for you. Almost everything should commence to stabilize and harmonize, both within and around you, before too long.

**MOTOCROSS** (see **COMPETITION** or **CONTEST**)

**MOTORBIKE** (see **MOTORCYCLE**)

**MOTORCYCLE**

The process of growing up may be arduous and painful, but there comes a time and a day when a person has to show some accountability and responsibility for their actions and deeds in life. An adult is supposed to be mature; unfortunately, this is not always the case. Would you believe that some children can be more mature than adults? In essence, this dream is trying to tell you to let go of the good old days, face your realities head-on, and start building your life with more dedication, substance, and purpose.

**MOTOR SCOOTER**

If you basically lead a good life, then a motor scooter reveals that happiness, success, and travel lie ahead for you. Your optimism and perseverance are the major factors which will weigh heavily upon the rewards yet to come. So, work hard, and these good things will come to pass.

If you are leading a degrading, uncaring, and pessimistic existence, then you can hardly expect much. What you will receive from life is no more and no less than what you put into life. Change your attitudes and outlook, pray, begin to help yourself, and then you will begin to see those winning successes you rightfully deserve!

**MOTTO**

Saying or hearing your favorite motto within a dream state infers that you actually live by that motto. You practice what you preach, and there are no ands, ifs, or buts about it. You accomplish what you set out to do, and you do it well! Those who know you admire you for your kindness, stamina, and courage—and, of course, your loyal dedication. Your future endeavours should bring you plenty of good luck, happiness, and an ample amount of prosperity.

## MOUNTAIN

Seeing a mountain or a chain of mountains in a peaceful sort of way means that you are a very dynamic, confident, and knowledgeable person. Even though your life has its many ups and downs, you still continue to strive diligently onwards until matters within and around you stabilize. You are to be admired and praised for your down-to-earth attitudes and actions. Is it any wonder people are attracted to your magnetic personality?

Seeing a mountain or chain of mountains in a sad or angered sort of way intimates that outwardly you are trying to be content and satisfied, but inwardly you appear to be depressed and quite alone. Whatever is troubling you, rest assured that you will master your problems before too long. Have you forgotten? Faith moved your mountain(s) before—and it will do so again!

If you see a mountain or mountains crumbling, vanishing in front of you, or being destroyed, then a recent plan or wish did not come true. Do not panic. Down the road a bit, you will fulfill some better plans and wishes.

## MOUNTAINEER (i.e., a person who climbs mountains, or lives near mountains)

Climbing up or looking up at a mountain indicates that you look to the brighter side of life. No matter what hardships you experience, you still see the possibilities of hope and faith turning everything around. And, you know—very often, they do! You are indeed a finely attuned, perceptive, and levelheaded individual. Your belief in yourself has no limits. This is why you are destined to make your existence upon this planet as meaningful and successful as you humanly can—and, rightfully so, you will!

Climbing, falling, or looking down a mountain intimates that you perceive life in a hopeless sort of way. Perhaps not always, but a good percentage of the time, you lack the faith and hope that things might get better. Yes, matters can get worse before they become better, but just think of the infinite, positive possibilities that can happen even when situations appear disappointing and futile. This dream advises you not to be so narrow-minded; rather, open your heart, mind, and soul to the panoramic view around you. Disband your tunnel vision attitudes and concepts; then, perhaps, you will begin to perceive the accessible potentials within you.

**MOUNTAIN PASS** (see **PASSAGEWAY**)

**MOUNTAINTOP** (see **MOUNTAIN**)

**MOUNTIE** (see **PEACE OFFICER**)

**MOURNING**

Being in a state of mourning or wearing the clothes of mourning within a dream infers that you are presently in a sad, depressed frame of mind. Whatever your reasons may be, rest assured that you will be happy and more active before too long. Life goes on, and you must too!

**MOUSE**

An active mouse (or mice) indicates that, in spite of your recent interruptions, setbacks, or annoyances, you know that you must carry on with speed in order to meet a deadline or carry out some plan or project. You will no doubt do this and much more!

A docile mouse (or mice) intimates that you feel stifled by, or penned in to, your present earthly circumstances (e.g., career, marriage, romance, education). Since you only feel this way, it does not necessarily have to be that way. Change matters around for yourself. If you think this is impossible, then you are strongly urged to seek outside help or assistance. You will be very surprised and pleased by the help you will receive!

A dead mouse (or mice) suggests you will finally settle, solve, or master an unfavorable, despairing problem that has been haunting you for quite some time (e.g., drugs, alcohol, harsh or foolish attitudes and outlook). It is consoling to know that you have finally decided to think about yourself and your future with a positive, more determined frame of mind. This time, you can succeed!

**MOUSETRAP**

You will try to expose someone whom you mistrust, or you will be exposed by someone who mistrusts you. Be wary of these circumstances, for truly there is a good and a bad way to approach matters of this order. If someone annoys you for some reason, then simply confront that person with maturity and diplomacy. In other words, say what you feel, and end matters there. Do not try to entrap or embarrass anyone in an awkward or aggressive way or in a crowd-filled room. You never know when your suspicions can backfire on you. Do not assail a friend; rather, prevail by understanding a friend's weakness or flaws with human logic and forgiveness.

## MOUTH

Seeing the mouth of a human or of an animal cautions you to be more aware of your verbal abuses or criticisms towards other people. It is totally unfair to gossip or condemn another person, especially when that person is not there to defend themselves. Unfortunately, there are far too many backstabbing, two-faced incidents among relatives, friends, and acquaintances which, sadly, create rifts and further hard feelings. The person whom you condemn may already be nailed to a heavy cross; do not make matters any worse than they are.

## MOUTH ORGAN (see HARMONICA)

## MOUTH-TO-MOUTH RESUSCITATION (see RESUSCITATION)

## MOVE (i.e., a change of residence, or removing an object from one place to another)

To move away or to move something within a dream state shows that you are alive, happy, and basically well. The mere fact of moving from one location to another or moving an object from one location to another intimates that you are capable of moving closer to your goal(s) or obstacles in life, and/or you are just as capable of moving away from your goal(s) or obstacles in life. A more mature, sensible individual would always strive to come closer to a goal and would strive to move away from an obstacle, if at all possible. An immature, uncaring individual might move away from a goal or aim because of a bad attitude only to come closer to a pending obstacle or difficulty. Basically, you have a free will and a free mind to improve your life or ruin your life; the choice is entirely up to you.

## MOVER (see MOVE)

**MOVIE** (see **MOTION PICTURE**)

**MOVING SIDEWALK**

Everyone appreciates a shortcut or two, especially if this saves them time and money. However, this dream advises you to stop, look, and listen before trying to take an easy way out of an obligation or situation within your life. A job half done is a job not done, so do not look for excuses, for alibis, or for simpler methods of doing something when, in fact, the job calls for thoroughness and thoughtfulness. When you have something to do, do it well; otherwise, you may have to start all over again.

**MOWER** (see **LAWN MOWER**)

**MUCK** (see **MUD**)

**MUCUS** (i.e., excretion by the mucous membranes from the nose or other parts of the body)

The sight of mucus within a dream can be just as repulsive as it is during your wake state. This, then, would imply that you or someone whom you know has a very offensive habit (e.g., nose picking in public, clipping fingernails by the table). Whatever your habit may be, it is entirely up to you to know the difference between what is right and what is wrong. Bad habits are bad manners!

**MUD**

There is trouble, mischief, or danger lurking in the background, so be very careful during this time. Having a dream of mud is like waking up on the wrong side of the bed and having a terrible week to show for it. Be calm, firm, and sensible with yourself and others during this trying period, and perhaps those lurking difficulties will be triumphantly mastered.

**MUFFIN** (see **FOOD**)

**MUFFLER**

Any one or several of the following definitions may be applicable to you: A) that you just bought a new muffler; or B) that you need a new muffler for your vehicle; or C) that you suspect something is wrong with your present muffler; or D) that you have attempted to repair your muffler, with or without success; or E) that you concentrate too much on speed rather than safety where your driving is concerned; or F) that you do not understand the mechanics of a vehicle too well but feel that there is something wrong with your car; or G) that this dream has little or no relevance to you at this time.

**MUG** (see **EARTHENWARE**)

**MUGGER** (see **BURGLARY**, **CRIMINAL**, or **THIEVERY**)

**MULE** (see **DONKEY**)

**MULTITUDE** (see **CROWD**)

**MUMBLER** (i.e., one who speaks or complains indistinctly such as with a partly closed mouth) (see *also* **DELIRIUM**)
    Being or seeing a mumbler within a dream state infers that you are dealing with some type of senseless, illogical, or no-win situation with yourself or with someone whom you know. Perhaps you are trying to be or act like someone totally alien to your ways and habits, or perhaps you had a foolish argument with a spouse or friend over something so trivial that you cannot bear to think about it, and so on. Do not despair. Your feelings, thoughts, or actions in this entire matter will soon wane; and, before you know it, everything will be forgotten.

**MUMMY** (i.e., a human body preserved by embalming as practiced by the ancient Egyptians)
    You are dealing with some narrow-minded individuals who could very well be within the family circle. You simply must resign yourself to the fact that there are some people on earth (relatives or otherwise) you will never change, no matter how convincing you may be; nor will you ever satisfy some of these people, no matter what you do for them. Realize that not everyone has your mentality, capabilities, and insight. When you talk, they hear you, but they do not listen or do not often understand you. Do not be vexed by these matters; rather, be more tolerant with all those whom you know.

**MUMPS**
    Any one or several of the following definitions may be applicable: A) that you presently have the mumps; or B) that you know of some-

one who has the mumps; or C) that you fear this disease, not only for yourself but for your loved ones as well; or D) that you know of someone who had severe complications with this disease; or E) that you had the mumps many years ago; or F) that this dream has little or no relevance to you at this time.

## MUNITIONS (see ATOMIC BOMB, BOMB, CANNON, DYNAMITE, GUN, HYDROGEN BOMB, or MISSILE)

## MURAL

As you go on in life you are, in fact, painting your own mural on the wall of your soul, and absolutely nothing is erased without His approval and forgiveness. So, if the mural you see is beautifully painted, then you can deduce that you lead a very good, wholesome, clear-conscience existence. However, if the mural you see is foreboding or shoddy, then it is time to do some serious soul-searching; there is obviously something very amiss with your thoughts, actions, and deeds. Find the problem, correct the problem, and then seek a better life for yourself.

## MURDER (see *also* GENOCIDE or KILL)

Any one or several of the following definitions may be applicable: A) that you abhor the thought of violence, crime, murder, or anything else that is wicked upon this planet; or B) that you know of someone who was murdered; or C) that you are haunted by some sordid past event which could have involved manslaughter or murder; or D) that you are extremely troubled at this time and could use some psychological assistance; or E) that you may have recently read something involving a murderous crime; or F) that you are appalled and disgusted by the high incidence of crime and murder; or G) that you feel there are a lot of sick, depraved people who fail to listen to their better instincts until it is too late; or H) that murder is not only a crime on earth, but it is a crime upon the soul, as well; or I) that this dream has little or no relevance to you at this time.

## MUSCULARITY (i.e., great physical strength with well developed muscles)

Any one or several of the following definitions may be applicable: A) that you are endowed with a well developed body; or B) that you wish you were more muscular, and you certainly intend to work towards this goal until you are; or C) that you would like to be more muscular but because of your busy schedule, this idea does not seem plausible at this time; or D) that you envy muscular people, or you are repulsed by muscular people; or E) that because of some sickness or bone structure problems, the possibilities of you becoming muscular seem far away and remote; or F) that you are happy to be the way you are, no matter what personal endowments others have; or G) that this dream has little or no significance to you at this time.

**MUSEUM** (see *also* **WAXWORKS**)

You can expect an abrupt change of events where your career or home life is concerned. This turning point is not of a negative nature; rather, it is a beneficial leap for you and for your loved ones. Your struggles, pain, and sorrows have not gone unnoticed; your faith will now bring you to an even higher plateau in life. Now it appears that some of your innermost wishes will come true!

**MUSHROOM**

To see an edible-looking mushroom means that someone will pose a very personal, thought-provoking question to you (e.g., sexual matters, marriage matters, romantic matters). Do your very best to assist this person. The end results will prove favorable if you give a direct, honest answer instead of musing over this serious matter in a vague, perhaps inhibited way.

A poisonous-looking mushroom (e.g., toadstool) denotes quarrelsome, antagonistic gestures on your part towards an elderly person and/or a younger person's negative behaviour towards you. Unfortunately, there is no comfort or reprieve forthcoming unless all parties concerned learn to get along with one another. This can be attained through less bickering and more appreciation for each other.

**MUSIC** (see *also* **CHOIR, COMPOSER, CONCERT, CONDUCTOR, INSTRUMENT, MUSICIAN, OPERA, ORCHESTRA, REHEARSAL, SINGER,** or **STUDIO**)

Beautiful sounding music intimates that you are a very inspiring, creative, knowledge-seeking individual. You always go to the heart of the matter to solve a problem simply because you want to know and understand as much as you can. Like good music that fills the heart, mind, and soul of many things, so you, too, are just as good, trusting, and attuned to the finer quests of life.

Hearing awful sounding, discordant music indicates that you have a deaf ear for wholesome music; you also seem to have a closed mind where your temperament is concerned. In matters of temperament, you would be wise to explore and perceive what true peace and harmony are all about. Know yourself better and, for the sake of a better road ahead, do not toil and trouble people with your rants and ravings. Instead, be more willing to listen to those beings who just might be a bit wiser than you.

## MUSICIAN (see *also* CHOIRMASTER, COMPOSER, CONDUCTOR, ORCHESTRA, ORGAN GRINDER, PERFORMER, POET, or SINGER)

Any one or several of the following definitions may be applicable: A) that you are, in fact, a musician who wouldn't trade places with anyone on earth; or B) that you recently joined a new music band; or C) that you would like to become a very famous musician in time to come; or D) that you are a famous musician and constantly strive to perfect your craft; or E) that you know of someone who is in a music band; or F) that you recently lost your job with a music band but hope to join another before too long; or G) that you would like to become a good musician someday but not necessarily on a professional level; or H) that this dream holds little or no importance for you at this time.

## MUSIC STAND

This dream symbolism indicates that you would like to do something rather special in life, but someone appears to be contradicting you or is trying very hard to dissuade you from your better wishes. Weigh the matter very carefully. If you honestly feel, beyond any shadow of a doubt, that your intentions, aims, or goals are matters of the mind and soul, then never turn back. Go for it all the way! However, if you have some doubts about what you want, then do not be too impetuous at this time. Reflect upon your needs and wants sincerely and diligently; and, before you know it, a well based decision will be made.

## MUSKEG (see SWAMP)

## MUSKRAT (see RAT)

## MUSTACHE (see HAIR)

## MUSTARD PLASTER

This dream could very well imply that you have been using a mustard plaster recently, or perhaps you need to use one. However, if this is not the case, then this symbolism suggests that you will be apologizing to someone before too long. This could pertain to something you said to someone in a joking manner or perhaps something you said or did to someone in an offending manner. Whichever the case, the important factor is that you will make things right, and that is commendable.

## MUTENESS (see VOICELESSNESS)

## MUTILATION (see INJURY)

## MUTINY (see DISOBEDIENCE or DISSATISFACTION)

## MYSTERY

Solving a mystery, puzzle, or riddle within a dream infers that you have a very perceptive, analytical mind. You obviously know where you are going in life, and wherever you go, you certainly will not lack friends. In time to come, you may be involved in a business venture which could amass a fortune for you. There is also happiness and world-wide travel ahead for you.

Being unable to solve a mystery, puzzle, or riddle means that you do not waste your time on trivial matters or incidental details, especially when there are more important things to do. You are a go-getter who rarely minces words needlessly with anyone. So often, you aim for something; and, before you know it, you attain it. You are unique, talented, and outstanding in so many ways one that could almost deduce that you were born to be successful. In truth, you are successful!

## MYSTIC (i.e., a person who understands the Universal Truths beyond human insight)

Never underestimate your human potential nor ignore your human weaknesses and flaws. When you allow shadows of doubt and other repressions to harbour within your mind, you are placing earthly limitations upon your soul's progress. The object of this life is for you to use your inspirational gifts, talents, thoughts, ideas, and actions in the greatest, most constructive way possible. If you must "waste" a moment, an hour, or a day, do your utmost to "waste" your time on some constructive measures—not lazy, uncaring measures. Always remember why you are on this planet: you are here to learn and to love life—not hate or destroy it. You have a Universal Opportunity to scale the highest mountains, to explore the greatest oceans, or to wing through star systems not even remotely seen on this planet; that is, when you are ready, willing, and able to attune your mind to the Love and Unselfish Devotion God has for you. Set your mind-sails to the furthest corners of the Universe until your love of all life becomes like that of the mystic.

**MYTH** (see **LEGEND**)

**NAGGING** (see **COMPLAINER**)

**NAIL**

You have been through quite a bit of pain, struggle, and sorrow in your life but, unfortunately—and perhaps through stubbornness—you have failed to learn some valuable lessons about yourself. Not everything you say or do is foolproof, yet at times you would like to believe that this is so. Along some of those highways and byways of life, you have forgotten how to really live and enjoy yourself with at least some peace of mind. The simple things in life are free and enjoyable, but you must take the time to observe this fundamental truth with an open mind and certainly with a brighter outlook. There are no earthly treasures in pride or selfish motives; when you learn to direct your mind to more peaceful waters, you will discover that much of your sadness and suffering will dissipate. For your own sake, start accentuating your positive thoughts and actions, instead of hindering your progress with self-pity and hopeless views.

**NAIL POLISH** (see **COSMETIC**)

**NAKEDNESS**

Being partially or totally naked within a dream state could imply any one or several of the following definitions: A) that you have no reservations about being naked—you are not shy or ashamed about your body, in any way; or B) that you would be somewhat reluctant to stand nude in front of a stranger or group of people; or C) that your sexual drive is normal and natural, and that nudity is the common expression with this drive; or D) that you find it difficult to restrain your overly active sexual drive, especially when you see a nude person; or E) that you are a very passionate person but, in spite of this, you are still able to control your emotional and sexual needs; or F) that you are not concerned about the naked body but feel that the good mind and wholesome character of an individual are far more important; or G) that this dream has little or no significance to you at this time.

**NAME-DROPPING** (i.e., the act of mentioning famous names in order to impress someone)

Being a name-dropper or seeing one implies that you are very excited about a recent happening, or you feel embarrassed or afraid about some past incident which haunts you now and again, or you harbour some mental conflicts about your own abilities to continue where your home, job, or career is concerned. Everyone has their ups and down from time to time, and you are no exception to the rule. Try not to become so frustrated and annoyed with every little situation that arises within your daily life. Learn to accept what comes your way; expect the unexpected from time to time; and, with common sense, begin to show more self-control and confidence. Being less hyper will indeed improve your corner of the world!

**NANNY**

You are trying to help someone who appears to be indifferent to your good, sound philosophy and help. So be it! In many respects, this person is like a prodigal son or daughter who must learn the hard way until some measure of character improvement and maturity is achieved. If you must, take a good breath of fresh air, grit your teeth, and begin to realize that there is very little you can do for this person other than to stand back and hope for the best. Silence on your part would be considered golden at this time. Perhaps someday you will receive the gratitude and praises you so rightfully deserve!

**NAP** (see **SLEEP**)

**NAPKIN** (e.g., a small cloth, towel, or piece of paper used at meal-time for wiping lips, fingers)

There is plenty of time and space to accomplish the many things you hope to attain in life; but, for the sake of everyone concerned, stop being a one-player baseball team! Know your limitations, do your work well, and help others from time to time, but do not feel that you have to carry the load of everyone's work on your shoulders. You can only do so much. Besides, it is up to the next person to show some initiative and responsibility where actions and deeds are concerned. You obviously have enough will-power and speed to satisfy an army; but even an army is managed by teamwork. For a change of pace, put your team to work, and have enough faith and trust that their efforts will be just as good as yours.

**NARCISSISM** (i.e., possessing a great amount of self-love such as interest in one's appearance, rank, comfort, abilities)

Think carefully before you speak; think just as cautiously before you act! Being narcissistic within a dream state pretty much reflects what you are like during your wake state. This attitude is pompous and lacks self-discipline! Avoid giving in to the temptations of egoistic pride and selfishness; your place in life should be more humble. Right now, it appears as though you are heading towards a collision course with yourself unless you are prepared to at least modify or rectify some of your "higher than life" attitudes. Come down from your ladder, and begin to accept yourself and all life around you with a more sane perspective. Instead of idolizing yourself, learn to restrain yourself, for in this manner you will at least be true unto yourself.

**NARCOTIC ADDICT** (see **DRUG ADDICT**)

**NARRATOR** (i.e., a person who tells a story)

Do not expect some miraculous results or great prosperity from some project, plan, investments, or anything else you deem highly important at this time. It appears that your timing is off and that there will be some annoyances, delays, and some confusion before you actually see these better wishes materialize. Do not let your hopes fade or your courage slip during this brief, stressful period. Be alert, be optimistic, and—above anything else—be logical and patient. When the time is ripe, your earthly interests and comforts will be satisfied.

**NATIONALISM** (see **PATRIOTISM**)

**NATIVITY** (i.e., the birth of Jesus)

Seeing the Nativity within a dream infers that you, too, are undergoing a new birth or change within your life. Someone or something has affected you, or else you have decided to turn over a new leaf which, by all standards, is good and wholesome. It is like coming out of a dark pit into the sunlight for the very first time and seeing newer beginnings and realities ahead of you. You can be sure of one thing: what lies ahead of you is far greater and awesome than what you are leaving behind.

**NATURALIST** (i.e., a person who studies nature, animals, and plants)

Dreaming of being or seeing a naturalist intimates that you are not a complex individual but one who believes in the so-called simple pleasures of life. Your direction is positive. Even though others may frown or misunderstand your motives upon this planet once in a while, the fact remains that you are a survivor and a pioneer-minded individual who has good taste, logical judgments, and plenty of courage. Who could possibly want or ask for anything more?

**NATUROPATHY** (i.e., a system of treating diseases in a natural way, without the use of drugs) (see *also* **HERBALIST**)

Any one or several of the following definitions may be applicable to you, where this dream is concerned: A) that you are in fact a naturopath; or B) that you believe some treatments used by naturopaths are amazing; or C) that you believe some treatments employed in naturopathy seem to work very slowly and are not always effective; or D) that you would prefer naturopathy treatments rather than drugs; or E) that you feel drug treatments and naturopathy treatments both have their flaws and weaknesses just like anything else—that nothing is always perfect; or F) that you feel far too many people use drug treatments when they should at least try more holistic measures to heal themselves; or G) that this dream has little or no relevance to you at this time.

**NAUSEOUSNESS** (e.g., carsickness, sea sickness, air sickness) (see *also* **SICKNESS** or **VOMIT**)

Having sensations of being nauseated within a dream state could imply that you are not feeling too well while you are asleep. However, if this is not applicable to you, then your dream symbolism implies that you complain too much but do very little to rectify the problem(s) at hand. You also give up too quickly and easily when matters around you appear challenging. This simply will not do; this is not the route to take! You are obviously dissatisfied and discouraged with your lifestyle and daily activities. Perhaps you do not receive enough credit for some of the things that you do strive to fulfill, or perhaps you just feel neglected, used, and unwanted by those who you feel should be more caring and understanding towards you. Whatever is troubling you, this dream counsels you to change your outlook a bit and not be so swayed by what other people say or do. You are responsible for your own attitudes and actions in life—you cannot account for anyone else's. Change your tune and tactics, and you just might discover an ample amount of love, courage, and understanding waiting to be awakened within your being.

**NAVIGATOR** (i.e., a person who plots the course for a ship, airplane)

Never let anyone tell you that you are not the master of your own ship in life for, in many respects, you are that and more! You know exactly who you are and where you are going; you know precisely what route to take in order to succeed. Being very special in the eyes of many already, it appears that your leadership potential will lead you on to greater realms of fortune and humanitarian triumphs.

**NAVY**

Any one or several of the following definitions may be applicable: A) that you are, in fact, in the navy and find this career most enjoyable and wholesome; or B) that you are in the navy now but hope to retire before too long; or C) that you are now retired from the navy; or D) that you would like to join the Navy, before too long, but have a few doubts or qualms about doing so; or E) that many members of your family work or worked for the navy and you certainly do not want to spoil this fine and admirable tradition; or F) that recently you received a promotion within the navy ranks; or G) that you know someone who is in the navy and, in many respects, you envy this person; or H) that you could not join the navy due to health problems or some other personal reasons; or I) that this dream has little or no significance to you at this time.

**NAZARENE** (see **JESUS**)

**NAZISM** (see *also* **STORM TROOPER**)

Any one or several of the following definitions may be applicable: A) that you cannot even remotely imagine the terror and horrors this political party created during the Second World War; or B) that you hope this world will never see the likes of Nazism again along with its false, ruthless, abominable theories and actions; or C) that you are presently writing a book or essay about Nazism; or D) that you have recently read a book about Nazism; or E) that you can never understand why the world sat back when this racist political party climbed to power; or F) that you know of someone who suffered or who died at the hands of Nazism; or G) that you are haunted by some thoughts of Nazism for very personal, very painful reasons; or H) that this dream has little or no significance to you at this time.

**NEANDERTHAL** (i.e., prehistoric man)
You are in a bit of an earthly rut, but you can come out of this situation, providing you keep your feet on the ground and remain levelheaded in this situation. It only appears that your overall life is caving in on you; in reality, you are the one who is falling to pieces or failing to face facts as they are. This storm will pass you by; but, for the moment, do not persistently feel that no one cares or that there is nothing you can do about it. Nothing is easy; but, by the same token, nothing is absolutely hopeless either. Pray, be positive, be active, and care enough to put your life back in order. If you cannot do these things, then you are strongly urged to seek some psychological or spiritual help.

**NEATNESS** (see **CLEANLINESS** or **PERFECTIONISM**)

**NEBULAE** (see **GALAXY**)

**NECKBAND** (see **CLOTHES** or **DECORATION**)

**NECKING** (see **KISS**)

**NECKLACE** (see **JEWELRY**)

**NECKTIE** (see **CLOTHES** or **DECORATION**)

**NECKWEAR** (see **CLOTHES** or **DECORATION**)

**NECTARINE** (see **FRUIT**)

**NEEDLE** (see **ENGRAVING, INOCULATION, KNITTING, RECORD PLAYER, SEWING, SYRINGE,** or **TOOL**)

**NEEDLEPOINT** (see **EMBROIDERY, KNITTING, LACEWORK,** or **DECORATION**)

**NEGLECTFULNESS**

Neglectfulness towards yourself or someone else, or having this action displayed towards you, intimates that you are somewhat intolerant and cold-shouldered towards several people whom you know. Perhaps your reasons are just; however, there is a nice way and a wrong way in handling such matters. If someone or something troubles you, your best course would be to go to the source of the problem. Do not hide from or skirt around a problem—face it head-on. Say what you feel, but say it in a calm, diplomatic, and truthful manner. In essence, this dream is advising you not to keep a person in midair with your offish attitude, but to say what you feel and get it over with, sensibly and maturely.

**NEGLIGENCE** (see **NEGLECTFULNESS**)

**NEGOTIATION**

Bargaining for anything within a dream state infers that a period of inactivity will beset you. Do not be too disappointed; simply accept this time to gently recoup your strength and stamina for better times to follow. In reality, this dream is a blessing in disguise! Your overzealous attempts to overwork and to downplay your busy schedule were slowly beginning to get you bogged down. Being argumentative and restless does not help matters much either. Enough is enough! When this restive period comes, enjoy it!

**NEIGHBOURHOOD**

Any one or several of the following definitions may be applicable: A) that you like the neighbourhood you are in now; or B) that you do not like your neighbourhood and would like to move away, as soon as possible; or C) that you recently moved from one neighbourhood to another, and now you find the same problem you escaped from also exists in your new neighbourhood; or D) that you get along with all your neighbourhood friends, except for one or two people down the street; or E) that it never pays to get mad or angry at a neighbour, if you can help it, simply because life can become unbearable under those conditions; or F) that you recently had a squabble with a next-door neighbour; or G) that your neighbourhood is quaint and very pleasant; or H) that this dream has little or no relevance to you at this time.

## NEPHEW

Seeing a nephew or niece who appears to be rather happy and pleasantly preoccupied within a dream indicates that you may be seeing your nephew or niece before too long, or else you will be hearing some very good news regarding this person shortly. All is well!

Seeing a nephew or niece who appears to be in some kind of difficulty or trouble indicates that this person is in some kind of emotional or physical quandary; or is too proud to ask for help and simply becomes more confused and frustrated; or could be involved with the law (drug abuse, drunkenness, etc.). If you can reach out to your nephew or niece in some manner, then you certainly would be doing a good turn for everyone concerned.

Seeing a nephew or niece who appears to be sick-looking or very exhausted could very well indicate precisely that situation. For some reason, this individual is not feeling too well and could get worse unless proper care is taken. Common sense should prevail; and, before too long, everything will turn out all right!

Seeing a nephew or niece who appears rather sad and perhaps waves good-bye to you within your dream state could indicate the sudden passing away of this individual (e.g., accident, sickness). There are troubled times around this person, so special care must be taken, otherwise there could be sad, trying times ahead. Pray for your nephew or niece, and contact this person, if you can, to make sure that everything is in order. Safety and common sense are prime factors in this dream; do your best to instill this attitude where this individual is concerned.

Seeing a nephew or niece who has passed on already indicates that this person wants a prayer from you. When you do say a prayer for this soul's well-being, do not forget to tell your nephew or niece to "ask for the Light"!

## NEPTUNE (see PLANET)

## NERVOUSNESS (see *also* DANGER or EVILDOER)

Being nervous or jittery within a dream state basically implies that you are faced with a problem or hang-up you do not wish to deal with or face. You must realize, however, that your situation will not vanish into thin air unless you are prepared to do something about it. This dream further reveals that you can master your problem or hang-up through self-examination and strong determination. This is entirely up to you.

## NEST

If the nest is intact and undamaged, then your everyday home activities and business affairs should be in order. There should be peace and harmony around you at this time. It also appears that you are looking forward to travel, to renovate your home, or to make some major purchase down the road. Your future looks promising, productive, fulfilling, and prosperous!

If the nest is very messy or damaged, then this dream intimates that you may be creating some big problems for yourself. You are being far too hasty with your decisions and actions lately; this could bring you remorse or trouble in due time. "Think before you act" is the motto advised by this dream. If someone or something annoys you, think twice before doing something foolish, reckless, or improper. You have a lot to be grateful for now; so, for your own sake, do not spoil the progress and happiness you have worked so hard to attain. Settle down, be more forgiving, and try to steer around your latent suspicions—which, in all likelihood, are senseless and groundless. If you truly want peace and order in your life, then hold on to it; don't push it away!

## NET (e.g., fish net, tennis net, hairnet, veil)

A new-looking, well-kept net means that you will be embarking upon a new experience, adventure, or career before too long. The wheels appear to be already in motion, so what you are seeking or wanting will be accomplished with amazing skill and fortitude. The horizons ahead of you are much brighter than you realize. Time will convince you that you are headed towards outstanding accomplishments and success.

An old-looking or torn net infers that on the surface you appear to be very calm, cool, and collected, but on the inside you are very insecure and are unsure about many things. You are not alone. There are many people like you who harbour fears, secrets, and weaknesses which they find too personal or too embarrassing to mention. What is vitally important here is that you have the intelligence and basic courage to master your inner weaknesses and anxieties through prayer. If you are too uneasy or shy to tell anyone about your hang-ups, what on earth should stop you from confiding in God? He will not only hear you; He will help you! By simply pouring out all your troubles to Him, you have in effect cleansed and purified your mind, heart, and soul. Now, since God is the Healer and Purifying Force of All Things, you must begin to accept and believe that a marvelous change has come upon you. In effect, it really has. But in order for this to work, you have to accept and believe that this is so. Some people, unfortunately, expect God to hit them on the head with a mallet and say: "You are healed!" God does not work that way at all! He works so peacefully and silently, that, in truth, you can hardly tell unless you are keenly perceptive, receptive, and open to His Will for you. Remember: you, as a child of God, belong to Him; and He, as your True Father, belongs to you.

**NETWORK** (i.e., radio or television network) (see *also*
**ANNOUNCER, NEWS ROOM, PROGRAM, RADIO, STUDIO,** or **TELEVISION**)
     Seeing or working for a radio or television network within a dream state infers that you are headed towards greater satisfaction and honour in life. Working hard, gathering vital experiences here and there, and showing gratitude for what you are doing will ultimately lead you closer to your visualized rank and success. Walk on each day as though there were an invisible pathway made especially for you; believe that your purpose in life is far greater than any outside interference could possibly hope to hinder or legislate. And, as you climb higher and higher in life, share your importance or greatness in the wisest, kindest way you can humanly master. If you fail in this light, you may be replaced by someone far greater than yourself.

**NEUROLOGIST** (see **DOCTOR**)

**NEUROSIS** (i.e., an emotional personality disorder)
     If you are in fact a neurotic, then your dream is merely projecting your behaviourial problems for you to see and perhaps rectify. However, if this does not apply to you, yet you see yourself acting in a neurotic sort of way, then this dream intimates it is far better for you to talk things out with someone when you are troubled, sort things out with yourself from time to time, and settle other matters of impor-

tance in a peaceful, harmonious, and logical way. Young adults and even adults who throw tantrums or who tend to be vexatious are, in fact, immature, selfish, and hind-sighted individuals who fear growing up. Do not be a poor loser, nor be a quitter in life; rather, accept your place on earth with dignity and honour among other compromising, caring, and struggling minds and souls.

**NEUTRALISM** (i.e., not taking part in anyone's argument or war)

This act within a dream state does not necessarily imply that you always take a neutral stand on issues, arguments, or discussions. What is basically implied with this symbolism is that you use foresight before you leap into any difficult or negative situation. This does not, in any way, imply that you are selfish or uncaring; on the contrary! You are willing to lend a hand to anyone or anything, providing there are a certain number of sensible possibilities open to you. If you are asked to be a peacemaker between two people, for example, you want to be absolutely sure that these two people are sincere instead of being back-slappers, and back stabbers, and time wasters.

**NEVER-NEVER LAND** (see **FAIRYLAND**)

**NEWLYWED** (see **MARRIAGE**)

**NEWSBOY** (see **PAPERBOY**)

**NEWSDEALER** (i.e., a retailer who sells newspapers, magazines) (see *also* **NEWSSTAND**)

You like to voice your opinions—which, on most occasions, are respected and appreciated. However, there are times when you say too much. This creates hardships and misunderstandings between you and whoever happens to be involved. Since your efforts are never really half-hearted, you are strongly urged to tone down or totally cease your forthright views and opinions, especially with caring, sensitive, and sometimes troubled people. Be more thoughtful and discerning with everyone; this at least will create no hardships or ill feelings.

**NEWSLETTER**

Mere whims, notions, or yearnings of the mind will not bring you into better times, but your courage and efforts certainly will. In other words, do not expect something for nothing. Good judgments and understanding, along with wholesome work and self-sacrifice, are all vital keys in getting ahead. When you place insurmountable barriers in front of yourself, you are in fact admitting that you have very little initiative and willpower to carry out your plans or concepts in the first place. Talk is cheap, but actions speak for themselves. You have greater capabilities than you are ready to admit to yourself. If you ever forge ahead, you just may discover it was really not as difficult as you thought it would be.

## NEWSPAPER

Reading a newspaper implies that your work and good efforts are very appreciated by others around you. You are a very active and busy person—this makes you feel happy and accomplished. Your mind is very disciplined and alert, allowing you to concentrate on and complete your tasks or goals with outstanding speed, accuracy, and efficiency. You are destined to forge ahead simply because you do not allow anyone or anything to stand in your way. Besides, you have enough electrifying determination to move many mountains—and will still do so.

Tearing up a newspaper or seeing one that is tattered, shredded, or damaged in any way intimates that you will have to clear the air with someone who appears to be badly misinformed about a topic or subject close to your mind and heart. This will be done today or very soon thereafter.

(*Note*: A repetitive dream about a newspaper "headline" or "article" could very well be a prophetic dream. In other words, having a dream of this nature quite consistently for a period of about a week or two could imply that what you are reading could eventually come true. If the headline or article appears to be of a devastating nature, then it might not be a bad idea to inform your local newspaper about what you have seen. You never know; maybe your dream's purpose was for you to forewarn someone in order to avert a catastrophe or to at least give people time to save their lives. Think about this carefully, and let your conscience be your guide.)

## NEWSPAPERMAN (see **EDITOR** or **JOURNALIST**)

## NEWSREEL (see **MOTION PICTURE**)

**NEWS ROOM** (i.e., a room for editing and writing news at a news-paper office, radio or television station)

New and exciting prospects lie ahead for you if you dream of a news room. With your diligence and farsighted mentality, your efforts and work will not go unnoticed. You will be in the limelight playing a vital role for your community, state, country, or the world, for that matter. Whatever it is that you are doing, it is a comfort to know that your venturesome journey in life will now be very rewarding, satisfying, and ultimately successful!

**NEWSSTAND**

Your candid nature and philosophy are wholesome towards some people, but not towards all. It appears that a friend, neighbour, relative, or co-worker is not on best terms with you due to your blunt statements. Basically, your standards of conduct are exceptionally high; however, there are times when you get carried away with gossipy overtones, only to later regret your biased phrases and prejudices. Your dream is a reminder for you to show more self-control in these matters, so that you will lead a more peaceful, clear conscience existence.

**NEW YEAR'S DAY**

A dream about New Year's Day intimates that you would like nothing better than to see a more promising, enlightened year ahead of you. Maybe last year was "the pits" where you were concerned. However, there are occasions when you will be isolated, dejected, and tested for a period of time until you have learned some valuable lesson about yourself and perhaps life in general. You have that God-given right to expect better times ahead, which inevitably will come to you sooner or later—hopefully, sooner! But before this can happen, you must commence to initiate, activate, and accentuate your most positve inner values, concepts, actions, and deeds with the highest frame of mind you can conceive. In other words, do not think or act despairingly or feel hopeless when, in fact, positive things can happen overnight, providing you have the right outlook and the willingness to believe that all things are possible.

**NICKELODEON** (see **INSTRUMENT** or **RECORD PLAYER**)

**NIECE** (see **NEPHEW**)

**NIGHT** (see *also* **MIDNIGHT**)

Do not feel so terribly alone in your hardships, nor be blinded in the truth of your harvest. Out of the darkness you will be guided into a new phase of your life filled with truth, compassion, satisfaction, and freedom. Like a sea whose mighty waves constantly crash upon the shoreline, so you, too, will have to create a new vision of self with deeper insight, a sense of belonging, and a shocking realization that you are not on earth for useless reasons. You have an opportunity to begin again with greater foresight and certainty; do not ignore this opportunity.

**NIGHTCAP** (see **CLOTHES**)

**NIGHT CLOTHES** (see **CLOTHES**)

**NIGHTCLUB** (see **CABARET**, **CAFÉ**, or **LIQUOR**)

**NIGHTMARE**

Most people are troubled when they experience a nightmare. They should allay their fears. A nightmare is a combination of various tensions and anxieties we all tend to suppress during our wake state, only to later release a barrage of nonsensical thoughts and actions during our sleep state. The suppression of hatreds, jealousies, vengeance, or just about anything that is unpleasant to the mind and soul will always surface in a nightmarish type of dream, sooner or later. These tensions and anxieties must come out, otherwise a person could become mentally and physically sick. Very often, people bring on a nightmare by overeating, drinking alcoholic beverages, arguing, or simply going to bed in an angry, frustrated mood. As well, waking up anytime during your sleep state and then going back to sleep a second or third time will automatically produce a nightmare or two. This second or third sleep state merely releases your tensions prior to your waking up. The conglomerate of symbolisms within a nightmare are mind-boggling and can, in many ways, be compared to preparing a huge pot of soup. Everything is thrown into the pot; just as everything you see or do is absorbed by your subconscious mind. You have your soup, you digest it, and you later release it! So, too, you have your bottled inner anxieties and frustrations which your subconscious digests and later releases via nightmares. The best thing to do is to simply ignore nightmares, if you can. Above all, remember that these tension-oriented dreams are basically a protective zone to release, control, and to ultimately combat certain fears and phobias we all tend to suppress and conceal from time to time.

(*Note*: If you are very troubled with nightmares, then this strongly indicates that you are not prepared to face up to some facts about yourself, someone else, or about anything else that haunts or troubles you. In many ways, you are not willing to "forget" or "forgive" what ails you. Unless you do, you will probably continue to have your nightmares until you begin to face your realities in a logical, sensible manner. By changing your outlook, you can automatically be free of nightmares.)

**NIGHT SCHOOL** (see **SCHOOL**)

**NIGHT WATCHMAN**
Do not let your complex nature make you outdo yourself right out of some happiness, the job market, or some other opportunities. The culprit in this case is your ego! In constantly trying to be someone you were long ago, you are failing to accept yourself for who and what you are today. If you truly want to progress in life, stop feeling so sorry for yourself, do not procrastinate, and begin to accept today's challenges as tomorrow's victories. Such is life. You must move forward with your thoughts and actions, not backwards with your memories and your might-have-beens. Otherwise, your foreseeable future does indeed look bleak and wasted.

**NIPPLE** (e.g., of a woman's teat, or a baby's bottle, or a teething ring)
Sadly, it appears as though you are lost in some time warp simply because of your inability to admit to yourself that many of your failings and heartaches in life were self-created. Somewhere in time, you have found it more expedient to maintain a double personality with your secretive, convincing manner rather than face the truth about yourself in a realistic, sure-footed manner. You have the right to muddle your own life—but surely not at the expense of those who really care for and love you. Take stock of this dream, for it is in the best interest of your future to begin to shape up and to rectify your selfish desires and actions. Face the truth about yourself, without pride or false pretenses, so that you can be able to move on to more worthy actions, which you are quite capable of undertaking.

## NIRVANA (see **HEAVEN**)

## NOBLEMAN

How strange life works! Just when everything appears to be caving in around you, something happens to change matters for the better; call it fate, luck, or whatever you wish. Still, it is gratifying to know that some of your S.O.S. signals have been heard and have been answered. Very soon you will hear a cry, a wail, a call for help, and you will be there to throw a lifeline of hope and comfort to a very dear, loyal friend. You will talk together, and you will cry together; and, somewhere in time, you will reflect back on this occasion with noble feelings and emotions.

## NOBLEWOMAN (see **NOBLEMAN**)

**NOD** (e.g., moving one's head up and down signifying yes or sideways signifying no, or slightly moving one's head to show a greeting to someone, or dropping one's head slightly forward indicating a state of extreme drowsiness)

To see the silent actions of a nod take place within a dream state infers that you are seeking an answer or explanation to something which puzzles you in a general, insignificant sort of way, and/or you are seeking an answer to a serious matter which took place quite recently. Be patient. The individual questions will be resolved shortly. One answer will surprise you; the other answer will shock you.

## NOEL (see **CHRISTMASTIDE**)

**NOISE** (see *also* **SOUND**)

Hearing a noise within your dream could very well mean that you did, in fact, hear some kind of noise while you were sleeping. If not, then this symbolism of noise signifies that you are harbouring hostilities towards someone or something in life. This could be towards a relative, friend, acquaintance, home, school, job or anything else you could possibly fathom. Venomous feelings can be poison to the mind and body! Hold no grudges towards anyone or anything; instead, be more sensible and realistic with your views and actions. There is a Universal Law to which everyone should adhere: If you fail to forgive someone who has done you wrong, then how can you expect divine forgiveness—be it on earth or on the other side of life? Without a doubt, it would be far better to make your peace while here on earth!

# NOMAD

You have been a bystander and a witness to many things in your life; now you must begin to put some of the pieces or puzzles of your life together. A great wail—a mighty prayer—is heard within the very denizens of your soul so that, at last, you may come forth with your gifts and talents. There are many great souls and martyrs who abound everywhere on this planet. In truth, you possess creative visions and mystical understandings of the life forces within and around you; so, in many respects, you have a duty to share your inner wisdom in your wanderings or wherever fate may lead you. Love, truth, and trust are three vital keys you should employ in order to gain confidence, respect, and understanding with those you meet and greet. Do so humbly and wisely!

# NO MAN'S LAND (see DESERT)

# NOMINATION (i.e., appointment to some public office, or naming a candidate for election)

You are a very competitive individual who simply hates to lose! However, as luck would have it, you do win on most occasions. This dream indicates you will always compete, learn, pursue, and achieve those aims and goals that are both challenging and fulfilling. Whether you win or lose is irrelevant; what is important is that you have the inner spirit to go after and to ultimately supercede your previous record, score, or mark in life. Your values and competitive outlook in life are quite intact; this will inevitably lead you towards enduring self-fulfillment and success.

# NONCHALANCE (see APATHY)

# NONCONFORMISM

If you are, in fact, a nonconformist during your wake state, then your dream about nonconformism merely alludes to the lifestyle you keep. Should this not be your case, then your dream indicates that you are a bit defiant and that you try to be a little bit different or unique, from time to time. This inner drive is basically common in people who seek some pleasure in being a bit unique, eccentric, or electrifying—or who simply want to mask their personalities for a brief period of time. In many ways, these nonconformist attitudes and actions are like play-acting. But, if it helps people to unwind or forget about themselves for a moment or two, then maybe nonconformism is more of a means to find oneself than a mask to hide oneself.

**NONCOOPERATION** (see **DISOBEDIENCE**)

**NONPERSON** (i.e., a person who is completely ignored as though being nonexistent)

Being a nonperson or seeing one intimates that you are over-spending, and/or you are doing something with the help of others, which may be self-defeating and futile. In matters of overspending, be careful. You never know when the well can run dry! In the second case, you would be wise to be more discerning and cautious with opportunities or schemes that appear promising, or you could real-ize much later that you are up against a brick wall. Verbal promises and activities are deceiving; practical efforts and activities tell the truth.

**NONRESISTANCE** (i.e., not using force to defend oneself or any-one else)

Nonviolence within a dream state could very well imply that you are basically a nonviolent person. However, there have been rare occa-sions when you have resorted to mild outbursts of temper or violence which were not long-lasting. In many respects, you would rather talk and compromise in a sensible manner than resort to any form of immature, senseless behaviour.

**NONVIOLENCE** (see **NONRESISTANCE**)

**NOODLE** (see **DOUGH** or **FOOD**)

**NOOSE**

If a noose is used for peaceful purposes such as for a rope for a fen-cepost, then someone will make peace with you before too long. It is always consoling to know that indifferent feelings can change to thoughtful, humble feelings.

However, if a noose is used for evil, harmful purposes, then some-one will have a confrontation with you; this could signal the end of a friendship or a personal relationship. Only time will tell. If you are to blame in this matter, then realize that you have affected someone very deeply. Apologize and hope for the best. If you are blameless in this matter, then do your very best to explain your situation honourably and truthfully. This is all you can do.

## NORMALCY

Being or acting normal within a dream state is basically common with all people. Most everyone tries to be as normal as possible in a dream, but this certainly is not always the case. Not by any means! One minute you can be sensible within a dream state, the next you could be doing something so outlandish that you would find it hard to believe that you were sane and normal. Within a dream state you can experience great moments of normalcy and great moments of almost anything else the mind could possible conceive. So being logical, sensible, and predictable within a dream state would mean that you are much the same during your wake state, though certainly not always! You could be illogical, absurd, and unpredictable during your wake state as well! Remember that a dream has limitless possibilities through the subconscious mind. However, during your wake state your conscious mind restricts or limits what you can do as a human being. Just be grateful to be alive, happy, healthy, and wise—and normal!

## NORTHERN LIGHTS (see AURORA BOREALIS)

## NORTH POLE

You are on the threshold of actually seeing some positive results from your worthy endeavours! It would be comforting, however, if your loved ones were more supportive or at least offered you a praise or two once in a while. You are not necessarily being ignored here; however, it just seems that some of your family members find it difficult to display emotions like love, affection, and concern. For the moment, you can discuss your feelings with them. Perhaps they will change their silent, aloof, or cold feelings towards you. If they don't, you must understand they still admire and like you in their own silent, secretive way.

## NORTH STAR (see STAR)

## NOSE

To see a nose actually implies that you have a complex about your nose, eyes, ears, or hair. Take your pick! Don't worry, though. There isn't a person on earth who does not feel something is wrong with their body. This does not necessarily mean that there is something actually wrong with the body; it simply means that people are sometimes vain and dissatisfied. To want to look your best is natural and normal, and you certainly are free to initiate any improvements which you deem necessary regarding your appearance. From this vantage point, however, you look just fine!

**NOSEBLEED**

Dreaming about a nosebleed could imply that you have had one recently or that you are very susceptible to getting nosebleeds, for some reason. If these are not applicable, then this symbolism suggests that you will be making some vitally important decisions before too long. However, before you do, you will intend to give up a habit which was brought to your attention quite recently. On both counts, you should be successful and happy!

**NOSE DIVE** (see **PLUNGE**)

**NOSE DROPS** (see **MEDICATION**)

**NOSE JOB** (see **SURGERY**)

**NOSE RING** (see **DECORATION**)

**NOSTALGIA** (see **BIRTHPLACE, HOME, HOMESICKNESS, REMEMBRANCE,** or **SADNESS**)

**NOSTRIL** (see **NOSE**)

**NOSY** (see **CURIOUSNESS**)

**NOTE** (see **MEMORANDUM**)

**NOTEBOOK** (see **BOOK** or **LOOSE-LEAF**)

**NOTICE** (see **ANNOUNCEMENT** or **OBITUARY**)

**NOTION** (e.g., a sudden idea, impulse, view, opinion)

Having a notion within a dream state is simply a natural instinct which allows the dreamer to either get involved in or get out of some good or bad situations. For example, if you are chased by some evil being, you may suddenly have a notion to fly away, climb a tree, or hide in order to save yourself; or you may have a sudden notion to run after the evil being, only to be caught and tortured. Whether you are dreaming or awake, notions can be good or bad, so a person should always strive to act upon a good instinct or notion. Bear in mind, however, that everyone makes mistakes now and then. If we didn't, we probably would not belong on this planet.

**NOURISHMENT** (see **FOOD**)

**NOVA** (see **STAR**)

**NOVEL** (see **BOOK**)

**NOVELIST** (see **AUTHOR**)

**NOVENA** (see **PRAYER**)

**NOVICE** (see **LEARNING**)

**NUCLEAR BOMB** (see **ATOMIC BOMB** or **HYDROGEN BOMB**)

**NUDITY** (see **NAKEDNESS**)

**NUISANCE** (see **ANNOYANCE, MISCHIEF, PERSECUTION**, or **PEST**)

**NUMBER** (see **MATHEMATICS**)

**NUMEROLOGY** (i.e., a practice of using numbers to calculate one's destiny)
　　Any one or several of the following definitions may be applicable: A) that you believe in numerology and its forecasts, where you are concerned; or B) that you do not believe in numerology; or C) that you are a practicing numerologist who has had outstanding success with your work; or D) that you are just beginning to learn about numerology and hope to be a professional numerologist in time to come; or E) that you find numerology is far too impractical or demanding where name changes or alterations are concerned; or F) that you can-

not understand how your name can possibly affect your life's pathway; or G) that you know of someone who did change their name through numerology, only to experience more trying times than before; or H) that you know of someone who did change their name through numerology followed by amazing results and success; or I) that this dream has little or no relevance to you at this time.

## NUMISMATICS (see COLLECTOR or MONEY)

## NUN (see CONVENT)

## NUNNERY (see CONVENT)

## NUPTIAL (see MARRIAGE)

## NURSE

If you are a nurse and dream of seeing or being one, then your dream is simply projecting the work that you do. Should this not be the case, then this symbolism implies that you have a very dominant personality which can be a blessing, in some ways; yet in other ways, this attitude can be upsetting and ineffective. You can make life more pleasant and workable for yourself, but first you must stop harbouring grudges or jealousies wherever you go. Do not be so critical towards others, for others can be just as critical towards you. If you intend to be kind and thoughtful, then do so without being demanding and hardheaded. Surrender your imperfect thoughts and attitudes to the wind; then you will see a brighter, more comfortable time ahead of you. As well, for your own sake, do not forget to smile or laugh once in a while; this is good for your mind and your soul.

## NURSEMAID (see NANNY)

## NURSING HOME

Any one or several of the following definitions may be applicable: A) that you are content to be in a nursing home; or B) that you are very unhappy about being in a nursing home and simply long to return back to your homestead or family; or C) that you are employed in a nursing home and like or dislike the work that you do; or D) that you wish your family would come to visit you more often, but—sadly—it seems as though they have forsaken you or simply abandoned you for their own selfish reasons; or E) that you know of someone who is in a nursing home; or F) that when you grow old, you hope that you will never have to go into a nursing home; or G) that it seems so sad that many elderly people had to struggle and suffer most of their lives, only to feel isolated and unwanted during the twilight years of their lives; or H) that you feel closer to a friend than you do to most of your family members; or I) that in many respects, life can be good, but in so many other respects, it can create anguish, bitterness, and so very much sadness for sickly people; or J) that this dream has little or no relevance to you at this time.

**NUT** (see **KERNEL**)

**NUTCRACKER** (see **UTENSIL**)

**NUTMEG** (see **SPICE**)

**NYMPH** (see **MAIDEN**)

**NYMPHOMANIA** (see **INTERCOURSE** or **SEX**)

**OAR** (i.e., a pole with a thin blade used to paddle or steer a boat, canoe, or other water vehicle)

Any negative thoughts or actions which you contemplate at this time may bear unwholesome results where your future is concerned. Do not be in such a hurry to run away from a situation which could heal itself through time and patience. Your demands upon several people are extreme; for your sake, you would be wise to be more pleasantly communicative, fair-minded, and forgiving. You are under the illusion that your words or demands must be adhered to no matter what someone else may say, think, or do. There are always two or more sides to a story, so be careful not to outdo yourself in these matters. Do not feel let down when people think for themselves. Your ideas may be good; but, by the same token, the next person has worthy ideas and contradictions, too. Compromise in a calm way, and you will slowly begin to vanquish the warlike atmosphere of your existence.

**OARSMAN**

Flaunting your superiority or importance towards people will not bring you closer to the truth of your own goodness, nor will this attitude bring you lasting peace of mind. You are creating your own detours and obstructions in life! Be a good listener, and begin to praise others, no matter what rank or position they may hold. Do not be vexatious or selfish for personal attention, but be humbly satisfied with your rank and financial gains in life. As well, be a better example to others by showing more faith, loyalty, and worthy actions towards God and life around you. Remember that pride can destroy a soul, whereas leading a sensible life nourishes the soul!

**OAT** (see **GRAIN**)

**OATH** (see **PROMISE**)

**OATMEAL** (see **FOOD**)

**OBEDIENCE**
Obeying something good and worthy within a dream state suggests that you are an outgoing individual or an introverted individual who inwardly panics and wilts when others tend to disagree with your concepts and ideas. Your self-imposed complexes and other personal hang-ups have deterred you from mixing calmly and soundly with small or large groups of people. Overcome your attitude by slowly realizing that you are basically no different or less unique than anyone else. Everyone on earth has some fears, faults, and personal hang-ups which they tend to bottle or display, from time to time. When you reach out to someone or to a group of people, always remember to be honest and sincere. Nobody will bite you, so do not be afraid to say what you feel, even if everyone happens to disagree with you, from time to time. Can you honestly say you agree with everyone all the time?
Obeying something evil, bad, or unworthy in a dream suggests that you may very well be an outgoing individual or an introverted individual who is easily led or swayed by unwholesome people. Do not let the outward appearance of someone deceive you! Not all people on this planet are sincere and honest. This dream counsels you to be more prudent, objective, and wise in your dealings with those whom you meet and greet and with those in whom you confide.

**OBELISK** (i.e., a four-sided tapering pillar whose top is like a pyramid)
You appear to be receiving some headstrong opposition from someone who finds your latest wish or desire to be more of a pipe

dream than a possible reality. Unfortunately, this dream does reveal that you are presently overshadowed by past mistakes and losses, thus leaving your credibility somewhat in doubt. Do not be too quick to gamble your time and someone's financing or blessing unless you, too, are now absolutely prepared to back up your side of the bargain. There is plenty of hope with this dream, providing you are sincerely willing to be persistent, courageous, practical, and completely honest with your new-found aim or goal. This time, do not squander your worth, but prove it—not only to yourself, but to others as well.

## OBITUARY

Seeing or reading an obituary intimates that you are conscience-stricken over some past or present action which seems to have involved you versus someone you know now or someone who has passed away. In essence, you feel guilty, ashamed, or sad for not making some peace or amends for whatever happened. So, what on earth should stop you from doing so now? If the person involved is still alive, then approach this person with human friendship so that at least some satisfaction or forgiveness comes your way. If the person involved has already passed away, then pray to God for forgiveness and for the well-being of that soul who was supposedly affected by you. Then, after you have made your peace, go forward in life with the firm belief that you have become wiser through this experience.

**OBJECTION** (see **COMPLAINER, CONTRADICTION,** or **HATRED**)

**OBLIGATION** (see **CONTRACT, PROMISE,** or **RESPONSIBILITY**)

**OBOE** (see **INSTRUMENT**)

**OBSCENITY** (see **IMMORALIST, LOW-MINDEDNESS, PORNOGRAPHY,** or **SEX**)

**OBSERVATION** (see **INSPECTION**)

## OBSERVATORY

Emotionally, mentally, and spiritually you are a very sound individual with enough self-esteem to carry you to limitless horizons on this earth plane. Your intelligence and actions are admirable! This dream simply compliments you for just being an outstanding individual whose assigned purpose on earth seems to be carried out with diligence and outstanding skill.

**OBSESSION** (i.e., preoccupation with an idea, wish, hope, person) (see *also* **MONOMANIA** or **POSSESSION**)

If you are in fact obsessed with something while awake, then it is very likely that you will dream about these same obsessions while asleep. Should your mind preoccupations be of a mild nature, then you probably have very little to worry about. However, should your mind preoccupations be centered upon out-of-control matters or negative, false, or evil matters, then indeed you are in a very serious mental bind. Being overly obsessed with anything in life can bring you trouble unless you have the wisdom and foresight to let go while you are still ahead in the game. If you are unable to snap out of your mental fixation or bind on your own, then you are strongly urged to seek professional help or guidance.

**OBSTRUCTION**

Some people are afraid of facing their obstacles, not only during their dream state, but during their wake state, as well. However, there are countless people who master their obstacles with great insight and endurance. An obstruction within a dream merely poses a challenge to you. Do you accept the challenge by doing something about it, or do you somehow reject the challenge by doing nothing about it? If you master the obstacle in front of you, then you certainly have your feet planted firmly on the ground, and you know exactly what you hope to attain in life. Should you fail to master an obstacle, then in many ways you are a defeatist, complainer, or procrastinator. The heartaches of your existence are pretty well self-induced. Unless you are willing to apply more logic and self-assertiveness along your way, your successes and happiness will continue to be limited and stifled.

**OCCASION** (see **CELEBRATION**)

**OCCUPATION** (see **CALLING, CAREER, EMPLOYMENT, LIFEWORK,** or **OWNERSHIP**)

**OCEAN** (see **WATER**)

**OCEANARIUM** (see **AQUARIUM**)

**OCEANOGRAPHY** (see **INSPECTION** or **WATER**)

**OCTOPUS** (see **MOLLUSK**)

**ODOUR** (see **SMELL**)

**OFFENSE** (see **ANGER** or **RUDENESS**)

**OFFERING** (see **GIFT**)

**OFFICE** (see **EMPLOYMENT** or **OWNERSHIP**)

**OFFICER** (see **AIR FORCE, ARMY, NAVY, LEADERSHIP,** or **PEACE OFFICER**)

**OFFICIAL** (see **CORONER, JUDGE, GOVERNOR, MAYOR, OMBUDSMAN, PRIME MINISTER, PRESIDENT,** or **SECRETARY**)

**OFFSPRING** (see **DAUGHTER, SON,** or **STEPCHILD**)

**OFFSTAGE** (i.e., the wings of a stage not visible to the public)
Recently, you have not been totally honest and sincere where your feelings are concerned. Nobody wants to hear incomplete truths or false flattery! This dream counsels you not to camouflage the unlimited goodness and wisdom that is within you. You obviously know better, but you seem to be masking or blemishing the truth perhaps to avoid hurting someone's feelings, pride, or ego. "Let the truth be known" is the best policy to uphold and by which to live. Do this gently and wisely; and you may be amazed at the positive response you will receive!

**OGRE** (see **GIANT** or **MONSTER**)

**OIL** (see **FUEL** or **LUBRICANT**)

**OIL WELL** (see **DERRICK** or **HOLE**)

**OINTMENT** (see **COSMETIC** or **MEDICATION**)

**OLD AGE**

Dreaming about old age could imply any one or several of the following definitions: A) that you are an elderly person who accepts this fact of life with calmness and ease; or B) that you are an elderly person who does not accept this fact of life with calmness and ease; or C) that you wish you could turn the clock back in order to start all over again; or D) that if you had your way, you would never want to grow old at all; or E) that you admire elderly people very much and wish that they had a greater voice within your society; or F) that you do not get along with old people and have very little respect for their knowledge and wisdom; or G) that you know of several people who disrespect their elderly parents; or H) that you would never do anything to annoy, disappoint, or upset the elderly people within your society; or I) that your job or career is to serve elderly people; or J) that you would like to see greater integration plans between old age homes and orphanages so that everyone could mingle with one another in order to feel more needed, wanted, and—above all—loved; or K) that this dream has little or no relevance to you at this time.

**OLD TESTAMENT** (see **BIBLE** or **GENESIS**)

**OLIVE** (see **FRUIT**)

**OLYMPIC GAMES** (see **COMPETITION** or **GAME**)

**OMBUDSMAN** (see *also* **INQUIRY**)

Seeing or being an ombudsman within a dream intimates that you or someone very close to you is ignoring a task, a duty, or some legal matters that require attention. If you are not careful, this oversight could set you back emotionally and financially at a later date. Perhaps you or someone close to you is planning to make a will but has for some reason put this plan aside, or perhaps some debt or tax matters are being ignored, and so forth. Whatever it might be, consider this dream a reminder to do something now in order to save yourself much grief down the road.

**OMELET** (see **EGG** or **FOOD**)

**OMEN** (see **FOREWARNING** or **PROPHECY**)

**OMNIPOTENCE** (see **GOD**)

**OMNIPRESENCE** (see **GOD**)

**OMNISCIENCE** (see **GOD**)

**ONION** (see **FOOD** or **PLANT**)

**ONLOOKER** (see **SPECTATOR**)

**OPENER** (see **UTENSIL**)

**OPERA**
Being highly intelligent is indeed one of your foremost trademarks. However, your boredom and impatience often give rise to anger and snobbish attitudes. You have refined and developed a shallow technique which seems to work for you, but certainly not for others around you. Whatever happened to down-to-earth courtesy and kindness? Remember that you are defeating your own purpose when you make other people sad and miserable around you; for then you are, in effect, making yourself more sad and miserable! A new aim and a better understanding of yourself are required before you can even hope to regain the respect you so richly deserve. Change your inner world, and your outer world will change for you!

**OPERA GLASSES** (see **BINOCULAR**)

**OPERA HOUSE** (see **OPERA**)

**OPERATION** (see **SURGERY**)

**OPERETTA** (see **OPERA**)

**OPINION** (see **NOTION**)

**OPPOSITION** (see **CONTRADICTION** or **ENEMY**)

**OPPRESSION** (see **DICTATOR** or **PERSECUTION**)

503                                                                                 *orator*

**OPTIMISM** (see **HOPEFULNESS**)

**OPTION**

Having a distinct option or choice within a dream suggests that you are finding it extremely difficult to make a decision concerning two people, two places, or two things. However difficult your task may appear to be, your dream reveals that you will inevitably make the right decision, though not necessarily overnight. Take your time, and the results will lead you towards happier times and greater fulfillments than you could even imagine. As well, this dream symbolism advises you to keep up your charitable objectives, your good work habits, and other talents which make you an exemplary citizen.

**OPTOMETRIST**

You will begin to work things out for yourself, providing you maintain a sensible, confident outlook. Do not be careless or overly pompous; otherwise, you could ruin your chances of fulfilling a deep and earnest desire to fulfill a long-awaited goal. Go each step of the way with a clear, positive mind so that this second chance will bring you the better world you seek.

**ORACLE** (see **CLAIRVOYANCE, MEDIUM,** or **PROPHECY**)

**ORANGE** (see **FRUIT**)

**ORANGUTAN** (see **APE**)

**ORATOR** (i.e., public speaker)

Any one or several of the following definitions may be applicable: A) that you are, in fact, a public speaker whose dream merely projects your likes or dislikes in what you do; or B) that from a personal point of view, you would be afraid to speak in front of a small or large group of people; or C) that you did speak in front of a body of people one time but felt very uneasy and unsure of yourself at the time; or D) that you know of someone who is an orator; or E:) that you recently had an opportunity to see and hear an orator; or F) that you feel you are not qualified to speak in front of a group of people; or G) that you would like to be an orator someday because of the work you do now or the work you intend to do in the future; or H) that this dream has little or no significance to you at this time.

**ORBIT** (i.e., the pathway taken by a heavenly body, satellite, or spacecraft around another heavenly body)

Seeing this spectacle within a dream truly augurs good news for the dreamer. A great gift or reward will be bestowed upon you shortly or in time to come. When the time does come (even if you feel this honour may be thirty years too soon or thirty years too late), it will nonetheless be appreciated, not only by you, but by others who know you well and who admire your kindness and worthy efforts.

## ORCHARD

Do not waste your precious time on hearsay, nor be influenced by mundane distractions and other shortcomings of those around you. You have better things to accomplish! You are a highly intelligent person capable of carrying out a plan or project without any outside interferences, disappointments, and trivialities. Follow the truth, and lead your own personal life with gratitude, fixity of purpose, and endurance for others to follow.

## ORCHESTRA

This dream advises you not to go beyond your worldly capabilities and expectations, otherwise pleasant situations can change overnight for you, and financial or material gains can be lost through foolish ventures and investments. This does not necessarily imply that you should turn your back on something that appears to be promising; just remember that not everything you do will turn out prosperous and successful. Sift, investigate, research, and reflect upon those plans, projects, or transactions which you feel you can handle instead of jumping headfirst into something you may later regret. In other words, show more restraint, common sense, and humility in all your earthly endeavours so that you may continue to grow and prosper wisely.

## ORDAINMENT

Any one or several of the following definitions may be applicable: A) that you were recently ordained into the priesthood; or B) that you know of someone who was recently ordained as a minister, priest, or rabbi; or C) that you would like to be ordained into the ministry someday; D) that you know of someone who would like to be ordained into the ministry; or E) that you get along with your clergyman; or F) that you do not get along with your clergyman at this time;

or G) that you recently read an article or book pertaining to ordination; or H) that this dream has little or no relevance to you at this time.

## ORE

Be more content with what you have, and be more sure about what you want. These are confident avenues of thought you should always pursue. Chasing rainbows and pipe dreams may be fulfilling to some people, but certainly most people have the insight and intelligence to know better. Study your thoughts and motives with greater spiritual insight so that you can recognize your wants and needs with greater control and foresight. You cannot have everything in life, but you certainly can attain many things—providing you settle down with sensible initiatives rather than scattered, nebulous initiatives.

## ORGAN (see INSTRUMENT)

## ORGAN GRINDER

If the organ grinder looks relatively peaceful and happy, then you can be sure that your courage and faith will carry you through some difficult situation which you happen to be experiencing at this time. The problem may, in fact, involve someone else more than it involves you. However, you do have a tendency to over-worry about everyone; in the long run, this is neither wise nor wholesome. Be at peace, for times are changing for you. Hopefully, you will begin to change a little bit with the times.

Seeing an organ grinder who is sad or hopeless or who appears completely out of touch with the work that he does intimates that everything appears to be getting progressively worse for you, rather than better. It is during these times that you should be drawing closer to God with your heart and soul instead of complaining about certain situations not to your liking. Do not be blinded by hopelessness when, in fact, you have been through similar situations in the past, and you mastered the situations most proficiently. Do not be narrow-minded either, at this time; rather, be open-minded and hopeful about your better tomorrows.

## ORGANIZATION (e.g., club, union, society)

Any one or several of the following definitions may be applicable: A) that you are presently content or discontent with an organization in which you are a member; or B) that you would like to join an organization before too long; or C) that you recently quit an organization due to some problems with its members; or D) that you have recently been elected or appointed to a high ranking post in an organization; or E) that you feel you could not possibly belong to any organization, for some reason; or F) that you are far too preoccupied with your own life and that joining an organization at this time would be tantamount to burning the candle at both ends; or G) that you feel most organizations are too biased, self-seeking, or politically minded for you to even think of belonging to one; or H) that you are neither a leader nor a follower and simply could not see yourself as belonging to any group whatsoever; or I) that this dream has little or no relevance to you at this time.

## ORGANIZER

Any one or several of the following definitions may be applicable: A) that you are, in fact, an organizer; or B) that you are not an organizer; or C) that you have a lot of courage and dynamic enthusiasm to become an organizer; or D) that you are a very orderly, organized individual who has more leadership potential than you care to admit; or E) that although you are a quick, systematic, and organized thinker, you could not possibly see yourself becoming involved in some historic cause, union, or organization; or F) that you would be delighted to be an organizer of great things in order to make life on this planet more peaceful and loving; or G) that you are a very unsettled individual who is totally disorganized, but you do envy anyone who has the ability to be a good organizer; or H) that you are having enough trouble organizing your own life; or I) that you feel far too many organizers tend to be biased, opinionated, or simply too unjust in their dealings with people; or J) that you are neither a leader nor a follower, at the best of times, so that you could not possibly see yourself as an organizer of anything or anyone; or K) that this dream has little or no relevance to you at this time.

## ORGASM (see **INTERCOURSE, MASTURBATION,** or **SEX**)

## ORGY (see *also* **SEX**)

Any one or several of the following definitions may be applicable: A) that you do, in fact, participate in sexual orgies; or B) that you do not, and would not ever, participate in this type of sexual activity; or

C) that you know of someone who has been to an orgy; or D) that you feel sexual orgies are no more and no less than base attitudes of depraved minds; or E) that you feel sexual orgies are both mentally invigorating and sexually stimulating to most people you know; or F) that you feel there is nothing wrong with an orgy, providing there is no harm done to anyone; or G) that you feel this form of sexual activity is not wholesome to the mind, body, or soul of anyone, but rather reveals the base outlook one has towards sex and towards true intimacy and affection between two loving people; or H) that anyone participating in this type of sexual activity is either a slave to their sexual desires and lusts or else is incapable of maintaining a satisfying relationship with one person; or I) that orgies may outwardly appear to give you sexual freedom, but inwardly entrap you with shame, guilt, sadness, and anguish; or J) that this dream has little or no significance to you at this time.

**ORNAMENTATION** (see **DECORATION**)

**ORPHAN**

If you are, in fact, an orphan, then your dream is merely reflecting upon your present state of being. No matter how difficult life may appear to you at this time, you still have the courage and faith to make your todays and tomorrows more fulfilling and greater than ever before. Should this not be applicable to you, then this dream intimates that sometimes you feel neglected, alone, and abandoned by those whom you truly love and admire. This symbolism shows that, although you may have these thoughts from time to time, you are still loved and admired. Whenever you feel left out, not listened to, or not heeded, for some reason, simply realize that the people who tend to ignore you just may be too busy to realize the effects of their attitude upon you. Talk to those who affect you so that some long-lasting compromises may be achieved. Indeed, they will be if and when you decide to share your true feelings in this matter.

**ORPHANAGE**

Any one or several of the following definitions may be applicable: A) that you are presently in an orphanage; or B) that you were in an orphanage many years ago; or C) that you know someone who is presently in an orphanage; or D) that you often contribute towards the welfare and well-being of an orphanage in your town or city; or E) that you work at an orphanage and enjoy your work very much; or F) that you feel an orphanage and an old age home should be side by side so that together there could be more mingling, appreciation, and love between young people and old people; or G) that you feel your government does not give enough assistance to orphans when, in fact, it should; or H) that many people who once stayed in an orphanage became very prominent and wealthy in their own right; or I) that it is still consoling to know that there are places like orphanages which can offer homeless children shelter, food, and education; or, J) that you read an article or book about an orphanage quite recently; or K) that this dream has little or no relevance to you at this time.

## OSCAR (i.e., Academy award)

Seeing or holding an Oscar within a dream state could very well imply that you are, in fact, in the entertainment business and that you have already received one, would like one, or feel you have an excellent chance of receiving this honour in time to come. However, if this is not applicable to you, then this symbolism implies that you are a very creative and inventive individual who certainly may reach the heights of success in the future. Who knows, maybe you are destined to achieve an Oscar or equivalent recognition for something you will yet do in life. Nothing is impossible. If you do not believe this, just ask someone who has already received an outstanding award!

## OSTRICH (see BIRD)

## OTTER

An otter represents sudden and drastic changes that could be either beneficial or disappointing to you (e.g., a promotion, a new job offer, losing a job, having to vacate your premises). Be careful! The winds are blowing from every direction, so you never know if a storm is brewing or whether this gust of wind is short-lived. Be highly optimistic at this time, but also be very cautious, levelheaded, and prepared for whatever ups and downs happen to come your way. Basically, you have the stability and courage to go forward, so if anything not to your liking happens within the next several days, just do your best to maintain a calm, cool, and collected attitude. Always bear in mind that you are a winner in life, not a loser—no matter what happens!

**OUIJA** (i.e., a device, supposedly used to contact souls from the other side of life, consisting of a planchette and an alphabet board with certain signs and symbols)

Any one or several of the following definitions may be applicable: A) that you do, in fact, have a Ouija board; or B) that you do not have a Ouija board simply because you do not believe in this device; or C) that you know of someone who does have a Ouija board; or D) that you recently read an article or book about Ouija boards; or E) that you feel anyone playing around with this board could be in for more trouble than they realize; or F) that someone around you is telling you half truths and half lies; or G) that you are telling someone half truths and half lies; or H) that you intend to buy a Ouija board before too long; or I) that quite recently you were playing with a Ouija board with little or no results, or with good results; or J) that this dream has little or no relevance to you at this time.

(*Note*: A Ouija board is considered very dangerous in many more ways than one! People buy this device with the hopes of communicating with a departed soul or just for the sake of entertainment. Well, they may be communicating with someone on the other side of life but, unbeknownst to them, it is not the soul they wish to contact. This force or soul working through the Ouija board is highly deceptive and is, without a doubt, situated in the nether regions, or hell state, on the other side of life. Yes, this so-called base soul can give you some of the answers you seek, but there will come a time when it becomes totally obnoxious, blasphemous, and possessive. Here, then, is where the trouble starts; an obsession can then become a possession! A Ouija board is not wholesome, spiritual, or worthy of anyone's valuable time, money, or efforts. Avoid this board like you would a plague; for, indeed, it can be considered a plague to the heart, mind, and soul of anyone foolish enough to believe otherwise!)

**OUTCAST** (see **BANISHMENT** or **NONPERSON**)

**OUTER SPACE**

You are very intelligent, serious-minded, and somewhat of an eccentric; this all adds up to a unique, gifted individual! There are many times when you feel as though you do not belong to this planet, or you may feel "spaced out" because of your novel thoughts and actions. You do belong to Earth; but, in many ways, you are ahead of your time! Your inner capabilities should lead you to inestimable heights of success and prosperity in time to come. Outer space may be beautiful and overpowering to the eyes and mind of the beholder; however, your inner space is just as challenging and awesome to behold!

## OUTHOUSE

Seeing an outhouse indicates that your self-esteem is at its lowest ebb. Your self-imposed loneliness and hopelessness are useless feelings, not worthy of your time and labour! Something is bothering you that could involve your appearance, speech, height, weight, or anything else that might place you in a despairing state of mind. Essentially, you have allowed yourself to be overpowered by what you believe or hear about yourself. If you are generally happy the way you are, then never mind what other people think, say, or do. If you are not happy with the way you are, then it is up to you to correct or modify your problem. You have been given a powerful lance in life, called free will, to do with as you see fit. Use it comfortably and wisely!

## OUTLAW (see CRIMINAL)

## OUTPATIENT (see PATIENT)

## OUTPOST (i.e., a military base stationed away from the home country)

It appears that far too many people around you (with sincere intentions, mind you) are telling you what to do with your life rather than giving you a fair chance to prove yourself one way or another. When God handed out talents in life, He did not expect everyone to become a blacksmith, or a doctor, or a farmer. On the contrary! All people are unique upon this planet and should be allowed to pursue what they are best suited to accomplish within their lifetime. You are no exception to the rule. If you must prove yourself, then indeed you will!

## OVATION (see APPLAUSE)

## OVEN

Be wary! Someone intends to bring up a topic about your past which could surprise, disappoint, or humiliate you. If you handle this matter with sincerity and diplomacy, you will succeed in dealing with this so-called busybody for all time. Unfortunately, busybodies do not see themselves as being troublesome or officious people but see themselves as open-minded, inquisitive people. In many respects, they are inwardly incapable of handling their own lives. As well, they often can handle criticizing others, but cannot handle criticism when directed at them; they can "dish it" but can't "take it".

**OVERALLS** (see **CLOTHING**)

**OVERCAST** (see **CLOUD**)

**OVERPASS** (see **BRIDGE** or **PASSAGEWAY**)

**OVERPRINT** (see **OVERWRITE**)

**OVERWORK**
      Any one or several of the following definitions may be applicable: A) that you are presently overworked; or B) that you are not presently overworked; or C) that you feel guilty because someone seems to be overworking on your behalf; or D) that you know of someone who does tend to work too hard, but no amount of persuasion can convince this person to rest or take a holiday; or E) that someone in your family worked too hard and is now quite ill; or F) that someone you know died of a heart attack because of overwork; or G) that you feel your work is very hard, but no one seems to care one way or another; or H) that no matter how hard you work, you are never given a raise, a rest, or a praise for the work that you do; or I) that you will quit your job before too long unless more help is received for the amount of work you have to do; or J) that you cannot tolerate employers who overwork and underpay employees; or K) that your job is to see that employees are treated fairly by their employers; or L) that you became very sick because of overwork, and now you have no choice but to slow down or else your heart or some other internal organ will simply give way; or M) that you do not mind a person doing your work for you simply because you are somewhat lazy and uncaring; or N) that you do not mind a person assisting you once in a while, but you would never use a person to do all your work for you; or O) that this dream has little or no relevance for you at this time.

**OVERWRITE** (i.e., to write over other writing)

To overwrite anything written or printed within a dream state reveals that you are either covering up for someone's wrongdoing, or you are trying to conceal your own wrongdoing from someone. You stand to lose on both counts! Sooner or later, the truth will be revealed, but not necessarily by you. The sad situation here is that when this does happen, your honesty and integrity will be in grave doubts for a long time thereafter. By making your wrongs into rights now, you could alter this revelation to your benefit and well-being. The choice is up to you!

**OWL** (see **BIRD**)

**OWNERSHIP**

Owning something within a dream state merely suggests that you wish to expand or increase your present prosperity (e.g., adding a new section to your present home, building another home, setting up a branch office to expand your present business). Your intentions are very sincere. Obviously, you are setting out to accomplish what you have planned to do for quite some time. No doubt you will do whatever your heart desires—and much, much more.

**OXYGEN TENT**

Seeing or being in an oxygen tent indicates that someone very close to you may have an allergy or two, and/or you may hear of someone being under an oxygen tent before too long. Where allergies are concerned, it appears that you may be living under some dry or damp atmospheric conditions which may be causing you a great deal of discomfort. Seeking medical attention in this matter would certainly be of help to you. Regarding the second definition, it appears that the person under the oxygen tent will recuperate. God, of course, will have the final word in this matter.

**OYSTER** (see **MOLLUSK**)

**PABLUM** (see **FOOD**)

**PACEMAKER** (i.e., a device implanted in the body to assist the beat of the heart)

You could very well be using a pacemaker. If so, then your dream is merely revealing this fact. However, should this not be applicable to you, then your dream indicates that you go from day to day just being grateful for being alive and well. You are a sure-footed, mature individual who accepts life for what it has to offer rather than becoming upset over every little problem that happens to come your way. This down-to-earth philosophy is both commendable and wholesome; it will no doubt carry you through years of significant betterment and peace.

**PACIFIER** (see **NIPPLE**)

**PACKAGE** (e.g., a parcel)
Good news from a distance is foretold in seeing a package within a dream. Also, before too long, you will be abandoning some plan or project for another which will turn out quite favorably for you.

**PACKET** (see **PACKAGE**)

**PACKING**
Packing something (e.g., a suitcase, box, trunk) suggests that you need more time to think things over to avoid making any rash, hasty, or foolish decisions. You may not be the happiest person on earth, but that is for you to remedy and solve, providing you are willing to do so. You are strongly advised to face some hard facts about yourself and about those around you before you decide to do something regrettably inconsistent with your better mind and judgment. Common sense should be your earthly guide at all times!

**PACKSACK**
Being more fair, compromising, and forgiving in your relationships with other people will allow you to realize that you cannot always have your own way. Life with all its blessings and tribulations should teach you that two wrongs do not make a right! Release your grudges, mind threats, or anger to the wind, for these negative thoughts are unworthy of your being. You may not have your way today because of someone's decision on your behalf; by the same token, another time will come when your wants, needs, or desires will be fulfilled to you. Be very patient with yourself and with others, for in so being, greater times and events can come to pass.

**PACKSADDLE** (see **SADDLE**)

## PACK TRAIN

Someone or something is bothering you. Do not press any panic buttons! Today you may want to grumble and complain about your problem(s), but tomorrow you may have an entirely different perspective, where these matters are concerned. In life you will come across obstacles which you must sift through and sort out until your mind is refueled with renewed strength and hope and a greater desire to move forward. Far too often people act impulsively, only to recognize their folly later on. Things have a way of working out right, providing you have the foresight and logic to recognize this possibility.

**PAD** (e.g., ink pad, stamp pad, writing pad, shoulder pad, seat pad)

Your confidence and courage have carried you through some bitter and trying storms; this reveals your winning attitude and character. Your future holds more promising interests and challenges ahead for you; however, this time you will fulfill one to two goals which will give you great satisfaction and profitable recognition. Always remember, though, that it is your hard work, your headstrong perseverance, and your ultimate belief in self and in what you do that will give you the realistic progress you so earnestly desire. There are no detours on this highway you are taking; it is long, straight, and narrow!

**PADDLE** (see **OAR**)

**PADDLE WHEEL** (see **BOAT**)

**PADLOCK** (see **LOCK**)

**PAGEANT** (see **PARADE** or **THEATRE**)

**PAGODA** (see **CHURCH**)

## PAIL

A pail indicates your intentions to begin something new in your life. This could involve graduating from a college and starting your career for the very first time, or getting married, or writing a book, or just about anything that you intend to accomplish for the very first time. There is happiness and a great deal of prosperity with this dream, providing your intentions are sincere, sensible, and honourable.

Kicking or dropping a pail symbolically describes your inner desires to be understood, to be accepted, and to have more loving communication with those around you. As well, you would like to pursue what you want to do in life, not what someone suggests, demands, or expects from you. You have enough ambition, talent, and fortitude to do whatever your heart desires, and you probably will, in many ways! In the interim, however, try to understand that not all people around you totally fathom your inner plans and aims. In fact, some people feel that you are going over your head or that you are fantasizing about what you hope for or wish to attain in life. Do not let others upset you. Simply recognize what you are capable of mastering within your own lifetime, and humbly set out to do so!

**PAIN** (see **ANGUISH, BACKACHE, BIRTH, BRUISE, CRUELTY, DISAPPOINTMENT, EARACHE, HEADACHE, INJURY, PERSECUTION, PREY, PUNISHMENT, SICKNESS,** or **TEETH**)

**PAINKILLER** (see **ANESTHETIC, ANTIDOTE,** or **MEDICATION**)

**PAINTBRUSH** (see **BRUSH**)

**PAINTER** (i.e., an artist who paints pictures)
    Painting pictures within a dream state shows your inner need to be in total command of yourself, at all times. However, you have a knack for creating demands and venting your frustrations on others, as well. Some people take you seriously; others who know you quite well simply take you with a grain of salt and perhaps a chuckle or two. You certainly are a person with a tremendous amount of vitality, sensibility, and reliability. You can accomplish many great things in your lifetime, if that is your true aim or purpose. On the other side of the spectrum, you can be just as happy and content leading a normal and natural existence.

**PAINTING** (i.e., a picture already painted, or the act of covering homes, fences, walls, furniture, and other surfaces with paint, varnish, or other substances)
    You are harboring many fears, prejudices and farfetched ideas, which should be dispelled. It appears that your upbringing has had such a traumatic effect upon your being that to even consider the pos-

sibility of change would be a miracle in itself. You are set in your ways; and, no matter what someone suggests, you are not about to listen to anyone but yourself. Even if you make countless mistakes and complain in the process, this experience will not alter either your thinking or your actions. Your overly practical views and insight are those realities you must live with, but it would be nice, on occasion, to be a bit more reasonable and understanding where other views and philosophies are concerned.

## PALACE

Your instincts to go that extra mile in whatever you do will never leave you simply because you were always meant to plod onwards with faith, curiosity, and an eagerness to learn. Such is the quest of your mind and soul whose worth is far more precious than all the things wealth could possibly buy.

The palace you saw within your dream state is the palace you harbour within your soul; it is indeed a mighty fortress of love, compassion, and courage. It is obvious that you will accomplish many fine things within your lifetime simply because you care enough to seek, to find, and to ultimately master your quests slowly but surely and one at a time!

## PALATE (see MOUTH)

## PALETTE (i.e., a small board used by an artist to mix paint colors)

There is something very special you would like to do which you seem to be harbouring in the back of your mind. However, you also seem to be putting this goal or aim aside because of some minor excuse, phobia, or qualm. Perhaps you are afraid of failing—or maybe you are afraid of succeeding? At this point in time, you would be wise to seriously scrutinize your thoughts and ideas with a greater amount of self-examination and determination. You can succeed in your innermost wishes and good desires, providing you put them into practice. Until then, no amount of wishful thinking will get you there.

## PALETTE KNIFE (see KNIFE)

## PALM (see HAND)

## PALMISTRY (see FORTUNETELLER)

**PALSY** (see **PARALYSIS**)

**PAMPHLET** (see **BOOK**)

**PANCAKE** (see **FOOD**)

**PANE** (see **WINDOW**)

**PANELIST**

Being or seeing a panelist implies that you are a shrewd, demanding, and self-centered individual. These habitual qualities you harbour are not wholesome, nor will they give you the humility or integrity towards which you should be striving. There is absolutely nothing wrong with your intelligence or your innovative ideas, for that matter; what is bothersome is your choice of methods and tactics! Everyone around you has something to offer, no matter who that person may be; the sooner you realize this, the better off you will be. Truly, you have a better role to play on this planet. Do not thrust your will upon others; compromise, harmonize, and begin to follow a more noble truth towards God, yourself, your loved ones, and your fellow man, as a whole. For your sake, do not waste your time and efforts on selfish behaviour. You should be setting a good example for everyone concerned!

**PANIC** (see **CONFUSION, DANGER, HYSTERIA,** or **STARTLE**)

**PANTRY** (see *also* **CELLAR**)

It appears that no matter how hard you try to say or do something really worthwhile, everything just seems to rebound right back to you with negative results! Are you jinxed, or is there some black cloud over your head which simply refuses to dissipate? No, you are not jinxed, nor is there a black cloud over you. However, you are going through some bitter realities and lessons in life; these will clear up for you before too long. For the moment, hold on to your high ideals, pray, keep busy, and be very confident that your tomorrows will be better. Out of the darkness and shadows of your life, you will emerge stronger, wiser, and certainly more open-minded to the rewarding realities yet awaiting you. Be at peace, for the mighty lessons of life are like a raging wind which cannot stop until the hour, the moment, is ripe. Soon the hour and the moment will be ripe for you!

**PANTS** (see **CLOTHES**)

**PANTSUIT** (see **CLOTHES**)

**PANTY** (see **CLOTHES**)

**PAPERBACK** (see **BOOK**)

**PAPERBOY**
You are an enduring, patient, and reliable individual who will make bold guesses in life. These will take you to the pinnacle of your chosen profession and draw satisfaction, praise, and respect. Keep smiling; do not forget to compliment others along your way; never forget how to laugh and share joys with family, friends, and strangers; never judge or show envy towards anyone on this planet; concentrate on how to love and respect Holy Earth more; be a Solomon in your thoughts, actions, and deeds; and, never rule, control, or injure another soul for the sake of your ambitions. This dream symbolism brings you no quarrel at all; it simply brings you great peace and a few truths for you to consider.

**PAPER CUTTER**
Some truthful matter will be revealed to you before too long. If this truth causes you to blame, hate, ridicule, or throw tantrums, then you will create more trouble and anguish for yourself. However, if you maintain your own personal dignity and honour, no matter how embarrassing, painful, ridiculous, or horrendous this entire matter may appear to be, then you will continue to carry on with positive direction and courage.

**PAPER KNIFE** (see **KNIFE** or **PAPER CUTTER**)

**PAPERWEIGHT**
Seeing or using this device within a dream indicates that you have some very special talents, but you are failing to reveal these talents for fear of being ridiculed by others (e.g., a six-foot male writing a love poem, a woman overhauling a car engine,). It really should not matter what your good talents may be, as long as you are ready, willing, and able to fulfill that inner need for self and for the benefit of others around you. Thomas Edison did not invent the light bulb just for him-

self, nor did Van Gogh paint a masterpiece just for himself. These men and thousands like them throughout history performed magnificent feats for the world to behold and cherish—even though they, too, may have been mocked and jeered by less understanding people. Do not be afraid of sharing your special abilities with anyone, for God wants you to be unique and different! In spite of what others may say or think about you, be happy to be who you are. Never be ashamed to be who you are or what you can do in life.

## PARABLE (see *also* BIBLE)

Your mental, physical, and spiritual disappointments are mainly the results of your unfounded fears, phobias, and newly adopted cynical attitudes about life in general. Perhaps life has dealt you a blow or two, or perhaps you have been tried and tested to the limits; but it is during these trying times that your hope and faith should be the strongest! Do not disappoint yourself by simply letting yourself go or giving up in hopeless feelings, concepts, or other associated distortions within your life. Your pessimism is nothing more than a frightful glance at your todays, without even remotely perceiving the positive prospects of your tomorrows. Be very thankful to be alive and to be given so many opportunities to wake up to the possibilities within and around you. To invariably alter your lifestyle for the betterment of all concerned, you must do something about it—before it does something to you.

## PARACHUTE

An unopened, unused parachute (on the ground) implies that you and/or a loved one are on the verge of carrying out a plan or wish that will have long-lasting effects. The results will prove to be positive, rewarding, and profitable!

To see an opened parachute (on the ground or in the air) predicts a challenge in team work lies ahead for you. In other words, you and a few other people will be working together on a project or plan that will require ample brain work, long hours, and an abundance of harmony in order to master this forthcoming challenge. The end results will be very gratifying, providing everyone involved stays together and works together with the one main goal in mind.

To see a parachute that fails to open, either on the ground or in the air, implies that a vitally important decision you have to make may disappoint you in more ways than one. Perhaps you want to marry someone you are not sure about, or maybe you plan to move away to another state, province, or country, or maybe you intend to quit school, or anything else you are not sure about. Whatever it is, you are strongly advised not to be too hasty at this time; instead, hold off temporarily until you are more settled and sure about what you wish to do. Since others around you may be affected by your decision, it is wise to pause and think twice before you rush into something you may never be able to retract.

## PARADE

You are leaving yourself wide open to criticism from other people. Perhaps it is what you say or do that makes them wary of your presence? Even though you are a likeable person in many ways, you nonetheless often say the right things at the wrong time or the wrong things at the wrong time. Whatever the problem may be, you are strongly urged to look more closely at yourself where verbal outpourings and bad habits are concerned.

## PARADISE (see HEAVEN)

## PARAKEET (see BIRD)

## PARALLEL BARS

You appear to be praying for or wanting better physical health and more peace of mind. Sometimes when people pray for better physical health, they are healed in the mind and soul, instead; or when someone prays for some deep-rooted mind or soul problem, they appear to be cured of a bodily problem, instead. No matter how God sees fit to cure you or help you, you must always be grateful for His Light upon you; and, above all else, you must learn to be calm and patient upon His Time, His Hour to cure or help you. A deep-felt prayer is like a golden, sealed letter to God; what you ask for, or what you give, should always reflect love, humility, and unembellished truth!

## PARALYSIS

Any one or several of the following definitions may be applicable: A) that you are paralyzed; or B) that you are not paralyzed but do feel very sad for anyone who might be; or C) that you know of someone who is paralyzed but, because this person is so mentally active, you can hardly notice the handicap; or D) that you are presently looking after someone who is paralyzed; or E) that someday you would like to help or work with people who are paralyzed; or F) that you often wonder what it would be like to be on a planet without sickness, disease, pain, etc.; or G) that you have often complained about many things in the past, but today your outlook is totally different, and you are so grateful for having a sound mind and body; or H) that for some reason, you have little or no respect towards people who are paralyzed; or I) that someday you hope man will create or invent a cure for anyone who is paralyzed; or J) that this dream has little or no relevance to you at this time.

## PARAMEDIC

It is up to you to make a clear distinction between who has your best interests at heart and who does not. If some people are taking advantage of your loyalty and kindness, then you must be honest with them by letting them know exactly how you feel. Be gentle but firm so that matters between you and these people can be more harmoniously settled. Remember, there are some people who will always try to take what they can, rather than give what they can, for jealous or selfish reasons. Luckily, most people do not act this way! In most instances, you should be able to trust people around you; but be wary, for there are always those small-minded individuals who only care about themselves.

## PARAMOUR (see **AFFAIR** or **MISTRESS**)

**PARANOIA** (i.e., condition characterized by delusions of grandeur or persecution complex)

If you suffer from paranoia during your wake state, you could very well see yourself behaving in a paranoid manner in you dream. The strife you hold within yourself can only be resolved by dispelling it from your life. You can create all types of horror stories, fantasies, or fixations within your mind, but the important thing is to replace these thoughts with some other activities. Unfortunately, you may be very self-centered and simply refuse to think of anyone else or anything else but yourself. This dream counsels you to pray, to keep very busy with different activities, and to begin to perceive life more openly, rather than believe in the untruths of your mind. If your problem seems too big for you to handle, then by all means seek professional help with the prime idea of listening to good advice, not ignoring it. There is ample hope for you, providing you are ready, willing, and able to change.

**PARAPSYCHOLOGY** (i.e., psychological investigation of psychic phenomena)

Any one or several of the following definitions may be applicable: A) that you are a parapsychologist whose work is far more interesting than people might believe; or B) that you are not a parapsychologist but certainly believe in the unknown forces of life; or C) that you would like to deal with parapsychology, in time to come; or D) that you are presently taking a course or two in parapsychology; or E) that you recently read a book or an article on parapsychology and found it to be interesting yet frightening, believable and yet incredible; or F) that you know someone who is a parapsychologist; or G) that you visited a haunted home a long time ago; or H) that your home appears to be haunted; or I) that you are a psychic who has the ability to hear or see souls from the other side of life; or J) that you often see things other people cannot see, or you hear voices other people cannot hear, and this either troubles you or fascinates you; or K) that a neighbour or a friend has had ghost or poltergeist problems at home; or L) that you believe almost anything is possible on earth, even though you personally have had no unusual or strange experiences in life; or M) that you have several psychic photographs in your possession now; or N) that you have the "psychic thumb", which allows you to take psychic photographs at random; or O) that a departed spirit once stood over your bed; or P) that you can astral travel or bilocate, or you know of someone who can; or Q) that you would like to levitate; or R) that this dream has little or no relevance to you at this time.

**PARASITE** (i.e., a person who lives at the expense of another individual without actually making any contribution in return, or an animal or plant that lives off another species) (see *also* **ANIMAL** or **PLANT**)

Seeing or being a human parasite could very well indicate that you or someone whom you know does behave in this manner of wanting something for nothing. However, if this does not apply, then this dream implies that you are dealing with someone who is very stubborn, demanding, and—at times—verbally abusive. The best advice shown here is for you not to feed this individual's ego with false statements or praises; if possible, advise this person to seek professional help. If this advice is refused, then perhaps you would be wise to seek some professional advice for yourself to at least help you understand why this person behaves this way.

Seeing an animal or plant parasite, on the other hand, suggests that a family member or someone else will want you to sign something or do something which you personally will not want to do. It appears that you will be given some great promises which you will not accept or believe. Your perception will be at an all-time high! This dream strongly urges you to hold your ground on such matters, otherwise you could be left with nothing more than the shirt on your back.

**PARASOL** (see **UMBRELLA**)

**PARCEL** (see **PACKAGE**)

**PARENT** (see **FATHER** or **MOTHER**)

**PARISH** (see **CHURCH**)

**PARK** (e.g., amusement park, ballpark, national park) (see *also* **PLAYGROUND**)

If the park you see is very natural and peaceful, then you will receive news or visitors from a distance, and/or you will send some good news via letter, telegram, telephone, or some other means to someone far away and travel a great distance, as well. In either case, there are emotional greetings and good tidings shown by this dream symbolism.

Seeing a park in shambles, or one that does not look natural in any manner, suggests that your efforts to understand or solve a present problem may be in vain. Trouble, by way of someone's possessiveness or indifference towards you, will continue to persist until some outside help is sought. It seems that a loved one would sooner be helped by a third party than by someone close to home—namely, you. Even if the third party gives this individual the same piece of advice you give, it just seems to sink in better when someone else reveals the same truths.

**PARKA** (see **CLOTHES**)

## PARKING LOT

A vacant parking lot signifies that you may be buying something very special, or you will be selling something very special in the near future (e.g., vehicle, boat, trailer, antique, home).

A parking lot with vehicles in it signifies a temporal financial setback due to overspending, mismanagement of funds, or loaning an excessive amount of money to someone who promised to pay you back. You will, however, come out of your setback just in the nick of time in order to settle your other wants, needs, or debts.

A parking lot in shambles suggests that you have had trouble with a vehicle, you will have trouble with a vehicle, or you know of someone who is having difficulties with a vehicle. In matters regarding your own vehicle, you are cautioned to be careful, otherwise you could have a vehicle breakdown when you least expect it.

## PARKING METER (see METER)

## PARLIAMENT (see GOVERNMENT)

## PARLOUR (e.g., beauty parlour, ice cream parlour) (see *also* HAIR, HAIRCUT, HAIRDRESSER, MANICURE, or MASSAGE)

Any one or several of the following definitions may be applicable: A) that you do work in a parlour of some kind; or B) that you do not work in a parlour but know of someone who does; or C) that you have plenty of self-esteem but lack the expertise in fulfilling something you would like to do or achieve; or D) that you have very little belief in yourself or others, for that matter; or E) that you have a personal problem or habit that is very difficult to eradicate due to your daily stresses and strains; or F) that you have a fear of being ostracized by others you work with or by some other people you happen to know; or G) that you often complain about something, but you fail to do anything about it; or H) that someone appears to be stopping you from progressing in life; or I) that you have mixed feelings about the people you happen to work with or about your work place as a whole; or J) that you wish to take an educational course or two in order to advance your status at work; or K) that this dream has little or no relevance to you at this time.

## PAROLE (see LIBERATION or PAROLEE)

**PAROLEE** (i.e., a person released from prison on condition of future good behaviour) (see *also* **REHABILITATION**)

Any one or several of the following definitions may be applicable: A) that you are, in fact, a parolee at this time; or B) that you are looking forward to being on parole before too long; or C) that you know of someone who is presently on parole; or D) that your life has taken you from bad to worse, for some reason or other; or E) that you have never received a fair break in your entire life and doubt very much whether you will; or F) that no one should be blamed for your troubles or problems in life but yourself; or G) that in spite of what people say or think, you know that you are innocent or guilty of some wrongdoing; or H) that you have been highly deceptive to some of your family members; or I) that some of your family members have not been treating you in a fair manner; or J) that sometimes you wish you were never born; or K) that someone tricked you into doing something you never wanted to do in the first place; or L) that you are not facing your realities in a down-to-earth, logical manner; or M) that your upbringing is the whole root of your hang-ups and problems; or N) that you accept life for what it is and now realize that you must change in order to be accepted and respected; or O) that you pray for courage and hope for better tomorrows; or P) that this dream has little or no relevance to you.

**PARROT** (see **BIRD**)

**PARSLEY** (see **FOOD** or **PLANT**)

**PARSNIP** (see **FOOD** or **PLANT**)

**PARTHENON** (see **TEMPLE**)

**PARTNERSHIP**

Any one or several of the following definitions may be applicable: A) that you are presently in a business partnership which you like or dislike; or B) that you have been asked to be a partner in some business but do not know whether to accept or refuse; or C) that you personally would never consider being a partner to anyone in any business arrangement, no matter how enticing the business prospects might seem to be; or D) that you know of several business partnerships that have failed due to economic reasons or simple misunderstandings;

or E) that you know of some partnerships that have been highly successful because of hard work, luck, and good, innovative ideas; or F) that you would sooner become a business partner to a good friend than to a relative; or G) that you are not in any financial position to consider any type of partnerships at this time or possibly in the future, for that matter; or H) that this dream has little or no significance to you at this time.

**PARTY** (see **CELEBRATION**)

**PARTY LINE** (see **TELEPHONE**)

**PASSAGEWAY** (i.e., a narrow place or room to move about, such as an aisle, corridor, hallway, mountain pass, underground passage, passage or underpass) (see *also* **ALLEY, ARCHWAY, BOARDWALK, BRIDGE, CANAL, CHECKPOINT, CROSS-ROAD, DETOUR, DITCH, HIGHWAY, ORBIT, PATH, RACE TRACK, RAMP, SHORTCUT, SIDEWALK, STREET, SUBWAY,** or **TUNNEL**)

You are a very daring person who has, it appears, taken far too many risks for your own good. However, such is the life of an adventurous spirit who cannot tolerate being unchallenged in some way. At this point, it seems that you need more time to yourself so that you can reaffirm your responsibilities and commitments in life. On the one hand, you would like to fly away to some exotic shore; on the other hand, you know that you may be facing a decision or two which may or may not be to your liking. No matter what obstacles you may be facing, you can be sure that your life will continue to offer you challenges you may find difficult to refuse. But this, then, is the life of an adventurous spirit. You may seem immature and inconsiderate to others, but to yourself you are no more and no less a person for wanting to see life in a realistic, raw, untamed sort of way.

**PASSENGER**

Whether you are a passenger on land, air, or water, this symbolism advises you to heed your better instincts where new ventures are concerned and/or where travel is concerned. If you feel good about what you want to do, or your inner instincts tell you to go for it, then by all means do so. However, if all signs and symbols within you tell you to back off, or you have great doubts about what you want to do, then you would be wise to postpone your plans, at least for a temporal period of time—until the dark clouds roll by! Many accidents, tragedies, and other losses have been averted by listening to that inner voice; right now you would be wise to do so!

## PASSION PLAY

Seeing a play that depicts the Passion of Jesus symbolizes the anguish you are presently experiencing, yourself. It seems like you are going around in circles trying to please everyone else but yourself. You must know, by now, that not everyone thinks the way you do, nor are they appreciative for the many things you have done for them. By the way, this is their problem—not yours! You still have enough compassion and love left in you to persevere and to hope that someday you will be respected and appreciated for simply being a kind, thoughtful individual. God knows who you are, your dream knows something about you; and now, may your family, friends, or anyone else, for that matter, be granted the wisdom and compassion to know you better!

## PASSOVER (i.e., a Jewish holiday celebrating the freedom of the ancient Hebrews from Egypt)

Dreaming about this serious yet happy occasion reveals you have shed many tears, experienced countless lonely moments, and certainly have had a broken heart on more than one occasion over the many burdens you seem to be carrying still. In all respects, you are such a good, wholesome individual that it literally stuns the mind into deep silence as to why you have suffered so profoundly! This dream, however, reveals that your love, courage, and actions are felt by many around you, and perhaps your good wishes for inner peace will not be long in coming. Visualize a better tomorrow; and, with steadfast faith, your past and present disturbances will slowly commence to diminish.

## PASSPORT

Your busy schedule sometimes leads you in very pleasant circles but keeps you away from what you would truly like to achieve or accomplish. In the very near future, you are slated to be more settled so that, at last, you can commence to carry out some plan or wish. In this particular soul cycle of your life, be aware that both luck and fate are on your side, all the way!

**PASSWORD** (i.e., a secret word or phrase for gaining entrance)

There are times when you are far too analytical, suspicious, and secretive for your own good. Those cloak and dagger mind games you play with yourself and others may be all right up to a point, just as long as you do not go overboard and try to be someone you are not. Some people become so engrossed with their fantasies, self-importance, and self-worth that they lose touch with reality itself; do not let this happen to you! Always strive to be the best person you can humanly be, and remember to humbly accept the truths and failings of yourself and others in the process.

**PASTA** (see **DOUGH** or **FOOD**)

**PASTEURIZATION**

Seeing the process of pasteurization take place within a dream state cautions you or a loved one to be wary of bad addictions (drinking of alcohol, drugs, etc.); poor food habits (junk foods, improper dieting, etc.); and misguided sexual activities (promiscuity, etc.) which could inevitably lead to future problems. Use your highest God-given intelligence, discretion, and self-control in any of the above-mentioned predictions, otherwise critical and unpleasant consequences could come to pass.

**PASTOR** (see **CLERGYMAN**)

**PASTRY** (see **FOOD**)

**PASTURE**

If the pasture looks relatively peaceful, without any signs of danger or obstructions on it, then you will be able to forge ahead with a clear mind and conscience. It seems that, far too often, you have been made to feel guilty or remorseful over something you said or did. There is always someone or something trying to hinder or stop you! The good news with this dream is that your tomorrows will be far less troublesome, cluttered, and disappointing. Ahead of you lie happiness, ambitious pursuits, and enough prosperity to last you a lifetime—and then some!

Seeing a pasture that appears ominous or has some evil or hopeless obstruction on it reveals that your happiness and basic progress is being thwarted by your own attitude(s), the lifestyle you keep, or by someone's misguided thoughts and actions against you. Whether your obstacles are self-created or not, the only way to improve your life is to employ your own logic and willpower in order to come out of your anguish or difficulties. You may think this is hard to do, but it is relatively simple when you finally concede to yourself that "enough is enough"!

**PATCHWORK** (see **DARNING**, **REPAIR**, or **SEWING**)

**PATENT** (see **DOCUMENT**)

**PATH**

A long, narrow path denotes that you are a sure-footed, responsible, and loving individual. You obviously strive very hard to make things better, both within and around you, always realizing that determination and hard work are the ultimate keys to success. That long, narrow path within your dream state is the actual pathway you have envisioned for your future's goals or aims. Obviously you want peace, harmony, and prosperity; and, if at all possible, you want your path in life to be very trouble free. With your sensibilities, you are bound to make your innermost dream, wishes, and hopes come true!

A winding path denotes that you are going around in circles, where your life is concerned. You are not being very emotionally, financially, or spiritually realistic at this time; this adds to your grief and pain. Settle down and begin to apply greater order into your life instead of scattering your thoughts and actions here and there, without actually accomplishing too much of anything. Be positive, be more assertive with yourself and others, and stop being so moody and fickle. The winding path you envisioned within your dream state is the arduous pathway you are actually taking in life. Why make life so complex and unnecessarily difficult for yourself and others when all matters within and around you could be so much simpler and better?!

A path that ends abruptly or has some type of obstruction on it reveals that you are about to call it quits in some matter of vital concern to you, and/or you are being far too stubborn and grudging with a loved one, your work, or just about anything else in your life. This dream cautions you not to be too foolishly headstrong and impulsive, otherwise you could lose more than you gain. Take it easy! By being less demanding and irrational in your ways, you could begin to live in peace.

Walking down a steep path indicates that your immediate plans, hopes, or wishes will not be fulfilled this time. Unexpected trouble is brewing from several sources which you must master before you can go on with your better desires. By using a bit of insight and common sense, you will be able to master this unexpected trouble rather admirably. If, on the other hand, you should decide to be critical and prideful in this situation, then your chances of being triumphant will be, and will remain, very minimal!

Walking up a steep path denotes an upward trend in all aspects of your daily life. In other words, just about everything should be going your way now and will continue to do so for quite some time to come. When you are happy and the world around you is relatively happy, peaceful, and productive, who could ask for anything more!

## PATIENT

Any one or several of the following definitions may be applicable: A) that you are a patient at this time; or B) that you are not a patient at this time, but you know of someone who is ill; or C) that you were a patient at a hospital, either this year or last year; or D) that a patient you knew died recently; or E) that you have never been a patient at a hospital and, with good luck, you never intend to become one; or F) that your job or career entails you to help patients; or G) that you are very grateful for being alive and healthy; or H) that you would rather pass away than be constantly unhealthy or be a burden to anyone on this planet; or I) that you were satisfied or dissatisfied with the treatment you received in a hospital; or J) that you will be having an operation in a hospital before too long; or K) that more people should look after their health rather than ignore it; or L) that if there was less stress in the world, there certainly might be fewer patients as well; or M) that you are, or someone you know is, a hypochondriac; or N) that this dream has little or no relevance to you at this time.

## PATIO

A neat, peaceful-looking patio indicates that you wish to drop or forget about some past or present topic which you find somewhat controversial and disturbing. Good! Do not dwell upon things that have already happened; rather, look forward and strive towards worthier things that can and probably will happen for you.

A messy, frightful-looking patio, on the other hand, denotes your unwillingness to change your complaints or pessimistic attitudes about your home life, place of work, romantic endeavours, or almost anything else that seems to bother you. Unfortunately, some people go through life viewing everything as being hopeless and useless without even realizing that they generally create their own chaotic upheavals through their own foolish, negative attitudes. This dream strongly urges you to modify, change, or control your bleak outlooks for more worthy thoughts, values, and endeavours. Nobody promised you a rose garden on earth; by the same token, you are hardly trying to create one! If you want a better, more productive and successful life, then view your life with hope—not with anger, sour grapes, or grumpy speculations.

**PATRIARCH** (i.e., a person regarded as the founder of a great business, colony, religion)

To see a patriarch or to be one within a dream state indicates your great strength of character and your ability to influence people with wholesome ideas, plans, and actions. You are vitally important to those around you simply because you have the innate ability to move forward with better, more productive, innovative concepts. A person like you never counts laurels nor sits back to vegetate, but rather is more inclined to create history while still alive on this earth plane. Many awards, honours, and plaudits await you as your future unfolds!

**PATRIOTISM**

To be loyal towards your country intimates that you are capable of teaching, leading, or directing others towards truth, happiness, and healthier attitudes about themselves. You are not afraid to speak the truth, even if this fact places you and your reputation on the line. You are a unique individual whose determination and service in life will continue to help, support, and uplift those beings less knowledgeable and less comforted than you. In many respects, you are like an angel of mercy, sharing your truths and wisdom wherever the cry for help is needed most.

**PATROL** (i.e., the act of guarding something)

Your analytical inspection of other people's work, actions, or verbal thoughts can be overdone, at times. Very often you have the tendency to redo what someone has already done for you, even if the job was considered complete and finished. Your perfectionist attitudes, actions, and phobias may be hard to eradicate unless you commence to see yourself through the eyes of other people. Some introspection is in order here, so that you can honestly begin to perceive and dispel some of those unnecessary, enslaved desires (or habits) which consistently hinder your progress in life. Let your good, wholesome mind guide you along the way; but, for your own sake, do not be ruled or guided by mind thoughts and actions considered to be unsound and unwholesome.

**PATRONAGE** (see *also* **ENCOURAGEMENT**)

Supporting, sponsoring, or encouraging a good cause within a dream state is a sure sign that you are trying to improve or correct some matters within your life. Something very special is happening to you simply because you have tapped into the infinite love within yourself which overcomes evil and ultimately creates good. One of the greatest privileges on this planet is to be able to find yourself through a deep sense of spiritual understanding and inner strength.

**PATRON SAINT** (see **SAINT**)

**PAUPER** (see **BEGGAR** or **POVERTY**)

**PAVEMENT** (see **HIGHWAY, SIDEWALK,** or **STREET**)

**PAVILION** (see *also* **TENT**)

Do not make promises or give guarantees you cannot fulfill. People who trust and respect you expect you to be honest and true to your word at all times, not just some of the time. Practice what you preach, be more punctual, and do not be ashamed to admit that you are not always right or perfect in your ways. If you truly wish to impress people, then do not take a cavalier attitude towards them, nor disappoint them.

**PAWN** (see **PAWNSHOP**)

**PAWNSHOP**

This dream could very well imply that you own a pawn shop, you work at a pawn show, or you were at a pawn shop not too long ago. However, if this is not applicable to you, then this dream intimates that you are being forsaken or abandoned by those you once helped or assisted. Your financial losses or other situations may be at an all-time low, or your friends may have abandoned you, at this time. However, in the very near future, you will recognize your losses as being gains. Soon, an event, a circumstance, or luck itself will reward you tenfold for your courage in not only believing in yourself, but believing in those remote possibilities that things might get better. Your testimonial in life will truly prove that a small seed of hope can actually create quantum changes for anyone who has the spirit to believe as you do!

**PAYCHECK** (see **INCOME**)

**PAY PHONE** (see **TELEPHONE**)

**PEACEMAKER**
   To bring peace to your fellow man, such as putting an end to war, starvation, privation, political or spiritual unrest, racism, and so forth, or to be able to calm a storm, hurricane, or other disaster within a dream state infers that you are indeed a child of peace, a child of fate, and certainly a child of Universal Understanding whose Cosmic Wisdom is not to be ignored. Having this power within a dream intimates that you have complete control over your life, in every sense of the word. In many respects, you are ahead of your time; in greater respects, your gifts and talents are needed now more than ever before! Your future holds a gamut of opportunities and experiences for you, but nothing that you could not control, rectify, or master in your life.

(*Note*: You may also have the pleasure of knowing that if, for example, you are experiencing a very negative dream but at the very end of your dream sequence or anywhere during your dream sequence you happen to see a peacemaker, then the symbolism of a peacemaker takes precedence over your entire bad dream. Consequently, you have nothing to worry about simply because the peacemaker acts as a "buffer zone" to anything negative within a dream.)

**PEACE OFFICER** (see *also* **DETECTIVE**)
   Any one or several of the following definitions may be applicable: A) that you are a peace officer who is happy or unhappy with the type of work you do; or B) that you have great respect for the work carried out by peace officers; or C) that you have very little respect for peace officers because of your present state of being or for some other per-

sonal reasons; or D) that you would like to become a peace officer; or E) that you have committed some crime or wrongdoing and fear you will be apprehended by a peace officer; or F) that you would be willing or unwilling to help a police officer if you were asked to do so; or G) that you know of someone who is a police officer; or H) that a police officer you knew lost his or her life in the line of duty; or I) that for some reason, you fear for your safety but refuse to seek help where the law is concerned; or J) that there was a time when you were assisted by a police officer, and you will never forget the kindness and help you received; or K) that this dream has little or no significance for you at this time.

**PEACH** (see **FRUIT**)

**PEACOCK** (see **BIRD**)

**PEANUT** (see **FRUIT**)

**PEANUT BUTTER** (see **FOOD**)

**PEAR** (see **FRUIT**)

**PEARL** (see **JEWELLERY**)

**PEARL DIVER** (see **DIVER**)

**PEASANT** (see **PEASANTRY**)

**PEASANTRY**

You may not necessarily have all the comforts some other people possess and cherish, but you certainly do enjoy life to the fullest in your own simple, thoughtful, and productive manner. In many inspiring ways, you realize that life's treasures lie not in wealth or materialistic gains, but rather in the truth, fairness, and dignity a person tends to uphold. Of course, some people will always strive to get something for nothing, but this sad philosophy does not apply to you, at all. You believe in carrying your load; in completing your tasks, duties, or obligations; and in accepting what is rightfully yours, and nothing more. You not only uphold a good philosophy in life, you fulfill it through your deeds and actions.

**PEBBLE**

Seeing these small stones in any manner suggests you will be beset with difficulties for a brief or a long period of time. This period's duration will depend upon your ability to cope with or to solve the problems at hand. These difficulties could involve finances, marriage, offspring, romance, or almost anything else in your life. You will survive the storms ahead, but not without learning some valuable lessons about the selfish needs and wants of others versus your own stubborn needs and wants. These unique but trying experiences can be both constructive and wholesome, providing the individuals involved commence to evolve from these trials and tribulations sensibly and maturely. Be wary, though, for not all people come through their personal storms any smarter or wiser than when they first started. As a matter of fact, some people simply refuse to forget or forgive anything in their lives, thus prolonging their agony. A poor attitude can bring you poor results; a good attitude can bring you beneficial results!

**PEDAL** (i.e., a lever pressed by the foot such as on a piano, organ, sewing machine, bicycle, automobile)

There are still many tomorrows left, so why all the agitation and eagerness to complete everything in a day? You are a workaholic! Such severity and stubbornness with self can affect you, if you are not careful. Do work and keep busy but, for your mental and physical well-being, strive a little harder to balance out your work time, your leisure time, and your sleep time with down-to-earth common sense.

**PEDDLER**

Something unpleasant and burdensome has been bothering you for quite some time; however, you do not appear to be doing too much to appease your thoughts or suspicions. Until you are honestly prepared to appraise or solve this matter more openly and sensibly, you will continue to wrest with the facts, fallacies, or fantasies as you see them. This dream symbolism merely wishes to remind you that the power of prayer can lead you towards worthier and nobler actions and solutions.

**PEDESTRIAN**

Seeing or being a pedestrian who acts in a calm, sensible, and perhaps cautious manner indicates that you, too, behave this way. You are a highly organized and determined individual who accepts the highs and lows of life with confidence. Rarely do you hassle or haggle with anyone; you prefer, instead, to do your job quietly and efficiently. Times are improving for you and will continue to do so for quite some time to come.

Seeing or being a pedestrian who acts in a nervous, foolish, wayward, or careless manner indicates that you behave this way, as well. The actions of your life are certainly weighed by the precarious attitudes you hold! When you decide to place your life in order by thinking rationally about yourself and about the things you supposedly hate, fear, or ridicule, then—and only then—will you commence to find the happiness you rightfully deserve. No one can help you until you commence to find and help yourself!

**PEDOMETER** (i.e., an instrument used by a walker for measuring distance)

Seeing or using this instrument infers that you are often preoccupied with out-of-the-ordinary interests and hobbies. Some people may admire your different interests but would not necessarily hop on the same bandwagon as yours. That is just fine—be unique! As long as you are happy in what you are doing, and there is no danger to yourself or to anyone else, then continue to be sensibly wise and unique!

**PEEK-A-BOO** (see **GAME**)

**PEEPHOLE**

For some reason, you have the strange notion that someone or something is constantly watching every little move you make. Fears of being followed or spied on, or mistrusting others no matter what they say or do, has become somewhat of an obsession with you. Yet, by the same token, you appear to be spying on someone you know, as well. What a coincidence! You will, however, be happy to know that your mind-fears and your spying will soon stop. A sudden inspiration or spiritual realization of self will help you in this matter. People can and do change for the better when they commence to see the futility of their vices and follies; you are no exception to this rule.

**PEEPING TOM** (i.e., a person who generally receives sexual or mental pleasure by watching others from a distance; a voyeur)

Any one or several of the following definitions may be applicable: A) that you are, in fact, a Peeping Tom; or B) that you are not a Peeping

Tom, but you know or knew of someone who is, or C) that you recently read a book or article about a voyeur; or D) that you are not a voyeur but think it would be interesting to be one; or E) that you feel a Peeping Tom is sick and mentally depraved, as well; or F) that you have inclinations towards being a Peeping Tom, but your better judgment holds you back; or G) that you read various sexual magazines or view sexually explicit video tapes which, to some degree, could imply that you are a voyeur; or H) that you were apprehended by the law for being a Peeping Tom; or I) that you know of someone who was apprehended by the law for being a Peeping Tom; or J) that you were once in a very embarrassing situation and later discovered that you were being observed by a voyeur; or K) that anyone who is a Peeping Tom should seek professional help or assistance; or L) that although you are sexually frustrated, you would never resort to being a Peeping Tom; or M) that this dream has little or no significance to you at this time.

**PEG** (see **PLUG**)

**PELICAN** (see **BIRD**)

**PELT** (see *also* **BEARSKIN**)
This dream advises you to bank some money for a rainy day. In fact, there is a storm brewing in the horizon for you; it foretells lean, difficult times. Ignoring this matter could invariably leave you in a future state of destitution and embarrassment.

**PEN**
Have you ever really noticed how fast time slips away when you are doing something you truly enjoy? Well, this dream wishes to inform you that you will either be starting or completing something of importance which might seem to take a long time to accomplish. Yet, before you know it, the task will be done.

**PENCIL**
You have placed many walls and barriers around yourself because of your indifference and stubborn refusal to listen to good, sound advice. In truth, you have unlimited potential, providing you commence to dispel your obstinacy with patience and understanding, and your hate with love. You are fighting a battle with yourself, and it seems so totally unnecessary! If you truly want peace, then you must

place your mind-weapons down, and commence to find your strength in God. In your case, the pencil is mightier than your sword, and your new-found strength will overcome your emotional weaknesses.

## PENDULUM

A vital decision you made recently could have been somewhat risky and quarrelsome for you; but, in the long run, you obviously made the right choice. This will be further revealed to you, as you slowly begin to realize and weigh the final outcome. The days ahead look exceedingly bright for you simply because you now have a greater concept about where you are headed and about what you hope to achieve.

## PENGUIN (see BIRD)

## PENHOLDER

Seeing a penholder without a pen reveals that you will be hiring some outside help to complete a project or task. Sometimes you spread yourself too thin by setting up deadlines you cannot meet or handle. This dream cautions you to be more selective in your dealings with people, strive for more quality in your work, and be more punctual in finishing what you start. Any unwarranted delays in what you do can, at times, create hard feelings, misunderstandings, broken contracts—and, of course, a tainted reputation.

## PENIS (see GENITALS)

## PENITENCE (see GUILT or REGRET)

## PENITENTIARY (see PRISON)

## PENLIGHT (see FLASHLIGHT)

## PENMANSHIP (see HANDWRITING)

## PENNANT (see FLAG)

## PENNY ARCADE

Many people refer to you as being a good worker, but sometimes you feel like a workhorse with little or no free time to do more pleasurable things. Right now you need a bit of a break from your workload; then, you will feel much better and a bit more satisfied with the things you do. This dream reveals that you will receive future recognition for your work and more admiration and appreciation from others for being so cooperative and dedicated in your beliefs and concepts. As well, a greater understanding with yourself and with others will be gained through your earthly experiences and self-sacrifices.

**PEN PAL**
Any one or several of the following definitions may be applicable: A) that you are presently writing to a pen pal; or B) that you had a pen pal many years ago; or C) that you would like to have a pen pal; or D) that you are looking forward to meeting your pen pal before too long; or E) that you married your pen pal; or F) that you recently read a newspaper or magazine that has a list of pen pals to write to; or G) that you are listed in a magazine as a pen pal; or H) that your parents were pen pals many years ago; or I) that this dream has little or no significance to you at this time.

**PENSION** (e.g., old age pension, military pension)
Any one or several of the following definitions may be applicable: A) that you are presently receiving a pension; or B) that you will be receiving your first pension payment before too long; or C) that you look forward to retirement and being a pensioner; or D) that you would like to take an early retirement but fear your pension payment will be too minimal to support you; or E) that you feel people in the work force should be able to retire early so that younger people would be given a better chance to become employed; or F) that you know of several people who are receiving a pension now—but, inwardly, they would prefer to go back to their former place of employment; or G) that many people who finally retire and receive a pension are not ready for this simply because they have no outside interests or hobbies other than their previous place of employment; or H) that when you retire, you intend to keep busy and, of course, traveling will be at the top of your list; or I) that far too many people wait for retirement to do some of those special things they always wanted to do, only to realize that their ambitions and interests change as they grow older; or J) that you misplaced your pension cheque not too long ago but found it later on; or K) that this dream has little or no significance to you at this time.

**PENSIONER** (see **PENSION**)

## PENTHOUSE (see APARTMENT, HOUSE, or LODGING)

## PEPPER (see SPICE)

## PERCEPTION

Whether or not you are endowed with great insight or intuitive abilities, this dream shows that you are very capable of rising over and above any difficulties you might encounter. You may be demanding and may complain at times; but, generally speaking, your judgments and opinions are sound, clear, and coherent. How you treat others is more or less how you would expect others to treat you. Should anyone fail to treat you right, then you merely express your feelings of disappointment to the person involved. As you courageously carry on with your faith, truth, and appreciation of all things, greater and better times are shown ahead for you (e.g., travel, a possible winning, new business interests or investments).

## PERFECTIONISM

Seeing yourself or someone else as a perfectionist within a dream state suggests that although you may be imperfect in many ways, in so many other ways you are "perfect" but intolerably dogmatic. The point is: do you admit your imperfections to yourself, or do you always strive to be faultless and blameless? Certainly strive to improve your imperfections but not to the point of being fanatically illogical about your good qualities. Birth and death can perhaps be considered perfect states on this planet; but what happens between birth and death is a gamut of good and bad experiences which have to be sifted, weighed, and ultimately accepted or conquered. Heavenly Beings are perfect; earthlings are "perfect-imperfect" beings who must work a little harder towards self-improvement.

## PERFORMER (see ACTOR, COMEDIAN, or MUSICIAN)

## PERFUME

Just as one is attracted to the sight and smell of anything pleasant, so it is in your life, too, that you strive for individual order, appreciation, and a natural understanding of your earthly existence. You are always there when needed and never have time to sit back counting your laurels when there is so much to do in an honest day's work. Whether you falter, fail, or succeed, you still have the honour and dignity to say you at least tried something your way—that is, full-heartedly and undaunted. As you already know, there can be no turning back in those lessons or experiences in life. With sensibility, you must move constantly forward in your thoughts and actions so that you can weave and create a better world, not only for yourself but for others, as well!

**PERIL** (see **DANGER**)

**PERIOD** (see **MENSTRUATION**)

**PERISCOPE**
   Seeing or using this device within your dream strongly warns you not to create any unnecessary trouble towards a family member, friend, or acquaintance just to appease your inner hatred or anger towards this individual. Nothing good will come out of this situation! God has forgiven you hundreds of times over; so you, too, should commence to be more tolerant towards others and more thankful for being alive and well. You have no enemies except yourself!

**PERJURY** (see **DECEPTION** or **LIAR**)

**PERMANENT WAVE** (see **HAIR** or **PARLOR**)

**PERMIT** (see **DOCUMENT** or **PASSPORT**)

**PERPLEXITY** (see **CONFUSION**)

**PERSECUTION** (i.e., being harassed or oppressed cruelly, such as in religious, political or racial persecution)
   Any one or several of the following definitions are applicable: A) that you are being persecuted by someone or by a system of life that is not of good order; or B) that you know of someone or a group of people who are being mistreated by a dictatorship government; or C) that several of your family members have been injured or killed because of some government's foul laws; or D) that you feel nobody should have the right to mistreat anyone on this earth plane; or E) that you feel some people deserve what they get, no matter how cruel and wicked a government system may be; or F) that you are most grateful to be living in a free society where persecution does not take place; or

G) that you are presently helping some people who have been persecuted by their government; or H) that you would never travel to or support any country which persecutes its people; or I) that far too many people blame God for their troubles when, in fact, it is man alone who creates his own woes and misery; or J) that some people on this planet are being persecuted practically on a daily basis; or K) that this dream has little or no relevance to you at this time.

**PERSEVERANCE** (see **DETERMINATION**)

**PERSISTENCE** (see **DETERMINATION**)

**PERSONNEL** (see **EMPLOYEE**)

**PERSPIRATION** (i.e., sweating)
Any one or several of the following definitions may be applicable: A) that you do have a perspiration problem; or B) that you conquered your perspiration problem through medical assistance, proper eating habits, and the intake of certain vitamins; or C) that you know of someone who has a perspiration problem but feel too embarrassed to tell this person; or D) that you once had a friend who had a perspiration problem; or E) that you are in the medical profession and often treat people with perspiration disorders; or F) that you are very self-conscious about your body and, from time to time, you have experienced body sweat or odor; or G) that some people who do perspire more than the norm are probably more mentally nervous than the average person; or H) that everyone perspires, but some people perspire more than others; or I) that this dream has little or no relevance to you at this time.

**PERVERSION** (see **IMMORALIST** or **SEX**)

**PESSIMISM** (see **DEFEATIST** or **HOPELESSNESS**)

**PESTILENCE** (see **EPIDEMIC**)

**PET**
Dreaming about your pet infers that you love and respect him or her. On certain occasions, a dream of this nature could imply that your pet may be sickly and/or is about to pass away.

(*Note*: The death of a pet can be just as traumatic and heartbreaking as losing a very dear, close friend. A pet, in the truest sense of the word, is a great friend too! There is an Animal Kingdom on the other side of life where the souls of pets and other animals abide. There is great peace and contentment in this Animal Kingdom, and when a person passes away, the deceased pet is there as well! Basically, loving a dear, loyal pet on this earth plane is no different than loving your pet in the hereafter.)

**PETITION**
Although you are very knowledgeable and intelligent in your own way, not everyone has the ability to understand or quickly grasp your points of view. It seems as though you become very impatient with people who are less knowledgeable than you. Bear in mind that there are many uneducated people on this planet who could impart more knowledge and wisdom from their life's experiences than one could possibly glean from any book. In essence, this dream symbolism is indicating that you should be more understanding towards all people, and do your very best to listen to more points of view, from time to time.

**PETROLEUM** (see **FUEL**)

**PETTICOAT** (see **CLOTHES**)

**PEW** (see **CHURCH**)

**PHANTOM** (i.e., apparition)
Your conscious and subconscious apprehensions are not only active during your wake state but during your sleep state, as well. This dream symbolism strongly infers that you are limiting your scope of learning and experiences because of your one-sided views about the unknown or unseen factors of life. Your upbringing may be at the very root of your limited views; someone may have indoctrinated you into believing that anything pertaining to the "unknown" is evil and wicked. Of course, this is not the case at all! You need not worry about the often exaggerated and misunderstood unknown sights, sounds, and forces of life. Rather, you should be more concerned about the so-called "known" forces of life which seem to abound on planet Earth (e.g., war, hatreds, drug abuse, physical violence). Many people who

have experienced a vision or two or who have actually seen something unexplainable have become more aware of their inner capabilities and were convinced that something does, indeed, exist beyond the five senses of the mind. There is more to Heaven and Earth "than meets the eye". Perhaps one day, as man becomes more finely attuned to the higher frequencies of life, the veil of the supernatural will be lifted, for all time.

## PHARMACIST (see CHEMIST or DRUGGIST)

## PHEASANT (see BIRD)

## PHILOSOPHER

You will never close your mind to any form of learning, be it of a higher or lower level; it appears that you simply must know the whys and wherefores as to what makes people "tick" and/or what follies and stupidities compel man to repeat the same mistakes over and over again (e.g., greed, vices, war) Your intelligence, understanding, and wisdom will no doubt lead you towards writing, teaching, advising, or lecturing others who are in need of your innate sense of worldly and universal concerns. In fact, philosophizing within a dream state intimates that you philosophize during your wake state, as well!

## PHONOGRAPH (see RECORD PLAYER)

## PHOTOCOPY

There appears to be very little diversity or outside interests in your present state of existence. Why? Because you fail to do anything about it! When you isolate yourself from meeting people, gaining new friends, or going out once in a while, then it is because you have created a sour grapes attitude about yourself and about life in general. There are many things for you to do if and when you are ready to meet and greet those new challenges in front of you. Do not complain about your present situation; instead, do something about your indifferent and impractical thinking!

## PHOTOGRAPH (see *also* FILMSTRIP)

If the photograph you see is relatively clear and concise, then you can be sure that others around you not only admire you but envy you, as well. You are not a pompous person, nor do you associate with negative or untruthful people. Basically, you see yourself as a person with sensibilities and weaknesses just like anyone else, but you do expect your loyalties to be reciprocated.

If the photograph you see is unclear, torn, or perhaps fades right in front of you then you have some cause for concern about your personality or about some particular habit that tends to annoy people around you. Obviously, you are not the most popular person to be around, but you can certainly change this matter for yourself, if you want to. Be aware, also, that sometimes when people shun away from you or tend to be overly critical towards you, it is because there is something about your personality that they find intimidating, demeaning, or repulsive. They may not tell you this directly; but, in their minds, actions, or verbal abuses, they are trying to tell you something about yourself. Look within your mind, and begin to see where your flaws and weaknesses might be; then, with a little bit of foresight and determination, commence to eradicate each problem, one at a time. Doing so will inevitably create a happier and better person within you.

### PHOTOGRAPHER (see *also* DARKROOM or STUDIO)

This dream symbolizes your willingness to carry on, in spite of some recent traumatic setbacks. As long as you maintain this sound, logical attitude in life, you will eventually see some of your greatest hopes, efforts, and ambitions fulfilled.

### PHYSICIAN (see DOCTOR)

### PIANIST (see MUSICIAN)

### PIANO (see INSTRUMENT)

### PICKAXE (see AXE)

### PICKET (see DEMONSTRATOR or STRIKER)

### PICKLE (see CANNING, FOOD or FRUIT)

### PICKLOCK (see THIEVERY)

### PICKPOCKET (see THIEVERY)

## PICNIC

If the picnic you see is relatively pleasant and appears to be in good order, then you can expect some pleasant surprises in the very near future (e.g., good news from a distance, better grades at school, marital harmony). Whatever it is, you can be sure you will be very pleased with the outcome.

Seeing a messy picnic or one where people tend to be disorderly strongly urges you to make peace with someone whom you have neglected or simply refuse to forgive. Failing to do so now could bring you great anguish and tears down the road.

Seeing a picnic which appears to be destroyed by man or nature advises you to take a closer look at your personality in order to see how you can overcome your feelings of pride and self-importance. This dream symbolism advises you to be more humbly grateful for your blessings rather than being boastful, overbearing, or snobbish. What you have, you can lose. You see, all things come from God, and ultimately all things belong to God. Tread lightly with your actions, for you are indeed walking on a tightrope, and you could fall.

A picnic appearing to be gloomy or perhaps mournful intimates that you or someone you know is very depressed over some recent event or occurrence. The clock cannot be turned back; one simply has to accept the sad or traumatic events which take place in life. Be strong and logical in all matters, and truly your tomorrows will seem far less upsetting than your todays.

A picnic with no one present reveals that you may be provoked by someone, or you may impulsively provoke yourself into doing something highly irrational and perhaps frightfully dangerous! One foolish mistake can cost you a lifetime. So, for your own sake, be very careful for the next week or two.

## PICTURE (see PAINTING or PHOTOGRAPH)

## PIE (see FOOD)

## PIER (i.e., dock or wharf)

If the pier appears to be intact and relatively safe to walk on, then this symbolism implies that you have made up your mind about something you wish to do or accomplish. Your better wishes can come true, providing you do not back down this time; success awaits you, providing you are willing to forge ahead.

To see a pier that seems to be dilapidated or relatively unsafe to walk on intimates that you are worried, overburdened, or overanxious about a certain matter or situation. This certain matter or situation can turn out in your favor. In the meantime, calm down. Everything of good order has its time and day. Await the good news with hope and courage.

**PIG** (see **HOG**)

**PIGEON** (see **BIRD**)

**PIGPEN** (see **BARN** or **HOG**)

**PIGTAIL** (see **HAIR**)

**PILL** (see **MEDICATION**)

**PILLAR** (see **MONUMENT** or **TOWER**)

**PILLOW**

You may be seeing a pillow within your dream state because the pillow you are sleeping on may be uncomfortable, or maybe you removed it from under your head, for some reason. If this is not applicable to you, then this dream symbolism indicates that in some aspects of your life, you are content; in other aspects, you are disillusioned and depressed. There just appears to be no happy medium for you. In order to find the key solutions to your problems, you have to be strong enough to admit your own weaknesses and failings. You are far from being perfect, so do not expect anyone or anything in your life to bring you happiness when you fail to give happiness. When you finally decide to let go of your "higher than life" expectations of self and of others and when you stop expecting life to cater to your every whim or notion, then you just might find the contentment and peace of mind you deserve. Expecting far more out of life than what you are willing to put in will bring you absolutely nothing. Change your attitude about what you think you deserve, and humble yourself; then maybe your tomorrows will begin to fulfill some of your better dreams, wishes, and aspirations.

**PILOT** (see **AERONAUT**, **AIRPLANE**, or **NAVIGATOR**)

## PIMP

Any one or several of the following definitions may be applicable: A) that you are a pimp; or B) that you were a pimp many years ago and now regret to God that you ever were one; or C) that you know of someone who is a pimp; or D) that you are presently working for a pimp but hope to get out of his clutches before too long; or E) that a pimp would like you to work for him; or F) that a pimp is like a parasite because he flourishes and grows rich from the mental anguish of others; or G) that you recently read a book or an article in a magazine or newspaper about a pimp; or H) that you recently met a pimp who appeared to be hiding behind a mask of contradictions and outright lies; or I) that a pimp may lead a secretive life in his own way, but God sees it all; or J) that this dream has little or no relevance to you at this time.

## PIN (see CLOTHESPIN or SAFETY PIN)

## PINEAPPLE (see FRUIT)

## PIPE (see *also* SMOKER)

Seeing a pipe within a dream state intimates that you are a very insecure person. Trying to impress others with your knowledge or experiences cannot bring you happiness, nor can pretending that everything is just fine when, in fact, everything is miserable and difficult! One deception leads to another and, before you know it, you have a mountain of trouble to contend with—namely, yourself! Be honest and realistic with yourself and others, and learn to accept the good times and the bad times with down-to-earth common sense. Do not be ashamed to admit when you are depressed or when you are penniless, for that matter. Honesty and logic can pave your way to a better, brighter future—but only if you have the wisdom to believe this truth!

## PIRANHA (see FISH)

## PIRATE (see THIEVERY)

## PISTOL (see GUN)

## PIT (see HOLE)

## PITCHFORK (see TOOL)

**PITY** (see **COMPASSION, CONSOLATION,** or **FORGIVENESS**)

**PIZZA** (see **FOOD**)

**PLACARD** (see **POSTER**)

**PLACENTA** (see **AFTERBIRTH**)

**PLAGUE** (see **EPIDEMIC**)

**PLAN** (see **AIM** or **DETERMINATION**)

**PLANE** (see **AIRPLANE** or **TOOL**)

**PLANET**
There are many times when you feel totally misunderstood and misrepresented by people around you; yet, in many ways, this dream intimates that you are triumphantly ahead of your time. It is feeling "out of place" from time to time that compels you to reach higher into the unknown realms of the Cosmic Universe and its many mansions or into the inner space within yourself to glean and expand upon your gifts and talents. Come what may, you are headed towards great quests and lasting successes in life!

**PLANETARIUM**
Were you ever angry or vexed over something simple or trivial, only to realize much later how foolishly or naively you behaved? Well, this symbolism intimates that another similar situation will arise again before too long. This time, however, you will stop in your tracks, remember this dream entry, and ultimately save yourself an embarrassing moment or two.

**PLANETOID** (see **ASTEROID**)

**PLANT** (see *also* **CACTUS, FARMING, FIELD, FLOWER, FOREST, GREENHOUSE, JUNGLE, LAWN, LEAF, MEADOW, MOSS, MUSHROOM, ORCHARD, PARK, PASTURE, PLANTATION,** or **SHRUB**)
Seeing plants within a dream reveals your love of growing things and of seeing wide open spaces of green growth. It also reveals your

inner desires to share your knowledge or expertise with others. Perhaps you have a green thumb; if not, you certainly admire anyone who does have this unique ability to make almost any plant thrive and grow. You are a very realistic individual who accepts the highs and lows of life. You always come out of various difficulties because of your outside interests and preoccupation with other attractions around you. Your busy schedules may thwart you in some ways now, but your future certainly reveals plenty of leisure moments to fulfill some of your greatest wishes, dreams, hopes, or plans.

## PLANTATION

You have taken the wrong turn on more than one occasion within your life and lost what you apparently felt you gained. It appears that now you are planning something which can turn in your favor, providing you do not dishonor anyone, hedge away from your responsibilities, or seek more than you rightfully deserve. Success in anything must be earned and nourished in order for it to be long-lasting and worthwhile!

## PLAQUE (see DECORATION)

## PLASTER

Seeing plaster that is firm (not parched or cracked) advises you that some past or present negotiations should turn out in your favor. This entire matter could be headed towards legal channels in order to be finalized, or it has already been conducted from a verbal and legal point of view. The end results should give you a few pleasant, satisfying surprises!

Seeing plaster that is parched, cracked, or is falling from a wall, ceiling, or partition strongly indicates your earnest desires to move away from your present location and/or your wish to resolve some of the unpleasantness you have been receiving at home or at work. "Patience, perseverance and self-sacrifice" has been your motto up to now; and, as you pass by the next year or so, you will find yourself happier and much more successful!

## PLASTER CAST (see *also* MOLDING)

This dream shows that many difficulties may be at your doorstep before too long because of misguided advice, unwise investments, broken contracts, gambling debts, or something else in which you may be involved. Whatever your troubles may be, the lesson is the same: you have failed to listen to your own wisdom and judgment. Some of your losses may eventually be regained, but not all. Sadly, there is a price to pay here; there is loss brought about by pride and lack of self-control.

**PLASTIC SURGERY** (see **SURGERY**)

**PLATE** (see **DINNERWARE**)

**PLATFORM** (see **STAGE**)

**PLATYPUS**

As rare as the platypus may be to you, this dream reveals that you, too, hold the distinction of being unique and exceptional, in your own right. Your personal magnetism, wit, and charm are great contributing factors towards your original abilities and ultimate successes. You are a very adaptable, creative individual who can inspire and capture the minds of many people. And rightfully so! There is a bit of leadership in everyone. But, in you there is no mediocrity or uncertainty—only the God-given wisdom to pilot your life with noble generosity and truth.

**PLAY** (see **GAME, MUSICIAN, PASSION PLAY**, or **THEATRE**)

**PLAYER** (see **ACTOR, GAMBLER, GAME, MUSICIAN,** or **RECORD PLAYER**)

**PLAYER PIANO** (see **INSTRUMENT**)

**PLAYGROUND**

If the playground you see is pleasantly active or peaceful, then your efforts to reach an agreement with someone or something will be shortly forthcoming. There are many winning events and opportunities ahead for you!

Seeing a playground that is somewhat foreboding or appears to be in shambles reveals that you are not being encouraged or motivated in a positive, sensible manner. It seems that someone or a group of people are either picking on you or putting you down, for some reason. Until times change—and they will—you are advised to use your own better judgment in doing what is right for you. Ignore your antagonist(s) and seek refuge with more understanding, compassionate people, places, or things.

A playground that is destroyed by man or nature denotes that you may be hindered from doing something because of someone's hardheaded, possessive attitude towards you. This person is very insecure and may require a certain amount of reasoning from you, otherwise matters can get out of hand. A reciprocal agreement can be reached, providing you communicate with pure, sound logic.

**PLAYING CARDS** (see **CARD**)

**PLEASURE** (see **HAPPINESS**)

**PLEBISCITE** (see **VOTE**)

**PLEDGE** (see **PROMISE**)

**PLIERS** (see **TOOL**)

**PLOT** (see **AIM**, **BOOK**, **GARDEN**, **GRAVEYARD**, **MAP**, or **MYSTERY**)

**PLOW** (see **TOOL**)

**PLUG**
You are holding yourself back from saying something important to a family member, friend, or someone else, and/or you are afraid of doing something for yourself because you fear you will be ridiculed or rejected. You are harbouring far too many troubled "ifs" and "buts" in your life instead of rising over and above your overly sensitive feelings. Sometimes people place themselves on a cross of anguish and despair only to realize that all they had to do was speak their mind or carry out their plan(s) and hope for the best! In reality, that is all anyone can do. Be more assertive; you just may discover a better world for yourself as a result.

**PLUM** (see **FRUIT**)

**PLUMBER** (see **PLUMBING**)

**PLUMBING**

Your unsettled personality today seems to stem from your confused, love-hate feelings about your past. Perhaps you were mistreated by your parent(s), or maybe you were wayward for some reason, or maybe you were attacked by someone. Whatever your reasons may be, this dream encourages you to settle down with your thoughts and actions so that you can at last bring some calmness and consistency into your life. You have been beating your drums far too long for anyone's satisfaction; this in itself can only lead to more sadness and hate. Discard your Peter Pan Syndrome, and face your realities with greater foresight and clearer thinking. You can either make your life work for you, or you can ruin everything in a day by being careless, thoughtless, and irresponsible. That vital choice is entirely up to you!

**PLUME** (see **FEATHER**)

**PLUNGE** (i.e., leaping downward or diving)

This dream forewarns you that you are about to take a "nose dive" in some matters of your life (e.g., marital misunderstanding, financial loss, making a wrong decision that could affect your happiness). Yielding to sudden whims, notions, or emotional outbursts could very well plummet you pell-mell into a battling situation you never remotely imagined could possibly happen to you. Be very careful at this time, especially where anger, hatreds, or vendettas are concerned. This is not the time to say or do something foolish; you may eternally regret it!

**PLUNGER** (i.e., a large suction cup to clear drains, and other channels)

Do not go out looking for trouble or feel you are justified in doing some wrongdoing for the sake of getting back at someone, yourself, or the world at large. Do not tarnish your reputation nor disgrace yourself or anyone else, for that matter. During these troubled times, think positively and act constructively so that your tomorrows can greet you with comfort instead of hardships!

**PLUTO** (see **PLANET**)

**POACHER** (i.e., one who hunts or fishes illegally)

You will be compensated for some financial or material loss, and/or you will receive an apology from someone who has done some injustice to you. This dream symbolism indicates that "a wrong will be made into a right"; it will pacify your mind or your pocketbook.

## POCKETBOOK (see PURSE or WALLET)

## POCKETKNIFE (see KNIFE)

## PODIUM (e.g., pulpit or rostrum)

You are an attention seeker! By being less aggressive and selfish in your ways, you just might find life to be far move satisfying and agreeable. Believe and admire other people around you; be more helpful and compassionate towards less fortunate beings; express your views truthfully, rather than in an annoying, exaggerated manner; and pave your life, not with self-obsessions, but with love and understanding for all things. Within you lies the greatest treasure of all—love and compassion—but you must bring this forth, not hide it!

## POET

You certainly are not like the average person, not by any means! In many ways, you are a character of many compulsions, eccentricities, and often misunderstood perceptions. However, this is the way you were created. You seek truth with deep-felt meaning, analysis, and passion. Life may be bittersweet to you, but this is what makes your world and your intellect or genius so remarkably unique. So, dreaming about seeing or being a poet implies that you either think and act like one, or you are one!

## POETESS (see POET)

## POISON

This dream forewarns you that bad tidings await you unless you commence to change your depressed, hopeless tune about yourself and about everything else in life. The mental and physical strains you are placing on yourself and others around you are not wholesome, nor will these solve your problems. Do not be guided by false notions, whims, or feelings of the mind; these disturbed thoughts are playing a game of Russian roulette with you. Letting yourself go in this matter could ultimately produce mental and physical impediments you would not conceivably wish upon an enemy! Seek help if you must; but, for your own sake, do something to suppress or conquer those anxieties and stresses festering within your being.

**POLAR BEAR** (see **BEAR**)

**POLE** (see **STICK** or **TOTEM POLE**)

**POLICEMAN** (see **PEACE OFFICER**)

**POLITICIAN**

Any one or several of the following definitions may be applicable: A) that you are an honest or dishonest politician; or B) that you are not a politician, nor do you have any desire to become one; or C) that you either trust or distrust politicians; or D) that you would like to become a politician someday, but if you ever do, you know that you would never become mercenary or corrupt in your ways; or E) that anyone who makes a false promise is a false person; or F) that most politicians are sincere, upright citizens who try to do their very best for their state or country; or G) that someone you know should become a politician by the way he or she speaks and acts; or H) that you were a politician who retired, resigned, or lost a seat during an election; or I) that you feel the politicians you elected to office are either doing their jobs well, or they are ignoring their tasks or duties; or J) that if you were ever elected to public office, you certainly would make some good changes; or K) that most politicians are very humble before being elected, but after they are elected, they become vainglorious and somewhat shortsighted; or L) that most politicians listen to their electorate, but some do not; or M) that this dream has little or no relevance to you at this time.

**POLITICS** (see **DOCTRINE, GOVERNMENT,** or **POLITICIAN**)

**POLL** (see **VOTE**)

**POLYGAMY** (i.e., the custom or practice of having two or more wives or husbands at the same time)

Any one or several of the following definitions may be applicable: A) that you live in a polygamous society and you do have more than one wife or husband; or B) that you do not live in a polygamous society, nor would you ever want to; or C) that you feel anyone who practices polygamy could not possibly know true love as in a monogamous marriage; or D) that you do not feel God ever intended anyone to be married to more than one wife or husband at a time; or E) that you often fantasize about having two wives or two husbands, but deep down you know that you would not go to this extreme; or F) that you would not mind having two wives or two husbands; or G) that anyone who has a mistress or lover while still being married is to some degree being polygamous, except that this is not morally recognized or endorsed; or H) that you are satisfied with your marriage and would not have it any other way; or I) that this dream has little or no relevance to you at this time.

**POLYGRAPH** (i.e., a lie detector)

Seeing or using this device supports your suspicions or beliefs about a recent situation or about someone you do not trust. Perhaps by following your hunches a step or two further, you will discover the ultimate truth for all time. You maintain a very high standard in life and do not have the time to dicker with anyone who is manipulative or deceptive. Honesty in self and in others means everything to you. Should anyone fail to comply with your high ideals in this matter, then rarely will you give that person a third chance to prove otherwise. Be it for better or for worse, such is life and its many lessons along the way.

**POMEGRANATE** (see **FRUIT**)

**POMPOM** (see **CHEERLEADER** or **DECORATION**)

**PONCHO** (see **CLOTHES**)

**POND** (see **WATER**)

**PONTIFF** (see **POPE**)

**PONTOON** (see **BOAT**)

**PONY** (see **HORSE**)

**POOH-BAH** (see **LEADERSHIP**)

**POOL** (see **FLOAT**, **SWIMMING**, or **WATER**)

**POOL TABLE** (see **BILLIARDS**)

## POORHOUSE

Any one or several of the following definitions may be applicable: A) that you are in fact destitute at this time; or B) that you have been impoverished for quite some time, but inwardly you somehow feel you will be coming out of this depressed state before too long; or C) that you fear you will be in the poorhouse before too long, unless your financial situation improves; or D) that you know of someone who is in the poorhouse now; or E) that many years ago your family was in the poorhouse—but, after much struggling, pain, and sorrow, they managed to come out of their depressed state with amazing results; or F) that you are presently bankrupt and do not know how you will ever make up for your great losses in life; or G) that you foolishly gambled all your savings and possessions away, and now you are walking the streets asking for handouts; or H) that you do not want to be in the poorhouse, but someone cheated you of all your wealth and possessions; or I) that a truly poor person is one who disbelieves in God; or J) that if you ever became poor, your whole world would crumble and shatter in front of you; or K) that a poor man is far more satisfied and less demanding than a wealthy man; or L) that being rich or poor in life is not what truly matters on this earth plane—having a healthy outlook is; or M) that this dream has little or no relevance to you at this time.

## POPCORN (see FOOD)

## POPE

Seeing yourself or someone else as a pope signifies that you would like more authority and freedom to finally unshackle yourself from the criticisms and other injustices that have been plaguing you for quite some time. Sadly, you are often misinterpreted by your family and friends. You must learn to let go of past quarrelsome situations, where your family or friends are concerned. Striving to be less defensive when you make a mistake and honestly admitting that you are not without fault would certainly begin to make life a lot more meaningful for you and for everyone else concerned, as well. Be fair in your dealings with all people—not just some chosen ones within your life—and strive harder not to be so overly superstitious in times of fear, fatigue, or sickness. Peaceful times are predicted ahead for you, but not without some self-sacrifices and positive actions on your part.

## PORCH (see **PATIO**)

## PORCUPINE

You need a push once in a while in order to get you going, otherwise some of your work could be waylaid for weeks on end! A scattered mind can produce scattered results—and somehow you seem to fit into this category. This dream wishes to remind you that if you want to get ahead in life, then do not just sit back and muse about it—do something about it!

## PORNOGRAPHY (see *also* **SEX**)

Any one or several of the following definitions may be applicable: A) that you are in the pornography business; or B) that you know of someone who is in the pornography business; or C) that you find most pornographic material mentally and sexually stimulating; or D) that you do not read or view pornographic material and find the entire concept of pornography shameful and disgusting; or E) that you have a vast collection of pornographic material in your possession; or F) that you feel the laws of your state or country are not strict enough to eradicate this human form of degradation, once and for all time; or G) that you feel that if a person is an adult, then it is up to each individual to either accept or reject pornographic material; or H) that you feel pornography is not an art, as some people claim it might be, but is something base and clearly immoral; or I) that you are sexually confused at this time and feel that pornographic material could not possibly assist you in any way; or J) that you feel anyone in the pornography business is either sexually confused or does not know the difference between what is morally right and what is morally wrong in life; or K) that you feel very few people are actually affected by viewing pornographic material; or L) that you feel it is the younger people of your society who become greatly affected by viewing pornographic material; or M) that you were very upset when someone recently showed you a pornographic picture; or N) that you recently read a book or article pertaining to pornography; or O) that you were caught reading or viewing pornographic material not too long ago; or P) that this dream has little or no relevance to you at this time.

## PORPOISE (see **DOLPHIN**)

## PORRIDGE (see **FOOD**)

**PORT** (see **HARBOR**)

**PORTER** (see *also* **JANITOR**)
You have been doubtful about a decision concerning a proposal, plan, or transaction made recently. In due time, you will realize that your decision was very eloquently correct! Right now you are on a powerful cycle of change which is both impressive and far-reaching. By looking at the clear facts around you, and by displaying your expertise during these changing times, you will commence to forge ahead with sure-footed speed and comfort. Those impossible dreams will now become realities, as you courageously move closer towards your windfall success!

**POSSESSION**
Many people who dream about being possessed by an evil spirit very often have great tendencies towards believing in all types of superstitions, old wives tales, curses, and so forth. In many respects, they frighten themselves sick over strange or odd incidents which could simply be coincidental or explainable. Of course, there are such things as possessions, curses, and so on, but this does not imply that you are or will be possessed or cursed in your life. Primarily, all this dream wishes to relate to you is that you must learn to be logical and more open-minded where matters of the unknown are concerned. You tend to accept frightful, ghoulish stories at face value without considering the possibilities or absolute probabilities that the author or authors of such material were very likely being overly imaginative. If you truly want to see someone possessed on this earth plane, then all you have to do is see someone who is totally drunk and obnoxious or see someone who is on drugs and spaced out. Essentially, anyone who is evil-minded on this earth plane can be subject to possession and can, in many respects, be possessed already! Innocent people can become possessed, as well, but only when they allow their inner attitudes and outlook to become weakened by what they read, see, or hear. An obsession with anything can become a possession! Always remember that Christ is your ally in these matters; the evil spirits are your foe. The less you concentrate on the evil forces, the better off you will be. Ignore them, rebuke them, and—of course—always pray for your guidance and protection.

## POSTAGE STAMP

To meet your earthly needs and wants and to satisfy your spiritual requirements in life, you must first begin to accept self-forgiveness as a major stepping stone in your enlightened quest. Far too often people tend to blame themselves needlessly, not realizing that they must inspect, adjust, repair, or refuel their earthly needs with love, self-esteem, and an inner recognition of self-worth. Just like a letter that must be signed, sealed, and delivered, so you, too, must have a stronger fixity of purpose until your concepts, ideas, and actions are signed, sealed, and delivered. In many respects, your dream is trying to tell you to stop punishing yourself for your thoughts, actions, or imperfections; instead, take charge of your life with sound, practical judgments. Self-forgiveness is your ultimate key to happiness!

## POSTER (see *also* ADVERTISEMENT)

Seeing a poster or creating one indicates that you are trying to impress others with your talents or expertise in order to gain something, and/or you are trying to persuade someone into joining forces with you in something you would like to do or achieve. However, as you will soon see, not everything can or will turn out in your favor. Nevertheless, if you still have unlimited patience and a great amount of willpower left, a better opportunity will arise before too long, giving you a chance to really prove yourself. Happily, you will do this and go on to bigger and greater ventures.

## POST OFFICE

Any one or several of the following definitions may be applicable: A) that you do, in fact, work at the post office; or B) that you do not work at the post office, but this dream certainly reminded you to mail a letter or overdue bill; or C) that you are expecting a parcel at the post office; or D) that your post office is presently on strike; or E) that you know someone who works at the post office; or F) that you are presently retired from the post office; or G) that a friend of yours resigned or got fired from the post office not too long ago; or H) that you recently applied for employment at your local post office; or I) that the post office recently lost a letter or cheque of yours, but it was finally delivered to you; or J) that you are expecting a vital letter, document, or contract through the mail before too long; or K) that you recently phoned the post office to complain about some matter regarding a letter, a package, or poor delivery service; or L) that you personally have no complaints about your post office simply because the workers there are very efficient; or M) that this dream has little or no significance to you at this time.

## POTATO (see **FOOD** or **PLANT**)

## POTHOLE (see **HOLE**)

## POTION (see **DRINK, LOVE POTION, MEDICATION**, or **POISON**)

## POTTERY

Before too long you will be approaching a close, intimate friend about a matter which seems to annoy you. You would prefer a conflict free situation, where this relationship is concerned, but it appears that you simply have to get something off your chest, otherwise your mind and conscience will give you no rest. Approach your friend in a gentle, mature manner. With dignity and foresight, you will receive the acknowledgements you seek.

## POTTY (see **BATHROOM**)

## POULTRY (see *also* **CHICK** or **CHICKEN**)

You have a great tendency to push yourself and others to the very limits where work is concerned. Not everyone has your high energy level or your high expertise in certain matters, so the input and output of others may not always meet your expectations. This dream is merely trying to remind you to be more lenient with yourself and with others where your work habits are concerned. Be a good worker, but do not be a slave driver! This fact was mentioned to you before, without results. Hopefully this dream will have the right effect on you now.

## POVERTY (see *also* **BANKRUPTCY, BEGGAR, DEBT, GHETTO, HOBO, POORHOUSE**, or **SLUM**)

To dream of poverty could imply that you are harbouring many feelings of being unworthy, inadequate, and possibly a total failure. These mental thoughts may hurt and haunt you—and will no doubt continue to do so until you are ready to rise over and above the wall of despair you have built around yourself. Note: you are NOT unworthy, inadequate, or a failure in God's Mind; you are a Child of God and have the ability and the worthiness to redirect your life towards outstanding prosperity and success! Do you lack education to get ahead? Then, get some education! Do you lack willpower or faith to move forwards? Then pray for willpower and faith! Do you feel uncomfortable or unhappy in what you do? Then look for other interests and activities, or consider a possible change in jobs! Is someone making your life miserable or refusing to let you be yourself or get ahead in life? Then be more assertive and seek some outside help in order to improve and ultimately fulfill your wants and needs! Do you feel like you are in an absolutely no-win situation, no matter what advice you have received thus far? Then wisely give all your troubles to God by speaking to Him candidly, openly, and trustfully. He will relieve you of your suffering, providing you have the true inner ability to believe without a doubt that He has taken your problems away. In doing this, be very patient! Forget your immediate problems (do not dwell upon them at all during this time), for God is preparing an answer for you in a very strange but simple way. Soon someone may approach you, or you might receive a letter, a cheque, a winning, a healing. Whatever He decides for you, you can be sure that He has assigned someone or something to help you. Be at peace!

**POWDER PUFF** (see **COSMETIC** or **PAD**)

**POWER PLANT**

You need to look no further in life for a hero—you are a hero! The trials and tribulations you have been through may appear endless; yet, in spite of your many letdowns, you remain a very compassionate, loving, and knowledgeable soul! People need you in their loneliest hour in order to find the strength and beauty in themselves. Reminding others to laugh, to not be afraid to fail or to succeed, and to express their feelings with truth, honour, and dignity are those philosophical facets you project to others. How could anyone fail to appreciate your good company? You possess an inner strength—a power house of insight—that will lead you towards bigger and greater events yet to come.

**POWWOW** (see **CONFERENCE** or **MEETING**)

**PRACTICAL JOKER** (see **COMEDIAN** or **MISCHIEF**)

**PRAISE** (see **ADULATION, COMPLIMENT,** or **CONGRATULATION**)

**PRAYER** (see *also* **BAPTISM, HYMN, LAST RITES, LENT, LITANY, MASS,** or **ROSARY**)

Praying to God within a dream state is always of good order. No matter how alone you may be at this time, you will not be alone forever. There is an abundance of hope, happiness, and prosperity ahead for you, providing you concentrate your earthly attention upon Him for the help and assistance you need. Your mental, physical, spiritual, or financial anguishes are not permanent; they will leave you. However, you must also be on guard against getting too comfortable or complacent in your ways. Prayer is a vital key to our human safety and spiritual salvation, at all times. With prayer all things can become possible.

(*Note*: You may also have the pleasure of knowing that if, for example, you are experiencing a very negative dream but at the very end of your dream sequence or anywhere during your dream sequence you happen to say a prayer, then this prayer symbolism takes precedence over your entire bad dream. Consequently, you have nothing to worry about simply because the prayer acts as a "buffer zone" to anything negative within a dream.)

**PREACHER** (see **CLERGYMAN**)

**PRECAUTION** (see **CAUTION**)

**PRECIPITATION** (see **HAIL, RAIN, SLEET,** or **SNOW**)

**PREDICAMENT**

Sooner or later, everyone gets into some predicament within a dream state—this is normal and natural. The question here is what actions do you employ in order to come out of your dream's predicament? For example, if you solve your predicament in a peaceful manner, this symbolizes that you are as much an introvert as you are an extrovert. These shy, outgoing personality traits can be a blessing to you at times, but not all the time. As well, you may be a perfectionist whose sensitivity is often misunderstood by practical, thick-skinned individuals. On the other hand, if you employ violence as a way to come out of your predicament, then you are either a peace-loving soul who tempers logic with justice and wisdom, or else you are an aggressive person whose thinking is based on indifference and hindsight. Now, if for some reason you are unable to come out of your predicament at all, this symbolism verifies your confusion and vexation in handling some wake state problem (e.g., marital or romantic problem, offspring difficulties, career or financial difficulties). However, this does not infer that this problem cannot be solved shortly or in due time; it can be, and it probably will be!

**PREDICTION** (see **PROPHECY**)

**PREFACE** (see **BOOK** or **INTRODUCTION**)

**PREGNANCY**
Any one or several of the following definitions may be applicable: A) that you are pregnant at this time; or B) that you would like to become pregnant but, for some reason, cannot at this time; or C) that you do not wish to become pregnant now or later on, for that matter; or D) that you are afraid of becoming pregnant for genetic or health reasons; or E) that you are single and think you might be pregnant; or F) that you have fathered a child but refuse to accept your responsibilities or obligations towards the mother or child; or G) that you are totally incapable of having children, for some reason, but would like to adopt a child or two someday; or H) that you are an alcoholic or drug user who fears for the safety of your unborn child; or I) that you have contracted some venereal disease which causes you to avoid pregnancy or causes you to fear for your unborn child; or J) that you accept motherhood or fatherhood as being very sacred and very dear to your good character and upbringing; or K) that you are about to be married and anticipate having children; or L) that this dream has little or no significance to you at this time.

**PREJUDICE**
Any one or several of the following definitions may be applicable: A) that you are not prejudiced towards anyone or anything, at anytime; or B) that you are a prejudiced person, for some reason or other; or C) that you were prejudiced towards a group of people long ago but do not feel this way now; or D) that over the years, you have witnessed many types of prejudices inflicted upon certain races of people, but

you do not believe that this is the way to create peace or harmony with anyone; or E) that you feel all races of people and their governments should harmonize more in order to maintain spiritual peace and brotherhood; or F) that you know we are all dependent upon one another on this planet, and to hurt someone in any way is tantamount to hurting yourself the most; or G) that you have no patience or pity for anyone who is less fortunate than yourself; or H) that you are envious and perhaps mock others who have more than you; or I) that you are dishonest and gossipy about your family, friends, acquaintances, or almost anyone you meet or greet; or J) that you are not a charitable person, nor do you believe that anyone should help you, either; or K) that you do not keep your promises or commitments to yourself or to others but would sooner stall, hedge, or complain about your earthly and spiritual duties in life; or L) that you are a victim of prejudice—which could be considered a living hell, in many ways; or M) that some people tend to blame God for all the prejudice taking place on earth when, in fact, it is man's pride, stupidity, and irreverence that is doing all this harm; or N) that no matter what color, race, or creed anyone happens to be, we all share "Holy Earth" together, and we all have the God-given right to be equal in every minute sense of the word; or O) that anyone who is prejudiced towards people on this earth plane is in for the most intense, rude awakening on the other side of life that one could remotely imagine; or P) that this dream has little or no significance to you at this time.

**PRELUDE** (see **INTRODUCTION**)

**PREMIER** (see **GOVERNOR** or **PRIME MINISTER**)

**PREMONITION** (see **FOREWARNING**)

**PRESCRIPTION** (see *also* **ANTIDOTE** or **MEDICATION**)
    This dream is a reminder for you to do something you have been wanting to do for quite some time; but, unfortunately, your fear or lack of self-confidence has kept you away from doing this task (e.g., physical check up, getting a driver's license, going back to school). Sometimes we employ illogical and unorthodox measures to wash our fears away; sometimes we face those fears courageously, with mature determination and sensibility. The basic prescription for a good life is to always be your high-leveled self in all matters and to seek those

inner and outer highways and byways in life with love, dedication, and gratitude for being a part of the Universal Consciousness.

**PRESENT** (see **GIFT**)

**PRESENTATION** (see **AIM, CELEBRATION, GIFT, PRIZE,** or **THEATRE**)

**PRESERVE** (see **CANNING, FOOD,** or **FRUIT**)

**PRESIDENT**

Your mental stresses and other burdensome factors around you will be mastered in due time. It appears as though you are caught between satisfying family members and satisfying other people you work with or know. The fact remains that it is almost impossible to satisfy or pacify all people at all times, no matter how much you may care about them. When family and friends become too demanding, then it is time to express your feelings in a calm, matter-of-fact tone, explaining your time, obligations, and limitations, as well. Love and friendship should be shared in a compromising manner, not in a possessive manner.

**PRESS BOX**

This dream symbolism suggests that you are striving towards one goal that is both logical and attainable; yet, on the other hand, you are striving towards another goal that is both illogical and unattainable. Common sense will guide you with the first quest. However, some hard luck and personal losses may be your lesson where the latter quest is concerned. Not everyone on earth was meant to be famous or rich, so be guided by the first quest. It is more down-to-earth and practical.

**PRESS CONFERENCE** (see **CONFERENCE**)

**PRESSROOM** (see **NEWSPAPER**)

**PRESSURE SUIT** (see **SPACESUIT**)

**PRETENSE** (see **MAKE-BELIEVE**)

## PREVENTION

Preventing someone from doing something or preventing something from happening within a dream is an indication of your strong willpower, courage, and innate ability to be a leader in your own right. You are in complete control of your life! Your inspiration can be a springboard—not only for yourself, but for others, as well—giving them wisdom and confidence to surge ahead in life. A word of warning, however: self-restraint can hold you back from reaching your deserved goals. Let your willpower pave the way!

## PREY (see *also* PROWLER)

You are battling a conflict within yourself regarding one or two people. The exchange of harsh words and the mixed emotions between you appear to be at the root of your inner conflict. Time and forgiveness will rectify this entire matter.

## PRIDE (see CONCEIT or SNOBBERY)

## PRIEST (see CLERGYMAN)

## PRIESTESS (see IDOLATRY)

## PRIME MINISTER

You are not handling a personal problem properly; you are skirting around the basic issues instead of zeroing in on the matter at hand. This dream symbolism reveals that failing to do something very constructive now could cause you regrets, later on, for not having followed your good intuition or desires. This dream also reveals that perhaps far too many people are telling you what to do, without giving you a fair chance to think and act on your own judgment and better faith. Sometimes, you must take a chance or two; and, whether you succeed or fail, you will have at least gathered something from that vast reservoir of human struggle, toil, and sweat. If you can visualize your life upon earth as a starting point in which you have to take charge, then it is here upon this Holy Earth that you should strive to reach your higher self through hope, prayer, and unlimited faith in all things, until the prophecy of your own life becomes a fulfilling reality.

**PRIMITIVISM** (i.e., the practice or belief of primitive living, ways, art, culture) (see *also* **NEANDERTHAL** or **STONE AGE**)

Once you make up your mind, there can be no turning back for you! You are a very distinguished individual whose intense ideas, concepts, and opinions are not only preached, but practiced, as well. You are a gifted explorer of truth in a poetic, religious, and literal manner of speaking. Just as a ripple on the water grows and grows, so you, too, will grow with greater compulsions to forge ahead. No matter how difficult life may appear to you at times, your spirit (force, drive, impetus) and your universal soul will guide you towards calmer waters and greener pastures.

**PRINCE** (see **ROYALTY**)

**PRINCESS** (see **ROYALTY**)

**PRINCIPAL**

Dreaming of seeing or being a principal suggests that you are capable of great achievements within your life span. Your intellect, imagination, and determination are all positive factors that can allow you to rise over and above the pits of despair around you. The immeasurable completeness and performance within your life are the "words" you fulfill and the "truth" you illuminate towards peace and inspired understanding. Indeed, you are a noble, giving human being whose destiny path will be rich, rewarding, and ultimately inspiring!

**PRINTING PRESS**

A printing press in good working order advises you not to be too distressed or confused about a recent change or occurrence in your life. This, too, will pass!

Seeing an unworkable, rusty, or damaged printing press reveals that your depression and loss of self-esteem may be due to someone's hardheaded attitudes towards you and/or due to a business matter which appears to be ill-fated due to financial losses. You could use a miracle right now; but, if matters get any worse, don't worry. This dream reveals that you will go on to greater, more rewarding ventures.

**PRINT SHOP** (i.e., printing office) (see *also* **PRINTING PRESS**)

This dream reveals that you are gaining great information and knowledge from books, from some educational course, or from some other form of mental pursuit or challenge. You are destined to travel extensively within your lifetime, but you are also destined to teach, preach, and no doubt write about your experiences in life. Your sensitive, compassionate feelings towards your fellow man are very wholesome and reassuring. You are destined to reach out to inspire many, many people. This old world is in great need of humanitarian, God-blessed souls like you!

**PRISM** (see *also* **SPECTRUM**)

The gamut of one's positive or negative emotions, wants, and needs may be expressed within this dream: you are very intelligent or endowed with average intelligence; you are productive or nonproductive; you are finding inner peace or you are creating trouble; you are truthful or you are dishonest; you are happy or unhappy; you are searching for inner truths in a logical manner, or else you are searching for inner truths in an illogical manner; you are easy to get along with, or you are a very stubborn, difficult person; you are a very ambitious person, or you are not so ambitious and perhaps a defeatist; you are famous, not famous, or infamous; you believe in God or you do not believe in God; and, last, you look for strength to find your inner worth, or you fall back with unachievable aims, hopes, and wishes. In many respects, this dream is likened unto having a child's mind within an adult's body or having an adult's mind within a child's body. The comparisons between people can be infinite, but the entire key to this dream is for you to do some serious introspection so that you can attune yourself to the higher spectrum of life within you. For example, if you know you have a certain problem or bad habit, then try to solve or master it; or, if you know you want to achieve something special in your life, then don't wait for the moon to turn blue—do it now! In essence, the prism is the pureness, understanding, and ultimate quests you can attain in life, providing you look within your inner world to weed out your negative qualities and to replant more wholesome, satisfying qualities.

**PRISON** (see *also* **CRIMINAL**, **GUARD**, **INMATE**, or **WARDEN**)

Any one or several of the following definitions may be applicable: A) that you are employed in a prison; or B) that you are an inmate in a prison; or C) that you were once employed in a prison, or you were once an inmate in a prison; or D) that you fear the thought of going to prison for some wrongdoing; or E) that you feel laws are too outdated where prisons are concerned; or F) that you feel there is not enough psychological or spiritual counseling provided in prisons; or G) that you know of someone who is in prison now or who was in prison quite some time ago; or H) that you have no sympathy towards inmates in a prison; or I) that you are planning some wrongdoing which could, in fact, put you in prison; or J) that the inmates of a prison may serve time on earth but, unless they sincerely ask God to forgive them, there will be another prison awaiting them on the other side of life; or K) that it is so very sad to know that some gifted and talented inmates in prison now have to waste their lives away because of their foolish, rebellious attitudes and actions; or L) that you feel a person is never born bad but rather acquires vengeful attitudes, habits, and actions while growing up; or M) that you feel the prisons are doing a good job or a bad job in rehabilitating criminals; or N) that if more people believed in God, there would be far less crime on this earth plane; or, O) that crime is a total no-win situation either on earth or in the hereafter, for that matter; or P) that this dream has little or no significance to you at this time.

**PRISONER** (see **CRIMINAL, HOSTAGE, INMATE,** or **PRISON**)

**PRIVATE EYE** (see **DETECTIVE**)

**PRIVATE PARTS** (see **GENITALS**)

**PRIVATE SCHOOL** (see **SCHOOL**)

**PRIZE**

Receiving or giving away a prize reveals this could actually take place, in time. However, this is not always the case. Essentially, this dream implies that you long for better luck, greater financial security, and emotional happiness within your life. Anything is possible for you; however, do not expect a miracle unless you are prepared to at least put sincere efforts and labour into your better wishes, wants, and needs. Pray and meditate; this will help you along your way.

**PRIZEFIGHT** (see **BOXING**)

**PRIZE RING** (see **BOXING**)

**PROBATE**

Probating a last will and testament within a dream state signifies that you are far too preoccupied with inconsequential earthly matters instead of putting your priorities in order. This dream advises you to "put your house in order", not for the sake of leaving this planet at this time, but for the sake of good common sense. Some important matter, plan of action, or document should not be ignored; it should be looked into now!

**PROBATION** (see **LIBERATION** or **PAROLEE**)

**PROBE** (see **SPACECRAFT**)

**PROCLAMATION** (see **ANNOUNCEMENT**)

**PROCREATION** (see **BIRTH**)

**PRODIGY** (see **GENIUS**)

**PROFANITY** (see **BLASPHEMY** or **LOW-MINDEDNESS**)

**PROFESSION** (see **CAREER** or **EMPLOYMENT**)

**PROFESSOR** (see **TEACHER**)

**PROGRAM** (e.g., agenda, list, or schedule; or a radio or television broadcast)

Sooner or later you will have what you want, but remember that your patience, generosity, and self-sacrifices will be the vital ingredients necessary to make it all happen. Always try to avoid being shortsighted, self-centered, or overconfident with yourself, otherwise you could thwart your wholesome chances for true success. Note: all good things come to those beings who reflect upon, examine, and pray for the eternal progress within and around their lives. And, from time to time, when you are being tested mentally, physically, and spiritually upon this earth plane, remember that your faith is being made stronger. You will travel extensively, you will study extensively, and you will prosper extensively as you move unselfishly forward with your faith.

**PROJECT** (see **AIM** or **DETERMINATION**)

**PROMISCUITY** (see **IMMORALIST, INTERCOURSE, ORGY,** or **SEX**)

**PROMISE** (see *also* **CONTRACT**)

Keeping a promise or oath in a dream suggests that you have enough direction and willpower to carry you through your lowest ebb to your finest hour. You finish what you start and will not settle for anything done in a careless manner. Your honesty and integrity are well aboveboard, as many people around you will attest. To you, a promise is sacred!

Breaking a promise or oath indicates that you feel distanced, isolated, or abandoned by those who you thought would be more supportive of you in times of great need. Unfortunately, not all family members, friends, or acquaintances will lend a helping hand or be supportive when it would be most appreciated. Yet, it is during these trying times that many truths about yourself and about others are revealed to you. Sometimes, when you walk all alone through your hardships, you begin to perceive a greater being within yourself; life then becomes a lot simpler, clearer, and more meaningful.

Not knowing whether to keep or break a promise or oath reveals that you are becoming disinterested in a friendship or two. Whatever the trouble may be, you are strongly advised to either make peace or part company on mutual terms—not angered terms. Without appreciation, understanding, and sharing, there can be no friendships.

**PROMISSORY NOTE** (see **MEMORANDUM** or **PROMISE**)

**PROMOTION**

Any one or several of the following definitions may be applicable: A) that you recently received a promotion; or B) that you did not receive a promotion simply because someone else did; or C) that it seems every time a promotion is due, your employer finds an excuse not to give you one; or D) that you recently quit your job in a company because they failed to recognize your credentials, capabilities, and good working habits regarding a possible promotion; or E) that you know of someone who recently received a promotion; or F) that sometimes your employer seems to pick the wrong people, where promotions are concerned; or G) that you do not deserve a promotion due to your negative attitudes and work habits; or H) that you recently declined the offer of a promotion for personal reasons; or I) that you hope to receive a promotion in due time—at least, you will try your very best to warrant one; or J) that you feel that a person who disagrees with the boss does not stand a chance of being promoted; or K) that a promotion should not be based on whom you know at work but rather on what you know about your work; or L) that this dream has little or no significance to you at this time.

**PRONG** (see **TOOL** or **UTENSIL**)

**PROPAGANDA** (see **DECEPTION** or **DOCTRINE**)

**PROPELLER** (see *also* **AIRPLANE** or **BOAT**)

Seeing a propeller alone in a dream signifies that an opportunity which passed you by once before will be made available to you again, before too long. The big question is whether you will accept or reject this opportunity. You must weigh your needs and wants sensibly at this time and ask yourself whether "nothing ventured, nothing gained" is still your favorite motto. You can say yes to this opportunity if the facts and figures are correct; you can say no if your doubts outweigh these figures. Whatever you decide, this dream reveals that you will make the right decision, as time will prove to you.

**PROPHECY**

To prophesy in your dream could very well mark a vital new beginning in your life! This dream has already given you some spiritual truths about yourself; now you should be able to shed some of those unnecessary stresses from within your being. Many doubts, questions, and disappointments about your life as a whole have plagued you for a very long period of time, thus leaving you no choice but to become somewhat cynical, pessimistic, and very likely uncaring. However, this dream reveals that you will now have more uniformity, satisfaction, and prosperity within your life. You see, God was there all along, but you had to reach higher and higher until the prophet in you touched that inner Light of Understanding within your soul.

**PROPHET** (see **PROPHECY**)

**PROPHYLACTIC** (see **CONTRACEPTIVE**)

**PROPRIETOR** (see **OWNERSHIP**)

**PROSECUTION** (see **LAWSUIT**)

**PROSECUTOR** (see **LAW** or **LAWYER**)

**PROSPECTOR**

Having the same routine, day in and day out, can be rather stifling. You would like to travel, and you certainly would like to be able to accomplish some other goals in your life. However, your obligations, time, and finances will not permit this now. Good news! In the very near future, your inner hopes and good desires will come to pass. For the moment, however, do the best you can in what you are doing. There is nothing but good luck ahead for you, so be trusting, calm, and patient till then.

**PROSPERITY** (see **ABUNDANCE**)

**PROSTITUTION** (see *also* **BROTHEL** or **PIMP**)

Any one or several of the following definitions may be applicable: A) that you are, in fact, a prostitute; or B) that you were a prostitute a long time ago, but not anymore; or C) that you would not dream about quitting this trade simply because your life is far too luxurious and comfortable; or D) that you cannot forget or forgive the harm that was done to you earlier in life, and now you have no recourse but to "get even" with someone by prostituting yourself; or E) that you either envy or despise people who are in this profession; or F) that you know someone who is a prostitute; or G) that someone asked to you to become a prostitute once, but you rejected this offer; or H) that recently you read a book or newspaper article about prostitution; or I) that you cannot condemn or cast any stones at anyone for you know that the life of a prostitute is not easy or safe, for that matter; or J) that you hire a prostitute, from time to time; or K) that you know God still loves these people, but they must strive a little harder to let their past go, so that they can seek a more worthy purpose in their lives; or L) that you are thinking about becoming a prostitute; or M) that you quit being a prostitute because you are about to be married; or N) that this dream has little or no significance to you at this time.

**PROTOCOL** (see **DOCUMENT** or **NEGOTIATION**)

**PROTRACTOR** (see **MEASUREMENT**)

**PROVISION** (see **FOOD**)

**PROVOCATION** (see **ANGER** or **ANNOYANCE**)

**PROWLER**
Seeing or being a prowler within a dream could imply that you are one. If this is not your case, then this dream shows that you fear being alone in disagreeable places (e.g., dark alleys, empty streets). Your anxieties are justified in that one never knows who or what to expect in deserted or seedy areas. The idea here is to avoid walking through any area which causes you concern or apprehension. Also, if you are afraid of being home alone, then become informed on all the possible ways to safeguard your home against possible intruders. Don't be neglectful; be prudent!

**PROXY** (see **AGENT**)

**PRUNE** (see **FRUIT**)

**PRY** (see **CURIOUSNESS**)

**PSALM** (see **HYMN**)

**PSYCHIATRY** (see **PSYCHOTHERAPY**)

**PSYCHIC** (see **MEDIUM**)

**PSYCHOANALYSIS** (see **PSYCHOTHERAPY**)

**PSYCHOKINESIS** (i.e., ability to influence objects or events by the mind)
Most people have this unique ability of psychokinesis within their dreams but cannot produce the same results during their wake state. For example, when you dream about something, you can will it away at random; or, when you want an object to move from one location to another, you can will this object to move at your mind's command. This, of course, would be very difficult to do during your wake state! The symbolism here is that your faith can move moun-

tains when you are ready, willing, and able to either climb over or walk around those mountains. In essence, you must believe in yourself before you can forge ahead. If you do have this inner belief, then obviously you see and know the results of your work. But, if you do not have this inner belief, then do not blame anyone for your failings but yourself!

**PSYCHOLOGY** (see **PSYCHOTHERAPY**)

**PSYCHOMETRY** (i.e., holding an object of a person in order to reveal something about that person)

The ability of psychometrics within a dream state may very well imply that you do, in fact, have this talent during your wake state. However, if this is not the case, then this dream strongly indicates that you wish to learn more about the power of the mind and soul and, of course, about psychic phenomena, as a whole. Anything that is unusual, hard to explain, or "stranger than fiction" phenomena has a great appeal for you. This is good and wholesome simply because you are opening up your mind thoughts to the realization that there is more to Heaven and Earth than meets the eye! And, indeed, there is. Carry on; the more you learn, the wiser you become!

**PSYCHONEUROSIS** (see **NEUROSIS**)

**PSYCHOPATH** (see **CRIMINAL** or **NEUROSIS**)

**PSYCHOSURGERY** (see **SURGERY**)

**PSYCHOTHERAPY**

Any one or several of the following definitions may be applicable: A) that you are in the field of psychotherapy; or B) that you are not in this field nor would you really want to be; or C) that you are presently seeing a psychiatrist or psychologist; or D) that you know of someone who could use the help of a psychiatrist or psychologist; or E) that psychotherapy actually saved your life; or F) that you feel some people are beyond help simply because they absolutely refuse to listen to good, sound advice or simply refuse to grow up; or G) that you feel some mental illnesses may be due to heredity and some through birth, but a vast number of mental illnesses may be due to shock, fears, personal loss, lack of love, drugs, alcoholism, accidents, or some other kind of negative behaviour attitudes people have about themselves and about the world in which they live; or H) that you feel most psychiatrists and psychologists are doing an excellent job; or I) that you feel most psychiatrists and psychologists are doing a very poor job; or J) that you know of someone who is mentally ill; or K) that you have loving, caring parents who bring out the best in you; or L) that you have loving, caring parents who try to bring out the best in you but, due to your wayward thinking, you do not give them half a chance; or M) that you feel if matters within and around you do not change before too long, you will have no recourse but to seek a psychotherapist; or N) that many mentally ill patients can come back to reality with time, patience, good guidance, prayer, and hope; or O) that you wish more people would be compassionate and understanding towards mentally ill patients; or P) that sometimes you fear you are becoming mentally ill, for some reason; or Q) that you feel there have been great strides made in curing mental diseases but feel someday there may be a total cure for all types of mental sickness; or R) that this dream has little or no significance to you at this time.

## PSYCHOTIC (see INSANITY)

## PUBERTY

This phase of life within a dream state merely projects your happiness or unhappiness at the present time. If you are happy and content with yourself and your lifestyle, then may God bless you and enrich you with greater happiness, prosperity, and peace. However, if you are not the peace loving, happy person you were always meant to be, then here is your dream's message: you cannot possibly hope to achieve anything in life without some sound, intelligent efforts on your part; you should not expect someone to do your job for you; you should not hold hatreds, grudges, or say foul words to anyone unless you see yourself as being totally perfect which, by the way, is not your case; you should commence to look more seriously within yourself to see whether or not you are willing to improve some of your ways and ideas before your future catches up to you; you should commence to mature and grow with the times, not rebel against yourself and the world you chose to live in; you should pray a little more earnestly for your peace of mind, and—last—look ahead with better dreams and wishes until they are inspirationally fulfilled to you. That is all!

**PUBLICATION** (see **ADVERTISEMENT, ANNOUNCEMENT, BOOK, BOOK REVIEW, EDITOR, JOURNALIST, NEWSPAPER, MAGAZINE, OBITUARY, POSTER,** or **PUBLISHER**)

**PUBLICITY** (see *also* **ADVERTISEMENT, AGENT, ANNOUNCEMENT, FAME,** or **SIGNBOARD**)

The act of making something known or available to the public, such as in publicity, basically infers that you have the innate ability to create, organize, direct, and ultimately achieve new concepts, ideals, or plans whenever the need arises. Your dynamic personality is one of a kind! Ahead of you lie greater ventures, opportunities, success, and travel. You not only deserve the best in life; but, in so many ways, you are and will continue to be the best at what you do! The so-called place at the top may have a vacancy for you in time, but only if this is what you want in life. If this does not apply to you now or later, then still be assured that your gifts and talents will carry you as far as you want to go.

**PUBLIC RELATIONS** (see **PUBLICITY**)

**PUBLIC SCHOOL** (see **SCHOOL**)

**PUBLISHER**

This auspicious dream sees you as a commander at the helm of your life! Your well-informed background, expertise, and leadership potential will carry you to outstanding honour and achievements, in time to come. From time to time, you may be misunderstood, misinterpreted, or simply ignored by others who fail to see the caring, world-minded thoughts within you. Patience, lucky speculative insights, and risks or guesses are truly your vital keys to success! In this world of "nutty-plus-eccentric-genius-type" individuals who have the extraordinary ability to shine above and beyond the average mind, so you, too, are likened unto such a mind—and you will constantly strive to make this world a better, richer, and wiser place in which to abide.

**PUDDING** (see **FOOD**)

**PULLEY**

What you think about yourself is far more important than what others may think or say about you. Do not let anyone get you down;

be strong and pay no mind to crass or rude people. Sometimes you have an urge to walk away from your present life, never to return. This, of course, is not your answer—nor will it ever be. This dream advises you to hold on to your higher ideals and good, clean living concepts; for, in the long run, you will be the winner, in many ways. Ahead of you lie greater peace, worthy changes, and an ample amount of luck to make your prosperity wishes come true!

**PULPIT** (see **PODIUM**)

**PUMP**

Closer attention should be paid to emotional and physical problems. Eat and exercise properly; rest when you are tired, but do not push yourself to extremes when you are working; and, last, be less demanding and more compromising with others. You are what you do to yourself and others; you are what you think and say; you are what you eat and drink; and you are who you are through your thoughts, actions, and deeds. Take care of yourself, for you only have one mind and one body on this earth plane—and neither is exchangeable or refundable!

**PUMPKIN** (see **FRUIT** or **JACK-O'-LANTERN**)

**PUNCH** (e.g., a paper punch or a machine for making holes)

You are creating some shortcuts in your life which may or may not be of benefit to you. Sometimes the shorter distance between two points may seem more appropriate or expedient, but there will come those times when you will have to take a longer route in order to learn or gain something perhaps very vital to your well-being on earth. Do not be careless or lazy, and do not be in such a hurry to go nowhere. In life, you must account for your logic, your time, your responsibilities, and your actions, not only to yourself and to others, but to God, as well. You have one life to live here; do your very best, at all times, while you still have the chance to do so.

**PUNISHMENT** (i.e., correction, discipline, penalty, or revenge)

Receiving a punishment within a dream state intimates that, on the one hand, you appear to be very content and hopeful with yourself and the world; but, on the other hand, you harbour fears, hatreds, and misunderstandings with self and with anyone else who happens to be around you at the time. The sad part here is that you are doing very little to change your attitudes and make them more pleasant and worthwhile. Compromise more, listen to good sound advice, believe in your own worthiness, normalcy, and sanity rather than listen to someone's criticism or disapproval of your sensitive being. The good things you do for yourself today will give you the boost and confidence you need for your tomorrows.

Giving a punishment to someone, on the other hand, indicates that you are very stubborn, often feeling that your ideas, concepts, or rules must be believed and carried out or else! Or else what? Or else you lose control with your thoughts and actions! Be careful what you say and do in times of stress, for you can say or do some wrong things you might forever regret. Measure and weigh your actions diligently; you just may be overdoing the punishment routine on someone close and dear to you. Sadly, if that life should suddenly be taken away from you, who would you be punishing then? God gives life, and God can just as easily take a life away, if He sees fit to do so. Be more loving, patient, and understanding in all things. Instead of venting your frustrations on someone, why don't you run around the block instead?

**PUP** (see **DOG**)

**PUPPETRY**

You tend to be too open and glib about yourself in front of others; later you become remorseful and embarrassed for the things you said or did. This dream symbolism is merely reminding you to be more calm, cool, collected, and sensible in front of people you see, meet, or greet. When in doubt, why don't you just be a wise listener, instead?

**PURCHASE** (see **INVESTMENT**, **MERCHANT**, **NEGOTIATION**, **OWNERSHIP**, or **STORE**)

**PURGATORY** (see **AFTERLIFE**, **PUNISHMENT**, or **REGRET**)

**PURPOSE** (see **AIM**, **CALLING**, or **DETERMINATION**)

**PURSE**

Merely seeing a purse within a dream state signifies that you would like to do something rather special; but, due to lack of funds or lack of time, this possibility becomes more remote by the moment. Another time will arise, however, when you will do something just a bit more special! Be at peace with yourself and with the world—everything will begin to improve for you very soon.

Finding a purse signifies that you are being rather extravagant when, in fact, you should be more frugal at this time. Carefree financial attitudes or "buy now, pay later" attitudes can bring you more difficulties than you rightfully deserve. Be prudent in these matters, and perhaps you can save yourself some grief down the road.

Losing a purse or having a purse stolen indicates that you are very frugal and seem to have fears about being robbed or cheated, for some reason. In many respects, you do not trust too many people—perhaps because of some past, traumatizing incident. Or perhaps your feelings stem from your childhood days, which may have been hard, difficult times. Being a little less dominant and stubborn could help create better changes for you. Many people trust you. Sometimes you have to bend a little bit by being a bit more trusting as well.

**PURSUIT** (i.e., the act of chasing, capturing or overtaking)

This dream reveals that you are sometimes angered and confused about the duties or requests others shower upon you. Being confident and efficient in what you do is perhaps one of the main reasons that family, friends, and others tend to rely so heavily upon your services and expertise. In many respects, you are trying to tell everyone quite subtly: "Give me a break!" Be assured that no one is trying to take advantage of you or your kindness. People like and admire you more than you realize; so, in a way, you are being complimented and praised for your need and worth upon this planet. After all, you need some things to do, except perhaps when you are a bit grumpy and tired. Cheer up! There is a pleasant surprise in the horizon for you. It will make your days ahead seem so much brighter and certainly worth admitting to yourself that, in many respects, you are special!

**PUS**

Seeing pus within a dream is not a very good omen. This augurs sickness, family difficulties, financial or career problems, and some anticipated plans that may have to be postponed or cancelled. These should pass by. However, when these trying times are over, you will learn a valuable, thought-provoking lesson about yourself and about those who truly love, respect, and support you.

**PUSHCART** (see **CART** or **WHEELBARROW**)

**PUSSY WILLOW** (see **PLANT** or **SHRUB**)

**PUTTY**

You are assuming too much. Everything within and around you is not really as good as you say it is, and being mysterious and secretive about your problems will not make them go away. Always face a crisis or problem in a head-on manner instead of running around in circles feeling guilty, angered, and mistrusting. The realities of this life and its trials and tribulations should be faced with truth and all the practical logic you can humanly muster. What would ever happen to you if you honestly had to face a major catastrophe in your life? Would you run and hide then; would you be putty in your own hands; or would you be honest and strong enough to face the challenge ahead of you? Be wary about this dream; in many ways it is trying to tell you not to become your own worst enemy when, in fact, you should be your own best friend!

**PUZZLE** (see **CONFUSION**, **JIGSAW PUZZLE**, **MYSTERY**, or **TOY**)

**PYJAMAS** (see **CLOTHES**)

**PYRAMID**

A new cycle of thought and action is in the horizon for you, thus making your road ahead more reassuring and meaningful than it has been for a long, long time. You have faced many difficulties in your life but, time and time again, you have pulled yourself and others out of the pits of despair, with undeniable victories! Now you are approaching a vital link, a mighty crossroads in your life, which will bring about the honour, recognition, and gratitude you so aptly earned and so honestly deserve. The angels sing for you today, such as the gods and masters of old, who were and still are, now bow to you. Be at peace.

**PYROMANIAC** (see **ARSONIST**)

**PYTHON** (see **SNAKE**)

**QUACK** (see **CHARLATAN** or **DECEPTION**)

**QUADRUPLET** (see **BIRTH**)

**QUAGMIRE** (see **MIRE, PREDICAMENT,** or **SWAMP**)

**QUAIL** (see **BIRD**)

**QUAKE** (see **EARTHQUAKE**)

**QUALIFICATION** (see *also* **CERTIFICATE** or **RÉSUMÉ**)
Being able to meet some qualification or requirement within a dream state (e.g., for a job, duty, plan) suggests that your strength of will and mind and aggressive tendencies to get ahead are well above-board. You obviously know what you want; consequently, you do something about it. You do not just sit on a good thought; you act upon this thought until you achieve your ultimate aims or goals.

Being unable to meet some qualification or requirement, on the other hand, suggests that you should commence to study your needs and wants more seriously and discreetly, stop feeling so sorry for yourself, and then, with a bit of courage, go after that aim or goal you want. You can do anything your heart desires, providing you have the determination to back you up. Be aware that you are on this earth plane to learn, to create, to discover, and to experience those decisions and conditions that will ultimately bring you closer to your highest perfected self and to your highest perfected actions. In essence, this dream symbolism is telling you that you were meant to progress, not regress, in life.

**QUALIFIER** (see **QUALIFICATION**)

**QUALITY**
Studying the quality of something within a dream state, whether it be good or bad, merely alludes to your pleasant or unpleasant thoughts and motives while you are awake. Everyone on this planet has the capabilities of thinking positively or negatively; but, it is the channeling of those positive ideas, concepts, and actions that truly is the most vital expression one should uphold, at all times. Fight your negative wants and needs; rebuke them until they disappear from the portals of your mind and heart! Everyone born to planet Earth belongs to planet Earth, but it is up to each individual to center or focus the life given to them with common sense and appreciation. The less you complain, the better off you will be!

## QUALM (see DOUBTFULNESS, FAINTNESS, or NAUSEOUSNESS)

## QUANDARY (see PREDICAMENT)

## QUARANTINE

You may have reached your limits with someone who appears to be making your life miserable and unhappy! When was the last time you smiled or laughed? You are much too fine an individual to simply vegetate and waste your life trying to please, appease, and console someone who practically does not even know you exist. Are you a glutton for self-punishment and pain? This heartbreaking situation will not disappear until you do something about it. Perhaps you will have to "quarantine" yourself—remove yourself—from this individual so that your absence could make the heart grow fonder. Professional help is not ruled out, either. But, failing all this, it appears as though the parting of the ways could become inevitable. Do not pine in this matter; rather, rejoice in the knowledge that you are finally getting your mind and courage together to create a better life for yourself!

## QUARREL

This dream strongly advises you to "say your piece" whenever you are troubled or whenever someone affects you. Why bother to inwardly quarrel or argue with yourself or have sleepless nights over matters you could have solved hours or days ago? In the end, you might find out that your mind-quarrels were totally uncalled for simply because the situation was not the way you assumed it to be, or the person involved did not mean for you to be slighted or hurt by what was said or done. Do not waste your mental, physical, and spiritual energies on silent resentments; rather, say what you feel, get it off your chest, and then carry on with greater pursuits in your life.

## QUARRY (see EXCAVATION, MINE, or PREY)

## QUARTERBACK (see GAME)

## QUARTZ (see ORE)

**QUASAR** (i.e., celestial star-like objects which emit great amounts of light and radio waves)

Dreaming of a quasar—one of the rarest of dreams—reveals that your gifts and talents belong to the world! You are a rare light, a one-of-a-kind individual whose mission appears finely attuned to the higher frequencies of time, space, and earth. Obviously, you are a deep thinker whose inner soul has a great longing to assist mankind in a very special way. Your mind is like a computer whose level of intelligence cannot be defined, measured, or perhaps understood at all times. God blesses us with special beings from time to time; somehow you just seem to stand a little taller, a little wiser, and a little greater than the rest. Carry on; and, whoever you may be, may you continue to bless us with your strength, your courage, and your unique wisdom!

(*Note*: You may have the pleasure of knowing that if, for example, you are experiencing a very negative dream but at the very end of your dream sequence or anywhere during your dream sequence you happen to see a quasar, then this quasar symbolism takes precedence over your entire bad dream. Consequently, you have nothing to worry about simply because the quasar acts as a "buffer zone" to anything negative within a dream.)

**QUEASINESS** (see **NAUSEOUSNESS**)

**QUEEN** (see **ROYALTY**)

**QUEEN CONSORT** (see **ROYALTY**)

**QUEEN REGENT** (see **ROYALTY**)

**QUEST** (see **AIM**, **EXPEDITION**, **HUNTING**, **PREY**, or **PURSUIT**)

**QUESTION** (see **DOUBTFULNESS** or **INQUIRY**)

**QUESTIONNAIRE** (see **INQUIRY**)

**QUIBBLE** (see **CONTRADICTION**, **COMPLAINER**, **CRITICISM**, or **QUARREL**)

**QUICKNESS** (i.e., speed, swiftness)

The pace of any action within a dream state, be it quick or slow, reveals your quick or slow thoughts and actions during your wake state. This particular dream about quickness merely indicates your skill in planning, managing, and directing your thoughts and actions with quality, speed, and excellent results. You are planning to do something and/or planning to finish something as though there were a time limit on it. Allay your fears; you will fulfill that wish! And, you can consider your wish as being a startling beginning to something better, greater and more emotionally satisfying.

**QUICKSAND**

Do not push your luck where emotional, physical, or financial matters are concerned! These vital areas of your life need more care, attention, and analysis before you can progress. You are responsible for yourself; no one else can account for your silent uncertainties and difficulties. What you do to yourself in a carefree or worrisome way could inevitably sadden and disappoint those who truly care about you, trust you, and ultimately love you. This dream strongly urges you to face facts as they are. Do not pretend that situations are in order when, in fact, they may be quite out of order! Accept your earthly responsibilities sensibly so that you can continue to carry on with dignity and freedom from nagging fears.

**QUICKSTEP** (see **MARCH**)

**QUILT** (see **CLOTHES**)

**QUITTER** (see **ABANDONMENT**, **DEFEATIST**, **DISAPPOINTMENT**, or **DISCOURAGEMENT**)

**QUIZ** (see **INQUIRY** or **TEST**)

**QUIZMASTER** (see **MASTER OF CEREMONIES** or **PROGRAM**)

**QUIZ PROGRAM** (see **PROGRAM**)

**QUOTATION** (e.g., the act of quoting something or using your favorite quotation)

Saying or hearing a quotation within a dream implies that you are studiously harnessing your energies towards some thesis, degree, distinguished achievement, plan, or action that will make you happy; or, you are deciding upon a career you wish to pursue in life. You have enough depth and willpower to follow any avenues in life and still come up smelling like a rose! The intimate understanding you have of yourself and of people around you gives you that extra edge—that leverage—to forge ahead with quantum leaps here and there. Your intellect and imaginative prowess will be met with success over and above your greatest expectations. Good luck, and may God guide you each step of the way.

**RABBI** (see **CLERGYMAN**)

**RABBIT**
    This dream confirms that a major decision to be made will eventually prove beneficial and rewarding for you. Right now, there is enough confusion and strife around you to last you a lifetime. However, with your sensibilities and self-control, you are bound to master your problems with pleasing success. You are headed towards many distinguished achievements and vast changes that could in due time compel you to move away. Note that an elderly person may be interfering, disputing, or simply attempting to rule your life. This, too, will be mastered wisely but firmly. You were always meant to be different, in your own way. If you have to go in other directions in order to prove yourself, then so be it—you will!

**RABBLE** (see **CROWD**)

**RABBLE-ROUSER** (see **DEMONSTRATOR**, **DISOBEDIENCE**, or **DISSATISFACTION**)

**RABIES**
    This disease symbolizes that someone whom you know and love (e.g., spouse, offspring, parent, friend) is unwilling to conform to a better way of life. Some people simply refuse to change until something traumatic happens in their lives. Some people are not willing to change at all, no matter what happens to them. You may in fact be dealing with a person who has a double personality. Professional help is in order here; however, it would be wise to control your emotions in this matter, at this time. Leave the doors of love and understanding open to this person at all times, but maintain a kind

of "tough love" in order to consummate the changes you so earnestly desire.

## RACCOON

This dream symbolism advises you to be more thoughtful, kind, and considerate towards all people whom you know and meet; and, for your sake, use more foresight in your daily actions. Your relationships with people around you seem to be rather precarious, at times, due to the fact that you suddenly become sarcastic, moody, and fickle, for no apparent reason. Basically, you are a good-hearted soul, but you must strive a little harder to show more sensitivity and self-control with your words and actions. Note that people tend to like you; however, up until now, they have found it difficult to truly understand you.

## RACE (see COMPETITION, CONTEST, GAME, HUMANITY, MARATHON, MOTOCROSS, QUICKNESS, or RUNNING)

## RACEHORSE (see HORSE)

## RACE TRACK

You are so supersensitive about what people say or think about you that you have on occasion accused others of being against you when this was not true at all. Your mistrusting nature is neither wise nor wholesome! In most cases, people have enough of their own problems and hang-ups to contend with, let alone be bothered with your shortsighted misgivings, as well. You are not being watched, followed, or monitored by anyone except by what is in the portals of your own mind. Those who know you certainly try to understand you, but you continually push them away with your prickly and unreasoning attitudes. When you learn to trust yourself more, then you will commence to trust others around you, as well.

## RACISM (see HATRED, PERSECUTION, or PREJUDICE)

## RACKET (see CONFUSION, GAME, or NOISE)

## RACKETEER (see CRIMINAL, CHEATING, DECEPTION, EXTORTION, or THIEVERY)

## RADAR

Just when everything appears to be going your way, something always seems to happen to upset your day. If it isn't one thing, it's another. However, that is a part of your life that you must contend with and master. It will not always be this way; in the interim, it would be wise to complain less and to be less stressful where your daily disappointments are concerned. There are numerous and varied improvements ahead for you, but first you must allay your inner fears about your todays and your immediate tomorrows. Think clearly and positively each day; then you will commence to conquer your minor obstacles with perhaps even a bit of humorous levity to lighten the way.

## RADIATION

Fearing radiation contamination, poisoning, or sickness within a dream state infers that you are concerned about some health problem (e.g., allergies, a rash, stomach pains). When you harbour great fears about what ails you, then you can in many ways sustain your ailment for a long time. Think healthy, and you will be healthy; think sick, and you can become sick! However, if you deem your problem to be more serious than you can handle, do seek some medical assistance.

## RADIATOR (see MACHINERY)

## RADIO (see *also* NETWORK)

Seeing a radio that is in good working order denotes that you will take a trip with one or two people. This trip will not take you that far, but it will give you the pleasure and enjoyment you seem to need at this time.

A radio that is not in good working order reveals that some ill-timed adventure or experience may cost you your time, some of your valuable money, and perhaps your self-respect. You will receive an inner warning to "not go" or "not do" something against your better judgment. The question is whether or not you will heed this warning.

Seeing a radio being repaired, being taken apart, or one that is totally unworkable suggests that you are analyzing or pondering over some recent event that upset you, or else you are refusing to compromise with, or forgive, someone you know. Use your better judgment, and wisely seek peace in both matters!

Changing the channel or dial on a radio suggests that you are beginning to change your mind about something, you are planning ahead for your future happiness, or you are beginning to be more perceptive and attuned with your inner self and with life around you. You will forge ahead in life with plenty of luck, creative thoughts, and positive actions, as well!

## RADIO ASTRONOMY (see ASTRONOMY)

## RADIOGRAM (i.e., a message transmitted by radio)

You are being discouraged or detained, or you are hedging from doing something rather special for yourself (e.g., making a special purchase, taking a once-in-a-lifetime trip, cosmetic surgery, tooth repair). Nobody can spoil you better than you can. Perhaps this time, though, you are not spoiling yourself but are just long overdue in treating yourself to something needed or something special! Many times, you have overlooked your own needs for the needs of others. This is a very fine thing to do, but there are those rare occasions when you should center your wants and needs for someone who deserves a pat on the back once in a while—namely, you!

## RADIOLOGY (see X-RAY)

## RADIOTHERAPY (see X-RAY)

## RADISH (see FOOD or PLANT)

## RAFFLE (see LOTTERY)

## RAFT

Seeing or being on a raft where the water is relatively clear and calm suggests that overall situations both within and around you should commence to improve drastically within the next several days to a week. Be at peace with yourself, and never lose your courage and faith. Your wants and needs will yet be fulfilled!

Seeing or being on a raft on mucky, muddy, and very choppy waters augurs some bitter times ahead for you where emotional, spiritual, and financial matters are concerned. Your demands and your ego are sometimes greater than you are. Do not assume anything at this time; rather, look more closely at your strong dislikes, your sense of self-importance, and other attitudes affecting your emotional wants and needs. Settle down, be calm, and be more levelheaded in everything you do. Then you will see some of your good wishes and hopes finally come to pass.

Seeing an abandoned raft on water or land suggests you are running away from some deep, hidden truth about yourself. The sooner you accept or admit this particular truth to yourself, the better off you will be. To free your conscience and clear the road ahead, you must be true unto yourself!

## RAG (see *also* CLOTHES or DISHCLOTH)

This dream advises you to be a good listener and to get your facts straight before you make any rash or harsh conclusions or decisions about anyone or anything in life. Far too often, you tend to hear your side of the story, without honestly listening to the other side of it in a fair and reasonable manner.

## RAGE (see ANGER)

## RAID (see INVASION)

## RAIL (see RAILROAD)

## RAILROAD (see *also* CONDUCTOR, STATION, or STATION AGENT)

If the train or any section of a train stands still or happens to be traveling on a more or less straight set of tracks, then you can be sure you are on track with your life. In many respects, just about everything should be going your way at this time. The culmination of your hard work and sincere efforts will eventually pay off, thus allowing you to enjoy your life more leisurely and comfortably.

Should a train or any section of a train be switched onto a sidetrack, then this implies that your lifestyle will be slightly altered by some good, wholesome events yet to come. Do not panic or worry about this matter; just realize that your spiritual and earthly prosperity will commence to grow when this alteration or change takes place.

Should a train or any section of a train be abandoned, derailed, demolished, or crash into another train or into something else, then you are essentially "off track" with your thinking and actions. This dream strongly urges you to discontinue some of your negative ways and habits so that your future can be more rewarding and meaningful for you. Failing to do this could ultimately and sadly minimize your chances for true, lasting happiness and peace of mind.

## RAIN

There is a cloud of indifference within and around you at this time. In other words, you do not seem to care too much about anyone or anything at this time, so other people merely project the same feelings back to you. If you don't care, they don't care either! If you truly want to be appreciated and understood, then stop being so doubtful and pessimistic about everything. Reach out to others with kindness and respect, and you will commence to come out of your emotional haze with optimism, courage, and common sense.

## RAINBOW

The rainbow you perceived within your dream state is, in fact, the rainbow you seek in life. That so-called pot of gold at the end of a rainbow truly exists, but it exists within you. This dream reveals that you are concentrating far too much attention on your own needs rather than what you can do for someone else from time to time. Share your wealth of knowledge, expertise, and kindnesses with everyone so that you can bring out that beautiful rainbow within you for everyone to see and appreciate. The happiness you seek is not here, or there, or beyond any rainbow; it is embedded within your heart, mind, and soul. Bring it forth; display it. You will be wiser and happier for having done so!

## RAINCOAT

Seeing a raincoat or wearing one advises you to think for yourself instead of depending upon someone to tell you what to do, where to go, how to live, and so forth. You have a good mind, so do not be afraid to use it—but, always use it sensibly. This is not to imply, however, that you should not heed someone's good advice. On the contrary! Heed good advice, but follow your own good instincts and logic, as well.

**RAINMAKER** (i.e., a person who attempts to make rain fall or a person who is associated in seeding clouds)

Seeing or being a rainmaker reveals that you are or you will be restoring or repairing something back to its original condition (e.g., repairing a car, a house, a boat, clothing, an ornament). Whatever it may be, you can be sure you will be happy with the results!

**RAINSTORM** (see **STORM**)

**RAINWATER** (see **RAIN** or **WATER**)

**RAISIN** (see **FRUIT**)

**RAKE** (see **TOOL**)

**RAMP**

Going up a ramp suggests that you are beginning to make some headway with your logical decisions and good financial management capabilities. It appears that you are at last beginning to see some positive results with your time, labour, and other efforts, as well. This high cycle will continue as long as you do not shirk your responsibilities or quit when the going gets a little rough, from time to time. Keep up the good work; you will be very proud of yourself in due time!

Going down a ramp, on the other hand, suggests you are experiencing some physical or emotional problems at home, at work, or at play. You will pass this tempest, but not without some wear and tear where your stubborn attitudes and habits are concerned. Compromise with yourself a little bit more, and be willing to heed the good advice given to you, from time to time. Take a rest, recuperate, and then see people, places, and things with a better frame of mind. A new outlook is the right outlook!

An unused ramp suggests that you are, or you will be, postponing some plan of action for a future date until things get better or at least until you feel more comfortable and secure in what you want to do. In the very near future, you will rekindle and fulfill this plan with positive results (e.g., travel, become a partner in a business, set up your own business).

**RAMPAGE** (see **ANGER**)

**RANCH** (see **FARMING** or **PLANTATION**)

**RANCHER** (see **COWBOY**, **FARMING**, or **PLANTATION**)

**RANGE FINDER** (see **GUN** or **CAMERA**)

**RANGER** (see **WARDEN**)

**RANSOM**
The act of paying a ransom or having to pay a ransom for the release of someone within your dream state indicates your own personal fears and distress for loved ones (e.g., family members, friends). Maybe you are in a country where kidnappings and ransoms are prevalent; if this happens to be the case, then caution should be exercised to the best of your ability. However, if this is not the case, then this dream suggests your fears are the products of extreme fatigue, of an over-imaginative mind, and perhaps of not receiving the attention you desire from those whom you love. Be patient, and continue to send out your love thoughts and actions towards those who might be indifferent to you. If given the right amount of time, space, and understanding, people can change, both in character and behaviour.

**RAPE**
Any one or several of the following definitions may be applicable: A) that you are a rape victim; or B) that you are presently receiving some kind of therapy because you were sexually assaulted and attacked; C) that you have raped someone; or D) that you know of someone who was raped; or E) that you feel not enough is being done to assist or counsel rape victims; or F) that a person should not walk alone in the dark or in some isolated areas where rape attacks could happen; or G) that you feel many rape victims got into trouble by either going to the wrong places with the wrong people or else tend to be too sexually suggestive around people; or H) that you feel those who rape others are repeating the same act that happened to them in their lives; or I) that you have great compassion for the rape victim and also harbour some compassion for the assailant and his sickly attitude towards the opposite sex; or J) that you have great compassion for the rape victim, but certainly not for the assailant; or K) that you feel there are many potential rape assailants who need psychological help, but they are too proud, unstable, or downright ignorant to seek the assistance they need; or L) that you fear for your children but also realize that they have been educated wisely on these matters; of M) that you recently read an article or book about rape victims or about behavioural patterns of assailants; or N) that you treat rape victims and are

aware that rape is not an act of sex, but of violence; or O) that this dream has little or no significance to you.

**RAPTURE** (see **HAPPINESS**)

**RASCAL** (see **CRIMINAL, DECEPTION, MISCHIEF,** or **THIEVERY**)

**RASH**

You are very self-conscious about your overall appearance and mannerisms in life. There is nothing wrong with you except for the way you feel about yourself. When you commence to accept your mind and body for what they are, then you will commence to realize that you are not an outcast after all. You are appreciated and admired by others; now it's time you had the same feelings about yourself!

**RASPBERRY** (see **FRUIT**)

**RAT**

This dream forewarns the dreamer to be very cautious where accidents are concerned (e.g., vehicle, motor bike, boat, skiing, skating, climbing a ladder). Be prudent for the next three weeks or so until this storm warning blows over. Carelessness could bring about unpleasant and dire consequences!

**RATTLE** (see **TOY**)

**RATTLER** (see **SNAKE**)

**RAVAGE** (see **DESTRUCTION**)

**RAVEN** (see **BIRD**)

**RAZOR** (see **HAIRCUT, SHAVER,** or **TOOL**)

**READING** (e.g., the act of reading a book, magazine, or other literature)

You are attempting to place your thoughts, values, and aims in perspective rather than settle for unorganized actions within your life. Whether in sleep or during your wake state, reading should inspire you to build your knowledge and wisdom with an open mind, to gain some food for thought here and there, and to perhaps discover some pertinent facts about yourself.

**REBELLION** (see **DEMONSTRATOR, DISOBEDIENCE,** or **DISSATISFACTION**)

**RECALL** (see **REMEMBRANCE**)

**RECEIPT** (see **ACKNOWLEDGEMENT**)

**RECEPTION** (see **CELEBRATION**)

**RECEPTIONIST**

If the receptionist is kindly and cooperative, then you are advised to follow suit by refining your thoughts, feelings, and actions towards other people. This action will bring you more loyalty and lasting friendships.

If the receptionist is ill-mannered and non-cooperative, then you should commence to combat your intolerance and irritability with calmness, courage, and down-to-earth rationality. Compassion and love for all things will bring you the comfort and peace you seek.

**RECIPE** (see **FORMULA**)

**RECITAL** (see **CONCERT** or **MUSIC**)

**RECLINER** (see **ARMCHAIR**)

**RECORD** (i.e., a flat disc played on a record player) (see *also* **BOOK, BULLETIN BOARD, CHRONICLE, DIARY, DOCUMENT, LIST, MANUSCRIPT, MEASUREMENT, MEMORANDUM, NEWSPAPER, PROGRAM, RECORD PLAYER, SIGNATURE,** or **TAPE RECORDER**)

You essentially hate any form of conflict within your life. However, you tend to be very obstinate when it comes to heeding good, sound advice from others who are perhaps more experienced and knowledgeable than you. You are advised to be a bit more flexible in your thinking and to respect all people for their experience and wisdom (e.g., parent[s], a good friend or teacher, an elderly person).

**RECORDER** (see **TAPE RECORDER**)

**RECORD PLAYER**

You are very easily swayed by what you read or hear. Not everything you read or hear is wholesome, so be very wary and discerning as to what is true and what is false. Be guided by logic, and do not be afraid to challenge those matters in life which seem ludicrous, gossipy, or completely "left field" or "off balance" where good, sensible thinking is concerned.

**RECOVERY** (i.e., regaining something that has been lost or stolen, or one's return to good health)

You have a very strong willpower, not only during your dream state but during your wake state, as well! It appears that you are not dependent upon anyone to tell you where to go in life, what to do, or how to do it. You have a mind of your own, that you obviously use very well and with positive and meaningful results! You are not a follower, nor are you necessarily a leader, but you are a born winner, in many respects!

**RECTOR** (see **CLERGYMAN**)

**RECUPERATION** (see **RECOVERY**)

**RED LIGHT DISTRICT** (see **PROSTITUTION**)

**REDUCTION** (i.e., to lessen something in weight, size, value; abridgement)

This act reveals that your inner depression and desolate feelings, due to some change within your life, should actually be a new beginning for you rather than a supposed end. God has not abandoned you; He has revealed that everything under His control has greater purpose and meaning than you wish to perhaps accept. Be strong, courageous, and faithful in this new time ahead for you, and you will know that you have not been forsaken or abandoned by anyone. All your life, you have offered hope and praise to others; now it is your turn to know that you are loved, needed, and wanted.

**REED** (see **INSTRUMENT** or **PLANT**)

**REEL** (see **FISHING TACKLE**)

# REFEREE

This dream cautions you not to interfere in family matters outside your own home (e.g., disputes between parents, offspring, a brother, a sister, a cousin). You may be called upon to settle a dispute or argument with a family member or relative who could in turn blame you for their problems if something goes wrong with the advice you give them. Be careful! If you must try to help, then take a neutral stand, thus giving them a chance to solve their own problems, as you do your own. Simply be a good listener, so that they can listen to themselves!

# REFLECTOR

This device reveals that you are expressing good will thoughts and perhaps actions towards someone who you feel is somewhat reticent about becoming a friend. Good friendships should be long-lasting, not just a temporal greeting and meeting of the ways. You obviously see something very special in this person, otherwise you wouldn't be thinking or acting the way you do. Your sincerity may bring about the true comradeship and/or companionship you desire. If you have something in common, then a friendship is already established!

# REFORMATORY (see PRISON or REFORM SCHOOL)

# REFORM SCHOOL

You often reflect upon why your life up until now has taken you through so much unpleasantness and hardship. Were you unwanted and unloved by your parents, or did something traumatic happen to you when you were young to completely change your attitudes about life? Whatever the problem may be, this dream reveals that you feel very much alone in your quest for love and appreciation. Do not give your disappointments and regrets any room in your mind and heart, but believe that hopeless matters can change to better situations, instead. Bear in mind, as well, that you cannot possibly expect love, praise, and respect from others unless you show these same qualities to yourself and to others. Take a good, hard look at yourself, and begin to realize that you, too, have a place, a purpose, a gift to share with your fellow man; but first you must erase your hopeless attitudes and feelings about your past, your present, and about your future. By the way, your future is a very promising one!

# REFRESHMENT (see DRINK or FOOD)

**REFRIGERATOR** (see **FREEZER**)

**REFUGE**

Seeking refuge from some danger or disaster or for some other reason within a dream state indicates that you are dissatisfied and vexed over certain plans, actions, activities, or verbal innuendos emanating from within the family core, outside the family core, or a combination of both. If someone troubles you, then the best avenue to pursue would be to say what you feel rather than to repress your confusion and anger. If those involved fail to listen or fail to be guided by your feelings or opinions in certain matters, then the best alternative is to leave them alone until they come to their better senses. Sooner or later, a lesson will be learned. Then you can say, "I told you so!"

**REFUND**

Adhere to good food habits, exercise, and rest. Neglecting these vital matters within your life can produce unpleasant anxieties and physical problems. Nourish your mind and body wisely so that you can be more functional and productive, the way God intended you to be.

**REGATTA** (see **COMPETITION** or **CONTEST**)

**REGIMENT** (see **BATTALION**)

**REGISTERED MAIL** (see **MAIL**)

**REGISTERED NURSE** (see **NURSE**)

**REGISTRATION** (i.e., enrollment)

Although your present state of being may be at times somewhat irritating and unexciting, it is highly improbable that you dwell upon these depressive states for lengthy periods of time. You are far too intelligent to whine over personal or outside problems that could be rectified, in some way. Your aim in life is to move on, no matter what obstacles beset you; and, so far, you have mastered the elements rather well! Your future looks very promising; your inner visualizations and goals should be fulfilled to you in due time, as well as your hopes to find more leisure time to continue some special work or task.

**REGISTRY** (see **REGISTRATION**)

**REGRET** (i.e., remorse; repentance)
Any one or several of the following definitions may be applicable: A) that you are feeling deep regrets over something you felt, said, or did recently or quite some time ago; or B) that you are regretful for participating in some wrongdoing or mischief against your community; or C) that you feel no remorse for doing something wrong to another person; or D) that you are too proud to admit that you were wrong or regretful for something you did towards someone or something in life; or E) that when someone criticizes you, you want an instant apology, but when you criticize someone, you do not offer any apologies or regrets; or F) that you could not care less what you say to others and rarely, if ever, have regrets for your actions; or G) that you basically have very few regrets in your life except for perhaps one or two prime incidents which were eventually rectified; or H) that to make a mistake is natural and normal, but to apologize for that mistake is noble; or I) that when you had a chance to make amends and apologize to someone special in your life, you refused, and now, sadly, it is too late to do anything about it; or J) that even though someone owes you an apology for something said or done against you, you are mature enough to forgive and forget the entire matter; or K) that you have great regrets for not having studied for an exam or for actually failing an exam; or L) that you have remorse for not marrying the person you once loved; or M) that you have regrets for not following your better instincts where your career is concerned; or N) that if you had more education, you would not be experiencing half the remorse you are experiencing today; or O) that this dream has little or no relevance to you at this time.

**REGULATION** (see **LAW**)

**REHABILITATION**
Any one or several of the following definitions may be applicable: A) that you are presently being rehabilitated; or B) that you are not being rehabilitated and hope that you never have to be; or C) that you know of someone who is being rehabilitated at this time; or D) that many years ago, after you were rehabilitated, your life changed for the better; or E) that you recently read an article on rehabilitation and feel that there is excellent progress being made in this field; or F) that to

be rehabilitated a person must think positively, sincerely, and faithfully about their daily progress; or G) that you feel many people who are supposedly rehabilitated often revert to their old ways when the going gets tough; or H) that you feel that many people who are rehabilitated do make sincere efforts to change and improve their ways in life; or I) that rehabilitated people can lead full and productive lives, providing they have the encouragement and courage to do so; or J) that this dream has little or no relevance to you at this time.

**REHEARSAL** (e.g., dance, music or drama rehearsal)

Rehearsing for something within a dream state indicates that you are unsure about a job, some plan of action, or about a course or two you may be taking or plan to take at school. Right now, you are experiencing some minor setbacks, which add to your confusion and lack of confidence. This dream advises you to talk to a friend or someone special in your life who could be in a better position to help you make up your mind. Hopefully, you will adhere to this advice so that you can finally settle your mind with the courage and understanding you so often display.

**REINCARNATION** (see *also* **KARMA**)

Any one or several of the following definitions may be applicable: A) that you believe in reincarnation; or B) that you do not believe in reincarnation, nor do you intend to ever do so; or C) that you have great doubts about the doctrine of reincarnation simply because there is no real, concrete proof of its existence other than in the minds and imagination of people; or D) that far too many people get on the reincarnation bandwagon without any foundation to back up their statements or beliefs; or E) that there are many people claiming to have been Cleopatra, Mark Anthony, or some other great notable in their supposed past life, but rarely does anyone claim to be the reincarnation of anyone insignificant or unknown in history; or F) that you feel when a person is hypnotized and supposedly regressed to a so-called past personality, what really happens is that this individual's spiritual cord opens up, and in pops a passing spirit, thus temporarily possessing the mind and imagination of the subject; or G) that the doctrine of reincarnation merely influences those people who are so insecure, depressed, or impoverished in their lives now that they somehow feel that, if they cannot have what they want today, they will be given another chance through reincarnation; or H) that this ancient doctrine is just another unexplained myth perpetrated to confuse mankind in some way; or I) that you personally know of some people who claim to have been reincarnated, but you do not know whether to believe what they say or not; or J) that you are presently studying or researching the theory of reincarnation and find it to be totally fascinating; or K) that you simply cannot believe that you were someone else in a past life but believe that you need to learn and do good upon this earth now so that your eventual eternity will be more rewarding and wholesome; or L) that you fail to understand why the so-called ancient ghosts reported in various parts of the world (e.g., castles, ancient tombs) still linger and haunt this earth if such a thing as reincarnation exists; or M) that you personally cannot see the necessity to come back to this earth plane when the heavenly planes or mansions have much more to share and offer; or N) that you often wonder why mankind fails, stumbles, and falls so consistently without improving inwardly— that surely by now mankind, with all its supposed reincarnated souls, should be in league with the angels and masters; or O) that you feel God is a forgiving Father so He would not continually send His Children back to earth to suffer when there are so many mansions on the other side of life to correct wayward souls and attitudes most effectively; or P) that you believe you pass through this world but once, and the good or bad you do upon this planet are those mighty judgment truths you take with you to the other side of life; or Q) that this dream has little or no relevance to you at this time.

**REINDEER** (see **DEER**)

**REJOICING** (see **HAPPINESS**)

**RELATIVE** (see **AUNT, BABY, BIRTH, BROTHER, BROTHER-IN-LAW, COUSIN, DAUGHTER, FAMILY, FAMILY TREE, FATHER, FATHER-IN-LAW, GODCHILD, GODPARENT, GRANDCHILD, GRANDPARENT, HUSBAND, MOTHER, MOTHER-IN-LAW, NEPHEW, PATRIARCH, SISTER, SISTER-IN-LAW, SON, STEPCHILD, STEPPARENT, UNCLE,** or **WIFE**)

**RELAY RACE** (see **COMPETITION, CONTEST, QUICKNESS,** or **RUNNING**)

**RELIABILITY** (see **RESPONSIBILITY**)

**RELIC** (see **ANTIQUE**)

**RELIGION** (see **BIBLE, CHURCH, DOCTRINE, GOD, HOLY MOTHER, JESUS, LOYALTY,** or **PRAYER**)

**RELUCTANCE** (see *also* **FOREWARNING**)
Showing reluctance within your dream infers that your mental disposition and overall character qualities show good moral strength, self-discipline, harmony, patience, and courage. Whenever you say yes, you mean it; whenever you say no, you mean this, as well! Knowing who you are and precisely where you are going in life is a most commendable trait that you consistently display. Because of your unselfish willingness to struggle for your beliefs, hopes, and aspirations, you are bound to experience a satisfying and prosperous life.

**REMAINS** (see **ASHES, CORPSE, DEATH, DESTRUCTION,** or **URN**)

**REMEDY** (see **ANTIDOTE, MEDICATION,** or **PRESCRIPTION**)

**REMEMBRANCE** (e.g., to remember something left behind or having some memory of something)
Very often, when people forget something during their wake state, they may have a memory recall while dreaming. Unfortunately, very few people can remember this fact when they wake up! Some people take a writing pad to bed with them; and, upon waking up, they quickly jot down their dreams, for a dream can be forgotten within seconds of waking up. Once forgotten, the dream sequence they are trying to remember rarely, if ever, comes back to the conscious mind's memory bank. So, in essence, your dream about trying to remember something within a dream state simply means that, whether you are awake or asleep, the mind computer can just as easily erase some thoughts and actions of your life as it can recall some thoughts and actions of your life. Like it or not, that is the way we are programmed, at least during this time in history. However, there will come a time when the human mind and brain will be completely functional; then nothing will be lost or ever forgotten from memory.

**REMINDER** (see **MEMORANDUM** or **REMEMBRANCE**)

**REMINISCENCE** (see **REMEMBRANCE**)

**REMNANT** (see **MATERIAL** or **RAG**)

**REMORSE** (see **GUILT** or **REGRET**)

**REMOTE CONTROL**

Your existence can be as interesting and exciting or as mundane as you want it to be. Do not blame others for your problems. Accept your own faults and failings, and recognize the drastic need to change for the better. This dream advises you to come out of your doldrums by finally doing something constructive, instead of pining or whining over something you hope to do, plan to do, or might never do! Life is not easy. Be a little prepared to work for what you want; then maybe you will gain what you want.

**REMOVAL** (see **MOVE** or **UNVEILING**)

**RENDEZVOUS** (see **MEETING**)

**RENOVATION** (see **REPAIR**)

**RENOWN** (see **FAME**)

**RENT** (see *also* **BORROWER**)

Any one or several of the following definitions may be applicable: A) that you are in the rental business at this time; or B) that you are presently renting something, such as a trailer, house, apartment, television, etc.; or C) that you have been renting a house or two for many years, but now you are planning to sell this property; or D) that you are planning to move away, and now you will have to find some place to rent; or E) that you are behind in your rent payments but hope that this problem will be solved before too long; or F) that you have complained to your landlord about your new rental increase; or G) that someday you would like to own an apartment building or a group of houses to rent; or H) that you are finding it difficult to rent some property; or I) that you will never go into the rental business again; or J) that you are presently paying rent for a suite in an apartment, but you are not happy with the tenants or the neighbourhood; or K) that you do not mind paying rent where you are living, but your landlady or landlord is a very snoopy person, where your private life is concerned; or L) that you recently moved from an apartment to a house or vice versa because the rent was much too high; or M) that this dream has little or no relevance to you at this time.

## REPAIR

The thought of repairing something, the act of actually repairing something, or the fact of actually seeing something repaired could mean that you will be, in fact, repairing something before too long. However, if this is not applicable to you, then this dream implies looking after someone who appears to need your guidance and good judgment from time to time. This person may fail to heed your good logic on occasion; however, continue to be as helpful as you can. One day you will be very thankful you did!

## REPENTANCE (see GUILT or REGRET)

## REPORT CARD

Any one or several of the following definitions may be applicable: A) that you are pleased or displeased with your marks on your report card; or B) that you passed or failed an exam and now wonder what effect your mark will have on your report card; or C) that you are a teacher who is presently working with report cards or who will be, before too long; or D) that even though you know you are gifted, you find school to be dull and boring; or E) that even though your marks in school were very outstanding, you cannot understand why it is so difficult for you to choose a career; or F) that your marks may have been very low in school, yet you have battled all odds to become very prominent and successful; or G) that this dream has little or no relevance to you at this time.

## REPORTER (see JOURNALIST)

## REPRIMAND (see ANGER or DISAPPROVAL)

## REPTILE (see ALLIGATOR, CROCODILE, DINOSAUR, DRAGON, LIZARD, SNAKE, or TURTLE)

## REPULSIVENESS (see HATRED or NAUSEOUSNESS)

## REPUTATION

Any one or several of the following definitions may be applicable: A) that as far as you are concerned, your reputation is well aboveboard; or B) that your reputation was tainted because of someone's gossip or false rumors about you; or C) that you know of someone whose reputation was recently tarnished because of some wrongdoing; or D) that you will always strive to have a good reputation, no matter what people say or think about you; or E) that your bad reputation caused you to be incarcerated; or F) that a family member once had a bad reputation, but now you would not even know it was the same person; or G) that basically you are a very intelligent person, but because of your mischievous thoughts and pranks, you are beginning to have a terrible reputation; or H) that because of your fighting habits, you are beginning to have a bad reputation around the neighbourhood; or I) that you have established an unsavory reputation because of your wild antics and parties; or J) that because of your attitude and poor working habits, you have created a bad reputation for yourself at work or somewhere else; or K) that you have established a fine reputation where you work; or L) that this dream has little or no relevance to you at this time.

## REQUEST (see PETITION or PRAYER)

## REQUIEM (see MASS)

## REQUIREMENT (see QUALIFICATION)

## RESCUE (see *also* LIBERATION, LIFEGUARD, LIFELINE, LIFE NET, LIFE PRESERVER, or RESUSCITATION)

To be rescued or to rescue someone or something within your dream basically reveals that you are quite capable of coping, managing, and ultimately mastering your present problems or difficulties with little or no discomforts. You are a very organized individual who knows precisely what to do and what not to do in times of distress. Your insight and dedication towards your higher ideals and concepts will carry you very far in life, thus enabling you to achieve almost anything your heart desires!

## RESEARCH (see INQUIRY)

## RESENTMENT (see ANGER)

**RESERVATION** (e.g., Indian reservation, military reservation, game reservation)

This dream urges you to put aside your bitterness, frustrations, and contradictions. Reorganize your thoughts and actions with sincere intentions and constructive endeavours. Be happy for just being alive, and realize that you can rise to greater opportunities when you put your mind towards positive goals. So many people have come out of their pit of despair and poverty, proving over and over again that where there is a strong will, there is a better way! Liberate yourself from the doom and gloom attitudes you have been harbouring. Remember that you, too, are important in God's Cosmic Plan of Life.

**RESERVOIR** (see **WATER**)

**RESIDENCE** (see **CAMPUS, HOME, HOUSE,** or **LODGING**)

**RESIGNATION**

Any one or several of the following definitions may be applicable: A) that you have resigned from a job or position quite recently; or B) that you intend to resign from your job or position, before too long; or C) that you do not intend to resign from your job or position, but you do know of someone who recently resigned; or D) that after you resigned from your last job, your life improved tremendously; or E) that after you resigned from your last job, your life simply went downhill; or F) that because of your instability or dissatisfaction in life, you have resigned from three to four jobs during the last year or so; or G) that you are far too stable and dedicated in your work to resign now or in the future, for that matter; or H) that if you were financially secure at this time, you wouldn't think twice about resigning from your employment; or I) that because your employer was picking on you, you had no choice but to quit your job; or J) that a very close friend of yours had to resign from her position because she was being harassed on the job; or K) that you had to resign from your job because of emotional or physical reasons; or L) that this dream has little or no significance to you at this time.

**RESORT**

Having a nice, pleasant time at a resort or seeing everything as being relatively peaceful there indicates that you are very consistent in your work, and you have complete confidence in carrying out your plans, aims, or aspirations. Being a reliable, well-thought-of individual merely adds to your already dynamic personality!

Having a dull, unpleasant time at a resort or seeing unpleasantness there reveals that you are attempting to pursue or achieve some goals that could very well be beyond your reach. Perhaps you could use some guidance or assistance here in order to further understand or evaluate your chances of succeeding. From your dream's point of view, your chances appear rather doubtful—but with a little bit of luck and hope, you never know! Situations can change overnight, and you could be on the road to something bigger and better.

## RESPECTABILITY (see REPUTATION)

## RESPONSIBILITY

Being responsible during your dream state infers that you are very responsible during your wake state, as well. You expect everyone to carry their load, but if they refuse, then you have no qualms about giving them an earful about your work ethics in life. Sometimes your expectations of others are fulfilled; sometimes they are not. Ahead of you lie greater commitments and challenges, which you will master quite admirably!

## RESTAURANT (see CABARET, CAFÉ, or CAFETERIA)

## RESTORATION (see REPAIR)

## RÉSUMÉ (i.e., a short summary of one's qualifications for a job application)

A good résumé implies that you are still trying to prove yourself to others in spite of their total acceptance of you already. Your insecure feelings about self and about others seem to be totally unfounded; the sooner you realize this fact, the better off you will be. When you begin to appreciate and respect yourself for who you are, then perhaps it will be much easier for you to accept others on a one-to-one basis.

A poor résumé implies that you are life-weary because of your boring daily routine, few outside interests, and some morbid anxieties about your future. Nothing will change for you unless you are willing to occasionally get away from your humdrum existence. For example, you could join a club, take a course or two at a school, do some charitable work, take up photography or some other hobby, and so forth.

Your life could be wonderfully exciting and certainly more rewarding for you if you would simply take that first step towards doing something more unique or different with your leisure time.

**RESURRECTION** (see **AFTERLIFE, CELESTIAL, GOD, HEAVEN, IMMORTALIZATION,** or **JESUS**)

**RESUSCITATION**

If you resuscitate someone within your dream, it implies that you are trying to prevail over or convince a person you know to heed your good, sensible advice. You are trying to get a point across to this individual who may or may not be inclined to listen or follow your logical thinking. At this stage, all you can do is hope for the best. On the other hand, if someone resuscitates you, then someone you know is trying to get a point across to you. The question is whether you will heed this person's sound advice. If you happen to dream of someone resuscitating another person within your dream, then you know of someone who is trying to get a point across to another person. That is all!

**RETARDATION** (see **MENTAL RETARDATION**)

**RETIREMENT**

Any one or several of the following definitions may be applicable: A) that you are presently retired and appear to be enjoying yourself very much; or B) that you are presently retired and appear to be at a complete loss with all your free time; or C) that you are about to retire and move away from your present location; or D) that you wish you could have retired earlier in life so you could have traveled or at least accomplished some other things that interested you; or E) that you were always an active person, and now, in retirement, you find it very difficult to even move around; or F) that in spite of your retirement, you plan to take an educational course or two and will continue to keep as busy as possible; or G) that if you had more outside interests or hobbies, your retirement would be so much better; or H) that you are about to be retired, but you have not been feeling too well recently; or I) that you are rather concerned about your parents who are presently retired or about to be retired; or J) that you intend to travel and live in a warmer country when you retire; or K) that if you had your way, there would be no such thing as compulsory retirement, at all; or L) that you feel far too many people assume that retirement simply means to retire from life when, in fact, it should be the beginning of a richer, better life for them; or M) that you have great fears about retirement because of loneliness, lack of money, or old age itself; or, N) that you intend to retire early in life so that you can achieve some other goals or aims you have had in mind; or O) that this dream has little or no relevance to you at this time.

**RETREAT** (i.e., a religious retreat)
You are not only asking yourself some soul-searching questions, but you are trying to seek humility, as well. From time to time, everyone should look within themselves so that they can find a more enriched purpose within their lives. The mind and soul certainly become more enlightened as a result.

**REVELATION** (see **BIBLE** or **PROPHECY**)

**REVENGE** (see **ACCUSATION, ANGER, HATRED,** or **PUNISHMENT**)

**REVEREND** (see **CLERGYMAN**)

**REVOLT** (see **DEMONSTRATOR, DISOBEDIENCE,** or **DISSATISFACTION**)

**REVOLVER** (see **GUN**)

**REWARD** (see **MEDAL** or **PRIZE**)

**RHINOCEROS**
This animal indicates that sudden changes, adjustments, or compromises will have to be made before too long; these may or may not be to your liking. In life, you must be prepared for almost anything. Hopefully, these minor or major setbacks will make you stronger and wiser for the experience or for the lessons learned. If you are sensibly mature, then these forthcoming changes, adjustments, and compromises may not be that difficult to handle. However, if you are immature and irresponsible, then you just may have a battle on your hands.

**RHUBARB** (see **PLANT**)

**RIBBON** (see **MATERIAL**)

**RICE** (see **GRAIN**)

**RICHNESS** (see **ABUNDANCE, BILLIONAIRE, FORTUNE, MILLIONAIRE**, or **OWNERSHIP**)

**RIDDLE** (see **MYSTERY**)

**RIDICULE** (see **ANGER, HATRED, MOCKERY**, or **RUDENESS**)

**RIDING SCHOOL** (e.g., a school for horseback riding)
  Your tolerance level is not up to par, especially where family members are concerned (e.g., children making noise, arguments created by minor incidents, financial difficulties which upset you). Whatever your problems may be, you are urged to tone down your anger and frustration, and begin to settle matters in a more rational, realistic manner. Exercise and a long walk certainly wouldn't hurt you, at this time. Note that the more you shout, the more unreasonable your demands become. The fewer demands you make, the better off you will be. Be patient with yourself and others so that time itself can heal resentments, calm your mind, and bring you closer to the comforts of everyone feeling wanted and needed.

**RIFLE** (see **GUN**)

**RIGHT-HANDEDNESS** (see *also* **LEFT-HANDEDNESS**)
  If you are, in fact, right-handed in life and dream about using your hand that way, then this action merely reflects your body's preference for being right-handed. However, if you are left-handed and dream about being right-handed, this symbolism intimates that you are trying much too hard and too quickly to settle or solve some pertinent matters within or around you. Your intentions are good and sincere, but the task ahead of you may take days, weeks, or even months to solve, rectify, or fulfill. Pull the reins on your mind, in this matter, go a little slower, relax, and you just may discover that it is not time that is of the essence here, but the quality of your thoughts and actions.

**RIGOR MORTIS** (see **CORPSE** or **DEATH**)

RING (see **BELL** or **JEWELLERY**)

RINGMASTER (see **CIRCUS**)

RINGSIDE (see **BOXING** or **CIRCUS**)

RINK (see **ICE** or **GAME**)

RIOT (see **DEMONSTRATOR, DISOBEDIENCE,** or **DISSATISFACTION**)

RIP CORD (see **BALLOON, DIRIGIBLE,** or **PARACHUTE**)

RIVALRY (see **COMPETITION**)

RIVER (see **WATER**)

ROAD (see **HIGHWAY, PASSAGEWAY,** or **STREET**)

ROADBED (see **HIGHWAY, RAILROAD,** or **STREET**)

ROADBLOCK (see **OBSTRUCTION**)

ROAD MAP (see **MAP**)

ROBBERY (see **BURGLARY, CHEATING, DECEPTION,** or **THIEVERY**)

ROBE (see **CLOTHES**)

**ROBOT**
Seeing a robot within a dream state infers that you sometimes feel like a robotic human being. In others words, your life may be too regimented and predictable or lacks the vitality and interest you might want it to have. Nothing can change for you unless you alone are prepared to create some diversity within your daily life. The keynote here is for you to "let your hair down" once in a while in order to see or to experience other interesting facets of living, instead of abandoning yourself to a shallow, narrow existence.

**ROCK** (see *also* **PEBBLE**)

One part of this dream symbolism implies that you may be creating some animosity because of your straightforwardness, naivete, or inquisitiveness into other people's lives. You appear to be very insensitive about the emotional feelings and personal affairs of other people. Be wary; what you give in life, you may also receive in life! People know who you are, so consider what you say or do simply because what goes around can also come around again. Then, you would have no one else to blame but yourself. The second part of this dream shows that you often feel you are not getting a fair break, enough attention, or equality where you live or where you work. Sometimes you feel completely left out of some activities, and this augments your grief and self-pity. In order to come out of your insecure state, you would be advised to generate more interest in your life, be less demanding, and learn to be more versatile and compromising with self and with others around you. Pining and whining about what you feel you deserve or should have may not necessarily bring you the comfort you think it will. Life is not a popularity contest. If you truly want to be appreciated and respected, then stop complaining, and commence to share your time and efforts more generously.

**ROCK-AND-ROLL** (see **DANCE, MUSIC, MUSICIAN,** or **SINGER**)

**ROCKET** (see **MISSILE**)

**ROCKING CHAIR**

There is no place like home, and there is no comfort like sitting in one's favorite rocking chair. This dream symbolism reveals that you are biding your time for some opportunity or circumstance that could perhaps make your life more interesting or, at least, more bearable. Be patient. There are two people who will express their views to you about the wisdom and/or the folly of your present plan(s). The wisdom of your quest is that you see vast improvements ahead of you, providing you do not sway or falter. The folly of your quest is that you may be wanting something out of your league at this time; you may be biting off more than you can chew financially.

**ROD** (see **STICK**)

**RODEO** (see **COMPETITION**)

**ROGUE** (see **CRIMINAL, DECEPTION, MISCHIEF,** or **THIEVERY**)

**ROLLER COASTER**
Your life may be going up and down just like a roller coaster because of the various stresses, demands, and activities around you at this time. Somehow, you will come out of this busy period to discover some valuable lessons about yourself and about people around you. As well, you will have learned from this experience that it pays to follow your own instincts and better judgments, rather than to heed some advice that is neither practical nor wise.

**ROLLER SKATE** (see **GAME** or **SKATE**)

**ROLLING PIN** (see **UTENSIL**)

**ROMANCE** (see **LOVE, BOOK, AFFAIR,** or **ADULATION**)

**ROOF** (see **APARTMENT, DOME, HOME, HOUSE, LODGING,** or **SHED**)

**ROOF GARDEN** (see **GARDEN**)

**ROOKIE** (see **LEARNING**)

**ROOMING HOUSE** (see **HOSTEL, HOTEL, LODGING, MOTEL,** or **RENT**)

**ROOSTER** (see **CHICKEN**)

**ROOT** (see **PLANT**)

**ROPE** (see *also* **CABLE** or **NOOSE**)
This dream advises you not to exaggerate or stretch the truth of any matter out of proportion. Stop being so melodramatic and glib, think twice before you speak, and ensure that your information is accurate and sincere before you speak. Strive towards being your finer, better self so that worthiness and goodness become the main theme in your daily life!

## ROSARY

Seeing or using the rosary reveals your inner understanding and spiritual strength to carry on in spite of your present needs, wants, or setbacks. What is life without trust and faith in God! As you pray, you become a greater being in seeking God, in sharing your free gift of love towards your fellow man, and in believing that your todays and tomorrows will be satisfying. The rosary is a powerful expression in the quest to emulate Christ's Passion, Faith, Hope, and Charity in all things.

## ROSE (see FLOWER or PLANT)

## ROSTER (see LIST)

## ROSTRUM (see PODIUM)

## ROTTENNESS (i.e., decay)

Anything that is rotten or spoiled within a dream is never of good order. This dream could imply sickness, accidents, deep depression, or even death. Whenever you see something rotten within a dream state, the best advice is to pray for comfort, peace, and protection so that whatever negative forces may be lurking around you will perhaps dissipate or disappear.

(*Note*: Having a repetitive dream about something rotten or spoiled forewarns the dreamer that something is afoot or about to happen. Prayer and caution are highly advised at this time!)

## ROUGE (see COSMETIC)

## ROULETTE (see GAMBLE or GAME)

## ROWBOAT (see BOOT)

## ROW HOUSE (see HOUSE)

## ROYALTY (see *also* MAHARAJAH)

Better tidings lie ahead for you if you see a king or queen within a dream. Much too often you have been drained emotionally, physically, spiritually, and financially, and this has taken its toll, especially where your confidence and faith in life are concerned. Be at peace. You are now entering a new phase or cycle which will not only astound you but shock others who perhaps felt you were a born loser. Good fortune, good will, and better times are forecast with this dream.

Seeing a prince or princess reveals your emotional loneliness, your lack of communication with someone special, and unwarranted criticism against you for simply being helpful to those around you. It will not always be this way, so do not feel so lonely and abandoned. In due time, you will be more content and inwardly fulfilled than a lot of other people whom you know. The courage you seek, you will find; the patience you seek, you will find; the compassion you seek, you will find; the understanding you seek, you will find; and the love you seek, you will find.

Seeing a duke or duchess reveals that you show good business or domestic management, you are hospitable and compassionate towards most people, and you have a deep appreciation for the creative talents of gifted individuals. In many respects, your life is like a story book; you are destined to achieve your utmost wishes in life, before you live happily ever after!

Seeing a count or countess denotes some physical or mental unrest due to your workload or due to your mental stresses pertaining to some personal or outside matters. Slow down! You are not a workhorse—you are a human being with certain physical limitations. Work if you must, but also rest when you must. As well, your worries seem so needless simply because the matters you are depressed about will be resolved before too long.

Seeing any other rank of royalty suggests that you need to let go of some personal hostilities towards someone or something in your life. No good can come from these feelings. Unshackle your thoughts from this matter, once and for all time. Ahead of you lie peace and prosperity; do not ruin this wonderful opportunity in your life by doing something unwise or foolish!

## RUBBER BAND

Seeing a rubber band in a dream is a reminder of something you should be doing but, for some reason, are not doing (e.g., a promise given or compromise made with someone which perhaps you refuse to keep, or a loan or debt which was to be paid but was not, or a job or obligation to fulfill without—procrastinating this time). Whatever it may be, this dream is simply trying to tell you to be more responsible; not only for yourself, but towards others who may be depending upon your honesty and integrity. Giving a feeble excuse does not rectify the failure to keep a promise.

## RUBBER STAMP

This dream symbolism reveals that you have or will have some misgivings about having signed a contract or document, and/or you will have buyer's remorse for having bought something perhaps beyond your means. There is a remote possibility that you may be able to pull out of this matter. Failing this, you may have to accept the inevitable consequences. You will at least have learned a very valuable lesson.

## RUBBISH (see DUMP, GARBAGE, or JUNK)

## RUDDER (see BOAT or AIRPLANE)

## RUDENESS

The act of being ill-mannered and impolite within a dream state implies that you also behave this way during your wake state. This does not imply that you behave this way all the time but during those periods when you are overtired or perhaps just plain grumpy for some reason. More self-control should be exercised where your emotional dislikes are concerned.

## RUG (see CARPET)

## RUGBY (see GAME)

## RUIN (see DESTRUCTION)

## RULER (see CAPTAIN, CHIEF, DEPUTY, DICTATOR, GOVERNMENT, GOVERNOR, JUDGE, LEADERSHIP, MAHARAJAH, MEASUREMENT, PATRIARCH, POLITICIAN, PRESIDENT, PRIME MINISTER, ROYALTY, or SHEIKH)

## RUM (see LIQUOR)

## RUMOUR (see GOSSIP)

## RUMP (see BUTTOCK)

## RUMPUS ROOM

A neat-looking rumpus room denotes order and stability in your life. You are very confident and thorough in your work. Your overall attitude makes you an excellent candidate for making a good marriage and special friendships and for achieving abundant success to keep you happy and prosperous.

A messy rumpus room shows that your stubbornness, fickle emotions, and lack of interest at home, at work, or at play have all deterred you from attaining the peace and prosperity you rightfully deserve. Since no one can honestly force you to change your ideas or outlook, and since you probably would not even listen at this time, this dream is reminding you that an occurrence or event yet to come will compel you to alter your attitudes about people, places, and things—and about yourself.

## RUNAWAY (see **ESCAPE** or **RUNNING**)

## RUNNING (see *also* **COMPETITION**, **MARATHON**, or **QUICKNESS**)

Running towards someone or something implies that you are very willing to accept your present challenges and that you are currently becoming more aware of your destiny or purpose in life. Your successes may be average and satisfying, or great and gratifying!

Running away from someone or something implies that you are discouraged about a person or some other matter; or you do not wish to go somewhere or do something you may find dull and boring; or you may be running away from some stark truth about yourself or about someone whom you know. If you are mature and responsible, then no doubt you will find the way and means to solve your problem(s) truthfully and wisely. However, if you are immature and irresponsible, then no doubt you will continue to run away from certain realities you do not wish to face.

## RUNWAY (see **AIRPORT**)

## RUST

Seeing rust within a dream is not a wholesome sign; it warns that anything from falling off a ladder to having a serious vehicle accident could happen. This is a very crucial warning! You are advised to be very prudent in whatever you do and wherever you go. Take nothing for granted, nor do anything foolish or daring at this time. This dream involves land, air, or water and shows little or no mercy to the unsuspecting victim. This warning, by the way, is not just for a day; it could last from a two-week period to a month.

(*Note*: A repetitive dream about rust merely adds to the urgency of you being very careful at this time. Something not to your liking is about to happen, but if you are careful and alert and, of course, have said a prayer or two for your guidance and protection, then hopefully this ill-omened time will pass you by.)

**RUT** (e.g., a groove, track, or furrow made by a wheeled vehicle)
This dream cautions you not to "make waves" against a friend or two who have apparently been very faithful to you. Be prudent in your words and actions, and life will become a lot more simple and easy for you to handle. Instead of acting before you think, why not change your tune and think before you act? If you expect your friends to be true to you, then it is only reasonable that you be true to them.

**RYE** (see **GRAIN** or **LIQUOR**)

**SABER** (see **SWORD**)

**SABER-TOOTHED TIGER** (see **TIGER**)

**SABOTAGE** (see **DESTRUCTION** or **MISCHIEF**)

**SACCHARIN**
Dreaming of this product cautions the dreamer not to overindulge in sweets, pastries, and so on and/or not to go on some self-prescribed diet plan which could well cause physical problems. Be wise and educated in these vital matters!

**SACHET** (i.e., a small bag with perfumed powder used to scent clothing in a closet or other items)
A pending move which could be against your better judgment, a sudden change of heart where marital or romantic harmony is concerned, or being envious of someone's good fortune are all characterized by this dream symbolism. The best advice here is for you to look deep within yourself and begin to sort out your rights from

wrongs. It is up to you to make things work out. Failing to do so will ultimately bring you deep regrets and hardships in the future.

**SACK** (i.e., a coarse cloth bag for holding foodstuffs, grain, sand, and other items)

Confusion, nagging mistakes, and self-quarrels are all revealed by this dream's symbolism. You seem to be harbouring some deep regrets or guilt feelings about something that has already happened. Your conscience will cease to haunt and embarrass you when you finally forgive yourself and anyone else who happens to be involved in this matter. Conquer your prideful attitude with inner strength and truth so that your tomorrows may be faced more peacefully and wisely.

**SACKCLOTH** (see **CLOTHES**)

**SACK RACE** (see **COMPETITION** or **CONTEST**)

**SACRAMENT** (see **PROMISE**)

**SADDLE** (see *also* **HARNESS**)

You are a highly opinionated individual who has a tendency, quite frequently, to say the wrong things at the wrong time. This habit has placed you in some awkward and embarrassing situations. Strive sincerely not to overstate your opinions; use a bit more foresight, gentleness, and silent sensibility before you speak. Your future looks very promising, but don't forget that the inner changes you create could make your todays and tomorrows far happier than they have been thus far.

**SADDLE HORSE** (see **HORSE**)

**SADISM** (see **ABNORMALITY** or **MASOCHISM**)

**SADNESS** (see **ANGUISH, CRY, DEPRESSION, HOMESICKNESS, HOPELESSNESS, KILL-JOY, LONESOME-NESS, MOAN, MOURNING, REGRET,** or **SORROW**)

**SAFE** (see **BANK** or **MONEY**)

**SAFECRACKING** (see **CRIMINAL** or **THIEVERY**)

**SAFETY BELT** (e.g., a belt used to support a window washer, a telephone lineman, a tree climber; or a seat belt used in an airplane or other vehicle)

When things get out of hand in your life or when someone accuses you of something, you tend to employ various excuses or alibis in order to wipe your slate clean. You are not, however, always honest and aboveboard, where your excuses or alibis are concerned. It seems that you cannot face any kind of trouble squarely, or you cannot tolerate being blamed for things you have done. When you run away from matters which tend to involve you directly or even indirectly, you are not accepting the realities of your thoughts and actions soundly and truthfully. Do not be afraid to admit that you are wrong, from time to time, for, in fact, on many occasions you are. Learn to accept your responsibilities and obligations with honour and dignity. Begin to realize, as well, that no one on this planet is infallible!

**SAFETY GLASS** (see **GLASS**)

**SAFETY PIN**

Whether your troubles happen to be big or small, this sign reveals that there is about to be a lull in, or a solution to, the difficulties you are presently experiencing. Sometimes you are overanxious for situations to change within or around you. However, not everything can or will change to your liking overnight; you must face this earthly fact. Be wise and ever so sensible in your trials and tribulations, for even your greatest problems can vanish into thin air, providing you have the patience and faith to see this transpire.

**SAGE** (i.e., a very wise man, or a Solomon)

Seeing or being a sage within a dream indicates that you are learning to embrace a deeper understanding about God, yourself, life on earth and beyond this earth, and about the many injustices on this planet that could be corrected with harmony and peace. An inner yearning to know the whys and wherefores of life's purpose itself should be explored through wholesome books, prayer, meditation, personal experiences, and extending your hand as a peacemaker to those around you. Who knows? In time, perhaps you will become the sage you appear to admire, honour, and emulate.

**SAILBOAT** (see **BOAT**)

## SAILOR (see NAVY or NAVIGATOR)

## SAILPLANE (see AIRPLANE)

## SAINT (see *also* MARTYR)

Seeing, meeting, or talking to a saint or actually being a saint within your dream state infers that your compassion and virtuous characteristics as a human being are aboveboard, and your zeal for earthly and spiritual perfection seems to be a never-ending quest. You mean well, and you certainly are on the right road in life. Do not be disillusioned by the criticisms, anger, or hate of others who fail to understand your inner needs. Carry on, and you will go beyond the smallness of others around you. A word of caution: do not get carried away with your gifts and talents, but courageously carry on in a humble, giving manner.

(*Note*: You may also have the pleasure of knowing that if, for example, you are experiencing a very negative dream but at the very end of your dream sequence or anywhere during your dream sequence you happen to see a saint, then the symbolism of a saint takes precedence over your entire bad dream. Consequently, you have nothing to worry about simply because the saint acts as a "buffer zone" to anything negative within a dream.)

## SALAD (see FOOD)

## SALARY (see INCOME or MONEY)

## SALE (see AUCTION, BAZAAR, CANVASSER, CARGO, CLERK, MARKETPLACE, MERCHANT, NEGOTIATION, PEDDLER, SALESMAN, or STORE)

## SALESMAN (see *also* CLERK)

Dreaming about seeing or being a salesman could indicate that you are a salesman who merely dreamt about your daily work. If this is not the case, then this dream suggests that you are either pleased or displeased with your present life conditions, and/or you are contemplating some drastic change that may affect your immediate family or friends. Sometimes you are looking here and there for happiness and peace of mind, when it is in fact lying dormant within your being.

Conquer your restlessness and your dissatisfaction. For your own sake, do not believe that the grass is always so green on the other side of the fence. Settle down for a while, and begin to accentuate the positive drive and impetus you already possess. Work towards one good goal in your life, and you will prosper; if you persist in looking for too many goals, you will falter and fail.

**SALESWOMAN** (see **SALESMAN**)

**SALIVA** (see **SPIT**)

**SALMON** (see **FISH**)

**SALOON** (see **CASINO** or **LIQUOR**)

**SALT** (see **SPICE**)

**SALTWATER** (see **WATER**)

**SALVATION** (see **LIBERATION** or **RESCUE**)

**SAMPAN** (see **BOAT**)

**SANCTUARY** (see **CHURCH, REFUGE, RESERVATION,** or **RETREAT**)

**SAND** (see *also* **DESERT, HOURGLASS,** or **SHORE**)
   All you can do is pray and hope that your loved ones begin to understand what you actually mean to them. Your mind and your heart may be heavy and sad at this time, yet this dream wishes to inform you that those who have mistreated you will return with better concepts and attitudes—not only about themselves, but about you, as well. Hold on! No one has lost you. By the same token, you have lost no one, either. Time will heal your wounds, and peace will come.

**SANDBAG** (see **SACK**)

**SANDBOX** (see **SAND**)

**SANDMAN** (see **LEGEND**)

## SANDPAPER

Some people see you as having an open mind; some people see you as being rather practical and extremely one-sided. Basically, you are a private, secretive individual who finds total solace in your own thoughts, actions, and deeds. You do not want people to dictate, to rule, or to control your life, in any way. More prosperity lies ahead of you simply because your hardworking efforts will bring you the results you hope to achieve. You not only stand by your words—you live by them!

**SANDSTORM** (see **STORM**)

**SANDWICH** (see **FOOD**)

**SAPPHIRE** (see **JEWELLERY**)

**SARDINE** (see **FISH**)

**SASH** (see **MATERIAL**)

**SATAN** (see **DEMON**)

**SATCHEL** (see **BAGGAGE**)

**SATELLITE** (see **MOON, SPACECRAFT,** or **SPACE STATION**)

**SATISFACTION** (see **HAPPINESS**)

**SATURN** (see **PLANET**)

**SATYR** (i.e., a deity having a man's body with horns, a tail, pointed ears, and the hind legs of a goat)

As imaginary and fictitious as this creature may be, it can surface within a dream, from time to time. The dreamer is advised to sort out and dispel any negative sexual perversions, fetishes, deviations, or other unnatural sexual habits that are demeaning to the mind and soul. No good can come from unholy attitudes or wanton desires of the flesh. If you are troubled, then pray to God for help. If necessary, seek professional assistance in order to set your mind straight, where unusual or unnatural sexual matters are concerned.

**SAUSAGE** (see **MEAT**)

**SAVAGERY** (see **CRUELTY** or **PRIMITIVISM**)

**SAVINGS ACCOUNT** (see **BANK**)

**SAVIOR** (see **GOD** or **JESUS**)

**SAW** (see **TOOL**)

**SAWDUST**

Sometimes, when you feel life is totally hopeless, someone reaches out to help you, or something happens to bring you back to reality. Life is full of those small or great lifelines which should allow us to forge ahead with renewed confidence and strength. Much too often, people rebel when things go sour and tend to feel victimized or too defenseless to carry on. They forget all about their reasoning faculties and seem to be unwilling to face their problems in a headstrong manner. This dream is telling you to never forget the power and glory within your being. You can master almost anything in life, providing you do not succumb to or give in to your inner foibles and weaknesses. Do not create more senseless and needless strife for yourself in dire times; instead, recognize your God-given ability to master your problem(s) with down-to-earth logic and common sense.

**SAWMILL** (see **MILL**)

**SCAFFOLD** (see **STAGE**)

**SCALD** (see **BOIL** or **INJURY**)

**SCALE** (i.e., a weighing machine or device)

You are weighing or balancing a vital decision or action in your life. What may appear, at first, to be a no-win situation will turn out to be both satisfying and, eventually, profitable for you. Be at peace! Luck—plenty of it—is riding in your corner and will continue to do so for a long period of time.

**SCARE** (see **STARTLE**)

## SCARECROW

There are times when you think you have failed not only yourself, but others around you, as well, for some reason or other. You are well thought of and admired. Recently, however, one or two people whom you know and care about seem to be acting somewhat aloof and indifferent towards you—or so it appears. You cannot put your finger on it and are blaming yourself for something you possibly said or did to create this negative atmosphere. Relax; this matter will settle itself soon. In the process, you will discover that even a friend or two can have a personal problem that must be solved quietly and alone.

**SCARF** (see **CLOTHES** or **DECORATION**)

**SCENT** (see **SMELL**)

**SCHEDULE** (see **CALENDAR, LIST,** or **PROGRAM**)

**SCHIZOPHRENIA** (see **INSANITY** or **PSYCHOTHERAPY**)

**SCHOLARSHIP** (see **GIFT**)

**SCHOOL** (see *also* **BLACKBOARD, BOARDING SCHOOL, CLOAKROOM, COLLEGE, CONSERVATORY, DROPOUT, FACULTY, FRESHMAN, GRADUATION, HOMEWORK, INITIATION, LEARNING, LESSON, PLAYGROUND, REFORM SCHOOL, REPORT CARD, RIDING SCHOOL, SCHOOLMATE, SCHOOLROOM, TEACHER,** or **UNIVERSITY**)

Any one or several of the following definitions may be applicable: A) that you are presently attending or working at a school; or B) that you find school both interesting and challenging; or C) that you find school dull, boring, and very meaningless; or D) that you wish you had attended school longer than you did; or E) that someone you know refuses to go back to school; or F) that you recall your school days with fond or bad memories; or G) that in school, you were dubbed as being "least likely to succeed"—but, in the end, you proved otherwise; or H) that if you had your way, the school system would be changed or altered to suit your needs and fancies; or I) that you are happy to be attending a certain school and find that most of the teachers and students there are easy to get along with; or J) that you are presently attending night classes at a school in order to get your diploma; or K) that you wish to get your high school diploma in order to go on to a higher education; or L) that you are either satisfied or dissatisfied with your present curriculum; or M) that you are having difficulty with a teacher or two and/or a student or two at school; or N) that you are having difficulty with a subject or two but hope to correct this matter, before too long; or O) that you feel if more students would take the time to realize how lucky they are to be attending school in the first place, they just might strive a little harder to upgrade their marks; or P) that you had to quit school many years ago, but you later returned to finish your schooling in order to go on to a higher education; or Q) that this dream has little or no relevance to you at this time.

## SCHOOLMATE

Any one or several of the following definitions may be applicable: A) that you are presently on good terms or on bad terms with a schoolmate; or B) that you wanted to be in the same classroom as your schoolmate but, unfortunately, this was not possible; or C) that you dreamt about a former schoolmate who passed away many years ago; or D) that you have just acquired a new schoolmate in your classroom; or E) that a schoolmate recently moved to another town or city; or F) that you will be attending a new school before too long and seem to be worried about whether your new schoolmates will be friendly or not; or G) that a schoolmate of yours was recently hospitalized; or H) that a schoolmate of yours became a president of a large corporation; or I) that you recently met a schoolmate whom you had not seen for years; or J) that at a recent school reunion celebration, you met most of your past schoolmates; or K) that a schoolmate recently quit school or was expelled from school; or L) that a schoolmate you knew about became a famous personality; or M) that most of your schoolmates are friendly except, perhaps, for one or two who are most unfriendly and uncooperative; or N) that this dream has little or no significance to you at this time.

## SCHOOLROOM

A schoolroom that is relatively neat, quiet, and orderly indicates that you are a highly appreciated and respected individual. You are always willing to share your innate knowledge and wisdom—spanning many fields and topics—with others. It also appears that both younger and older people are attracted to you. They seem to appreciate and admire the quality of your work and accomplishments. Presently, you seem to be building a foundation towards earthly and spiritual happiness, success, and prosperity. Your quests and wants on planet Earth will be satisfied, and your successes will be great and bountiful!

A schoolroom that seems to be in shambles, is noisy, or is totally disorderly indicates that you are at times very careless, argumentative, and somewhat lazy. Will you change? Possibly yes, possibly no. This dream advises you to stabilize your thoughts and actions, show more compassion towards others, and begin to realize that it is not what life gives to you that counts, but what you can contribute to life. Life does not owe you a living! Be more caring and productive in what you do; don't just sit back and hope for the best. There will be no best of anything unless you are prepared to work hard for what you want or hope to achieve. Try not to be so demanding and wanting; be more giving, instead. This positive action should commence to place you on the right track in life.

**SCHOOLTEACHER** (see **TEACHER**)

**SCHOOLWORK** (see **HOMEWORK** or **SCHOOL**)

**SCHOOLYARD** (see **PLAYGROUND**)

**SCIENTIST**

Seeing or being a scientist in a dream indicates that you have influence over other people. Perhaps it's your personal magnetism, your charisma, or your position in life, but, whatever it is, one can only hope that your authority or power over people is used wisely and fairly. Failing to do so can ultimately lead to being exposed, shamed, and regretful.

**SCISSORS**

If the scissors are relatively new-looking and workable, then several of your immediate plans or wishes will come true. Be patient. Everything of good order has its moment, its hour, and its day.

If the scissors are old-looking and unworkable, then someone or something will disappoint you before too long (e.g., a trip not transpiring, a contract being broken, a house not being built). Whatever it is, you will be strong enough to accept the facts as they are given to you. However, in the future, you will be more inclined to believe that actions speak louder than words!

**SCOLD** (see **ANGER** or **DISAPPROVAL**)

**SCOOTER** (see **MOTOR SCOOTER** or **TOY**)

**SCORN** (see **ANGER, CONTEMPT, HATRED, MOCKERY,** or **RUDENESS**)

**SCORPION**

Seeing a calm or a busy scorpion reveals that you are hypercritical of yourself because of some foul experience or disagreement that you had recently. The first step here is to settle down, and begin to relax your mind, for you seem to be getting worked up for nothing. Allay your fears and doubts! What happened, happened; you cannot retrieve or necessarily retract what transpired. Just hope for the best, and remember that your own fears can bring about precisely what you fear the most.

To kill a scorpion or to see an aggressive or a dead scorpion indicates that you will pass a very trying time with common sense and courage. This is not a death dream but rather a dream that reveals an enormous number of challenges and questions of the heart, mind, and soul that have to be answered. This could involve some type of anguish at home, at work, at school, with a friend, and so on, or any other matter that outwardly appears hopeless, yet inwardly appears hopeful. If all goes well, you should come out of this stormy episode of your life with a greater blessing and understanding about yourself, about your needs and wants, and about life in general.

**SCOUNDREL** (see **CRIMINAL, DECEPTION, MISCHIEF,** or **THIEVERY**)

**SCOUT** (see **DETECTIVE, ESPIONAGE, GUARD,** or **PATROL**)

**SCRAP** (see **JUNK**)

**SCRAPBOOK**

Your positive, enthusiastic, and independent nature are all harmonious character qualities that will inevitably assist you in life. Shortly, you will embark upon a new venture which should lead you towards an accomplished and worthy goal (e.g., attending a university, college or specialized school; starting a new business venture; writing a book; starting up a music band). Whatever it may be, you can be sure it will be a stepping stone for something bigger and greater in your life.

## SCREAM

To hear a scream within your dream implies that you are actually hearing yourself or someone else scream outside your dream state. If this is not the case, then your dream suggests that you are either your own best friend (i.e., liking who you are and what you do in life) or else you are your own worst enemy (hating who you are and creating trouble for yourself). Hopefully, you are your own best friend. However, if for some reason you are not, then this dream urges you to do some serious soul-searching, at this time. Nobody expects you to be one hundred percent perfect in everything you do, nor should anyone condemn you for every little mistake you make. But to deny yourself the opportunities for self-improvement is tantamount to not really caring one way or another. In life you should care, for it is you and you alone who will have to account for your soul and the precious time you waste upon this planet. If you truly want to see a better reflection of yourself in the mirror, then commence to revamp your self-image with confidence; begin to control your desires, actions, and habits with sound logic; and commence to examine your heritage, abilities, and self-worth with respect. Fulfill your gift of life with all the hope, courage, and successes you can humanly muster. For your own sake, do not waste your life on senseless thoughts, actions, and self-pity. You have only one life to live on earth, so do a good job of it. There is no second chance!

## SCREEN (see **AWNING, CURTAIN, HIDING, INVISIBILITY,** or **MOTION PICTURE**)

**SCREW** (e.g., a machine screw, wood screw, lag screw, set screw)

There should be no room for excuses when things have to be done. This dream advises you not to shirk your duties, chores, activities, studies, promises, or other things which require immediate attention. If everybody decided to be lax in life, this world would come to a complete standstill. Everyone is dependent upon one another, in some way. Realize that your excuses for not doing something can in fact have a great impact and effect on others around you. Do not expect the next person to do something for you that you should be doing for yourself!

**SCREWDRIVER** (see **TOOL**)

**SCRIBE** (see **AUTHOR**)

**SCRIMMAGE** (see **GAME**)

**SCRIPT** (see **DOCUMENT** or **MANUSCRIPT**)

**SCRIPTURE** (see **BIBLE**)

**SCRIPTWRITER** (see **AUTHOR**)

**SCROLL** (see **BOOK** or **MANUSCRIPT**)

**SCROOGE** (see **MISER**)

**SCUBA** (see **AQUALUNG** or **DIVER**)

**SCULPTOR**
At this time, you appear to be held back from progressing or from undertaking something you would like to do. Perhaps you lack financial funds or a good education, or perhaps you are living in a bad environment? Whatever your obstacles might be, this dream indicates that you will fulfill your purpose or mission in life, sooner or later. What you cannot attain today, you will have other opportunities to fulfill, at a later date. Be patient in all things, and your thirst for adventure, inspiration, knowledge, and wisdom will yet be satisfied.

**SCULPTURE** (see *also* **SCULPTOR**)
If the sculpture is intact, clear, and concise, then this dream infers that you are a highly intelligent, skilled, or gifted individual. You always try to express originality in what you say or do, implying you are a creative person (e.g., sculptor, author, poet, artist). As well, your knowledge about the fine arts, various philosophies in life, and about life itself is most interesting and appealing to those who know and understand you.

Seeing a sculpture that is weathered, broken, or destroyed reveals that you are trying to put the pieces of your life back together by keeping quite busy, or you are trying to mend or repair some difficulties between you and another person. In either case, you will not only be successful in your efforts, but you will also be extremely happy and proud for listening to your better instincts!

**SEA** (see **WATER**)

**SEA ANCHOR** (see **ANCHOR**)

**SEA CALF** (see **SEAL**)

**SEA ELEPHANT** (see **SEAL**)

**SEA GULL** (see **BIRD**)

**SEA HORSE** (see **FISH**)

**SEAL**

You may be experiencing some mental frustrations and stresses, at this time. The reasons for this may be attributed to the fact that you find it very difficult to cope with new situations or sudden changes which happen to occur within and around you, on occasion. Life will not stand still for you, nor must you stand still for life! Always be prepared for events or circumstances which could alter your daily activities in a minor or major way. Do not be upset when things suddenly happen to you. Rather, be prepared to challenge and master those events with determination and harmony within self and by adopting a greater sense of humor. Laughter can wash away your stresses one at a time. Try it—it really works!

**SEAMSTRESS** (see **DRESSMAKER**)

**SÉANCE**

If the séance appears to be calm, loving, and not frightening in any way, then you are an open-minded individual who is fascinated by curious customs and stranger-than-fiction concepts and ideas. People are automatically attracted to you for your great insight (which appears to be far-reaching and true) into matters of life and death.

Seeing a séance that is both frightening and unbelievable reveals that you are a strong-minded individual who does not necessarily believe everything some people claim to see or hear (e.g., flying saucers, ghosts, hearing the voice of a departed soul, miracles). Sometimes, in spite of your own uncertainties, you can discover some wondrous revelations and truths about life, when you least expect it to happen! By letting go of your earthbound thoughts for a moment or two, you might discover that there is more to heaven and earth than meets the eyes or ears of any Doubting Thomas on this planet—even the Doubting Thomas within you.

**SEAPORT** (see **HARBOUR** or **PASSAGEWAY**)

**SEAQUAKE** (see **EARTHQUAKE**)

**SEARCH** (see **EXPEDITION, INQUIRY,** or **PURSUIT**)

**SEARCHLIGHT** (see **FLASHLIGHT**)

**SEASHELL**

If the seashell is intact, then be prepared to be visited or entertained by unexpected company; it could be relatives, friends, or others. This occasion should be enjoyably humorous and emotionally tender for all concerned.

Seeing a seashell that is broken or damaged suggests that you are upset or unsure about attending some special gathering or celebration such as an anniversary, wedding, birthday party, or other event. This dream reveals that you will attend the gathering or celebration and that you will be very pleasantly surprised by the royal treatment you will receive.

**SEASHORE** (see **SHORE**)

**SEASICKNESS** (see **NAUSEOUSNESS**)

**SEA SNAKE** (see **SNAKE**)

**SEASON** (i.e., spring, summer, autumn, or winter)

Dreaming about any season which appears to be natural looking and relatively calm and peaceful suggests that you are overzealous about a certain matter. Be calm, be patient, and certainly hope for the best, but do not be too disappointed if things do not turn out exactly as you mentally envisioned them or mentally surmised they should. Not everything happens the way we want things to happen. Sometimes we simply must accept the bitter with the sweet and accept humbly and gratefully what is given to us.

Dreaming about the four seasons in quick succession, and/or seeing a mixture of seasons together, such as a winter scene combined with a summer scene or a summer scene combined with a fall scene, reveals that you are in some type of anguish or despair about a personal matter or a trying situation involving a family member. Face the truth that is within you, and you will be able to face the truth that is around you, as well. Today your troubles may seem insurmountable, yet tomorrow—another day—may bring you the hope and courage needed to master your present difficulties. You eventually will!

**SEASONING** (see **SPICE**)

**SEAT BELT** (see **SAFETY BELT**)

**SEA URCHIN**
This dream counsels you to study or analyze your motives and attitudes in life with an open, caring mind. Do not feel that everything you say or do is aboveboard when, in fact, it is not. You cannot ignore the fact when you offend or hurt someone in an emotional way; nor can you ignore the fact that your pride, domineering attitudes, and exaggerations are doing you harm. You possess some unique insights into life, in general; but, for your future's sake, it might be wise to look more deeply into the portals of your own heart, mind, and soul for the best qualities within you. When you find these qualities, accentuate them and live by them. You will prosper this way!

**SEAWEED** (see **PLANT**)

**SECLUSION** (see **ISLAND, QUARANTINE, REFUGE, RETIREMENT**, or **RETREAT**)

**SECRET** (see **CONFIDENCE** or **MYSTERY**)

**SECRET AGENT** (see **ESPIONAGE** or **INQUIRY**)

**SECRETARY** (see *also* **RECEPTIONIST**)

Any one or several of the following definitions may be applicable: A) that you are a secretary who either likes or dislikes the work that you do; or B) that you recently left your secretarial job for another position or for something else; or C) that someday you plan to be a secretary in a large corporation; or D) that you know of someone who is a secretary; or E) that you are presently attending secretarial school; or F) that your employer is always complaining or is dissatisfied with your secretarial work; or G) that your employer praises your secretarial work; or H) that you feel your employer or other staff members are trying to take advantage of your good personality and work habits, so they give you most of the work to do; or I) that your employer is harassing you in some way; or J) that you are planning to take a refresher course, where your secretarial career is concerned; or K) that you would like to travel more, where your job as a secretary is concerned; or L) that you are trying to find a job as a secretary but, unfortunately, there does not appear to be any position open to you, at this time; or M) that you feel you deserve a raise in pay as a secretary, but your employer thinks you do not; or N) that you recently received a raise in pay which makes your work as a secretary seem so much more worthwhile than before; or O) that you recently retired from work as a secretary; or P) that this dream has little or no significance to you at this time.

**SECRET SERVICE** (see **ESPIONAGE** or **INQUIRY**)

**SEDATIVE** (see **MEDICATION**)

**SEDUCTION** (see **DECEPTION, EVILDOER,** or **INTERCOURSE**)

**SEED** (see **GRAIN, KERNEL,** or **PLANT**)

**SEER** (see **CLAIRVOYANCE, MEDIUM,** or **PROPHECY**)

**SEESAW**

Sometimes people take advantage of your abilities or skills, but you still tend to respect them, in spite of their flaws and weaknesses. Those who are more aggressive than you could certainly learn a thing or two from you about unselfishness. In many respects, you have a heart of gold;

your true friends will attest to this reality. Quietly and peacefully, your future will be paved with wise decisions and opportunities which will make your life more pleasurable and much more financially rewarding.

**SEGREGATION** (see **GHETTO, HATRED, PERSECUTION, PREJUDICE,** or **QUARANTINE**)

**SEIZURE** (see **ARREST, EPILEPSY** or **FIT**)

**SELF-ABASEMENT** (see **HUMILITY** or **MASOCHISM**)

**SELF-ABUSE** (see **ACCUSATION, DISAPPROVAL, HATRED,** or **MASOCHISM**)

**SELF-ADMIRATION** (see **NARCISSISM**)

**SELF-CONCERN** (see **NARCISSISM**)

**SELF-CONFIDENCE** (see **CONFIDENCE**)

**SELF-CONTROL** (see **PREVENTION**)

**SELF-DEFENSE** (see **JUDO** or **KARATE**)

**SELF-DENIAL** (see **FAST, LENT, MARTYR,** or **PREVENTION**)

**SELF-DISCIPLINE** (see **PREVENTION**)

**SELF-ESTEEM** (see **BRAGGART, CONCEIT, CONFIDENCE,** or **SNOBBERY**)

**SELF-EXAMINATION** (see **INTROSPECTION**)

**SELF-GOVERNMENT** (see **GOVERNMENT, INDEPENDENCE,** or **LIBERATION**)

**SELF-SACRIFICE** (see **MARTYR** or **SUICIDE**)

**SEMEN** (see **INTERCOURSE, MASTURBATION** or **SEX**)

**SEMIDOME** (see **DOME**)

**SEMINAR** (see **INQUIRY, LEARNING,** or **LECTURE**)

**SEMINARY** (see **SCHOOL**)

**SENATE** (see **GOVERNMENT** or **LAW**)

**SENILITY** (see **OLD AGE**)

**SENSE** (see **SMELL, SOUND,** or **TOUCH**)

**SENTRY** (see **GUARD** or **PATROL**)

**SEPULCHER** (see **ALTAR** or **GRAVE**)

**SEQUIN** (see **DECORATION**)

**SERGEANT** (see **AIR FORCE, ARMY,** or **NAVY**)

**SERIAL NUMBER**
Seeing a serial number indicates that you would like to win a major prize in some lottery or contest. Maybe you will win in time; if you do, thank God for His abundance and blessings to you.

**SERMON** (see **CLERGYMAN, BIBLE, LEARNING,** or **LECTURE**)

**SERPENT** (see **SNAKE**)

**SERVICE STATION** (see **GAS STATION**)

**SEWER**
Seeing or being in a sewer predicts troubled times (e.g., accident, sickness, failing at something)! Pray to God for guidance and protection, look after your health, avoid unnecessary travel, if possible, and do not do anything in a foolish, mindless manner. Hopefully, this mighty storm brewing around you will leave you totally unscathed!

# SEWING

Seeing yourself or someone else sew indicates that you will be attending a gathering (which could be happy or sad) with family members and friends, or you will solve a personal problem which has been troubling you for quite some time, or you will be annoyed with a family member or friend who tends to be very bossy, gossipy, and troublesome. You are a survivor of many trials and tribulations already, so whether there is difficulty or happiness ahead for you, you have learned to accept life for what it is and for what it brings. This is a good, wholesome attitude to uphold and maintain! If more people thought the way you do, this world would be a lot less troublesome.

# SEWING MACHINE (see SEWING)

# SEX (see *also* ADULTERY, AFFAIR, BESTIALITY, BISEXUALISM, BROTHEL, EXHIBITIONISM, FRIGIDITY, GIGOLO, HAREM, HOMOSEXUALITY, IMMORALIST, IMPOTENCE, INCEST, INTERCOURSE, LOVE, MASOCHISM, MISTRESS, ORGY, PEEPING TOM, PORNOGRAPHY, PROSTITUTION, PUBERTY, RAPE, TRANSSEXUAL, TRANSVESTITE, or SICKNESS)

Sexual dreams are universally common in all human beings simply because we are all sexual beings. Some sex oriented dreams may be more bizarre than others, but this does not necessarily imply that a person is sexually perverse or sick. If you lead a good life and have a healthy outlook towards yourself, sex, the opposite sex, and other people as a whole, then rest assured that your sexual dreams are no more than your conscious or subconscious projections concerning your sexual likes, dislikes, or fantasies. A good, sane attitude about sex during your wake state simply means you have a good, sane attitude about yourself and about life in general. However, if you actually do have a perverse, sickly attitude about yourself, sex, the opposite sex, and about life as a whole, then your sexual dreams can actually haunt you, taunt you, or perhaps leave you even more confused than you are already. A sickly, perverse attitude about sex during your wake state simply means you have a sickly, perverse attitude about yourself and about life in general. You may be living in your own little world of Jekyll and Hyde. This can get progressively worse unless you seek some kind of professional help. Your sexual problems no doubt started earlier in life; and, unless this area of your life can be tapped, sifted, and literally wiped out of your mind, you will continue to harbour your sexual confusions, frustrations, and base attitudes for years to come— or perhaps for as long as you are alive on this earth plane.

(*Note*: The entire concept in having sexual dreams is to simply allow each individual an opportunity to release their sexual and emotional wants, needs, and suppressions via the conscious and subconscious mind through a dream. There is no need for concern in this matter unless a person has a sick or perverse attitude about themselves, about sex, and about other vital matters of life. Again, if your sexual desires are wholesome and loving in life, then you are on the right road to happiness and satisfaction. However, if your sexual desires are lustful, perverse, or simply downright unsound, then professional help is strongly urged and advised.)

**SEXLESSNESS** (see **FRIGIDITY** or **IMPOTENCE**)

**SEXTANT** (i.e., an instrument for measuring angular distances such as the location of a ship)
    What you do with your time is entirely up to you. So often, people waste energies on foolish thoughts and actions, only to regret this fact much later in life. No matter how rough the road in life may appear to be to you, you should always strive to be constructive and willing to improve your mental, physical, and spiritual outlook. It is far more important to go forwards in life than to simply sit back and wait for something wondrous to happen to you, or to sit back and do nothing, or to sit back and count yesterday's laurels. Too much idleness can breed contempt in life. Keep busy, and you will discover a greater purpose to your worth upon this planet!

**SEXTUPLET** (see **BIRTH**)

**SHACK** (see **CABIN** or **HOUSE**)

**SHADOW**
    Seeing your own shadow or that of someone else forewarns you of some pending difficulties with something or with someone who appears to be unstable, unreliable, or simply untrustworthy (e.g., a vehicle, an appliance, a tool, a family member, a friend, a stranger). Be careful! If you are sensibly mature, then no doubt you will be able to

handle this matter with shrewd, sound logic. However, if you tend to be foolish and uncaring, then you may be asking for more trouble and grief than you deserve!

**SHAME** (See **GUILT** or **REGRET**)

**SHAMPOO**

You will very soon reach some final decision or understanding concerning some bothersome situation that has troubled you for quite some time. It appears that you have been harbouring some doubts and anguish concerning this matter, but now you want some inner peace. You shall have that inner peace within a fortnight of this dream.

**SHARK** (see **FISH**)

**SHAVER** (e.g., a razor, electric shaver)

You will diffuse some of your fearsome attitudes and commence to carry out some long-awaited aims, plans, or proposals. Do not be afraid to do things alone. The only obstacle you can possibly have in front of you now is yourself. So, for your own sake, make that quantum leap that you have been dreaming about, praying for, and visualizing.

**SHED** (e.g., storehouse, warehouse, depository, workshop, lean-to)

Seeing a shed indicates that you will be apologizing to someone about an emotional, physical, or financial matter, and/or you are becoming obsessed with a doctrine or belief that could be false and misleading. You are urged to go onto other, more important, matters and avenues of your life. Admittedly, it is far easier to make a mistake than it is to correct that mistake, but we must all learn to accept our blunders with honesty and intelligence and ultimately realize that we are never too young or too old to learn a valuable lesson or two in life.

**SHEEP**

Sometimes you fail to realize how fortunate you really are to be alive and well and to have someone or know someone who loves and cares about you. Taking these factors of your life for granted is like having a beautiful potted plant and forgetting to water and nourish it. This dream wishes to remind you to never forget the needs and wants of those very dear and close to you; nor should your loved ones forget your needs and wants. You certainly may count sheep before you sleep; but, in a dream state, seeing or counting sheep simply means count your blessings!

## SHEET (see CLOTHES)

## SHEIKH

You have not been facing some matters of importance (e.g., health, finances, investments, marriage, romance) in a practical, logical manner recently. Someone has already given you some good advice; however, you are failing to heed it! You should not ignore anyone's kindness and common sense at this time—or at any other time, for that matter. Do not be so stubborn and illogical. Rather, face the truth in front of you. Nothing is permanent here, and your losses and gains are simply what you make them out to be. You can solve your problem(s) overnight, but you must be willing to forget your wants and needs for the moment, and faithfully face the stark realities of what life is all about. You were born on earth to learn; now you have a wonderful opportunity to learn something about yourself. Do so wisely, and you will profit from this experience.

## SHELLFISH (see MOLLUSK)

## SHELTER (see DUGOUT, HOME, HOUSE, or REFUGE)

## SHEPHERD (see HERDSMAN)

## SHERIFF (see PEACE OFFICER)

## SHIP

Seeing a ship that is docked or sailing reveals that you will be asked to solve a problem or two where a younger person is concerned. Your advice will be heeded, and positive results will be achieved by this younger person.

A ship that appears to be in danger (e.g., being destroyed, colliding, sinking) reveals that you often see the futility of worrying and fretting over others around you, but it is a part of your nature to be concerned about your loved ones, in one way or another. Be wary about being over-stressed with certain matters which may unduly affect you. Do not forget to look after yourself, as well. This is not being selfish; this is being logical. Your loved ones need and love you as much as you need and love them. Learn to be more calm, placid, and inwardly trusting whenever it rains and storms in your life. With this attitude, you will experience a more peaceful ending to a troubled story.

**SHIRT** (see **CLOTHES**)

**SHOCK** (see **ANGER, DANGER, EARTHQUAKE,** or **STARTLE**)

**SHOE** (see **FOOTWEAR**)

**SHOEHORN**

Seeing this implement means that you will come out of a financial slump, or you will come out of some physical disorder, with great relief. A brief period of confinement may be in order for you, but you will pass this time in peace and comfort. As well, you will take a lengthy journey, in due time, to an island where palm trees abound and/or to a region where snow is prevalent. Happier, healthier, and better times are ahead for you.

**SHOELACE** (see **FOOTWEAR**)

**SHOEMAKER**

You alone will have to decide whether or not you wish to overcome some personal bad habit and/or a sexual problem bothering you at this time. Perhaps through self-control or self-persuasion, you will be able to conquer those contrary and difficult conflicts within your being. It certainly is not an easy task to be "perfect" on this earth plane, especially when disappointments, trials and tribulations, temptations, and a host of other conflicting emotions get into the picture. However, you must at least try for betterment in life, and hope that you can stay in the right direction without giving in to vain hopes, fears, and despair.

**SHOESHINE** (see **FOOTWEAR**)

**SHOP** (see **STORE**)

**SHOPPING CENTER** (see **STORE**)

## SHORE

From time to time, you tend to suppress your affections towards others simply because of outside pressures and difficulties. This is quite normal and natural. Everyone has their moods, their notions, their ups and downs, their good days and bad days; and these have a great bearing on their feelings. This dream is trying to tell you that you are not unusual or uncaring, but rather a human being who is trying to be pleasant, fair, and just on most occasions. Now and again, you will succumb to difficult pressures beyond your control, which will ultimately make you feel miserable, distant, and aloof. The mighty waves of a sea come and go; so it is with your high and low feelings. They come… and they go; they come… and they go.

## SHORE BIRD (see **BIRD**)

## SHORE PATROL (see **COAST GUARD, GUARD, NAVY,** or **PATROL**)

## SHORT CIRCUIT

To witness a short circuit within a dream implies that an alarming amount of strain, nervousness, and melancholy has beset you lately. Someone or something continues to trouble you, and/or your physical health is not up to par, for some reason. It seems as though you are ready to throw your hands in the air in total despair and defeat! Be at peace! There is plenty of hope and comfort for you down the road; but, in the interim, you must alter your downhearted spirit with hopeful thoughts and visualizations. The more depressed you are, the worse situations appear to be for you; the more optimistic you are, the greater your ability becomes in coping and mastering your problems at hand. Don't give up on anything, now or later; but look ahead, and forge ahead with all the human understanding and confidence you can conceivably muster within you! You can do it, and you can make it. First, repair that short circuit (lack of self-confidence) within yourself!

## SHORTCUT

Taking a shortcut in a dream implies that you will be taking a shortcut in some matter of saving time, labour, cost, and so on during your wake state. Will it work for you? Maybe; maybe not. How many times have we all attempted to take a shortcut in life, only to see the folly of our ways? We had to backtrack and spend more time, effort, and energy on that one task than it was worth! This does not imply that shortcuts should not be utilized and respected. When you map out a strategy where a shortcut is concerned, then you are probably on the right track. To take a shortcut without foresight, however, could cost you more time, energy, and money than you remotely imagined possible.

## SHORTHAND
This form of speed writing suggests that you are a quick thinker and are very capable of handling most of your problems with speed and efficiency. Basically, you are a no-nonsense kind of person. If someone says something wrong to you, then you quickly correct or broach that person, right on the spot! You are very loyal to your true friends and expect the same consideration in return. And, why not? You work very hard to maintain your honesty and dignity. If you can do it, others around you should be able to do it, as well!

**SHOTGUN** (see **GUN**)

**SHOUT** (see **CALL** or **SCREAM**)

**SHOVEL** (see **TOOL**)

**SHOWBOAT** (see **ACTOR, BOAT,** or **THEATRE**)

**SHOW BUSINESS** (see **ACTOR, MOTION PICTURE, TELEVISION,** or **THEATRE**)

**SHOWER** (see **BATH** or **RAIN**)

**SHREW** (i.e., a mouse-like animal)
Sometimes you think the right thing to do may be the wrong thing to do, or the wrong thing to do may be the right thing to do. Be at peace! Everyone experiences this human frailty practically on a daily basis. Don't be afraid to be confused and frustrated from time to time, for this too helps you to revitalize and reorganize your thoughts and actions in a sensible, practical manner. Soon, you will be experiencing a difficult emotional period in your life. You will feel

alone, forgotten, and totally forsaken by others whom you know. However, you will not be alone in this storm! A very special person will be there with you to guide you and protect you as you wander here and there in search of an answer to your needs, wants, and prayers. You will find your answer, and you will be made stronger, for indeed Jesus, the Christ Light, will be by your side each moment of the way. Your tomorrows will come and you will tower above many things past.

## SHRIMP

You do not always keep secrets. You give some away, and on certain occasions in the past, this has created various problems for you. Be careful! Someone will be approaching you before too long wanting you to "keep a big secret". This dream advises you to be very diplomatic and truthful to this person, stating that you do not wish to hear any so-called secrets. Now, if you should decide to ignore your dream's forewarning, then you must be prepared for some backlashes, complaints, or rebuke from this individual who will assume that you "spilled the beans".

## SHRINE (see ALTAR, BURIAL, CHURCH, GRAVE, or MAUSOLEUM)

## SHRINKING (see REDUCTION)

## SHROUD (see BURIAL or MATERIAL)

## SHRUB (e.g., a bush, creeper, vine)

You mistrust someone or someone mistrusts you. Perhaps your reasons seem just and fair to you; but, in the long run, unless you learn to at least forgive your enemy, there can be no peace in your heart, mind, and soul. Hate creates anxieties, and anxieties can create further stresses not to your liking. It all adds up and, when you least expect it, you could become sick over this prideful matter. You have better things to do with your time and thoughts, so do so wisely!

## SHUFFLEBOARD (see GAME)

## SIAMESE TWINS (see BIRTH)

**SICKNESS** (see *also* **BLOOD POISONING, CANCER, COLD, DELIRIUM, ECZEMA, EPIDEMIC, EPILEPSY, FIT, INFECTION, INSANITY, LEPROSY, MALARIA, MUMPS, PARALYSIS,** or **RABIES**)

Any one or several of the following definitions may be applicable: A) that you are presently sick but hope to recover before too long; or B) that you recently recuperated from some sickness; or C) that you know of someone who has a curable or an incurable disease; or D) that you are worried about a family member or friend who is presently sick and perhaps in a hospital; or E) that as a child you were very sickly, but today you are very healthy; or F) that you have some type of sickness your doctor cannot seem to pinpoint or cure at this time; or G) that you know you can actually become sick by merely telling someone you are sick when you are not; or H) that you feel most, if not all, diseases on this planet will be eradicated in time to come; or I) that you believe in miracle cures where some presently incurable diseases are concerned; or J) that you have some constant fears about becoming sick, but you are doing your best to ignore these thoughts; or K) that you know a healthy mind and outlook are the best remedies to cure yourself whenever you are sick; or L) that you feel illness can be created through stresses, depression, hatreds, anxieties, anguish, or the feeling of being totally unwanted and unloved; or M) that you feel God and prayer are the two greatest healers in your life; or N) that this dream has little or no relevance to you at this time.

**SIDESADDLE** (see **SADDLE**)

**SIDEWALK**

If the sidewalk is straight and natural-looking, then you can be sure that your earthly and spiritual affairs are being handled properly and sensibly. You have your feet firmly on the ground and certainly make no bones about working for your aims and goals. Your perceptive thinking and positive work ethic will bring you the comfort and satisfaction you seek in life.

A sidewalk that is not straight or natural-looking or one that ends abruptly implies that you are not happy with your lifestyle, and/or you are creating unnecessary grief for yourself and for others around you. This dream symbolism advises you to get a grip on yourself; begin to find out who you are, what you are actually giving in life, and what you actually expect from life. Are your demands greater than your compromises, or are your compromises greater than your demands? Are you unwilling to admit your mistakes or at least make some efforts to correct your mistakes? How hard do you honestly try to improve your life? Do you just sit back and hope for the best, or do you make countless efforts and sacrifices to make matters within and around you better? Do you like yourself, or do you hate yourself? If you like yourself, then you should have enough courage and stamina to come out of your present quandary. However, if you hate yourself, then do not expect anything to change for you unless you change within yourself.

**SIEVE** (see **STRAINER**)

**SIGN** (see **AUTOGRAPH, COAT OF ARMS, INITIAL, PROPHECY, SIGNATURE, SIGNBOARD, SIGNPOST**, or **SYMBOL**)

**SIGNAL** (see **BEACON** or **FLAG**)

**SIGNATURE** (see *also* **INITIAL**)
Accept your past and present accomplishments with fond memories, but lay greater importance upon those things you have yet to accomplish. The wisest souls amongst us never reflect upon their past or present glories or greatness but diligently strive to be inspired on a daily basis. Life is far too short on this planet to do everything one hopes to accomplish. Doing your best is all that is required of anyone. God knows this and accepts this; you should also! In youth, there are always those new, vital times ahead with great aims and goals to look forward to; but when a person grows old, the sounds of life may become misty and dusty. Yet, the song of twilight and age can be the most precious, the most noble unfolding of Man's service and worth upon this planet. Carry on, for someday your service and worth will be judged and recorded as you sign your name on the scroll of life.

**SIGNBOARD** (i.e., billboard)
You have a calm, secure outlook in life, or else you have an uneasy, insecure outlook in life. Obviously, if you are a mature, calm and secure individual, then you accept your existence on earth in a respectful, trustful manner. You know who you are and where you are going and quite naturally adapt to new ideas, concepts, and challenges. However, if you are a difficult, insecure kind of individual, then your

existence on earth can be rather painful and disappointing. Harbouring disinterests, anxieties, and self-pity will not bring you any peace on earth. Since you cannot live your life over again, it only seems wise and practical that you begin to turn things around for yourself. How can you be happy? Well, stop harbouring so many grudges against—and doubts about—people, places, and things. Your existence on earth is a once-in-a-lifetime experience, so make the best of it. Begin each day with a hopeful, brighter outlook. Just tell yourself that you are going to have a marvelous day today, and you probably will! And, don't forget to pray for peace of mind and unselfishness.

**SIGNPOST** (e.g., a stop sign, a guide post)

Recently, you have been somewhat careless and absent-minded in your daily activities (e.g., poor driving habits, leaving an appliance on when it should be turned off, failing to mail a vital letter). You probably have too much on your mind, or you are mentally and physically exhausted. This dream merely wishes to remind you to either focus your attention on what you are doing, or else take a break, get a grip on yourself, and then go about your daily chores, feeling awake and alert.

**SILHOUETTE** (see **PAINTING**, **PHOTOGRAPH**, or **SHADOW**)

**SILK** (see **MATERIAL**)

**SILO** (see **TOWER**)

**SILVERWARE**

You seem to be able to give people very good advice; but, when you run into a similar problem, you tend to forget or ignore your own sound judgment. Forgetting what you preach is one thing; ignoring what you preach is altogether different. This dream advises you to be more consistent in your thoughts and actions, rather than falling to pieces when matters fail to work for you. If you can help other people, then you certainly can help yourself, as well! In times of trouble, just sit yourself down and begin to reflect deep into the portals of your heart, mind, and soul. An answer will come, but you must have the patience and courage to see it through. Your perception in life is exceedingly high; don't be afraid to use it when the need arises.

**SIMMER** (see **BOIL**)

**SINGER** (see *also* **CAROLER**)
If you are a professional singer in life, then your dream is merely revealing the type of work you obviously enjoy. However, if this is not the case, then this dream advises you to be on guard where one to two people are concerned. A conflict is brewing which could break up a long standing friendship between you and the others involved. Be careful; you may regret saying or doing something which you might never be able to retract! Strive for peace within your house, not war!

**SINK**
Being single-minded in certain matters is one thing, but failing to get another person's approval or consent in matters that require mutual consent or approval is an open invitation to trouble (e.g., buying an expensive car without your wife's approval or vice versa, making a large investment without your partner's approval). You may have a mind of your own, but you should not undermine the next person who perhaps was meant to be an integral part of your life, such as a spouse, relative, or a friend. You just may wind up selling the kitchen sink in your sudden impulses! Don't be so mind bent in having your own way—true relationships and partnerships cannot, and probably will not, survive in this manner.

**SIPHON**
Be wary of the company you keep! Although your true friends or acquaintances may never create mischief or trouble for you, there can always be a weed among the flowers. Remain at arms length from any friend or stranger who may attempt to lure you into some den of iniquity or wrongdoing for the sole purpose of smearing your good name and reputation. There is a great storm brewing; so, for your future's sake, do not degrade yourself through anyone's ignorance and stupidity!

**SIREN** (see *also* **SOUND**)
You may actually be hearing a siren outside your dream state (e.g., a fire engine, ambulance or police vehicle nearby). However, if this is not the case, then this dream shows that you are very sensitive to loud sounds, and you are very fearful about possible events that could affect you and your family—such as war, accidents, sickness, and other

calamities. No one promised you a rose garden; in this life, you must be prepared for almost anything. But if you truly believe in God, in yourself, and in life's opportunities, successes, and failings, then you are on a healthy road to understanding yourself and the world around you a lot better. At the moment, your anxieties are totally unwarranted. In the future, however, there will be trying times that you will have to surmount.

## SISTER

If your sister is pleasant, happy, or helpful to you within your dream, then you are headed towards many happy, prosperous, and adventurous experiences. This dream also alludes to the fact that you do get along with your sister and other family members.

Seeing a sister who is greedy, unpleasant, or just plain cruel reveals that you are trying to bring some reason and logic to others around you, but they are just not willing to listen. You can only hope and pray that these people will come to their better senses someday and finally realize that you were that "voice in the wilderness" begging them to put aside their hatreds and indifferences.

Seeing a sister who is very sad and who waves good-bye to you within a dream reveals an illness, accident, or possible death to the sister you see. This ill omen may be averted by alerting your sister to take good care of her health, to watch where she travels, and to be very careful in all aspects of her life for the next month or so. A prayer for her guidance and protection is strongly advised!

Seeing a sister who has already passed away reveals that she wants or needs a prayer from you. Say a prayer for her; she will be most profoundly grateful. Remember, when you say a prayer for the dearly departed, they are saying a prayer for you, as well! In your prayer, do not forget to tell your sister to "ask for the Light"!

## SISTER-IN-LAW

Seeing a sister-in-law who is happy and perhaps helpful to you suggests that you should continue to be optimistic where family matters or personal difficulties are concerned. Very soon, there will be a lull or break in the storm(s) you and your family seem to be experiencing. In time, you will prosper from the fruits of your labour!

Seeing a sister-in-law who is unhappy for some reason suggests that your stubborn pride and selfish attitudes are detaining you from getting ahead in life. By simply letting go of these negative attitudes, you will commence to be more motivated, productive, and happy!

Seeing a sister-in-law who has already passed away reveals that she wants a prayer from you. Say a prayer for her and advise her to "ask for the Light"!

**SITAR** (see **INSTRUMENT**)

**SIXTH SENSE** (see **CLAIRVOYANCE** or **PERCEPTION**)

**SKATE** (e.g., ice skate, roller skate)

If you or someone else skate without falling, then you can expect some wonderful surprises, events, and socializing for the next week or two. Having a dream of this nature is like admitting to yourself that everyone and everything is "going my way"!

To fall while you skate reveals that for the next week or so you will be experiencing some very trying times with almost everyone you know and everything you do. Having a dream of this nature is like admitting to yourself that "nothing is going my way"! Be patient; everything will straighten itself out before too long. Sometimes we have to go through a brief trying period in order to find some greater values and truths within ourselves. You are lucky—you will come out of this period a little wiser and much braver than you have ever been before!

**SKELETON**

You are worried about someone or something, and/or you are frightening yourself sick about some morbid "doom and gloom" thoughts about life and death. In either case, you are harbouring some inner anxieties and fears about something not turning out right for you, about a loved one, about a friend, or someone else about whom you are worried. Allay your fears! Your imagination is working over-time, and the false visions you are concocting within your mind are certainly not in keeping with your worthy personality. Just snap out of it! Nothing is wrong anywhere except what you are creating within your mind. Be strong, rebuke your mind, and learn to accept all matters of your life with love and hope—not fear and despair.

**SKEPTICISM** (see **DOUBTFULNESS**)

**SKETCH BOOK** (see **BOOK**)

**SKI** (e.g., snow ski, water ski)

Skiing within a dream infers that you may be living in the fast lane of life, you are living far beyond your means, or you are experiencing some emotional setback at this time. Slow down and smell the roses! Going beyond the boundaries of good judgment and down-to-earth common sense can lead you down a garden path you never anticipated. Tread lightly; live calmly and truthfully. Life will bring you those earthly and spiritual comforts you seek, but first you must settle down within yourself and begin to show honour and respect for your God-given life!

**SKI JUMP**

Seeing a ski jump or going down one suggests that you are tempted, or someone is tempting you, to do something you may later regret. Be careful! The outcome could prove shameful, painful, and extremely regrettable. If possible, use your stubbornness and intelligence to guide you away from this temptation. Solve your emotional conflicts with prayer and reason; solve your outside dealings with logic and unselfishness. Go through your destiny with liberty, joy, and peace, and you will be a very happy person for heeding this dream's lifeline to you.

**SKIN DIVING** (see **DIVER**)

**SKIPLANE** (see **AIRPLANE**)

**SKIRT** (see **CLOTHES**)

**SKULL AND CROSSBONES**

Beware of this sign within a dream! Be very vigilant in what you do and where you go. There is trouble and mischief around you at this time. Be extremely cautious of anyone who might spike what you are drinking; do not accept a free ride from a total stranger who could harm you beyond repair, and so on. A dream of this nature has no limits where sadness and horror are concerned; the dreamer must use the greatest care and wisdom in avoiding any type of trouble at this time. The life you save could be your own!

(*Note*: The abovementioned symbolism is not meant to frighten the dreamer. However, danger of a paramount order is lurking about. If you, the dreamer, can be forewarned ahead of time, then for all that is good and glorious, heed this advice! Do not become paranoid over this matter; but, wisely, do not go anywhere you do not belong nor talk or ride with any stranger at this time, and so on. This forewarning is for about a month's duration. Please, for your own sake, think twice before you decide to do anything rash, foolish, or unwise!)

## SKUNK

Dreaming of a skunk implies that, no matter how hard you try, you do not have a very high opinion of yourself regarding perhaps your appearance, attitude, surroundings, failings, and so on. You are urged to look more closely at your needs and wants in life. Even though you are not the perfect person you would like to be, you are a person nonetheless. There is not a person on earth who can truly claim to be totally happy. Some people complain about their bodily features, others complain about their successes, and still others complain about anything they have a yen to complain about, no matter how life treats them. You are not alone in your complaints. Sooner or later down the road in life perhaps you can make those great changes you desire; or perhaps, with time, you will learn to accept and love yourself for who you are.

## SKY

A clear, calm sky reveals that you are a very openhearted individual who would assist anyone in time of need or trouble. You have obviously been through some pretty rough times yourself, so you know what it is like when difficulties strike. Your well admired thoughts and actions have far reaching effects. As you forge on, your future will be filled with much success, happiness, and a surprising amount of good luck.

A dark, foreboding sky reveals some imminent hardships are ahead for you (e.g., sickness, financial problems, family difficulties, discarding a bad habit). You will survive this ordeal and go on to bigger and better measures.

## SKY DIVING

Your unsettled, free-spirited attitudes and actions have created some major difficulties for you in life. This dream is merely a reminder for you to put your priorities and obligations in order. Doing so will simply allow you to plough on with greater gains instead of greater losses. Long ago you had great ambitions; but today, you are afraid to face the realities of your existence. Uphold your promises and obligations, and you will truly commence to prosper.

## SKYWRITING

You cannot solve an immediate dilemma or problem without revealing some pertinent facts to someone who appears to have your best interests at heart. The writing is not on the wall this time; it's written in the sky! Be honest and logical in this matter, and you will be assisted with a great amount of compassion and understanding. Remember: the truth within you will set you free.

**SLANDER** (see **ACCUSATION** or **LIBEL**)

**SLAP** (see **PUNISHMENT**)

**SLATE** (see **ROCK**)

**SLAUGHTER** (see **GENOCIDE**, **KILL**, or **MURDER**)

## SLAVERY

Sometimes you feel like a slave; not only to yourself, but to everyone and everything around you. This dream advises you to gain a stronghold within your mind and spirit so that you can at last commence to sort out those rights and wrongs within your life. Your attitudes, concepts, suppressed emotions, and your loneliness will not change unless you are prepared to appraise your weaknesses and accentuate your inner forces. Life may be like a "wear and tear" routine to you, but this is what you have created for yourself. There is no sense in complaining or blaming someone else for your difficulties when you alone have allowed people to take advantage of your good work, expertise, and good nature. You need more time for yourself. Find this time, use it well, and do not be afraid to say no to anyone who expects you to cater to their sudden whims or notions, in the future. You have a good mind; say what you feel to your slave drivers, and you will feel much better for having said it, instead of having bottled it.

## SLEDDING

At last you are commencing to take charge of your life with greater insight and determination. Now, you are beginning to focus your mind on earthly and spiritual matters that will make a difference in your future (e.g., going back to school for a better education, making peace with a family member, being more charitable). Whatever the improvements you are actually creating within yourself, you can be sure that your new outlook will bring you more happiness and fulfillment than you have ever before achieved. Carry on; you have other mountains to climb and conquer!

**SLEEP** (see *also* **DREAM** or **SLEEPWALKING**)

To see yourself or someone else sleep within a dream state infers that you are annoyed about losing time or about being detained from accomplishing some task, plan, or project. Allay your fears. This delay is a hidden blessing! Very soon, order will prevail and you will be able to not only pursue your course of action with speed and good will, but you will also integrate more quality into your work.

**SLEEPING BAG**

Your stubbornness and adventurous, rugged spirit have led you through some precarious and dangerous situations in life. But, this is your nature—to explore and discover your world with raw courage, no matter what risks might be involved. All this dream wishes to relate to you is that you are, in many respects, a lionhearted individual who accepts earthly challenges with gutsy actions instead of feeble attempts. To some people you may be considered a hero; but to yourself, there is an inner desire, a greater destiny to gather your down-to-earth experiences single-handedly.

**SLEEPING PILL** (see **MEDICATION**)

**SLEEPWALKING**

If you do sleepwalk in life and dream about this action, then your dream is merely reflecting upon your sleepwalking habit. However, if this is not the case, then this symbolism indicates that you are very worried, angered, or confused about some matter within you or around you. With your strong will and hardheaded attitudes, you are bound to solve or master this situation before too long. Try not to take your troubles to sleep with you; don't go to bed in a frenzy or in an argumentative mood. If you want a peaceful sleep, go to bed with a peaceful mind!

**SLEET** (see **HAIL**, **ICE**, **RAIN**, or **SNOW**)

**SLING** (i.e., a large piece of cloth suspended from the neck to support an arm)

Your attitude, conduct, or character requires more support and praise from those around you. Perhaps you are not being encouraged by your parents, or maybe your spouse never praises you for something you do, or maybe your employer fails to notice your good work, and so forth. Whatever it may be, this dream urges you to communicate with those who affect you so that some compromises or fair dealings may be initiated. Heeding this dream's advice is the precise encouragement you need!

**SLINGSHOT**

You appear to be riding on someone's laurels or hard work without attempting to do more for yourself. Those lazy, hazy days may be comforting to you but not necessarily wholesome to your duties and achievements. There are literally thousands upon thousands of people who would do anything to go back in time to correct some uncaring attitude which inevitably placed them on a difficult, struggling road in life. Take care; be more self-assertive and productive with your time, otherwise you could be the one to struggle in time to come.

**SLOGAN** (see **MOTTO**)

**SLOOP OF WAR** (see **BOAT**)

**SLOPPINESS** (see **NEGLECTFULNESS**)

**SLOTH**

This dream advises you to be more punctual with your appointments and more sincere with your promises. You are not always measuring up to your words! People can be affected by your tardy actions and simple excuses; so, for your own sake, try to be more caring and reasonable with other people's time, energy, and sincerity.

**SLOUGH** (see **SWAMP**)

**SLOWNESS**

The pace of any action in a dream, be it quick or slow, reveals your quick or slow thoughts and actions during your wake state. This particular dream about slowness merely intimates your doubts, delays, and sometimes careless efforts in planning, managing, and directing your thoughts and actions. You presume to have all the time in the world to complete an assigned task or job when, in fact, you do not. This dream strongly urges you to be more caring and alert in your work and with other activities, as well. These actions will help you reach the speed and efficiency you are quite capable of achieving.

**SLUG** (see **MOLLUSK**)

**SLUM** (i.e., a densely populated area of a city where poor conditions abound) (see *also* **GHETTO**)

Any one or several of the following definitions may be applicable: A) that you live in a slum area of a city or town; or B) that many years ago you lived in a slum area, but you were determined to get out and did; or C) that you know of someone who is living in slum conditions; or D) that a relative of yours recently moved out of a slum apartment; or E) that you feel there should be no slum conditions anywhere and that each government is responsible for correcting this matter, justly and fairly; or F) that you feel many people create their own slum conditions because of an uncaring attitude or due to spending their money on some had habits such as alcohol, drugs, etc.; or G) that you feel very insecure about where you live or where you work; or H) that you feel very insecure about someone whom you know; or I) that although you are not living in a slum area, you feel your home or lodging is no better than a slum; or J) that you feel most people living in slum conditions do not want to live this way, but because of their lack of money, education, and work, they have absolutely no choice—otherwise they would be living on the streets; or K) that there is no crime in being poor, but there is a crime when society turns its back on the needs of poorer people; or L) that you feel many towns and cities are beginning to rectify the matter of poor housing conditions and that in due time many slum areas will be a thing of the past; or M) that although you do not live in a slum area, you are ashamed to bring your friends over to your house because of poor living conditions; or N) that you often wonder how many people on this planet go to bed hungry and crying; or O) that this dream has little or no relevance to you at this time.

**SLUMBER PARTY** (see **PARTY**)

**SLUMLORD** (see **LANDLORD** or **SLUM**)

## SMASHUP (see COLLISION or INJURY)

## SMELL

The smell or odour you dream about is precisely what you are smelling while you are asleep. For example, you could be smelling a flower in your room, or you could be smelling an old pair of socks by your bedside, or you could be smelling some bodily odour or household odour, and so forth. Whether you choose to sleep indoors or outdoors, your "dream smell" is the actual smell or scent around you while you are asleep. That is all!

## SMOCK (see CLOTHES)

## SMOKE

Seeing smoke that is whitish and perhaps peacefully drifting here and there implies that you are resourceful, quick-witted, and tend to be extremely independent in your actions. You cannot tolerate anyone telling you what to do with your time or your life simply because you are a go-getter! You require no coaching from anyone to get something done; you simply do what you have to do and then go on to other matters of importance. Your splendid attitude is very commendable. You can be sure that there will be many honours and surprises for you down the road in life.

Seeing smoke that is black, gray, or simply unnerving to the mind of the beholder implies that some outstanding honour or tribute will be given to you in life. Fame for you is certainly not out of the question, for it appears that you are someone very special on this earth plane. You must, however, go through some very trying experiences before you can realize the measure of your worth and importance. Be at peace! You are undoubtedly the captain of your own ship; you will not only master your problems, but you will eventually guide or teach others in a wise, Solomon-like way.

## SMOKER (see *also* PIPE)

Any one or several of the following definitions may be applicable: A) that you are a smoker who has no intention to quit at this time; or B) that you are a smoker who does intend to quit very soon; or C) that you are not a smoker, and you are not about to start, either; or D) that you have tried almost every conceivable method to quit smoking but, because of your nervousness, you just cannot seem to let go of this habit; or E) that you are a nonsmoker who simply detests others smoking around you; or F) that you are a nonsmoker who does not mind when others smoke, provided they do not blow smoke in your face or in your direction; or G) that you were a heavy smoker many years ago and hope never to smoke again; or H) that you recently quit smoking but have very strong urges to start again; or I) that you help, instruct, or teach people how to quit smoking; or J) that someone you know is encouraging you to stop smoking or to start smoking; or K) that you have become ill through smoking and would encourage others to stay away from this physically and mentally addictive habit; or L) that you know of someone who has died from smoking; or M) that you know of some active smokers who are over ninety years old; or N) that you are concerned about your parents, friends, or relatives who smoke; or O) that your doctor recently told you to quit smoking; or P) that you were recently caught smoking by a parent, relative, teacher, or friend; or Q) that you recently paid a fine for smoking in a nonsmoking area of a building or public place; or R) that this dream has little or no significance to you at this time.

**SMOTHER** (see **CHOKE**)

**SMUGGLER**

Any one or several of the following definitions may be applicable: A) that you are, in fact, in the smuggling business; or B) that you are not in the smuggling business; or C) that you recently read an article or book about a smuggler; or D) that you work for a law enforcement agency who apprehends smugglers; or E) that you know someone who is a smuggler; or F) that you want to smuggle something into another country but are afraid of being detained, fined, or incarcerated; or G) that many years ago or quite recently you stole something and later resold the item(s) to another person; or H) that you know of someone who was caught trying to smuggle something into another country; or I) that this dream has little or no relevance to you at this time.

**SNAIL** (see **MOLLUSK**)

**SNAKE**

Sexual superstitions, fears, phobias, and frustrations are strongly suggested with a snake dream. Some cruel, hateful thoughts concerning the opposite sex are indicated here. These haunting, mistrusting thoughts can deter you from finding happiness unless you try to rectify your feelings in these matters. Who can help? Start with a prayer or two and, if you are strong enough, try to dispel your hate, anger, stubbornness, and ignorance concerning the opposite sex. However, if your stubbornness is greater than your will, then professional help is highly recommended.

(*Note*: Seeing a snake go through a hoof of a cow, horse, and so on could very well imply that someone you know is very inwardly depressed and could be considering suicide as a way out! If you do know of someone at this time who is behaving in a strange, inward, very indifferent, depressed manner, then for all that is good and glorious, do not hesitate to communicate with that person and to strongly recommend professional help. Do not take no for an answer; just consider this person's problem[s] as extremely critical!)

## SNAKE CHARMER

You are playing with fate if you dream about seeing or being a snake charmer. You are purposely avoiding some solution to your problem(s). This will not help you; it will inevitably bring you greater tensions and unhappiness. Get a grip on yourself, and commence to face the realities of life within and around you. There is no easy answer(s) to anything in life, so be prepared to struggle for what you want. You fought so desperately hard to come into this world, and now you are looking for escape routes from this world. This will not solve your difficulties; it will create greater ones! Don't look for feeble excuses in life—simply face yourself and life around you with common sense and dignity.

## SNAKE PIT (see HOLE or SNAKE)

## SNAKESKIN

You are merely skimming the surface where your needs and wants are concerned. A certain amount of mental, physical, spiritual, and sexual frustration and ignorance is indicated by this dream. Do not be too smug or complacent in your attitudes, nor feel you are beyond the age of improving yourself. Everyone stands to be corrected, from time to time; you are no exception. Always strive for improvement and dig a little deeper for your answers instead of assuming this is right or that is wrong when, in fact, you are not too sure about many things.

**SNAPSHOT** (see **PHOTOGRAPH**)

**SNARE** (see **TRAP**)

**SNOBBERY** (see *also* **CONCEIT**)
   The act of snobbery within a dream state implies that you either endorse this behaviour in life or you detest it. It is really that simple! People who are snobs will eventually discover that their so-called rank or importance is based on pride and self-deception. Individuals who are snobbish in life are like snowballs rolling down a mountainside, creating their own avalanche! People who refrain from this "greater than thou" attitude, however, are more sensibly attuned to the right vibrations of life.

**SNOOZE** (see **SLEEP**)

**SNORER**
   Snoring within a dream implies that you or someone within your household is actually snoring while you are asleep. In essence, what you hear outside your sleep state is precisely what you combine in thought, action, and deeds within your dream state. In actually hearing someone snore, you could be creating a scene within your dream state such as an oncoming train, airplane, ship, or anything else that might sound similar to a snore. For anyone familiar with snoring, the sounds can be unique, laughable, and exhausting!

**SNOW**
   Dreaming of snow is a very good omen. It symbolizes a type of purification; not only within yourself, but about life in general. This dream should bring out the best in you. You desire changes that are complimentary to your daily activities, instead of changes that are detrimental to your daily life. Success, as you see it, means to be happy, comfortably secure, and at peace within yourself and life around you. And so it shall be!

**SNOWBALL** (see **SNOW**)

**SNOWFLAKE** (see **SNOW**)

## SNOWSHOE

You appear to be fearful about some reprisals against you from a person or a group of people for something you did either in your past or quite recently. Allay your fears! If you have to face the music for something you said or did, then you will do so both admirably and soundly. As well, your future looks both promising and uplifting, and you will go forward with liberated truths, thoughts, and actions.

**SNOWSTORM** (see **STORM**)

**SNOWSUIT** (see **CLOTHES**)

**SOAP** (e.g., hand soap, lye soap) (see *also* **DETERGENT**)

You are either going to wash your hands clean of some episode or affair, and/or you are going to settle some financial or gossipy matter, for all time. Whatever your choices may be, creating a clean slate for yourself is the right beginning for a greater, happier future!

**SOAP OPERA** (see **PROGRAM**)

**SOAPSUDS** (see **DETERGENT** or **SOAP**)

**SOCCER** (see **GAME**)

**SOCIETY** (see **ORGANIZATION**)

**SOCIOPATH** (see **NEUROSIS**)

**SOCKET WRENCH** (see **TOOL**)

**SODA FOUNTAIN** (see **FOUNTAIN**)

**SODOMY** (see **INTERCOURSE, BESTIALITY, HOMOSEXUALITY,** or **SEX**)

**SOFTWARE** (see **COMPUTER**)

**SOLAR ECLIPSE** (see **ECLIPSE**)

**SOLAR SYSTEM** (see **UNIVERSE**)

**SOLDIER** (see **ARMY**)

**SOLDIER OF FORTUNE** (see **MERCENARY**)

**SOLITARY CONFINEMENT** (see **PRISON** or **PUNISHMENT**)

**SOLOMON** (see **SAGE**)

**SOMBRERO** (see **HAT**)

**SOMERSAULT** (see **ACROBAT** or **EXERCISE**)

**SON**

Seeing a son who is happy and perhaps pleasantly busy implies that he will be very constructively productive and successful in life. Be proud of him, but also be understanding and loving if, from time to time, he should fall by the wayside, for some reason.

An unhappy or angry son implies that although he is very intelligent, he is also very independent and stubborn. These qualities will allow him to excel in life at his own pace, in his own time, and in his own way. He loves you, but you must give him room to think, to feel, and to sort out his philosophy and actions in life. You can be very proud of your son, providing he accepts and feels your love and security as a parent. However, should he fail to accept or feel your love and security at this time, then do not fear or panic. Some raw experiences in life will teach him lessons—and then your prodigal son will return to you more humble and wise.

Seeing a son who waves goodbye to you within a dream state could imply a sickness, an accident, or even death. Great caution is advised where his health conditions are concerned or where any type of vehicle, motor bike, boat, hang glider, and so on are concerned. This is not the time for him to be ignoring some health problem(s) or for him to be careless or daring at home, at work, at play, or anywhere else he happens to be. Hopefully, with prayer and with the exercise of good common sense, nothing will happen!

To dream about a son who has already passed away implies that he wants a prayer from you. While saying a prayer for him, he will be saying a prayer for you, as well. Be at peace! When you do say a prayer for him, remember to tell him to "ask for the Light"!

**SONS** (see **MUSIC** or **SINGER**)

**SONGWRITER** (see **COMPOSER** or **POET**)

**SON-IN-LAW**

If your son-in-law appears to be happy and perhaps somewhat helpful to you within a dream state, then you can be sure that some family matters will be resolved before too long. You tend to over-worry about many things concerning your family members. In the future, try not to live another person's life. Everyone needs time and space to grow. So, for your own sake, try to be more giving and less demanding where others are concerned; you will then find the peace of mind you seek.

If your son-in-law appears to be unhappy, greedy, or somewhat demanding in your dream state, then the harmony and happiness you seek within your family circle will not be immediately forthcoming. Pride, selfishness, and hate are the key ingredients both within and around you that are bringing you trouble. By adopting a more serene, loving attitude towards yourself and others, peace will come! Don't be a know-it-all; learn to accept another person's point of view, from time to time.

Seeing a son-in-law who has already passed away infers that he wants a prayer from you. When you do say a prayer for him, remember to tell him to "ask for the Light"!

**SON OF GOD** (see **JESUS**)

**SOOTHSAYER** (see **ASTROLOGY, CLAIRVOYANCE, MEDIUM,** or **PROPHECY**)

**SORCERY** (see **BLACK MAGIC, EVILDOER,** or **WITCHCRAFT**)

**SORORITY** (see **ORGANIZATION**)

**SORROW** (see *also* **ANGUISH, MOURNING,** or **REGRET**)

The sadness, grief, or mental heartache you feel during your wake state could be precisely how you feel during your sleep, as well. These emotional upheavals will lift from the very yoke of your heart, mind, and soul—providing you give yourself an opportunity to let go of your harboured burdens. This may be a lot easier said than done; however, nothing is impossible to you if your willpower and general outlook is strong, hopeful, and faithful. The best known remedy to forget your troubles and woes is to keep busy with the things you like to do or to concentrate on the needs of others less fortunate than you.

**SOUL-SEARCHING** (see **INTROSPECTION**)

**SOUND** (see *also* **SMELL** or **TOUCH**)
Basically, the external sounds you hear while you are asleep are those sounds you bring into your dream state. For example, you may be hearing a vehicle pass by your home, only to instantly find yourself driving a vehicle within a dream; or you may be hearing an airplane fly overhead, only to find yourself in an airplane in your dreams; or you may be hearing someone snore, the wind blowing outside your home, or a dog barking, and so on, which could also produce a variety of sound related dreams. Your conscious and subconscious mind can retain literally hundreds or thousands known sounds you have experienced in life thus far; it may then release these sounds within your dreams when the opportunity arises. Even if you are dreaming in a soundproof room, where no outside noise is able to enter, you may hear the sound of a foghorn, an air raid siren, a whale, or other sound, because—at some time in your life—you heard that sound. Your mind is merely playing it back to you within a dream.

**SOUP** (see **DRINK** or **FOOD**)

**SOUVENIR**
The humanitarian light that shines through you reveals that you were meant to serve your fellow man in some big or small way. Whatever you do in life, continue to carry on your good, deserving work. Never look back on your laurels; rather, create new ones each day, so that others may see and follow your good example.

**SPACECRAFT**
You are not an ordinary individual; you are one whose quest is to enlighten, to improve, and to teach the world around you. A rich, rewarding destiny awaits you but not without the sweat, toil, and tears that so often accompany the journey of special, noteworthy people. From time to time, you may find yourself between the forces of

Heaven and Hell, but the wise judgments you make will be the fountain of your success. Remember that your many rewards in life will be the earthly and spiritual gifts from God, who wishes to reveal His Pleasure in you.

## SPACEMAN (see *also* CELESTIAL)

Seeing or being a spaceman within a dream simply reveals your keen interest in, knowledge of, or expertise on outer space matters. Perhaps you actually wish to travel from planet to planet or to other star systems in order to explore the greatest frontier of all time, outer space. Perhaps your wish will not be realized within your lifetime; perhaps it will. Nonetheless, you will be happy to know that people will eventually colonize other star systems; and then humankind, too, will be as the "gods" of old.

## SPACEPORT (see *also* LAUNCH PAD)

You will be given an opportunity to display your gifts or talents to a group of people or to someone who will be instrumental in helping you in life (e.g., an agent, talent show, literary contest, song writing contest, science fair). In many respects, you are a winner already simply because you know who you are and exactly what you wish to attain in life! When God handed out talent, He meant for it to be used patiently and sensibly; when He handed out gifts, however, He meant for them to be used wisely, humbly, and compassionately for the benefit of all His children.

## SPACE STATION

There appears to be an obstacle or two facing you at this time. However, your highly disciplined mind will carry you through this trauma with flying colors. It appears that you never fail to amaze others around you because of your fortitude and innate knowledge about so many things. You often venture where most people fear to tread! Your future reveals much travel, intellectual pursuits, and perhaps writing, lecturing, composing, or becoming involved in some scientific endeavours involving outer space.

## SPACESUIT (see CLOTHES)

## SPADE (see TOOL)

**SPAGHETTI** (see **DOUGH** or **FOOD**)

**SPANKING** (see **PUNISHMENT**)

**SPARROW** (see **BIRD**)

**SPATULA** (see **UTENSIL**)

**SPEAR** (see **ARROW** or **MISSILE**)

**SPECIMEN** (i.e., a sample of urine, blood, sputum, etc. for medical analysis)

Far too much emphasis is placed on your physical activities and appearance; hence, you are putting little or no effort towards mind or spiritual development. Much too often, people become attuned to one area of their life, and nothing else seems to matter. It does matter! The body may develop and prosper in your outside activities, but your thinking processes and growth towards God simply wanes and wavers. Have your exercise, play your games, look after your body; but don't forget to read good books once in a while, or to pray, or to think of others, and so forth. Try to harmonize your activities so that your body, mind, and soul may all be attuned to your earthly and spiritual quests or goals. You will prosper this way!

**SPECTATOR** (see *also* **AUDIENCE** or **CROWD**)

Seeing or being a spectator in a calm or excited sort of way reveals that you are a very active person and are honest and loyal to the core. You expect others to treat you fairly; but, should they fail in any manner, then they could lose you as a friend. You are not a spoilsport; you simply believe that honesty and integrity go hand in hand. Ultimately, you stand by your words!

Seeing or being a spectator who is rowdy, obnoxious, or plain foolish reveals that you are somewhat self-centered and obnoxious during your wake state. Basically, you are not a negative person; however, you tend to say and do things without realizing the consequences of your sudden whims, notions, and actions. You have a good mind; but, unfortunately, you sometimes hide it behind a facade of jostling or horsing around people, places, and things, where you do not belong. If you wish to be impressive in life, then use your God-given talents wisely, for the time you waste now is the time you may later lament.

## SPECTRUM

Seeing the spectrum of colors within your dream state reveals your moods, notions, habits, your ups and downs, and just about anything you might be doing right or wrong. In our conscious state, the colors of the spectrum are violet, indigo, blue, green, yellow, orange, and red. However, in our sleep state, the spectrum of colors are revealed as follows: gold, white, purple, blue, pink, green, orange, yellow, brown, red, grey, and black.

Gold is not only the highest colour of the spectrum, it is by far the greatest colour in the Cosmos. This colour belongs to celestials, gods, angels, and masters of the Universes. Seeing this colour indicates that your mind and soul frequencies are attuned to the Godhead of Life.

White is the colour of purity. Seeing this colour indicates that you are very good, helpful, and certainly faithful to God and all life around you. You forge ahead peacefully, masterfully, and wisely!

Purple is a spiritual colour. This colour reveals harmony with God, with yourself, and with the world, as a whole. Prayer, meditation, and attuning oneself to the higher frequencies of life are revealed by this colour. You go out of your way to be helpful, compassionate, and consoling to those around you.

Blue reveals your basic determination, courage, strength, and wisdom. The darker the blue, the greater your determination becomes; hence, your chances of having a better future are revealed right here. This colour also reveals some of your basic weaknesses, along with your likes and dislikes in life (e.g., eating too much, failing to keep on your diet, failing to be thoughtful and helpful towards others, wanting to succeed but being somewhat reticent in striving towards this end). This colour is exceedingly helpful in that it really tunes in to you, your inner self, and to your soul, in many ways.

Pink reveals health problems or your need for mental, physical, or spiritual healing. You are either receiving help in this matter, or you are neglecting to get the help you need.

Green is your basic attunement to earth. Your many materialistic wants, needs, and failings are revealed by this color. You may be greedy, or you may be extremely kind and inspiring to those around you. You may want more than you deserve, or you may deserve more than you want!

Orange is a very possessive color. Your demanding ways and actions may get you what you want in life, but more emphasis should be placed on kindness and gratitude for what you already have. This aggressive colour can lead you in many directions, so you have to be very careful not to outdo yourself or go beyond your limits in life. A colour of this nature advises you to use common sense in your life!

Yellow is a highly argumentative color. It reveals that you are going around in circles with your arguments; this is getting you nowhere in life. Be calm and still. Enjoy your life, and stop being such a complainer.

Brown reveals your strong hatreds and vendettas and your ability to create mischief through your gossip. Be careful! Seeing this colour reveals that unpleasant difficulties lie ahead of you because of your sudden whims, notions, and actions against someone or something. This colour also reveals the strength of your honesty or dishonesty in life. Are you truthful, or do you merely deceive yourself into believing you are?

Red reveals caution, trouble, and danger! Whatever you are doing at this time or intend to do, be very careful, for this colour is trying to tell you to "stop, look, and listen" before you do something you may regret forever. Look within yourself for this answer, and be sure to heed this colour warning!

Grey reveals sickness, pain, discomforts, and great depressions of the mind and body. A good percentage of your trouble is created by your base outlook and jealousies. In many respects, you could be highly troublesome—not only to yourself, but to others around you, as well. Do not create mischief for anyone; just gently mind your own affairs in life. Seeing this colour is likened unto trying to climb a mountain backwards. You are not flowing with the grain of life—you are flowing against it!

Black is the colour of great sickness, accidents, death. It reveals sadness, hardships, and strife. However, with prayer and faith, many things can be avoided; so do not ignore these greater cures and possibilities given to you. Do not be careless or foolish in life; instead, use your God-given talents and wisdom to the best of your abilities. Do not think or act in a hopeless manner; think positively and faithfully in everything you do.

(*Note*: The abovementioned colour interpretations only apply to the entry **SPECTRUM** or to the observation of myriad colors within a dream state.)

**SPEECH** (see **LECTURE**)

**SPEECH DISORDER** (e.g., stuttering, aphasia)

Dreaming about a speech disorder could imply that you or someone whom you know has a speech problem at this time. However, if this is not the case, then this dream shows that you are reaching out to someone who is presently experiencing some mental or physical difficulties. Your understanding and assistance in this entire matter is both consoling and angelic. Carry on; we need more people like you on this planet!

**SPEED** (see **QUICKNESS**)

**SPEEDBOAT** (see **BOAT**)

**SPEED TRAP** (see **QUICKNESS** or **RADAR**)

**SPELL** (see **CURSE, OBSESSION,** or **TALISMAN**)

**SPELLING**

Your mind is very quick and active; your actions, however, are sometimes scattered and without order. This dream advises you to show more control, planning, and stability in your thoughts and actions. Realize that a job unfinished is a job not done. Unless you commence to show more fixity of purpose, you will continue to struggle with your inner anxieties, arguments, and conflicts.

**SPHINX**

Seeing this majestic figure within a dream reveals your feelings of being repressed because of where you live, what you do, or not having the means to forge ahead. At this moment you may feel frustrated and vexed about your present condition. Times will change for you; and, in the process, you will change, as well. Be at peace! Ahead of you lies a journey of success and good fortune. In the interim, be willing to reach out to God and to your inner self for the strength, courage, and patience you seem to lack at this time. Do not undermine the power within your own being, for faith can move many mountains!

**SPICE** (e.g., clove, cinnamon, ginger, nutmeg, pepper, salt)

How can anyone be content if what they do in life brings them unhappiness? This unhappiness will not go away unless changes are made and one is willing to rise over and above one's earthly obstacles.

This dream encourages you to either be happy in what you do and stop complaining, or do something about what troubles or ails you so that you can be happy and productive once more. Nothing will come to you on a silver platter. You must work towards your happiness, interests, and good direction in life.

## SPIDER

This dream symbolism reveals that you appear to be in a "half-win, half-lose" situation. Whatever it is that you appear to be struggling with, you are strongly urged to do your very best. If the tide should turn in your favor, then be grateful for small miracles; if the tide should turn against you, then accept the fact—and still be grateful for having had the experience. There will be other times and other situations where you will win with flying colors! Perhaps in this situation you would not be losing a battle, but actually winning a war.

## SPIKE (see NAIL)

## SPINACH (see FOOD or PLANT)

## SPINET (see INSTRUMENT)

## SPINNING WHEEL

This dream reveals that you feel completely and thoroughly abandoned by those whom you love and admire (e.g., family, friends). You could perhaps speak frankly to these people in the hopes that they will change. However, if this fails, then you are urged to seek new people, places, and things. Always leave the door of love open to them in the hopes that they will eventually grow up or broaden their ideas about what respect and appreciation is all about. Nonetheless, you are urged to get a breath of fresh air, look within yourself, and—with a great sigh of relief—begin to do more for yourself and for others around you. You will prosper this way! You are not alone; God is beside you!

## SPINSTER

Dreaming about seeing or being a spinster could imply that you are a spinster—an unmarried woman. However, if this is not the case, then this dream reveals that you fear becoming a spinster in life. Not everyone should get married for the sake of marriage. As long as you are a happy, productive person, then may you continue on your pleasant journey in life. However, if it is marriage you want, then it is probably marriage you will get. However, do not expect Prince Charming to knock on your door—especially if he doesn't even know you exist! There are many introductory agencies today that are willing to help you out, but be sure that these agencies are aboveboard, decent, and law-abiding. Many are; however, there may be a few that are not. Check them out carefully. Then the rest is up to you.

**SPIRE** (see **CHURCH, MOUNTAIN,** or **TOWER**)

**SPIRITUALISM** (see **AFTERLIFE, CHURCH,** or **MEDIUM**)

**SPIT**

Spitting at a person within a dream implies that you are fed up with someone's behaviour and actions (e.g., base demands, gambling, drinking, fighting). This matter may or may not clear up unless this individual agrees to change, seeks help, and is finally willing to accept the responsibilities and obligations deemed necessary. Do not expect any great miracles here, though. It appears that you are the one who will be making some sudden, beneficial changes for the sake of your future and for the sake of your sanity.

Spitting on the ground or in the air implies that you are agreeing to something where a promise or agreement is concerned—but deep down, you are actually disagreeing! It may be that you do not have the courage to say what you honestly feel. Do not be afraid to say yes or no, but do your very best to remember that a no answer can also be a very wise answer.

Spitting at someone or something or into the air and realizing that your spit has returned back to you reveals that you have a very low opinion about yourself, your family, your surroundings, your work, and just about anything else that bothers you. Accept your life with more faith and foresight! By being so judgmental and self-abasing, you are hindering your earthly progress, in many different ways. A time will come when you will be out of those turbulent waters of your life, but you must be willing to accept the virtue of humility before you can achieve the rewards of prosperity.

**SPLASH-DOWN** (see **SPACECRAFT** or **WATER**)

## SPLINT

You will benefit by slowing down, by being more resolute with your thoughts and actions, and by ignoring the irrational remarks and acts of others around you. Learn to distinguish between those matters that are good for you and those that are bad for you so that in the future you can avoid plundering into some emotional or physical entrapments or difficulties (e.g., drinking, drugs). Do not be swayed by difficult or negative people. Instead, use your own good judgments, and life will bring you the rewards and happiness you so rightfully deserve!

## SPLIT PERSONALITY (see INSANITY or PSYCHOTHERAPY)

## SPOILAGE (see ROTTENNESS)

## SPOILSPORT (see KILL-JOY)

## SPONGE (e.g., a plantlike animal; or a sponge-like pad made of plastic or rubber)

You may be feeling someone or something is slipping through your fingers because you have lost control over some argument or agreement or perhaps over some financial matters. This dream counsels you to strive more towards mutual concerns and harmony, rather than make great demands with anger and bad humor. Success in anything is not achieved through negative temptations or conflicts in life; it is attained through peace and determination. Settle down and commence to think about your contradictions, misunderstandings, and disappointments until you actually perceive and understand the rights and wrongs of your ways. Then, with sound logic, make your compromises, and bring order into your life.

## SPONSORSHIP (see PATRONAGE)

## SPOOK (see DANGER, EVILDOER, GHOST, PHANTOM, or STARTLE)

## SPOON (see SILVERWARE)

## SPORT (see GAME)

**SPORTSWEAR** (see **CLOTHES**)

**SPORTSWRITER** (see **JOURNALIST**)

**SPOT** (see **STAIN**)

**SPOUSE** (see **HUSBAND** or **WIFE**)

**SPRAIN** (see **INJURY**)

**SPRAY** (see *also* **DEODORANT, DEODORIZER, SPRINKLER,** or **VAPORIZER**)
 The act of spraying someone or something denotes that you feel somewhat neglected by those for whom you care and love. From time to time, you too require an uplifting, a praise, or an inspired word for your good work, kindness, and generosity. This dream symbolism tells you that what you seek, you can have; however, you must say what you feel, rather than bottle what you feel and need. A little reminder from you about kindness and gratitude certainly would assist your loved ones—and you, as well! Try it; it will work for you!

**SPRING** (i.e., a coil of a wire used as a spring in clocks, or a leaf, helical, or expansion spring used in vehicles) (see *also* **GEYSER, HOT SPRING, JUMP, SEASON,** or **WATER**)
 The symbolism of a spring indicates that you would like to do something inspirational, innovative, and constructive; however, you are afraid of making a big mistake, wasting your time and energy, or having to borrow money for this plan or venture. Many people are afraid to take chances or risks unless they know, more or less, the prospects of success ahead of them. Yet, these prospects can be very unpredictable, at times. A person can win or lose with any chances or risks in life. But isn't life a risk, no matter how you see it? This dream advises you to use common sense, tact, and good judgment when fears upset your better direction and purpose in life. Fears will not bring you success; courage will!

**SPRING CLEANING** (see **CLEANLINESS** or **HOUSECLEANING**)

## SPRINKLER

Seeing or using one or more sprinklers reveals that you require more time to yourself. It seems that you are surrounded by people most of the time and never seem to have your own space, time, or freedom to accomplish something especially for yourself (e.g., reading a good book in silence, inventing or building something, listening to good music). A sprinkler shows that you will have your time to think and sort things out. In the process, you will discover some marvelous truths and better feelings about yourself and about life in general. Everyone needs their privacy from time to time; you are no exception.

## SPUTUM (see SPIT)

## SPY (see ESPIONAGE)

## SQUADRON (see AIR FORCE, ARMY, BATTALION, or NAVY)

## SQUARE DANCE (see DANCE)

## SQUASH (see FRUIT or GAME)

## SQUID (see MOLLUSK)

## SQUIRE (see OWNERSHIP)

## SQUIRREL

You do not seem to be so troubled about your past or present any longer, nor are you so nervous or fearful about the prospects and possibilities in your future. The calm changes within you are a sight for sore eyes; and it is wonderful to see that your laughter and confidence are finally back with you again. Let us hope these good signs stay with you for a long, long time to come. Ahead of you lie the appreciation, knowledge, and travel you seek. Be at peace! A greater destiny yet awaits you—one with many surprises, rewards, and good luck!

## STAB (see INJURY or KNIFE)

## STABLE (see BARN)

**STADIUM** (see **COLISEUM**)

**STAFF** (see **CANE, EMPLOYEE,** or **MACE**)

**STAG** (see **CELEBRATION** or **DEER**)

**STAGE** (i.e., platform or scaffold)
You are propelling yourself much too fast in wanting to gain or achieve something. Slow down, and everything your heart desires will no doubt come true! With your intelligence and know-how, you should be the pilot of your life, at all times. For your own sake, do not try to break the sound barrier, otherwise you could miss those vital gains and successes you seek. Remember that everything of good order takes time, and do not be too disappointed if your better hopes and wishes do not come true immediately. In due time, you will have everything you could conceivably hope for or want—and more!

**STAGECOACH**
With your mental concentration, determination, and painstaking efforts in life, you are bound to overwhelm even the most hardened skeptics around you! You are a born winner, and no matter what you do or where you go, you will always strive to better your previous ideas, concepts, and actions. Great events and opportunities yet await you. As you succeed here and there you will slowly but surely reach the pinnacle of success. And, who said the last could never come first?!

**STAGE FRIGHT** (see **NERVOUSNESS**)

**STAIN** (i.e., discoloration, streak, spot, or mark)
This dream intimates that you feel guilty or regretful for some past or present wrongdoing, and/or you are trying to solve and forget about a personal matter which has been haunting you for quite some time. Two wrongs do not make a right. You will simply have to make peace with yourself, with God, and—of course—with whomever you affected. Regarding the second definition, you are advised to face the facts as they are rather than look for some hidden meaning or underlying truth to the matter. The answer is quite clear: accept the honesty, integrity, and fairness that has already been shown to you, and let the rest go! Be at peace with yourself, and carry on with more important, useful pursuits in your life.

**STAIR** (i.e., staircase; flight of steps)

Merely seeing a staircase or flight of stairs indicates that you are a very cautious, deep thinking individual who plans each situation beforehand. This sure-footed strategy is both wise and wholesome simply because you value your time and energy. Why be foolish and careless in life when there is so much more to see, to do, and to achieve! Quite clearly, you will do that and more.

Going up a flight of stairs indicates an overall improvement where happiness and financial matters are concerned. You have been through some hectic, emotional times; now these forthcoming improvements should be very welcome!

Going down a flight of stairs reveals an overall downward trend where your happiness or financial matters are concerned. It seems as though you have your back pinned to the wall at this time, and there is very little you can do about it, other than hope and wait for better days ahead. Times will be better for you, but do not expect improvements to happen overnight. Hopefully, when better times do come, you will have become wiser and more humble from your experience.

To fall, to jump, or to dangle from a staircase, or to be pushed off a staircase, implies that a cash decision in something vitally important to you or to a member of your family could create personal stress and anguish for months to come. Be careful! Be very careful with your words and actions at this time; and think twice before you say yes or no to someone or something you are not too sure about.

Seeing a staircase that is destroyed, is about to be destroyed, or appears old and unreliable shows that you are deciding to quit something (e.g., organization, employment), or you are deciding to abandon some bad habit or attitude (e.g., smoking, drinking). Whatever you choices may be, it is sincerely hoped that you will find the happiness and peace of mind you seek. This dream certainly suggests you will!

**STAMP** (see **POSTAGE STAMP** or **RUBBER STAMP**)

**STAMPEDE** (see **CONFUSION, DANGER, HYSTERIA, QUICKNESS,** or **STARTLE**)

**STAPLER**

This device or machine indicates excessive or extreme demands are being made by you on someone else or by someone else on you. The anxiety and impatience revealed here should be stopped or at least questioned so that some form of earthly peace and satisfaction can be achieved. If you are the one making these great demands on someone, then study your reasons and motives for trying to characterize yourself as an ogre or a slave driver. Once you have found your answers logically and sensibly, then enough guilt on your part should commence to change you into someone more kind and likeable. On the other hand, if you are the victim of someone's incessant demands on you, then study your reasons and motives for allowing yourself to be used and manipulated in such a manner. You may require some professional help or assistance in guiding you away from your possessive and aggressive antagonist.

## STAR (see *also* COMET, CONSTELLATION, GALAXY, METEOR, or SUN)

You are a very intelligent and dedicated individual who strives very hard to make life within and around you more meaningful and purposeful. You are fascinated by the heavens, but you are also very interested in, and concerned about, the welfare of this planet. This dream reveals that you certainly are doing your part to make your corner of the world a little brighter and better through your humanitarian and peacemaking ways. Your horizons may bring you some sudden challenges and disappointments, but you will master these admirably. You can also look forward to some glowing achievements and rewards.

## STARDOM (see ACTOR, FAME, MOTION PICTURE, or THEATRE)

## STARFISH (see FISH)

## STARGAZER (see ASTROLOGY, ASTRONOMY, STAR, or UFOLOGIST)

## STAR OF DAVID (see SYMBOL)

## STARS AND STRIPES (see FLAG)

## STARTLE

Danger, anxieties, and fears can bring about "dream shock". The frequency of being startled within a dream depends upon how sensitive and impressionable you are in life. Many young children often experience this shock syndrome while they dream or sleep; as they grow older, however, they tend to lose some of their childhood fears, but they do not lose all their anxieties, fears, and phobias. Many adults, as well, still get startled within their dreams and perhaps will continue to do so as long as there are frightening, nightmarish experiences to contend with during one's sleep. Whether you are in a dream state or wide awake, to be startled or shocked by anyone or anything is not a pleasant experience. Somehow, though, we still manage to carry on and survive. This helps us learn to be more alert and strong when unforeseen events and storms happen to cross our pathway, now and again.

**STARVATION** (see **FAMINE, HUNGER, MALNUTRITION**, or **POVERTY**)

**STATESMAN** (see **GOVERNMENT** or **POLITICIAN**)

**STATION** (i.e., a railroad station) (see *also* **GAS STATION, GUARDHOUSE, RAILROAD**, or **SPACE STATION**)

If the station is natural-looking, relatively busy, and perhaps appears somewhat exciting to you, then you can look forward to some very busy, productive times ahead. In the midst of these busy times you will encounter a problem or two which will appear insurmountable at first; however, it will be handled superbly. Travel, improved financial status, and peace of mind are also indicated by this dream.

If the station is abandoned, destroyed, untidy, or just looks totally unnatural, then someone will say or do something that will disappoint you for quite some time (e.g., spouse, offspring, relative, friend, employee, employer). It is sincerely hoped, however, that you will find it more wise to be forgiving rather than harbour prolonged hatreds in this matter.

**STATION AGENT** (see *also* **RAILROAD**)

Seeing or being a station agent indicates that your workload and other demands made upon you just never seem to end. When you do ask for help, everyone around you appears to be too busy to look your way. Be at peace! It will not always be this way. Ahead of you lie greater rewards and comforts, but not for the moment. This dream advises you to be a bit more demanding with those around you so that the wear and tear you are experiencing can be alleviated. If you can, do your best to get away from your busy schedules for a while in order to regain your sanity and peace of mind!

## STATIONERY (see ENVELOPE or LETTER)

## STATUE (see MONUMENT, SPHINX, or STATUETTE)

## STATUE OF LIBERTY (see MONUMENT)

## STATUETTE

This dream reveals that, when you are very depressed and feeling all alone, you are just about ready to give up on everyone and everything in your life. All types of negative thoughts beset you, along with feelings of being unwanted, unloved, and disrespected by those whom you know and tend to love. Your self-pitying ideas, whims, and notions about yourself and about life in general are unwholesome and unwise. Do not expect everyone to cater to you; rather, learn to disband your opposing thoughts with prayer and foresight. Adopt a brighter vision of yourself, of your loved ones, and certainly of God—who will help you.

## STEAL (see CHEATING, DECEPTION, KLEPTOMANIA, or THIEVERY)

## STEAM BATH (see BATH)

## STEAMBOAT (see BOAT)

## STEAM ENGINE (see MACHINERY)

## STEAMROLLER

Seeing this heavy-duty piece of equipment within a dream implies that you are a very talkative, domineering, self-centered person. These habits you display can be curbed whenever you are ready, willing, and able to do so. Consider this dream a very dear, close friend to you. Be at peace; your new-found friend is very discreet and thoughtful and certainly cares enough about you to suggest that you consider rectifying your ways, a little bit here and a little bit there.

**STEEL BAND** (see **MUSIC** or **MUSICIAN**)

**STEEPLE** (see **CHURCH** or **TOWER**)

**STEPCHILD**

Any one or several of the following definitions may be applicable: A) that you have a stepchild or two whom you love and adore; or B) that you have a stepchild or two who are not too easy to get along with; or C) that you are contemplating a marriage with someone who has one to two children, but you are worried whether or not this marriage will work out because of these children; or D) that you were recently married and now have some adjustments to make regarding a stepchild or two; or E) that your stepchild was recently sick but is feeling much better now; or F) that a stepchild or two have been making your life rather miserable lately; or G) that your stepchild has some emotional problems which require immediate attention; or H) that you do not seem to have privacy and happiness in your marriage because of a stepchild's interference or jealousies; or I) that you still have close ties with a stepchild or two from a previous marriage; or J) that you have disassociated yourself from a stepchild or two for personal reasons; or K) that you feel your stepchild or stepchildren are closer to you than your own children; or L) that you recently dreamt about a stepchild who passed away but realize that this individual wishes good thoughts and prayers from you; or M) that you believe a marriage with stepchildren can work providing everyone involved is willing to adopt a close, loving friendship with one another; or N) that you are a stepchild and feel that your upbringing was extremely trying and disappointing, in many ways; or O) that you are a stepchild and feel that your upbringing was good and wholesome; or P) that this dream has little or no relevance to you at this time.

**STEPPARENT**

Any one or several of the following definitions may be applicable: A) that you like and admire your stepparent; or B) that you cannot tolerate your stepparent; or C) that you have never received any love and support, from your stepparent, that you can ever recall; or D) that you are not living with your stepparent anymore and are most grateful for this fact; or E) that as you reflect back, you have not been kind and understanding towards your stepparent; or F) that you take advantage of your stepparent's kindness and generosity; or G) that you are more close to your stepparent than to your biological parent(s); or H) that you appear to be in the middle of some conflict between your biological parent(s) and a stepparent; or I) that you fail to see what your biological parent has in common with your new stepparent; or J) that when you were young, you never really appreciated your stepparent, but later on in life, you realized how good and kind your stepparent actually was towards you; or K) that you have a friend who has a stepparent; or L) that your stepparent recently passed away; or M) that a stepparent recently visited you from another state or country; or N) that you recently telephoned or wrote a letter to your stepparent, or your stepparent recently telephoned or wrote a letter to you; or O) that this dream has little or no relevance to you at this time.

**STEREOSCOPE** (i.e., an instrument used for viewing two pictures, giving a three-dimensional effect)

Seeing or using this old-fashioned instrument signifies that you are actually seeing two images of yourself. In other words, you can be happy yet feel unhappy, successful yet feel unsuccessful, productive yet feel you are not doing enough, and so forth. This dream merely alludes to those areas of your life which you feel you can improve upon but, for some reason or other, tend to ignore or leave these matters of concern for another day or another time. No one is absolutely, one hundred percent content on this earth plane, but we must at least strive a little harder to improve upon those matters or situations which seem to bother us now and then. If you weigh the positive and negative areas of your life, you can pretty well deduce where you stand and where you can possibly correct and better matters for yourself. Note that improvements in your life can be effected, providing you have the realistic courage and determination to get things done. Actions are far more satisfying than procrastinations!

**STEW** (see **FOOD**)

**STEWARD** (see **STEWARDESS**)

**STEWARDESS**

This dream indicates that a special duty or task will be required of you, where your career or home life is concerned. It appears that you will have to go over and above the call of duty in this matter in order to achieve precisely what you want. This will depend entirely upon your willingness to accept this worthy challenge and opportunity, which will be shortly forthcoming. A tip: difficult decisions and ultimatums with self should be made with a clear mind, not with a doubtful mind!

**STICK** (e.g., a pole, rod, or club) (see *also* **CANE** or **PUNISHMENT**)

Seeing or using a stick indicates delaying or canceling some event, personal plans, or travel plans because of some threat, danger, or harmful possibilities associated with these areas. Sometimes we must be guided by our own impulses, intuition, or just plain common sense when situations around us or anywhere on earth appear to be unsettled and troublesome. Be guided by your inner voice, and back off or stay away from people, places, or things that could bring you grief and anguish beyond your wildest imagination!

**STICKER** (see **LABEL**)

**STIGMATISM** (see *also* **BLOOD** or **CRUCIFIX**)

Seeing or being a stigmata within a dream implies that you have very strong convictions about what you say or do in life. Whether your thoughts and actions involve religion, politics, or the humanities, this dream symbolism reveals your intense awareness of earthly life and its thirst for cooperation and lasting peace. If you could rule the world for a day, the ultimate vision of your love and courage would no doubt bring the world a little closer together.

**STILLBIRTH** (see **FAILURE**, **FETUS**, or **MISCARRIAGE**)

**STINK** (see **SMELL**)

**STINK BOMB** (see **MISCHIEF** or **SMELL**)

**STITCH** (see **DARNING**, **REPAIR**, or **SEWING**)

**STOCKBROKER** (see **STOCK EXCHANGE**)

**STOCK EXCHANGE**

You just may be a gambler at heart, but this dream appears to be telling you that you are counting your gains and losses in life. No matter how you place people, places, and events in your life, you can be quite certain that your gains far supersede your losses, with plenty to spare. You may complain for a moment or two when situations do not go your way, but you have a knack for re-channeling your thoughts and actions towards more promising, fulfilling ventures. The truth and courage in your life is worth far more than all the riches in the world!

## STOCKING (see FOOTWEAR)

## STOCK MARKET (see STOCK EXCHANGE)

## STOCKPILE (see STORE)

## STOCKYARD

A stockyard devoid of animals implies that you are worried about some personal health problems and about the welfare of a family member or friend. Improvements are forthcoming, so just carry on with prayer, hope, and far less anxiety. Your worries are totally unnecessary!

Seeing a stockyard with animals in it reveals that several people you know are displaying a certain amount of anxiety and anger or are being highly deceptive about certain matters. Be cautious for, in some way, you just may be used by these people, who apparently only think about themselves. Jealousies and immaturity appear to be at the root of their attitude. They may create some mischief for you; if that happens, be very tactful and truthful about how you feel towards them and their actions—perhaps this will help. Hopefully, they will commence to at last mature.

## STOMACH

Seeing the stomach of a person or animal indicates that you are experiencing some annoyances, nervousness, and perhaps ridicule at home, work, school, travel, or in some other area of your life. These negative tensions you are bottling will leave you, providing you try not to take everything so seriously and sensitively. If someone annoys you, simply realize that you do not have a problem—your antagonist does! You would be amazed at how many people go out of their way to aggravate others just for a lark, not realizing the offense or effect they create upon others. Don't lose your sense of humour with some people, no matter how ridiculous they may appear to you. You know, more smiles and laughter on your part could quite easily baffle and cool down your offender(s) in an amazing, ingenious way!

## STONE (see **PEBBLE** or **ROCK**)

## STONE AGE

Dreaming about the Stone Age simply infers that you would like to go back to the good old days when things were perhaps better and happier for you. This, however, is not possible. Life goes on with or without us; we must all learn to cope, adjust, and harmonize with those great changes, both in the present and those yet to come. Keep busy, learn new things, and constantly strive to share your love and understanding with those around you. Remember that you were meant to progress and to do good things upon this earth plane, not hide behind personal fears and self-pity. Be strong, carry on, and— with great peace in your mind—create a chain of love with people whom you know and meet.

## STONEHENGE (see **MONOLITH**)

## STORE (see *also* **BAZAAR, BOOKSTORE, CONFECTIONARY, MALL, MARKETPLACE, MERCHANT,** or **STOCK EXCHANGE**)

If the store you see is abandoned or devoid of people, it indicates that you wish to make a major purchase or do something quite constructive, but your financial resources seem to make your good wishes somewhat impossible to fulfill at this time. Be patient! There are plenty of wonderful opportunities ahead of you; there is also much good luck to eventually help you attain all your better dreams and wishes!

If the store you see is crowded or spooky, or just seems unusual in some manner, then be wary of signing a contract or document you are not too sure about; be careful not to overspend at this time; and think twice before you decide to borrow money from, or lend to, someone. You may otherwise have to face some personal regrets or difficulties you never bargained for or anticipated. Right now, your financial situation appears rather precarious. Be patient; don't do anything rash or regrettable. There are financial improvements ahead for you. Then you will have the peace of mind and security to go ahead with your many plans or actions.

Seeing a store in utter chaos or in a shambles means that you may have regrets for having bought something beyond your means or having made an agreement you feel you cannot possibly honour. This dream is reminding you to show more self-restraint and logic when buying something or planning something. Doing things impulsively and then later thinking about your mistakes will not solve anything for you. "Think before you leap" should be your motto from now on; it could save you a lot of wear and tear in the future!

**STORK** (see **BIRD**)

**STORM** (e.g., hailstorm, gale, rainstorm, sandstorm, snowstorm, windstorm) (see *also* **BLIZZARD, HAIL, HURRICANE, LIGHTNING, MONSOON, THUNDER,** or **TORNADO**)

Seeing a storm within a dream could imply that you are experiencing a storm of some nature within your wake state (e.g., emotional, physical, financial). If you are an optimistic individual, you stand a better chance of coming through your tribulations— wiser and perhaps healthier from your experiences. If you are a pessimistic individual, you probably will still come out of your storm, but not necessarily any better or wiser. This dream is advising you to learn from your experiences, to grow from your experiences, and to impart to others the knowledge and wisdom of your experiences. Your storm is not permanent. Always remember to be confident in God, in yourself, in others, and in the world around you. These positive measures can ease or cease your trials and tribulations!

**STORM TROOPER** (i.e., any Nazi or Hitlerite)

To see or to be a storm trooper (a "brown shirt") within your dream reveals that you or someone you know is getting carried away with some doctrine, belief, or habit that could be both troublesome and dangerous, as time goes on. This is a no-win situation; you would be well advised to turn away completely from anyone or anything that gives you something but expects to receive more in return than you can conceivably offer! Don't sell your time, your mind, or your soul for something you were never meant to do or believe in. Use your God-given mind and talents for higher and greater purposes and ideals— not for false, base ideas and actions.

**STORYBOOK** (see **BOOK**)

**STOVE** (see **APPLIANCE**)

**STRAINER** (i.e., a device used for filtering, sifting; a sieve or filter)

This dream symbolism suggests that you are filtering or sifting certain facts and ideas which could be to your benefit, in time to come. Your plans seem very wholesome and constructive; given the time and patience, you will surmount your present obstacles to go on to bigger and greater ventures. Yes, you will be very productive, successful, and happy in your lifetime!

**STRANGULATION** (see **CHOKE**, **KILL**, or **MURDER**)

**STRAP** (see **BELT** or **PUNISHMENT**)

**STRAW**

Some sudden changes around you compel you to make some drastic decisions, which you may or may not like (e.g., move, bankruptcy, divorce, selling something you like). Whatever the problem may be, it appears that there is no way to counteract this decision, but to simply go along with the tide of events, as they appear to be. Chances are that everything will turn out all right for you, in the end. Realize that time is the ultimate healer of all inner conflicts, wounds, and sadness that we supposedly must bear in this life! No, nothing is easy; but, nothing is permanent, either!

**STRAWBERRY** (see **FRUIT** or **PLANT**)

**STRAW MAN** (see **SCARECROW**)

**STREAM** (see **WATER**)

**STREAMER** (see **FLAG** or **NEWSPAPER**)

**STREET**

If the street you see is relatively quiet and peaceful, then you are finally putting your foot down in order to do something you always wanted to do, or you are hoping to make a change or two that will give you the time and freedom to forge ahead. When people succeed in life, it's because they are courageous and persistent in their beliefs and actions. When people fail in life, it's because they either lack faith in themselves and their work, or they are just too eager to quit when times become difficult and despairing. Is this how you feel?

A busy street indicates that recently you have been somewhat slack, lazy, or uncaring where your attitudes and obligations are concerned. Essentially, you are a very good worker; however, when someone criticizes you or even offers you constructive criticisms, you tend to become very inward, depressed, and uncaring. Be a bit stronger within yourself. Realize that the dividends of your good work are far more appealing to others than seeing you whine or suffer because of someone's resentment towards you and your excellent work habits. Carry on; you have many things to do and many places to visit within your lifetime.

A street that is being constructed, renovated, or destroyed reveals that you have a love-hate relationship with many things around you. You never seem to be too happy or satisfied with anything. When you are flustered, frustrated, sad, or disappointed with someone or something, don't complain so much. Instead, simply realize that not everything can be as perfect as you might want it to be. Nothing is perfect, so try not to demand perfection!

Seeing a portion of a street, seeing one which appears hazy (like a mirage), or seeing one which sinks into the earth reveals that you are experiencing some emotional, physical, or spiritual fears and anxieties, at this time. Sometimes you place yourself on a "worry cruise" which is headed absolutely nowhere! Break away from your mind fears, pray, and do not lose touch with the realities around you. Visualize better times ahead of you; hopefully, you should be able to come out of this stressful time with a little bit more faith in yourself and in the world around you.

## STREETCAR

What you hope to attain and what you will actually attain in life are two different things. Actions speak louder than self-promises and words; if you truly want something, you will find a way to achieve it. There is a moral to this dream symbolism: Do not expect something for nothing in life—rather, expect what you deserve from the sweat of your brow!

## STREETWALKER (see PROSTITUTION)

## STRETCHER (see *also* AMBULANCE)

You seem to have great qualms and difficulties in accepting the stark realities about life on earth. You fear sickness, injury, and death. Most people on earth have these fears, but these fears are to no avail. On the one hand, God gave us a door to enter this planet, through birth; on the other hand, He gave us also another door to leave this planet, through death. What you do between birth and death is entirely up to you. However, it would be advisable to live your life with a good and clean heart, mind, and soul. When your conscience is clear, and you are attuned to God through prayer and faith, then you don't have to ponder over the heartaches, hardships, and stark realities of life. Those stark realities of life are facts of life that you can either accept or reject. They will be there, in either case.

**STRICTNESS** (see **MORALIST** or **OBEDIENCE**)

**STRIKEBREAKER** (see **DISOBEDIENCE** or **STRIKER**)

**STRIKER**
To be a striker within your dream displays your anger and frustration concerning a family member or two, a roommate or two, or about some unpleasant work matters. The way to solve things in life is to be prepared to listen to the other side, compromise with the other side, and harmonize with the other side. Stubbornness and pride will get you absolutely nowhere. Do not expect to win out in these matters without being realistic and wise!

To be a strikebreaker, on the other hand, reveals that you would sooner follow someone's scattered thoughts and actions than listen to your own sensible thinking. Do not follow anyone who might cunningly lead you down a garden path. You have a good, wholesome mind; use it wisely and comfortably in life! Bad company can bring you bad times. For your own sake, be guided by your own good instincts instead of someone else's foolish whims and notions.

**STRING**
Seeing a piece of string or a roll of string indicates that you are walking a very fine line where some people's attitudes about you are concerned. Perhaps you are "pulling too many strings" behind doors, or perhaps you are creating false stories about people. Whatever it is, you are strongly urged to be more honest and sincere in your ways; otherwise, your enemies and pitfalls may far outnumber your blessings.

**STRIPTEASE** (see **BURLESQUE**)

**STROKE** (see **BELL, CARESS, FIT, HEART ATTACK, MASSAGE, PARALYSIS,** or **SICKNESS**)

**STUBBORNNESS** (see **DETERMINATION**)

**STUDENT** (see **FRESHMAN, LEARNING,** or **SCHOOLMATE**)

**STUDIO** (e.g., artist studio, photographic studio, dancing studio, music studio, motion picture studio, radio or television studio, recording studio)

You have a very progressive spirit and earnestly want to be at the top of the ladder in some chosen field or profession. However, your more exalted thoughts about becoming instantly rich and famous are short-sighted daydreams, for the moment. You will see accomplishment and prosperity within your lifetime, but only after you learn that love, courage, and determination are the vital keys required to lead you there. If you are prideful, selfish, and hateful or attempt to step over anyone for your own selfish reasons, then you will instigate your own downfall. The notion that this is a "survival of the fittest" world is nothing more than a silly, arrogant, one-sided attitude about life. It is foolish and groundless! Be careful. Tread gently upon your road to success, and when you achieve it, remember that there is always someone out there who would gladly trade places with you.

**STUMP** (see **CONFUSION, FOREST, LOG, MYSTERY,** or **PLANT**)

**STUNT MAN** (see **ACROBAT** or **DAREDEVIL**)

**STUPIDITY** (see **ABSURDITY**)

**STUTTERER** (see **SPEECH DISORDER**)

**SUBMACHINE GUN** (see **GUN**)

**SUBMARINE** (see *also* **MISSILE, NAVIGATOR, NAVY,** or **TORPEDO**)

Seeing a submarine suggests that you are harboring a misconception about someone, and/or you will have a disagreement with someone who has been loyal to you for many years. Be wary of your actions, at this time. Realize, as well, that sometimes a friend may say something that appears offensive but, in fact, no harm whatsoever was intended. Follow your better instincts in these matters; do not pre-judge someone or misjudge someone who has your best interests at heart.

**SUBPOENA** (see **SUMMONS**)

**SUBSCRIPTION** (see **CONTRACT, DOCUMENT, PRESCRIPTION**, or **SIGNATURE**)

**SUBWAY**
Sometimes you envy and copy others because of their appearance, riches, or power without honestly recognizing the wealth of your own existence. There are some outstanding qualities in you that some people will never attain on this planet; unfortunately, your love-hate relation-ship with yourself will not give you the rightful opportunity to be your natural self. Love and accept yourself for what you are rather than who you would like to be. Not everyone was meant to be rich, famous, or beautiful. When God created you, He created a miracle of love and hope within you so that your communion with life itself would be wise, ful-filling, and giving. One's appearance, status, or rank on this earth plane is superficial; doing good upon this planet is eternal!

**SUCCESS** (see **ABUNDANCE, COMPLETION, CONQUER, DETERMINATION**, or **HEROISM**)

**SUCKER** (see **CANDY**)

**SUFFOCATION** (see **CHOKE**)

**SUGAR** (see **CANDY, FOOD**, or **SACCHARIN**)

**SUICIDE** (see *also* **DEATH, KILL**, or **MURDER**)
Any one or several of the following definitions may be applicable: A) that you know of someone who has committed suicide; or B) that you of someone who has attempted suicide; or C) that you per-sonally prevented someone from attempting this tragic act; or D) that you know of someone who is suicidal, but fortunately this person is

receiving excellent professional help; or E) that long ago you were contemplating suicide, but something within you begged you to stop, and you did; or F) that you tried to commit suicide, but fortunately someone stopped you just in time—and to this very day, you thank God for it; or G) that you are a professional counselor who knows that anyone who is lonely, depressed, feeling totally useless to themselves and the world, or anyone who openly advertises their intention to commit suicide is a prime candidate for this tragic act; or H) that you feel no one should attempt or commit this act (no matter how hopeless and meaningless life may appear to be) but should seek professional help and counseling, when the need arises; or I) that you feel there is absolutely no reason, cause, or excuse for anyone to commit this tragic deed against themselves simply because the "spark of life" belongs to God, and no human being has the right to extinguish it or assume His Authority; or J) that you feel people who commit suicide are foolish defeatists who cannot even fathom the difficulties that await them on the other side of life as a result of their act; or K) that you feel anyone who does contemplate suicide should look beyond their despair with courage, faith, and hope instead of wallowing in self-pity and grief; or L) that people who do commit suicide are basically self-centered individuals who never imagined the anguish, mystery, and disappointments they inflicted upon those who truly loved them; or M) that to throw the gift of life back in God's Face is a transgression; or N) that this dream has little or no significance to you at this time.

**SUITCASE** (see **BAGGAGE**)

**SUMMER** (see **SEASON**)

**SUMMONS** (i.e., a subpoena to appear in court)

Seeing or receiving a summons within your dream suggests that some of your brave ideas, inclinations, aims, concepts, actions, and so on may be ridiculed by some people. Their motives could stem from jealousy, hate, revenge, ignorance, or some other form of dissatisfaction with you as a person. Don't be alarmed by this revelation. Simply realize that some people just fail to see anything beyond their nose. People who are ahead of their time are often attacked and ridiculed by ignorant beings and blind critics who are simply too smug and prideful to praise someone's inspirational work when they see it. Forge on; your day—your time of glory—will come!

## SUN

This auspicious dream reveals that you are headed towards some very busy, rich, full, and rewarding experiences before too long. How lucky you are to have this dream! You have the potential to fulfill some of your greatest wishes and desires on this earth plane, and it is quite obvious that you will. In many respects you are like a time traveler whose intelligence and supernatural awareness far outshine that of the average individual. Ahead of you lies an important destiny which you can fulfill, providing your will and purpose are in the right place. Serve your fellow man in some manner, and you will be on the right road! The sun you saw within your dream is the light you emanate towards others.

## SUN BATH (see BATH)

## SUNBONNET (see BONNET)

## SUNDIAL

This dream advises you to be wary of sudden arguments with an aggressive individual, or to be careful not to say something very offensive and depressing to a person more sensitive than you. You know these people, so you should be able to identify with the above. On the positive side, this dream reminds you to learn from your past experiences in these matters, instead of falling prey to repeated weaknesses and mistakes.

## SUNFLOWER (see PLANT)

## SUNLAMP (see LAMP)

## SUNRISE

This favorable dream symbolizes good health, compatibility with your fellow man, and travel to faraway places you have longed to see. What more could one possibly ask for in life? Your philosophy is not complex; you just know that one of the greatest axioms in life is to remember to be thankful for all your blessings. Whether in good times or hard times, your complete trust and hope in your Creator is that simple, secret ingredient that has made your life so fulfilling, purposeful, and rewarding! Others could gain from your wisdom in life, if they would only learn to give praise and thanks for all things bright and beautiful. You have.

# SUNSET

This auspicious dream reveals that you are beginning to express your feelings, wants, and desires with more openness. Your insecurities, fears, and despair are now gone. You are much happier now than you have ever been before, and rightfully so. You are doing something or attaining something that is very meaningful to you. It could perhaps be just as meaningful to others around you. You are not only finding the beauty and wisdom within you, but around you, as well. You are likened unto a person who has wandered through a forest many times before; but now, for the very first time, you are beginning to acknowledge the beauty and purpose of life within and around you. Welcome home!

**SUPERMARKET** (see **STORE**)

**SUPERNOVA** (see **STAR**)

# SUPERSTITION

There are old wives tales and beliefs that bear no logic to one's supposed higher intelligence and logic. Many times, the superstitions you believe during your wake state will be just as forceful and believable during your dream state. Basically, if you have a sensible, mature outlook, then you should be able to weed out the truth from the fiction in a superstition, no matter how convincing those hand-me-down stories, fables, and warnings may appear to be. Fears about the unknown forces are prime reasons why people create superstitious beliefs and attitudes, in the first place. What they do not know or understand, they automatically label as evil, bad, wicked, and so on—and so a superstition is born. Hopefully, you have a searching, investigative kind of mind which will allow you to eliminate those unwarranted, ignorant superstitions and fears which tend to surface in dreams now and again.

**SUPERVISOR** (see **CARETAKER**, **FOREMAN**, or **MANAGER**)

**SUPPER** (see **MEAL**)

**SUPPER CLUB** (see **CABARET**, **CAFÉ**, or **LIQUOR**)

**SUPPOSITORY** (see **MEDICATION**)

**SURFBOARD** (see **SURFING**)

**SURFING**

You are a very versatile individual who makes the best out of life, even under the worst conditions. Others admire you for your charisma and for your unusual ability to surpass treacherous obstacles with astonishing skill and wonder. The future looks very bright and promising for you; you are secure enough within yourself to attain those goals or aims you so choose; in many respects, you are the master of your own destiny. It appears that your free-spirited individualism is bound to lead you towards the limelight.

**SURGEON** (see **DOCTOR**)

**SURGERY**

No one can appeal to your better judgment and wisdom unless you are prepared to listen. Your stubbornness knows no limits, but your intelligence does! This dream foretells of sickness that can perhaps be avoided through rest, through good nutrition, and by maintaining a good, clear, positive mind. You are not a machine, nor can you expect to work beyond your limits indefinitely. Burning the candle at two ends is not your answer, but it certainly could be your undoing. Respect your time, body, mind, and soul so that you can at least enjoy your life, once in a while. Less stress in your life could be the beginning of a whole new chapter for you!

**SURRENDER** (see **ABANDONMENT**, **OBEDIENCE**, or **SLAVERY**)

**SURREY**

To see or to ride in this old-fashioned pleasure carriage reveals your freedom, peace, and joy for some recent accomplishment or for personally conquering a negative habit. You certainly have the right to be proud of yourself! This new, unselfish beginning will lead you towards more rewarding inner victories and graces.

**SURVEYING** (see **INSPECTION**)

**SUSPENSION BRIDGE** (see **BRIDGE**)

**SWALLOW** (see **BIRD**)

**SWAMP**

There is a certain amount of disharmony around you regarding ownership of something, regarding a boorish relative, and regarding a very demanding friend. Stubbornness, jealousies, and foolishness appear to be at the root of this situation. This situation will not be resolved until there is some peace and compromise with everyone concerned. Unfortunately, some problems are never resolved or handled wisely simply because some people refuse to listen to good, sound logic. Deal with this situation as best you can. If you cannot strike some sort of a bargain with your antagonists, then politely walk away until they commence to see the light of day.

**SWAMP BUGGY** (see **BOAT**)

**SWAN** (see **BIRD**)

**SWASTIKA** (see **NAZISM** or **SYMBOL**)

**SWEARING** (see **BLASPHEMY, LOW-MINDEDNESS,** or **PROMISE**)

**SWEATING** (see **PERSPIRATION**)

**SWEEPSTAKES** (see **LOTTERY**)

**SWIMMING** (see *also* **DIVER, FLOAT, PLUNGE,** or **WATER**)

The act of swimming simply symbolizes "keeping your head above water" until your present difficulties pass. Do not press any panic buttons at this time, nor make any hasty or cash decisions you may later regret. All is well, providing you maintain your courage and strength to see you through this trying time. Right now things may be a little tough on you; but, before you know it, this will pass, and you will go on to bigger and greater challenges and ventures.

**SWIMMING HOLE** (see **FLOAT, SWIMMING,** or **WATER**)

**SWIMMING POOL** (see **FLOAT, SWIMMING,** or **WATER**)

**SWINDLER** (see **CHEATING, DECEPTION**, or **THIEVERY**)

**SWING**

Boredom, fear, and nervousness appear to be at the core of your inner troubles. Unless you commence to dispose of those unwanted attitudes, you will continue to sway back and forth with your decisions and plans in life. You make up your mind one day, only to change it the next day, and so forth. Be more consistent in your life, and do not be afraid to forge ahead even if you do fail once in a while. We all do! If you try hard enough at anything, then you are bound to reap the rewards of your labour. This dream is a small reminder to you that you do not try hard enough to reap those rewards which you so rightfully deserve. Why don't you? You just might be surprised; it is not as difficult as you make it out to be.

**SWING BRIDGE** (see **BRIDGE**)

**SWITCH** (see **STICK** or **PUNISHMENT**)

**SWITCHBOARD**

Your communication with others around you appears to be at a complete standstill. This dream urges you to reevaluate your likes and dislikes of self and others in a peaceful, forgiving manner. When you nourish and cultivate a friendship, for example, you can expect far greater results than if you were to neglect or ignore friendships or if you were to give way to faultfinding, for some reason or other. Verbalize, harmonize, and respect those around you and people whom you know; you never can tell when a loved one or a friend is suddenly taken away from you.

**SWORD**

Sometimes life can be very difficult and disappointing, in spite of the changes and concessions you have already made. Yet, it is precisely at this "no win" kind of crossroad that you should commence to see yourself in the clearest, soul-searching way. You will discover that the soul is indeed mightier than the sword; and you, being a soul, are simply trying to remove some of those earthly obstacles through trial and error. Do not be sad or disappointed at this time. Be happy and encouraged that you have the will and the mind to persevere, to challenge, and to ultimately conquer those obstacles. Very soon, you will!

**SWORDFISH** (see **FISH**)

**SWORDPLAY** (see **FIGHT, GAME,** or **SWORD**)

**SYMBOL** (e.g., emblem, Star of David, badge, sign, swastika)

A symbol itself within a dream state reflects upon your personal feelings, emotions, observations, attempts, experimentations, and so on as well as your overall reactions and reflections about some of your experiences in life. Whether your experiences are good or bad, these events, tests, or trials in your life make you who you are and what you are today. The dangers of being too confident, prideful, or selfish can lead you towards temptations and obstacles that are very difficult to surmount. Always strive to be mature, farsighted, virtuous, appreciative, and loving in all that you do so that the curiosity within you will turn into fearless joys and happiness.

**SYMPATHY** (see **COMPASSION** or **CONSOLATION**)

**SYMPHONY** (see **MUSIC, MUSICIAN,** or **ORCHESTRA**)

**SYMPOSIUM** (see **CONFERENCE**)

**SYNAGOGUE** (see **CHURCH**)

**SYPHILIS** (See **INTERCOURSE, SEX,** or **SICKNESS**)

**SYRINGE**

When you commence to feel good about yourself, you will then commence to feel much better about everything else. Begin to realize that you will derive the greatest pleasure from your life through patience, humility, consideration, and respect for all things—not just a select number of things. By putting your "house" in order (e.g., attitudes, feelings, concepts), you will then be able to forge ahead with greater peace of mind, liberty, and happiness. Nothing is impossible to you or for you. As you strive to progress, realize that the efforts you put into life are more or less the results you will receive from life. Do not expect something for nothing; be prepared to work more passionately and sincerely for your quests and wishes.

**TABERNACLE** (see **CHURCH**)

**TABLE**

If the table is neat and new-looking, then your future will be much better than your past. Forthcoming changes and inspired attitudes will allow you to forge ahead like you have never done before! In many respects, you will feel as though there were a time limit with the work you wish to accomplish. There will be no time limit, per se; however, this attitude will certainly allow you to complete your future plans with personal satisfaction and prosperity. You will make up for lost time as you energetically enter your future.

If the table you see is untidy, old-looking, or is damaged, then you are advised to alter some of your old concepts and actions in order to see a better future. Personal doubts, hang-ups, habits, fears, and other attitudes are holding you back from looking ahead with a clear mind. You are being far too pessimistic for your own good, and unless you disband some of your hopeless views, you will not see the futuristic progress and happiness you so rightfully deserve. Feeble excuses will get you nowhere; inspirational changes will open many new doors for you.

**TABLE LINEN** (see **MATERIAL** or **NAPKIN**)

**TABLESPOON** (see **SILVERWARE**)

**TABLEWARE** (see **DINNERWARE**, **GLASSWARE**, or **SILVERWARE**)

**TACK** (see **NAIL**)

**TACKLE** (see **FISHING TACKLE**)

**TAG** (see **GAME** or **LABEL**)

**TAILOR** (see **DRESSMAKER**)

**TALISMAN**

You despise exaggeration and melodramatic behaviour and actions from people around you; yet, recently, you seem to be doing the same things yourself. This is not very becoming a person of your caliber and intelligence. This dream is reminding you to practice what you preach and to not preach unless you can live by your words.

**TAMBOURINE** (see **DRUM** or **INSTRUMENT**)

**TANK** (see **VAT**)

**TANKER** (see **SHIP**)

**TAPE RECORDER**

You are fretting and fussing about some matter that troubles you. The more you dwell upon this matter, the longer the anguish persists. You can simply record your trouble within your mind without actually doing anything about it, or you can decide to peacefully solve your trouble and then ultimately erase it from your mind, for all time. The difficulties you had five years ago are now all solved. You worried about those problems too! What makes your immediate problem any different? This, too, will pass when you face your trouble with foresight and courage.

**TARANTULA** (see **SPIDER**)

**TARGET** (see **AIM** or **BOWMAN**)

**TASSEL** (see **DECORATION** or **LACEWORK**)

**TASTE** (see **FOOD, SMELL,** or **SPICE**)

**TATTOO**

A series of events could create shame and dishonor for you, if you are not careful. This blemish or mark upon your character can perhaps be avoided through honesty and by admitting your faults and failings when the need arises. Do not exaggerate or hide behind deceitful words, especially when others around you know differently. You can discover a greater person within yourself by showing more humility— which, up to now, you have pridefully ignored.

**TAVERN** (see **CASINO, HOTEL,** or **LIQUOR**)

**TAX** (e.g., income tax, property tax, sales tax)

Dreaming about this happy or sad event concerning taxes could very well be precisely what you are experiencing at this time, such as receiving a tax rebate, paying taxes, or not having enough money to pay your taxes). However, if this is not the case, then this dream indicates that you are being weighed down or taxed by certain demands, regulations, or put-downs from other people around you. Also, your workload has created a great strain upon your mind and body. Prayer, seeking some good, sound professional advice, if necessary, and believing and fighting for your human rights and dignity are all important factors which can assist you in your present plight and predicament. You will survive, and you will surmount your present difficulties very soon!

**TAXICAB** (see **CAR**)

**TAXIDERMY**
There is a great love of nature and music in your mind and soul! You are very self-conscious, conservative, and unselfish; and you make a very loyal companion and friend to those who know and respect you. Your wishes for the future will be granted, but not without first making a few mistakes here and there so that your self-confidence and outlook will grow and prosper.

**TEACHER** (see *also* **COACH, GURU,** or **MAHARISHI**)
If the teacher you see is kindly, pleasant, helpful, and so on, then rest assured that your enthusiasm, concentration, and efforts will lead you towards the recognition you rightfully deserve. You are slated for many rich and rewarding experiences in life. Ahead of you also lie happiness and a spirit filled with curiosity and truth.

If the teacher you see is unpleasant, angry, or quite frightful for some reason, then you are cautioned to be more aware about your contradictions, overconfidence, and reckless attitudes in life. Your rash thoughts and actions can lead you towards difficult times! Commence to correct some of your shortcomings and limitations with deep introspection and down-to-earth logic. Always strive to be fair, just, and compassionate in your dealings with self and others around you, if you truly want to prosper on this earth plane.

Seeing a teacher who is unhappy, doubtful, confused, surprised, fearful, or simply silent reveals that you can make your life as successful or as disappointing as you want it to be. What you do with your aims and efforts is squarely up to you. The legacy of this dream symbolism is that you must be determined and enterprising in order to find your true purpose and appreciation on earth. Do not expect too much of something for nothing; this attitude will collide with you in time to come. However, if you are willing to work hard for what you want in life, then, in most instances, you will be gratified and satisfied with the overall outcome.

**TEAMWORK** (see **COOPERATION**)

**TEAR** (see **CRY**)

**TEASING** (see **MOCKERY**)

**TEASPOON** (see **SILVERWARE**)

**TEDDY BEAR** (see **TOY**)

**TEENAGER** (see **ADOLESCENT**)

**TEEPEE** (see **TENT**)

**TEETERBOARD** (see **SEESAW**)

**TEETH**
Healthy looking teeth reveal that you are overanxious to complete a task or to do something that will give you more peace of mind and happiness in life. Whatever your reasons may be, this dream indicates that you will simply continue to follow the dictates of your mind and heart until all your plans or goals are fulfilled. You will settle for no more and no less!

Teeth that are loose or unclean, or experiencing a toothache within your dream, forewarns of sudden sickness or trouble that will take time to heal and correct. The power of prayer, faith, courage, and laughter are the key ingredients to carry you through this forthcoming, difficult period.

Teeth that are decayed, bleeding, falling out, spitted out, chipped, or broken indicates a mental, physical, and financial strain upon you and some members of your family, at this time. Overexertion or being reckless in any manner can bring about further troubles and strife (e.g., accident, sickness, death). Be extremely prudent during these trying times! The key words for you and your loved one's guidance and protection are prayer, caution, and self-restraint.

**TELEGRAM**

A written telegram indicates that news from a distance will bring you happiness or sadness, or a journey to a distant place will bring you happiness, confusion, or sadness. Such is this life and its many bitter, happy, and sad times. However inspirational or painful this symbolism may seem to you, the fact remains that you have the courage to accept life for what it is and for what it has to offer. Hopefully, your news or your trip will be peaceful and rewarding for you—only time will tell.

A blank or torn telegram reveals that you are worried about a younger or an older family member. This could pertain to someone's wayward attitude or someone being sick at this time. Whatever the problem may be, it is sincerely hoped that with time, love, and prayer, everything within and around you will improve. Be patient; miracles have a way of surfacing when you least expect them to do so!

**TELEGRAPH** (see **MORSE CODE, TELEGRAM,** or **TELEX**)

**TELEKINESIS** (see **MEDIUM**)

**TELEPATHY** (see **CLAIRVOYANCE, MEDIUM, MYSTIC, OUIJA, PARAPSYCHOLOGY, PERCEPTION, PROPHECY,** or **SÉANCE**)

**TELEPHONE**

You are not giving yourself half the credit you deserve in life. Such fine potential and talent should not be wasted; it should be utilized to the best of your ability. Why are you hiding it? Why are you ignoring it? Don't be afraid of what is within you. Gently come forth and show us the spark, philosophy, and communication hidden within your being. You are so rich and wise with your thoughts and actions. The world needs another sound, another truth; come forth gently and wisely, and share your talents with us.

**TELEPHONE BOOK**

This book or directory implies that, rather than being guided by your own better instincts, judgments, and common sense, you are more worried about what people will say about you. Sometimes you have to completely ignore the reaction people have towards you and courageously do what is best for you. You recently made a very wise decision; stick with it, no matter what people say! Besides, people will

say what they want to say, no matter what you say or do; it really does
not matter! So be true unto yourself at all times; you will prosper this
way!

## TELEPHONE BOOTH (see **TELEPHONE**)

## TELESCOPE

There appears to be a certain amount of emotional confusion
within you, at this time. Your insecurities could be based on someone
ignoring you. Whatever the reason, do not fret so much or take everything so seriously. You have been through worse situations in your life,
yet you managed to resolve them. Your problem now is no different.
Calm your mind, and you will free yourself from your supposed hopeless situation. Your tomorrows will come, and the love and harmony
you seek will come with them!

## TELEVISION (see *also* **NETWORK**)

Seeing a television set that works or changing the channel on one
intimates that you have the fortitude and determination to beat the
odds in your life. With your logical, analytical mind and your willingness to forge ahead, even under difficult circumstances, you are bound
to succeed in your own time and in your own way.

Seeing a television that does not work, is damaged, or is being
damaged by someone or something reveals inner discord with self and
with others around you. You are a very moody person and are difficult
to know and understand. This dream advises you to calm down and to
begin to realize that you are creating anxieties in people around you.
No good can come from your difficult moods and notions, so you are
strongly advised to stop feeling so sorry for yourself, stop trying to get
a reaction out of people with your sudden, rude outbursts, and strive
a little harder to progress, rather than regress, in life. A little bit of
kindness from you could go a very, very long way. Why don't you try
it sometime?

## TELEX

Seeing a telex message or using a telex machine reveals that you are
a very determined, progressive-minded individual. Sometimes you go
over and above the call of duty in order to help someone or to get
something done, and you finish what you start. Some immediate surprises may inspire you to go on a brief journey, to make a major

purchase, to alter your future plans, or to take some educational course in order to assist you. Your future will be as bright as you want to make it—and make it, you will!

**TELLER** (see **CLERK**)

**TEMPLE** (see **CHURCH** or **ORGANIZATION**)

**TEMPTER** (see **DANGER, DEMON,** or **EVILDOER**)

**TEN COMMANDMENTS** (see **BIBLE** or **MOSES**)

**TENNIS** (see **GAME**)

**TENT**
Far too much emphasis is placed upon money and materialistic matters. Being selfish or greedy in these matters will never bring you the happiness, love, and truth you seek. If you are rich already, then do your very best to share some of your prosperity with those less fortunate than yourself; God will bless and reward you in many different ways. If you are poor, then do your very best to share what you have with those around you; God will bless and reward you in many different ways.

**TERMITE** (see **INSECT**)

**TERRACE** (see **BALCONY, LAWN,** or **PATIO**)

**TERRORISM** (see **CONFUSION, CRUELTY, DEMONSTRATOR, DESTRUCTION, DISOBEDIENCE, HATRED, INJURY,** or **MISCHIEF**)

**TEST** (e.g., school test, or quiz, or medical test) (see *also* **EXPERIMENT**)
Any one or several of the following definitions may be applicable: A) that you recently passed a test with flying colors; or B) that you are worried about a test you had recently; or C) that you have great qualms about having to take a test before too long; or D) that you dread failing anything in life, and this troubles you, from time to time; or E) that you have happy or sad memories where school exams are concerned; or

F) that you would like to take a course or two at school but fear the thought of failing any future exams; or G) that you always found school exams to be easy but never realized that life's experiences could be so harsh and difficult; or H) that your textbook knowledge and exams were somewhat antiquated in comparison to the stark realities of your job; or I) that you know someone who either passed or failed a test recently; or J) that you are in the educational system or medical profession and give tests to people; or K) that medical tests are not always foolproof, as you have already experienced more than once; or L) that you feel the raw experiences in life are the true tests for everyone on this earth plane; or M) that you cheated on a test; or N) that before an exam you can remember just about everything, but when you are actually writing the exam, you tend to forget many things; or O) that you recently wrote your final exams at school; or P) that you look forward to writing your final exams at school in the very near future; or Q) that this dream has little or no relevance to you at this time.

**TESTAMENT** (see **BEQUEST**, **BIBLE**, or **GENESIS**)

**THAW** (see **MELTAGE**)

**THEATRE** (see *also* **ACROBAT**, **ACTOR**, **AGENT**, **ARENA**, **AUDITORIUM**, **AUTHOR**, **BALLERINA**, **BALLET**, **BURLESQUE**, **CABARET**, **CALVARY**, **CIRCUS**, **COLISEUM**, **COMEDIAN**, **COMEDY**, **DANCE**, **MANAGER**, **MINSTREL SHOW**, **MONOLOGUE**, **MOTION PICTURE**, **OFFSTAGE**, **OPERA**, **PASSION PLAY**, **PERFORMER**, **PUPPETRY**, **REHEARSAL**, **STAGE**, or **STUDIO**)

You sincerely want to make some justifiable changes within your life. However, it appears that you are receiving some mixed reviews and answers from people who tend to be non-supportive and unsympathetic to your cause. What is important here is that you should be acting on your own initiative and courage instead of being dependent upon people who fail to understand your needs and wants in life. Be very strong, and do your very best to ignore the misunderstandings and ridicule you may be receiving at this time. You can succeed, but this will depend solely upon your attitude and strength to overcome your present obstacles and conflicts. Ahead of you lies the ultimate teacher of all things: your experience. This will allow you to persevere and grow until your earthly ambitions are achieved. Good luck!

**THEFT** (see **THIEVERY**)

**THEORY** (see **DOCTRINE, FORMULA,** or **NOTION**)

**THERAPY** (see **ASSISTANCE, ANTIDOTE, MEDICATION,** or **PSYCHOTHERAPY**)

**THERMOMETER**
    Using or seeing this device within a dream state reveals your level of tolerance or intolerance with self and with people around you. Sometimes you are calm, open-minded, and extremely easy to get along with; at other times, you are highly demanding, argumentative, and totally unforgiving. Many people behave this way—you are not alone. What this dream symbolism is trying to tell you, however, is to strive a little harder to control your temper and anger when matters not to your liking take place. You will have these up and down experiences in life many times, so why bother getting an ulcer or high blood pressure over some things that turn out to be more laughable in the end than you care to admit! Smile, laugh, be tolerant, and be as happy as you can on this earth plane. This attitude will cure your impatience and unreasonable demands.

**THERMOSTAT**
    This device reveals your level of happiness or unhappiness in life. If you are a happy individual, then may you be blessed with even more happiness! If you are unhappy, then you must get to the source of your trouble. Why are you unhappy? Who or what is creating your unhappiness? Can you do anything to solve your problem so that peace might be forthcoming? Have you tried to solve your problem, or did you merely skim the surface, hoping matters might change for you? Are you a forgiving person, or do you hold grudges against others and life itself? Do you wish to have a better life, or do you merely "whine and pine" and daydream about better times ahead? Are you willing to change now or later? Have you prayed earnestly for your peace of mind and happiness? Have you heeded the good advice given to you lately, where your unhappiness is concerned? Are you afraid to move forward in life in order to truly find yourself and succeed in your own way? Do you believe in God, or do you feel you can get along without Him? If you truly love God, then realize that some forthcoming changes ahead of you will be to your benefit and well-being. However, if you are

blaming God, or someone else, or something else for your problems in life, then wisely seek your God; He will give you all the rest and happiness you need.

**THESIS** (see **AUTHOR, BOOK,** or **MANUSCRIPT**)

**THIEVERY** (see *also* **BLACKMAIL, BURGLARY, CHEATING, CRIMINAL, DECEPTION, EXTORTION, FORGERY, KIDNAPPING, KLEPTOMANIA, MAFIA, POACHER, PROWLER, RANSOM, RAPE,** or **SMUGGLER**)

Any one or several of the following definitions may be applicable: A) that you are a thief; or B) that you are not a thief, but many years ago you did take something that did not belong to you from someone; or C) that you are distressed and conscience-stricken about some of your hidden habits, sexual preferences, and general actions in life; or D) that you have a fear about being cheated or robbed; or E) that a thief recently stole some of your valuable possessions; or F) that you know of someone who is a thief; or G) that you were tempted to steal something once, but your better instincts held you back; or H) that you know of someone who was incarcerated for thievery; or I) that you feel thievery is not only a sin, but can be a sickness for attention, as well; or J) that you recently protected your home with burglar alarms and other devices to keep thieves away; or K) that you are intending to protect your home with burglar alarms and other devices in order to keep thieves away; or L) that a neighbour was recently robbed; or M) that you recently saw some thieves in your neighbourhood; or N) that you apprehended some thieves recently; or O) that this dream has little or no significance to you at this time.

**THIMBLE** (see **SEWING**)

**THIRST**

Experiencing thirst within a dream state could imply that you simply are thirsty. If this is not the case, then this symbolism reveals that you are a very well balanced, well admired individual. You have the innate ability to assist people without getting upset or emotional about their problems. In your final analysis or judgment with people's problems, you are both fair and impartial; this is most comforting to know. Have you ever thought of yourself as being a sage? In many respects, you are! Your wisdom is one to behold and cherish. You are loved and appreciated in more ways than you realize!

**THISTLE** (see **PLANT**)

**THORN** (see **PLANT**)

**THREAD** (see **SEWING**)

**THREAT** (see **BLACKMAIL, BULLY, DANGER, EVILDOER, FEAR**, or **FOREWARNING**)

**THRESHING MACHINE** (see **MACHINERY**)

**THUNDER**

Hearing the sounds of thunder could be precisely what you are hearing during your dream. However, if this is not the case, then this dream implies that you are somewhat impractical and misdirected in situations that call for more logic and prudence. Do not be blinded by false information handed down to you by word of mouth; nor be tempted to act bad, foolish, or unusual on someone's insistence or urgings. Think twice before you attempt to do something you may regret. You have a good mind; use it wisely, at all times!

**TICKET** (see **ACKNOWLEDGEMENT, CERTIFICATE, LABEL, LICENSE, LIST, MEMORANDUM, SUMMONS**, or **VOTE**)

**TICKLE** (see **HAPPINESS, LAUGHTER**, or **TOUCH**)

**TICK-TACK-TOE** (see **GAME**)

**TIDDLYWINKS** (see **GAME**)

**TIDEWATER** (see **WATER**)

**TIGER**

A peaceful-looking tiger indicates that some business matters and/or personal negotiations between you and someone else will allow you to carry on your work without any emotional and financial setbacks. You are on the right road, and you will prosper by your work!

To see a ferocious tiger or one that is wounded or about to attack you reveals that you are angered about someone's attitude or actions and/or about some embarrassing situation that occurred quite recently.

Even if you are right and justified most of the time, strive harder to give and take a little bit here and a little bit there; life will offer you more this way. Remember, as well, that not everyone or everything in life can meet your high thoughts and standards. Learn to let go of matters beyond your control, and wisely reach out to others with love and understanding. You will ultimately prosper this way!

**TIGHTROPE** (see **ACROBAT**, **CABLE**, **CIRCUS**, or **ROPE**)

**TIMBER** (see **FOREST** or **LUMBER**)

**TIME CAPSULE** (see **CAPSULE**)

**TIMEKEEPER** (see **CLERK**, **EMPLOYEE**, or **EMPLOYER**)

**TIMETABLE** (see **CALENDAR**, **LIST**, **MEASUREMENT**, or **PROGRAM**)

**TIN** (see **CAN**, **METALWORKING** or **ORE**)

**TINSEL** (see **DECORATION**)

**TIPTOE** (see **CAUTION**)

**TISSUE** (e.g., tissue paper, toilet paper, disposable handkerchief, wrappings) (see *also* **NAPKIN**)

The amount of interest you create in your daily life depends entirely upon you. Right now, it appears that you are bored sick with your day to day obligations, activities, or idleness (e.g., housecleaning, routine at work or school, being unemployed). Even though you may despise your lifestyle, it is up to you to generate those greater feelings and changes that are possible to you. Right now, you are your own worst enemy. How hard have you tried to actually make your life more interesting? Have you honestly taken the time to have a fun day just for yourself? Have you made any attempts to meet or welcome new friendships into your life? Have you sincerely taken the time to introspectively glean the boundless love and understanding within you, or do you find it easier to complain and whine about your present state of being? Have you considered taking up a hobby or two or perhaps joining a club or nonprofit organization just to get away from the humdrum, mundane routine of your life? Do you know how to relax, or are you a workaholic who is finally beginning to realize that there is more to life than work itself? Do you believe in exercise and long walks? How about reading a good book once in a while, or why don't you consider writing one? Are you afraid to forge ahead in life in order to explore what is within and around you? Well, this dream advises you that you should not be bored or sick with your life! There are literally hundreds of new things for you to do, if you take the time to find them. Why don't you?

**TOAD** (see **FROG**)

**TOADSTOOL** (see **MUSHROOM**)

**TOAST** (see **BREAD**)

**TOASTER** (see **APPLIANCE**)

**TOBOGGAN** (see **SLEDDING**)

**TOE**

    Seeing a toe itself within a dream state reveals that there are some vital decisions that you will have to make within the next several months or so. One decision, however, will guide you towards inner peace, happiness, and probable future success (e.g., a move, marriage, changing jobs). You are in the throes of leaving old things behind and ushering in new prospects and adventures into your life. You will! But, in the interim, do your best to dispel those doubts about yourself, your potential, and your future. Here's a tip for you: your optimism and courage will bring you the things you seek in life; your pessimism and self-pity will diminish your chances.

**TOGA** (see **CLOTHES**)

**TOILET** (see **BATHROOM** or **OUTHOUSE**)

**TOILET PAPER** (see **TISSUE**)

**TOLLBOOTH** (see **CHECKPOINT**, **MONEY**, or **TAX**)

**TOLL BRIDGE** (see **BRIDGE, MONEY,** or **TAX**)

**TOMATO** (see **FRUIT** or **PLANT**)

**TOMB** (see **BURIAL, CATACOMB, CENOTAPH, GRAVE, MAUSOLEUM,** or **MONUMENT**)

**TOMBSTONE** (see **BURIAL** or **GRAVESTONE**)

**TOOL** (see *also* **AXE, CHAIN, DERRICK, FORCEPS, HATCHET, HOE, JACK, KNIFE, LEVER, MALLET, NAIL, OAR, PULLEY, SCISSORS, SCREW, SWORD, TWEEZERS,** or **UTENSIL**)

Using or seeing a tool within a dream may very well represent the tool(s) you actually use at home or at work. If this is not the case, then the dream implies that you are unsettled and somewhat disorganized in life. You may be charming and interesting to some people, but you are failing to question your tunnel vision attitudes and actions towards those who know you very well. You are a very stubborn individual! Even when you make a mistake or two, you are not about to change or admit it—not if you can get away with it. But woe to anyone else who makes a mistake! You are the first person to notice these matters and certainly the first person to complain about these matters, as well. Unless you change some of your one-eyed views and concepts about yourself and about life, you will continue to feel neglected, suspicious, and impractical in your ways. If you are following the example of a parent, grandparent, aunt, uncle, or someone else around you, it is not because you have to—it is because you want to. You know that old attitude: "It was good enough for my grandfather, so it is good enough for me!" Maybe so, but highly unlikely! A change within you is in order. This depends entirely upon you.

**TOOTH** (see **TEETH**)

**TOOTHACHE** (see **TEETH**)

**TOOTHBRUSH**

Using or seeing a toothbrush indicates that you are a generous, bighearted individual who often gets upset and disoriented over unimportant, trivial matters; however, you are very capable in handling important, vital matters with ease and comfort. Whenever you are confronted with minor problems in life, simply commence to relax, study the problem at hand, and then peacefully master it. Do not make any big deal over small, unimportant things. What is important is that you are capable of handling the bigger challenges within and around you. Consider this a big blessing, but be thankful for small blessings in life, as well!

**TOOTHPASTE** (see **TOOTHBRUSH**)

**TOOTHPICK**

You are being far too complacent in a vital matter that may soon require your undivided attention (e.g., health, finances, marital or off-spring difficulties). Whatever it is, this dream reminds you to "wake up and smell the coffee" before matters get totally out of hand. Do not ignore what is in front of you; rather, peacefully solve it. There is a mighty storm brewing in your horizon; but it can be totally avoided if you begin to solve this matter of importance, at this time.

**TOOTH POWDER** (see **TOOTHBRUSH**)

**TORCH** (see **BLOWTORCH**, **FIRE**, or **FLASHLIGHT**)

**TORMENT** (see **ANGUISH**, **CRUELTY**, **DISAPPOINTMENT**, **PERSECUTION**, or **PUNISHMENT**)

**TORNADO**

A tornado forewarns of troubling times with lasting scars and lessons. So often in life, it is the innocent victims who have to suffer the bitterness and anguish created by other, less caring individuals. At this time of your life, more than ever before, keep your strength in God, and pray for peace and comfort around you. Just about anything can happen with this dream symbolism, so be extremely prudent in what you do and where you go. Danger is lurking at every crossroad, highway, and byway; this is not the time to be foolish, daring, or absentminded!

**TORPEDO** (see **BOMB** or **MISSILE**)

**TORTILLA** (see **FOOD**)

**TORTOISE** (see **TURTLE**)

**TORTURE** (see **ANGUISH, CRUELTY, DISAPPOINTMENT, PERSECUTION,** or **PUNISHMENT**)

**TOTEM POLE**

This dream strongly indicates your need to be recognized as a person with feelings, hopes, dreams, and wishes—just like the next person. Sometimes you feel left out or abandoned by others who appear to be more versatile with their time and actions. However, the quality of being your natural self at all times is far more important than envying others who appear to be more outgoing and fun loving. What attempts have you honestly made to come out of your inner shell or to express your desires to join forces with those whom you envy? The things you do for yourself are basically those vital bridges you cross for your own satisfaction, learning, and betterment. However, if you fail or refuse to cross those vital bridges from time to time, then ultimately you have no one to blame but yourself.

**TOUCH**

The actual sensation of touching yourself, someone, or something within a dream can be related to actually touching yourself, someone, or something while you are asleep. For example, you may be unwittingly touching some part of your body while sleeping, only to find yourself dreaming about some sexual or amorous situation; or you may be touching your loved one during sleep, only to simultaneously dream about some loving situation; or you may be touching some part of your bed or bed clothes, only to dream about touching a car, a tree, and so forth. However, this is not always applicable. Your conscious and subconscious mind can remember the sensation of touch from the time you were born and can release the sensations to you while you dream. There is no mystery here; it simply is that way!

**TOUCHDOWN** (see **GAME**)

**TOUPEE** (see **WIG**)

**TOURIST**

Being or seeing a tourist within a dream denotes your need for a retreat, leave of absence, or holiday from your busy and sometimes monotonous schedule. Although this inner need may not become an immediate reality, it is shown that you will eventually break away from your course of activities to some remote hideaway for peace of mind and leisure. Thus far, your life has been rather noble and complimentary. As you forge ahead, you will commence to fulfill some of your latent wishes and hopes with fine accomplishments and personal satisfaction.

**TOURNAMENT** (see **COMPETITION, CONTEST**, or **GAME**)

**TOWBOAT** (see **BOAT**)

**TOWEL** (see **MATERIAL, NAPKIN**, or **TISSUE**)

**TOWER**

This symbolism reveals your magnificent attempts to stay "above water" amidst your present setbacks and disappointments. Sadly, you have been through some very depressed, uncertain, and unhappy situations which would have compelled another person to give up. But not you! Basically, you do not ask for too much except for a roof over your head, good health, and perhaps some success in your lifetime. It is shown that your tolerance and courage will bring you peace, and your insight and faith will bring you an opportunity which will allow you to rise over and above your despair. Be at peace! Soon, your tomorrows will tower over you with such good luck that you will find it hard to believe you are living on the same planet. But you will be—and you will prosper in many different, unique ways.

**TOWLINE** (see **CHAIN** or **ROPE**)

**TOWN**

Seeing a town that appears relatively peaceful and natural reveals that you are a very stable, intelligent individual. Your common sense and persistence will lead you towards greater challenges and events with admirable results and many financial blessings!

Seeing a town that does not appear peaceful or one that appears unnatural denotes your basic discouragement, boredom, and somewhat scornful outlook in life. A part of you simply wants to escape from the chaotic turmoil within and around you; another part of you appears to fear new concepts and drastic personal changes. You will remain in a no-win situation unless you let go of your old, antiquated ideas and fears. Where you are is where you will continue to be many years from now unless something—more miraculous than this dream—changes your narrow, fearful outlook.

**TOWROPE** (see **ROPE**)

**TOY**

If a child dreams about a toy, then this symbolism merely reflects upon that child's keen awareness and perhaps fears in life. The child is behaving normally and naturally, according to age and development. However, if an adult dreams about a toy, then this symbolism indicates that you tend to become childlike and helpless when you think that everything has failed you in life. It is during these "helpless" situations that many people commence to see their faults and failings with greater insight; it is at this crossroads that many people commence to part company with old habits, desires, and nonsensical hang-ups. Such are the trials and tribulations of growing up, seeking new objectives, and perhaps finally settling down to the realities of life. This dream urges you to look at yourself more seriously by commencing to accept all your responsibilities with down-to-earth common sense, instead of rebelling or being immature. No one expects you to be perfect in life; by the same token, it certainly wouldn't hurt to try to do your best.

**TRACK AND FIELD** (see **COMPETITION** or **CONTEST**)

**TRACTOR** (see **MACHINERY**)

**TRADER** (see **AUCTION, BAZAAR, MARKETPLACE, MERCHANT, NEGOTIATION, PEDDLER, SALESMAN, STOCK EXCHANGE**, or **STORE**)

**TRAGEDY** (see **MISFORTUNE**)

**TRAILER**

Your moods shift like the wind. This could be the result of some emotional repressions you tend to harbour; you are a very insecure individual, at times. This dream symbolism strongly urges you to stabilize your thoughts and actions with more trust and faith—not only in yourself, but in life as a whole. Your sudden anxieties and fears are often groundless. They appear to be tricks and deceptions that your mind concocts against you. Your imagination is working overtime, so do your utmost to ignore any base or unwholesome thoughts which tend to annoy or aggravate you. Plant you feet firmly in the ground, and begin to focus your mind-thoughts towards calm, pleasant, and more wholesome ventures. You will be in a win-win situation if you do.

**TRAIN** (see **RAILROAD**)

**TRAITOR** (see **BETRAYER** or **DECEPTION**)

**TRAMP** (see **BEGGAR** or **HOBO**)

**TRAMPOLINE** (see *also* **ACROBAT** or **JUMP**)
Your high expectations of someone or something may not always be met with satisfaction. Your own perfectionism can be your worst enemy, if it is not harnessed and controlled. In life, you will discover that your disappointments should be an excellent source of character building—not character weakening! Don't be so hard on yourself and on those around you. It's perfectly normal and natural to want things to turn out in your favour and to your specifications, but there are times when things do not pan out the way you expect them to do. Shatter your myths about having things "my way or no way". Instead, strive a little harder to be more open-minded when disappointments happen to come your way. You will become wiser this way!

**TRANCE** (see **FAINT, HYPNOTISM, MEDIUM, MYSTIC, SÉANCE,** or **SLEEP**)

**TRANSFORMATION** (see **METAMORPHOSIS**)

**TRANSFUSION**
It appears as though you need all the encouragement you can humanly muster! So often, you are set back by either misunderstandings, neglect, or misdirection from others that life itself becomes a daily chore or, at best, a daily challenge. This dream wishes to inform you that when you are misjudged in life, the best outlet is prayer, faith in God and yourself, and keeping yourself pleasantly busy. Time will heal your wounds. In the interim, never mind what people say or do.

Go about your business, and you will eventually radiate amongst those who willfully made your life seem luckless and unhappy.

**TRANSLATOR** (see **INTERPRETER**)

**TRANSMITTER** (see **ANTENNA, MORSE CODE, RADIO, TELEPHONE, TELEVISION,** or **TELEX**)

**TRANSMUTATION** (see **ALCHEMY**)

**TRANSSEXUAL** (i.e., a person who is more inclined to identify with the opposite sex, or a person who undergoes a sex change)
Any one or several of the following definitions may be applicable: A) that you are a transsexual who has already undergone a complete sex change; or B) that you are a transsexual who is thinking about the possibilities of having a complete sex change in the very near future; or C) that you know of someone who is a transsexual; or D) that you are not a transsexual but often wonder what it would be like to be of the opposite sex; or E) that you feel people have no right to tamper with the laws of nature, no matter how cruel the circumstances may be; or F) that you feel if nature made a mistake in the first place and the sex change technology is available, then a person has that God-given right to make their stay on earth as comfortable as possible; or G) that you feel no one has the right to judge or condemn others in a situation such as transsexualism unless they personally have experienced the trauma and anguish that these people often experience; or H) that you read an article or book about transsexualism quite recently; or I) that you feel most transsexuals do not get a sex change for sexual reasons or on a whim, but rather for their sanity's sake so that their thoughts and feelings can harmonize with their bodies, as well; or J) that this dream has little or no relevance to you at this time.

**TRANSVESTITE** (i.e., a person who receives satisfaction from wearing clothes of the opposite sex)
Any one or several of the following definitions may be applicable: A) that you are a transvestite who is happy or unhappy with the lifestyle you maintain; or B) that you are a transvestite who is considering therapy for your problem(s); or C) that you know of someone who is a transvestite; or D) that you feel a woman wearing male clothes could be seeking the love of her father or a man wearing woman's clothes could be seeking the love of his mother; or E) that you feel the

fetish to wear clothes of the opposite sex can be overcome through professional help and guidance; or F) that you feel these people are essentially mentally sick and should be institutionalized so they can be helped; or G) that you have great compassion towards any group of people who may require help and understanding; or H) that you are in the medical profession and deal with transvestites quite frequently; or I) that you recently read a book or article about transvestitism, or you saw a movie about this subject matter; or J) that this dream has little or no significance to you at this time.

**TRAP** (see **AMBUSH, DECEPTION, DECOY, HUNTING, NET, NOOSE, MOUSETRAP,** or **QUICKSAND**)

**TRAPEZE** (see **ACROBAT, CIRCUS,** or **ROPE**)

**TRASH** (see **GARBAGE**)

**TRAWLER** (see **BOAT**)

**TREASON** (see **BETRAYER** or **DECEPTION**)

**TREASURE** (see **ABUNDANCE, GOLD,** or **PRIZE**)

**TREATMENT** (see **ANTIDOTE, ASSISTANCE, MEDICATION,** or **PSYCHOTHERAPY**)

**TREE** (see **CONE, FOREST, ORCHARD, PLANT,** or **SHRUB**)

**TREE HOUSE**
You will be faced with the personal dilemma of being alone and terribly lonely unless you take hold of your present situation with maturity and firm action. Hiding behind a facade of indifference and uncaring will not diminish your problem(s); it will augment them! This dream symbolism advises you not to run away from yourself or from the truths you must face realistically. Your life can be better if and when you are ready to acknowledge the necessity to love and appreciate those who truly care about you. The love and compromises you require are within them and within you. The steps you make for peace will be long lasting; but the steps you take to avoid peace will be the saddest measures of your entire life. Time will reveal this truth to you!

**TREMOR** (see **EARTHQUAKE**)

**TRENCH** (see **DITCH**)

**TRIAL** (see **EXPERIMENT, LAWSUIT, PREDICAMENT,** or **TEST**)

**TRICK** (see **DECEPTION, DECOY,** or **MISCHIEF**)

**TRICYCLE**
You expect quite a bit of service from other people around you, but what exactly are you giving in return? If you can honestly say you are reciprocating in all your affairs with others, then may God richly bless you and reward you. However, if you cannot say this, then it is time you begin to see matters of fairness in a clear, objective way. Do not be selfish or expect to be served hand and foot without showing some measure of gratitude. Politeness and basic kindness can open many, many doors for you, if you have the foresight and wisdom to see the truth in this simple matter. Do not expect someone else to do your bidding when you are lazy and indifferent; you can do your own bidding just as well. You have a mind, two hands, two feet—use them! Be honest with yourself and others, and this, too, will carry you through many treasured highways and byways in life. Be proud to be a child of God, but be sure in your mind and conscience that He can be proud of you, as well!

**TRIGGER** (see **GUN**)

**TRINKET** (see **DECORATION, JEWELLERY,** or **TOY**)

**TRIP** (see **JOURNEY**)

**TRIPLANE** (see **AIRPLANE**)

**TROLL** (i.e., supposed dwarf-like or giant-like supernatural beings of ancient time who lived underground or in caverns)
This symbolism indicates your base feelings about yourself or about someone else in your life. If you are mad at yourself or someone else, for some reason, then do you not you think it is about time to let bygones be bygones? Sometimes you think and walk proud and tall; at other

times you think and walk shortsighted and small. Planet Earth may not be the exact paradise you expected, but you must learn to brighten your own little corner of the world, from time to time. Self-pity and self-centeredness are two strong negative forces you can do without! Reach up to the highest regions of your being through prayer and meditation. When you get there, you may commence to see the beauty and wisdom that even a troll, contrary to mythological belief, once possessed.

**TROMBONE** (see **INSTRUMENT**)

**TROPHY** (see **COMPETITION, CONTEST,** or **PRIZE**)

**TROUBADOUR** (see **MUSICIAN, POET,** or **SINGER**)

**TROUGH** (see **MANGER**)

**TROUSERS** (see **CLOTHES**)

**TROWEL** (see **TOOL**)

**TRUCK**
Driving a truck or seeing a moving, parked, or stalled truck indicates that you will go ahead with some long-awaited plans (e.g., a move, a trip, marriage, entering a college or university). Whatever your plans may be, the outcome should be both rewarding and beneficial to you and to your loved ones, as well!

Seeing a truck that is wrecked and abandoned denotes that you will be exasperated and disappointed over some emotional or financial matters before too long. It will seem as though you are in a "no-win", deadlock situation. However, some bold changes are pending for you; they will allow you to rise over and above your emotional or financial uncertainties.

**TRUCKER** (see **TRUCK**)

**TRUMPET** (see **INSTRUMENT**)

**TRUNK** (see **BAGGAGE** or **BOX**)

**TUBA** (see **INSTRUMENT**)

**TUBERCULOSIS** (see **SICKNESS**)

**TUGBOAT** (see **BOAT**)

**TUG OF WAR** (see **COMPETITION** or **CONTEST**)

**TULIP** (see **FLOWER**)

**TUMBLER** (see **ACROBAT**)

**TUMBLEWEED** (see **PLANT**)

**TUMOR** (see **LUMP**)

**TUNIC** (see **CLOTHES**)

**TUNING FORK** (see **INSTRUMENT**)

**TUNNEL**

A tunnel denotes your courage or your fears in accepting your trials and tribulations and other challenges that may confront you, from time to time. If you are a strong-minded, determined individual, then no doubt you are very prepared to meet your challenges in a head-on manner, on most occasions. However, if you are not so strong-willed and determined, then you will have those hidden fears that will surface in times of difficulty. Don't be fearful about "struggling times"; they are a way and a means of making you a bit stronger and certainly a bit wiser. As well, do not forget that the meek can be strong, and the strong can be meek in these situations, just as well. You are not alone! No one really appreciates troubled times. Of course, they do crop up now and again. They do not simply vanish into thin air; they must be faced courageously and wisely!

**TURBAN**

This symbolism indicates a feeling of self-importance. This may be, but you must never forget the importance of others around you, as well. No matter what rank or position you hold in life, never feel that you are any better or wiser than the next person. Treat others equally, and you will be treated with respect; treat others unfairly, and you will experience disrespect and injustice!

**TURNIP** (see **FOOD** or **PLANT**)

**TURTLE**

This symbolism cautions you to be extremely careful where poorly installed electrical outlets, plugs, wiring, or appliances are concerned (e.g., home, office, vehicle). Carelessness in these matters can create considerable harm, damage, or loss—not only to you, but to your home or vehicle, as well. Special attention should be given to small children (especially within the home) who could inadvertently expose themselves to serious electrical injury.

**TUTOR** (see **COACH**, **SCHOOL**, or **TEACHER**)

**TWEEZERS**

According to this symbolism, you will say something to someone without foresight and later regret it, and/or you will go ahead with some ill-advised plan and later regret it. Unfortunately, you may not want to believe your dream until it is too late. If you refuse to learn the easy way, then perhaps the hard way will show you the truth.

**TWILIGHT** (see **SUNSET**)

**TWISTER** (see **STORM** or **TORNADO**)

**TYPEWRITER**

You exert a great influence upon others! Your ability to express, teach, or show the higher values and concepts about this world and about life in general are wholesome beginnings to a greater life ahead of you. Your future will be filled with many wonderful surprises, honours, and successes as you carry on with your spirit of courage and good hope. Your overall life and your business, professional, or creative endeavours deserve much praise and encouragement. Carry on!

**TYPHOID** (see **SICKNESS**)

**TYPHOON** (see **HURRICANE**, **STORM**, or **TORNADO**)

**TYRANNY** (see **DICTATOR** or **PERSECUTION**)

**U-BOAT** (see **BOAT**)

## UFO (see FLYING SAUCER)

## UFOLOGIST

Perhaps you are a ufologist. If so, then you are visibly facing the future—not only in a dream state, but during your wake state as well. You are to be admired for your worthy and commendable outlook in life. If you are not a ufologist but dream of being or seeing one, then the symbolism implies that a part of you wants to believe in the possibilities of extraterrestrial beings visiting this planet, but another part of you is held back by simplistic earthly theories and notions that this could not be possible. In life, all things are possible! God did not create other star systems for Earth to simply wonder whether or not there is life on other planets. Of course there is life on other planets! There was, there is, and there will always be life on other planets! Not necessarily in our solar system, but beyond our system and planets, there are life forms a million years beyond our intelligence. UFO beings have been here from the beginning of time and will continue to be here until mankind is ready for the Cosmic Union of Planets. We, too, must be as the gods of old, and that connection is with our friendly cousins in space. May God bless them as they slowly teach us the way, in "invisible silence", to find our pathway to the stars. They are here now, so whenever you meet or greet a stranger, you may never know whether this person is an earthling or a celestial from the heavens above. The mystery of their presence will continue for a while, but there will be a time forthcoming when everyone on this planet will know who these celestials are, where they come from, and of their God-given purpose to seed star systems—Earth having been no exception this the rule!

## UKULELE (see INSTRUMENT)

## ULCER (see SICKNESS)

## UMBILICAL CORD (see BIRTH)

## UMBRELLA

This symbolism foretells the birth of a child within the family circle (perhaps a relative) and/or the birth of new thoughts, actions, and deeds where you personally are concerned. These changes you may be experiencing should give you the force, drive, and impetus to finally carry out some plans or actions you always had in mind (e.g., writing a book, early retirement, travel, lecturing) Whatever it may be, you are now being elevated to a higher soul cycle so that your knowledge and experiences thus far can be put to better use. You came to this planet to be helpful; now you will commence to find and fulfill your greater purpose!

**UMPIRE** (see **REFEREE**)

**UNBELIEVER** (see **AGNOSTIC** or **ATHEIST**)

**UNCLE**

Dreaming about an uncle who is presently alive indicates your actual thoughts and feelings towards him. If you get along with him, then your feelings towards him will reveal kindness and respect. If you do not get along with him, then your feelings indicate unkindness and disrespect. Try to patch things up; you will feel a lot better for taking this course of action!

Dreaming about an uncle who has passed away indicates that he wants a prayer from you. Say a prayer for him and remember to tell him to "ask for the Light"!

**UNDERBRUSH** (see **FOREST, ORCHARD, PLANT**, or **SHRUB**)

**UNDERCARRIAGE** (see **FRAMEWORK**)

**UNDERPASS** (see **PASSAGEWAY**)

**UNDERSCORE** (i.e., a line drawn under a word, passage, sign, etc., to stress importance)

You are forgetting to fulfill some personal commitment to yourself or to someone else, and/or you are not striving hard enough to get rid of a habit that appears to trouble you from time to time. This dream reminds you that your neglect in these matters may have a greater effect upon you, in time to come. Your general attitude and maturity will ultimately determine whether or not you will fulfill the abovementioned goal(s).

**UNDERSKIRT** (see **CLOTHES**)

**UNDERSTUDY** (see **ACTOR** or **AGENT**)

**UNDERTAKER** (see **BURIAL, FUNERAL HOME,** or **MANAGER**)

**UNDERWEAR** (see **CLOTHES**)

**UNDRESS** (see **CLOTHES, BURLESQUE,** or **NAKEDNESS**)

**UNEMPLOYMENT**
Dreaming of being jobless could very well imply that you are presently unemployed, or you are worried about becoming unemployed. If this is not applicable to you, then this symbolism implies that you are not happy with your domestic duties, obligations, or vocation in life. It is up to you to make your life more bearable and purposeful. Happiness is not given to anyone on a silver platter; it must be earned through initiative, personal satisfaction, and personal fulfillment within your lifestyle. Complaining will not help; doing something constructive about your present quandary will!

**UNHAPPINESS** (see **DEPRESSION** or **SORROW**)

**UNICORN**
Seeing this so-called mythical horse-like animal reveals your inner belief in self. No matter what trials and tribulations you have experienced thus far, nobody can say that you have had an easy life. You wept many times, and you prayed many times, until your call for help was answered. You have undoubtedly been through some very trying and traumatic experiences, yet your todays and tomorrows are not as uncomfortable and fearsome as they once appeared to be. You are not afraid any more—and rightfully so! You have paid your dues in many ways. As your future gently unfolds, you will be endowed with the freedom and confidence you need to fulfill your better wishes and plans. Note, as well, that "Lady Luck" will be riding with you all the way!

**UNIFORM** (see **CLOTHES**)

**UNION** (see **ORGANIZATION**)

**UNIVERSE** (see **ASTEROID, ASTROLOGY, ASTRONOMY, CELESTIAL, CELESTIAL NAVIGATION, CIVILIZATION,**

COMET, CONSTELLATION, EARTH, GALAXY, GENESIS, HEAVEN, HUMANITY, METEOR, MOON, OBSERVATORY, ORBIT, OUTER SPACE, PLANET, QUASAR, SKY, STAR, or SUN)

**UNIVERSITY**
Any one or several of the following definitions may be applicable: A) that you are, in fact, attending a university; or B) that you hope to attend a university before too long; or C) that your future career may compel you to attend more than one university; or D) that you know someone who is presently attending university; or E) that you are a professor or employee working at a university; or F) that in time you would like to work at a university; or G) that you are presently working towards your Master's Degree at an outstanding university; or H) that you completed your university many years ago and certainly have no regrets for going this route in life; or I) that you quit university but hope to go back someday; or J) that you are finding a course or two at the university rather difficult to handle; or K) that you feel that unless you shape up with your studies and marks, you will be compelled to leave the university that you are presently attending; or L) that you recently failed a university course; or M) that you recently graduated from a university; or N) that this dream has little or no relevance to you at this time.

**UNVEILING** (i.e., removal of a covering from a monument, statue, or other object)
The act of unveiling something within a dream state signifies that you do not appear to have enough liberty and privacy in your life. As much as you would like doing more things by yourself, it just seems that someone or something always disrupts your daily work and good intentions. This kind of situation can be trying at times but should be treated with tact and diplomacy. Let others know exactly how you feel. If you can divide your schedule into blocks or sections of time, then perhaps you might have the space for yourself and the time for other things, as well.

**UPRISING** (see **DEMONSTRATOR**, **DISOBEDIENCE**, or **DISSATISFACTION**)

**URANUS** (see **PLANET**)

## URCHIN (see ADOLESCENT, DECEPTION, ELF, MISCHIEF, SEA URCHIN, or THIEVERY)

**URINAL** (i.e., a container used by the bedridden, or a fixture used by men in a public restroom)

The peace and happiness you create on this earth plane is, in truth, the peace and happiness that will allow you to grow and prosper in life. You will find the respect and appreciation you so rightfully deserve when you cease to be unfriendly, antagonistic, and petty in your earthly affairs. This dream urges you to elevate your mind towards higher opinions and beliefs about yourself and about others and to adopt a more wholesome attitude towards your obligations and duties in your corner of the world.

### URINATION

The act of urinating within a dream indicates that a busy schedule is in store for you, especially one project which will require your undivided attention. Procrastinating at this time is not advisable at all, unless you wish to experience some verbal backlashes and disappointments from others around you. If all goes well, the end result reveals a job well done!

(*Note*: There is also the possibility that a person who dreams of urinating may also actually urinate or be urinating on the bed.)

**URN** (i.e., a container used to hold the ashes of a cremated body)

Do not be overzealous in starting something that may, in time, bring you bitterness and displeasure! There are warning signs all around you cautioning you to hold back from some impulsive, short-sighted plan which could backfire on you, when you least expect it to do so. You may be doing this to spite someone or to prove a point; however, there will be no point to prove! Greater scrutiny and research is needed to thoroughly investigate the pros and cons of your plan or scheme. Your dream is simply issuing this strong advice to you so that you might begin to see things in a clearer and peaceful frame of mind.

### USHER

Being or seeing an usher indicates your willingness or unwillingness to partake in some contest, competition, or ceremonial affair in the very near future. You might have to contend with some strong opposition if you refuse to participate; however, you will still be understood and respected for your better wishes. Listen to the dictates of your better judgment and conscience in these matters; then you will be bound to make the right decision for all concerned.

**UTENSIL** (see *also* **EGGBEATER, SILVERWARE,** or **STRAINER**)
You have a very low tolerance level to loud sounds or noises and to people who tend to be chatty, exaggerating, and false in their ways. Sometimes people say or do things at the top of their heads, honestly not realizing the negative effect they create upon others. This dream advises you to be especially cautious not to offend or hurt others, where your strong dislikes are concerned. Be kind and tactful so that the point you make will be clearly understood and respected.

**VACATION** (see *also* **CELEBRATION, LIBERATION, RESORT,** or **TOURIST**)
Any one or several of the following definitions may be applicable: A) that you are planning to take a vacation before too long; or B) that you are presently on vacation, and your dream merely projected the enjoyment or stresses you are presently undergoing; or C) that you are planning to visit some friends or relatives in the very near future, if all goes well; or D) that you recently returned from a vacation with misgivings or fond memories; or E) that a friend or relative is visiting you now; or F) that you are planning a vacation with a group of friends, but someone else wishes to join company with you, and you are not too sure about this person; or G) that for your next vacation, you do not intend to go anywhere, but stay home and relax; or H) that you had your wallet or purse stolen during a vacation; or I) that you feel you never really know someone until you go on a vacation with them, and then the true colors of their personality come through; or J) that you will never go with certain people on a vacation again because of some negative or traumatic experiences you had with them; or K) that you have traveled extensively but still intend to go on vacations, as long as you can; or L) that you recently met someone on a vacation, and now you are corresponding with that friend; or M) that no matter where you have gone, your vacations have always been exciting and rewarding, in many ways; or N) that you would like to go on a vacation but, due to financial setbacks or other reasons, this is not possible at this time; or O) that you envy anyone who can afford vacations whenever they

please; or P) that this dream has little or no relevance to you at this time.

**VACCINATION** (see **INOCULATION**)

**VACUUM CLEANER** (see **APPLIANCE**)

**VAGABOND** (see **HOBO**)

**VAGRANT** (see **GYPSY** or **HOBO**)

**VALEDICTORY** (see **GRADUATION** or **LECTURE**)

**VALENTINE** (see **CARD** or **LOVE**)

**VALET** (see **BUTLER**)

**VALISE** (see **BAGGAGE**)

**VAMPIRE**

You are a very restless, high-strung individual. You often become aggravated by, and suspicious of, the actions of others around you. No one wishes you any harm, nor is anyone talking about you in front of you or behind you, for that matter. Do not waste your time on misguided and foolish mind notions which prompt you to make rash judgments towards others. Your jealousies are neither wholesome nor wise. Instead of succumbing to an inferiority and persecution complex not befitting a fine person like you, stop, look, and listen to the good spirit within you.

**VAMPIRE BAT** (see **BAT**)

**VAN** (see **TRUCK**)

**VANDALISM** (see **DESTRUCTION** or **MISCHIEF**)

**VAPORIZER**

Stick to your better instincts and intentions instead of clogging your pathway with unnecessary thoughts and actions. Even though life may be unbearable at times, you should not wallow in self-pity, laziness, and foolish ventures. By being more mindful of your earthly and eternal life, you will slowly commence to see the importance of your time and space upon this planet. Cherish your beautiful moments here on earth like the majesty of an eagle in flight, have more trust in the virtues of hope, and be more grateful for who you are.

**VASE**
There is no greater human love upon this planet than the innocent love of a child! Many people, however, fail to maintain the truth and innocence of their childhood simply because they are too busy with everyday temptations, self-deceptions, and other worldly matters. Far too many people are much too eager to seek and uphold useless distractions and theories instead of maintaining inner qualities such as love, faith, truth, patience, humility, gratitude, and other positive traits which can make them strong and whole. Whatever you put into your life is what you will receive in return; what you sow, you will reap. This thought, though ancient and old, is nonetheless true! Bear in mind, as well, that the meek and innocent spirits on this planet are indeed those beings we should all emulate.

**VAT**
You can make your life on earth a paradise if you honestly believe in yourself and your talents, or you can squander your life away on superficial hopes and wishes. Tomorrow can be a very beautiful and rewarding day for those who are happy and appreciative, in spite of their troubles and woes in life. They somehow know that with strong determination, prayer, and hope their losses can eventually turn into greater experiences and successes. And, eventually this does happen! On the other side of the spectrum, people create their world of desolation and failure when they think and act negatively, or when they assume their purpose in life is totally meaningless and hopeless. God's children and God's abounding life are not meaningless or hopeless, at any time! The spark within you is the ultimate key that can create the positive energy or impulse that can guide you towards a better today and a much greater tomorrow.

**VAULT** (see **BANK, BURIAL, CAVE, CELLAR, GRAVE,** or **MAUSOLEUM**)

**VEGETABLE** (see **FOOD** or **PLANT**)

**VEIL** (see **CURTAIN, HIDING, INVISIBILITY, MASK,** or **NET**)

**VEILING** (see *also* **CURTAIN** or **NET**)

You are a very private person who expects others to respect your better wishes in this regard. Most people do! It appears that from time to time, however, someone intrudes into your personal affairs, thus creating an enemy in your secluded camp. Nobody should trespass upon anyone's private life unless invited to do so. Do not hate your enemies; pray for them, but do not mingle with them.

**VELVET** (see **MATERIAL**)

**VENDING MACHINE**

So often, people place their good energies upon wrong ideals, hopes, and actions. They thus head towards a collision course with themselves and with life in general. At times, life can be very generous for those who respect their everyday blessings, but when gambling, greed, pride, or envy step into the picture, be very cautious, for it is at this crossroads that monetary and materialistic gains and pursuits can slip through your fingers. Nothing belongs to us on this planet—not even our breath! This all belongs to God. We are all here on borrowed time, and it is what you do with your time that counts. Use it wisely, and you will prosper!

**VENETIAN BLIND**

Happiness, pleasant surprises, and agreeable profits are foreseen for the dreamer who sees open venetian blinds within a dream. Hold a steady course towards your goals and aims in life, and you will eventually reach the great rewards awaiting you!

Seeing venetian blinds that are closed reveals that you are not making the necessary efforts to fulfill your better thoughts and decisions in life. You give up much too easily, without utilizing your God-given courage and determination. Perhaps for selfish, morbid, or superstitious reasons, you are afraid to forge ahead for fear of being disappointed! This dream strongly urges you to revamp your attitude and views with an encouraged, open mind instead of with a closed, fearful mind.

**VENOM** (see **ANGER, HATRED,** or **POISON**)

**VENTRILOQUISM** (see *also* **PUPPETRY**)

Either you or someone you know is being evasive about a pertinent matter concerning a recent incident or occurrence. Whoever it is, there are only two ways to handle this situation: face the matter head-on and get it out of your system, or simply chalk it up to experience and continue on with your life. That is all!

**VENUS** (see **PLANET**)

**VERANDA** (see **PATIO**)

**VERDICT** (see **ADJUDICATION, COURT, DETERMINATION, JUDGE, JURY,** or **LAWSUIT**)

**VEST** (see **CLOTHES**)

**VESTMENT** (see **CLOTHES**)

**VETERINARIAN** (see **DOCTOR**)

**VIBRATOR** (see **MASSAGE**)

**VICAR** (see **CLERGYMAN** or **DEPUTY**)

**VICE-PRESIDENT** (see **LEADERSHIP** or **PRESIDENT**)

**VICE SQUAD** (see **PEACE OFFICER**)

**VICTIM** (see **PREY**)

**VIGILANTE** (see **GUARD**)

**VILLA** (see **HOUSE**)

**VILLAGE**

A peaceful-looking village indicates that you are basically content with your life and with the hardships (challenges) that go with it. You are not one to mince words with anybody; when something has to be done, you do it, and that is that! Because of your many experiences in life, you could probably write a best-selling book; each chapter of your life is filled with a glowing example of your ingenuity, your overpowering determination, and your indomitable faith in conquering unbelievable obstacles. You truly have the spirit of a great human being whom others should emulate and follow.

A village that appears to be unusual or foreboding cautions you not to create any unnecessary arguments with those near you and not to become involved in someone else's arguments. You are offended much too easily! Basically, a good percentage of what you hear is not meant to offend you. However, you have a tendency to misunderstand or take things the wrong way. You would be wise to simply follow your better instincts by ignoring what you hear, from time to time. This will at least give you the peace of mind you require. What you do not hear will not hurt you.

**VIRGIN MARY** (see **HOLY MOTHER**)

**VISA** (see **PASSPORT**)

**VOCATION** (see **CALLING, CAREER, EMPLOYMENT, LIFEWORK,** or **OWNERSHIP**)

**VOICELESSNESS** (i.e., having no voice, or being mute)

Perhaps you are mute in life. If this is so, then your dream is simply pertaining to your present state of being. However, if this is not applicable to you, then this dream symbolism indicates that you are fearful of someone or something, or you are creating some mischief or trouble around you. Your fears should be looked into, but no help can be forthcoming unless you actively seek the help you require. For the second definition, scare tactics or threats of any type are quarrelsome and base, to say the least! You are strongly urged to be more silent and understanding so that you can move on in life with greater insight and logic. Always strive to be sensible and compassionate in your dealings with others!

**VOLCANO**

Whether the volcano is active or inactive, this symbolism advises you to pay heed to mental and physical stresses, at this time. You may not necessarily be the happiest person right now, but common sense should dictate to you that it is not wise to simply let yourself go because of someone's indifference towards you or because you are experiencing some other type of hardship beyond your control. When you commence to feel better, you will certainly begin to think and act better!

**VOLLEYBALL** (see **GAME**)

**VOMIT**

You are very unstable and nonchalant in many areas of your life. Unless you settle down in your ways, there may be many upheavals and obstacles down the road which will be almost impossible to handle or master. Keep the promises you make to yourself instead of falling prey to the same faults over and over again! If you truly want to see some progress in your life, then become more attuned to your aims and goals, without changing your mind so frequently. Consistency in your thoughts and in your work will bring you success in life!

**VOODOO**

You are easily affected by the words and actions of those whom you know. However, this should not necessarily hinder you from being better and smarter! If others around you wish to be untrue, immature, and foolish, then they will have to pay for their mistakes—not you. You will progress in life only through your own good actions and deeds. Ignore those uncaring, insensitive, and troublesome individuals who personally couldn't care less whether you succeed, fail, fall, or disappear. Keep your faith, intelligence, and sanity above water, and you will banish your present myths and illusions just like a cloud which dissipates in the sky.

**VOTE** (see *also* **CAMPAIGN, NOMINATION,** or **OPTION**)

Voting for someone, something, or some cause within a dream state denotes your determination and free will to uphold your thoughts and actions, no matter what others may think about you. If your vote or cause is of good order and is geared towards the truth, then you have the right to instill food for thought in others around you. However, if your vote or cause is towards something chaotic or violent, or it shows disrespect towards your fellow man, then you should be aware that something you are doing is not of good order. Violence begets violence; peace begets peace! Any changes you wish to instill in others should be revealed with human truth, love, compassion, respect, and wisdom. No more and no less will do.

**VOYAGE** (see **JOURNEY**)

**VOYEUR** (see **PEEPING TOM** or **SEX**)

**VULGARITY** (see **BLASPHEMY** or **LOW-MINDEDNESS**)

**VULTURE** (see **BIRD**)

**WADING POOL** (see **FLOAT**, **SWIMMING**, or **WATER**)

**WAFFLE** (see **FOOD**)

**WAGON** (see **CART**, **CHUCK WAGON**, **BUGGY**, **SURREY**, or **TRUCK**)

**WAGON TRAIN** (see **CONVOY** or **GUARD**)

**WAIF** (i.e., a homeless child, or stray animal)
Seeing or being a waif reveals your compassion or indifference towards anyone or any living thing which may be less fortunate than you. If you are a loving, caring kind of person, then may you be blessed with many comforts and rewards within your life; you deserve the best! In time, you will receive that and more. Now, if you happen to be a laid-back, unconcerned kind of individual in these matters, then you would be very wise to consider where your services could be utilized. Don't waste your life in a prideful, selfish manner! Look around you, from time to time, and lend a helping hand whenever the need arises. Those times are here and now! Someday, your needs will come; then who will hear your call and your cry for help?

**WAITER** (see **CARHOP**, **HOSTESS**, or **STEWARDESS**)

**WAITRESS** (see **CARHOP**, **HOSTESS**, or **STEWARDESS**)

**WALKY-TALKY**
You must think and do more for yourself instead of expecting others to pave a way for you. When people are afraid to learn and grow from their past and present experiences and mistakes, they simply slip, fall, and tumble headfirst into the future. Don't let this happen to you! Have you ever heard the static sounds of a walky-talky? Well, this is

quite symbolic of the static harmony and progress you have thus far created for yourself. Your troublesome past has affected your unhappy present, and your unhappy present will now affect your uncertain future, unless you change. More determination, foresight, and common sense are the essential ingredients required to make life ahead of you more progressive and meaningful. Will you change? That is the vital question you should be asking yourself at this time.

**WALL** (see **ENCLOSURE**)

**WALLABY** (see **KANGAROO**)

**WALLET**

To see or to find a wallet within a dream state reveals a need to budget your time and money and to use more discretion and diplomacy in your daily life. You may be busy, and you may have a tendency to spend more than you make at times. Furthermore, your thoughts and actions are often scattered. In the midst of all the hustle and bustle, you tend to become somewhat moody and edgy. Hence, the people around you become affected by your uncalled-for, snide remarks. Calm down and strive to put more order and kindness into your life. These actions will assist you towards a more meaningful and prosperous future!

To lose a wallet or to have one stolen reveals that you actually have a fear about losing your wallet or having it stolen. You also tend to be somewhat miserly and mistrusting. This phobic insecurity is not worth your time and efforts. Adopt a more loving, sharing attitude in your daily life; this, in itself, will allow you to dispel some of your unwarranted fears and suspicions. Right now you are playing cloak and dagger with yourself. No one wishes you any harm, now or later!

**WALRUS**

Life can be so hard, fruitless, and demeaning at times that you often wonder if struggling onwards is worth your time and effort. Of course, it is! Absolutely no one is immune to pain, sorrows, and struggles on this earth plane, no matter what rank or position one holds. Your place on earth is to rise over and above those personal struggles with prayer, faith, strength, and timeless hope! You are a survivor, in many ways. Someday, when you leave this planet for a better place, you will know, without a doubt, that your earthly struggles were all a blessing in disguise.

**WALTZ** (see **DANCE** or **MUSIC**)

**WAMPUM** (see **DECORATION** or **MONEY**)

**WAND** (see **DIVINING ROD, ILLUSIONIST**, or **STICK**)

**WANT AD** (see **ADVERTISEMENT**)

**WAR** (see **BATTLE, BATTLEFIELD, CHEMICAL WARFARE, FIGHT**, or **QUARREL**)

**WARDEN** (e.g., a forest ranger, game warden, fire warden, a prison warden)
 Seeing or being a warden within a dream reveals your shrewd, sharp-witted observations about people, places, and things. It also reveals your tunnel vision stubbornness, which either holds you back in life or allows you to progress with amazing results. Basically, you choose to be persistent and more or less tolerant in your aims and ideals; hence, you are quite competent in finishing what you set out to do. This is good and wholesome. However, your future could be more enriched if you were more flexible and open-minded with some of your more practical thoughts, notions, and actions. Not everything is as black and white as you sometimes think it is. Colors can change and vary; so should you!

**WAREHOUSE** (see **SHED** or **STORE**)

**WARHEAD** (see **BOMB** or **MISSILE**)

**WARLOCK** (see **BLACK MAGIC, EVILDOER**, or **WITCHCRAFT**)

**WARRANT** (see **DOCUMENT, LICENSE, PASSPORT**, or **PROMISE**)

**WART** (see **LUMP**)

**WASHBOWL** (see **BASIN** or **BATHROOM**)

**WASHCLOTH** (see **MATERIAL** or **TISSUE**)

**WASHING MACHINE** (see **APPLIANCE**)

**WASP** (see **INSECT**)

**WASTELAND** (see **DESERT**)

**WATCH** (see **CLOCK, GUARD, MEASUREMENT,** or **PATROL**)

**WATCHTOWER** (see **OBSERVATORY** or **TOWER**)

**WATER**

To see clear water is always a good dream! Presently, you are moving towards a more mature pinnacle within your life, thus gaining a greater understanding about yourself and about everything else around you. As you slowly seek the truths within and around you, you will commence to plant those truths in other people. Some people will listen to you and follow your good counsel; others will not. Do not be disappointed with those who do not—they must learn another way. What is vitally important here is that you are reaching inward and outward in order to help your fellow man. Whether your help is major or minor is highly irrelevant. The important thing is that you are doing something constructive and positive with your earthly time! Your good thoughts and actions will bring you other, greater discoveries and successes as you gently walk sure-footed into the future.

To see dirty, muddy water or unclear water indicates that you are, or you will be, undergoing some personal difficulties which will eventually settle. However, you must maintain inner calmness, love, truth, and justice before you finally see the dramatic change or turnabout in your life. The peace and order you long for will eventually come to pass, but not without first experiencing some mental, physical, and spiritual anguishes and regret. Such are the stark realities of this life; yet you have the heart, mind, and soul to master these things, and much more. And, prophetically, you will!

(*Note*: You may also have the pleasure of knowing that if, for example, you are experiencing a very negative dream but at the very end of your dream sequence or anywhere during your dream sequence you happen to see clear water, then this clear water symbolism takes precedence over your entire bad dream. Consequently, you have nothing to worry about simply because the clear water acts as a "buffer zone" to anything negative within a dream.)

**WATERFALL** (see **WATER**)

**WATERHOLE** (see **HOLE** or **WATER**)

**WATERING CAN** (see **CAN**)

**WATERMELON** (see **FRUIT**)

**WATER PISTOL** (see **TOY**)

**WATER POLO** (see **GAME**)

**WATER RAT** (see **RAT**)

**WATER SNAKE** (see **SNAKE**)

**WATERWEED** (see **PLANT**)

**WATER WHEEL**
Essentially, you are a highly intelligent person who could achieve almost anything you want; however, because of your changing moods, notions, and ambitions, you have become your own worst enemy. No one has hindered you in life as much as you have hindered yourself! Through self-assurance and through spiritual introspection, you could mend your ways and habits for a better and brighter future. Will you take the time to alter the course of your destiny constructively, or will you continue to flounder here and there until there is no destiny to alter? That vital decision faces you now.

**WAXWORKS** (e.g., wax figures in a wax museum, figurines)
You are venting your frustrations in a most uncaring manner by foisting your demands and threats upon others around you. These negative actions will get you absolutely nowhere in life. Right now, the biggest obstacle facing you is yourself! This dream urges you to adopt the virtues of prayer, respect, patience, humility, and unselfishness so that you can at last find that inner peace and happiness you so rightfully deserve. Remember that you cannot bring your yesterdays back, but you certainly can improve upon your todays and tomorrows! Do so wisely.

**WAYBILL** (see **LIST**)

**WEALTH** (see **ABUNDANCE, BILLIONAIRE, FORTUNE, HAPPINESS, MILLIONAIRE,** or **OWNERSHIP**)

**WEAPON** (see **ATOMIC BOMB, BOMB, CANNON, DYNAMITE, GUN, HYDROGEN BOMB,** or **MISSILE**)

**WEASEL**

Beware of some unscrupulous, deceitful individual who may attempt to cheat, harm, or rob you and/or someone whom you personally know. If you are wise and careful in your daily life and travels, then perhaps you have very little to worry about, where this dream symbolism is concerned. However, if you are unmindful of the dangers that lurk about, then you may become a victim of your own carelessness and pride.

**WEATHER VANE**

You are an intelligent, complex individual whose thoughts, moods, attitudes, and actions tend to change like the weather. Although you are shrewd and independent in many ways, you often appear to be outwitted by your own overconfidence. This dream counsels you to be more dedicated in your work, show more love and gratitude towards God for all your blessings, and learn to be calm and patient when things go sour in your life. Remember that those inner changes and wholesome resolutions you make today or tomorrow can be the ultimate keys for a happier, more victorious future!

**WEAVING** (see **HANDICRAFT**)

**WEB** (see **COBWEB, CONFUSION, LACEWORK, MATERIAL, NET,** or **TISSUE**)

**WEDDING** (see **CELEBRATION** or **MARRIAGE**)

**WEED** (see **PLANT**)

**WEEPING** (see **CRY**)

**WEIGHT LIFTING** (see **BARBELL, COMPETITION, EXERCISE, GAME,** or **MUSCULARITY**)

**WELL** (see **HOLE, FOUNTAIN,** or **WATER**)

**WET NURSE** (i.e., a woman hired to suckle another woman's baby)
You have the heart of an angel! Unfortunately, many around you fail to see or acknowledge this truth. You always find the time to serve the needs of others in a peaceful, caring manner; this makes you a very special individual. Giving of the heart, mind, and soul freely is, indeed, the purest form of service you could possibly perform on this earth plane. This dream merely wishes to remind you that, in spite of your trials and tribulations with those around you, your place on earth is one to be admired and respected. And soon, in many different ways, you will be!

**WHALE**
You are a knowledgeable individual with unlimited potential. Sooner or later the success you dream about will be fulfilled to you, but not necessarily without experiencing some vast inner and outer struggles all great men and women must endure. You will endure, and you will prosper by the fruits of your ingenious, determined efforts!

**WHALEBOAT** (see **BOAT**)

**WHARF** (see **PIER**)

**WHEAT** (see **GRAIN**)

**WHEEL**
To merely see a wheel or half a wheel, or to see a wheel suspended in midair, or to see one rolling downhill indicates that you wish more love and attention from someone whom you know (e.g., a parent[s], other relatives, a friend, an acquaintance). You obviously admire and look up to this individual in a great way, but you seem to be reticent in communicating your true feelings towards this person. This dream strongly advises you discard your fears by taking the time and effort to establish a one-to-one line of communication with this individual. It will work for you; you will at last have the friendship and rapport you seek.

Seeing a wheel rolling uphill or on a leveled surface indicates that you are a very dependable, hard-working individual. Greater improvements and satisfaction are soon forthcoming, along with some leisure time that seems long overdue. Your immediate future shows travel, entertainment, and a major purchase. Your distant future shows greater prosperity, a possible move, and continued happiness.

**WHEELBARROW**
Seeing or using this pushcart reveals that some plan or workload ahead of you may be creating some worrisome fears or doubts within you. Sometimes your fears and worries are justified; other times they are not. In this case, you can remove your baseless anxieties by looking to the brighter side of things. Allay your fears, for the direction in which you are now headed can only bring you the comfort and success you seek.

**WHEELCHAIR**
If you do, in fact, use a wheelchair in life, then your dream simply reveals your present state of being. In other words, you may be happy, sad, vexed, or feel limited and restricted in the many things you would like to do. There is no magical answer to your problems or to the whys and wherefores of your life; but, by accepting your life for what it is, you will slowly commence to adjust and prosper. However, if this is not the case, then this dream's symbolism indicates that you have adopted a very cavalier attitude about your mental and physical attributes and endowments in life. There are many people who cannot talk, see, hear, or walk; yet, these people have learned to cope in life with admirable stability and progress. Much too often, healthy people fail to realize just how fortunate they are to be able to talk, see, hear, and walk. This dream is a reminder for you to count your blessings on a daily basis for being mentally and physically able to do the many things some other, less fortunate people merely envision.

**WHIP** (see **BELT** or **PUNISHMENT**)

**WHIRLPOOL** (see **WATER**)

**WHIRLPOOL BATH** (see **BATH**)

**WHIRLWIND** (see **HURRICANE, STORM,** or **TORNADO**)

**WHISKEY** (see **LIQUOR**)

**WHISTLING** (see **SOUND**)

**WHOLESALE** (see **SALE** or **STORE**)

**WICKET** (see **WINDOW**)

**WIDOW**

Any one or several of the following definitions may be applicable: A) that you are, in fact, a widow (or widower); or B) that you are not a widow (or widower) but know of someone who is; or C) that you personally hope never to become a widow (or widower) but realize that this choice is not yours to make; or D) that you cannot possibly conceive of the inner trauma, sadness, and despair a widow (or widower) must feel in losing a loving partner; or E) that recently you became a widow (or widower) and know that you must plod on, no matter how difficult situations may appear to be; or F) that you were a widow (or widower) many years ago, but since then you have remarried, and now you are quite happy and content; or G) that you recently read an article or book about a widow (or widower); or H) that this dream has little or no relevance to you at this time.

**WIDOWER** (see **WIDOW**)

**WIFE**

Any one or several of the following definitions may be applicable: A) that you are a good husband to your wife and family; or B) that you often feel unloved, unworthy, and unwanted because of your wife's or children's attitudes towards you; or C) that you would like to have a more loving relationship with your spouse, but there are far too many difficulties standing in your way for this to transpire (e.g., alcoholism, drugs, infidelity, physical abuse); or D) that you are very hopeful matters between you and your spouse will clear up, before too long; or E) that you realize you married prematurely, and now there is a very high price to pay in an emotional, social, and financial way; or F) that you feel your spouse has not been faithful to you; or G) that you have very much in common with your spouse; or H) that you have very little in common with your spouse; or

I) that you recently had a very serious talk, then argument, with your wife; or J) that whenever something goes wrong between you and your wife, you still are man enough to apologize and ask for forgiveness; or K) that you regret the way you treat your wife or the way you once treated your wife; or L) that you feel that without your wife, you would be a nobody today; or M) that you recently dreamt about your wife who has, in fact, passed away. Say a prayer for her from the depths of your soul, and do not forget to tell her to "ask for the Light"!; or N) that you are grateful beyond words to be married to your wife; or O) that this dream has little or no relevance to you at this time.

## WIG

Perhaps you do use a wig; if so, then this dream symbolism merely reflects upon your inner need to use a hairpiece for personal, satisfying reasons. However, if this not applicable to you, then this symbolism indicates that you have some type of a "quirk" or "hang-up" concerning your appearance and body (e.g., teeth, nose, eyes, hair, nails, feet, hands, height, weight). You must realize that many people on earth would like to have a "body perfect" but this, we know, is not possible. There is always something to complain about where one's body is concerned. Count your blessings for what you have and try very hard not to be so overly concerned or self-conscious about your appearance. If, however, your situation is too embarrassing or too traumatic for you to handle, then you are strongly advised to seek some professional help to alleviate your problem (e.g., your doctor, plastic surgeon, dental surgeon).

## WIGLET (see WIG)

## WILL (see BEQUEST, DETERMINATION, DOCUMENT, INHERITANCE, PROBATE)

## WINDFALL (see FORTUNE or OWNERSHIP)

## WINDMILL

No one stands to gain more from your mistakes in life than you do. A wise person will always learn from mistakes, whereas a stubborn, foolish individual simply ignores the lessons and goes on to make more mistakes until some are learned. Sooner or later, the lessons are learned!

We learn, we fall, we stumble, we crawl, we get up, we try again, we fall, we fall again, we try again... and then we learn. We fall, we stumble... and on and on it goes. Such is life and our many trying experiences on this planet. The measure of learning, however, holds no bounds, and no matter how many times we must struggle, we should always strive to glean something from our experiences, no matter how big or how small they may be. Learning from your mistakes and experiences in life is like reading a good book for the second time around—only to comprehend its meaning more fully and wisely this time. So, as you go on to greater plateaus and cycles of your life, remember that it is the summation of your lessons (mistakes) and experiences (wisdom) that has placed you there. A mistake can bring you wisdom, or a mistake can be your downfall. It all depends what you learn from it.

## WINDOW

An open window reveals having an open mind to new concepts and changes in your life. In other words, you are not afraid to move forward, no matter what obstacles happen to be in your way. You are in many ways a progressive, determined thinker who gets things done quickly and effectively.

A closed window reveals you have a mind closed to new concepts and changes in your life. You have very little desire to change inwardly or to improve anything around you, for that matter. You see no necessity to forge ahead with new ideas, concepts, and actions simply because you believe the old ways should never change. But there is no choice in the matter; as long as man has the determination and the brain to create new concepts and ideas, changes will be inevitable—with or without you.

A broken window advises you to be more clear-sighted, patient, and confident about some matter that will solve itself before too long. Do not jump to any drastic conclusions at this time, otherwise you might regret your words and possible actions.

## WINDSTORM (see HURRICANE, MONSOON, STORM, or TORNADO)

## WINE (see LIQUOR)

## WINE CELLAR (see CELLAR)

## WINK

Winking or seeing someone wink denotes that you are deceiving yourself about some emotional or physical matter, and/or you are being evasive about some matter of importance which you do not wish to reveal to someone whom you know. It might be a good idea to solve or settle this matter now instead of prolonging the fear of being caught red-handed. The outcome may not be as bad as you think. The longer you wait, however, the greater the consequences may become!

## WINTER (see SEASON)

## WIRETAP

Being wiretapped or using a wiretap within a dream reveals a strong feeling of misunderstanding and mistrust which you harbour towards someone, and/or someone harbors towards you. The dark clouds of pride and contradictions appear to be at the root of this problem. This dream symbolism advises you to question your motives and intentions with greater clarity, honesty, and maturity. If these shortsighted hostilities you harbour bother you so much, what on earth will you do when you are faced with a major problem? Look for peace in your life, not for misjudgments or revenge.

## WITCHCRAFT (see *also* BLACK MAGIC or EVILDOER)

The practice of witchcraft within a dream state strongly urges you to see life in a more harmonious, loving way, rather than in a futile, depressive, revengeful way. It is what you can give to life that counts, not what life can give to you! No amount of revenge, hate, or cursing can bring happiness to anyone on this earth plane, no matter how hard they try. It is very sad that some base people on this planet attempt to play God by abusing, misusing, and defying His Laws for their own purpose, power, and gain. It is these same people who eventually stumble and fall into their own web of pride, foolishness, and evil deceptions.

## WITNESS (see SPECTATOR)

## WIZARD (see BLACK MAGIC, EVILDOER, ILLUSIONIST, or WITCHCRAFT)

# WOLF

You are being somewhat irresponsible in some vital areas of your life (e.g., marriage, offspring, romance, home, career, education, health matters). Regardless of what is troubling you, taking vital matters of your life for granted is like throwing away a part of your good destiny into the sea. When people run away from their obligations and problems, they are, in many instances, running away from the truth about themselves. They may run as long as they like, but they can never escape themselves—either in this world or the next! A change of attitude about yourself, your responsibilities, and your obligations is strongly urged so that you can face your todays and tomorrows with sensible progression, not irresponsible regressions.

## WORKSHOP (see SHED)

## WORM

You are strongly advised to show greater respect and concern for your mind and body. Ignoring poor health conditions or abusing, misusing, or overworking the mind and body can bring you stressful anxieties and self-inflicted trouble. Know your limits in life because overindulgence in anything can create mental and physical havoc beyond repair.

## WORSHIP (see BURNT OFFERING, CALVARY, CHRISTMAS-TIDE, CHURCH, EASTER, HUMILITY, IDOLATRY, KNEEL, LOVE, LOYALTY, PRAYER, or RELIGION)

## WRAPPING (see TISSUE)

## WREATH

If the wreath is well made and extremely colorful, then you can expect better times ahead (e.g., a prosperous move, a good career, a special project fulfilled, an award). Hard work, determination, and a great amount of gutsy courage are the ingredients you possess to make your future more meaningful and successful.

If the wreath is decayed, discolored, and not well made, then be prepared for some trying times ahead (e.g., sickness, financial setbacks, loss of a family member). This dream is very serious and should not be taken for granted. Warning signs are indicated, so be very prudent at this time. Prayer, positive thinking, courage, and hope are the essential ingredients that should help you through those pending, difficult times.

**WRENCH** (see **TOOL**)

**WRESTLING** (see *also* **COMPETITION, CONTEST, EXERCISE, FIGHT,** or **JUDO**)

Perhaps you are a wrestler. If so, then your dream is merely reflecting upon the work that you do. If you are not, then this dream symbolism reveals the possibility of you being accused of some wrongdoing by someone who may be trying to victimize you for some base, revengeful reasons. Be wise! Don't be caught in anyone's trap! Be careful, but be prepared to have a sound alibi should this negative revelation come to pass.

**WRITER** (see **AUTHOR**)

**WRITING** (see **ALPHABET, BRAILLE, GRAPHOLOGY, HANDWRITING, HIEROGLYPHICS, MISSPELLING, OVERWRITE, SHORTHAND, SIGNATURE, SKYWRITING,** or **SPELLING**)

**XEROGRAPHY** (see **PHOTOCOPY**)

**X-RAY**

Dreaming about an X-ray tube, an X-ray photograph, or X-ray therapy reveals your inner need to know what makes people like yourself "tick or click" in life. Sometimes you feel sane and normal; at other times, you feel somewhat abnormal because of the foolish thoughts, moods, and actions you sometimes display. Don't be so hard on yourself—everyone gets carried away now and again, later realizing their conduct or behaviour was not exactly up to par. Have you ever heard someone say: "I made a complete fool of myself!"? Well, we all do, now and again. This dream symbolism is telling you not to dwell so much on your pointless or careless character mistakes, but to try to be more diligent so as not to make the same blunders over and over again. That is all!

**XYLOPHONE** (see **INSTRUMENT**)

**YACHT** (see **SHIP**)

**YAM** (see **PLANT**)

**YARDSTICK** (see **MEASUREMENT**)

**YEARBOOK** (see **BOOK**)

**YOGA** (see **EXERCISE** or **MEDITATION**)

**YOUTH** (see **ADOLESCENT**)

**YOYO** (see **TOY**)

**ZEBRA**

No one knows you better than yourself. Nonetheless, strive to know yourself just a little bit better. Utilize some of your stubbornness and "far-fetched" ideas and concepts to create something wise and concrete for all to share. When you lock your gifts or talents within your being, you ultimately become confused and bitter and consequently fall prey to self-doubt. One of the saddest things on this planet is to see someone with a gift or talent give it up because someone or something discouraged them or influenced them to do something else. Know your "worth" through self-belief, your "potential" through introspection, and your "purpose" through faith, experience, and encouragement; then you will discover that your "way out" intelligence or genius is not something to merely brush aside. No! You must follow your better instincts, and you must gently come forth into the world with your created masterpieces and visions for all to see and share. The world needs you, so do not neglect what is within you; rather, wisely and gently share your purpose, your mission, your goals with us. The world needs you…!

**ZIPPER**

This symbolism reveals that you are too possessive, overprotective, and demanding towards those who know you and love you. You appear to be working against the wind by actually mistrusting those who want to love and trust you the most. You may mean well in all that you say or do; nonetheless, you are failing to bring peace and satisfaction into your life. There will be no sweet music in your life unless you commence to alter some of your personal insecurities and weaknesses with logic and deep introspection. Place your feet firmly on planet Earth, and begin to appreciate those precious joys given to you. No one is here forever, so make your life as meaningful and as purposeful as you can humanly muster! Love those who love you, and peace will come.

**ZITHER** (see **INSTRUMENT**)

**ZODIAC** (see **ASTROLOGY**)

**ZOMBIE** (see **VOODOO**)

**ZOO**

There is a great satisfaction in knowing that you are very capable in making your world a better place in which to live. As you plod onwards with an open mind and free will, you will discover easier and simpler ways to make your existence less cumbersome. Such is the state of man's progress upon this planet, both now and into the future! This dream symbolism, representing Mankind, advises you to personally function on the highest level of spiritual, emotional, and physical oneness that you can humanly muster! By doing good for yourself and for others, you can build a good base—a good foundation—for others to emulate and follow. As time goes by, you may have the immeasurable satisfaction in knowing that your earthly road was paved with good intentions and winged thoughts of Love, Respect, and Peace of Soul. Reach out to help your fellow man with great peace and self-sacrifice, and never look back; rather, continue on and on until every vestige of your being is immersed in God's Love. Then one day, when you are no longer here, your soul will gaze back upon this planet, wave good-bye, and cry out, "Oh, Remembered Earth!"

# TABLE OF CONTENTS

*mountain*

Voyeur (see Peeping Tom
or Sex)
Vulgarity (see Blasphemy
or Low-mindedness)
Vulture (see Bird)
Wading Pool (see Float,
Swimming, or Water)
Waffle (see Food)
Wagon (see Cart, Chuck
Wagon, Buggy, Surrey, or
Truck)
Wagon Train (see Convoy or
Guard)

Waiter (see Carhop, Hostess,
or Stewardess)
Waitress (see Carhop, Hostess,
or Stewardess)
Wall (see Enclosure)
Wallaby (see Kangaroo)
Waltz (see Dance or Music)
Wampum (see Decoration
or Money)
Wand (see Divining Rod,
Illusionist, or Stick)
Want Ad (see Advertisement)
War (see Battle, Battlefield,
Chemical Warfare, Fight,
or Quarrel)
Warehouse (see Shed or Store)
Warhead (see Bomb or
Missile)
Warlock (see Black Magic,
Evildoer, or Witchcraft)
Warrant (see Document,
License, Passport, or
Promise)

Wart (see Lump)
Washbowl (see Basin or
Bathroom)
Washcloth (see Material or
Tissue)
Washing Machine (see
Appliance)
Wasp (see Insect)
Wasteland (see Desert)
Watch (see Clock, Guard,
Measurement, or Patrol)
Watchtower (see Observatory
or Tower)
Waterfall (see Water)
Waterhole (see Hole or
Water)
Watering Can (see Can)
Watermelon (see Fruit)
Water Pistol (see Toy)
Water Polo (see Game)
Water Rat (see Rat)
Water Snake (see Snake)
Waterweed (see Plant)
Waybill (see List)
Wealth (see Abundance,
Billionaire, Fortune,
Happiness, Millionaire,
or Ownership)
Weapon (see Atomic
Bomb, Bomb, Cannon,
Dynamite, Gun, Hydrogen
Bomb, or Missile)
Weaving (see Handicraft)
Web (see Cobweb,
Confusion, Lacework,
Material, Net, or Tissue)

MEMBER OF SCABRINI GROUP

Québec, Canada
2006